£12·95.

Introduction to British Politics

Second edition

D1150603

Introduction to
British Politics

Analysing a Capitalist Democracy

Second Edition

John Dearlove and *Peter Saunders*

Polity Press

First published 1984 by Polity Press in association with Blackwell Publishers
Reprinted 1985, 1986, 1987, 1988 (twice), 1989

Second edition first published 1991
Reprinted 1992, 1993, 1994

Editorial office:
Polity Press, 65 Bridge Street,
Cambridge CB2 1UR, UK

Marketing and production:
Blackwell Publishers, the publishing imprint of Basil Blackwell Ltd
108 Cowley Road, Oxford OX4 1JF, UK

Basil Blackwell Inc.
238 Main Street, Cambridge, MA 02142, USA

ISBN 0 7456 0599 0
ISBN 0 7456 0600 8 (pbk)

British Library Cataloguing in Publication Data
A CIP catalogue record for this book is available from the British Library.

Library of Congress Cataloging in Publication Data
Dearlove, John,
    Introduction to British politics: analysing a capitalist democracy / John
Dearlove and Peter Saunders, — 2nd ed.
      p.   cm.
    Rev. ed. of: Introduction to British politics. 1984
    Includes index.
    ISBN 0–7456–0599–0   ISBN 0–7456–0600–8
    1. Great Britain — Politics and government — 1979-   2. Great Britain —
Economic Policy — 1945-   I. Saunders, Peter R.   II. Dearlove, John.
Introduction to British politics.   III. Title.
JN231.D4   1991   90–1233
320.941–dc20   CIP

Typeset by Colset Private Ltd, Singapore
Printed and bound by T. J. Press, Padstow, Cornwall

Printed on acid-free paper

Contents

Introduction to the Second Edition

For the most part reviewers of the first edition of this book have been kind and it sold well. However, these selfsame reviewers were often frustrated because we failed to come to 'decisive conclusions' as to how the system really worked and as to which theoretical tradition was the best of the lot in making sense of things. Reviewers liked the fact that we presented 'a very complex picture which attempts to incorporate several points of view within the plan' but they also felt that 'rocking the boat is not enough' because without a proper 'synthesis' of the divergent theories and a clear presentation of our own perspective the 'likely end result for most students is a confused rather than a sophisticated understanding of the world of British politics and a conviction that all theory is futile'. In effect, we were told that we did a good job in presenting and assessing a variety of points of view but, in striving to make 'a virtue of the theoretical inadequacy and complexity' that our analysis revealed, we did a bad job in wrapping things up and in letting people know precisely where we stood as to the best theory and the overall functioning of the British political system. How do we answer these kind of charges?

We still hold to the view, expressed in the introduction to the first edition, that 'there is no single simple key which can unlock the complex reality that is British politics, and no single theory can provide all the answers'. This being the case, we are no nearer to advancing our very own perspective on British politics which we feel should be *the* theory on the subject and which should dominate academic discourse. Put another way, we still do not look for certainties in an uncertain world; we still do not seek simplicity where we see only complexity; and we still do not see the need for the anchor of a settled analysis in a sea of political changes. Having said all that, we do take seriously the charge that we did not advance 'decisive conclusions' in the first edition and so our new concluding chapter sets down the basic propositions found in each of the chapters as well as summary statements that we think capture the fundamental lessons to be drawn from the chapters in question.

In terms of the nuts and bolts, we have two entirely new chapters. Chapter 3, 'Explaining voting behaviour', explores three different perspectives on voting choice in the light of the increased electoral volatility of the last twenty years. This chapter also deals with the geography of voting at the same time as we stick our necks out and assess the prospects for the parties at the polls. Chapter 8, 'Liberalism, conservatism and the "New Right" ', not only reviews the ideas and philosophies that lay at the heart of Thatcherism but also highlights the extent to which these ideas dominated the whole of the political agenda of the 1980s. Although the Prime Minister who gave her name to 'Thatcherism' resigned in 1990, the influence of these ideas is still marked and it is impossible to understand British politics in the nineties without understanding the sea-change which occurred in the eighties.

All the other chapters have been extensively rewritten in order to take into account developments in British politics since 1984 *and* changes in our understanding of the various theoretical positions as they have struggled to make sense of these developments. For example, Charter 88 has breathed new life into the debate about the need for a written constitution; the Labour Party has advanced new and 'realistic' sets of policies in the light of three electoral defeats; the brave new mould-breaking SDP has now gone from the scene; the Conservative Party is struggling to develop a dis-tinctively post-Thatcherite political philosophy; corporatism looks to be a dead duck; large chunks of British industry have been privatised; the *Spycatcher* and Ponting trials have thrown more light into the dark corners of the secret state; local government has been rocked by a variety of developments – not least the furore over the 'unfair' (or is it the fairer?) poll tax; and all the while the powers of the European Community have been encroaching at the same time as the East and West power blocs have been crumbling.

Notwithstanding the detailed specifics of change, at this point in our understanding of British politics, we are mindful as to the importance of two things. First, we want to stress the sheer power of the British state over and against the kind of 'informal' political processes that have absorbed the energies of political scientists and sociologists for well over three decades. Academics have spent far too much time worrying about parties and pressure groups, and not enough time studying the state and the importance of constitutions. Second, we are also increasingly alive to the seeming demise of all nation states in an age of international organisations and an integrated world economy. Not surprisingly, therefore, we conclude this edition with the observation that 'for good or bad, British politics can no longer be contained within the increasingly anachronistic boundaries of the territorial nation state, and so narrow books on British politics seem destined ultimately for the dusty shelves of the antiquarian bookshops'. In this book we have dwelt on structures of power and policy-making within Britain, but have alluded to the importance of international politics; future editions could well need to reverse this balance.

John Dearlove and Peter Saunders
Brighton, 1990

Works Cited

McBride, S. (1985) 'Review', *Canadian Journal of Political Science*, 18, 647–8.

Punnet, R.M. (1985) 'Adversarial political studies: mainstream versus Marxist', *Parliamentary Affairs*, 38, 114–17.

Tivey, L. (1988) *Interpretations of British Politics*, London, Harvester Wheatsheaf.

Introduction to the First Edition

British Politics Today

British politics have been undergoing some quite dramatic and fundamental changes and upheavals over the last few years. As the country's economy has lurched into recession, and as different sections of the population have posed different and often irreconcilable demands across a variety of issues ranging from the deployment of nuclear weapons to the future of the welfare state, so long-established political arrangements have begun to crack under the strain. New patterns of political alignment, new types of political organisation, and new sources of political conflict have emerged.

One manifestation of these changes has been the erosion of the two-party system. In 1981, the Social Democratic Party was formed, and just over 2 years later, in alliance with the Liberals, secured over 25 per cent of the popular vote at a general election. This result was not reflected in Parliament, however, where the Alliance won just 23 seats (the Labour Party, with 2 per cent more of the vote, won 209 seats!). The Alliance complained about the inequities in the electoral system and called for a new, written, British constitution to include proportional representation.

The 1983 general election was no less traumatic for the Labour Party which recorded the worst defeat in its history. Almost as many working-class people voted Conservative as voted Labour and the party (together with many political analysts) was at last forced to recognise that it had no automatic support base among manual workers, many of whom were now avowedly anti-socialist in their views and sentiments.

Labour's defeat also nailed once and for all the fallacy, so common on the Left, that when capitalism gets into a mess, the masses will fall in behind a radical socialist alternative. Throughout the 1970s and early 1980s, Labour's rank and file activists had pushed the party away from the 'middle ground' to embrace the explicitly socialist programme of state intervention which proved electorally disastrous. Meanwhile, during this same period, the Conservatives had been moving off in the opposite (free market, anti-state) direction under the zealous Right-wing leadership of Margaret

Thatcher with the result that party politics had become polarised to an extent unprecedented in the post-war years.

By the early 1980s, both major parties had, in their different ways, come to reject most of the basic principles by which governments had attempted to run the country since the Second World War. Neither Labour nor the Conservatives were any longer content to support the so-called 'mixed economy', for while the former urged a massive extension of public ownership, the latter set about privatising many of the major nationalised industries. Both parties similarly rejected the economic policies which had been adopted following the end of the war as the means for ensuring continued growth and relatively full employment. Labour came to place its faith in greater economic planning by the state while the Conservatives embraced a monetarist, anti-state strategy which brought inflation under some kind of control but at the cost of driving unemployment to new record levels. Finally, while Labour increasingly criticised the inadequacies of the welfare state, the Conservatives busied themselves with dismantling it.

As unemployment rose, social services deteriorated, and the plight of large sections of the population grew steadily worse, so the Conservative government became increasingly concerned about the possibility of social unrest. The police and the army were strengthened and legislation limiting civil liberties was pushed through Parliament. In the summer of 1981, riots broke out and spread through many English cities resulting in damage estimated at £45 million. The Home Secretary immediately announced increased expenditure on more effective riot-control equipment and police pay was again increased as unemployment continued to rise.

While some groups took to the streets in direct and angry confrontation with the police, others developed alternative modes of airing their grievances. The peace movement re-emerged from hibernation and women mounted a long and weary vigil outside the Greenham Common airforce base in protest at the deployment of Cruise missiles under the control of the American government. This protest in turn reflected the growing vitality of the women's movement, and throughout the 1970s and 1980s, this and many other movements – ranging from tenants' associations to the gay-rights campaign – sprang up to give voice and expression to interests and concerns which could no longer be contained within the straitjacket of conventional party politics, interest-group politics, or class-based movements.

The development which more than any other struck at the very heart of the established system of state power was the growth of nationalist movements in Scotland, Wales and Northern Ireland. While the threat posed by Scottish and Welsh nationalism was (temporarily) overcome at the end of the 1970s, the question of Northern Ireland has proved intractable. British troops were deployed in the province in 1969 and have remained there ever since, while the minority nationalist population has continued to demonstrate its resolute hostility to continued British rule by, among other things, electing Sinn Fein candidates, one of whom starved himself to death in a British military prison in Belfast.

The sovereignty of the United Kingdom state was also under threat during this period. In 1973, the UK joined the European community and ceded certain crucial powers to the European bureaucracy in Brussels. This, together with the growing dependence of the British government on an American-dominated military alliance and the weakness of the British government in the face of pressure from the International Monetary Fund, led many commentators to doubt whether Britain was any more in control of its own destiny.

All of these tendencies help to explain why, from the 1970s onwards, democracy itself came to be questioned from a number of different quarters. For those on the Right, 'mass' democracy began to look like a luxury which the country could no longer afford. Politicians, political scientists, military personnel, and police chiefs began to complain about 'elective dictatorship' and 'adversary politics'. They wondered whether government was not becoming 'overloaded' by democratic demands, whether trade unions could any longer be allowed to disrupt the pursuit of profitability, and whether it was necessary to curtail established rights in order to defend the established social and economic power structure. Those on the Left by contrast came to see aspects of liberal democracy as little more than a sham. They saw the potential in participatory democracy and constrasted this with the reality of the non-responsive power of multinational corporations, the machinations of the banks and finance companies, and the secrecy of the various state agencies over which ordinary people had virtually no control. On both Right and Left, therefore, democracy came to be seen as a problem: there was too much for the Right, and not enough for the Left.

This brief review of contemporary developments indicates the extent to which British politics have been in turmoil over the past few years. We attempt to make sense of these changes in this book for we believe that the turmoil in British politics has caught existing accounts wrong footed. What then do we see as the limitations of the existing textbooks on British politics?

The Limitations of the Established Literature

It is not possible to generalise about texts on British politics as there is no single tradition of writing on the subject. Having said that, the dominant, mainstream, political science texts have tended to focus almost exclusively on the democratic aspects of British politics. For most of this century, the emphasis has been on the liberal-democratic constitution and the formal institutions of Parliament, Cabinet and Prime Minister. More recently, political scientists have come to deal with the process of policy-making taking into account the significance of parties and interest groups. Yet despite this development a narrow view of politics and power has continued to prevail. Too much has been taken for granted. Too much has been ignored because it does not fit within a democratic perspective. British politics have been defined either as being about describing the institutions of the state (with the presumption that power is somehow *in* those institutions), or as involving an explanation of the process of public policy-making through an emphasis upon the role of parties and interest groups.

In this mainstream literature, therefore, no real attention was paid to the non-democratic aspects of British politics; no attention was paid to the substance of public policy so as to deal with just who benefited from government action (and inaction); no attention was devoted to the implications which flowed from the fact that Britain possessed a capitalist economy that was operating in a world market; and there was no recognition that power was caught up in 'private' matters, dull routines, and inaction as much as in the more public arena of governmental institutions and formal political participation.

Texts of this kind tended to be complacent, and they are characterised less by their explanatory rigour than by their unthinking praise for, and commitment to, the system of democracy in Britain.

In the 1970s, teaching texts articulating the conventional and orthodox wisdom about representative and responsible government continued to emerge, but at the same time they were becoming increasingly out of step with informed opinion as to the 'reality' of our politics and problems. Established political scientists could be heard expressing their unease about the drift of democratic politics in Britain. Instead of praising the British constitution as a sweet success it was increasingly seen as a sour problem that was the root cause of our economic ills and in need of change. Part and parcel of this critique was the recognition that the conventional wisdom was at odds with reality and so could no longer explain it. Political scientists were telling us that we had to break out of the conventional wisdom in order to make any kind of sense of the sorts of changes in British politics which we discussed above. Instead of talking about responsible party government, these critics came to talk of adversary politics, and instead of seeing interests groups as contributing to a cosy pluralist democracy they saw them as leading to a dangerous overload of demands and to a crisis of governability itself. Leading political scientists slowly dumped the conventional wisdom and took on a New Right perspective that was critical of big government and mass democracy because of the damage they were apparently causing to Britain's economic performance.

In fact, all the ballyhoo about the need to break out of the conventional wisdom conceals the essential continuity between that wisdom and the New Right accounts of British politics that have assumed a key place in the political science of British politics *and* in British politics itself. Although there is a change in the assessment of British politics, the system is still characterised as democratic above all else. In effect, political scientists have chosen to look at our political economy with an eye fixed only on politics, and on democratic politics at that. They have failed to focus on capitalism and take it seriously because the mere mention of capitalism has been dismissed as a coarse ideological irrelevance. In consequence, political scientists have continued to overlook the political significance of economic power. Where they have considered economic interests, their analyses have been limited to simple studies of the 'links' between government and industry which go no further than tracing the 'backgrounds' of those involved in politics and the interest-group organisations of business and labour.

Of course, texts defining British politics as democratic politics are not the be all and end all of the literature. A smaller, rival, tradition of critical writing, inspired by a Marxist perspective, is particularly attentive to capitalism and class. This perspective tries to place the institutions of the British state within the larger social and economic context, stressing the functions they perform in the defence of a class-based and divided society. There are considerable merits in this body of work, but there is often the presumption that British politics can be explained and simply 'read off' from a knowledge of Marxist theory backed up by a cursory glance at the underlying realities of economic power in Britain without the need for any concrete research into the messy stuff of politics itself. Moreover, if mainstream political scientists have failed to take capitalism seriously, then Marxist analysts have failed to take democracy seriously. From the Marxist perspective, democracy in Britain has been seen, all too easily, as mere 'bourgeois democracy' – as democracy for the capitalist class and the denial of democracy for the working class. Democracy, and even politics itself, is regarded as so snugly contained by, and fitted to, the essentials of capitalism that it offers no real prospects for change. Democracy simply buttresses (often by concealing) the power of the economically dominant class. It then follows from this that democracy can safely be ignored by the 'serious' student of British politics since *real* power lies not in parliaments or local councils but in company board rooms and (when the time is ripe) on the streets.

In many ways the Marxist accounts are the opposite side of the coin to the mainstream and New Right political science accounts. Marxist accounts are attentive to capitalism and economics to the detriment of a sustained concern with democracy, whereas mainstream and New Right accounts are attentive to democracy and to a narrow conception of politics to the detriment of a serious concern with the political implications of capitalism. Each tradition has its blind spots. Each tradition tends to operate in dismissive ignorance of the rival tradition: many political scientists have seen Marxist accounts of British politics as 'biased', value-loaded, and inattentive to the 'facts', and most Marxists have seen 'bourgeois' political science as offering accounts that simply mystify reality, legitimise the status quo and deal only with unimportant facts and the surface froth of democratic politics.

So, the texts on British politics have been polarised in a way that has reflected the increasing polarisation within British politics itself. More than this, authors have rarely been self-critical of the ideas they have been putting forward, and many have not been clear as to the theory guiding their work and the selection of the facts which they present. By and large *both* traditions of scholarship are over-confident, static, partial, and ahistorical and too eager to presume that politics today can be explained through a reliance on either liberal-democratic theories or Marxist theories, both of which have their roots in the experience of the nineteenth century.

In fact contemporary developments in the world of British politics and the turmoil and change which abound have rocked *both* traditions of scholarship and their advocates know it. In consequence the rival perspectives on British politics are increasingly uncertain of their explanatory grip on a political reality that seems to defy any simple appreciation and which mocks the attempt to apply nineteenth-century nostrums to late twentieth-century issues. Some say we are witnessing a crisis of capitalism, others that we are experiencing a crisis of democracy, but in an intellectual world in which theories compete, few are prepared to suggest that the situation is a complex mix of problems to do with capitalism *and* democracy – and much else besides.

It is here that we see the distinctive contribution of this book. We are not exclusively committed to any one theory or perspective; we do not feel a need to take simple sides with respect to the different traditions of scholarship; and we consider that the rival traditions are as much complementary as competing. To be a good political scientist you must be keenly alive to the Marxist tradition, and to be a good Marxist you must know 'bourgeois' social science. British politics are complicated and it makes no sense to see all wisdom as residing within one perspective.

Theories and Methods

Our concern is to liberate the student of British politics from the blinkers of the conventional textbook wisdoms *and* the increasingly conventional radical alternatives to those wisdoms. The first and crucial step towards such a liberation lies in the recognition that the study of politics entails the analysis of power in all its aspects. To achieve this, it is necessary to consider critically the insights which derive from a number of rival traditions including mainstream political science, the New Right, Marxism and neo-Marxism and political sociology.

No one perspective enjoys a monopoly over explanatory wisdom; nor can understanding be advanced it we are constrained by the limits of any single discipline. There is no single simple key which can unlock the complex reality that is British politics, and no single theory can provide all the answers. This is because theories, perspectives and even disciplines often differ in what it is that they are trying to explain.

There are different views as to the *essentials* of politics and power which means that the focus of attention is different in various traditions of work.

These traditions also differ in the *levels* at which they attempt to generalise about political power which means that some approaches are more specific in terms of time and place than others.

For example, if you consider that politics are essentially to do with the business of government' and the elected part of the state machine, then theories pertaining to elections and democratic procedures will clearly be central to your approach. If, however, your view of politics is broadened somewhat to include, say, the wider process of *public* policy-making by government and state, then your theoretical focus will also need to be wider since you will wish to consider the activities of interest groups as well as many other parts of the state system. And if your concern is with *private* power as it operates not just in and on the state but throughout the economy and society, and if you see this as the very essence of politics, then you will not wish to devote much attention to the analysis of elections, or Parliament or even the Civil Service, but will rather seek to focus on the significance of 'private' organisations and interests which may never be seen in the Palace of Westminister and which thus rarely feature in other kinds of theories.

None of these approaches is necessarily 'wrong'. Nor can we say that one approach is 'better' than another because it embraces a broader focus, for such judgements will depend on what it is we are interested in explaining at the time. Certainly there is no reason to assume that, if we draw on one of these perspectives this rules out the possibility of drawing on any other. Although academic debate and argument among those who are committed to different theories often proceed as if their approaches were mutually incompatible, it is clearly the case that different theories which focus on *different* questions posed at *different* levels of generality may in fact turn out to be *to some extent* complementary.

We should, however, be wary of simply cobbling together different theories in an attempt to develop a fully rounded picture. Just as we cannot develop a comprehensive understanding of Western art by focusing exclusively on Picassos or on Constables, so too our political analysis cannot be limited to any one tradition. Moreover, if it is the case that our understanding of the art world is likely to become very confused if we simply stitch together fragments from 'Guernica' and 'The Haywain', then so it is with our theoretical understanding of political power. Some theories are, to a greater or lesser extent, incompatible with each other, and if this is the case we cannot expect to achieve analytical clarity by sticking them together.

It is therefore one thing to say, as we do, that few theories are ever entirely wrong (or for that matter entirely right), but it is quite another to suggest that the truth of the mater can, therefore, somehow be attained by mixing them all together. Some theories *are* more valid than others in respect of specific questions which they address, and *the task is to sort out which sorts of issues are best explained by which sorts of theories*.

This, however, is easier said than done! Any social scientist will tell you that theory-testing is an extremely hazardous business, mainly because there is invariably a dispute over what is to constitute a 'fact'. Not all facts are problematic – it is a 'fact', for example, that the Conservatives achieved a parliamentary majority at the 1979 and 1983 general elections – but most of the 'facts' which we need to draw upon in order to start explaining things can be and are disputed by people who are committed to different theories. This is because we tend to see the world through our existing theories.

It is our theories which tell us what we are looking for and, in many cases, what we are looking at, and this means that different people wedded to different theories all too often end up disputing each other's interpretations of the evidence or simply talking past one another.

If 'facts' are to a large extent dependent upon our existing theories then there are obviously real problems involved in trying to evaluate competing theories against them. Nevertheless, it remains the case that some theories do seem able to explain certain problems more plausibly or more comprehensively than others and so the critical and self-aware observer does not have to accept that any theory is as good as any other at explaining a given problem. We can offer no simple acid test of theoretical validity, but it is possible to go some way to evaluate different perspectives in terms of their logical consistency and their explanatory power with respect to specific aspects of politics at particular moments of history.

In the chapters that follow, we set down some of the major perspectives which have been advanced to account for developments in British politics, and we attempt to evaluate them against each other *and* against historical evidence of what the British state has done, how it has done it, and with what consequences for different groups in the population. In particular, we shall be evaluating the various theories we encounter in terms of what they tell us about the organisation and use of power in and on the contemporary British state.

We begin the book with a critical assessment of those constitutional theories which see political power as lying within particular democratic state institutions. As we proceed through the book, however, we gradually expand out from the institutions of the state and formal constitutional, or institutional, approaches to power. We recognise that the non-elected institutions of the state exercise substantial power. We argue that political power is also caught up in the behaviour and activity of political parties and interest groups in particular issues and policy areas. However, we also recognise that this 'obvious' behavioural, action-oriented perspective on power does not go far enough since it is also vital to attend to the power that is caught up in inaction and non-decision-making in society and economy as well as just in government and politics. In effect, as you read through the book you will be moving away from simple statements about *where* power lies (be it in the institutions of the state, in parties, pressure groups, or particular social classes) in order to consider more complex and abstract themes bearing on *how* power is used (and not used) and to *whose* particular advantage given the actual substance of state activity and the balance of public and private provision for social needs in Britain.

The Plan of the Book

In chapter 1 we look at the historical development of the British constitution and of constitutional theory in terms of the interests caught up in trying to change and defend the formal rules of the British political game. The constitution and constitutional theory are important because the former is *in* politics and the latter is *about* explaining politics.

In chapter 2 we explore three perspectives on party politics in Britain. First we explore the mainstream model of responsible party government; second, we consider the New Right argument about adversary politics; and finally we deal with the Left perspective which is critical of the Labour Party and sees party politics itself as irrelevant of major consideration.

This is then followed in chapter 3 with a discussion of the world of interests and groups from three points of view. First, we set down the essentials of pluralist democratic theory; second we deal with the New Right assessment about an overload of interest-group demands leading to ungovernability; and finally we look at the Left perspective on interests in British politics which sees pluralism as wrong and which talks instead about the dominance of business groups in the system. As well as dealing with these three perspectives we also explore community action at the local level and the alleged trend to corporatism at the central level of the state.

Chapter 4 examines the argument that the established constitution is in crisis because it no longer explains things and secures support for the system. We go on to explore three packages of proposals for a new constitution: that of the (essentially Conservative) constitutional authorities; that of the Liberal/SDP alliance; and that of the Left of the Labour Party.

In chapter 5 we attend to the power and significance of the non-elected parts of the state machine, much of which is uncontrolled by the elected government of the day, and all of which is poorly considered from within the mainstream and New Right perspectives. We pay particular attention the the Civil Service, and the nationalised industries, the judiciary, the police, the security services and the military.

Our focus is expanded still wider in chapter 6 where we turn from an analysis of the organisation of state power to consider a sociological perspective on power in British society as a whole. In this chapter we discuss the domination which groups can achieve in our society through ownership of capital, through professionalism, and through closing off opportunities to others on the basis of gender and race. All of this leads us to consider whether or not there is some elite group which effectively controls our society from behind the scenes.

In chapter 7 we are concerned to deal centrally with Marxist perspectives on British politics, paying critical attention to two of the most influential

Marxist theories of recent years – those of Ralph Miliband and Nicos Poulantzas. In this chapter we not only evaluate this debate in theoretical terms, but we also consider its significance for the British Labour Party in the contemporary period.

The next three chapters focus on particular aspects of state activity in order to bring earlier theoretical themes and arguments to bear upon empirical and historical examples of what the state has actually done.

In chapter 8 we concentrate on the attempts by successive British governments to arrest the decline of the country's economy over the last 100 years or so. We show how economic policy has come full circle back to a kind of *laissez-faire* in an ever-more desperate search for remedies following the failures of Keynesian demand-management and the limitations of half-hearted attempts at 'socialist' planning.

This is followed in chapter 9 with an examination of the history of social policy, and we consider the different explanations which have been offered to account for the growth (and more recently, the erosion) of the welfare state.

In chapter 10, we discuss the role of the state in securing social order, and trace the shift of emphasis which has occurred in recent years between 'soft' control agencies such as schools and the media, and 'hard' control agencies such as the police and the military.

We move in chapter 11 from a focus on what the state does and why, to an analysis of the levels at which the state apparatus is organised on a geographical or territorial basis. First we consider the local level; second, we attend to the almost hidden regional agencies; third, we consider the national question and the particular problem of Northern Ireland; and finally, we look at the International Monetary Fund, the North Atlantic Treaty Organisation, and the European Community – international organisations that do so much to control and constrain British politics and policy-making.

The book ends with a conclusion in which we draw together the theoretical arguments and historical evidence reviewed in earlier chapters in an attempt to clarify the nature of the changes which are currently affecting British political life. The particular focus of this concluding chapter is on the emerging tension between capitalism and democracy in Britain – a tension that has been exacerbated by the long-term decline in the country's economic performance.

In his bleak novel *The Grapes of Wrath*, set in the American mid-west during the depression years of the 1930s, John Steinbeck reports a conversation between a poverty-stricken tenant further farmer and the driver of a bulldozer who has been sent to clear the tenant off the land. The driver, staring down the barrel of the tenant's rifle, claims that he is not responsible for the tenant's plight:

'It's not me. There's nothing I can do . . . You're not killing the right guy.'

'That's so,' the tenant said. 'Who gave you orders? I'll go after him. He's the one to kill.'

'You're wrong. He got his orders from the bank. The bank told him: "Clear those people out or it's your job".'

'Well, there's a president of the bank. There's a board of directors. I'll fill up the magazine of the rifle and go into the bank.'

The driver said: 'Fellow was telling me the bank gets orders from the east. The orders were: "Make the land show profit or we'll close you up".'

'But where does it stop? Who can we shoot? I don't aim to starve to death before I kill the man that's starving me.'

'I don't know. Maybe there's nobody to shoot . . .'

Fifty years on, with the economy again in crisis, many of us are just as bewildered as Steinbeck's farmer about who, if anybody, is culpable. Indeed, our economy and society have become even more complex in the intervening period such that it is now more difficult than ever before to pin down the source of the power which reaches out to touch all our lives. In such a situation, it is the task of political analysts to try to unravel the tangled web of power and domination in our society. The chapters which follow are an attempt to explore precisely this puzzle.

John Dearlove and Peter Saunders
Brighton, 1984.

"The heart of the constitution or a powerless rubber stamp?" (Reproduced by kind permission of The House of Commons.)

Chapter 1

The Changing Constitution

Everyone knows that the British constitution provides for a system of representative and responsible government.
A. H. Birch (1964) *Representative and Responsible Government*,
London, George Allen and Unwin, p. 13.

In 1953, I heard an eminent man of the left say, in utter seriousness, at a university dinner, that the British Constitution was 'as nearly perfect as any human institution could be', and no one even thought it amusing . . .
E. Shils (1972) *The Intellectuals and the Powers*. Chicago.
University of Chicago Press, p. 37.

Constitutional theory always has and always will emerge from the hard facts of politics rather than from the text-books of professors.
The Times 24 December 1985.

Introduction

This is a book that is concerned to make sense of contemporary British politics and so some of you may wonder why we are choosing to devote our opening chapter to the dry old stuff of the British constitution. We can understand your eagerness to get to grips with political power, with issues, and with all those 'fundamental' things that you think are *really* important. This being the case, we need to state clearly why we think that the constitution is really important since this is the basis on which we urge you to explore something which you may see as an old-fashioned irrelevance that simply hides the essentials of British politics today. Once we have suggested *why* you should study the constitution then we need to say just *what* is the constitution before going on to suggest *how* we think you should go about studying it. When we have got these matters out of the way we can plunge in to making sense of the changing constitution since the eighteenth century, as without this knowledge of constitutional and political history we are all ill-equipped to understand the constitution of today.

Why study the constitution?

There are three main reasons why we think you need to study the constitution if you are serious in your concern to make sense of British politics.

1 The established constitution and the rules and resources that are part of it operates *on* politics and provide a constraining and enabling context within which much politics occurs. From this perspective, the constitution is almost outside and above politics. It constitutes a kind of shell that regulates public access to, and the behaviour of, the various institutions and officials that make up the state (such as the Prime Minister, the Cabinet, the House of Commons, the Civil Service, the judiciary, and so on) – institutions and officials which, in their different ways, possess authority and the right to exercise public power, if necessary through the use of physical force, throughout the United Kingdom. For example, a general election for the House of Commons must be held at least every five years but only certain people have access to the vote and, in the absence of proportional representation, not all votes are of equal power in sending chosen candidates up to the Commons; the House of Lords (once a powerful state institution) has been constrained and can now only delay certain bills passed by the Commons; the Prime Minister must come from the Commons but resources attach to the office which enable the office-holder to exercise increasing power and authority; civil servants should be responsible to ministers and should not disclose information to Parliament, the media or individuals; and it is 'expected' that a government will resign and call a general election if it is defeated in a vote of confidence on the floor of the Commons.

2 The constitution is frequently *in* politics and a political issue in its own right. All constitutions are political constitutions and not just legal documents and so all constitutional arrangements tend to reflect and entrench the balance of political forces from the era when they were established. This being the case, no constitution can forever stay above the rough and tumble of politics; all constitutions may become the focal point for fundamental conflicts; and no constitution is immune from change by political action. Put another way, people may be constitution-*takers* for much of the time but no constitution is ever wholly external to human action and reason and so, on occasions, people may band together and through politics become constitution-*makers* eager, and perhaps able, to reshape the established rules of the political game – that is the constitution itself – to their own advantage. In this chapter we will be identifying two periods of decisive constitutional change and in chapter 5 we will deal with the substantial pressures for change with respect to the contemporary constitution.

3 Constitutional theory (itself a key aspect of the constitution) is *about* politics and provides a perspective on the location of power and the structure of relationships within the state, and on the relationships between the state and individuals, organisations and associations in society at large. Constitutional theory aims to tell us how state institutions and official positions hang together within a *system* of rule, and the established constitutional theory sits in a position of political and intellectual prominence as the 'official' view of British politics and, in consequence, tends to dominate the public discussion of politics

and many of the accounts that appear in the mass media. We may not agree with this official view, but that does not mean that we can avoid coming to terms with it precisely because it is a view of importance within the system itself. All things considered, constitutional theory is of importance because it seeks to provide us with answers to fundamental political questions about who governs and how; about who should govern and how; and about the respective rights of ordinary people and the propertied in British politics. It should not be ignored by those who are keen to explain British politics nor by those who are interested in social and political theory.

Taken together, these three points highlight the importance of thinking constitutionally if we are to make a start to understand British politics, the nature of public authority and the development of democracy. Of course, political practice is never wholly at one with constitutional theory but this does not mean that the British constitution is merely a mask hiding and legitimising the true reality of rule by the capitalist class – or by any other grouping. Let no one tell you that an understanding of the constitution and constitutional theory is a boring irrelevance. The issue is not *whether* we should study the constitution, but the problem is one of deciding just what *is* the constitution at the same time as we have to determine *how* best to understand and study it.

What is the British constitution?

The British do not have a constitution in the narrow, formal sense of the term in that our constitution is not written down in a single legal document which enjoys a special political status above the ordinary law even though much *is* written down in a host of laws of constitutional significance that bear on such matters as the franchise and the powers of the House of Lords. The absence of a single written document does not mean that the British constitution does not exist as we have a constitution in the broader sense of the term in that there are rules and arrangements relating to the organisation of the British system of rule but much is vague and outside of the law. This uncertainty which surrounds the British constitution is partly a function of the fact that the constitution is not in a single legal document because none of our constitutions has ever been 'made' from a fresh start, and also a function of the fact that the constitution is 'flexible' and is currently in flux, in politics, and the subject of political dispute. In this state of affairs, to answer the question, 'What is the British constitution?' is to say a number of rather different things.

1   In the most direct sense, we can say that the British constitution is simply the 'set-up', or system, *as it is*. This embraces, first, the various institutions that make up the state – the House of Commons, the Cabinet, the Civil Service and so on – and, second, the constitutional theory that links up these institutions

and gives them a coherence so that we can locate authority within the state and understand the basis for the representation of interests and the legitimacy of the political order itself. The trouble with this formulation is that it does not suggest *how* we can be sure as to just what is the constitutional set-up, and this is a particular problem once we recognise that the authority of particular state institutions is subject to change and that there are disputes as to what is (and should be) the constitutional set-up. To some extent uncertainty has been contained because some scholars have written books on the constitution that have endured to be regarded as so authoritative that they have defined the parameters of acceptable constitutional debate and almost the very constitution itself.

2 So, we can suggest that the constitution is what the constitutional authorities, or experts, *say it is*. In a country without a proper written constitution, the work of Bagehot and Dicey has actually become the written codification of the customs, conventions, traditions, and theory that have never been set down in a single legal document. The trouble with this formulation is that we need a basis for identifying just who are the constitutional authorities, and we also have to recognise that the authorities of a particular constitutional epoch might not continue to have a grip on the system if that system changes as a result of political action breaking the old shell.

3 It also makes sense to say that the British constitution is what the authorities *say it should be* because their views on what is constitutional and unconstitutional help to police everyday political practice, pulling it into line with the constitutional theory which they themselves advance as the proper way to conduct political affairs. Britain does not have a supreme constitutional court and a 'legal' constitution and so matters are deemed unconstitutional – against the spirit of the constitution – not when they are contrary to law but when they are contrary to conventions and the views of the constitutional authorities and so these views may have an impact on the actual practice of politics itself. The trouble with this formulation lies in the fact that it probably exaggerates the extent to which the views of the experts, as to what is constitutional and what is unconstitutional, actually come to have an effect on the practice of politics itself.

How, then, can we go forward to study *the* British constitution in a situation in which there are three rather different perspectives on what it is that we should be studying? Much hinges on the extent of political and constitutional stability. In times of stability there is likely to be rough agreement on constitutional fundamentals and in this state of affairs the set-up as it 'really' is, as it is said to be and as it is said it should be, will be pretty much one and the same thing. But in times of political crisis and upheaval, political practice (how the system 'really' works) and established constitutional theory (how the authorities say the system works) are likely to be out of step and there will also be limits as to what the constitutional authorities can do to shape political behaviour (and how the system should work). With political change, the established constitutional authorities are in a situation where they have to come to terms with new and emerging patterns of political power that are *outside* (but pressing in on) the established constitution that is supposedly made sense of through their theories. Political behaviour is not contained within the established system and rude *power* is out of mesh with the established patterns of constitutional *authority*. In this situation, established constitutional theory is worn out as a guide to practice; there will be disputes as to what should be the constitution; and there is even likely to be doubt as to just what is the constitution. If the established set-up survives the pressures for change then the established constitutional theory will continue to be of use as a guide to political and governmental practice. But if that set-up is broken then the established theories will be beached by change and new constitutional theories will come to assume centre stage. In periods of fundamental change political practice makes all the constitutional running and established theory gets swept aside as of no importance in shaping political behaviour – or in enabling us to understand it. In studying the British constitution we have to attend to the dynamic tension between constitutional theory and political practice, and to change over time. This has a direct bearing on how we should study the constitution.

How should we study the constitution?

For most of this century the British constitution has been applauded as the best in the world in providing for a system of representative and responsible government. The liberal-democratic constitutional theory provided by Dicey has been seen as *the* theory to make sense of our system of rule. The commitment to Dicey in combination with the praise for the system and the tendency to take the constitution for granted as a settled force *outside* of (but not *in*) politics has meant that a critical, political and historical perspective on the constitution has not pushed to the fore. Constitutional scholars have rarely been attentive to the tensions between constitutional theory and political practice, and so have failed to recognise that they are dealing with a changing, working political constitution. The bulk of scholarship on the British constitution has tended to settle into the dull constitutional approach to understanding. This approach takes the constitution for granted as fixed (but flexible) and the basic contentment with the overall set-up has meant that constitutional study has tended to tumble into the detailed description of particular state institutions, with institutional relationships explored in a highly stylised way that sucks them out of the larger political context within which they take on meaning. Exploring, explaining and analysing the actual working of the overall set-up in a self-conscious, critical and systematic way has tended to slip from concern. Most of those who have studied the twentieth-century constitution have failed to see it as a living thing *in* politics that has to be studied historically in relation to interests in society as a whole. There has been a failure to admit the possibility of a serious disjuncture between theory and practice, constitution and politics; there has been a failure to recognise that interpretations of the constitution are always relative to time, place and our position as observers; and so there has been the simple view that the constitutional set-up as it is, as it is said to be and as it is said it should be, are all as of one. In effect, those who operated from within the confines of the constitutional approach froze the constitution and presumed that the perspective advanced by Dicey in the nineteenth century could continue to capture the essentials of the constitution *and* politics into the twentieth century. As the constitution has entered a crisis stage in the late twentieth century – as a gap has clearly opened up between constitutional theory and political practice – so those locked into the constitutional approach have become increasingly ill-equipped to handle a constitution that is now an issue *in* politics. Consequently they have tumbled into carping critiques of political practice whilst advancing packages of constitutional reforms to set matters aright.

In fact, few political scientists have been in the forefront of constitutional study in this century and the study of the constitution has been left to the energies of constitutional lawyers. But their legal approach has been no more effective in enabling us to advance an adequate perspective on the constitution as they have chosen to cling to the certainties offered by Dicey; they have been particularly inattentive to the importance of political context and the insights of political science; and they have tended to draw arbitrary lines between matters political and matters legal, providing us with a very sterile, legalistic and apolitical perspective on what they are reluctant to see as a political constitution.

There is no good intellectual reason why the study of the British constitution should have slipped into the static sterility of the constitutional approach or into the grip of the perspective offered by lawyers. This being the case we hope to break out into a critical, historical and political approach that is crushingly attentive to the dynamic interaction between political practice and constitutional theory. Bogdanor is right to remind us that 'the study of constitutions cannot be divorced either from history or from politics' precisely because 'constitutions cannot be understood without looking at what lies behind them – at the political processes which gave them birth and at the historical thinking which conditioned the thinking of their founders'. To understand the constitution of today we need to make sense of the nineteenth-century constitution, but we need to look at this in the context of the eighteenth-century constitution which it replaced when the practice of politics was rapidly getting out of mesh with the then established theory of that constitution.

The Balanced Constitution

The established theory of the eighteenth-century constitution was provided by Sir William Blackstone. In his view:

the true excellence of the English constitution [is] that all the parts of it form a mutual check upon each other. In the legislature, the people are a check upon the nobility, and the nobility a check upon the people; by the mutual privilege of rejecting what the other has resolved: while the King is a check upon both, which preserves the executive power from any enroachments. And this very executive power is again checked and kept within bounds by the two houses, through the privilege they have of enquiring into, impeaching, and punishing the conduct (not indeed of the King, which would destroy his constitutional independence; but, which is more beneficial to the public), of his evil and pernicious counsellors. Thus every branch of our civil policy supports and is supported, regulates and is regulated, by the rest.

The mixed constitution of checks and balances may have been the *theory* of the constitution, but the *practice* of eighteenth-century politics fleshed these niceties out. True, executive power – the power to set state policies and to implement laws – was in the hands of the King, but the means for carrying this out had to be provided by the Houses of Parliament. Left to itself the House of Commons might well produce members of an independent spirit who could make the King's Government impossible by refusing to grant the money needed to execute his policies for the state. If clashes, deadlock and instability were to be avoided then ways had to be found to avoid the constitutional checks and ensure political harmony. This meant that the House of Commons had to be 'managed' and the King and the Lords could do this because they were able to use their patronage to exert 'influence' over the composition of the Commons, oiling the relations between the King and the representatives of the people and cementing the parts of the constitution into some kind of working whole. Crudely expressed, corruption was of the political essence and was the practical counterpoint to the constitutional theory of balance. The King exerted his will, not just because forty or fifty MPs held government posts, but because others in the Commons looked to him for financial help in fighting elections or else wished to secure contracts, pensions and favours for friends. For its part, the Lords was able to exert influence over the Commons in the context of a restricted franchise and a distribution of constituencies that bore less and less relation to the actual distribution of the population. In 1793 it was estimated that 400 members of the Commons (out of a total of around 530) were nominated or dependent on Lords to such an extent that they were likely to lack the chance to display any real independence in their parliamentary behaviour; in 1830, 70 English boroughs had 100 or less voters; Old Sarum and Dunwich were uninhabited constituencies.

The authorities on the eighteenth-century constitution tended to defend the set-up, the restricted franchise and the unreformed House of Commons. No one in authority seriously considered that the labouring masses had any political rights and there was the fear that if they secured the vote then they would destroy the delicate balance of the constitution – and much else besides. The conception of the political community which underlay the restricted franchise, coupled with the idea that corporate bodies (rather than individuals) should be represented, meant that supporters of the eighteenth-century system held to the view that every legitimate interest *was* represented in Parliament – if not directly then at least 'virtually' through the broad mix of members from different places and of varying backgrounds.

The ideology surrounding the constitution was one thing but in hard 'power' terms the balanced constitution was essentially aristocratic. At its worst it may have been a parasitic racket representing only itself to the detriment of all, but on the larger canvas of society it gave state power to a narrow group of substantial landowners in loose alliance with merchants and the small towns which were able to return members to the Commons. The constitution worked and held up only for as long as little in society changed, but by the end of the century new groups had come into prominence which were outside of the established set-up. The middle classes, based on manufacture in the emerging industrial towns of the north, and a working class that was being 'made' out of these self-same developments, gained a consciousness of the fact that they were unrepresented and politically disadvantaged within the eighteenth-century constitution. Manchester, Birmingham and Leeds returned no members to the Commons. Long before the eighteenth century closed pressures were building up for constitutional change *and* for more profound changes in the social and economic system itself. The writing was on the wall for the old system: it was doubtful whether the established constitution could hold in the face of the political pressures for constitutional change.

The Liberal Constitution

On the immediate constitutional front, corruption was attacked; 'virtual' representation was no longer seen as enough; and whilst some attacked the rights of *landed* property in politics (urging the principle that every man of substance should enjoy representation) some went further, denying the rights of *all* property and arguing for the 'rights of man', complete equality and a democratic republic based on the true sovereignty of all the people regardless of their income or wealth. There was the recognition that 'society was on the brink of a great struggle between property and population'. One thing was very clear, the limited eighteenth-century political contest between the ins and outs to government *within* Parliament was being transcended by a more fundamental division *outside* Parliament, in society between those who wished to change the set-up to their advantage and those who were determined to defend the status quo, the eighteenth-century constitution and the established basis of representation that had served them so well. In concrete terms, the reform of the House of Commons became *the* central issue dividing supporters from opponents of the established constitution. The Great Reform Act of 1832 stands as some kind of landmark constitutional development since it broke the essentials of the eighteenth-century constitution at the same time as it established a new principle of governmental organisation. The passing of the Act was associated with massive political unrest and a campaign of civil disobedience hovered over its passage through Parliament. The Act itself grew out of uneasy tensions and alliances between middle-class and working-class reformers and the entrenched aristocratic interest, but in a situation in which the tie-up between class interests and political action was anything but neat and tidy.

The middle classes faced both ways and walked a tightrope. On the one hand they resented the power of the landed aristocracy within the established set-up. On the other hand they were fearful of a change if it empowered the working class within a new set-up. They wanted a reformed House of Commons to represent *their* class (for, as one reforming MP put it in 1830, 'there has arisen in the minds of the wealthy and enlightened middle classes of the country a conviction that there did not exist between them and the legislature a sufficient link') and they wanted liberty and a liberal constitution with limited state intervention. But they certainly did not want a democratic constitution geared to the pursuit of equality since such a set-up might enact legislation that would threaten their position of power and privilege in the economy. All things considered, it was seen as essential to set a financial qualification for the franchise that would give the vote to 'decent' farmers and shopkeepers whilst excluding the lower social orders who, it was feared, might use their votes to elect MPs who would then plunder the public purse through the enactment of legislation of advantage to their class of constituents but at a cost to be borne by the new middle classes of substance.

For their part, although the die-hard aristocratic opponents of change were anxious about opening the floodgates, they nevertheless came to see that the price of outright opposition was becoming too high and might even bring disaster and revolution. As they were forced to respond to the pressures for constitutional change these established interests saw a glint of light at the end of the tunnel and came to entertain the hope that if the middle classes were allowed a subordinate share of power then they just might turn from poachers to gamekeepers of the system and so side with the aristocracy in helping to keep the working classes in order and outside of any new constitutional settlement. In other words, if it were possible to remove the grievances of the middle classes against those *above* them, then it might be possible to nip off the danger of an alliance between the middle classes and the working classes *below* them. There was the hope that modest constitutional change might attach the middle classes to the established institutions of the state if those changes meant that the House of Commons could be seen as an arena where middle-class grievances could be represented, discussed and perhaps even remedied.

Naturally enough, these constitutional machinations placed working-class organisations in a cruel dilemma. Would the reform of the franchise end the old system or, in giving the middle classes representation, merely add to the strength and number of working-class oppressors?

It is impossible to pass a pat judgement on the political implications of the 1832 Act. In the long run, a measure which drew a line between the middle classes with the vote and the working classes without the vote was almost bound to increase the consciousness of the latter in ways that would encourage their political aspirations and desire to be represented. In the short run, however, the property qualifications for the franchise *did* effectively exclude the working class from political participation through the ballot box. In fact, however, it needs to be remembered that the franchise itself was only increased by some 220,000 in England and Wales. Of greater significance was the redistribution of seats in the Commons. Small boroughs lost 141 members whereas the newly developed industrial areas of the north and Midlands secured representation through the creation of 65 new seats. In simple terms, the British constitution was being adjusted to the changed realities of economic power in the country at large.

The Act changed the working of the system in a number of ways.

1 The old politics of patronage lingered on, but with a larger franchise it was no longer possible for a small number of Lords to control the composition of the Commons, and so the Lords was forced to give way.
2 The power of the King was also reduced and was no longer as decisive in government. The effective choice of the Prime Minister and of his leading Cabinet colleagues passed out of the King's hands and onto the floor of the House of Commons.
3 In providing for the 'representation of the people', the act admitted of a new principle of linkage between state and society which gave power and legitimacy to the Commons. The House of Commons was no longer to reflect the ancient idea and represent 'whole' boroughs, county communities and corporate interests, but was to be representative of unorganised masses of individual men.
4 The Commons was at the centre of things, had a new independence and became a representative assembly of independent members chosen by individual electors whose right to the franchise gave them the opportunity to enjoy government based on their consent and *indirect* choice. The Commons *as a body* was independent of Lords and King. The members *within* the Commons enjoyed an independence of action inside the chamber: they were no more instructed delegates of their constituents than they were at the mercy of party whips.

The cumulative implications of these political developments destroyed the reality of the balanced constitution and hence the credibility of the established constitutional theory. This was noted by all manner of contemporary commentators but it was Walter Bagehot who provided *the* account of the new set-up in his study of *The English Constitution* published in 1867.

In observing the 'contrast' between 'the living reality' and 'the paper description' of the British constitution – in observing, that is, the gap between political practice and constitutional theory – Bagehot did two things of importance. Negatively, he shot down the eighteenth-century accounts of British politics as 'quite wrong' when used as descriptions and explanations of how things worked in the nineteenth century. Positively, he provided us with a new theory as to the essential reality of governing in the classical period of parliamentary government when members of the Commons enjoyed a brief golden age of independence between the fall of patronage and the rise of highly disciplined political parties. How, then, did Bagehot describe and explain the essence of the British Constitution: who governed and how?

Bagehot distinguished the 'dignified' from the 'efficient' parts of the constitution. The dignified parts (that is, the parts that were *seen* as powerful) merely 'impressed the many' and secured public support for the system, whereas the efficient parts (those that were *not* seen as powerful) actually had the real power so that they 'governed the many' in practice. Identity the efficient parts and you can say who governs; identity the dignified parts and you can see how the 'who' can get away with imposing their rule over the people. Bagehot argued that the King and the House of Lords had ceased to exercise power and had become simply dignified parts of the constitution since the Lords could only delay and revise legislation, and in our 'disguised republic' the constitutional monarch could only act on the advice of ministers responsible to the Commons. It was the House of Commons, and the Cabinet and Prime Minister that came from the Commons, that Bagehot saw as the efficient working parts of the constitution. Bagehot argued that 'the relation of Parliament, and especially of the House of Commons, to the executive government is the specific peculiarity of our Constitution', and he made the point that 'the efficient secret of the English constitution may be described as the close union, the nearly complete fusion, of the executive and legislative powers'. Bagehot saw this fusion as taking place in the Cabinet which he said was a committee of the legislative body chosen by the Commons to be the executive body and rule the nation. The House of Commons had a number of functions, but it was this elective function of making and unmaking Cabinets that was the 'most important' and which led Bagehot to argue that 'the ultimate authority in the English constitution is a newly elected House of Commons'. 'We are', said Bagehot, 'ruled by the House of Commons' even though he recognised that the Cabinet had a capacity to unmake the House of Commons since it enjoyed the right to ask for a dissolution of Parliament and after the election it could look for support from amongst members in a new House of Commons. In fact, it was precisely the subtlety of the relationship between Cabinet and Commons that led Bagehot to make the point that 'the English system . . . is not an absorption of the executive power by the legislative power; it is a fusion of the two.'

So, around the mid-nineteenth century, Britain was seen to have acquired a new liberal constitution – a constitution where there was an

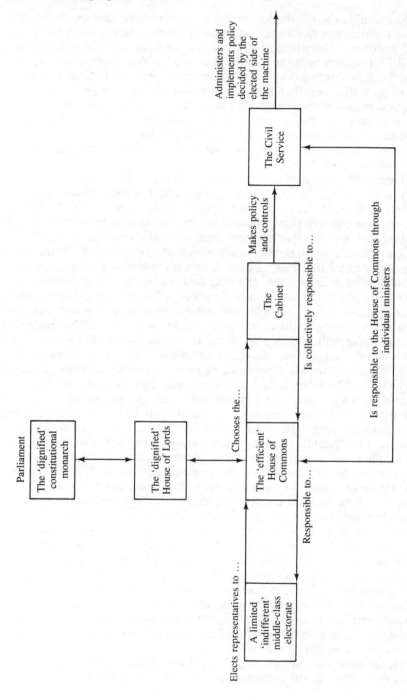

Figure 1.1　The Liberal Constitution of Parliamentary Government

executive responsible to a directly elected parliamentary assembly chosen by a small middle-class electorate, and where all those involved in the system were committed to individualism, a restricted franchise and limited government intervention in the market economy.

Informed contemporary commentators would tend to have described and explained the working of this constitution in the following terms. A limited, but well-informed, middle-class electorate (composed of less than one in six adult males) enjoyed the right to elect persons of calibre and substance to represent their opinions and serve the national interest in the House of Commons. Constitutionally, and in theory, Parliament as a whole was sovereign since the Commons was but a part of Parliament and for a bill to become law the assent of Lords, Crown and Commons were all needed. Politically, and in practice, however, the Commons was the real working guts of Parliament and it alone had the job of selecting (and checking) the Cabinet as the executive to govern the country. The Cabinet, for its part, had to put policy before Parliament and had to supervise the implementation of legislation through the control and coordination of the civil servants working in the various departments of state. The Civil Service itself was obscured from view within this perspective on the constitution. It was simply composed of *servants* who were charged with administration and implementation (not the making) of policy, and who were controlled by their elected political masters. Within this liberal constitution of parliamentary government everything flowed to and from the Commons and responsibility was of the essence: individual ministers were responsible to the Commons for the actions of the civil servants within their departments and ministers could be forced to resign if the Commons disapproved of the conduct of their departmental officials; the Monarch only acted on the advice of ministers responsible to the Commons; the Cabinet was collectively responsible to the Commons and if defeated on a major issue then it would either resign (as happened five times between 1852 and 1859) or else ask for a dissolution of Parliament in the hope of being able to secure the support of a new House of Commons; and the Lords were increasingly finding themselves in a position where they had to give way to the legislative views of the Commons.

Most authoritative commentators on British politics in the period between the Reform Acts of 1832 and 1867 did not just describe and explain the working of the constitution. They also applauded the system of responsible parliamentary government at the same time as they approved of the middle-class nature of the franchise and the absence of democracy. The 1832 Act gave the 'middle orders' in society political influence, but Bagehot probably exaggerated when he described the middle classes as 'the despotic power in England' even though the balance of power did tilt away from the large landowners in the Lords and towards the industrialists who were represented in the Commons. However, industrialists never 'took over' the state since they were partly absorbed into the ethos of the aristocracy, and landowners and industrialists alike were united in a shared unease about the pressures for change that were still coming from the lower social orders within society. Men of substance could come together within this liberal constitution but the possibility of a truly liberal-*democratic* constitution, with the threat of a working-class takeover of the state through the ballot box and the inevitability of their using the state to intrude into the rights of property and the liberties of the middle classes, seemed to be quite another matter. Political commentators and politicians were forced to ponder on the implications of allowing, or not allowing, the enfranchisement of the working class in a situation in which either course of action seemed to be fraught with dangers.

The Liberal-democratic Constitution

Defending the 1832 settlement involved justifications which talked about the rights of those with a propertied 'stake' in society with the related, and defensive, gloss that education was a necessary prerequisite for the 'responsible' exercise of the franchise. Intellectuals of the age believed in parliamentary government, not a democratic system; in liberty, not popular government; and the spectre of equality was seen as the darkest side of the claim for adult suffrage. Would not democracy inevitably interfere with the operations of capitalism and – as businessmen considered – for the worse? Would it not threaten free trade in Britain to which all parties were attached? Would it not threaten sound finance and the gold standard, keystone of all respectable economic policy? And would it not threaten the very survival of society as then constituted? All thoughtful Victorians were alive to the implications of a rampant industrialism. They knew that their society was riding a tiger and that an increasingly class-based politics could break out. They were conscious of the ups and downs of working class agitation for political rights, for the vote – and for more.

In theory and in the long run, liberals, such as J.S. Mill, were prepared to argue that representative government based on the votes of all adults was the best form of government since the political participation involved would promote the virtue, intelligence and 'development' of the people – the fundamental end of government. But in practice and in the short run (and given the need to conduct the business of government as 'efficiently' as possible), they saw the need for government by the 'fittest' and this objective would only be frustrated if all and sundry had the right to vote. Moreover, although liberals were keen to protect the governed from governmental oppression, they were also anxious about the legislative implications of majority rule for minority liberties, fearing that a system of one man one vote would tumble into the chaos of working-class domination over all other interests in society. Some were keen to shunt popular participation into the civic training ground of local government where there was the hope that too much government would not do too much damage. But no matter what, the fear remained that excluding the working man from some kind of involvement in the national political system could itself make for problems. Maybe the working man would entrench himself in his own institutions and, in isolation, be a danger to the unity and strength of the whole nation; maybe prolonged intransigence to working-class demands would break down the divide between the labouring classes and the 'dangerous classes', causing the popular forces to unite and assume a truly menacing character that would be beyond concessionary control; maybe, just maybe, the working class was loyal and could be trusted to display goodwill and deference to their betters; and maybe there was even the possibility of party advantage to be gained from seizing the initiative on the further reform of the franchise.

Democracy – *the* fundamental problem for bourgeois society in the nineteenth century – gradually came to be seen as something which was inevitable and could no longer be postponed even though extending the franchise to the working class was not viewed with any enthusiasm by the governments that introduced the legislation. The Reform Act, 1867, made working-class males a majority of the electorate in the country at large and the Acts of 1867 and 1883 almost quadrupled the electorate. By 1886 two in three adult males – almost 4.5 million people – had the vote in England and Wales, whereas some 50 years earlier the electorate had stood at little more than 650,000.

We can forever agonise over what is *really* meant by the term democracy. However, if we think about representative democracy and about a political system of 'government by the people' in which many adult males have the right to vote for representatives in a parliamentary assembly and an indirect right to choose the government of the day, and if we add the further gloss that the concept of 'the people' embraces the poor, then we can say that the British liberal state was grudgingly democratised towards the end of the nineteenth century. But this is not the whole story. True, the liberal state was democratised, but those in authority and power who recognised the inevitability of democracy were nevertheless eager to manage democratic politics, to limit it and to entrench a 'conservative democracy'. There was a concern to iron out direct participation, 'popular government', the whole struggle for equality, and 'collectivism' and socialism in favour of a pattern of limited (or *liberal*) democracy that would work with and within the prevailing economic system and informal distribution of political power. None of this could be guaranteed – and that was the fear – but with the uneasy liberalisation of democracy, democracy itself slowly ceased to embody the cry from below for the overthrow of the liberal state and the competitive market society. It came instead to embody the more limited claim that the working class had the right to a limited involvement within the established state institutions where there was a clear expectation – and hope – that the state would not be used to intervene in society to effect fundamental changes. No reformist working-class party immediately burst upon the scene to dance on the floor of Parliament – still less did a socialist movement arise that refused all compromise with the bourgeois state. The politics of deference (whereby working-class people seemed to *accept* the leadership of their social 'betters') held change in check and ensured that the Liberal and Conservative Parties retained their grip on things. Politically, the democratic aspirations of the popular-radical tradition were effectively contained within a Liberal movement dominated nationally by middle-class and aristocratic elites, and the Conservative Party was not slow to mobilise many working-class Tories into their camp. Put succinctly, democracy did not deprive the upper classes and the Liberal and Conservative Parties of political leadership. They still carried the ball, but the people moved from being spectators to doubling as occasional umpires as well. Contrary to the hopes and fears of those who had taken sides on the issue of democracy, political practice suggested that liberal democracy and a class-divided society could fit together without disaster and the overthrow of that society by democratic excesses. Here was cause for surprise and celebration. There was a need for a new constitutional theory that would ease the liberal orthodoxies aside as at odds with the developing facts of democratic political practice. By the last quarter of the nineteenth century the time was ripe for the acceptance of a liberal-*democratic* perspective as being of the essence of the British constitution.

If the accounts of British politics between 1832 and 1867 pointed to the sovereignty of Parliament, then the accounts that came to the fore after that period made the additional point that the sovereignty of the *people* was behind this and was of the constitutional and political essence. If liberal accounts saw the House of Commons as at the centre of things, then liberal-democratic accounts saw the Commons as a dignified part of the constitution that lacked power in the face of the power of the people and the constitutional implications of disciplined political parties within the heart of the state machine. If Bagehot's *The English Constitution* has been regarded as the authoritative constitutional account for the golden age of parliamentary government between 1832 and 1867, then Albert Venn Dicey's *Introduction to the Study of the Law of the Constitution*, published in 1885, has come to be regarded as the authoritative text for the period of parliamentary democracy since then and his account still occupies the high ground of British constitutional theory today. How, then, did Dicey describe and explain the essence of the British constitution?

Dicey was concerned to deal with the three 'guiding principles' which he considered pervaded the modern constitution of England. He centred his attention on the sovereignty of Parliament, the conventions of the constitution and the rule of law.

1 *The sovereignty of Parliament* meant that Parliament could make and unmake any law whatsoever; there was no higher legislative authority; and no court was in a position to declare properly passed Acts of Parliament invalid or unconstitutional. Having said that, Dicey went on to note that there were both 'internal' and 'external' limits to the actual exercise of this sovereignty. The internal limits derived from that 'nature' and 'character' of the sovereign.

The external limits were seen as of especial significance in the context of a democratic polity and to this end Dicey distinguished legal sovereignty (which was with Parliament) from political sovereignty (which was with the electorate). Put another way, Dicey welded the new *practice* of democratic politics onto the established *theory* of parliamentary sovereignty so creating the new constitutional theory of liberal-democracy.

2 *The conventions of the constitution* were unwritten rules that were seen as of crucial significance since they secured 'in a roundabout way what is called abroad the "sovereignty of the people" ' thus making for a governmental system in which 'the will of the electors shall by regular and constitutional means always in the end assert itself as the predominant influence in the country'. The conventions of the constitution, in ensuring the supremacy of the House of Commons, have 'one ultimate objective. Their end is to secure that Parliament, or the cabinet which is indirectly appointed by Parliament, shall in the long run give effect to the will of that power which in England is the true political sovereign of the state – the majority of the electors.' Dicey felt able to boil the British Constitution down to 'one essential principle': 'obedience by all persons to the deliberately expressed will of the House of Commons in the first instance and ultimately to the will of the nation as expressed through Parliament.' In his book on *Law and Public Opinion in England*, Dicey made the point that 'the English constitution has been transformed into something like a democracy' going on to argue that 'in a democratic country the laws which will be passed, or at any rate will be put into effect, must be the laws which the people like'.

3 *The rule of law*, Dicey argued, embraced at least three distinct though kindred conceptions. First, it stood for the idea that law excluded the exercise of arbitrary official power over individual citizens; second, it stood for the equality of all persons before the law – be they citizens or officials, rich or poor; and third, there was the idea that the constitution was not the source of citizens' rights but the general principles of the constitution were the result of the benefits and liberties conferred on individuals by the judicial decisions and remedies provided by the ordinary law of the land in particular cases. The rule of law was seen as an important *value* in the British political system. It was a vital principle of constitutional morality because it served as a shorthand phrase that was all about limited government and limiting the arbitrary, excessive and naked power of officials in order to protect and preserve the liberties and freedoms of individuals in the face of the power of the state.

Since Dicey, there has been no real room for rival perspectives on the British constitution and although we will be attending to Harold Laski's 'economic interpretation' in an appendix to this chapter it is important to recognise that most constitutional authorities have been content to follow in Dicey's footsteps even though there have been some lively disputes *within* liberal-democratic constitutional theory, one of which we will be considering in the second appendix to this chapter. For the moment, however, it is important to note that liberal-democratic constitutional theory has endured and has been seen as of the constitutional essence. Moreover, because the constitution has not been seen as something *in* politics (but has simply been seen as a force outside of politics that somehow operates *on* it and controls it), liberal-democratic constitutional theory has been seen as at one with political practice and hence it has also served as *the* theory to describe and explain British politics. Established constitutional theory has made sense of the British constitution *and* of British politics in the following way and this has constituted the 'official' view of British politics – a view that has been put across by the media, by established politicians and by a good few politics textbooks as well.

All adults enjoy the right to vote in free general elections that must be held at least every five years. The extension of the franchise created a situation in which the electorate had to be organised and persuaded as never before. Political parties came to assume a role of major significance, competing for votes on a mass scale and endeavouring to ensure that their candidates got elected to the House of Commons. In the context of a mass electorate it was no longer possible for parties to buy votes through corrupt electoral practices and the offer of ale to the lucky few. Moreover, the electorate itself was less open to these bribes and less inclined to attend to the calibre and standing of candidates. It was instead more attentive to the programmes of policies offered by the parties – programmes that were designed to secure popular support at the same time as they were to serve as blueprints for governmental action if a party was able to win a general election. Within the British constitution a party wins a general election – that is it is able to form a government – if it has secured a majority of the seats in the House of Commons as, by convention, the Monarch sends for the leader of the majority party in the Commons and asks him or her to become Prime Minsiter and form a government.

The Prime Minister forms a government by appointing party colleagues from the Commons and the Lords to ministerial posts, the most important of which sit with the Prime Minister in the Cabinet. In theory, the Cabinet as the executive is still collectively responsible to the Commons, and it is possible for a government to be defeated on a motion of no confidence in that House so that it would be forced to resign and face popular judgement at the polls. This is the liberal theory of things. In practice, however, this is very, very unlikely to happen in our liberal-democratic constitution because of the implications which flow from the powerful presence of disciplined political parties. Parties do not just organise the electorate, they also organise their members in the House of Commons. The fact that the Prime Minister is the leader of the majority party in the Commons, coupled with the tradition of strong party discipline, serves to ensure that the leadership of the party forming the government will be practically guaranteed the support of its parliamentary majority in the Commons. In this state of affairs, the liberal-democratic account of the constitution completely *reverses* the liberal account of the relationship between the Commons and the Cabinet. Instead of the Commons controlling, checking and making and unmaking the Cabinet, as was the case during the golden age of parliamentary government within the liberal constitution, the Prime

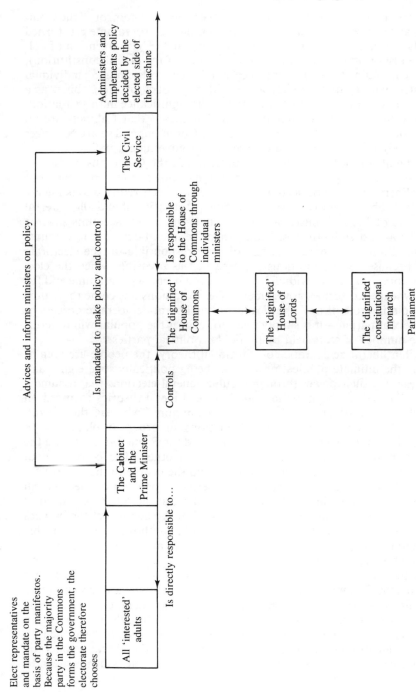

Elect representatives and mandate on the basis of party manifestos. Because the majority party in the Commons forms the government, the electorate therefore chooses

All 'interested' adults

Is directly responsible to...

The Cabinet and the Prime Minister

Advices and informs ministers on policy

Is mandated to make policy and control

The Civil Service

Administers and implements policy decided by the elected side of the machine

Controls

Is responsible to the House of Commons through individual ministers

The 'dignified' House of Commons

The 'dignified' House of Lords

The 'dignified' constitutional monarch

Parliament

Figure 1.2 The Liberal-Democratic Constitution of Cabinet, or Prime Ministerial Government within a Parliamentary Democracy

Minister and the Cabinet are now seen as very much in control of the Commons and so are able to ensure that their legislative programme gets turned into law with the minimum of parliamentary fuss. The convention of collective responsibility (so central to the essence of the liberal constitution), whilst continuing to be of importance as a device for disciplining individual ministers who cannot publicly agree with the policy of the Cabinet as a whole, inevitably gets drained of much of its significance in this situation. The crushing reality of party discipline has meant that Cabinets are no longer defeated on the floor of the House of Commons and so are no longer collectively responsible to the Commons for government policy.

In the liberal perspective on the constitution, the Commons was at the very centre of things and assumed a position of power and 'efficiency'. But in the liberal-democratic accounts, the Commons gets reduced to being the dignified rubber stamp of decisions made by the efficient and all-powerful executive of Prime Minister and Cabinet. If the liberal accounts saw the Cabinet as chosen by the Commons, then the liberal-democratic accounts see the Cabinet as chosen by, and directly responsible to, the electorate itself because general elections are regarded as occasions when the electorate votes, not for individual MPs, but for a party, a programme and for a party leader to form a government. The Commons has come to assume no mediating role of any significance in the liberal-democratic process of Cabinet formation – it is simply there to register the popular will in terms of the number of seats held by particular political parties.

Within liberal-democratic constitutional theory, the people are seen as having the ultimate political power – as being politically sovereign – and they exercise their power through regular general elections that assume a place of massive constitutional significance. Liberal theories focussed on the almost free-floating power of the Commons, whereas the liberal-democratic accounts bypass the Commons in order to place a twin emphasis on the government (the Cabinet and the Prime Minister) and the people in special relationship each with the other. The constitutional authorities see a transmission of orders from the people to the controlling few in the government whereby votes inserted at one end of the political system become popular public policies and laws at the other. An electoral chain of command pushes demands *up* so that the people get the policies and laws they want at the same time as those in authority are responsible *down* to the people through a general election. In an upward direction, the people choose the government and the government is mandated to carry out the policies on which it fought the election and is able to do so because it controls the Commons and the Civil Service. In a downward direction, the government is responsible to the people through a general election and the Civil Service is held responsible to the Commons through the convention of individual ministerial responsibility which is supposed to keep the permanent side of the state machine on its toes. From the liberal-democratic perspective on British politics (notwithstanding the role which is given to the Commons in the context of the convention about individual ministerial responsibility), everything tends to flow to and from the Cabinet and the Prime Minister. It is they who govern, but in the last analysis we are seen as enjoying a system within which the people have the right to choose the government and practically determine the politics which it will put into effect.

Liberal-democratic constitutional theory when shorn of legal jargon is quite simple: the British constitution provides for a system of Cabinet or prime ministerial government within a parliamentary democracy in which Parliament is legally sovereign and the people are politically sovereign.

Conclusion

In this chapter we have pointed to the importance of the British constitution and to the importance of constitutional theory. We claim that no one who is seriously interested in making sense of British politics can sensibly dodge the study of the constitution because it is both a force acting *on* politics at the same time as it is a force *in* politics. And since constitutional theory is *about* politics, it provides us with an explanatory perspective on the British system of rule and deals with the location of political authority within the state. Having said all that, we have nevertheless rejected the explanatory utility of the dominant constitutional approach to understanding the British constitution and we have also pointed to the limitations of a constitutional law perspective. The constitution needs to be studied, but it needs to be studied historically, politically and critically. We ourselves, in looking at the British constitutions from the eighteenth century onwards, were mindful of the need to explore possible tensions between constitutional theory and political practice because this could be a signal that constitutional change was on the way. We also highlighted the limitations of established constitutional theories making good sense of political practice. In situations where political practice is not contained within the established constitutional shell we cannot possibly expect the established constitutional theory to be of use in making sense of that practice.

In concrete terms, we explored the tension between theory and practice with respect to the 'balanced' constitution and the liberal constitution, and we also showed how those constitutional theories were overtaken by political events so that they could no longer make good sense of the changing practice of politics itself. But what can we say about liberal-democratic constitutional theory? So far we have only described the essentials of the theory. If we are to hold good to our commitment to advance a historical, political and critical understanding of constitutional matters then we need to posit four questions for which we provide brief answers because many of these matters will be picked up more fully in later chapters.

Is liberal-democratic constitutional theory still the established
theory of the contemporary constitution?

The theory advanced by Dicey 'still occupies the high ground of British constitutional theory' and so Harden and Lewis are correct when they go on
to state that 'Dicey's terms of debate still constitute the ruling paradigm:
they are the point of departure, the standard against which to judge constitutional propriety.' There is no alternative perspective on the British constitution that commands more respect or is more authoritative and so
Dicey's elegant simplification has an enduring influence even though it has
been attacked; looks threadbare; and there is a crisis with respect to its continued credibility. The liberal-democratic constitution described by Dicey
a hundred years ago still remains in uneasy existence.

Is there a tension between liberal-democratic theory and the practice of contemporary British politics?

Since the late 1960s it has become very clear that a tension exists between
constitutional theory and political practice. A 'gap' was seen to have opened
up between the favourable tone of the established theory and what were
increasingly defined as the horrors of the day-to-day political practice of
political parties and interest groups. In the 1950s both parties and groups
were seen as supportive of liberal democracy. By the 1970s, however, party
and interest-group practice came to be seen as at odds with liberal-
democratic theory and so the practice was condemned by many of those
who were our experts on the constitution. We will provide a fuller account
of all this in chapters 2 and 4 when we assess different perspectives on
the parts which political parties and interest groups play in British
politics.

Does liberal-democratic constitutional theory 'fail' to explain
British politics today?

Politics is never wholly contained within the shell of a constitution and so
explaining the politics of any country is always going to involve more than
simply attending to the perspectives advanced by constitutional theorists.
In the British context, the fact that we have no written constitution makes
for additional explanatory uncertainty and the fact that political practice
is increasingly bursting out of the established constitutional shell is bound
to mean that a theoretical perspective geared to the constitution alone will
be of only limited utility in enabling us to make sense of the full richness
of British politics. If constitutional theory was *all* we needed in order to
make sense of British politics then we would not need to attend to the
theories that we will be discussing and assessing in many of the other

chapters in this book. But, equally, if those theories were adequate on their own then there would have been no need for this chapter and yet we have already made clear why we see a knowledge of the constitution and constitutional theory as of importance for an understanding of British politics.

Is the established constitution in crisis and is a 'new' constitution a political possibility?

In chapter 5 we will argue that the constitution is in crisis and we will be exploring the prospects for a new constitutional settlement. We give little away at this point if we say that the future development of the British constitution depends on the play of political forces, as all constitutions are ultimately political constitutions that are *in* politics as much as they bear down *on* politics.

Appendix I: Harold Laski on the Constitution

For much of the nineteenth century many politicians and most businessmen were fearful about the democratisation of the British constitution because they felt this would eat into the rights of property and destroy the prospects for business. These fears were matched by those who hoped that democracy *would* lead to a more equal society. The fact that the introduction of a kind of democracy did not overturn the economic order dashed the fears and hopes of those who had taken sides on the issue of democracy. Liberal-democratic constitutional theory emerged to celebrate the unlikely combination of a democratic polity working within a capitalist economy. In the twentieth century, the dominat tradition of constitutional scholarship has forgotten about the nineteenth-century insights that saw democracy and capitalism as in tension, and so students of the constitution have been content to work within the confines of liberal-democratic theory and have made no attempt to visualise democracy within the context of the capitalist system. This failure to attend to the economic dimension of the British constitution has been one of the major limitations of the established perspective on the constitution. Harold Laski recognised this, and his study of *Parliamentary Government in England* has provided us with an 'economic interpretation' of the British constitution.

Laski was on the left of British politics and an active member of the Labour Party. He argued that Britain was a class-divided society; he was alive to the 'contradiction between our economic power and our political power . . . a contradiction between our political democracy and the hierarchical character of our social system'; and he recognised the need to explore the constitution beyond Parliament and behind appearances because 'it is vital to realise that all the pivotal positions in the judiciary, the civil service, the defence forces, the police, are occupied by members of the governing class'. At the most fundamental level, Laski was of the opinion that 'a political democracy which rests upon capitalist foundations has war, open or secret, in its midst' because 'a political democracy seeks, by its own inner impulses, to become a social and economic democracy. It finds the road thereto barred by the capitalist foundations upon which the political democracy is built. The validity of those foundations therefore becomes the central issue in politics.' Laski dealt with the *conditions* that he saw as necessary for the success of parliamentary democracy and so did not trouble himself overmuch with a detailed *description* of the principal institutional features of the British constitution. He saw democracy as a fragile flower and he felt it could only survive if there were tolerance; if all classes were included in the exercise of political power; and if there was a fundamental unity on the part of the people – a unity which Laski felt was contingent upon economic success. He was led to wonder 'whether the uneasy marriage between capitalism and democracy is psychologically possible in the period of capitalism's decline' when the 'better classes' no longer felt able to concede.

In the 1970s, nineteenth-century fears about the dangers of democracy were revived as those on the right of British politics blamed the economic decline of Britain onto the excesses of democratic politics. Constitutional reforms were called for to limit democracy and so ensure a better fit between the polity and the 'needs' of the economy. We will be exploring these reforms in chapter 5, but for the moment it is sufficient to note that the concerns of the 1970s surely highlight the relevance of Laski's observation that there exists an 'uneasy marriage between capitalism and democracy' and we can perhaps better appreciate the need to break out of the established perspective on the British constitution in order to gain an understanding of the constitution in the larger context of the British economy.

Appendix II: Disputes *within* Liberal-democratic Constitutional Theory: Cabinet Government or Prime Ministerial Power?

Our sketch of the established liberal-democratic constitutional theory in the body of this chapter was deliberately painted with a broad brush because we were concerned to capture the agreement on fundamentals that has united the views of the experts on the constitution. Honesty forces us to admit that such a sketch is partial: it did not reveal the disputes that have existed *within* the liberal-democratic perspective on the British constitution. Scholars have debated such matters as the role of the monarchy; the position of the House of Lords and the House of Commons and the nature of parliamentary sovereignty; the precise status of constitutional conventions (including those to do with individual and collective responsibility); the reality of the rule of law; the role of the Civil Service and the relationship between civil servants and ministers; and the extent to which prime ministerial power has – or has not – swept aside the reality of Cabinet government. We will be dealing with many of these disputes in chapter 5 and we will explore the relationship between ministers and civil servants in chapter 6, but we will attend to the dispute as to whether we have Cabinet government or prime ministerial power in this appendix.

In the period of parliamentary government in the liberal constitution between 1832 and 1867, a variety of factors served to mean that there was a delicate balance between the Commons and the Cabinet – between the legislature and the executive – so that each could be said to enjoy a measure of state power. With the coming of the liberal-democratic constitution after 1867, the rising power of party changed the relationship between the Commons and the Cabinet: the power of the Cabinet increased and the Commons came to be seen as but a dignified part of the constitution. In this system of Cabinet government, the Prime Minister was regarded as *primus inter pares*, as first among equals, and as just the leading member of the Cabinet. In the period since the Second World War, it has been argued that the power of the Prime Minister has increased to such an extent that it makes sense to see the Cabinet as yet another dignified part of the constitution and to talk of prime ministerial government. This argument about prime ministerial power has taken on a new lease of life since Margaret Thatcher moved in to 10 Downing Street. But what exactly are the powers of the Prime Minister and how cogent is the thesis about prime ministerial government?

The powers of the Prime Minister

Power over the party

The Prime Minister is leader of the majority party in the Commons and Margaret Thatcher presided over a party machine outside of Parliament that had become increasingly centralised under her control. Parties want success in politics and will give loyal support to a Prime Minister who looks well-placed to lead them to victory in the next general election. The fact that a Prime Minister is in a position to make over 100 ministerial appointments gives him or her an enormous 'hold' over party colleagues in the Commons who are keen to make a political career for themselves at a ministerial level.

Power over Parliament

Parliament makes laws and consists of the Commons, the Lords and the Monarch, even though the Commons is recognised as the pre-eminent part of Parliament. In a situation in which party organises the Commons the Prime Minister's power over the party also gives him or her power over Parliament. Since a Prime Minister without a majority in the Commons is an impossibility, he or she is seen as in a position to make any law he or she sees fit.

Power over the people

The mass media simplifies and personalises politics and so places any Prime Minister in the public eye as a prominent national leader. The fact that Margaret Thatcher was Prime Minister for more than a decade made her seem as if she was *the* government. Margaret Thatcher, her press officer and the Conservative Party's advertising agents, all showed themselves to be uniquely skilled in managing the media to her advantage. Moreover, she adopted a high-profile and populist style of leadership and was able to enhance her position as a national leader through her capacity to present herself as a world leader consequent upon her attendance at summit meetings with various other heads of state.

Power over the Civil Service

As government has expanded so has there been an increasing need to co-ordinate the administrative side of the state machine and the Prime Minister is best placed to do this as he or she is at the centre of things and is free of day-to-day departmental responsibilities. The Prime Minister has the power to instruct the Civil Sercice on the conduct of business; key civil servants look to the Prime Minister in order to gain a sense of where their departments should be going; and the Prime Minister is able to decide which civil servants will hold the most senior positions. Margaret Thatcher took a particular interest in the Civil Service, its size, its management and its overall efficiency, and she attempted to assert a more effective political control in order that it could better serve as a tool to implement her goals. She abolished the Civil Service Department (the department responsible for the central management of the Civil Service) and had its functions transferred to the Cabinet Office; and she appointed Derek (later Lord) Rayner of Marks & Spencer to the Cabinet Office and his Efficiency Unit set in motion a whole series of scrutinies that were geared to securing a smaller, more 'efficient', Civil Service. Moreover, the Prime Minister's formidable appointing powers were extended as promotion to senior positions increasingly came to depend on whether Margaret Thatcher judged the candidate to be 'one of us'.

Power over the Cabinet

The Prime Minister appoints ministers to the Cabinet, and can dismiss them and promote them. The Prime Minister chairs the Cabinet and has control over the machinery of the Cabinet; determines the agenda of the Cabinet; decides how issues will be dealt with at Cabinet and can announce the decision of a Cabinet without troubling to take a vote. A variety of factors have encouraged Prime Ministers to bypass the Cabinet altogether in favour of informal talks with individual ministers; a keen reliance upon an inner-cabinet, or kitchen cabinet, of particularly trusted and sympathetic colleagues; and the extensive use of a whole network of well over 100 Cabinet committees whose existence, composition and chairmanship are the responsibility of the Prime Minister. The growth of Cabinet committees has been one of the most significant constitutional developments of this century as they have undoubtedly served to weaken the collective role of the Cabinet itself even though they have been kept secret from the public. The Prime Minister is at the centre of this complex executive territory and at the very heart of the whole business of government. Under Margaret Thatcher, the Cabinet met less frequently; discussed fewer formal papers; and was presented with more *faits accomplis*, and all because the Cabinet probably felt constrained to go along with her view that they 'could not waste time having any internal arguments'.

Power over ministerial conduct

In addition to powers of appointment, dismissal and promotion, all new Prime Ministers issue a personal minute of procedure for ministers which lays down a whole range of requirements for behaviour. The Prime Minister can determine the responsibilities of a particular minister, and can take over particular ministerial responsibilities either informally or by adding them formally to his or her own responsibilities.

Other powers of patronage

In addition to prime ministerial patronage with respect to ministers and civil servants, the Prime Minister is in a position to create peers, dispense honours, appoint ambassadors, chiefs of staff and the heads of the security services, and has a key role with respect to top jobs outside of Whitehall, be they in the nationalised industries, the BBC, or the NHS.

Power to decide the date of a general election

The Prime Minister enjoys this power because it falls to him or her to ask the Monarch for a dissolution of Parliament. There is the suggestion that this power might serve to keep both the party in Parliament and the Cabinet in line since those in seats that are less than safe might be reluctant to face the country at a general election.

Prime ministerial government?

Critics of the prime ministerial government thesis do not deny that the powers of Prime Ministers have increased over the years, and they are not unmindful of the impact of Margaret Thatcher, but they do suggest that the thesis exaggerates the true position.

1 The thesis fails to recognise that the factors which contribute to prime

ministerial power can also serve to weaken it if circumstances change. For example, the Prime Minister has power over the party, but the party expects things of him or her if support is to be retained, and Prime Ministers have been dumped if they get to be seen as an electoral liability; the Prime Minister has power over Parliament, but just as his or her party in the Commons may cause trouble so the Lords can be a thorn in the side and it is difficult to get a precise measure as to the impact of the Monarchy; the Prime Minister has power over the people, but exposure brings vulnerability and danger if things go wrong and is no guarantee of popularity; the Prime Minister has power to appoint top civil servants but this may be resented and resisted as at odds with the tradition of a non-political service; and the Prime Minister has power to appoint, dismiss and promote ministers to the Cabinet but can hardly do this at will as senior ministers have their own political standing. Moreover, the Prime Minister needs allies, is dependent on the support of colleagues at the same time as he or she is constrained to 'bring on' younger members and has to give positions to leaders of factions within the party in the hope of softening their opposition.

2 The prime ministerial power thesis tends to suck the Prime Minister out of the larger institutional context within which he or she operates and so suggests that he or she can run the government and determine policy single-handed, without the help and support of others – and hence without the constraints that inevitably come with such help and support. The Prime Minister does not even have his or her own Prime Minister's Department. It is true that Margaret Thatcher increased the size of her personal staff, but it is still relatively small at between 70 and 80 people and most of these are caught up in dealing with the party and the press rather than with Whitehall and public policy matters.

3 The prime ministerial power thesis is naive in the way in which it chooses to think about power. It tends to see power in personal and zero-sum terms as something which the Prime Minister 'has' and which others, such as the Cabinet, do not have – or have very much less of. Such a perspective fails to recognise that power is a *relational* concept that is only meaningful if we also attend to followers, and it also fails to recognise that much of what is of importance when we attend to power and authority cannot easily be observed if we only choose to attend to action, dissent and conflict. For example, the fact that the majority party in the Commons invariably follows the lead of the Prime Minister and supports his or her government's policies does not 'prove' that the party is docile and powerless. Support may have been won by the leader being in tune with the party's conception as to the proper direction of government policy and by the leader *anticipating* their reactions to *possible* policies so that he or she 'chooses' to write certain policies off the governmental agenda rather than risk their rejection. And if the party has an impact in this way, then so may the public, as evidenced by the fact that Margaret Thatcher was 'forced' to say that the National Health Service was safe in her hands just before the 1987 general election in spite of her own views as to the most appropriate way of delivering health care.

The 'Thatcher effect'

It has to be recognised that Margaret Thatcher was a 'conviction' politician with a clear sense as to where she wished to lead the country. In the absence of a powerful counter-ideology to that of 'Thatcherism' – in the absence, that is, of a visionary basis for opposition – she was able to lead from the front and assert a highly personal power over the country, the Civil Service and the Cabinet, making a political virtue out of her stubbornness and preparedness to 'go it alone' against opponents and supporters. She was not afraid to sack popular ministers and she was often able to use some of the conventions of Cabinet government to enhance her own political power. For example, there is little doubt that the *disciplinary* side of the doctrine of collective responsibility that constrains ministers to go along with the policy of the Cabinet (or the Prime Minister?) was strengthened under her premiership and many ministers were forced to 'resign'. However, the *consultative* side of the doctrine which contains the idea that cabinets collectively formulate policy in a way that serves to constrain a Prime Minister was probably weakened under Margaret Thatcher as Cabinets came to be less involved in the collective determination of government policy consequent upon the rising importance of Cabinet committees, *ad hoc* ministerial groupings, and the various executive offices surrounding the Prime Minister herself. We had in Margaret Thatcher a high-profile Prime Minister who gave a new twist to the argument that we have prime ministerial government and the demise of the Cabinet. But, for all that, it is unlikely that the change of prime ministerial style carried with it quite as large a change of substance and we should not forget that Thatcher was pushed from office precisely because she often chose to do it her way without Cabinet support – the office of Prime Minister *was* more powerful under Margaret Thatcher, but her fall from power reveals that the Cabinet still has the power to bite back.

Conclusion

As in so many of the debates on the nature and location of power in Britain it is not possible to come to a firm and lasting conclusion as to the 'reality' of prime ministerial power when compared to the position of Cabinet government. Margaret Thatcher boosted the prime ministerial power thesis, but it is important to remind ourselves that the whole debate is on a very narrow terrain since it is only concerned with *executive* power *within* the state and on the *democratic* (or elected) side of the state at that. This debate as to the powers of Cabinets and Prime Ministers has occurred within the confines of agreement about the importance of the liberal-democratic constitution and the institutions of the state. In consequence, the economic and social context of politics and the constraints which this imposes on Cabinets *and* Prime Ministers alike has fallen outside of the framework of discussion even though we ourselves will be taking these matters on board in subsequent chapters.

Works Cited and Guide to Further Reading

Bagehot, W. (1963) *The English Constitution*, edited and with an introduction by R. H. S. Crossman, London, Fontana.
The classic account of the liberal constitution in the period 1832 to 1867. Of more than historical interest because his distinction between the 'dignified' and the 'efficient' parts of the constitution forces us to attend to the realities of rule and legitimation, and Bagehot's unease about democratic government finds an echo in New Right writings on the constitution over a 100 years later.

Benn, T. (1982) 'The case for a constitutional premiership'. In C. Mullin (ed.), *Arguments for Democracy*, Harmondsworth, Penguin.
A statement as to the immense powers of contemporary Prime Ministers and a powerful case for their being limited.

Blackstone, Sir W. (1809) *Commentaries Upon the Laws of England*, 15th edn, 4 vols, London, T. Cadell and W. Davies.
Includes the classic account of the balanced constitution of the eighteenth century.

Bogdanor, V. (ed.) (1988) *Constitutions in Democratic Politics*, Aldershot, Gower.
All the essays highlight the political importance of constitutions. Bogdanor argues that 'the study of constitutions cannot be divorced either from history or from politics' and his essay on the British constitution recognises that the constitution is now an issue *in* politics.

Brock, M. (1973) *The Great Reform Act*, London, Hutchinson.
Useful account of the factors leading up to the passage of the Reform Act, 1832 which gave more people the vote and gave seats in the House of Commons to expanding towns at the same time as constituencies with few inhabitants lost their right to representation.

Crossman, R. H. S., Introduction to Bagehot, *The English Constitution*.
Lively discussion of Bagehot and his ideas. Crossman argues that 'the post war epoch has seen the final transformation of Cabinet Government into Prime Ministerial Government'.

Dicey, A. V. (1885) *Introduction to the Study of the Law of the Constitution*, London, Macmillan.
The classic account of the liberal-democratic constitution from 1867 till today. Still in print; still widely used in courses on constitutional law; and still *the* book on the British constitution.

Dicey, A. V. (1914) *Law and Public Opinion in England During the Nineteenth Century*, 2nd edn, London, Macmillan.
Deals with the close connection between the laws passed by Parliament and public opinion. By the time the second edition was published Dicey's commitment to individualism and liberty led him to regard democracy and collectivism (or socialism) as grave threats to the country.

Griffith, J. A. G. (1979) 'The political constitution', *Modern Law Review*, 42, 1–21.
Perspective on the contemporary constitution which sees it simply as the overall set-up shaped by the shifting fortunes of power.

Hanham, H. J. (ed.) (1969) *The Nineteenth Century Constitution 1815–1914*, Cambridge, Cambridge University Press.
Full account, but not very 'political' or critical.

Harden, I. and Lewis, N. (1986) *The Noble Lie: The British Constitution and the Rule of Law*, London, Hutchinson.
They recognise that Dicey 'still occupies the high ground of British constitutional theory' but they try to knock him off his perch. They see a gap between constitutional theory and political practice and argue that major reforms are needed if the rule of law is to be the guiding spirit of the British constitution today.

Hennessy, P. (1986) *Cabinet*, Oxford, Blackwell.
Not deep, but stuffed with the views of insiders and geared to the contemporary scene. Hennessy argues that Margaret Thatcher has 'subjected the conventions of Cabinet government to their greatest hammering since David Lloyd George refashioned the Cabinet system at the height of the First World War'.

Himmelfarb, G. (1966) 'The politics of democracy: the English Reform Act of 1867', *Journal of British Studies*, 6 97–138.
Discusses the background leading up to the enfranchisement of the male working class and the implications of that development. Sees the Act as of decisive significance in British politics.

Jennings, Sir I. (1941) *The British Constitution*, 4th edn, Cambridge, Cambridge University Press.
Schoolkids book on the constitution. All the liberal-democratic myths are there, lovingly laid out for the uncritical reader to see as the reality of British politics.

Jones, G. W. (1965) 'The prime minister's powers', *Parliamentary Affairs*, 18, 167–85.
Puts the case against the prime ministerial government thesis.

Jones, G. W. (1985) 'Cabinet government and Mrs Thatcher', *Contemporary Record*, 1, 3, 8–12.
Continues to assert the power of Cabinet; rejects the view that Mrs Thatcher is a presidential figure and asserts that she has not supplanted the reality of Cabinet government.

Laski, H. J. (1938) *Parliamentary Government in England: A Commentary*, London. George Allen and Unwin.
Knocks constitutional orthodoxies and nudges towards a Marxist perspective on politics as concerned to see the British constitution, parliamentary government and 'the operation of democracy in the framework of the capitalist system'.

Mackintosh, J. P. (1977) *The British Cabinet*, 3rd edn, London, Stevens and Sons.
Full account of the development of the Cabinet. Argues that Cabinet government existed from the 1830s to the 1870s but, following a period of transition, sees a form of prime ministerial government assuming a fairly definite pattern from the late 1930s.

Madgwick, P. (1986) 'Prime ministerial power revisted', *Social Studies Review*, 1, 5, 28–35.
Takes on board recent developments that have been part and parcel of the Thatcher era and concludes that 'there has been a shift away from Cabinet power and towards prime ministerial power'.

Marshall, G. (1971) *Constitutional Theory*, Oxford, Clarendon.
Marshall, G. (1984) *Constitutional Conventions*, Oxford, Clarendon.
A political scientist who has followed in the footsteps of Dicey and kept the study of the constitution at the forefront of his work. If you want to dig deeper into the British constitution then you will need to read these two books even though you will probably find them pretty heavy going and possibly uninspiring.

Mill, J.S. (1861) *Considerations on Representative Government*, London, Everyman's Library, 1964.
The classic liberal case for representative government, but tinged by Mill's fear of popular participation and a working-class franchise.

Rees, J.C. (1977) 'Interpreting the constitution'. In P. King (ed.), *The Study of Politics*, London, Cass.
A delightful essay that critically assesses the interpretations of the constitution offered by Sir Ivor Jennings, Sir Ernest Barker, Leo Amery and Harold Laski.

Wass, D. (1984) *Government and the Governed*, London, Routledge and Kegan Paul.
Retired top civil servant argues that the British system of government is neither efficient nor responsive and so challenges many of the constitutional orthodoxies developed by Dicey and set out in the standard government textbooks.

Chapter 2

Perspectives on the Party System

The democratic process ensures that there will be a periodic opportunity for the electorate to review the record of the decision-makers who currently hold office; and, if the electorate wishes, it may replace them with an alternative team. The competing teams usually offer broad declarations of policy . . .
R. T. McKenzie (1963) *British Political Parties*, 2nd edn, London,
Heinemann, p. 646.

I concluded that since 1964 or thereabouts this party system, which I along with countless others had been accustomed to applaud, had become positively dysfunctional *to the British system of government.*
S. E. Finer (1980) *The Changing British Party System, 1945–1979*,
Washington, DC, American Enterprise Institute, p. xiii.

Under the present electoral system the most likely outcome of the continued fragmentation of the opposition to Conservatism is Conservative domination of British politics for a long period.
A. M. Gamble and S. A. Walkland (1984) *The British Party System and Economic Policy, 1945–1983*, Oxford, Clarendon Press, p. 182.

Introduction

In the period after the Second World War, British political science slowly came into its own as a discipline distinct from the study of constitutional law or philosophy. Political scientists who were in the intellectual vanguard chose to pay less attention to the constitution and to constitutional theory, and there was a growing consensus that the constitutional approach blocked an adequate understanding of the reality of British politics. There was the call for a more scientific and empirical approach to the study of British politics that would develop positive theories to explain matters. These theories would only be developed if political scientists dug beneath and beyond the institutions of the state and the boring formalities of the constitution and out into the harder practice of informal politics, political behaviour and the process of public policy-making itself.

CONSERVATIVE

Liberal
Democrats

''The parties of today but are there rivals waiting in the wings?'' (Reproduced by kind permission of The Labour Party, The Conservative Party and The Social and Liberal Democrats.)

Central to much of this new wave of work was the increased attention that was paid to political parties and interest groups. New theories that focused on parties and groups were advanced to explain (and praise) British politics, although these theories have since been countered by rival perspectives that have doubted the extent to which parties and pressures have enhanced the quality of democracy in Britain. In the next chapter we will try to explain voting behaviour because we recognise that the changing nature of the British party system is partly determined by the choices made by voters at the polls; in chapter 4 we will look at different perspectives on the part played by interest groups within the British system of rule; but in this chapter we will be exploring different perspectives on the nature of the British party system – perspectives which have been in conflict each with the other at the same time as they have tried to grapple with real changes with respect to the party system itself.

1 For much of the period since the Second World War, mainstream political science praised the part played by political parties as enhancing of democracy in Britain. The theory of responsible party government was developed and it has been the dominant theory of party politics, and almost of British politics itself. This theory constitutes the political science equivalent of the Westminster Model beloved of constitutional theorists. Most of the rival perspectives on party politics in Britain are a critical reaction to this theory.

2 In the late 1960s, and in response to the 'failures' of the Labour Party in government, a Left and Marxist perspective on British politics came to the fore which, among other things, criticised the reality of the responsible party government model on the grounds that the two parties did not offer a real choice to the electorate and that Labour did not actually implement its socialist programme.

3 Up to the 1960s, the political science of British politics had very little to say about women, but the entry of women into the discipline encouraged the development of a feminism that challenged the sexist 'malestream' within the discipline at the same time as it provided us with a critical perspective on the representative quality of party politics in Britain. Similar criticisms of the party system could be made from the point of view of a black perspective on that system.

4 During the 1970s, the resurgence of electoral support for the Liberal Party and the nationalist parties bruised the responsible party government model precisely because that model had always been anchored around there being just two parties, the party in government and the party in opposition. The heightened development of centre party support in the 1980s gave further sustenance to the view that we had ceased to enjoy responsible party politics. 'Realistic' political scientists suggested that the British were being forced to endure a system of adversary party politics, and they called for electoral reform to enhance the representation of third parties.

5 When Labour was in office in the 1970s, the New Right also picked up on the problem of adversary party politics and electoral reform but all this was rather set aside once a radical Conservative government was elected in 1979. Having said that, the New Right is not without a perspective on the party

system because Public Choice theory is critical of democratic party politics, arguing that it encourages politicians to 'bid' for popular support and to engineer political business cycles in ways that are seen as detrimental to the long-term health of the British economy.

Responsible Party Government

The theory

Political parties have often been attacked as bad things for the health of a polity because they are said to encourage division at the same time as they restrict free debate. In the 1950s, however, a particular *kind* of party system came to be regarded as utterly indispensable for the democratic control of government and that kind of party system was seen as best established within British political practice. What, then, were seen as the essential elements of the British party model, and how do these elements pull together so as to make for responsible party government and the popular control of public policy?

1 A *two-party system* with free and fair regular elections.

2 *One party forms the government*. The other party forms the opposition; criticises the government in Parliament and the country; keeps its ear to the ground of public opinion; and stands ready to form the government should it win the next election.

3 *The parties are in close competition* each with the other. Neither party can expect to be in permanent government or permanent opposition in a situation in which each party is able to 'swing' in and out of office over time. This close competition is seen as important for the health of a democracy. First, it keeps the governing party on its toes and sensitive to the public's views as to appropriate policies. Second, it means that the opposition party will be prepared to play by the established, rules of the party political competition, confident that its time will come to form a government, and so it will not have to resort to unconstitutional methods to secure office. Third, it serves to ensure moderation and contain political conflict to manageable proportions. Finally, it also helps to sustain the legitimacy of the system of rule so enabling law to be enforced with minimal levels of policing and force.

4 Parties compete for the support of the electorate, that is they aim to win an election and become the governing party, on the basis of *programmes of policies*, or manifestoes, that are set before the electorate. In effect, the parties organise and simplify the policy alternatives into policy packages that give the voters a meaningful and effective choice, so ensuring that the electorate is consulted at general elections with regard to fundamental legislative changes.

5 The fact of close electoral competition, and the crucial role of party programmes in that competition, means that the two parties try to draw up *popular programmes* of policies that will appeal to, and secure the electoral support of, a majority of the voters.

6 *Individual voters give the parties 'programmatic' support*. Put another

way, voters are seen as rational, informed and self-interested, and so they will vote for the party which has the policy programme that best advances their own individual interests, although any assessment of programmes will be tempered by the voters also attending to the records of the parties when they have been in office.

7 The party which wins a majority of seats in the House of Commons then forms the government and has a *mandate* to put its programme of policies into legislative effect.

8 Each party is a cohesive team under a strong leader where there is sufficient *party discipline* to ensure that once a party is in office it is in a good position to push its programme of policies through the House of Commons, onto the statute book and into effect in the country at large. There is no room for maverick and independently-minded Members of Parliament within this theory. MPs are in the House of Commons because they have stood in the name of a party; they owe the party everything; and so they are best seen as collectively responsible to the electorate as part of their party team in a way which should preclude their exercising individual judgement and voting according to their own views on a policy.

If a party system is in accord with these eight points then it is argued that parties serve as the crucial mechanism linking the people through to the kind of popular public policies which the majority wish to see passed into law. So, where there are two parties each putting forward programmes which they are pledged to carry out if elected to government, and which they are able to carry out because they are disciplined organisations, then the electorate in choosing a programme (and a programme at that which has been drawn up to be popular and appeal to their interests) mandates a party to carry out its programme at the same time as that party can expect to be held accountable for its implementation at the next election. If, at that election, the electorate considers that the governing party has broken the promises contained in the original party programme and failed to deliver of its mandate, or if the opposition party has since worked out more popular policies, then that electorate will vote out the established governing party and give the opposition a chance. If this kind of cycle obtains over the years, then it is argued that government will be controlled by the people so that public policy will be in line with the wishes of the majority of the electorate for most of the time.

The practice

How adequate is the responsible party government perspective on party politics in Britain? In order to form a view we have to attend to the evidence with respect to five broad areas. First, do we have a two-party system and close competition? Second, do we have single-party government? Third, do the parties actually put forward popular programmes of policies that are 'different' and offer a real choice? Fourth, do winning parties implement

their programmes once in office and, if not, is this because they are not sufficiently disciplined? Finally, do voters vote for parties on the basis of the
programmes that are put before them, or can we offer a better explanation
to make sense of voting behaviour and the nature of public support for
parties?

Is Britain a two-party system?

We need to be careful in providing a snap answer to this question.

First, we have to attend to the facts with respect to different periods in
our politics. Two-party dominance was at its greatest between 1945 and
1970 when the Conservative and Labour Parties won all but 8 per cent of
the vote and 2 per cent of the seats in the Commons, and when the competition between the parties was such that both parties were able to enjoy
periods when they could form the government as the 'floating voters' gently
shifted their support between the parties at elections. The model of responsible party government was born of this experience and it has tended to
elevate the politics of the moment into a law of nature that has distracted
attention from the more fluid aspects of Britain's political history. For
example, in the 1920's, before Labour replaced the Liberals as a viable
party of government, three parties were all getting substantial shares of the
popular vote. And again in the 1970s, the two-party model looked less than
valid and Britain took on the appearance of a multi-party state in the context of a situation where third-party candidates from territorially based
nationalist parties (Plaid Cymru and the Scottish National Party) and from
a nationally based centre-party grouping were able to secure 25 per cent of
the vote. For a time at least two-party politics and one-party government
went out of the window and for a few months in 1974 and again from 1976
to 1979 the country was ruled by a minority Labour government. The election of 1979 seemed to mark something of a return to the 'normal' two-
party model as third parties had their vote cut back to less then 20 per cent
(and they were only able to secure 27 seats), but in the elections of 1983 and
1987, third parties bounced back to secure around 30 per cent of the vote.
After the 1987 election, the demise of the SDP and the low standing of the
Liberal Democrats in the polls once again prompted pundits to see two-
party politics as the norm. Such a perspective is dangerous. First, it
minimises the volatility of the voters and the lack of secure support for the
two major parties. Second, it is inattentive to the continual undercurrent
of nationalism and to the rise of new movements that are outside of the old
mould of the capital/labour divide. For example, in the 1989 election for
the European Parliament the Green Party secured 15 per cent of the vote
and we will have to wait and see whether this is a pointer for further support
in the future.

Second, we should be mindful of the fact that the two-party dominance
of the Commons has not always reflected the pattern of electoral support in the country at large. The first-past-the-post electoral system has

frustrated 'fair' representation and made it difficult for third parties to break through into Parliament in proportion to their support in the country – the more so if they lack the kind of precise geographical base enjoyed by the nationalist parties. For example, in the 1987 election the Liberal/ SDP Alliance secured well over seven million votes (22.6 per cent of the UK total) but just 22 seats in the Commons (3.4 per cent of the total). If that election had been fought under some kind of proportional system then the Alliance would have secured 147 seats; the Conservatives would have been unable to govern alone; and some kind of coalition government would have been on the cards, almost certainly without Margaret Thatcher as the Prime Minister. In the 1989 Euro-election, the Green Party secured 15 per cent of the vote but not a single seat in the European Parliament.

In bald terms and in 1990, Britain can be characterised as a two-party system (in the Commons); as a multi-party system (in the country); and as a dominant party system (in the corridors of power) because the electoral system and multi-party politics have together enabled the Conservatives to monopolise the control of the state for more than a decade in a way that has mocked the close competition between the parties in the country at large. Not surprisingly, the centre parties, the nationalist parties and now major elements within the Labour Party, have all been pressing the case for electoral reform. We will be discussing this in chapter 5 when we deal with a variety of challenges to the established system of rule in Britain as the constitution has tumbled into some kind of slow and grinding crisis.

Does Britain have single-party government?

Since 1900, Britain has been governed by outright, formal coalitions of two or more parties for seven years between 1915 and 1922, for 1 year from 1931 to 1932, and for five years between 1940 and 1945. Between 1910 and 1914, 1930 and 1931, and 1977 and 1979 (the period of the 'Lib-Lab Pact'), the party of government lacked a majority in the House of Commons but was maintained in office by a tacit agreement with one or more of the smaller parties. From 1932 to 1940, Britain was governed by a National government which, although predominantly Conservative, was by no means wholly so. For a total of three years, in 1924, from 1929 to 1930, and from 1976 until the Lib-Lab Pact of 1977, a minority government succeeded in holding office without even a tacit agreement with another party. In other words, Britain has been ruled by a government of what is generally regarded as the 'normal' British kind – a single-party government with a clear majority in the House of Commons that is capable of getting its policies onto the statute book without open or tacit agreements with any other party, still less the need for a coalition – for roughly 60 of the 90 years of this century.

Single-party government may have been the norm for most of the period since the Second World War but it has not been the sole reality with respect to our past and we should be wary about predicting this pattern of government into the future, the more so if the electoral system is eventually changed.

Do the parties put forward programmes of policies that offer a meaningful choice?

In 1834, Peel was appointed Prime Minister. He issued the famous Tamworth Manifesto, nominally addressed to his constituents, but actually communicated to the London daily press so as to serve as a programme for the electorate as a whole. Since that time, and first fully developed by the radical wing of the Liberal Party, it has been normal for parties to fight elections on the basis of a manifesto of policy promises. Over time, the manifestoes have tended to become longer and more specific. Blondel, in his study *Political Parties: A Genuine Case for Discontent?*, claims that 'in the great majority of cases programmes are unclear, often limited in scope, and not closely connected to the goals which the party proclaims' and he goes so far as to assert that 'on balance parties do not really have programmes'. This certainly overstates the situation as in the context of universal suffrage parties have little choice but to compete for support through general programmes of policies. They are in no position to bribe individual voters with beer at the same time as the secret ballot has restricted the scope for candidates intimidating 'their' voters (their tenants or workers) at the polls. Having said that, party leaders like to keep as free a policy hand as is possible and so they will try to attack opponents and invoke positive symbols in preference to dealing with the specifics of what they would do if elected to office even though convention and necessity ultimately force them to state where they stand on many of the major issues of the day.

It is one thing for the parties to put programmes before the electorate, it is another matter as to whether those programmes offer a choice, but if a choice is not made available to the electorate then it could be argued that this restricts the extent to which the people can somehow choose to determine the course of government action for the next five years. Left academics have consistently held to the view that the electorate has no 'real' choice at the polls. They lament the fact that a proper socialist alternative has never been offered by the Labour Party, claiming that the leadership has somehow 'sold-out' on the membership and the voters because of a limp concern to manage capitalism better when they 'should' have been campaigning to abolish the capitalist system itself. Notwithstanding this assessment, most Left academics and activists have chosen to vote Labour (excusing this by saying that they do so 'without illusions') perhaps signalling by their actions that they do see some kind of meaningful choice at the polls. In fact, the extent of choice at the polls is not a settled given and it is important to divide the post-war period into four distinct periods:

1 The 1945 election would be regarded as some kind of high point in terms of the choice offered: Labour was out to create a new socialist Britain

whilst the Conservatives were still rooted in the Old Toryism of empire and unregulated capitalism.

2 The twenty years from the early fifties was the period of 'consensus politics' and limited electoral choice: programmes differed little between elections and the parties themselves were agreed as to the need for a welfare state and a mixed, but managed, economy that would gently soften the rough edges of capitalism. The Labour Party, under the leadership of Hugh Gaitskell, was dominated by a 'revisionism that edged away from socialism and dropped a commitment to the nationalisation of private industry. The Conservative Party, under the intellectual leadership of R. A. Butler, came to terms with the changes wrought by Labour during 1945–51 and adjusted to the new mood in the country so that it grudged towards state intervention in support of some kind of equality. This, then, was the age of 'Butskellism' – the age of political consensus based upon a certain kind of social and economic stability.

3 The political turbulence of the seventies, born of economic failure and increasing unemployment, destroyed consensus and brought 'conviction politics' and real choice back to the fore with a vengeance. The Conservatives rediscovered old roots in their opposition to state intervention and in their commitment to the market and to freedom; Labour swung to the Left and rediscovered socialism; the specifics of nationalist sentiment ebbed and flowed in unpredictable ways; and although the Liberal/SDP Alliance tried to recreate the kind of moderate consensus politics and policies that had characterised the fifties they failed to break the mould.

4 In the late eighties, after the Conservatives had won three elections in a row, the rival parties were forced to come to terms with the Thatcher revolution since the Conservatives were making all the political and intellectual running. As a new mood of 'realism' gripped a Labour Party that was hungry for electoral success; as the Conservatives trimmed policies (in a way that disappointed their New Right radicals); and as the centre parties continued to muddle away over policies, so a new and uneasy kind of right-of-centre consensus politics came to the fore. This consensus has taken on board crucial elements of New Right thinking, but the thrust has been tempered by the Green agenda and by the recognition that the state has some kind of role to play, albeit one that is far removed from anything remotely akin to 'old-fashioned' socialism and planning. Once again, the electorate seems to be in a position where it is left without a 'real' choice at the polls. However, if this is what the electorate truly wants then perhaps there is sufficient choice within the system for it to be called 'responsible', the more so if we can also argue that the electorate is able to help make the issues, shape the agenda of politics and so have an input into the party programmes themselves.

Do winning parties implement their programmes and deliver of their mandate once in office?

Many important policies have been introduced without their ever having been set before the electorate for their approval. This was the case with respect to the repeal of the Corn Laws in 1846; the passing of the Trades Disputes Act in 1927; the departure from the Gold Standard in 1931; the decision to opt for a nuclear defence policy after the Second World War; the decision to apply for entry into Europe in 1961; the passage of the Commonwealth Immigration Act in 1968; the privatisation programme of the Thatcher governments in the 1980s; as well as a whole host of defence and foreign policy matters over the years. More than this, the very stuff of electoral competition and the media coverage of our politics revolves around the issue of 'U turns' and 'broken promises', with politicians confessing (but excusing and explaining) the gap between election promise and ruling performance – programme and policy – with talk about being 'blown off course' by circumstances, accidents and the pressure of unanticipated world events beyond their effective grasp and control.

In concrete terms, the 1970 Conservative manifesto stated: 'we will stop further nationalisation', but this did *not* stop the Conservative government nationalising Rolls-Royce just eight months into office. That manifesto also stated: 'we utterly reject the philosophy of a compulsory wage control' but such a policy *was* introduced in 1972, even though it did collapse into failure. For its part, the Labour government of 1964–70 did a 'U turn' on a number of pledges (most notably by restoring charges for the health service), and although the party entered office in 1974 with a series of clear policy commitments more radical in tone and aspiration than any that the party had endorsed since 1945, the promise of industrial regeneration and social justice was not followed through with concrete policies to put these promises into effect. The contrast between the aspirations of the party in opposition and the actual development of policy once the party was in government could not have been starker. Indeed, it is the existence of this 'gap' between promise and performance that has served as a crucial basis upon which the Left has continually criticised, not just Labour, 'labourism' and 'parliamentary socialism', but the whole reality of responsible party government and democracy in Britain. In effect, Left critics of Labour have argued that the party's exclusive reliance on the parliamentary road (or means) to the goal (or end) of socialism has shut off the very possibility of actually implementing a socialist programme precisely because the parliamentary road overestimates the power of party and the democratic side of the state at the same time as it underestimates the importance of rival centres of power and minimises the moderating implications of the whole parliamentary process. Put another way, Labour, through an electoral victory and a majority in the House of Commons, may form a government and be in 'office' but it will not be fully in 'power' because real power resides in the secret state, the economy, and in the international market system itself. This Left claim that centres of power lie beyond the effective reach of an elected Labour government has led to the more general claim that party responsibility to the electorate is itself a myth precisely because an elected government working through Parliament and the established system is without the resources to be able to deliver of its mandate and promises to the electorate.

In 1979, a Conservative government entered office under the leadership of a conviction politician who 'was not for turning' but who was committed to turning the country around. The Thatcher government promised the electorate that it would reverse Britain's economic decline and restore incentives for enterprise through the creation of a free economy, and it would do this by relying upon a monetarist policy regime involving limited state intervention and reduced public expenditure. The Party also promised the electorate that it would strengthen the state so as to better uphold the rule of law, support family life and secure Britain's defences. In reality, it has been hard for the government to translate all its objectives and promises into practical policies and we will be discussing this more fully in chapters 8 through 11. In bald terms, however, it is clear that the government has not always been clear about its own objectives (or the means required for achieving them), and implementation has proved to be tricky in the context of a situation where the objectives themselves have often been at odds each with the other. More specifically, the government has found it difficult to implement the commitment to make deep cuts in public expenditure; holding down the rate of inflation has proved to be difficult; and disputes abound as to whether the government has delivered of its major promise and reversed Britain's economic decline through an economic miracle.

What, then, are we to make of the records of parties in government and the implementation of party programmes? Blondel has claimed that implementation is 'spasmodic and half-heated' so that the influence of programmes on policy-making is 'rather weak', but Rose, in his study *Do Parties Make a Difference?*, paints a more complex picture. He argues that 'the 1970–74 Heath government fulfilled at least 80 per cent of its manifesto pledges, and showed some evidence of action in another 10 per cent of cases', going on to note that 'the 1974–79 Labour government . . . acted unambiguously upon 54 per cent of all its manifesto commitments and gave some evidence of action upon a further 19 per cent'. Rose makes a more general point when he notes that 'the gap between what governments can do and what the public (and for that matter, the government) wants to do is greatest in the management of the economy'. In effect, governments are able to implement the 'small scale "do-able" policies' and so 'fulfill most of their pledges', but the production of the all-important promised 'economic benefits . . . appear to lie beyond the reach of either party' because Britain's economic performance reflects factors rooted in the past. In combination with the impact of international events, all this serves to place constraints on what parties can do when they are in government.

Do voters vote for parties on the basis of the party programmes?

It is easy to berate parties and governments for their failures and shortcomings in developing and implementing programmes of policies, but for responsible party government to be a reality the electors *themselves* should be informed about party policies and should choose to support a party on

the basis of a keen assessment of the programmes on offer. We will be dealing with these concerns more fully in our next chapter on voting behaviour
and so at this point in the discussion we need offer only some general and
preliminary observations about the nature of public support for parties in
Britain.

In the nineteenth century, when the country was caught up in debates
about extending the franchise to the working class, views were expressed
about the basis on which that class might come to support parties. Writers
like Bagehot hoped that any new working-class majority would be 'deferential' (and ignorant), disturbing little by simply voting for the established
class of rulers in the established political parties. However, those anxious
about the working-class franchise were fearful that deference might break
down. The working class might develop a keener sense of their own collective interests and form a view as to what they wanted of the parties and the
political system. This could force the established parties to develop programmes that would serve as the basis on which they would 'bid' for the
support of the working man. It could even prompt the rise of a working-
class party that could press a socialist programme through Parliament at
a cost to be borne by men of Bagehot's class.

In the years since those heated debates, the growth of academic work on
voting behaviour has provided us with more solid information on which to
explore the hopes and fears of those who took sides on the issue of
democracy at the same time as we are provided with information to check
out the reality of a key element of the responsible party model. So, just how
informed are the voters, and do they support parties on the basis of the programmes or are sentiments like deference still of importance? There are no
simple and unambiguous answers to these questions because students of
voting behaviour cannot agree amongst themselves.

In 1963, in the first major academic sample survey of the electorate,
Butler and Stokes chose to 'challenge any image of the elector as an
informed spectator', noting how 'understanding of policy issues falls away
very sharply indeed as we move outwards from those at the heart of
political decision-making to the public at large', and how public attitudes
are formed towards even the best-known issues to only a 'limited degree'.
Butler and Stokes took the view that working-class voters and middle-class
voters naturally 'identified' with Labour and Conservative respectively.
Voters expressed loyal support for 'their' party without much knowledge of
politics or regard for the particular policy programmes, with some voters
supporting their party, not because of its policies, but in spite of them! At
one time this kind of perspective constituted the conventional wisdom
about voters because it seemed to 'fit' the facts of a stable electoral situation
where modest swings of support between the two major parties were only
disturbed by occasional 'protest votes' for the Liberals, and where there was
little to divide the parties in terms of their policy programmes.

In the 1970s, however, the growth of third-party voting in general elections suggested that party identification and party loyalty were at less of a

premium because fewer people were voting for their 'natural' parties. Rival perspectives have been advanced to make sense of voting behaviour in the more volatile times of today. The Issue Voting–Rational Choice model suggests that voters *are* informed on the issues and *do* act as rational consumers in politics, using their vote as an 'instrument' to purchase the party programme that they see as most likely to advance their interests should the party win the election, form the government and set about implementing its programme of policies. This perspective clearly gives sustenance to those who are looking for data to support the responsible party government model and it tends to constitute the new conventional wisdom about voting behaviour. Having said that, this perspective does not stand alone as it has been challenged by a newer 'radical approach' which rejects the whole focus on individual voters at the same time as it also rejects the idea that voters are genuinely informed about the issues and knowledgeable about their 'real' interests so that they can use their vote as a rational instrument to better their situation.

We cannot tease out a settled view from these conflicting perspectives, but it is probably reasonable to suggest that most voters most of the time are not fools. They are perfectly capable of passing 'rough judgements' at the polls about which party will govern 'better', making their judgements in the light of past performances in government and the promises contained in the programmes and in the context of a 'feel' as to their own sense of economic well-being at the time of an election. Put another way, voters are more informed and are more likely to actually choose a party than Butler and Stokes have argued. However, the evidence nevertheless suggests that individuals vote less on the issues than the Issue Voting–Rational Choice model would have us believe, and it is also vitally important to recognise that individuals form 'their' views about interests, issues and programmes in a constraining social context which disturbs any simple individualistic view about the responsibility of parties to rational individual voters.

In the 1950s and 1960s, the model of responsible party government was the political science orthodoxy about British politics. The model cannot be simply and glibly dismissed. It has been (and still is) true in parts; it did have a good grip on a crucial aspect of British politics for a reasonable period of our history; and it still serves as a foil against which party politics and governmental practice tends to be judged by those who are eager to advance a viable democracy in this country. However, the model is no longer seen as *the* key to unlock the essence of British politics because its credibility tended to crumple in the 1970s in the face of changes in 'the facts' and in the face of a series of intellectual and political challenges. The Left saw responsible party politics as a sham because the parties did not offer a real choice and Labour did not implement its programme; feminists saw the parties as 'unrepresentative' in a way which limited their capacity to be truly responsible; and the centre parties and New Right theorists asserted the reality, and danger, of adversary party politics at the same time as they pushed the importance of Public Choice theory as a way of better understanding the system of party politics in Britain. Let us, then, move on to explore the cogency of the arguments about adversary party politics, taking on board those elements of Public Choice theory that apply to party politics.

Adversary Party Politics and Public Choice Theory

The theories

For much of the period since the Second World War the responsible party model was at one with the informed 'commonsense' as to the workings of our democratic system. More than this, the conditions of the fifties meant that it was 'natural' for praise to be heaped onto the party system because it seemed to be doing a good job in encouraging consensus, in helping to organise electoral choice and in making government effective and responsive to the people at the same time as the parties in government had been able to solve some crucial problems. On the one hand, capricious economic forces had been effectively managed by the governing parties so that slump and unemployment were things of the past, and on the other hand, a welfare state had been created and sustained by both the parties so ensuring that wealth and poverty (and hence any material basis for class conflict) had also been cast into the dustbin of history. Things were looking good; the party system was fine.

In the late sixties, however, the smug mood of buoyant self-satisfaction gave way to a mood of self-doubt and angry introspection. On the all-important economic front, there was a growing awareness that we just could not 'modernise' in order to get adequate growth out of our stagnant economy and so we were doing increasingly badly when compared to our neighbours in Europe. On the welfare front, poverty was rediscovered when it 'should' have been eliminated by the welfare state, and this not-withstanding the growing (and worrying) amounts of public expenditure that were being devoted to health and welfare provision. The concern to solve the central problem of our relative economic decline in the context of a competitive world situation from which we could not escape encouraged politicians and pundits to search for explanations for that decline in the hope that matters could then be set to rights. Scapegoats were swiftly identified in the unions and to a lesser extent in management, but there was also a more sophisticated discussion which sought to explore the relationship between the poor performance of the British economy and certain features of the British political system.

By the seventies, and part and parcel of the demise of consensus and the rise of conviction politics, the New Right had grown and was in a position of political and intellectual prominence. From their Public Choice perspective, the two-party system in particular (and democratic politics in general) was *the* problem and the prime cause of all our economic ills. By the mid-seventies, many political scientists came to share this kind of gloomy perspective on the party system, and they were joined (and perhaps led) by the 'informed' commentators in the quality press and by the growing numbers that were swelling the ranks of the Liberal Party and, later, the newly formed Social Democratic Party. 'Realistic' experts on our politics no longer chose to praise the responsibility of the party system but instead talked of, and roundly condemned, our system of irresponsible 'adversary party politics' where an 'electoral auction' was said to lead to the election of an unrepresentative 'elective dictatorship' which then went on to govern and manage the economy in such as a way as to create an injurious 'political-business cycle' that simply served to hinder our long-term prospects for sustainable economic growth. At one and the same time, we were being provided with a new characterisation of the British party system that challenged the cogency of the responsible party government model; we were being provided with a particular kind of explanation for economic policy-making; and we were also being offered an explanation for the decline of the British economy. These were ambitious claims and they demand our reasoned consideration. What, then is the precise nature of the adversary party politics thesis and what are the key elements of Public Choice theory that are relevant to the nature of party politics in Britain; how adequately do these perspectives make good sense of British party politics; and how adequately do they account for the development of economic policy and the poor performance of the British economy?

Adversary party politics

Gamble and Walkland are right to argue that 'the adversary politics thesis is concerned with the relationship between the state and the economy. It argues that the way in which the political system works and the kind of public choices that emerge from it in the form of government economic policies have had significant and harmful effects on the overall performance of the economy.' This, however, is a very bare description, but in order to go further we have to face the fact that we are dealing with a highly politicised piece of political science. Description, explanation and analysis of the 'reality' of the party system are all tangled up with a critique of that system at the same time as the adversary theorists have invariably been concerned to prescribe reforms that would destroy adversary politics and secure the 'fair' representation of the centre parties and hence the heightened probability of moderate policies that would survive over time in a way which the theorists think would better serve as the basis for our sustained economic recovery.

So, the adversary party politics thesis embraces description and analysis, criticism and prescriptive reform, and it can best be spelled out in the following catalogue of points:

1 The adversary system is based on a party duopoly of seats in the Commons and a party monopoly (or an elective dictatorship) of the government.

2 The duopoloy cannot be broken because third parties are quite unable to secure representation in the Commons in proportion to their votes in the country as a result of the workings of the first-past-the-post electoral system.

3 The adversary system serves to ensure that the 'extremists' secure undue influence over policy-making and the party leadership (and hence over government itself), because the activists want it that way and because the leadership is unable to get a firm grip on the party rank and file.

4 In an adversary system, where each of the parties is led by extremists and where each party is based on a particular social class, it is inevitable that the policies of the two parties will be extreme, polarized and mutually antagonistic.

5 The problem of extreme policies is seen as all the more alarming and 'undemocratic' given the fact that the electorate itself is invariably more 'moderate' than the activists within the two major parties. The electorate's views are seen as stable and centrist but, in the context of an electoral system that bolsters the two-party system and blocks the fair representation of third parties of moderation, the House of Commons is always divided into two warring camps that are both 'unrepresentative' of the policy positions of the population at large.

6 When one of the parties comes to form the government after winning an election it will claim a popular mandate to implement its manifesto of policies. This is seen as problematic for a number of reasons. First, the policies themselves will have been drawn up by the extremists with little regard for the views of the ordinary voter or for the practicalities of the situation a government will find once in office. Second, in order for the government to implement its manifesto it will have to repeal the policies that have been laid down by the previous party of government and this in itself is a problem. But, third, all of this repealing and radicalism will soon prove to be counterproductive and so the government will have to embark on a 'U-turn' and adopt sensible and pragmatic policies at the instigation of the Civil Service and under pressures from outside interests, particularly in the City. The government will only be able to pursue these 'sound' policies for a while because just as they come to bear fruit it will be time for another general election and it is likely that the other party will win to start the whole disastrous cycle of radicalism, repeal, 'U-turns' and eventual sensible pragmatism all over again.

7 The Commons can do nothing to break into this cycle and check a government bent on implementing its manifesto. Instead of reasoned opposition based on an honest assessment of the merits of the policies under scrutiny, the Commons is caught up in raw partisan opposition for opposition's sake and the mindless negation of government; the over-simplification of complex issues into two (but only two) conflicting alternatives; and the grand clash and confrontation of the cult of yaa–boo macho debates that are tempered only by constant petty squabbles that in themselves solve nothing of any consequence.

8 The whole adversary system is said to crush consensus and co-operation, and to destroy any basis for stable, moderate and pragmatic policies that survive beyond the lifetime of one party government. Left of centre policies alternate with Right of centre policies violently, rapidly and on the basis of

ideological considerations that are quite unrelated to the real needs of the situation. The system has resulted in huge discontinuities in government policy and in frequent reversals in economic policy in ways that have been costly for the whole health of the British economy.

9 The adversary system has also proved to be politically costly because the bouts of 'manifesto madness', U-turns, broken promises and policy reversals have all conspired to disillusion the public with party politics so that governments tend to lack authority, ungovernability becomes a problem and the legitimacy of the whole system gets called into question.

10 Electoral reform is needed to secure the fair representation of third parties. This would destroy the adversary contest between the two parties that currently dominates the Commons; it would restore the independence of Parliament; and it would encourage the formation of coalition governments that would build consensus and ensure policy continuity in a way that would enhance the prospects for the British economy.

11 Adversary theorists who are more gloomy about democracy urge reforms that would reduce the extent to which elected politicians are themselves caught up in the whole process of managing the economy and determining economic policies.

Public choice theory

Public Choice theory, or the Economics of Politics, seeks to apply the model of individual behaviour and the method of science integral to neoclassical economics to the material of politics. It constitutes a body of theory that tends to be sharply critical of the practice of democratic politics at the same time as it celebrates the workings of the unfettered market economy. Public Choice theory has fed into the frothy literature on adversary politics but it also has a more enduring integrity of its own, and two fields of Public Choice theory are relevant to any discussion of democratic party politics within a cpaitalist system.

(1) *The Economic Theory of Democracy.* Downs', *An Economic Theory of Democracy*, is the classic abstract Public Choice account of party competition within a democratic political system. Only a government, parties and voters inhabit the political scene. The government is made up by the party which maximised votes at the last general election. Political parties are assumed to be completely united behind their leaders and solely concerned to maximise votes as their only goal is to reap the rewards of holding governmental office. To that end it is rational for parties to be flexible and adopt whichever policies will secure votes and advance electoral success. In Downs' world it is not rational for parties to be committed to policies and to be active in persuading voters to give them their support. For their part, voters see elections as a chance to choose a government, and because they too are assumed to be rational and self-interested individuals, they will vote for that party which they consider will offer them the best policy package at the lowest tax cost.

This economic theory of democracy quite clearly parallels the neoclassical picture of the economy. Voters are political consumers using votes as money to demand policies, and parties are entreprenours in the business of supplying policies to win votes and secure the fruits of government office. The party that is most successful in judging what the public wants, wins the election and supplies the popular public policy goods the voters have demanded at the polls at the same time as it gains the rewards of office for itself.

On the surface, a system working like this looks to be good, but the *practical* effects of the electoral competition for votes have often been judged as problematic by Public Choice theorists. In the context of a situation in which the name of the game is winning votes to secure governmental office, it is suggested that elections all too easily become crude policy auctions in which the parties, through their manifestoes, bid for popular support and the highest (and most irresponsible) bidder wins all. On the 'supply' side, the parties will always be tempted to 'bribe' the electorate with the promise of more popular policies than they can ever safely deliver after the votes are in the bag and they are in the government. On the 'demand' side, party competition will tend to generate 'excessive' and 'unrealistic' expectations of government on the part of the electorate, which will also have every incentive to vote for more government services because they do not necessarily pay for them directly and individual tax payments may bear no relation at all to the benefits derived from particular services. In other words, the 'vote motive' and the whole system of competitive vote bidding can act like a ratchet, encouraging ever more government services and hence ever higher government taxes to pay for those services (and this notwithstanding the adverse implications of these taxes for incentives, investment and economic growth) at the same time as it promises to penalise a government that is prepared to take 'tough' decisions. Those decisions may hit particular interests in the short run even though they may work to the advantage of all in the longer run.

(2) *Political business cycles.*   The basic idea that political parties are geared to producing popular policies to win elections is seen as having particular implications for the way in which governments manage the economy and devise economic and monetary policies. This insight has been developed in the literature on political business cycles, a literature which embellishes the common-sense view that governments try to manipulate the economy to improve material conditions in time for the next election.

The Public Choice perspective rejects the idea that benevolent governments manage demand in the economy so as to iron out the booms and slumps that are said to be a part of the capitalist system. It is argued instead that *governments* introduce booms and slumps into what is a naturally self-regulating system, and they do this because they are selfish in wanting to manage the economy so as to enhance their own re-election prospects. When governments try to manage the economy they have to work out a trade-off between inflation and the level of unemployment. They have to do this because it is difficult to secure low inflation and a high level of employment, because the former requires a low level of demand whereas the latter requires a high level of demand. The trouble is that governments manage the economy, the level of demand and the inflation – employment trade-off with electoral considerations uppermost in their minds.

Public Choice theorists quite reasonably assume that voters make the government responsible for their own economic well-being and for the health of the economy, and that they vote according to their judgement of the government's success in these matters. They further suggest that voters dislike both unemployment and inflation, but in a situation in which it is difficult for a government to secure both full employment and low inflation at one and the same time, the public will tend to prefer the quick fix of boom, full employment and growth. With voters adopting this short-term perspective, and with governments geared to winning elections, then as an election approaches it is rational for a government to pump money into the economy to engineer a boom in the hope that the inevitable (and unpopular) inflation will hit only *after* the election is won and they are safely back in government. Once the election is out the way then the government can afford to be less concerned about its electoral prospects and can introduce sounder economic policies that bear down on the long-term problem of inflation, even if these policies do exacerbate growth and the problem of unemployment in the short term. However, in the run up to the next election, the whole political business cycle starts all over again and the government will have to think about the electoral implications of slow growth and high unemployment. So, in a situation in which governments are always having to respond to the next election and to the political short run, they are continually oscillating between two sets of economic policies: a policy to master inflation and secure sustainable and steady growth that is in the best long-term interests of us all; and a policy that is geared to the production of short-lived booms at election times, that is in the electoral interests of the government even though it does subvert the attainment of sustainable and steady growth.

The political business cycle is seen as bad because it led Britain and other countries to an accelerating inflation and eventually to a far worse slump and level of unemployment than would otherwise have been necessary to restructure the economy to meet world competition. More than this, state intervention in the management of the economy is itself to be deplored precisely because it introduces short-run political considerations into economic affairs in a way which serves to shift the economy away from 'natural' long-run optimal levels of steady growth.

Public Choice theorists have never been shy about offering policy advice, and proposals have been put forward to eliminate political business cycles. It has been suggested that states be required by law to balance their budgets; that the exact timing of an election should be determined by some kind of random process so that politicians, in being robbed of the knowledge as to the date of the next election, would be free to develop sound long-term economic policies that were not grounded in the need to respond to short-term electoral considerations; that scope for the 'political control' of the economy should be reduced by giving increased policy powers to central banks; and that the electors themselves should be educated to be less short-sighted, to be more critical of governmental attempts to buy votes by way of unsustainable expansions, and to stop holding governments responsible for the state of the economy which should be left to manage itself.

The practice

The theories about the party system that we have just been discussing provide us with perspectives that sensitise us to certain features of the system
(and to the problems which that system is supposed to pose for the health
of the British economy) but that tend to be too gross and general to be
simply tested against the facts of the system itself. Moreover, the fact that
the theories were always something of a right-of-centre *political* response
to the pressing politics of the 1970s tempts us to suggest that the theories
themselves are somehow too 'biased' to be treated seriously as political
science at the same time as they are now too 'out-of-date' to be relevant of sustained consideration. Indeed, many commentators now choose
to characterise the British party system, not in terms of adversary party
politics (still less in terms of responsible party government) but rather in
terms of it being a dominant party system with multi-party politics waiting
in the wings.

The fact that the Conservatives have been dominant for more than a
decade, and the fact that they have made a fetish out of *not* intervening in
the economy, of *not* bidding and bribing for votes and of *not* engineering
pre-election booms to secure their own election because they have been
prepared to take the kind of 'tough' decisions that are needed to secure the
long-term interests of the country as a whole, tempts us to set the adversary
politics thesis and Public Choice theory to one side. They now seem to be
wrong and at odds with the facts. But having said all that and recognising
that it is important to push beyond the rhetoric contained in the theories
and the rituals that are themselves a part of the party political battle, it is
also important to avoid easy talk about continued Conservative dominance
at the same time as we should avoid taking the Conservative record on its
own terms. Put another way, it *is* important to take the theories we have
set down in this section seriously, and so it is worthwhile exploring three
broad areas of concern where we can assemble a certain amount of hard
evidence.

First, to what extent has there been massive discontinuity and a series of
'U-turns' in economic policy as a consequence of adversary party politics?
Second, what is the evidence with respect to political business cycles in Britain and is it, as Finer has suggested, 'a matter of proven fact that governments try to manipulate the economy to improve material conditions in
time for the next election'? Third, can the economic decline of modern Britain be attributed to adversary party politics (any more than the 'recovery'
can be attributed to the fact that we now have a dominant party system
within which the Conservatives are supreme)?

With respect to the first question, Gamble and Walkland (in *The British
Party System and Economic Policy: 1945–1983*) have been specifically concerned to see how many economic policies were actually reversed by an
incoming government, and which areas of policy were left untouched,

over the period 1960–81 during which time four changes of government took place. They claim that the adversary theory 'generalises from a few instances to the whole of economic policy' and that it also fails to recognise the need to distinguish between the three main areas of economic policy. First, there is foreign economic policy involving the relationship of the British economy to the world economy and to Europe; second, there is stabilisation policy and the problems of using monetary and fiscal measures both to raise the necessary public finance for state activities and to promote a stable economic environment that encourages growth and minimises disruption; and third, there is industrial and commercial policy covering all those aspects of governmental responsibility for the economy aimed at improving long-run efficiency, output and productivity. According to Gamble and Walkland 'it is difficult to sustain the adversary politics thesis without substantial qualifications. The evidence that there have been significant discontinuities in economic policy-making caused by the adversary positions adopted by the parties seems to be limited to industrial policy' where the two parties have been sharply divided on industrial relations law, the size and operation of the public enterprise sector, planning and land policy. However, the 'major issues of foreign economic policy have been marked by continuity', and although the crucial issue of our membership of the European Community hovered on the edge of becoming subject to adversary politics it never did, and the divisions *within* the parties have continued to be of more significance than the differences *between* the parties when they have been in office. And with respect to stabilisation policy, 'the evidence for continuity is rather more plain than the evidence for discontinuity'. Of course, a major shift in the policy framework for managing the economy *did* take place. But the shift from Keynsianism to monetarism did *not* take place as a result of adversary politics and the election of a tough Conservative government in 1979, since Labour was converted to the 'need' for this approach in 1975–6 and quite outside of any policy-making pressures consequent upon the electoral cycle or adversary politics. It would be silly to pretend that the parties have agreed on all aspects of economic policy over the years. There are divisions and differences within society on these matters; democratically-based parties exist to give policy expression to these differences; and so it should not surprise (or alarm) us to discover that the two major parties have been divided on such important matters as the treatment of tax on high earners, incomes policy, nationalisation and privatisation, and the whole field of economic planning. But for all that, many of the other major issues of economic policy have rarely entered the adversary debate at all, and when economic policies have been changed these changes have not always been attributable to the adversarial contest between the parties but to the impact of events and actors from outside the whole framework of party politics itself. Moreover, the idea that every government is caught up in a policy-making cycle so that it is forced to perform a 'U-turn' on economic policy midway through its term (as it moves away from its silly ideological manifesto and confronts the realities of the situation with sensible and pragmatic economic policies), is itself largely a generalisation based on the experience of the Heath government of 1970–4. Gamble and Walkland point out that it was a generalisation that was not particularly well-founded even then.

Second, what are the facts of the situation with respect to political business cycles in Britain? Nordhaus has looked at the evidence in nine countries over the period 1947–72. He found that although the coincidence of business and political cycles was 'very marked' with respect to the United States, New Zealand and the economically highly-successful West Germany, this was *not* the case with respect to Britain because the continual need to take pressing action on the balance of payments swamped the possibility of there being a cycle of economic policy-making revolving around elections. Alt's study of *The Politics of Economic Decline* explored the nature of political business cycles in Britain alone and dealt with the possibility that governments might run the economy to their own electoral advantage through manipulating the rate of inflation, disposable incomes and unemployment in such a way as to rally short-run popular support at election time. He found no real evidence of any government attempting to hold down the rate of inflation in the short run in order to promote its own popularity at election time. Before the elections of 1964, 1966 and 1970 real personal disposable income *was* rising at more than double its normal rate of growth – so supporting the political business cycle thesis – but Alt suggests that these 'short pre-election spurts may not do the government of the day all that much good, and there is no evidence that they do (at least if short term enough) the economy any particular harm'. Alt further suggests that there is little evidence that any British government ever managed the unemployment rate simply with a view to winning the next election. Alt is wisely tentative in his conclusions, given the nature of the available data and the looseness of the thesis he is exploring, but he is prepared to argue that there is 'no evidence that any British government in the period [since 1964] . . . believed it could "steal" an election by mortgaging the future in the interest of an economically better present'. The thesis that governments attempt to win electoral support through the creation of mini-booms just before an election clearly accords with common-sense views about the behaviour of (self-serving) politicians, but it is a thesis that is not well-supported by the facts. Moreover, the thesis itself is overly 'economistic' in that it attempts to deal with the popularity of governments and the nature of public policy-making *solely* on the basis of a consideration of economic variables alone, so ignoring the part played by non-economic factors in contributing to electoral support and success. Even if a government were to attempt to manipulate the economy to win electoral support this does not mean it would be successful in either manipulating the economy as it intended or in securing support as result of its endeavours. After 1959 and until 1983 government changed hands every five years and no government was re-elected after serving a full term. The inability of governments to manage the economy was much more in evidence than their success, and each party while in government was rejected by the electorate on two occasions – the Conservatives in 1964 and 1974, Labour in 1970 and 1979. Of course, the Conservatives did go on to get re-elected in 1983, and they did so without even attempting to create a mini-boom (and with over three million unemployed) but with a little help from enemies in Argentina at the same time as multi-party politics in combination with the electoral system played into their hands as it did again in 1987.

Third, is there evidence to support the grand suggestion that the economic decline of modern Britain was caused by the adversarial nature of our party system? The decline of Britain has been a topic of concern right back to the end of the nineteenth century; the problem itself has spawned an enormous literature; and political and ideological divisions run through this literature as partisans to the debate have struggled to find *the* cause of decline and *the* key to revival. The perspective which sees in the contemporary history of adversary politics the cause of our decline (at the same time as destroying adversary politics will be the key to our revival) is one amongst many, and it is a perspective that even now looks dated at the same time as it lacks much credibility. First, the fact that the British economy has been in relative decline compared to the rest of the world for a hundred or more years should caution us about accepting an explanation for decline that is rooted in the experience of party politics over the last twenty or thirty years. Second, to single out political parties for blame fails to recognise that parties are only a *part* of the political system; they are not even in sole control of the British state and public policy; and they are certainly not the masters of Britain's economic destiny precisely because the forces determining the direction of the British economy are forces far stronger than parties alone. Third, and related to the last point, the focus on parties as the powerful political actors wrecking economic havoc also fails to explore the extent to which parties in government are themselves subject to all manner of constraints (quite apart from those which come from their supporters and the ballot box), constraints which need to be explored because they limit the capacity of parties in government to achieve the goals which they set themselves and which are set for them by supporters and the electorate at large.

Conclusion

Everybody would agree that no account of British politics would be complete if it did not attend to the part played by political parties and so all textbooks devote (too) much space to the subject. However, nobody can quite agree how to assess the worth of parties for the functioning of democracy and for the efficient discharge of public affairs, and disputes also abound as to how best to describe the British party system.

When it was thought that the system was in crisp accord with the responsible party government model just about everyone praised it, but when the two-party system was seen as having 'degenerated' into adversary party politics then the whole system was condemned as a travesty of democracy and as an appalling basis from which to develop economic policy and deal with public affairs. Both these conflicting perspectives on party politics have shared the view that Britain is best described as a two-party system. In the late 1980s, however, it became fashionable to suggest that we lived in a system of one-party dominance. But there was also the suggestion that we were 'really' a multi-party system – albeit one that would only come into flower if Parliament were to legislate for a 'fair' electoral system which gave seats in the House of Commons in direct proportion to votes and popular support in the country.

We have no wish to repeat what we have said in the body of this chapter as to the worth of these various suggestions, assessments and perspectives on parties, because we are concerned to conclude this chapter with some fairly terse observations about the British party system.

1 The two old parties are in decline in terms of their capacity to attract votes; in terms of their capacity to attract members; and in terms of their capacity to respond to new interests and new issues which lie beyond the old capital/labour divide on which they are based.

2 The party system, in combination with the established electoral system, is now quite clearly a poor basis from which to 'represent' the citizens of this country, and this notwithstanding the precise meaning we choose to give to the term representation. Women and blacks have cause to bemoan the extent to which they are under-represented in parties, in Parliament and in government, and third parties continue to be in a position where they cannot translate votes into seats. Electoral reform (which we will be discussing in chapter 5) could go some way towards making the system 'more' representative but there are limits as to what this would achieve if the parties themselves are less than representative and democratic in the ways in which they choose to organise their internal affairs.

3 The problems with respect to representation run through to cause problems with respect to the 'responsibility' and 'accountability' of party government. We say this without needing to take on board the wild excesses of the adverary politics thesis and without condemning the responsible party government model as utterly at odds with the facts.

4 All of the above problems 'matter' to anyone interested in the health of our democracy precisely because party in government matters in that the two parties each have a somewhat different impact on public policy and therefore on the direction of the state itself. Even at the level of local government, Newton and Sharpe have argued that parties 'matter in the sense that quite strong relationships emerged between party control and expenditure distribution. . . . In short, Left parties do tend to spend more on redistributive and ameliorative services, and Right parties do spend more on police and highways.'

5 Although 'parties do make a difference in the way Britain is governed', Rose is right to go on to stress that 'parties make less difference in reality than they claim in their rhetoric' and this is because parties in government are subject to major constraints and because parties are only one part of the political

system. Put another way, we should not ignore the role of parties in policy-making but neither should we overplay the part which they perform and the independent impact which they can have on policy. So, because it matters which party is in government it is important to study parties and to try and explain voting behaviour since this can provide us with pointers as to why parties win elections. But because parties are constrained and only a part of the system it is important to attend to the constraints at the same time as we do not underplay the role of other bodies and institutions. We will try to explain voting behaviour in the next chapter, and in the rest of the book we will be dealing with the other parts of the British political system, attending to the importance of constraints all along the way.

Works Cited and Guide to Further Reading

Alt, J. E. (1979) *The Politics of Economic Decline*, London, Cambridge University Press.
Detailed consideration of a mass of survey data on the public response to the economic decline of the 1960s and 1970s. Chapter 7 deals with 'Political business cycles in Britain'.

American Political Science Association, Committee on Political Parties (1950) 'Toward a more responsible two-party system', *American Political Science Review*, 44, Supplement.
Classic presentation of Britain as the happy home of responsible party government.

Blondel, J. (1978) *Political Parties: A Genuine Case for Discontent?* London, Wildwood House.
Not a particularly powerful study, but flags the future when he suggests that 'parties will die on their feet in the West'.

Butler, D., and Stokes, D. (1969) *Political Change in Britain*, London, Macmillan.
The pioneer study of voting behaviour in Britain. Stresses the importance of party identification and highlights the tie-up between class and party, but ill-equipped to deal with change and overly dismissive of the extent to which voters are not fools.

Downs, A. (1957) *An Economic Theory of Democracy*, New York, Harper and Row.
Classic Public Choice account of party competition within a democratic political system.

Epstein, L. (1980) 'What happened to the British party system?', *American Political Science Review*, 74, 1–22.
Discusses the changing assessment of the 'British party model' by American political scientists. Could usefully be subtitled 'From responsible party government to adversary politics'.

Finer, S. E. (ed.) (1975) *Adversary Politics and Electoral reform*, London, Anthony Wigram.
First in the field with the adversary politics thesis and a powerful case for electoral reform which at that time was supported by many Conservatives, including Wigram himself.

Finer, S. E. (1980) *The Changing British Party System, 1945–1979*, Washington, DC, American Enterprise Institue.
Attack on the adversarial nature of the British party system and a plea for reform.

Fitzgerald, M. (1987) *Black People and Party Politics in Britain*, London, Runnymede Trust.
Points to limited black involvement in mainstream politics and notes how the parties have 'managed "race" issues by keeping them off the main political agenda'.

Gamble, A. M., and Walkland, S. A. (1984) *The British Party System and Economic Policy, 1945–1983*, Oxford, Clarendon Press.
Crushing critical assessment of the adversary politics thesis.

Ingle, S. (1987) *The British Party System*, Oxford, Blackwell.
Basic descriptive stuff, but weak on analysis and explanation.

McLean, I. (1987) *Public Choice*, Oxford, Blaclwell.
Good and accessible introduction to Public Choice theory that also has a critical edge.

Newton, K., and Sharpe, J. (1984) *Does Politics Matter? The Determinants of Public Policy*, Oxford, Clarendon Press.
Concerned to explain the expenditure patterns of local authorities. Dated data, but concludes that parties do make a difference.

Nordhaus, W. D. (1975) 'The political business cycle', *Review of Economic Studies*, 42, 169–90.
Looks at evidence with respect to political business cycles in nine countries over the period 1947–72.

Randall, V. (1987) *Women and Politics: An International Perspective*, 2nd edn, London, Macmillan.
Full and excellent feminist perspective on politics and political science which includes information on women's under-representation within the party system.

Rose, R. (1984) *Do Parties Make a Difference?* 2nd edn, London, Macmillan.
Concentrates on what parties do in office. Argues that they do make a difference but not as much as they claim because they are but a part of the system and are often hemmed in by constraints – especially with respect to economic policy-making.

Chapter 3

Explaining Voting Behaviour

Political science orthodoxy, the party identification model, was first challenged by an economic or public choice theory of voting and, at the end of the 1970s, by the emergence of a radical-structural explanation.
P. Dunleavy and C. T. Husbands (1985) *British Democracy at the Crossroads*, London, Allen and Unwin, p. 3.

Introduction

The systematic study of elections and electioneering has a relatively brief history in Britain. Since 1945 Nuffield College at Oxford University has sponsored a study of each British general election and David Butler has been an author of these since the early days. These Nuffield Studies have tended to focus on the election campaign; the issues that have been part of each contest and the way in which these were presented by the party leaders and the mass media; and on the organisational efforts of the parties nationally and locally. They have also described the final outcome and provided readers with a full statistical appendix of results. The studies are useful guides as to how informed contemporaries saw a particular election but they do not really 'explain' an election outcome as they tend to range too widely in a fairly journalistic fashion. Put another way, the studies emphasise the leadership politics of campaign strategy and the public face of election campaigns but they do not provide us with a theory of voting behaviour because the ordinary voters do not really feature in the studies.

During the 1950s and 1960s a small number of *local* election studies were undertaken in such constituencies as Bristol and Greenwich. These studies tended to follow a common pattern. They were preoccupied with the significance of class and invariably found an association between social class and party choice at the polls. They were also concerned as to how voters 'should' behave in an election and so tended to bemoan the political ignorance of the average voter who did not live up to the high ideals of the informed and active citizen beloved of so much democratic theory. But these studies were also of limited use in enabling us to make good sense of

"No matter who you vote for the Government always gets in!" (Reproduced by kind permission of Rex Features. Photograph: Nils Jorgensen.)

general election outcomes because few voters were actually interviewed and it was inevitably difficult to generalise from one constituency to the electorate as a whole. Moreover, the studies tended to neglect both the relationship between local and national behaviour and the place of an election in a historical context as well as the working of the political system as a whole.

Voting behaviour research was somewhat different in the USA where researchers had long seen the importance of getting to grips with a sample of ordinary voters through extended interviews, and interview surveys had been a feature of every presidential election since 1948. Initially, the research emphasis was on the voter as a rational consumer and the vote was regarded as an *instrument* that was used to advance self-interest through politics. Later research conducted out of the University of Michigan downplayed this perspective on voters. Instead of seeing elections as opportunities for choice and decision, the Michigan researchers saw voters as 'party identifiers' who used elections as fairly unthinking opportunities to *express* their loyalty and partisan commitment to a party and its candidates.

British researchers eventually picked up on the American insights and theories, and on the importance of interviewing a large sample of voters on a number of occasions. The first academic nationally representative sample survey of the electorate was conducted in 1963 by David Butler, author of the Nuffield Studies, and Donald Stokes, from the University of Michigan. These two academics continued to direct the ongoing British Election Survey until 1970. Their study of the 1964 general election, *Political Change in Britain*, was modelled on the Michigan party identification theory of voting and they explored the general election from this point of view coupled with an intense (and very British) interest in the electoral significance of class. The two elections of 1974 and the election of 1979 were surveyed by Ivor Crewe and Bo Sarlvik from the University of Essex. Their study, *Decade of Dealignment*, explored the Conservative victory of 1979 mainly from the perspective of issues, but their discussion of electoral trends gave wide currency to the idea of partisan dealignment and class dealignment. The 1983 survey was conducted by Anthony Heath, Roger Jowell and John Curtice and reported in their *How Britain Votes* – a study which challenged the argument about class dealignment as well as the argument about the centrality of issue voting. Heath, Jowell and Curtice have also gone on to survey the electorate at the 1987 general election. Broadly speaking, the aim of the British Election Survey series has been to explore the changing determinants, both sociological and political, that have been regarded as of importance in shaping the vote and in accounting for variations in the patterns of voting behaviour in contemporary Britain. It is a series of major importance for anyone interested in exploring and explaining voting behaviour in Britain and the books that report and reflect on the findings of the series must serve as the bedrock of this chapter.

In the last chapter we explored different perspectives on the British party system. We cannot easily predict how this system will develop, for much will depend on just how the electorate votes in future general elections. This being the case, we can surely advance the prospects for our understanding future possibilities if we try to explain voting behaviour. This is our concern in this chapter where we will set down and assess three different approaches to the explanation of voting behaviour. In the course of this assessment we will also have to respond to the challenge of electoral change, because change has bruised the Party Identification model at the same time as it has led to the Issue Voting–Rational Choice model bouncing into prominence even though this model has been challenged by a new Radical-Structural explanation. Focusing on the three different approaches to voting behaviour and grappling with electoral change means that we will also be dealing with the significance of political socialisation and class cleavages, and taking a view as to the reality of class dealignment and partisan dealignment at the same time as we attend to the possible importance of sectoral cleavages in relation to the vote. We will also have to come to terms with the importance of issues and rationality in voting choice, and we will have to decide whether the way people vote is conditioned by a set of dominant ideological messages. In three appendices we will provide some facts and figures from the 1987 general election (as this will enable *you* to assess the three approaches in the context of a specific election); we will then deal with the geography of voting; and finally, we will offer our own brief assessment as to the future prospects for the parties at the polls.

The Party Identification Model and the Importance of Social Class

The concept of 'party identification' was developed by Angus Campbell and his associates at the University of Michigan who saw in attachment to party the key to accounting for voting behaviour, so challenging that perspective which saw voting as an individual act of rational choice by voters who were akin to consumers in the marketplace. Although Butler and Stokes' *Political Change in Britain* contains no explicit model of voting behaviour, we can nevertheless derive the essence of the Michigan model from this work at the same time as we are provided with a basis for predicting election outcomes and making sense of voting behaviour in Britain.

The model

The essence of the Party Identification model can best be set down if we provide answers to four basic questions.

What is party identification?

The concept of party identification denotes the long-term feelings of positive attachment which many electors develop for a political party. Over 90 per cent of Butler and Stokes' first interview sample expressed an attachment to a particular political party. This encouraged the view that little research attention needed to be devoted to the 'floating' voters since these were seen as a tiny minority who lacked an enduring commitment to a party and who were generally seen as fairly ignorant of political affairs. Party identification obviously varies in direction as people can identify only with the one party. It also varies in intensity as some people have a 'very strong' identification whereas others are rather less committed to a particular political party. By and large party identification tends to get stronger as people get older since during their lifetimes people tend to seek out information that reinforces an early, but possibly tentative, attachment. Party identification has been seen as the most enduring and important feature of a voter's political attitudes and behaviour.

How does party identification develop?

People are socialised into their partisan identification in much the same way as they learn to accept any other set of values and beliefs. Put another way, people come to acquire their partisan identification as a result of a process of social learning within a variety of social institutions that exist in a particular kind of society.

The early home environment is crucial as most voters tend to inherit their partisan self-image from their parents – the more so if both parents are strongly attached to the same party and if the child does not experience any social mobility later in life. But to say that children tend to inherit their partisan self-image from their parents does not tell us exactly *what* party they come to identify with. This is where class comes in. The fact that there is sufficient evidence that party allegiance has followed class lines more strongly in Britain than anywhere else in the English-speaking world highlights the importance of attending to the social class of the head of the household. Simply expressed, the middle-class home is more likely to raise children who go on to become Conservative voters, just as working-class homes will produce future Labour voters.

Although the inheritance of a party identification from parents is fundamental, Party Identification theorists recognise that political socialisation – even childhood political socialisation – is not confined to the home alone. Schooling is of importance as well. At the time Butler and Stokes undertook their first survey of electors there was an important distinction between grammar schools and secondary modern schools (only a small proportion of the school population attended private schools). For a variety of reasons children from middle-class homes tended to be overrepresented in the grammar schools just as they were underrepresented in the secondary modern schools, and the reverse pattern held for children from working-class homes. All this was seen as important to party identification theorists because they recognised that each type of school tended to have a particular 'ethos' and a particular set of expectations for their pupils which tended to 'reinforce' the socialising effect of the home environment. However, there was the recognition that the school did not always reinforce the home, and Party Identification theorists developed the notion of 'cross-pressures' to deal with situations in which voters were pulled in different directions by different socialising experiences. At the childhood level, for example, a working-class child was seen as experiencing 'cross pressures' if he or she were in a grammar school. The expectation for these pupils to secure a midddle-class career was seen as very much at odds with the expectations of the working-class home where leaving school early to get a blue-collar job was held to be the norm.

Childhood years were seen as particularly important in forming partisan attachments – give me the child and I will show you the adult – but Party Identification theorists recognised that political socialisation did not stop at sixteen and was not confined to the home and the school. Once people left school and the family home and entered the world of work (or unemployment) they then encountered a new range of face-to-face contacts that were seen as having implications for political attachments and identifications. The occupation that a person takes up will be affected by the home and educational background but, notwithstanding the route to a career, a job will bring people into contact with others who have particular political views which may well rub off on those that are part of the work milieu. Moreover, a particular job may contain expectations for union membership, and Party Identification theorists tended to argue that this could well reinforce a working-class occupational ethos and so increase the likelihood of Labour voting.

Finally, where people live and the type of housing that they occupy, although again conditioned by class and income considerations, has been seen as having implications for political socialisation and hence for the development and reinforcement of an individual's partisan self-image. By and large people tend to live in proximity to others in situations similar to their own and the social contacts this involves tend to reinforce the socialising effects of home, school and work. But individuals may occasionally live alongside people very different from themselves. In this state of affairs people may well adopt the dominant partisanship of the area in which they live and this notwithstanding their own social standing. For example, a working-class person living in a retirement resort on the south coast is far more likely to vote Conservative than the same type of person living in a northern industrial town because the south coast resident will be more likely to have friends and contact with people who are themselves solid Conservative voters. We will be assessing the importance of this 'neighbourhood effect' in an appendix to this chapter.

Party Identification theorists have not been indifferent to the significance of a whole variety of 'cross-pressures' in the political socialisation process but they have tended to see the socialising impact of childhood home, school, work, type and place of residence as normally pulling in one direction in a way which 'reinforces' the partisan attachment which is formed very early on in the family home

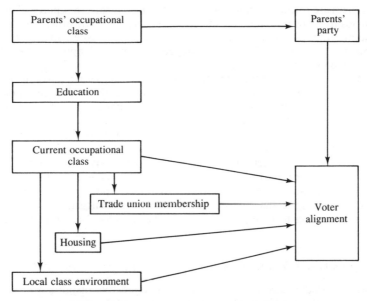

Source: Dunleavy and Husbands (1985) p. 6

Figure 3.1 The Party Identification Model

What is the function of party identification?

According to the doctrine of responsible party government and most democratic theorists, voters should give keen attention to the issues and to the programmes of the parties before they make an informed choice at the polls. In reality, party identification theorists suggest that all this is just too complicated and demanding for the average voter who is seen as poorly informed, lacking in understanding of political issues, and possessed of policy preferences that are weak and unstable and that do not hang together in a consistent pattern. In this state of affairs, the fact that the vast majority of voters identify with a political party makes for handy shortcuts that ease the burden of decision on election day.

1 The fact that voters know where they stand means that they engage in 'selective perception' in the way in which they relate to information and the media. Without necessarily being conscious of it, voters tend to seek out information and information sources which reinforce rather than undermine the predispositions and prejudices which come from a particular party identification. This perspective on information searching suggests that the mass media is very much less influential in shaping attitudes and political predispositions than certain other theorists have claimed.

2 The fact that a party loyalty develops early in life, *before* policy

preferences are formed on a whole range of issues, means that party identification tends to shape our views on specific issues (and *not* the other way around) and so provides us with a basis for responding to new issues. In effect, we are equipped with a party 'line' which we can follow and apply to new issues without the need for thought.

3 Most directly, the fact that voters tend to identify with a party means that they already know which party to vote for long before the date of an election and the onset of a campaign with all the talk of issues and choice. Put another way, many people actually choose to define themselves as a 'Labour person', as a 'Conservative loyalist', or as a 'Liberal protester'. In this state of affairs elections provide opportunities for voters to *express* their loyalty and commitment to 'their' party. Elections are not seen as occasions when voters make an *instrumental* choice. Party Identification theorists recognise that on occasions we may 'protest' and abstain (or even vote against the party with which we identify) but they argue that we normally retain our partisanship because we possess a 'homing tendency' that leads us back to 'our' party at subsequent elections.

What predictions follow from the Party Identification model?

Numerous predictions, expectations, and suggestive insights are part and parcel of the Party Identification model – indeed no other model or theory of voting behaviour offers more.

1 Party identification is seen as the strongest predictor of vote choice at an election: know which party a person identifies with and you should know how he or she will vote.

2 The stronger a voter's partisan self-image then the greater the stability of party choice over a series of elections (because people committed to a party are highly selective with regard to the information they take on board) and the greater the likelihood that they will actually turn out to vote.

3 Although parental partisanship is strongly associated with the direction of a voter's partisanship (because of the powerful socialising implications of the early home environment), a voter's party identification is predicted to depart from that of his or her parents if the parents were of Liberal, mixed or no strong party allegiance; if the parents were politically 'deviant' and identified with the party which obtained the minority of support within their social class; or if the voter went on to move out of the class of the parents so that early attachments no longer 'fitted' the new social situation.

4 Because party identification is usually self-reinforcing we can expect it to strengthen with the length of time it is held and so can predict that the newly enfranchised and young voters will be weakly attached to a party just as older people will be more strongly attached.

5 Most fundamental of all, because it relates to the development of the party system and to the prospects of electoral success for the Labour and Conservative Parties, Butler and Stokes predicted the maturing and strengthening of the established two-party system that was so much a feature of the party political scene in the 1950s and 1960s. This prediction derived directly from

their theory of political socialisation. Before the Labour Party was established, working-class voters were already integrated into support for the Conservative Party and the Liberal Party. The working-class could scarcely support a party which did not exist but once the Labour Party was established it did not immediately secure the mass support of the working class because both Liberal and Conservative attachments tended to linger on (and were *passed* on by families) in ways which restricted the development of Labour Party partisanship among the working class. However, as the Liberal Party slowly slipped from centre state during the inter-war period and as the Labour Party came to prominence so the electorate came to be increasingly composed of people who were socialised by parents who were *themselves* brought up in an era of Conservative and Labour dominance. In effect, Butler and Stokes considered that the process of socialisation caused partisan attachments to linger on so that change was lagged and delayed but not completely blocked. They predicted the continuing decline of Liberalism and the decline of working-class Conservatism. They also predicted that the Labour Party would go on to seize more and more of its 'natural' class base amongst manual workers so strengthening the significance of the class alignment in party politics; the extent of class voting; and the dominance of the two-party battle between Labour and the Conservatives.

The essence of the Butler and Stokes model

Butler and Stokes presented us with a simple two-class two-party model of Britain and its politics.

1 The Conservative and Labour Parties together were seen as commanding the electorate's overwhelming allegiance. Government swung from one party to the other on the basis of movements of votes that were nationally uniform but exaggerated by the electoral system.

2 The country was seen as simply divided into a middle class of non-manual (or white-collar) workers, and a working class of manual (or blue-collar) workers.

3 A tie-up was identified between class and party. The Conservative Party secured the bulk of the middle-class vote (70 per cent in 1955) just as the Labour Party secured the vote of the majority of the working class (69 per cent in 1966).

4 The Liberal Party was not exactly ignored, but the small size of the Liberal vote (just 5.9 per cent in 1959) and the fact that it was interpreted as an unstable protest that was not based on any class meant that its significance did not disturb the power of the two-party two-class paradigm.

5 In a similar way, cleavages besides those of class were not ignored but they too did not disturb the class-based perspective of Butler and Stokes. Certain cleavages were seen as of decaying and weakening significance, as was the case with respect to the religious cleavage, regional differences or local political traditions. Other cleavages were minimised because they were seen as basic corollaries of class that normally reinforced the basic class cleavage, as was the case with respect to level of schooling, type of housing and trade union

membership. In effect, the view was taken that a working-class job invariably 'went' with poor schooling, trade union membership and occupancy of a council house, just as a middle-class occupation 'went' with better education, home ownership and the absence of union membership. Of course, there was the recognition that certain individuals might break out from the normal reinforcing mould (be working class but own a house; be middle class but belong to a trade union) but these were seen as exceptions to the rule and they would have to endure uncomfortable 'cross-pressures' before deciding how to vote.

Working-class Tories and middle-class socialists

During the 1950s and 1960s the tie-up between class and party – between the working class and Labour, and between the middle class and the Conservatives – was seen as so obvious, so natural and so complete as not to need any explanation at all. We all somehow 'knew' that the Labour Party was 'for' the working class (since the Party itself told us so at the same time as the Conservatives berated Labour for being sectional and uninterested in the well-being of the nation as a whole) and it was not seen as necessary to explain just *why* and how the Labour Party secured working-class votes. In a similar way, we all too easily accepted the Labour Party view that the Conservative Party was the party of business and the suburban middle class and so saw no need to say *why* the middle class supported that party. Explanatory effort did not centre on making sense of the voting behaviour of the majority who supported the 'correct' class party but rather dwelt on those 'class deviants' who broke ranks and supported the 'wrong' party. Explaining the working-class Tories and accounting for the middle-class socialists absorbed an enormous amount of research energy during the 1960s precisely because these alignments were seen as odd given the grip of traditional class analysis on political sociology. In our view, this explanatory effort occurred to the detriment of adequate research attention being devoted to making sense of the prevailing class and party alignments. Notwithstanding this, however, it is still important for us to come to terms with the explanations for the voting behaviour of the 'class deviants' because this has been a core field of research within the British psephological tradition.

Working-class Tories

1 Marxists were of the opinion that no one from the working class 'should' vote Conservative (or even Labour!) since it was seen as correct for the working class to be rebels in red committed to the cause of socialist revolution. From this point of view, working-class Conservatism was explained by pointing to the power of a dominant ideology which shaped the consciousness of working people so that they were led away from any belief in the need for action that would work for the destruction of the capitalist system and the creation of a socialist society that alone would serve their 'real' long-term interests. The mass

media was seen as particularly important in this process because it carried the dominant ideology and so was crucial in leading an unthinking and uncritical working class into a false appreciation of where their real, or objective, political interests lay. Instead of seeing the need for action to attain socialism, working class people were duped by the media into support for the Conservative Party against their real interests and long-term needs. This suggestion that there is a dominant ideology in Britain and that it is important in enabling us to explain voting behaviour has been taken up more recently by Dunleavy and Husbands in their Radical Approach and we will be assessing this approach later in the Chapter.

2 Right back to the nineteenth century there were those who hoped that the working class would not rock the boat once they secured the vote but would be deferential and support the established leaders in the established parties, leaving them to govern the nation as only they knew best. This line of argument about 'deference' was picked up by mainstream social scientists in the 1950s and 1960s and used as an explanation for the existence of working-class Tories amongst those who were old, or who lived in the country or who worked in traditional craft jobs in close relation to their employers who were presumed to display a paternalistic concern for their workforce in a way which massaged the sentiments of employee deference.

3 Other theorists concerned to make sense of the working-class Tory vote pointed to the importance of 'self-assigned class'. In effect, if people who were 'really' working class nevertheless *thought* of themselves as middle class then they would be more likely to identify with the Conservatives because that was the party that somehow went with that class and that image.

4 There was also the view that the presence of authoritarian sentiments amongst the traditional working class explained their support for the Conservative Party because these sentiments somehow followed through into support for the party that was strong on law and order, traditional morality, the defence of the nation and (of course) the control of immigration.

5 As the 'You've never-had-it-so-good' and 'I'm alright Jack' decade of the 1950s bit into popular imagination so it was suggested that working-class people were abandoning support for the Labour Party simply because they were becoming more affluent. With private affluence, working people were seen as having less need of public services and so they had less interest in supporting the Labour Party – a party that was committed to state provision *and* to the high levels of taxation that were necessary to sustain that provision.

6 More subtlely, it was suggested that a process of *embourgeoisement* was at work whereby as working-class people became more affluent so they also took on the trappings of a more individualistic, privatised, home and family-centred, and consumer-oriented life-style. This was seen as important politically because it involved the adoption of new *values* that involved a break with the solidaristic loyalties of workplace and neighbourhood that in themselves were seen as having sustained an identification with the Labour Party regardless of the simple reality of poverty or affluence on its own.

We have to question many of these explanations for working-class Conservatism. The Marxist explanation exaggerates the power (and even the existence) of a dominant ideology at the same time as it is patronising in choosing to see the working class as duped fools. The argument about deference almost certainly exaggerates the extent to which this value pervades working-class thinking and works to the advantage of the Conservative Party. The argument about affluence and *embourgeoisement* presumes that there was once some kind of 'Golden Age' of collectively solidaristic working-class communities where common deprivation and poverty served to produce real fraternal values and Labour Party attachments. In reality, this view tends to be romantic and always portrays a community a generation or so before the time of the person referring to it. Moreover, early research on 'affluent workers' suggested that they actually retained a sense of solidarity and a commitment to the Labour Party. Finally, we also have to question that view which suggests that a concern with family matters, domesticity and materialism is both new to working-class experience and subversive of collective action since not only have sections of the working class long been preoccupied with status, position and materialism, but family values can often serve as a basis for mobilising workers into collective action. Pahl and Wallace's research on the Isle of Sheppey 'discovered neither the solidarity of workers intent on smashing the capitalist system (the rebels in red), nor the deferential privatised worker (the angels in marble)' but emphasised instead the multifaceted sources of social consciousness and the complex mosaic of social experience out of which working people construct their social identities and political allegiances. They further suggested that the Labour voters of the post-war years should be seen less as class warriors and more as pragmatic opportunists, selecting the best available strategy to get better health, housing, education and so on. Frank Parkin's contribution to the debate on the working-class Tories has had the wit – and the wisdom – to turn explanatory orthodoxy on its head. In suggesting that 'political deviance, examined from a national or societal level, is manifested not in working-class Conservatism but rather in electoral support for Socialism on the part of members of any social stratum', he not only highlighted the need to specifically make sense of the dominant patterns of class support for parties – working-class Labour; middle-class Conservative – but also challenged an implicit but all-pervasive vulgar Marxism which saw working-class support for the Conservative Party and all cross-class voting as anomalous, somehow wrong, and as so strange as to demand explanation above all else.

Middle-class socialists

The middle-class Labour voter has not received the same amount of academic attention as the working-class Tory. In part this is because the middle class have been more loyal to 'their' party, the Conservatives, but also because, we suspect, academics have been reluctant to turn the research spotlight onto themselves. There are, however, at least three distinct perspectives on the 'problem'.

1 There has been an emphasis on the psychology of the educated middle class in the caring professions who were seen as getting the emotional satisfaction of expressing values in action when they pressed for social reforms for *others* through support for the Labour Party.
2 More recently, the fact that middle-class employees in the public sector are more likely to vote Labour than their counterparts in the private sector has been explained by pointing to the *self-interest* of those who want to see a party in government which is committed to expanding the public sector and hence their job security and quite possibly their pay.
3 Some students of voting behaviour and class suggest that an element of the non-manual middle-class vote for Labour is best seen as a 'working class vote in disguise'. This view is based on the fact that much white-collar work is dull, routine, poorly paid and undertaken by those who may well have come from a working-class home and who may continue to choose to see themselves as working class – albeit workers by brain rather than by the hard graft of hand.

We will be discussing the importance of sectoral cleavages and the problems of defining class later in this chapter, but for the moment we can criticise much of the work on middle-class socialists by noting that it tends to be bedevilled by the same limiting assumptions that run through the literature on working-class Conservatives. Both working-class Conservatives and middle-class Labour supporters are defined as 'problems' to be explained precisely because writers are using a simple model which presumes that there is, and should be, a neat causal chain whereby people in a particular position in the class structure should have a particular form of social consciousness and should then go on to display a distinct pattern of political behaviour. Put more concretely, the conventional model presumes that the manual worker should be conscious of the need for socialist change and so support the Labour Party at the same time as the white-collar employee should want to preserve the status quo and so support the Conservative Party. This model is limited in its capacity to capture the complexity of social structure; limited in its capacity to explain the development of consciousness; and limited in its concern to derive political action from structure and consciousness. It is not the case that voters can simply be divided into a middle class of non-manual workers and a working class of manual workers as if that is the end of the matter with respect to what we need to know about social structure in order to explain the vote. It is also too simple to presume that an individual's consciousness and political action can be read off from knowledge about employment alone. Matters are vastly more complex than this. Consciousness does not come in the pay packet and a person's world view and identity is shaped by more, and less, than his or her position in the class structure. To say that class cannot explain everything we need to know to make sense of voting behaviour does not mean that we subscribe to the view that class can explain nothing. However, it does mean that we need to avoid being trapped in the use of simple models and outmoded concepts.

Assessing the Party Identification model

There is no doubt that the Party Identification – two-class two-party – model fitted the rough essentials of the electoral situation in Britain from 1945 to around 1970. It did a good job dealing with electoral stability and continuity. There are, however, niggling weaknesses within the Party Identification model as well as more fundamental problems that bear on its capacity to handle electoral change and volatility.

At the niggling level, the model tended to exaggerate the importance of early socialisation and failed to explain just how values and partisan attachments were formed and transmitted. Put another way, the model tended to have an 'oversocialised' conception of voters and so tended to presume that voting behaviour was explained if attention were devoted to the social situation of masses of voters irrespective of how individual voters thought about themselves and about politics. This emphasis meant that the model probably exaggerated the extent of voter ignorance and disinterest in politics and issues, and so failed to attend to the significance of issues and party policies in voting behaviour and in election outcomes. Predictions were a key feature of the Party Identification model but the predictions with respect to the fortunes of the Conservative and Labour Parties have proved woefully at odds with reality as third-party voting has increased and as new parties have come into being. Simply expressed, loyalty to a party is important but it is not unconditional and whilst it may act as a brake to slow change and shifts in support it can scarcely stop change altogether and forever.

It is this reality of change in many guises that has provided the fundamental challenge to the Party Identification model. That model placed its emphasis on class and on party identification and it has not been able to cope with changes in social structure and class, still less with the volatility that has become such a feature of electoral behaviour in Britain in the last two decades. To 'see' social structure simply in terms of class and to 'see' class simply in terms of a distinction between a middle class of non-manual workers and a working class of manual workers has shown itself to be insensitive to the more complex and developing realities of contemporary British society. Moreover, in a situation of electoral volatility where people are clearly *not* identifying with parties in the kind of stable and committed way that is the hallmark of the expectations integral to the Party Identification model then the model itself becomes problematic and unable to cope precisely because crucial matters are falling outside of its frame of reference. *The* problem for the Party Identification model lies in the fact that fundamental change *has* become a feature of society and electoral politics in Britain and the theory has had no real purchase on this. Many observers have argued that the 1970 election marked the close of a quarter-century of stable two-party voting at the same time as it opened a decade of dealignment.

These kind of observations invite two questions, both of which need to be answered if we are to better understand voting behaviour in Britain today: first, what are the electoral changes of significance that have occurred since 1970, and second, if the Party Identification model cannot make good sense of these changes are there alternative theories, or perspectives, that are better able to help us explain things?

Electoral Change: Partisan Dealignment and Class Dealignment

Butler and Stokes saw the overwhelming bulk of voters as partisans who were keenly aligned to (or identified with) either the Conservative Party or the Labour Party. They also saw the bulk of the working class aligned to and voting for the Labour Party just as the midle class were seen as aligning themselves to the Conservative Party at the polls. In contrast to this stable picture of partisan alignment and class alignment many observers have since noted that we have entered a new era of partisan *de*alignment and class *de*alignment.

Partisan dealignment refers to a trend of two-party decline – a trend whereby fewer and fewer voters feel attached to the Labour and Conservative Parties in ways that can be measured on various dimensions. Class dealignment refers to the decline of class voting – to the weakening association between occupational class and voting for the Conservative and Labour Parties. What, then, is the evidence with respect to these trends of change, and how can we best explain these developments in electoral politics?

What is the evidence with respect to partisan dealignment?

We can provide statistics on changes with respect to the two-party share of the vote; the two-party share of the electorate; and party membership; and we can also deal with the changing extent of party identification itself. All of this information is suggestive of partisan dealignment.

Table 3.1 makes clear that from 1945 to 1970 Britain came nearest to being a pure two-party system. Cracks began to appear in the election of February 1974 when the two-party *share of the vote* fell from 89.5 per cent (in 1970) to 75.1 per cent (in February 1974) – a fall which was obviously, and necessarily, mirrored in rising support for third parties. The 1979 election saw something of a return to 'normal', but the share of the vote secured by the Labour and Conservative Parties in 1983 and 1987 was still the lowest since 1923. We can also see from the table that Labour's electoral decline has been somewhat steeper than that of the Conservatives. Moreover, the Conservatives have had some 'ups' as well as some 'downs' in their vote share whereas this has been less the case with respect to the trend of change in the Labour share of the vote.

Table 3.1   The Parties' share of the vote: 1922–87

	Con	*Lab*	*Lib/All*	*Other*	*Con + Lab*
1922	38.5	29.7	18.9	12.9	68.2
1923	38.0	30.7	29.7	1.6	68.7
1924	46.8	33.3	17.8	2.1	80.1
1929	38.1	37.1	23.6	1.2	75.2
1931	55.0	30.8	6.5	7.7	85.8
1935	47.7	38.0	6.7	7.5	85.7
1945	36.2	48.0	9.0	6.8	84.2
1950	43.5	46.1	9.1	1.3	89.6
1951	48.0	48.8	2.6	0.6	96.8
1955	49.7	46.4	2.7	1.2	96.1
1959	49.3	43.9	5.9	0.9	93.2
1964	43.4	44.1	11.2	1.3	87.5
1966	41.9	48.1	8.5	1.5	90.0
1970	46.4	43.1	7.5	3.0	89.5
1974 Feb	37.9	37.2	19.3	5.6	75.1
1974 Oct	35.8	39.2	18.3	6.7	75.0
1979	43.9	37.0	13.8	5.3	80.9
1983	42.4	27.6	25.4	4.6	70.0
1987	42.3	30.8	22.6	4.3	73.1

Source: Heath, Jowell, and Curtice (1985) p. 3.; Butler and Kavanagh (1988) p. 283

Table 3.2 sets down the figures with respect to the two-party *share of the electorate*. This statistic takes on board the impact of abstention, of not voting for any party, and reveals a picture of uneven decline for the two major parties since 1951. In that year nearly 80 per cent of *electors* turned out to vote Conservative or Labour, but by the election of 1983 those parties had been dumped by nearly 30 per cent of the electorate and the pickup in support in 1987 has done little to restore the solid two-party pattern.

Figures with respect to *party membership* need to be treated with a pinch of salt since all parties have an interest in massaging their own membership upward. But the individual membership of the Conservative and Labour Parties has fallen dramatically from a peak in 1953, of 2,800,000 for the Conservative and 1,500,000 for Labour, and at a rate far faster than the fall in the two-party share of the electorate. By the early eighties Conservative Party membership was down to 1,200,000 and individual membership of the Labour Party dropped below 300,000.

Finally, and perhaps most telling of all, academic surveys of the electorate since 1964 have provided us with concrete information on the strength and direction of the electorate's *party identification*, and this is set down in Figure 3.2. In 1964, 81 per cent of the electorate identified with the Conservative or Labour Parties and 40 per cent were 'very strong' identifiers. By 1979 the figures were down to 76 per cent and 19 per cent, and in 1987 the figures stood at 67 per cent and 24 per cent. This weakening of partisan attachments has been a phenomena of all ages and of both sexes

Table 3.2 Share of electorate for each Party: 1945–87

	Con	Lab	Lib/All	Con + Lab
1945	29.1	35.4	6.7	64.5
1950	36.3	38.6	7.6	74.9
1951	39.3	39.9	2.1	79.2
1955	38.2	35.6	2.0	73.8
1959	38.8	34.5	4.6	73.3
1964	33.4	34.0	8.6	67.4
1966	31.8	36.4	6.4	68.2
1970	33.4	31.0	5.3	64.4
1974 Feb	29.9	29.3	16.6	59.2
1974 Oct	26.1	28.6	15.8	54.7
1979	33.3	28.1	10.4	61.4
1983	30.8	20.0	18.4	50.8
1987	31.8	23.2	17.0	55.0

Source: Butler and Kavanagh (1988) p. 283; Sarlvik and Crewe (1983) p. 6

and classes, but among young voters with a higher education partisan attachments have declined at a particularly sharp rate.

We clearly cannot predict from this information because nothing about an uneven trend ensures its continuation into the future. However, taken together with information about electoral volatility; uneven support for party policies; and the increasing extent of negative and tactical voting *against* parties (in place of positively voting for 'your' party) we do have evidence suggestive of a steady erosion of commitment to the Labour and Conservative Parties. Put more directly, we are able to support the proposition that there has been partisan dealignment in Britain. British general elections are no longer largely straight contests between two party giants. Having said that, our electoral system has prevented this development finding expression in the membership of the House of Commons where we continue to have two-party domination, and it is always possible that a pattern of two-party politics could reassert itself in the country at large.

What is the evidence with respect to class dealignment?

In dealing with this question we are trying to see whether the tie-up between class and party has broken down and whether there has been a decline in class voting, or whether the class basis of party support and 'class politics' itself is as strong as ever. This matter is hotly disputed. Much depends on how we define class and on how we choose to measure class dealignment. We will be attending to the various definitions of class that have been used within the literature on voting behaviour later in this section. For the moment it is important to be alive to the fact that there are three definitions of class dealignment.

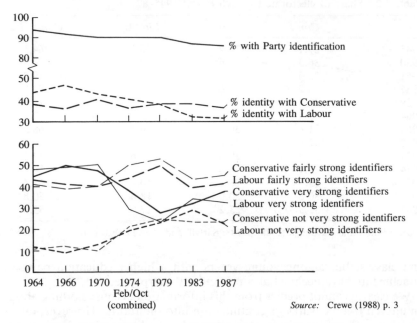

Figure 3.2 Incidence and Strength of Conservative and Labour partisanship 1964-87

Absolute class dealignment

Traditionally, class dealignment has been defined as a decline in *absolute* class voting. On this criterion we need to see whether Labour's share of the working-class vote has fallen; whether the Conservative share of the middle-class vote has fallen; and whether the overall level of class voting – middle-class Conservative and working-class Labour as a proportion of all votes – has fallen. Figure 3.3 shows the pattern of class voting since 1945. Throughout the 1950s and 1960s nearly two-thirds of both classes voted for their 'natural' class party. From 1970, however, there has been a striking decline in class voting. In the election of 1983, for the first time since surveys began, the majority of voters declined to vote along the 'correct' class lines, and this pattern of 'deviant' electoral support has continued to hold for the 1987 election. If class dealignment is defined as fewer middle-class people voting Conservative and/or fewer working-class people voting Labour then such a process *has* been taking place.

Relative class dealignment

There is a more exacting criterion of class dealignment which takes issue with the reasoning that is caught up in the first definition. From this second

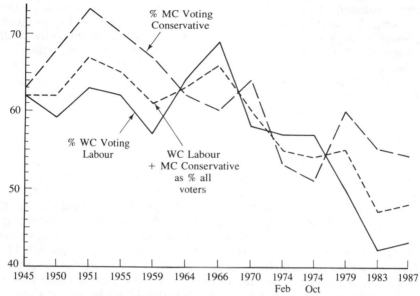

Source: For 1945-83, Heath, Jowell and Curtice (1985) p. 30; for 1987 MORI poll in the Times and Sunday Times, 13-14.6.87

Figure 3.3 History of Class Voting 1945-87

point of view what really matters is whether a party's support from a given class has changed *relative* to its support from other classes. Heath, Jowell and Curtice in their analysis of the 1983 selection survey take this view. They argue that to see the proportion of each class that votes for its 'natural' class party as a measure of class voting is misleading because it runs the risk of confusing a decline in Labour's electoral fortunes with a change in the class basis of voting. These authors make the point that if a class party like Labour does badly at the polls it is almost true by definition that a smaller proportion of the working class will have turned out to support their natural class party, and given the large size of the working class this in turn is likely to mean that the overall level of class voting will have fallen too. In their view, the traditional measure of class voting simply tells us how well the parties have done at the polls. They are of the opinion that class dealignment can only be said to have occurred if *cross-class* voting increases with the two classes voting *against* (rather than for) their respective natural class parties. Relative class dealignment will have occurred if, for example, Labour loses votes among the working class whilst gaining votes among the middle class. In this state of affairs the ratio of its working-class to its middle-class vote will have fallen and it will have become relatively stronger in the middle class than it was previously. Put another way, Heath, Jowell and Curtice do not see a decline in the working-class vote as a measure of class dealignment but look to see if there has been an increase in the working-class *anti*-Labour vote. They claim that Labour has lost as much ground in the middle class as in the working class and fared badly in all classes in 1983. Having said that, they argue that the party remained relatively stronger in the working class than the middle class – in other words it remained a class party but had become an unsuccessful class party. Not surprisingly, they feel able to conclude that 'the class basis of politics . . . shows no good evidence of secular decline'.

'Intuitive' class dealignment

This meaning of class dealignment tries to get away from specialised psephological constructs. It argues that class dealignment exists if the non-manual and manual classes have become more similar, or less contrasted, in their voting patterns over time. From this point of view the growth of Liberal voting from the mid-seventies onwards constitutes powerful support for the class dealignment thesis precisely because it shows that voters are detaching themselves from support for their 'natural' class parties. The fact that people are now choosing to vote Green in the late eighties is also of significance precisely because all third-party voting can *itself* be viewed as a measure of class dealignment. Hence it should not be seen as a factor which must be discounted in advance of assessing trends in class voting because of a preoccupation with a two-class two-party model more appropriate to earlier times.

Once we attend to the debates about class dealignment it is all too easy to get bogged down in definitional problems but a number of points need to be made before we can move on to explore the explanations that have been advanced to account for this, and other trends of change in voting behaviour.

1 Class itself is a contested concept. There is disagreement as to what precisely the term means: there are disputes as to how precisely to divide the population into different classes; and epitaphs are regularly written for the very concept of class. For the most part, students of voting behaviour have been content to follow the lead of Butler and Stokes and have adopted a two-class model of the class structure so that the population is simply divided into a working class of manual workers and a middle class of non-manual, or white-collar workers. The limitations of this two-class model are now widely recognised. Sarlvik and Crewe adopted the 'social grade' schema which divides the population into six groups based on differences in incomes and life-style. Heath, Jowell and Curtice reject this perspective, and in arguing that the focus on life-style has led political scientists to believe that rising living standards would erode the class basis of British politics, they highlight the extent to which perspectives on class dealignment are partly dependent on the way in which class itself is conceptualised. For their part, Heath, Jowell and Curtice focus not on income levels as such but on 'economic interests'. They distinguish five

classes. They take the view that wage labourers have different interests from
those of the self-employed or from those of salaried managers and professionals; they recognise that the self-employed category cuts right across the
conventional manual/non-manual distinction; and they are mindful of the
importance of distinguishing routine non-manual workers from the salaried
managers and professionals at the same time as they distinguish foremen and
technicians from the working-class proper. In their view, these distinctions are

(a) Social grade*

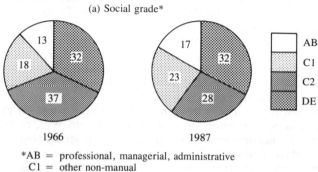

1966   1987

*AB = professional, managerial, administrative
 C1 = other non-manual
 C2 = skilled manual
 DE = semi-/unskilled, on state benefit

(b) Class composition of the British electorate 1964-87

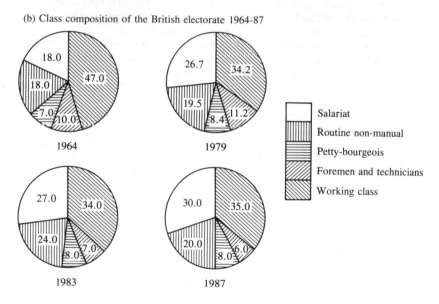

Source: For 1964 and 1983, Heath, Jowell and Curtice, (1985) p. 36; for 1979, Dunleavy
(1987) p. 418; for 1987, private letter from John Curtice who recognises that these figures
cannot be simply compared with those in Heath, Jowell and Curtice (1985)

Figure 3.4 Changing Class Composition

important because the fact that these five classes are in different positions in the labour market provides the basis for their differing values and political allegiances.

2 Notwithstanding the disputes about class, there is broad agreement that Britain has been transformed from a blue-collar society into a white-collar society in a way that has involved upward social mobility and a decline in the sheer *size* of the manual working class. This is revealed in the pie charts that make up figure 3.4. Attending to this transformation enables us to put debates about class dealignment into some kind of larger perspective. To focus on the declining *share* of the working class voting Labour is like rearranging deck chairs on the Titanic once we take on board the electoral significance of changing class *sizes* as well. Simply expressed, almost half of the decline in support for the Labour Party that occurred between 1964 and 1983 can be attributed to the decline in the size of the manual working class – a decline that has nothing whatsoever to do with class dealignment.

3 In a situation in which at least a third of voters have not voted for their 'natural' class party in every election since the Second World War, contemporary talk about class dealignment should not lead us to set up some past golden age of crisp class alignments. Occupational class on its own has never been a particularly secure base from which to *predict* the direction of party choice as the polls – still less has the preoccupation with class been able to really *explain*, or make sense of, voting behaviour.

4 Labour *is* securing a smaller share of the working-class vote than was once the case and this decline in absolute class voting holds true whether or not the Labour vote is rising or falling amongst the middle class.

5 The non-manual, middle-class alignment with the Conservative Party has also been breaking down. Although this has often been ignored because of the preoccupation with Labour's electoral fortunes, it demands attention and explanation and this will involve our having to attend to the significance of sectoral cleavages and to self-interested voting at the polls.

6 The growth of third-party voting, be it for the nationalist parties in the 1970s or for the Liberals and other centre parties in the 1970s and 1980s, is itself indicative of a weakening of the class–party connection at the same time as it suggests the significance of alternative bases of partisanship in regions and localities. We will be discussing the geography of voting in an appendix to this chapter.

The established explanation of voting behaviour in Britain was erected on the twin pillars of party identification and class voting in a two-party system: individuals were loyal to their party, and the working class was Labour just as the middle class was Conservative. The messy reality of partisan dealignment and class dealignment has cracked the pillars that supported the established explanation. Students of elections have recognised the need to devise alternative models of voting behaviour that are better geared to making sense of voting behaviour in volatile times.

Those attentive to the erosion of partisan loyalties point to the rise of issue voting by voters who are making informed and rational choices at the polls. Those more attentive to the declining electoral significance of class cleavages have found new sectoral cleavages to be of electoral significance and Dunleavy and Husbands have devised a radical approach in the attempt to make sense of things. What, then, do these two newer perspectives have to say about voting behaviour in Britain, and how far do they make good sense of voting in volatile times?

The Issue Voting–Rational Choice Model: the Importance of Political Issues and Individual Choice

Early work on voting behaviour in the party identification tradition tended to see the voter as poorly informed on issues; with weak and unstable policy preferences; and without any kind of coherent ideology. The conventional wisdom held that the majority of voters were ignorant of the specific policies of the party they supported. More than this, it was even suggested that some voters actively disagreed with the policies of their party – as was the case with Labour voters, many of thom were hostile to nationalisation. Observers concluded that issues and policies just did not matter. The view was taken that long-established and deeply-rooted party identifications came first and so served to shape issue-attitudes and policy preferences and not vice versa. Put another way, voters were said to form their views on issues *because* of their attachment to a particular party and they did not work the other way around and attach themselves to a party *because* they had well-established views on issues and policies which they wished to see advanced by any party.

More recently, the weakening of habitual party and class loyalties (and the realisation that there are many, many floating voters) has opened the way for a new literature on voting. This literature suggests that voters are not fools. Issue-related perceptions and attitudes are now seen as very much more important in the electoral process than earlier studies had suggested. Instead of seeing the vote as an emotional, unthinking expression of allegiance to a party and to a class, the vote is increasingly being seen as an *instrument* that is used rationally by individuals who choose to 'purchase' the package of party policies that will best advantage their own self-interest. In concrete terms, for example, explanations for the working-class Tory are now less likely to centre on the significance of deference and are much more likely to see this pattern of support as a self-interested and issue-oriented response to a party that taxes less and encourages the spread of home ownership at the same time as it has popular policies with respect to defence and law and order. Rational Choice theories that draw attention to the significance of issue voting argue that issues do matter precisely because policy preferences determine the direction of vote choice and not vice versa as Party Identification theorists have claimed. Not surprisingly, the role of party identification has been re-evaluated. Advocates of the Issue Voting–Rational Choice model of voting claim that party identification is not an *independent* influence on voting behaviour and does not add to our ability to predict electoral choice once the voters' policy preferences are known and taken into account. Himmelweit and associates, in *How Voters Decide*, see party identification as a confusing concept and argue that 'it is as likely that the stability of "party identification" across elections is a result of a good fit between individuals' views and a particular party's platform as an indication that identification with a party has affected the voter's views.

In attending to the Issue Voting–Rational Choice perspective on voting behaviour we are dealing with a perspective that has become highly pervasive but without a text which presents the perspective as powerfully as Butler and Stokes presented the earlier Party Identification approach. Having said that, it is important to explore and assess the pure theory of Anthony Downs before we deal with the applied research of Hilda Himmelweit and then take a stance on the more common-sense position which suggests that people now vote on the issues in order to put a party into office which will give them what they want.

An Economic Theory of Democracy and the problem of rationality

An early, but still influential, study of democracy and voting from the point of view of Rational Choice assumptions was provided by Anthony Downs in his *An Economic Theory of Democracy*. Downs applied the economic model of rational, maximising, self-interested man to the world of democratic politics. Political parties were seen as firms in the business of selling packages of policies in return for votes. Because parties were eager to maximise their share of the vote they sought to devise popular policies and this, combined with the process of electoral competition, produced a consensus politics as both parties struggled to win the mass of votes in the centre ground. For their part, voters were regarded as political consumers using votes as money to demand and buy policies. Downs assumed that voters knew what they wanted and were every bit as rational and self-interested as the leaders of the political parties. Voters were not seen as party identifiers tied to a party and they were not seen as possesed of enduring class or group loyalties since they were assumed to be rational, maximising, lone *individuals* geared to the attainment of their own best interests as they saw them. Given these assumptions, voters were free to shop around, attend to the past performance of the governing party and to the promises of the opposition, before eventually choosing that party which offered them the best policy package at the lowest tax cost.

In theory all this is fine, but Rational Choice theorists have always been troubled by the fact that voting clearly involves 'costs' for an individual. He or she has to bother to get information and go to the polls in a situation where the 'benefits' from voting are practically non-existent given the fact that one vote is neither here nor there in terms of its effect on the final election result. Put another way, Rational Choice theorists have difficulty in explaining just *why* a rational individual should bother to vote at all. One way around the problem is for theorists to argue that it makes sense for rational people to minimise these costs by not trying to be particularly rational voters! In other words, instead of attending to the issues and to the details of party policies and government performance, it makes rough-and-ready sense for voters to take short cuts, attend more to the ideologies of the parties, rely on the judgements of other people and make the most of the free information that comes by way of the media and informal conversations. But in saying all this, we are presented with a picture of the real-life 'rational' voter behaving in ways that are also recognisable from the Party Identification perspective. The truth of the matter is that in order to explain why large numbers of people do vote we are driven to recognise the importance of habit, duty and the social conventions that surround the importance of voting in liberal democracies. This takes us into matters and concerns that fall outside of the Issue Voting–Rational Choice framework at the same time as they challenge the credibility of that perspective on voting.

How Voters Decide and the problem of autonomous individuals

The most important British study of voting behaviour from the Issue Voting–Rational Choice perspective is *How Voters Decide*, by Hilda Himmelweit and a team of social psychologists. The study was written on the basis of repeated interviews over the period 1959–74 with a very small sample of British men drawn from the Greater London area. The authors placed all their emphases on the 'responsive', 'active', 'individual voter' and his 'cognitions'. They developed a 'consumer model of vote choice' so as to emphasise that the principles held in voting were the same as those which guided the individual in purchasing goods. In effect, 'the individual purchases a party' in that 'the individual searches for the best fit or least misfit between his or her views and preferences and the parties' platforms'. In doing this, however, the voter is affected by two 'variable and weaker influences' namely the habit of voting for a party ('brand loyalty') and the example of others – and here Himmelweit and associates 'draw an analogy to the influence of spouses, friends and colleagues whose purchases at times influence our own'. Notwithstanding the presence of these two weaker influences, the emphasis is on the policy preferences of the voter here and now, choosing afresh at each election and endeavouring to put into office a party 'which seems most likely to implement policies which they favour and whose style of government they can respect.'

Earlier studies of voters may have presented them as ignorant, ill-informed and non-ideological, but Himmelweit 'obtained a picture of the voter as someone who, though little interested in politics, is still accurately informed about many of the parties' platforms and holds definite views on a range of political issues'. She also found that the views of British voters were 'organised . . . along certain "ideological" dimensions which relate meaningfully to the individual's party choice'; she showed that knowing an individual's attitudes and values was a more accurate basis for predicting that person's vote choice than was knowledge about an individual's past vote; and she suggested that attitudes relevant to the vote (on issues and policies) did not merely reflect the individual's social group membership so that vote choice was not seen as closely linked to social determinants. In saying that 'attitudes matter more than past vote' Himmelweit was knocking the explanatory power of the Party Identification model and pointing to the extent of partisan dealignment. In refusing to see attitudes as a simple function of social group memberships and in arguing that people in the same social class do not tend to hold similar views Himmelweit was challenging the value of a perspective on voting behaviour that centred all attention on class; she was challenging the simple view of the class–party tie-up that bypasses the need to explore the *beliefs* that do (or do not) link class to party in the voter's mind; and she was highlighting the importance of class dealignment. In bald terms, Himmelweit pointed to the 'decrease in the role of social determinants in vote choice' and to 'the increased importance of voters' assessments of policies, parties and their leaders'. The portrait of the voter that emerges from Himmelweit's study is of someone 'who is not simply conforming to his or her own past or following other people's example, but makes up his own mind'.

The great merit of *How Voters Decide*, and of issue-oriented perspectives more generally, lies in the extent to which this body of work brings both thinking individuals *and* politics back into the study of voting behaviour. In the Party Identification model individuals, politics and issues were virtually ignored. The emphasis was on classes, and the concern to set down an association between class and party tended to bypass politics and failed to deal with politics and issues in the voters' minds. When theorists of voting behaviour found out that the majority of the working class voted Labour and that the majority of the middle class voted Conservative they invariably stopped their analysis at that point. They rather assumed that simply to set down this class–party tie-up was *of itself* enough to explain it and hence the voting behaviour of *the* working class and *the* middle class. Issue Voting–Rational Choice theorists reject the whole logic of this. They deny that a tie-up between a class and a party is any kind of explanation for it and they therefore insist on exploring the beliefs that actually link individual people within a class to a particular political party and vote choice. More than this, they refuse to see individuals as pressured products of a particular class background that coldly determines their views and political allegiances, but instead see individuals as thinking, calculating people who do make a rough attempt to attend to the issues in politics before voting. Theories of this kind make the effort to explain voting behaviour precisely because they deal with *mechanisms* and with politics. Put another way, they attempt to connect people to their vote through an exploration of the attitudes which people have about issues. In attending to these things they avoid the danger of seeing voting as some kind of apolitical act that is somehow explained, by social and economic determinants. Of course, the fact that class and party do not tie-up to anything like the same extent has made the Issue Voting–Rational Choice research agenda all the more relevant – the more so as the emphases on attitudes, issues and politics is better geared to dealing with electoral change than is the more static Party Identification approach.

Notwithstanding the explanatory merits integral to the issue voting perspective, *How Voters Decide* contains a number of defects which must caution us against too quick an acceptance of the analysis and conclusions.

1 The interview sample was small and unrepresentative. The study grew out of a non-political study of individual aspirations and started with over 600 respondents but only 178 people were successfully recontacted at every stage of the interview process. Moreover, only 31 of the final sample were manual workers whereas nearly 80 per cent were in the 'upper-middle' or 'middle-middle class' which is in no sense a representative sample of the electorate as a whole.

2 This perspective almost certainly exaggerates the extent to which voters do think about politics as individuals at the same time as it exaggerates the extent to which voters are open-minded on the issues and are thoughtful and informed on how to vote at an election.

3 The claim that attitudes were more important influences on voting behaviour than were social background influences is itself problematic. Not only is it always difficult to get at people's 'real' attitudes on political issues, but Himmelweit did not have enough social background variables for these to have a fair chance of showing their true importance: in particular neither housing situation, trade union membership nor employment status were among the variables measured.

4 This individualistic perspective on voting behaviour fails to provide an account of the origins of the political attitudes of those interviewed. This lack of interest in the origins of voters' attitudes and values, and the tendency to take voters' preferences for granted as 'givens', means that the attitudes themselves are seldom explored – still less located – in the larger social context, an understanding of which can go some way towards making sense of the values and attitudes held by different individuals in particular social locations. Rational Choice perspectives on voting tend to suck individuals out of the social context within which they are brought up, live and learn, and so see them as more isolated and autonomous than is probably the case. If it is important to see voters as individuals, it is also important for us to recognise that they are participants in society with all that this involves. Harrop and Miller are surely right to remind us that 'the era of the rational voter, unconstrained by ties of loyalty and fellow feeling, is still a long way off'.

Issue voting and the puzzle of Conservative success

Superficially, the easiest possible explanation for any election result is to say that on the most important issues in an election it was the winning party that had the popular policies. Such a perspective not only endows the election result with a special legitimacy – the winning party was in touch with public opinion – but also presents the voters in a flattering light as informed on the issues and thoughtful about their own (and the country's?) interests. With respect to the 1979 election, Sarlvik and Crewe pointed out that 'with one possible exception – the public's wish to maintain the standard of public services – the prevailing mood in the country was broadly in line with the Conservative's programme for economic recovery . . . and there was strong overall support for almost every plank in the Conservative platform'.

With respect to the 1983 election, however, Heath, Jowell and Curtice's analysis challenges the consumer theory's contention that the policies of the parties on the important issues determined the election result. They found that the issues of unemployment, inflation, taxation, government spending and defence were the dominant ones around which the election seemed to turn 'but on none of them was the Conservative Party clearly in the lead'. If the electorate had voted for the party they said they preferred on the single issue they said mattered most then the result would have been a deadheat. The same exercise in 1987 would almost certainly have placed Labour ahead – indeed, Crewe has made the point that 'had electors voted solely on the main issues Labour would have won' and yet they were only able to secure 30.8 per cent of the vote and just 23.2 per cent of the electorate in that election. Opinion polls and surveys, such as the British Social Attitudes surveys, deny the triumph of individualism. They suggest that the public has not been converted to Thatcherism and Thatcherite values on either the economic or the moral plane, and has consistently opposed a whole range of Thatcherite policies and decisions. More than this, these surveys suggest that the public has edged to the Left since 1979 and there has been a halting advance for tolerance and collectivism in a way which suggests that the 'new realism' of Thatcherism has not taken hold. That the Conservatives won the election in 1987 is not in doubt (even if they did only secure the support of less than a third of the electorate) but the evidence seems to suggest that they did this not so much because of their policies as in spite of them. This being the case a model of voting behaviour which attends to the importance of issue preferences and party policies does not give us much of a basis for making sense of the general elections of the 1980s. Even if the evidence with respect to the extent of issue voting was less ambiguous we would still face a problem in trying to construct a viable model of voting around the importance of issues and individuals since it is far from clear what constitutes an 'issue'. And it is not easy to discover how issue preferences convert into partisan support in the context of a situation where parties are presenting whole packages of policies about which the voters often know very little indeed. More then this, there are those who question whether the whole emphasis upon individuals and their own issue preferences can ever get to adequate grips with voting behaviour since it ignores the way in which people in society form their preferences and gain a sense of themselves and their interests. Instead of seeing individual voters as basically free to choose on the issues, the Radical Approach sees voters in groups as prey to influences which they cannot resist but which have to be regarded as central to any explanation of voting behaviour.

The Radical Approach: the Importance of Sectoral Cleavages and a Dominant Ideology

Dunleavy and Husbands' *British Democracy at the Crossroads* is unique in that it is the only study that advances what they see as a 'Radical Approach' to voting behaviour – an approach that is critical of both the Party Identification model and the Issue Voting–Rational Choice model.

The Party Identification perspective is rejected for two main reasons. First, it is viewed as based on an oversimplified and anachronistic model of British social structure that is only attentive to occupational class in a crude way; it sees the electorate as simply divided into a middle class of non-manual workers and a working class of manual workers. The consequence of this is that new *sectoral* cleavages that Dunleavy and Husbands see as significant in structuring political alignments and votes are either ignored, underestimated or reduced to mere corollaries of class that are not explored as significant in their own right. Second, the Party Identification perspective is seen as wrong in arguing that patterns of group partisanship are formed by a process of childhood socialisation and adult social contacts. Dunleavy and Husbands argue that the emphasis should be placed on the continuing and immediate *interests* of social groups – interests which derive from the position which a group occupies in the social structure even though the experience of those interests is seen as mediated through a dominant ideology which may mask a keen perception of what Dunleavy and Husbands see as the 'real' interests involved.

The Issue Voting–Rational Choice perspective is also rejected for two main reasons. First, the emphasis on individuals is seen as failing to deal with the shifts of party support in a mass electorate. Dunleavy and Husbands take the view that we can only make sense of why voters acted as they did at the polls if we place the emphasis on how social cleavages come to manifest themselves as political cleavages. Second, the perspective fails to get to grips with the reality and significance of a dominant ideology which Dunleavy and Husbands see as of massive significance in conditioning and shaping individual attitudes, interests and political alignments.

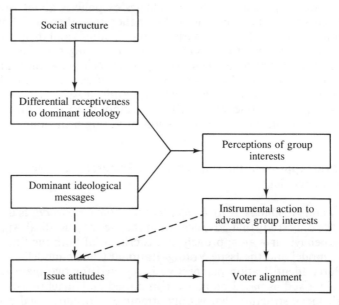

Source: Dunleavy and Husbands (1985) p. 19

Figure 3.5 The Radical Model

The essence of the Dunleavy and Husbands' model

Dunleavy and Husbands accept the widespread view that there has been a breakdown of class voting. However, they refuse to go along with the new conventional wisdom which talks of the rise of issue voting by rational individuals. They choose instead to focus on the influence of a changing social structure in shaping new political alignments, and on the role of dominant ideological influences and of party competition in structuring the way these social groups of voters view their interests. They argue that people's political and voting alignments are a product of five influences.

1 The first is their position in a complex social structure of inequalities and conflicts of interest. Class is seen as a line of social cleavage that has been losing its political and electoral significance. Dunleavy and Husbands argue that a new 'fault line' has emerged around sectoral cleavages to do with production and consumption that have developed as a result of increased state intervention in economic and social matters. Put more directly, there is a division between employees in the public sector and employees in the private sector; there is a division between those who depend on public services (principally for housing and transport) and those who rely on private provision through the market (home owners and car owners); and there is a division between those supported by the state, be they pensioners or the unemployed, and the rest who are either in work or in receipt of an adequate private pension. These sectoral cleavages

are seen as important precisely because they cut through the more established line of class cleavage and have the potential to assume significance in shaping political alignments. Health and education are (at least at this point in time) not especially significant in this regard because most people rely upon public provision so reducing the political impact of the cleavage between public and private sector consumers. But housing and transport are another matter precisely because they divide the electorate more evenly and cut through the working class in a way which fragments its fragile unity so contributing to the breakdown of the tie-up between the Labour Party and the working class. Simply expressed, many working-class people who own a car and a home and who work in the private sector have a material interest in low taxation and a smaller state and so are amenable to being mobilised into the Conservative camp. In a similar way, middle-class people employed in the public sector might be increasingly available to support the Labour Party whilst that Party continues to be geared to extending public provision, and secure public-sector employment in the face of a Conservative government that is bent on rolling back the state.

2 Consumption influences and the fact of a particular class or sectoral location do not of themselves tell us how people will line up and vote. Dunleavy and Husbands argue that 'the way in which people vote is conditioned by a set of dominant ideological messages'. These messages are seen as mainly formulated by a mass media which not only disseminates political (mis)information but which also defines acceptable political views and even 'the facts' themselves. This is said to form people's 'political consciousness'. Dunleavy and Husbands see this constructed consciousness as leading working people away from their longer term (but less visible) class interests and towards alignments based on less substantial (but more visible and immediate) sectoral interests. All of this is seen as working for the long-term interests of the dominant class because it works against and disorganises the whole working class from taking collective action for a fundamental change in the capitalist system itself.

3 'Out of the interaction between the first two influences people in different social locations form (collective) perceptions of how the interests of their location are integrated into the process of party competition'. For example, owner-occupiers are aware of the stake they have in the issue of mortgage tax relief and are encouraged to have a perception of the party that will best advantage their interest, just as social workers and teachers have a stake in well-funded state services and a sense as to the party which is geared to that cause.

4 'Within these perceptions most people most of the time act instrumentally . . . to promote the collective interests of their social location, as these have been defined in their society'.

5 'Finally, in this account, attitudes are formed simultaneously with alignments and as a result of the same influences' and so do not constitute important causal factors in structuring the way in which people vote.

Assessing the radical approach

Dunleavy and Husbands' emphasis on the electoral significance of sectoral cleavages arising out of state involvement in production and consumption is important. It gets us away from the simple class perspective on society that has tended to dominate most studies of voting behaviour in Britain. Nowadays, most students of voting behaviour are attentive to the electoral significance of sectoral cleavages and we can thank Dunleavy for this even though disputes abound as to the precise implications of these cleavages for patterns of voting within and between classes. In our view, the weight of evidence suggests that production-sector cleavages to do with work do operate within the middle class as public-sector managers and professionals are more likely to vote Labour than are their counterparts in the private sector. However, consumption-sector cleavages are of less electoral significance. True, they have a very limited effect on the working-class vote, but the emphasis on car owning as a key feature of a consumption sector is of itself ludicrous in that it focuses excessive attention on just one consumer good that most families now possess and perhaps even enjoy.

Whilst it is important to explore the electoral implications of sectoral cleavages, the *way* in which Dunleavy and Husbands go about this is open to challenge.

On the surface, what connects people in different social locations to a particular political party seems obvious enough once we take on board information about the policy positions of the parties and see people as fairly rational in the pursuit of their own interests. For example, the fact that a working-class person who lives in the south, owns a house, does not belong to a trade union and is employed in the private sector is more likely to vote for the Conservative Party than for the Labour Party could be explained simply by suggesting that the *experience* of the person concerned leads them to the conclusion that a Conservative government and Conservative policies will best advantage their interests. A similar, issue voting–rational choice explanation might also be used to explain why someone in the 'traditional working class' living in the north, housed as a council tenant, belonging to a trade union and working in the public sector is more likely to support the Labour Party. And a similar logic could be said to help us to understand why the Conservative vote amongst the private-sector middle class remained high and stayed solid in 1987 at the same time as it was much lower and fell amongst the public sector administrators and professionals who may well have felt threatened by a party that was eager, and willing, to roll back the state – and with it their jobs.

Dunleavy and Husbands seem to accept the plausibility of this kind of explanation since they themselves argue that 'most people most of the time act *instrumentally* to further the interests of their social location'. However, they pull dramatically back from this position when they argue that people are only able to promote their interests 'as these have been *defined* in their society'. In saying this, Dunleavy and Husbands are asserting the existence and power of a dominant ideology. They also give the mass media a crucial role in shaping this ideology and, in consequence, a crucial role in shaping political alignments in ways that Dunleavy and Husbands see as working against the 'real', or best, interests of working people. Now a case

can be made out for the impact of ideas and institutions on individual consciousness (as all of us tend to live out our lives through borrowed mean-
ings), and no one would deny that the mass media is powerful, can set
agendas and can influence what people think about. It is, however, quite
another matter to argue that there *is* one dominant ideology and that the
media ('the Tory press') *is* omnipotent, biased and able to shape people's
political consciousness over and against their own experience and interests.
We will be discussing all of this more fully in chapter 11, but for the
moment it is important for us to assert that if Dunleavy and Husbands
choose to explain voter alignments by giving weight to arguments about
ideology and the media then they need to assemble supporting evidence
about how this impacts on individual voters, and this they fail to do.

We have already suggested that the Issue Voting–Rational Choice model
can be criticised for taking voter preferences as 'given'; for simply assuming
that voters know their own best interests; and for arguing that individuals
do vote on the issues. However, such criticisms of an individualistic mode
of analysis need not lead us into support for the opposing 'structuralist'
position of Dunleavy and Husbands. This position, in asserting the existence of a dominant ideology pushed by a mass media, sees individuals as
pressured products of society who cannot reflect on their own experience
in order to come to a sensible appreciation of where their own interests lie
in the party political battle. In saying all this we are entering deep and dark
waters in the field of social theory where there has been a long-standing
dispute as to the importance of individuals or society. We clearly cannot
resolve this matter here even in the limited and applied context of making
sense of voting behaviour. However, we can say that it is quite impossible
to squeeze individuals out of the picture if we are to make good sense of
how people vote even though we recognise that it is also important to attend
to the larger societal context and to how this may (or may not) impinge on
individual consciousness about interests, issues and politics in ways that
affect the vote choice. The trouble is that Dunleavy and Husbands, in their
concern to dismiss individuals, ignore attitudes and bypass voters in the
rush to deal with 'aggregate social phenomena' and the political alignments
of sectoral groups, never ever feel the need to deal with the mechanisms that
serve to link real-life individual voters to their partisan choice – a choice
that is always and necessarily an individual act which can never be properly
explained if we only choose to focus on how groups line up at the polls. This
problem is compounded in *British Democracy at the Crossroads* because
Dunleavy and Husbands refuse to countenance the significance of socialisation and social contacts shaping distinctive voting patterns. Socialisation
theory of the kind advanced by Party Identification theorists is important precisely because it does provide a particular kind of explanation for
voting behaviour that, in connecting individuals to groups, goes some way
towards making sense of how many individuals vote and why, and does so
without relying on the overly individualistic viewpoint that Dunleavy and
Husbands condemn. Dunleavy and Husbands are part of that tradition

of scholarship which has sought to bury thinking individuals under the blanket of social pressures, and which has sought to read off politics from social and economic structures. But individuals do matter and do need to be taken into account in the study of voting behaviour, and the assumption that voting must somehow be rooted in, and explained by, social structure rather underestimates the extent to which voting may float free of social anchors in an era of increasingly political voting that is subject to a variety of short-term influences.

Conclusion

The three theories of voting behaviour that we have discussed in this section are very different in their starting assumptions and broad perspectives on voting. Theorists in the Party Identification tradition dwell on the importance of early socialisation; emphasise the stability and continuity of voting; see individuals as using the vote to express generalised support for a party; and argue that whole classes tend to align themselves to partic- ular political parties. Issue Voting–Rational Choice theorists downplay the importance of socialisation; see the vote as an instrument that is rationally deployed by individuals to advance their interests; are mindful of the extent of electoral volatility; and do not see individuals, still less classes, as aligned to particular political parties in an enduring fashion. For their part, Radical theorists refuse to focus on individual voters; see ideology and media power as all-important in shaping consciousness and political alignments; and are attentive to the electoral significance of sectoral cleavages in the light of social changes and the reality of class dealignment.

In our discussion of each of the theories we not only explored some of the evidence and how far the theories fitted the facts, but we also attended to the validity of the arguments and the assumptions that were integral to each perspective. In bald terms, the cogency of the Party Identification perspective was bruised by the demise of stable alignments and by the increasing reality of class dealignment and partisan dealignment. These developments in the real world of electoral politics opened up space for rival perspectives on voting that were better geared to making sense of voting behaviour in volatile times and changed social circumstances. The Issue Voting–Rational Choice perspective has come to assume a prominence. This perspective is important in that it brings politics and individuals back into the picture but it tends to assume that individuals are more rational and more autonomous than is the case, and the evidence suggests that individ- uals vote less on the issues than this perspective would have us believe. The Radical Approach is important in drawing attention to sectoral cleavages and to the role of ideology, but Dunleavy and Husbands are recklessly overambitious and offer us no solid empirical evidence to back their claim that production influences and consumption influences are important determinants of voting alignments. Their model does not attend to 'mechanisms' and so offers us no handle on the link between the perceptions of electors and their action as voters; and their argument about the importance of a dominant ideology is left unsupported by any evidence at the same time as their discussion of the media is weak.

These are all rather grim concluding assessments. We are suggesting that the Party Identification model has become increasingly unable to get an explanatory grip on voting behaviour, but we are further suggesting that Rational Choice models have not proved to be much more illuminating – and Dunleavy and Husbands' efforts to refute issue accounts yield a no more intelligible account of voting.

Notwithstanding the limitations of *all* the theories of voting behaviour, it is tempting at this particular point in the discussion to be bold and plump for one particular theory as the best of the lot. If this is seen as impossible then we may need to think about how we can advance understanding by trying to put the theories together using the best parts of each. And if it is difficult to combine rival and conflicting perspectives then maybe there is a case for psephologists trying to find a new approach that is better geared to explaining voting behaviour today.

Although purists might want us to plump for the one best theory in order to discover our view as to *which* theory has the explanatory edge we do not see this as sensible or possible since the theories are doing slightly different things which give them a relevance at different points in our electoral history. In a situation of electoral change we are better advised to try to explore *when* particular approaches are more, rather than less, useful than we are in trying to build on the insights of just one perspective alone. In broad terms, the Party Identification approach provides a static perspective on voting but it coped fairly well with the stable alignments that were so much a feature of electoral politics in the 1950s and 1960s; the Issue Voting–Rational Choice model had a better handle on change and provided a powerful perspective on the decade of dealignment in the 1970s when there was a freer-floating pattern of voting with voters responding to politics and engaging in a measure of informed choice consequent upon the breakdown of old loyalties; and if British politics is to realign around new sectoral cleavages then the sociological aspect of the Radical Approach might prove to contain useful insights. So, in our view you should not expect a single theory of voting behaviour to make sense of changing and highly fluid electoral situations.

But it is not just a matter of the time when a particular theory is more rather than less useful. Explaining voting behaviour is *always* going to be a matter of dealing with a complex and tangled situation. Voting behaviour involves rational choices and dull habits, where thinking individuals are subject to social pressures and the pull of powerful group loyalties. In this state of affairs it is highly unlikely that any single perspective will be cogent on its own precisely because it is inevitable that each perspective will be emphasising particular *facets* of the voting situation, but only at the cost of less attention being devoted to other matters of significance that may well be picked up in rival work. For example, if a theorist dwells on individual voters choosing on the issues at the polls it is unlikely that this theorist will be as eager to pick up on the importance of social structure, the significance of ideology and the dull habit of voting. In a similar way, theorists who are concerned to look at the social situation of the voter can all too easily forget that it is individuals who actually do the voting. This suggests to us that irrespective of the time *when* a particular theory best fits the facts you would be well-advised to think of trying to *combine* the insights of the different theories. However, there are problems caught up in this endeavour and the fact that the different theories are based on starting assumptions that are often in conflict each with the other limits this possibility. Rational Choice theorists of voting behaviour see individuals and their free choices as of the essence whereas Radical theorists reject this starting point and focus on social determinants and the role of ideology. Notwithstanding the problems of combining the insights caught up in the different theories of voting behaviour we see a need for theories that will attent both to individuals *and* to society – that will attend, that is, to the psychology of vote choice and to the context of that choice and hence to the larger sociology of voting. No theory of voting behaviour can be considered as complete which does not try to identify the patterns of social support for parties at the same time as it also attends to politics in the voters' mind. Making sense of voting behaviour and election outcomes is not a matter of attending to individual interests *or* party images, rational choices *or* ideological manipulation. Explaining voting behaviour involves attending to the interaction of interests *and* images where we recognise that individual voters *do* make choices (on the basis of direct experience for sure, and also on the basis of mediated experience and limited information where the media does assume a position of significance) *but* where the summation of those individual choices often reveals the underlying significance of a social patterning that should force us to shift our focus away from isolated individuals and their attitudes and towards a keener interest in the larger workings of society as a whole.

Having pointed to the need for a psychology and a sociology of voting we are also struck by the need for a more genuinely political theory of voting – for a theory which recognises that voting is a political act and which therefore attends to the effects and influences of long- and short-term political events. Be they events to do with the government's management of the national economy, or to do with domestic crises, the ramifications of international politics or the more mundane implications of changes in party leadership and images. Harrop and Miller are right when they remind us that 'the absence of such a theory is the major gap in our understanding of contemporary electoral behaviour' and this is the crucial area of research for the future.

Appendix I: the 1987 General Election

Table A.1(a)   The 1987 general election result

	% Votes	% Electorate	No. of seats	% Seats
Conservative	42.3	31.8	375	57.7
Labour	30.8	23.2	229	35.2
Alliance	22.6	17.0	22	3.4
Other	4.3	3.3	24	3.8
	100.0	75.3	650	100.0

Electorate: 43, 181, 321; turnout: 75.3%

Table A.1(b)   The new divisions in the middle class

	University educated		Works in public sector		Works in private sector	
	1987 %	1983–7 % change	1987 %	1983–7 % change	1987 %	1983–7 % change
Con	34	−9	44	−4	65	+1
Lab	29	+3	24	—	13	—
All	36	+4	32	+4	22	−1

Table A.1(c)   The new working class

	Lives in south	Owner-occupier	Non-union	Works in private, sector
Con	46	44	40	38
Lab	28	32	38	39
All	26	24	22	23

Table A.1(d)   The traditional working class

	Lives in Scotland/north	Council tenant	Union member	Works in public sector
Con	29	25	30	32
Lab	57	57	48	49
All	15	18	22	19

Source: Crewe, *The Guardian* 15.6.87

Table A.2(a)   How Britain has changed after eight years of Thatcherism

	1979	1983	1987	% change
Housing				
Owner-occupier	52	58	66	+14
Council tenant	35	29	27	−8
Private rent/other	13	13	7	−6
Share ownership				
Own	7	7	19	+12
Not own	93	93	81	−12
Trade union				
Member	30	24	22	−8
Non-member	70	76	78	+8
Employment				
Nationalised industry	5	4	4	−1
Central/local govt.	13	13	9	−4

Source: MORI, *British Public Opinion*, May 1987, p. 4

Table A.2(b)   How did these growing (and declining) groups vote in 1987?

	Con	Lab	All
Housing			
Owner-occupier	50	23	25
Council tenant	22	56	19
Private rent/other	39	37	21
Shareowners*	56	19	23
Trade union member	30	42	26
Employment			
Private sector	46	31	22
Public sector	38	37	22

* MORI sample of 16,025 in 180 constituencies interviewed as to voting intentions over period Nov 1986–March 1987.
Source: *MORI, The Times* 13.6.87; *The Sunday Times* 14.6.87

Table A.3(a) Question: Which two or three issues will be most important to you in helping you to decide which party to vote for at the general election?

	12–14 May	*20–1 May*	*27–8 May*	*3–4 June*	*Change*
	%	%	%	%	%
Unemployment/jobs	45	51	51	51	+6
NHS/health care	32	37	39	42	+10
Education/schools	26	35	42	44	+18
Defence	16	19	29	27	+11
Law and order	14	17	19	18	+4

Source: MORI, *British Public Opinion* June 1987, p. 5

Table A.3(b) Question: 'I am going to read out a list of problems facing Britain today. I would like you to tell me whether you think the Conservative Party, the Labour Party or the Liberal/SDP Alliance has the best policies of each problem.

	12–14 May %	*20–1 May* %	*27–8 May* %	*3–4 June* %	*Change* %
Unemployment					
Conservative	27	28	33	30	+3
Labour	35	34	34	35	0
Alliance	16	17	19	20	+4
Don't know/none	22	21	15	15	−7
Education/schools					
Conservative	31	33	32	30	−1
Labour	29	30	33	33	+4
Alliance	17	17	19	21	+4
Don't know/none	23	20	15	15	−8
NHS					
Conservative	24	24	27	27	+3
Labour	42	42	41	40	−2
Alliance	15	16	18	20	+5
Don't know/none	19	18	14	13	−6
Defence					
Conservative	48	49	52	50	+2
Labour	21	22	23	24	+3
Alliance	13	14	15	16	+3
Don't know/none	18	15	10	9	−9
Law and order					
Conservative	45	42	43	43	−2
Labour	18	22	25	25	+7
Alliance	11	12	15	15	+4
Don't know/none	26	23	17	17	−9

Source: MORI, *British Public Opinion*, June 1987, p. 6

Appendix II: the Geography of Voting

Do localities matter?

The widening economic, social, and political disparity between the north and south of the country became the focus of intense debate during the course of the 1980s. The result of the 1983 election revealed that Labour support was higher in the north and lower in the south and that its percentage-point losses of support since October 1974 had also been lower in the north. In 1987, only a few election results had to come in before pundits were once again suggesting that there was a deepening north–south divide in politics that was itself a reflection of more profound underlying realities to do with wealth and poverty – them and us – in a two-nation Britain. In bald terms, there was clear evidence of a broad division between north/west Britain, consisting of Scotland, Wales and the north of England, where Labour advanced strongly, and the south of England and the Midlands (except for Devon and Cornwall) where the Conservatives were doing better than in 1983. Labour was boxed into territorial heartlands of support in the declining north (and the inner cities) and could not break out, at the same time as the Conservatives were the party of the shires and the suburbs without any real purchase on the cities and possessed of a disaffected fringe in Wales and in Scotland. If the elections of the eighties suggested the denationalisation of British politics and highlighted the importance of a regionalisation of electoral trends, then this decade also destroyed the reality of a national two-party system and put in its place two two-party systems. True, there were familiar Conservative–Labour contests in urban and northern seats but in the rural and southern seats there was the novelty of Conservative–Alliance contests, even though Alliance strength only succeeded in skirting the peripheries.

The established literature on voting behaviour that we reviewed in the last section has not been geared to seeing, still less to explaining, this geography of voting. Localities just have not mattered for those who chose to focus on party identification, political issues and sectoral cleavages. Britain was viewed as an homogenous political culture – as one nation – and politics was seen as increasingly nationalised so that little attention was given to spatial variations in voting behaviour. Older cleavages to do with religion, regions and local political cultures were seen as squeezed out by the overbearing reality of the class cleavage in British politics. There was the presumption that an elector in Cornwall would tend to vote the same way as an elector from a similar class in Glasgow regardless of national or locational differences. What a person did for a job was seen as all-determining and where a voter lived was not seen as an especially relevant influence on electoral choice. Butler and Stokes felt able to talk of a 'national uniform swing' where to know the swing in Devon was to know within a percentage or two the swing in Wales or the Highlands. And a review of Sarlvik and Crewe's more recent study of electoral trends in the seventies suggested that 'the biggest gap lies in the failure to explore the relationship between geography, class and political affiliation'.

Now this failure to have attended to spatial variations in voting is regrettable because although the north–south divide in electoral behaviour has become starker and more polarised in recent elections it is not new and, at any event, such a gross perspective on spatial considerations fails to recognise variations within regions, urban–rural differences, and an emerging centre-periphery cleavage with the Conservatives doing better the closer a constituency is to London. At almost every election since 1959 Labour has done better in the north of Britain than in the south, while the opposite has been the case for the Conservatives. Put another way, the geography of voting in 1987 represents a continuation of a well-established pattern that some see going back to the 1930s. Labour may have succeeded in winning a large number of seats in the south and east of England for the first time at the 1945 election but it lost most of these by 1970 at the same time as its support was substantially eroded in many other constituencies in the south of the country.

In the past, political scientists may have been inattentive to locational issues in voting but increased attention is now being given to the significance of non-class cleavages in British politics. More than this, there has been a revival of a political and electoral geography that is centrally concerned to demonstrate that localities do matter and do affect vote choice. It is increasingly clear that spatial considerations need to be understood if we are to provide satisfactory accounts of voting behaviour precisely because the *patterns* of party support are not even across the country and neither are the *changes* in party support – the swing or shift of votes between elections – the same in all parts of the country. It is, however, one thing to describe spatial differences and to set down statistics which show that localities matter, but it is quite another thing to suggest just *why* it is that localities matter. How, then, can we best explain spatial variations in voting and so account for the concentration of partisanship in particular regions and localities?

Two lines of explanation immediately suggest themselves since they derive from two of the theories that we set down in the last section. First, it might be argued that spatial variations in voting are a simple function of spatial variations in the class composition of different regions and localities. Second, it might be argued that parties attract greater support in particular localities because they are advancing policies that are seen to be of particular advantage to the individuals living there. Let us explore each of these arguments more fully before we go on to examine further perspectives on the problem.

The most obvious sociological explanation for geographical differences in a party's support across the country appears to lie in the geographical distribution of those social groups and classes that are most inclined to support that party. The working class, on any definition, is more numerous in the northern regions and in the big cities than it is in the towns and rural areas of the south (excluding London) and so one might expect a larger Labour vote in the former areas and a larger Conservative vote in the latter areas. Butler and Stokes' work in the 1960s found that the ratio of working class to middle class was roughly three to one in the north but only two to one in London and the south-east. In Heath, Jowell and Curtice's 1983 survey 41 per cent of the Scottish respondents were working class as compared with 24 per cent in the south, and while 54 per cent of Scottish respondents were council house tenants only 20 per cent of the southern respondents occupied this form of housing. If it is the case that regional differences in party support merely reflect differences in the social composition of the regions then there is no real geographical aspect to voting at all since it is not where people live but what people do and possess that is basic and decisive. Two things need to be said in response to this. First, the differences between the north and the south in terms of their social composition are not as clear as is popularly believed. For example, the proportion of working-class people in Scotland is lower than it is in the Midlands; owner-occupiers are as common in Wales as in the south of England; and the proportion of people who were either themselves unemployed during the mid-1980s or had an unemployed spouse was only slightly higher in Scotland than in the Midlands. But second, and notwithstanding this, the differences in patterns of party support across the regions are *greater* than one would expect given knowledge about the social composition of the different regions. Class and housing differences are only part of the story. In 1964, Labour's share of vote was 11 per cent higher in the north than it was in London and the south-east whereas the working-class proportion of the population was only 8 per cent higher in the north than in the south-east. In 1983 there was an actual 31 point difference in Conservative voting between Scotland and the south but the hypothetical gap that would be expected to follow from the regional differences in class and housing was only 11 points. In other words, class and housing explained about a third of the political difference between the two regions. Johnson's studies of the elections of 1979, 1983 and 1987 led him to argue that knowledge of the pattern of voting by occupational class derived from national surveys did not allow for very exact predictions of the distribution of votes between the parties in the individual constituencies as constituencies differed substantially in the ability of parties to win and retain votes from the different occupational classes. In bald terms, Johnson highlighted the geographical variability in the pattern of the class cleavage and argued that 'it is clear that people in the same occupational class voted differently in different places'. Although differences in the social composition of regions and localities go some way towards explaining the differences in party support across the country there is more to it than this. The explanation of Britain's electoral geography is not entirely social but is social *and* spatial as people are influenced in their choice of party by their environment, by the people they live among and by the economic and social conditions in their localities.

But what of the geographical variations in the *changes* in each party's share of the vote? The division into two political nations has become steadily more important and more pronounced over the past thirty years. We may not be able to explain spatial variations in the pattern of party support by attending to spatial variations in the distribution of social groups alone, but can we explain the intensification of spatial patterns of party support by focussing on changes in the spatial distribution of different social groups? Economic growth and decline and the associated processes of migration and social mobility may have altered the social composition of regions and constituencies in ways which enable us to make sense of the deepening entrenchment of Labour and the Conservatives in particular parts of the country. There is little doubt that the tendency for urban Britain to move towards Labour, and rural Britain to move towards the Conservatives has been matched by congruent changes in the spatial distribution of classes. Indeed, Curtice and Steed 'conclude that a large part of the geography of voting in 1987 must reflect such fundamental changes as the long-term decline of the north's economic base and the social processes, such as middle-class migration, which that has produced.' In effect, the areas that have become more pro-Labour have suffered population decline and it is suggested that out-migration is probably dominated by upwardly mobile individuals who aspire to success in London and the south-east in a way that has protected Labour's social and electoral base in the north and west. But whilst social structure has moved in the Conservative's favour to a greater extent in the south than in the north and Scotland, it is doubtful if social change alone can account for the whole of the political change that has occurred in the recent fortunes of the parties in the different regions, if only because electoral change has been of a greater magnitude than could possibly be explained by regional differences in the rate at which social structure has changed. The reality of different social mixes in different regions and the fact of change in these social mixes goes a good way towards making sense of regional patterns of voting behaviour and of changes in the patterns, but it is clearly not the whole story.

What, then, of the significance of issues and policies – is Labour and Conservative support strong in particular parts of the country because the parties are espousing different policies that find favour, and curry disfavour, with distinct regional and local electorates? Put more directly, have the Conservatives done badly in the north because voters there are blaming the government for their relative economic distress? In 1983, the Conservative vote declined among all social classes the greater the level of unemployment in a constituency whereas the Labour vote and the rate of non-voting increased. More than this, the higher the level of unemployment in a constituency, the lower the loyalty to both Conservative and Alliance in all social classes and the greater the loyalty to Labour, the greater the shifts to Labour, and the smaller the shifts to Conservative and Alliance. In 1987, too, there was a tendency, albeit a weak one, for the Conservatives to do less well in seats with high unemployment. This information would seem to support an Issue Voting–Rational Choice perspective on regional variations in party support and provide us with an explanation for the north–south divide in politics. It is certainly the case that attitude surveys reveal that people in the north have less confidence in the operation of the free market, believe it generates too much inequality, and favour state intervention to advance equality. Such a position is more in line with support for Labour than support for the Conservatives. However, we should beware of seeing the strikingly varied verdict of the voters in June 1987 as a simple comment on the policies of the Conservative government precisely because the divide long pre-dates Mrs Thatcher's election as Prime Minister. Moreover, although the Labour Party has been the most successful in forging a clear regional electoral base it is open to question whether that Party has successfully advanced the cause of those areas when it has been in office. Voter assessments of party policies must clearly be a part of any explanation for the geography of voting (and they are likely to be of especial importance in accounting for short-run changes) but we need to see these, and this whole line of explanation, alongside the implications of the social geography of Britain at the same time as we also explore the significance of the neighbourhood effect, local political cultures and the growing salience of local labour and housing markets as bases of stratification and political mobilisation.

The neighbourhood effect, or contextual effect, is the most studied geographical influence in voting. It involves the idea that the way an individual votes is not just a function of his or her own social characteristics or views on particular policies but is influenced by the social environment in which they live. How people vote is seen as dependent on how people around them vote. There is the suggestion that this social context may pressure individuals to vote with the majority in their constituency against their own personal predispositions (or those which derive from their particular class position) in a way which would tend to accentuate prevailing patterns of support around the country. In bald terms, the neighbourhood effect argues that individuals tend to adopt the dominant partisanship of the area in which they live regardless of their own class position and political views. For example, in their 1960s survey, Butler and Stokes showed that whereas 91 per cent of working-class residents voted Labour in mining constituencies, only 48 per cent of working-class residents voted Labour in resort constituencies. In the 1983 general election, both the Conservative and the Labour Parties won more votes amongst all social groups in the areas where their support was greatest and all three parties were best able to retain support in 1983 in the constituencies where they were strong in 1979. And in the 1987 general election the most distinctive feature of the whole of north/west Britain, consisting of Scotland, Wales and the north of England, was that Labour did best in the more working-class constituencies, especially those with most skilled workers. Interestingly, Heath, Jowell and Curtice's work on the 1983 election led them to conclude that the neighbourhood effect was more important for working-class individuals living in middle-class wards than it was for middle-class individuals who displayed less of a tendency to vote Labour when they lived in working-class wards.

It is one thing to demonstrate that how you vote may depend on how the people around you vote, but it is another matter to explain just why this should be so. The most common explanation suggests that voting is 'contagious' and spreads through social contacts within the local environment but few studies have captured the mechanisms of personal influence at work and we should not assume that political alignments brush off simply as a result of people rubbing shoulders in the street or the pub. Some commentators suggest that context effects merely reflect the tendency for people who live together to have a similar sectoral position with respect to housing, consumption and work. Put another way, it is the shared sectoral position, rather than contagion, which is said to produce the so-called context or neighbourhood effect but this perspective on the problem of localities and the vote has been disputed. Self-selection of a residential area may well be of some importance in explaining the neighbourhood effect. For example, the (working-class) miner's son who qualifies as a (middle-class) teacher and then returns to teach in his home area is choosing to live in a Labour constituency *because* he votes Labour and not vice versa. Notwithstanding our capacity to come up with colourful examples like this, these patterns of self-selected residential locations are unlikely to have occurred on a scale sufficient to explain the workings of the neighbourhood effect across the country. In trying to account for the impact of locality on individual voting we should not minimise the significance of political factors. A party that is well-supported locally can build on this, fight good campaigns, attract good candidates and assume a prominence in local council politics that may well enable it to develop policies that have an effect on the nature of the area itself. And all the while the rival parties become demoralised and a spiral of their decline sets in so that they cease to be identified with the locality in any meaningful way. Over time, these kind of developments conspire to mean that local political traditions may well get built up – traditions that defy any easy economic interpretation; which may outlast social changes within a locality; and which serve to challenge that argument which suggests that British politics has assumed an increasingly national form in a way that has squeezed out any scope for a truly autonomous local politics. Against this position, Savage suggests that ideas about local political cultures and the political traditions of a place do not appear to help in explaining voting behaviour once social structure has been taken into account and we attend to the importance of local labour and housing markets. For example, a working-class owner-occupier in an expanding affluent area stands to make large capital gains from house price inflation. This combined with feelings of optimism which may derive from living in a locality which is performing well *vis-à-vis* the nation as a whole will help to give people a political sense which may explain their support

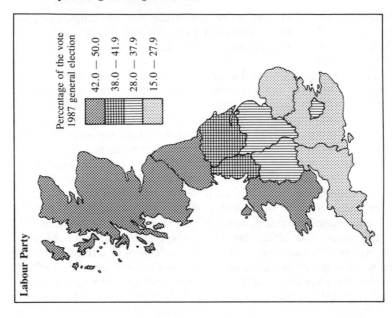

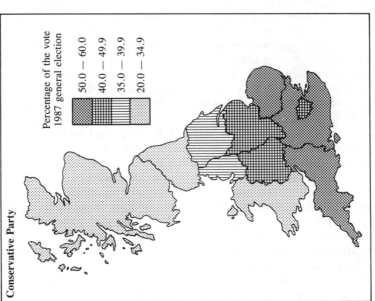

Source: Times Guide to the House of Commons

Figure 3.6   Mapping the Political Divide

for a Conservative government – and this without our needing to invoke the alleged importance of the neighbourhood effect. Much the same sort of logic could be used to suggest why a self-employed shopkeeper in a depressed region might vote Labour if that Party was committed to a policy of state intervention to promote the health of depressed regional economies, notwithstanding the challenge which this policy poses for the free enterprise, low tax ideology that finds general favour with the self-employed.

We know that partisanship is becoming more spatially concentrated but we lack an adequate explanation for this trend. Conventional wisdom about the importance of neighbourhood effects has been revived and joined to perspectives which centre on the class composition of localities and the impact of government policies on regions but we are forced to conclude that much work remains to be done before we will be equipped to make good sense of the geography of voting in British politics.

Table A.4 Regional results: share of votes cast 1987 and change since 1983

	Con	*Lab*	*All*	*Nats*
England	46.2 +0.2	29.5 +2.6	23.8 −2.6	
South	51.8 +1.2	20.9 +1.1	26.8 −1.9	
Midlands	47.8 +1.0	30.0 +1.9	21.8 −2.7	
North	36.6 +1.8	42.1 +5.4	21.0 −3.5	
Wales	29.5 −1.5	45.1 +7.5	17.9 −5.3	7.3 −0.5
Scotland	24.0 −4.3	42.4 +7.3	19.2 −5.3	14.0 +2.3

Source: Butler and Kavanagh (1988), p. 284

Appendix III: Party Prospects

Must Labour lose; can the Liberal Democrats break through; or will the Conservative Party continue to form governments for many years to come?

The Labour Party

Any commentary on the electoral prospects for Labour must first take a stand on the debate as to the viability of 'class politics' and the feasibility of full-bloodied socialism serving as the basis for a recovery at the polls. We will be discussing this more fully at the end of chapter 7, but we have no doubts that Labour faces a dilemma: it needs to retain the support of the traditional working class but it also needs to attract support from outside of that class. We think it will prove very difficult to devise an electoral strategy, an image and a set of policies that will do both jobs at one and the same time. Having said that, we are sceptical as to the viability of a pure 'class politics' strategy, and we are sceptical because the manual working class is shrinking in size and is now less than a third of the electorate; because the share of the working class that has chosen to vote Labour has steadily fallen; because a variety of policy changes implemented by the Conservative governments of 1979–87 have served to fragment the working class and reduce the size of the predominantly pro-Labour groupings within that class; and because class is but one factor giving people a sense of their own political identity and so cannot be overplayed by politicians to the detriment of all else. Irrespective of all this, there is also a geographical aspect to Labour's problems. Can the Party appeal to those in the north and to those in the south, or will the north–south divide find expression in the Labour Party itself – not least over the issue of a class politics versus a more populist strategy? Moreover, although Labour is well entrenched in the north and west of the country it must box its way out of this regional base precisely because this base is just too small for overall victory. But this problem is compounded by population movements out of Labour's declining regions and cities and into the heartlands of Conservative support in the south of England. This matters because new constituencies will be opened up in the growth areas that have been traditionally safe for the Conservative Party at the same time as safe Labour constituencies will be abolished in the areas of decline in the north and the inner cities. The next boundary review will be implemented in 1993 and it could 'give' the Conservatives between 20 and 25 seats. Of course, this kind of perspective on Labour's electoral prospects is overly sociological and deterministic. It dwells on social trends and geographical patterns to the exclusion of any consideration of issues and politics over which the Party has some control. For sure, Labour lost the elections of 1979, 1983 and 1987 and a variety of social trends were working against support for the Party, but optimists argue that the Party can lift its electoral prospects by changing its policies and attending to politics. In fact, Labour was in front on most of the important issues in 1987 (and even in 1983) but faced a problem with its image of extremism, weak leadership and lack of unity. In this situation Labour finds itself in something of a political bind: it has less electoral need to change its policies than its image, but it has less capacity to change its image than its policies. Moreover, the rush to abandon 'old-style' socialism and endorse policies favouring the market and individual choice has involved the Party accepting the ideological integrity of Thatcherism. This not only gives increased credibility to the Conservative position but could also lose the support of the 'traditional' working class that has been left behind by the Thatcher revolution. Labour's electoral prospects may well hinge as much on politics as on social structure, but when social trends are working against a party and when a party loses the ideological initiative it is very difficult to get the politics right. We may have painted a gloomy picture of Labour's electoral prospects but pundits who wrote off the Labour Party after the three election defeats of 1951, 1955 and 1959 had to eat their words when Labour won the elections of 1964 and 1966. So we should be wary about predicting a long-term trend of decline for Labour consequent upon the three election defeats of 1979, 1983 and 1987. Far more hinges on what the Conservatives do in government than what Labour does in opposition.

The centre parties

The Liberals last formed a government in 1915. The share of the electorate voting for the Liberal Party never reached into double figures at any election between 1931 and 1970 except in 1964 when the Party returned nine MPs. In the period of Conservative and Labour dominance after the Second World War, Liberal voters were seen either as middle-of-the-road hangovers from a past period of alignments or as disaffected protest voters who were voting negatively against the failings of the party with which they 'naturally' identified. The resurgence of the Liberal vote in the two elections of 1974; the creation of the SDP in 1981; and the alliance between the Liberals and the SDP in the 1983 election – an alliance which secured 25.4 per cent of the vote but just 2.8 per cent of seats in the Commons – forced psephologists to attend rather more closely to the centre party vote. Heath, Jowell and Curtice's analysis of the 1983 general election led them to conclude that the Alliance vote was no longer just a protest drawn from the different social classes since they detected that the Alliance had at last secured 'a social base in the salariat, particularly among its educated professional and technical wing.' True, this base was small and the Alliance parties had not established themselves as *the* party of the professional and technical worker, but the base was an expanding one. If votes were simply to follow the drift of social change and be grounded upon social structure then we could well expect the Alliance vote to be on a steady upward trend. Centre-party optimists have sometimes sought to present their future in these rosey terms but the salariat is an insufficient social base for electoral victory. Moreover, the lack of a geographical base has meant that the centre vote has rarely 'bunched' in particular constituencies and so it has been hard to translate votes into seats. This in itself is a problem because if a party continues to fail to translate votes into seats then it faces an uphill battle in translating support into votes because of voter anxiety about wasting a vote for a party that is doomed to lose. Of course, proportional representation would clearly help the electoral fortunes of the centre parties but the Conservative Party is against this change; Labour is divided; and the centre parties are in no position to implement the electoral system of their choice precisely because they lack political power. And there are other political problems that face the centre parties. The fact that these parties tend to occupy the centre ground of British politics means that they are standing on an ideological terrain that is always vulnerable to takeover by the Conservative and Labour Parties in a way that makes it difficult for them to establish a clear and lasting political identity in the minds of the voters. To some limited extent political parties hold their electoral fortunes in their own hands but it is all too easy for parties to score own goals at the polls. If the Labour Party manifesto of 1983 was the longest suicide note in history then it has to be said that the Alliance did little to advance its electoral fortunes in the 1987 election and the subsequent concern to create a new party out of the Liberal Party and the SDP led to months of damaging infighting that pushed the parties down in the polls. The Social and Liberal Democrats (later to be known as the Liberal Democrats) was eventually launched as a new party in 1988. But David Owen's Campaign for Social Democracy refused to die and the SDP was relaunched as an independent party in its own right although it failed to take off and ground to a complete halt less than a year later. None of this served to rally members or to improve confidence amongst potential centre-party voters and in the absence of electoral reform the Liberal Democrats face difficult times ahead – the more so with Labour moving away from the Left and across to the centre ground of British politics.

The Conservative Party

The factors that we set down as bruising of the electoral prospects for Labour and the centre parties can be flipped over and seen as working to the advantage of the Conservatives. For example, Labour has been strongest amongst social groups that are contracting in size whereas the Conservatives have been strongest in groups that are expanding; boundary changes that work against the Labour Party will probably work for the Conservatives; the centre parties are disadvantaged by the established electoral system just as the Conservative Party is advantaged by this system; and the opposition parties are disadvantaged by the divisions amongst themselves at the same time as these divisions strengthen the Conservative position to such an extent that they secured office in 1983 and again in 1987 against the wishes of the majority of the voters. Many social trends may be running the way of the Conservatives (even though sections of the middle class are running away from 'their' party), but the Conservative capacity to form governments in the 1980s has been a function of a divided opposition combined with a first-past-the-post electoral system. The Conservatives will not change the electoral system; the opposition parties will find it difficult to enter into electoral pacts in the foreseeable future; little can be achieved by individuals who choose to vote tactically; and it is unlikely that the centre parties will shrivel to such an extent that we see a return to two-party politics. But for all this the immediate electoral prospects for the Conservatives hinge less on social structure (since this changes rather slowly) and less on the machinations of the opposition parties and more on popular feelings as to personal prosperity and the state of the economy in combination with assessments as to the competence and 'style' of the party in government in handling a series of political problems. It is easy for all of us to follow long-term social trends and the slowly-changing structures of British society and these things do matter, but so too does politics and shorter-term political events and these can come from out of the blue to hit a governing party in a way which can take away all the advantages that come from a simple deterministic assessment of the run of social trends. In 1990, the furore surrounding the poll tax threw the Conservative government into disarray; it enabled the Labour Party to rise in the polls to a lead of well over 20 points; it pushed Margaret Thatcher's rating to the lowest of any Prime Minister since 1938 (and she was out of office by the end of the year); and all of this in the context of a situation where the government is left with but little time to get matters 'right' before the next election. We should never forget that a week is still a long time in politics and governments can do far more to lose elections than oppositions can ever do to win them. Our concluding comment in the body of this chapter stands: we need a more genuinely political theory of voting that takes us into matters that lie beyond the concerns of those who have advanced psychological and sociological perspectives.

Works Cited and Guide to Further Reading

Alt, J.E., Sarlvik, B., and Crewe, I. (1976) 'Partisanship and policy choice: issue preferences and the British electorate, February, 1974', *British Journal of Political Science*, 6, 273–90.
Rejects the older conventional wisdom which held that voters were ignorant of issues and policies, and suggests that issue-related perceptions and attitudes are rather more important in the electoral process than earlier studies had suggested.

Alt, J.E., and Turner, J. (1982), 'The case of the silk-stocking socialists and the calculating children of the middle class', *British Journal of Political Science*, 12, 239–48.
Interprets the fact that public-sector employees are more likely to vote Labour than private-sector employees as a function of either ideological self-selection or self-interest.

Butler, D. and Butler, G. (1986) *British Political Facts: 1900–1985*, 6th edn, London, Macmillan.
Exactly what it says it is. Tends to stick to the established political system, but useful facts and figures on social conditions and the economy as well.

Butler, D. and Kavanagh, D. (1988) *The British General Election of 1987*, London, Macmillan.
The latest in the long line of 'Nuffield' studies of British general elections. Useful appendix of statistics and an excellent analytical appendix by Curtice and Steed.

Butler, D. and Stokes, D. (1969) *Political Change in Britain*, London, Macmillan.
The pioneer study of voting behaviour in Britain. Stresses the importance of party identification; highlights the tie-up between class and party (working class is to Labour as middle class is to Conservative); but not geared to explaining electoral change and overtaken by the reality of voting in volatile times. For a review see

Crewe, I. (1974) 'Do Butler and Stokes really explain political change in Britain?' *European Journal of Political Research*, 2, 47–92.

Crewe, I. (1984) 'The electorate: Partisan dealignment 10 years on'. In H. Berrington (ed.), *Change in British Politics*, London, Cass.
Useful and clear update on the changing nature of public support for the two major parties.

Crewe, I. (1987) 'A new class of politics' and 'Tories prosper from a paradox', *The Guardian* 15 and 16 June 1987; 'Why Mrs Thatcher was returned with a landslide', *Social Studies Review* 3, 1, 2–9.
Analysis of the 1987 general election result based on a survey commissioned by BBC television and conducted by Gallup.

Crewe, I. (1988) 'Voting patterns since 1959', *Contemporary Record* 2, 4, 2–6.
Basic presentation of facts and figures to do with party identification, class and party and electoral geography, but also considers more intangible matters to do with ideological change.

Crewe, I., Sarlvik, B. and Alt, J.E. (1977) 'Partisan dealignment in Britain, 1964–1974', *British Journal of Political Science* 7, 129–90.
Puts the term 'partisan dealignment' onto the intellectual agenda and examines the decline in both Labour and Conservative partisanship over the decade.

Curtice, J., and Steed, M. (1982) 'Electoral choice and the production of government: the changing operation of the electoral system in the United Kingdom since 1955', *British Journal of Political Science*, 12, 249–98.
Seminal article pointing to the widening spatial variation in voting patterns; to the related fall in the number of marginal seats; and to the problems of minor parties securing seats in proportion to votes. Along the way makes a powerful 'academic' case for electoral rerform.

Downs, A. (1957) *An Economic Theory of Democracy*, New York, Harper and Row.
The classic economic, rational choice, perspective on democracy: political parties as firms competing to supply public policies; voters as self-interested consumers of those policies; and votes as a kind of political money used to buy packages of policies at an election.

Dunleavy, P., and Husbands, C.T. (1985) *British Democracy at the Crossroads*, London, Allen and Unwin.
Analysis of the 1983 election in which the authors advance their own 'radical approach' to explaining voting behaviour and party competition. Useful discussion of the electoral significance of sectoral cleavages but less convincing in asserting the importance of 'dominant ideological messages'. For a review see A. Gamble (1985) 'The political agenda of the 80s', *Marxism Today*, July.

Franklin, M.N. (1985) *The Decline of Class Voting in Britain*, Oxford, Clarendon.
Careful discussion of changes in the basis of electoral choice over the period 1964–83. Argues that the decline of class voting (class dealignment) opened the way for the rise of issue voting and sees '1970 as the year when a new basis for British electoral choice became established'.

Harrop, M., and Miller, W. L. (1987) *Elections and Voters: A Comparative Introduction*, London, Macmillan.
The best textbook on the subject with a good discussion of the different models of voting behaviour, but because it deals with Western liberal democracies it is inevitably a bit thin on the detail of elections in Britain. If you buy just one book from our guide to further reading in this chapter, then make it this one.

Heath, A., Jowell, R., and Curtice, J. (1985) *How Britain Votes*, Oxford, Pergamon.
The analysis of the 1983 general election. Argues against class dealignment; rejects both the 'expressive' (Party Identification) theory of voting and the 'instrumental' (Rational Choice–Issue Voting) theory of voting in favour or an 'interactionist interpretation' that 'tries to combine the insights of both schools'. Considers that 'Labour might be able to revive whilst remaining a class party'. For a review (and a heated debate) see Crewe, I. (1986) 'On the death and resurrection of class voting: some comments on *How Britain Votes*', *Political Studies*, 34, 620–38; Heath, A., Jowell. R., and Curtice, J. (1987) 'Trendless fluctuation: a reply to Crewe', *Political Studies*, 35, 256–77; and Dunleavy, P. (1987) 'Class dealignment in Britain revisited', *West European Politics*, 10, 400–19.

Himmelweit, H., Humphreys, P., and Jaeger, M. (1985) *How Voters Decide*, Milton Keynes, Open University Press.
A longitudinal study of political attitudes and voting over the period 1959–74 which focuses on the individual voter and issues; advances a 'consumer model of voting'; and rejects the importance of party identification and the idea that vote choice is socially determined. For a review see Dunleavy, P. (1982) 'How to decide that voters decide', *Politics*, 2, 2, 24–9.

Johnson, R. J., Pattie, C. J., and Allsop, J. G. (1988) *A Nation Dividing?* London, Longman.
Geographers explore the increasing north–south divide in the British electorate and tease out the political implications of their analysis for party prospects at the polls in the future.

MORI (1987) *British Public Opinion*, June.
Analysis of the 1987 general election which pulls together various polls and surveys, of which the MORI/*Sunday Times* panel survey is of especial importance. If you cannot get hold of this then check out *The Times* and *The Sunday Times* 13 and 14 June 1987.

Pahl, R. E., and Wallace, C. D. (1988) 'Neither angels in marble nor rebels in red: privatization and working-class consciousness'. In D. Rose (ed.) *Social Stratification and Economic Change*, London, Hutchinson.
Based on research on the Isle of Sheppey. Did not discover either rebels in red or angels in marble amongst the working class. Rejects any simple view of the links between social structure, social attitudes, and political action in favour of a perspective which emphasizes the complex mosaic of social experience out of which people construct their social identities.

Parkin, F. (1967) 'Working class Conservatives: a theory of political deviance', *British Journal of Sociology*, 18, 278–90.
Refusing to see working-class Tories as 'deviants' opens up the whole question of the need to really explain the relationship between class and party support.

Parkin, F. (1968) *Middle Class Radicalism*, Manchester, Manchester University Press.
Classic, early study that deals with the social bases of the Campaign for Nuclear Disarmament and which bears on the question of the middle-class 'deviants' who support the Labour Party.

Sarlvik, B., and Crewe, I. (1983) *Decade of Dealignment*, London, Cambridge University Press.
The study of the 1979 general election. Does not really contain a 'new' model of voting behaviour; a bit long-winded; but attentive to the importance of issues and makes the case for both partisan dealignment and class dealignment. For a review see Berrington, H. (1984) 'Decade of dealignment', *Political Studies*, 32, 117–20; and Peake, L. J. (1984) 'How Sarlvik and Crewe fail to explain the Conservative victory of 1979 and electoral trends in the 1970s', *Political Geography Quarterly*, 3, 161–7.

Savage, M. (1987) 'Understanding political alignments in contemporary Britain: do localities matter?' *Political Geography Quarterly*, 6, 53–76.
Explores three explanations for the increased regional variation in British voting patterns since the 1950s. Critical of those explanations that centre on the changing geography of social class or the supposed revitalization of local political cultures and plumps for a tricky explanation to do with 'the growing salience of local labour and housing markets'.

Chapter 4

Perspectives on Interests and Groups

It is now widely recognised that the exercise of political influence through organised groups is a dominant feature of British government.
B. Smith (1976) *Policy-Making in British Government*, London, Martin Robertson, p. 61.

In the last fifteen years the concept of corporatism has made a dramatic impact on the field of political studies. It . . . revitalised the topic of interest group studies. . . .
A. Cawson (1986) *Corporatism and Political Theory*, Oxford, Blackwell, p. 1.

The riots were essentially an outburst of anger and resentment by young black people against the police
Lord Scarman, (1981) *The Scarman Report: The Brixton Disorders 10–12 April 1981*, Harmondsworth, Penguin, 1982, p. 78.

Introduction

At one time, not so long ago, no serious student of British politics chose to see interest groups as of much importance within our political system. For most of this century attention centred on the constitution, and after the Second World War the growing entrenchment of the theory of responsible party government – 'the Westminster Model' – blocked the rise of new perspectives on British politics at the same time as it encouraged political scientists to try and explain voting behaviour. American political scientists had long been prepared to recognise that pressure groups were of importance within their system, but these groups were seen as strong precisely because the American party system was weak and the fact that Britain possessed a strong party system was thought to preclude scope for a strong group involvement in the British political process. By the early 1960s, however, no British political scientist who was worth his or her salt doubted the fact that interest groups provided the key to unlock the real workings of British politics in ways that promised to take us behind the formalities

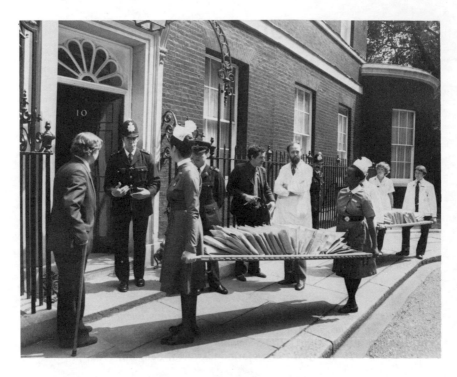

"Pressure on the Prime Minister or a pointless gesture of political powerlessness?"
(Reproduced by kind permission of The Hulton Picture Company.)

of the constitution and the dull rituals associated with the party political battle. In effect, the intellectual centre of gravity within the discipline of politics slowly moved from political parties to interest groups and a new theory – pluralism – emerged that quickly gained wide acceptance as *the* theory to make sense of British politics.

In the 1960s, a wave of pluralist writing claimed that the 'group process' dominated modern British politics in a way that was supportive of democracy; in the 1970s, Marxists, feminists and the New Right offered different challenges to the pluralist perspective but all of them cast doubt on the extent to which interest-group politics enhanced the quality of democracy within Britain; and then in the late 1970s, social scientists focused on corporatism, arguing that business and labour had come to work so closely with the interventionist state in the field of economic policy that they had become governing institutions in their own right. So, in this chapter we will set down the essentials of pluralist democratic theory and assess the cogency of this work as a way of making sense of British politics. This will inevitably lead to our going on to explore the value of the rival perspectives on interest-group politics in Britain.

Pluralism: Perfect Competition

The first wave of work on interest groups in Britain involved case studies of strong successful groups – such as the Confederation of British Industry, the National Farmers Union or the British Medical Association, or else it involved the study of group competition within the context of a particular issue – such as capital punishment, commercial television, rent control or legislation with respect to race relations. In all of this work, it was customary to define interest groups and distinguish them from political parties at the same time as readers were offered a way of categorising groups.

Interest groups, like political parties, were regarded as important informal political organisations which sought to influence public policy and the direction of the state but they were seen as different from parties in terms of their scope and objectives. Political parties were defined as broad governing coalitions that had the job of 'aggregating' interests and a whole package of policies into programmes. These programmes were then put before the electorate by candidates with a view to their party winning the election and actually undertaking the direct government of the country on the basis of the party programme. For their part, interest groups were seen as assuming a rather more modest role in that they had the job of 'articulating' a single interest or policy. Because of this narrowness of interest they could not (and did not seek to) form a government but had to be content to exert pressure on the government in the hope that, indirectly, they might be able to shape but a facet of public policy to their own group's advantage. Having defined pressure groups in this way, and having recognised that the distinction between parties and groups was blurred once attention centred on the minor parties that had no hope of office, it was customary for early students of the new group politics to categorise groups as either 'interest' or 'promotional'. Interest-groups proper (such as employers organisations and trades unions) were caught up in trying to advance the immediate material, sectional and 'selfish' interests of their own members, whereas promotional groups (such as Shelter, the Society for the Protection of the Unborn Child, and Greenpeace) were involved in furthering particular causes that were not simply in the selfish interests of their own members. Research further suggested that promotional groups tended to mount one-off campaigns targeted at Parliament, the media and public opinion, but that sectional interest groups were more likely to be in regular day-to-day contact with ministers, government, and the permanent and administrative side of the state machine.

The fact that early work on interest groups in British politics was based upon single-case studies of groups or issues tended to mean that theory to explain just why and how groups were influential in shaping public policy to their advantage was not well developed. Easy talk about the exertion of 'pressure' – as if that really said anything – only sidestepped the whole explanatory problem. However, once new textbooks began to appear in the 1960s it was clear that some political scientists felt able to pull the case studies together in a way which involved the adoption of an implicit theoretical perspective that bore on groups at the same time as it was designed to make sense of British politics as a whole. 'Pluralism' rapidly established itself as the new theory of British politics. Those who subscribed to the explanatory value of this theory held to the view that it was important to explain the process of public policy-making (since this was the very stuff of British politics); they saw interest groups as the all-powerful actors in that process; and they regarded the activities of groups as enhancing of democracy in Britain. These, then, are the three bare defining elements of pluralism, but in fuller form the pluralist perspective on politics embraces the following elements:

1 The chief characteristic of society is that it is 'open' and made up of many interests that freely and automatically form themselves into a variety of different groups. Moreover, because an individual is likely to be a member of more than one interest ('cross-cutting ties') and more than one group ('overlapping membership') this will soften or moderate their commitment to any single interest. This view of society clearly rejects the perspective of blacks and feminists who talk in terms of 'closure' consequent upon the existence of institutionalised racism and patriarchy. It also challenges the Marxist perspective which sees society as made up of just two classes, with class itself as the only 'real' line of cleavage.

2 Individuals on their own are not particularly significant in politics. They do not participate directly in the policy-making process and they are not well-

informed. Put another way, the pluralist perspective rejects the ideal of a participatory democracy as a utopian dream, and it regards the expectations for citizens integral to liberal-democratic constitutional theory and the theory of responsible party government as quite unrealistic.

3 Elections and party politics are rather less significant in securing democracy and representative and responsible government than was once thought to be the case. After all, general elections occur only once every five years, and because the parties can only attend to the broad lines of policy they do not represent particular interests in a meaningful way.

4 Interest groups, then, and not classes, individuals or parties, are the crucial building blocks of the British polity. Individuals (who are rational and know where their own best interests lie) participate in politics through groups and are effectively represented by groups.

5 No interests are left outside of the group world. Even those interests that are unorganised still have the 'potential' to organise should the need arise. Even the inactive and apathetic citizens enjoy an 'indirect' influence if only because elected politicians have to 'anticipate' their wishes in order to win elections so that they can get back into office to bargain with the more active and organised interests.

6 No one interest group is dominant in the policy process: there is balance, equilibrium and fair competition. This view contradicts rival perspectives on the world of interest-group politics. First, and contrary to the Marxist perspective (to be discussed more fully in chapter 7), business groups do not dominate the policy process, in part because they are divided amongst themselves; in part because they face the 'countervailing power' of organised labour; and in part because they face general competition from other groups, including consumers. Second, and contrary to the New Right perspective (to be discussed later in this chapter) organised labour has never been the dominant interest in British politics, and group politics works 'for' democracy and the interests of individuals and not against them as Public Choice theorists have claimed. Third, and contrary to the perspective of blacks and feminists, it is not the case that either white groups or male groups dominate the policy process to the exclusion of the interests of blacks and women.

7 Political power is 'fragmented' because the resources that are the basis of power and influence are widely dispersed and 'non-cumulative'. For example, an interest group may be rich but it may be so ill-organised that it fails to punch its political weight, just as a poor group may enjoy political power simply by virtue of the extent to which it is active and well-organised in politics. In fact, pluralists see much political power attaching to action, participation and skill in the political marketplace itself, and so they challenge the Left perspective on groups which tends to see money and wealth – 'economic power' – as the only solid basis for political power. Pluralists tend to see politics as analogous to an idealised economic marketplace of free and fair competition where all groups have a good chance to get in on the act of shaping public policies to their advantage.

8 There are many issues that are actually in politics and an infinite range of potential issues that could be in politics. However, because the political system is 'open' to all there is nothing to stop any issue coming onto the governmental

agenda for action and decision. If an interest group wants to press an issue onto the agenda of government then all it has to do is to organise that issue into politics.

9 Although an interest group may be active and very influential within a limited range of issues that are of pressing concern to it, such a group will take no part in a whole host of other issues where different groups will be active and influential. Power in one sphere of policy is unlikely to carry over into power in other spheres.

10 Because there are many interests and groups in society; because groups can come and go as they wish; and because they all enjoy some measure of influence in particular issues, politics itself is fluid and ever changing and the policy process is best characterised as one involving bidding, bargaining, negotiation, accommodation, compromise and checks and balances.

11 Competition (and not class or racial conflict) is the name of the political game. Moreover, this competition is kept moderate and restrained because of all the implications which flow from cross-cutting ties between groups; from the existence of potential groups on the sidelines of political activity; from the rules of the political game; from the role of the state; and from the whole context of pluralist politics. We need to elaborate on some of these latter points.

12 All political activity within a democracy takes place within the context of 'public opinion'. Pluralists tend to argue that the British political system is grounded in a kind of consensus so that the rules of the interest-group game are set by society in order to ensure 'fair play' and free access for all those legitimate interests that want the ear of government.

13 Pluralists talk less about the state than about government and they have a weak theory of the state but they nevertheless see the whole state system as open, neutral and fragmented. Put another way, pluralists see the state as divorced from the interests of any one class, gender or racial grouping and so it is not regarded as the cohesive 'instrument' of the economically powerful, or of men or of whites. Neither is the state seen as a biased establishment serving only itself, and the very fragmentation of the state is seen as providing multiple access points that give all groups the opportunity to exert political influence. Government and state exist to provide the 'arena' where all major interest-group disputes are debated and resolved. More than this, the government also acts as the 'referee' of the group struggle. It holds the ring and secures the public interest by restoring the balance and moving in when one group goes too far, at the same time as it is prepared to protect the interests of the inactive and inarticulate. This kind of perspective on the nature of the state and the government is at odds with all the rival perspectives on interest-group politics which see the state in a much less benign light.

14 The outcome of interest-group activity and of the political process itself is roughly equitable. Every legitimate group secures its fair share, and the equilibrium of interest-group interaction makes for public policies that are a reasonable approximation of society's preferences. Consequently the general interest is secured at the same time as the overall system is rendered stable and legitimate. Put another way, interest-group politics makes for a democratic political system. Of course, pluralists recognise that Britain is not a democracy of the kind envisaged by those nineteenth-century theorists who focused on the

active and informed citizen, and so it is not a democracy that is in accord with, or can be explained by, the 'old-fashioned' liberal-democratic theory of the constitution. From the pluralist point of view, traditional liberal-democratic theory is 'wrong' precisely because it is unrealistic and at odds with the facts and the possibilities of government in an age of complexity. Pluralists argue that interest-group competition is all-important in making for a good working democracy and so they take the view that democratic theory needs to be adjusted to the realities of governing Britain in the twentieth century. Once this is done, then it is argued that interest groups are at one and the same time the key to making sense of the political process and the defining essence of what a viable and realistic democracy is all about.

What are we to make of the pluralist perspective on interest groups in particular and on British politics more generally?

The recognition of interests and groups in society, and the concern to see them in relation to government and the development of public policy represented an important breakthrough in the study of British politics. There was a developing awareness that politics went beyond the constitution and the institutions of the state, and that the connections between state and society involved more than attending to the formal implications of regular general elections and the play of party politics. Politics came to be seen as a social and collective activity which rose above the individual but which somehow fell short of the ideal of the nation or the whole community. At first blush, the pluralist perspective on British politics seems to be at one with a rough common-sense appreciation of the facts and many people would be prepared to accept the pluralist definition of politics, thinking that it is just about public policy-making by the government, at the same time as they would share the pluralist assessment that interest groups are good for democracy. More than this, it is clear that there are many interest groups in Britain and it is a travesty to pretend that all interests can be boiled down and lumped into two conflicting classes; it is also clear that on many issues (and at certain levels of the state) we can discover a pattern of competitive interest-group politics in which no one group appears to be overwhelmingly dominant; and on occasions the state does simply 'referee' the group struggle and is content to ratify the outcome of the balance of competing forces. But for all that, pluralism has been challenged by rival perspectives on the world of interests and groups in British politics and we need to set these perspectives down for two main reasons. First, and negatively, they enable us to get a better critical handle on the limitations of pluralism. Second, and positively, these perspectives pull facts into focus ignored by pluralists and so they provide us with a different view, not just of interests and groups, but of British society and politics itself at the same time as these rival theories involve different assessments of the value of interest groups for democracy.

Marxism and Feminism: Imperfect Competition

Marxists and feminists have argued that pluralism is a theory at odds with the facts of British politics because it adopts a restricted frame of reference and takes too much for granted so that it ignores important phenomena in relation to interests, groups, power and the state.

The pluralist conception of politics is too narrow

Pluralists actually define British politics as being all about public policy-making. They treat the public policy process as an end in itself and see politics as somehow 'explained' once they tell us how policies are made as a result of the activities and pressures of various interested groups.

Marxists and feminists see two main things as wrong with this conception of politics:

1 The fact that pluralists are only interested in explaining *public* policy-making means that they confine their attention to those issues that involve government and the state in a very direct way. This means that they rule out of consideration power and policy-making in the *private* sphere at the same time as they blandly accept the whole public/private distinction. Marxists are conscious of the politics and power caught up in decision-making in the 'private' economic sphere; feminists are crushingly attentive to the exercise of male power in the 'private' domestic sphere; and both reject the public/private distinction as ideological at the same time as they reject the idea of a self-contained and autonomous politics that operates outside of economic and domestic arrangements. If politics is defined as being all about public policy-making, then Marxists and feminists claim that political scientists will simply ignore the decisions made by businessmen in private enterprise and the power exercised by men in the domestic sphere. And this in spite of the fact that these things have political implications every bit as important as those which follow from public policy-making itself.

2 Pluralists are centrally concerned to identify who participates in politics and are eager to explain the *making* of public policies. This means that they emphasise inputs into the political system to the detriment of a serious consideration of public-policy outputs. Put another way, they tend not to explore what difference it makes who takes part in the public-policy process, or else they simply assume that the beneficiaries of public policy can be 'read off' from information about group participation because of uncomplicated assumptions about all groups participating in a way which inevitably advances their own best interests. Marxists and feminists argue that pluralists ignore the more fundamental question of who actually benefits from public-policy outputs and wrongly assume that participation in politics is the same thing as power in politics.

Simply expressed, and taking these two points together, pluralists are charged with asking the wrong question (who participates instead of who benefits) about just public policy-making (so that they ignore the 'private' aspect of power and policy).

The pluralist perspective ignores the problem of group formation and the problem of consciousness

Pluralists adopt an individualistic viewpoint and assume that every individual is the best judge of his or her real interests. Because of this they tend to see a simple one-to-one relation between interests and group organisation: individuals know their interests and form themselves into groups in order to advance those interests. The interest-group world is taken as a given that arises 'naturally' in a way that calls for no complicated explanation.

Marxists and feminists reject this as inadequate. They argue that not all interests are organised into groups and in order to best explain this they see it as important to consider two phenomena ignored by pluralists:

1 There is the problem of information. For example, all of us have a stake, or an 'objective' interest, in a healthy environment (whether or not we have a 'subjective' awareness of this interest) but we may have no information about the ways in which the environment is being polluted to the detriment of our health. But if we lack the kind of information that is vital in enabling us to gain a subjective awareness of our own real interests then we are hardly likely to be in a position to get together to organise into groups.

2 The issue of group formation goes beyond the simple matter of information, because not all interests are 'allowed' to develop a sense of their own collective identity. For example, the poor and the unemployed are largely outside of the interest-group world. This is best explained, not by suggesting that they do not have interests in common or that they are satisfied with things as they are, but by attending to the crushing significance of ideas in society which tell us that to be poor is an individual's own fault and that unemployment can be solved if individuals get on their bikes and look for work without organising together to press for changes in the very fabric of society. In a similar way, feminists have sought to explain women's lack of participation in the public sphere of group politics by pointing to the policing importance of those ideas which suggest that women 'should' be in the home looking after their children – ideas which bite into the very consciousness of women themselves. And for homosexuals to organise involves their coming to terms with themselves in the context of a society which has certain views as to what is 'normal' and proper with respect to sexual behaviour – views which do not make it easy for gays to come out, still less to come together to organise for public political activity.

So, the formation of interest groups cannot be taken for granted but has to be explained. This involves our attending to the factors that shape the consciousness of individuals, factors which give individuals a sense of what their interests are and how they can best be advanced. The pluralist perspective is not a lot of help in dealing with these kind of problems because it is more interested in observable political behaviour than in the role of ideas in society and the formation of political consciousness.

The pluralist perspective provides a partial perspective on political interests and political inactivity

Pluralists tend to assume that people know where their own best interests lie; they assume that people will automatically participate in politics if those interests are threatened; and they assume that all interests possess the 'potential' to organise and be influential in politics. These assumptions mean that pluralists consider that people will squeal politically if their toes are trodden on, and so political inactivity gets interpreted as a sign of satisfaction with the prevaling order of things.

Marxists and feminists, and those speaking for blacks within our society, whilst recognising that some political inactivity can sensibly be construed as a measure of satisfaction and even political power, nevertheless argue that this is not the case for all interests. They take the view that in many cases political inactivity can best be regarded as symptomatic of a power-lessness and fatalism which renders any organised political activity pretty pointless. In bald terms, they refuse to see a simple relationship between participation and power; between action (or inaction) and the satisfaction of interests in society. For example, in a capitalist society such as Britain, the interests of private capital will invariably and necessarily be taken into account in the development of public policy without those interests needing to participate in politics. So, we should not expect to see business leaders standing on a soapbox anymore than we should expect to see those who enjoy the ear of government organising on the streets. However, there are groups outside of the mainstream, such as black youth, who do not organise to press their views on the state. This is not because they do not need the state and not because they are not alive to the possibility of their lot being improved as a result of state action, but because they are mindful of their own powerlessness to change things through political activity. This inactivity can hardly be interpreted as indicative of satisfaction but is best regarded as a 'rational' response to a position of powerlessness on the part of those who are making rough-and-ready calculations as to the likely response to their views and demands. If people sharing certain interests in common anticipate no response from the state, a blunt refusal or even an attack on their very integrity, then it makes good political sense for heads to be kept down below the level of activity. Simply expressed, there is no point in organising to talk politics to the powerful if you are powerless and cannot force those in government to listen and act on what you have to say.

For groups in this position the right to take part in politics represents little more than the right to whistle in the wind and their inactivity should not be construed as as a sign of political satisfaction.

The pluralist perspective exaggerates the extent to which all groups enjoy some influence

Far from the interest-group world being one of perfect competition, Marxists and feminists claim there there is imperfect competition with business and male interests assuming a dominance over the best interests of the working class and women. Marxists recognise that their are certain issues of no moment to business but within their particular sphere of concern business is overwhelmingly influential and trade unions (in particular) are seen as in a wholly inferior political position. We will be exploring the arguments which are advanced in support of this position in chapter 7.

The pluralist perspective studies only one 'face' of power

Pluralists see political power as caught up in participation in decision-making in issues that are within the public arena of politics and government.

Many critics of pluralism reject the idea that political power is only embodied in participation in decision-making and is specific to particular issues and concrete policy situations. These critics see power as 'structured' beyond and behind public participation in particular issues, and they point to other 'faces' of power. For example, power is involved when certain interests are able to organise issues out of politics, off the political agenda and beyond pluralist decision-making. Likewise, interests are advantaged (and therefore those interests have power) consequent upon the fact that other issues may never get onto the political agenda even though the interests so advantaged have not needed to come together to organise to keep them out of politics. We are challenged to go beyond decision-making and the pluralist perspective on power and are forced to recognise, first, that power is also involved in non-decision-making, in inaction and in non-participation, and, second, that interests are advantaged and disadvantaged by the fact that certain issues are not on the governmental agenda. The latter is due to complicated reasons that take us behind the scenes of the public face of policy-making and into the murky waters of the constraining role of ideas in society.

The pluralist perspective is wrong in seeing the state as neutral

Marxists reject the idea that the state is neutral as to the different interests in society and so they deny that the state 'referees' the group – for Marxists read class – struggle. The Marxist literature on the state is complicated (and will be discussed in chapter 7) but the dominant line of argument within that tradition of discourse has seen the state as a biased 'instrument' of capital that might enjoy a certain 'autonomy' but only so that it is better able to work for the long-term advantage of capital as a whole. For their part, feminists have argued that the British state has frequently acted to reinforce women's oppression because the concern to secure political order and stability has encouraged the state to develop policies that 'use' the family in ways that have kept women dependent and powerless within the domestic sphere.

Pluralists themselves have been biased in the way they have approached the facts

The pluralist perspective on British politics was built up by political scientists who were predisposed to provide an account which presented interest-group politics in a good, democratic light. The research dice were loaded in favour of pluralist conclusions.

1 Pluralists have tended to study successful groups and the early emphasis upon the powerful, house-trained group going about things the proper way built up a picture of group influence within the context of the play of a moderate and restrained politics.
2 When pluralists studied issues in British politics they then tended to latch on to issues that generated controversy and a highly-visible politics of action and participation. Issues such as the abolition of capital punishment or the legislation on abortion inevitably revealed a picture of an open, competitive pattern of politics where the state was often content to sit back and referee the group struggle. These studies were not 'wrong' to present a pluralist picture, but it is wrong to conclude that this pattern of interest-group politics holds for all issues.
3 The pluralist emphasis on groups, issues, policy-making and action tended to suck research attention away from the more unchanging aspects of British politics, from non-issues and non-groups and from the winners and losers of the outcomes of public policy. All of this suggests a picture somewhat at odds with the fair and equal pluralist heaven here on British soil.
4 Pluralists have chosen to interpret the significance of political inactivity in a way supportive of a perspective which sees power as fragmented and detached from those of wealth. So, pluralists argue that if those of economic wealth are not directly involved in public policy-making then this is some kind of 'proof' that they lack political power. But if poorer people are not directly involved then it is suggested that they are really satisfied and enjoy power because politicians are eager to 'anticipate' their concerns and they themselves possess the 'potential' to organise for their own advantage.

Pluralism is an ideology

Marxists in particular assert that pluralism is best regarded as an ideology: it masks power in Britain and so helps to legitimise and sustain a system of rule that, in reality, is grounded in inequality and an absence of fair play. Pluralism provides a top-down view of British politics. In dealing with the surface politics of the moment and with the politics of participation and satisfaction it tends to reproduce the bias of the system under scrutiny because it provides a description and an assessment that is couched in terms set by the system itself. The pluralist perspective makes no attempt to criticise British politics. It tends to bend democratic theory in a conservative direction so that it justifies and defends the established system as it is in spite of the fact that the system is at odds with the kind of democracy that involves widespread participation and individual development. Pluralism is insensitive, and inattentive, to the view from the bottom; to the politics of the powerless; to the ill-organised and unincorporated politics of movement, protest and riot; and to the power of government and the state to rebuff demands for change and to destroy certain groups.

Those of a pluralist persuasion might well be tempted to suggest that the Marxist and feminist critique is itself ideological; the product of bigoted minds disaffected from the established order and inattentive to the facts. There is some truth in this view as all perspectives select out facts from a complex reality, and that selection is bound to be conditioned by the politics of the researcher concerned. But for all that, it has to be recognised that many of the points of critique that we have just set down are substantial. Not only have Marxists and feminists pulled important things into view that have been ignored or underplayed by pluralists, but their points of critique and their more positive suggestions as to the nature of interests and groups in British politics have often been backed up by solid research into the concrete world of pressure politics. Research on interests in local politics and research on the 'third world' of groups at the national level with only limited and sporadic access to government, has revealed a picture of interest groups (and non-groups) and political decision-making (and non-decision-making) that is starkly at odds with the rosy optimism integral to pluralism. Let us, then, set down some of these research findings since we ourselves were caught up in disputing the pluralist perspective in our research in Kensington and Chelsea, and in Croydon.

In the 1960s, in response to changes in social structure and expectations of government, and in the context of a party and interest-group world that would not embrace new interests and new demands, substantial numbers (frequently female) of inner-city residents formed themselves into loose 'community action' groups to press for changes in local public policies. Contrary to the kind of expectations integral to the pluralist perspective, these groups were anything but successful in securing a positive response to their demands. They were invariably regarded with hostility by Conservative *and* Labour councils and found themselves to be in a 'Catch 22' – no-win – situation in so far as their own political action was concerned. If these groups were relatively inactive and presented their demands through what the councillors defined as the proper (private) channels then their demands rarely secured a favourable response. But as soon as the groups concerned moved on to a more public and active presentation of their demands the councillors condemned this activity as improper; the demands themselves were ignored; and the groups were held up to public ridicule as a threat to democracy and the general interest. Relatively powerless groups of underprivileged people were frequently ignored by councillors when they played by the rules of the game, and were vilified when they did not. For many groups, public protests were not signs of their power but were testaments to the frustrated powerlessness of those who could not get the ear of government, still less their positive action and this no matter what they did or did not do. The rules of the game, then, far from being set by society so as to ensure fair play for all, seemed to be set by the local authorities themselves and they served to protect established policies (*and* the easy access of those groups and interests advantaged by them) at the same time as groups urging change were ruled out of court by a whole series of exclusion devices which frequently served to crush the groups out of their fragile existence.

On the one hand, interests in line with the prevailing policies and ideology of a local council were able to secure effective access and substantive policies that advanced their interest without any *need* for activity and organisation. For example, in Croydon, big-business interests were influential in local politics but their involvement was personal and informal and their influence was rarely in evidence in overt action on policy-making as the local authority was already keenly sensitive to their concerns without any need for pressure-group prompting from outside of the council chamber. But on the other hand, poorer residents *in spite* of their organisation and activity, could often do very little to press their demands through to a successful policy outcome. They were frequently left out in the cold and were fobbed off with symbolic concessions – such as a tatty 'adventure' playground instead of a decent nursery. If these groups persisted in their protests then were were often drawn into sham 'participation' exercises with the local council that experience showed did more to neuter their dissent than to advance their real interests. No matter what, the basic fundamentals of council policy were left quite untouched and much pressure-group activity came to nothing.

Research into interest groups, power and policy-making at the local level of the British state rather suggested that there was a dual political system. One system involved interests that were inactive, close to the council and powerful in that they got the council action (and inaction) which advantaged them. The other was active and noisy, far removed from the council and powerless in that the groups concerned could not budge council policy. Neither of these systems of interests and politics gets pulled into clear focus from within a pluralist perspective because that perspective cannot cope with too much raucous political activity, anymore than it can even 'see' (still less sensibly interpret) political inactivity.

The New Right: Demand Overload and the Problem of Collective Action

At much the same time as Marxists and feminists were disputing the pluralist perspective and offering their own account of the part played by interests and groups in British politics, more mainstream political scientists were also being forced to ponder on the extent to which pluralism was adequate to some of the developing facts of British politics.

In February 1974, the Conservative government called an early general election: their incomes policy was in tatters and their attempt to legislate on industrial relations had been beaten back by action on the factory floor and on the streets. The country as a whole was on a three-day working week and the mineworkers were solidly in favour of strike action in support of their pay claim. The election was fought on one issue: 'Who runs the country, the government or the trade unions?' The Conservatives lost; Labour scraped into office with a quarter of a million fewer votes than the Conservatives; the miners secured a 30 per cent pay rise; and the Industrial Relations Act was repealed. The quality press was horrified and questioned whether Britain was still governable in the context of a situation where the trade unions could bring down a government and then secure legislation to their advantage against the general interest. It was clearly time for 'realistic' political scientists, who were not tainted by the ideology of Marxism or feminism, to reassess the pluralist perspective.

Most political scientists quickly dumped the favourable tone integral to the pluralist perspective, arguing instead that the group system was out of control and undemocratic as some groups were too powerful in a way which made for a dangerous 'overload' of demands. Four reasons were advanced for this state of affairs.

1 *The public* as a whole had fallen victim to the revolution of rising expectations and displayed a lack of 'realism' as to the constraints that bore on the capacity of government to provide ever more services. These expectations were nurtured by the adversarial nature of the party system, but the welfare state (in entrenching the ethic of equality) had itself contributed to the lobby for more and better public services.

2 *The bureaucrats and officials* within the state, who were involved in welfare and public-service provision, were themselves a powerful lobby for more state activity. They had a personal stake in improving their own pay and conditions (and were aided in this by the growth of powerful public-sector trade unions) and they also had a 'professional' commitment to improve the lot of the clients of their services. Both factors meant that bureaucrats had every incentive to try to maximize the budgets for their own service without any

regard to the larger implications of this for the scale of state activity and public expenditure.

3 *Local authorities* in the major urban areas were frequently in the grip of Left-wing Labour councils. They were also faced with demands for services from a variety of new local-interest groups. Local government as a whole lacked sufficient rate income to service all these demands and so they were forced into becoming interest groups themselves, pressing the central government for more grant income. In so far as they secured a satisfactory response to their demands they then simply succeeded in lifting their own fiscal crisis up to the level of the central state.

4 *The trade unions* in particular were too powerful. They were pre-eminent within the interest-group world and they were unchecked. They had a tight financial and historical grip on the Labour Party, and hence on any Labour government. But, regardless of which party formed the government, the post-war commitment to full employment had increased the bargaining power of workers and the unions representing their interests; the strike weapon could be used to disrupt and exert pressure on employers and governments alike; and as inflation came to be seen as *the* problem (and as a problem caused by 'excessive' wage demands) so trade unions found themselves in a new position of strategic importance and power. To try and preserve industrial peace and control wage inflation governments were forced to adopt a carrot-and-stick approach to the trade unions. However, the limitations of the stick forced governments to try and secure voluntary co-operation through concessions and 'social contracts'. The experience of the 1960s and 1970s led many political scientists to conclude that the trade unions were the lads on the top and the force in British politics.

Taken together, these four factors were said to have made for an expansion of participants in the interest-group system and for an expansion of 'unreasonable' demands on government. In effect, the New Right wisdom of the time was telling us that we were having too much of a good thing. The moderate pluralism of bargains, balance and compromise within rules of the game, designed to ensure fair play and fair shares for all, was one thing. But this had been transformed into the perverted and self-defeating hyperpluralism of a few strong groups facing weak governments where there were no rules (only a free-for-all where might was right) so that all governments got overloaded and could no longer cope or even govern with any authority. More than this, political scientists and pundits sensitive to the problem of overload detected a vicious downward spiral at work between political and economic factors. They recognised that a weak economy heaped increased demands on government as more people were in need but that this occurred at a time when government itself was weak and lacked the financial slack to be able to respond. Inevitably, therefore, government failed to deliver the goods as demanded, as expected (and sometimes even as promised!) and this failure undermined governmental authority and weakened the legitimacy of the whole political system. There was no easy way back and out of the spiral because if a government attempted to buy back public support in order to alleviate the 'political' problem of governability then this overtaxed the economy and gave a twist to inflation so further exacerbating the 'economic' problem of sustaining steady growth.

What are we to make of this perspective on British politics?

It cannot be glibly dismissed as 'wrong' because it deals with phenomena of real importance. However, because it is a perspective that was very much at one with the mood and political circumstances of the 1970s it does not sit comfortably in the changed circumstances of the 1990s. Local authorities and public-sector employees might still exert pressure on the government for more, but the 'strong' Conservative governments of the 1980s did succeed in getting a legislative grip on the power of the trade unions and the public was re-educated to be more 'realistic'. Consequently, less came to be demanded of government at the same time as the Conservative governments themselves had more authority to be able to rebuff the demands coming from 'sectional' interest groups. The overload perspective was caught up with the frothy politics of the 1970s and so it should not surprise us to find that it has had a somewhat limited shelf-life as an explanation for British politics.

But even at the time, the overload perspective was less than adequate for two main reasons:

1 It shared many of the limiting assumptions integral to pluralism itself in that the emphasis was restricted to a narrow conception of politics and to interests overtly organised for political action. And this occurred to the detriment of any sustained and deeper consideration being given to the implications of inaction; the problem of ('objective') interests forming themselves into groups; and the entire context of politics and power in both the economy and the secret state. We have already set down the Marxist and feminist challenges to the pluralist position on these points and so we do not need to repeat them again here.

2 The overload thesis was always an intensely partisan political perspective. Put another way, it was always more politics than political science in that the theorists concerned were more eager to *criticise* trade-union power and weak (Labour) governments than they were to advance a rigorous description and explanation of British politics itself. Those political scientists who advanced the overload perspective were party to the 'realism' of the view from the top and they were keen to feed their analyses (and themselves!) into politics itself. They displayed an eagerness to put forward a series of policy prescriptions that would cut back the activities of the state; change the nature of the political system; and even change the party in control of the government. The fact that the party in control of government did change in 1979 and the very success of the New Right *in* politics in the 1980s did much to change things in ways which undermined the description and explanation *of* politics which the New Right advanced when the Conservatives were out of power in the 1970s. Not for the first time was the political science of British politics undermined by the cruel realities of practical politics out in the real world of British politics.

The overload thesis is but a part of the New Right perspective on interest groups and so before we close this section and move on to consider the corporatist viewpoint we need to consider the less frothy Public Choice perspective associated with the work of Mancur Olson.

Olson's *The Logic of Collective Action* highlighted how difficult it is for certain interests to organise to lobby government if potential group members are behaving in clear accord with a rational appreciation of their own self-interest. Olson's basic argument is simple enough. The rationale for interest-group organisation lies in the capacity of a group to lobby for government policies. However, in a situation in which a government policy is a public good which is indivisible and available to everybody (whether or not individuals have actually contributed to the lobby for the policy) it is always tempting for potential group members to 'freeride' and not contribute to the group effort. Any one individual's contribution is invariably too small to affect the success of the group lobby and so if the group is successful an individual can enjoy the benefits without paying, but if the group is unsuccessful the strategy of non-contribution is still rational since one additional contribution would be unlikely to have changed things and made the group successful. So, although all the potential members of a group have a common interest in obtaining the collective benefit of a favourable government policy, they do not have a common interest in paying for the cost of lobbying for that policy. The problem is that if some members of the potential group freeride then the good will be underprovided and if all of them freeride then the good will not be provided at all! Olson's claim that rational self-interested individuals will not act to achieve their common or group interests leads to his arguing that successful interest groups will be those which can find ways of solving the freerider problem so that they can attract a larger percentage of the potential group to actual membership. Exerting moral pressure on non-contributors (calling non-strikers 'scabs'); delivering selective benefits to members (access to discounts at stores) and selective 'harms' to non-members; or securing some kind of legal sanction to enforce group power (the legally enforceable 'closed shop') are all ways around the problem. However, Olson makes it clear that collective action is easier to effect amongst a smaller potential group just as it is easier to effect where the gains from a public policy are expected to be large. Olson's second volume, *The Rise and Decline of Nations*, takes a more pessimistic view of interest groups. Producer groups are seen as best able to organise because they are small and have much to gain from government, but in lobbying for political privileges for their members (in 'rent-seeking') they tend to secure transfers of wealth and an unfair share of resources for themselves at a cost to the dispersed mass (of consumers) who are very much less able to organise. Olson argues that the whole process of lobbying not only generates social waste but can lead to 'sclerosis' in old industrial societies if, for example, loss-making industries are effective in securing government subsidies or the shield of protective tarrifs against the larger public interest. In bald terms, Olson is telling us why it is that certain

interests might not form themselves into lobby groups, but he is also arguing that the producer interests that are most likely to organise will press for
their sectional interests at the expense of consumers and against the larger
public interest in ways that are at odds with the benign presumptions of
pluralist analysis.

This kind of perspective on the formation of interest groups and the costs
of group activity is important and well worth following up even though
only limited progress has been made in applying the insights of Olson to
the British situation. Having said that, we know that producer groups such
as farmers have been able to exert a very powerful influence over the
policies of the Ministry of Agriculture through the National Farmers
Union, at the same time as doctors have been able to block changes in the
National Health Service consequent upon their active involvement in the
British Medical Association. Much of this group activity has occurred to
the detriment of the consumers of food and medical services. Moreover, the
fact that governments have chosen to bail out large firms such as British Leyland and Rolls-Royce (whereas many small businesses have been
left to go bankrupt) is explicable from within the Public Choice framework because it is clear that large firms are already organised and find
co-operative action easy and relatively inexpensive. Small firms, by way of
contrast, cannot organise themselves into an effective interest group to
secure the ear of government and so it is always going to be tempting for
those who run small business to opt out of any group involvement.

But this kind of perspective on groups, important though it is, runs the
danger of sucking individuals out of their social and cultural context.
Clearly, it has difficulty coping with the fact that many thousands of people
do choose to involve themselves in 'promotional' groups geared to a variety
of altruistic causes that are quite unrelated to securing material gains for
the members who give so freely of their time and effort. However, if you
are thinking of rejecting the Public Choice perspective on groups as simply
selfish and 'Right wing' then you should ponder on the fact that the problem of collective action by rational individuals has also been taken up by
'Rational Choice Marxists'. These scholars have departed from the struc-
turalism central to orthodox Marxism in favour of a reliance upon the
insights integral to methodological individualism and rational choice with
a view to better explaining why it is that classes do (or do not!) emerge as
important collective actors in politics. By all means be scathing as to the
lasting virtues of the overload thesis, but ignore the Public Choice perspective on interest groups at your peril; it has teeth.

Corporatism: Closed Competition

By the middle years of the 1970s there were few political scientists who any
longer subscribed to the optimism about groups that was integral to the
pluralist perspective. But students of interest-group politics just could not

agree to the facts of the situation – still less on how to interpret them. On the one hand, New Right theorists bemoaned the overbearing power of the trade unions, but on the other hand, Marxists saw the unions as weak, arguing that business dominated the world of pressure politics. In the latter part of the 1970s, corporatist theory emerged and offered an uneasy way out of this clash of perspectives. Corporatists accepted the widespread critique of pluralism, arguing that not all groups had (equal) influence within politics. But they refused to side with either Marxists or the New Right on the question of whether it was business *or* the unions that dominated the system since corporatists argued that both unions *and* business were the influential interests in British politics within a system of tripartite arrangements that also involved the government. Not surprisingly, political scientists of many political persuasions felt able to join in the debate as to the meaning and precise implications of corporatism.

One of the main limitations of the corporatist debate has been the lack of agreement, among those taking part in it, about what the term actually means. Some see corporatism grandly as a novel system of political economy, different from capitalism and socialism; others see corporatism as a form of state within capitalist society which emerges alongside, and then dominates, the parliamentary state form. But the dominant and most fruitful approach has seen corporatism as connoting a particular system of interest-group politics and representation that is distinct from the systems pictured by the other perspectives that we have considered in this chapter. These latter corporatists share with pluralists the belief that the basic building blocks of the political process are groups formed around interests and that these have somehow taken over from the significance of representation through elections, political parties and parliaments. However, corporatists are sharply critical of the pluralist perspective in so far as that perspective sees the interest-group system as competitive, 'democratic', equal and open to all, so that it leads to policy outcomes that give fair shares to everyone. Put another way, corporatists 'see' pluralism as at best partial and at worst wrong because it presents a picture of interest-group influence that is at odds with some or all of the facts of a situation. Corporatists argue that certain groups actually enjoy a monopoly of political influence within a system of closed competition that is sanctioned by the state in return for the insider groups concerned being willing to help the state to implement public policies and secure support. Far from the play of group politics leading to fair shares for all, corporatists see it as leading to a situation in which some groups are 'in' and influential whereas others are 'out' and without any influence.

Writers within the corporatist tradition do not emphasise only the extent to which the pattern of interest representation is structured in ways which defy competition and favour certain groups over other groups that are left 'unincorporated' out in the cold. These writers also make the point that this pattern of interest-group politics has itself served to contribute to more extensive state intervention in the workings of the economy and in meeting social needs. In effect, powerful interest groups prompt state intervention but this intervention has had implications for the representation of interests and each development has reinforced the other in ways which have led to an increasingly closed and tight pattern of interest group/state relations.

Corporatists have further suggested that the growth of state intervention and the development of a corporatist system of interest representation have to be understood within the larger context capitalist development. In the early days of competitive capitalism the role of the state was limited, but this era was not to last and as democracy developed and as faith declined in the self-regulating virtues of unfettered monopoly capitalism so the search was on for a 'better' way of handling political and economic affairs. Big business prompted the development of big unions. Large and powerful interest groups organised 'their' people, and the state came to involve itself more and more in economic management and in meeting a variety of social needs. In the course of these developments, corporatists have argued that the competitive and open pattern of pluralist politics passed into comparative insignificance. The state's involvement in managing the economy and in organising a welfare state enabled certain interests to secure exclusive access and an inside track to the ear of government as well as a permanent relationship to the administrative side of the state machine. The peak associations of business and labour in particular were seen as of especial importance in the economic sphere because they controlled resources that were needed by government if public policy was to be effective and capable of implementation and enforcement. In this state of affairs, these major interests were no longer in a position of having to press in on government from the outside. The very fact that they were needed by the state meant that they were actually drawn into government and asked to give advice at the same time as they came to act as agents through which state policy was actually implemented. Authors on the Left, however, considered that trade union involvement was tokenal and best regarded as a ploy through which capital/state interests tried to co-opt labour movement leaders into sustaining capitalism against the 'real' interests of the workers they were supposed to be representing. There may have been disputes as to which interests have been advantaged by corporatist arrangements but there has been the broad recognition that certain interests – but only certain interests – came to enjoy a quasi-legal status so that they almost became a part of the state and governing institutions in their own right. Other lesser interests may have continued to exist but they were excluded from effective influence in crucial areas of public policy because interest-group influence was monopolised by those on the inside whose support was needed by government even though that support was bought at a cost which limited the decisional autonomy of government itself.

Within the literature on corporatism, then, there is the suggestion that it is possible to link the growth of corporate forms of interest representation to developments with respect to the interventionist state in the specific context of advanced, or late, capitalism. It is these three points about interests and their representation, state intervention, and the problem of managing the late capitalist economy, that serve as the cutting edge and the defining essence of the corporatist perspective.

The insights into politics derived from a corporatist perspective have been best applied to Britain by Keith Middlemas in his important book on *Politics in Industrial Society* which carefully explores the experience of the British system since 1911. Middlemas recognises that 'the accepted version of the constitution . . . has become inadequate'; he asks 'is it possible to discover a hidden code which explains more fully the behaviour of political parties, other institutions and government?'; and he argues that it *is* possible to 'establish a theory . . . of British "governance" in the first half of the twentieth century'. In bald form, Middlemas argues that around the time of the First World War the nineteenth-century political system had broken down under the weight of the antagonisms and conflicts within industrial society. In consequence, a deep change took place in the nature of government. Parliament and party became increasingly irrelevant as trade unions and employers' associations came into positions of greater political prominence. Indeed, 'the main theme' of the book is the argument that the triangular pattern of co-operation between government and the two sides of industry built up a new form of harmony which lasted to the mid-1960s and led to the trade unions and employers' associations being elevated to a new sort of status so that they became 'governing institutions' sharing some of the political power and attributes of the state itself. In this 'process of corporate bias', what had once been merely interest groups crossed the political threshold and became part of the extended state. The control which state and interest groups together could exert over the social and economic life of the nation contributed to a uniquely low-level of class conflict for much of the twentieth century so ensuring a political stability that reached its zenith during the period from 1945 to 1965. Middlemas concludes by arguing that 'the nineteenth-century concept of the state is wholly outdated, even when the modifications of early pluralist theory are taken into account.'

What can we make of the corporatist perspective on the part played by interest groups in British politics, and just how stable is the structured pattern of group representation suggested by those who point to close collaborative arrangements between particular interests and the state in pursuit of ever more state intervention?

There is no doubt that the corporatist literature is important: it is ambitious; it is sensitive to the tie-up between politics and economics (in a way which pluralism never was) and it is attentive to major developments with respect to interest politics, state intervention and the development of the economy; it deals not just with the process of public policy-making but with the susbtantive outcomes of that process as well; it is keenly alive both to the clashes of interests *and* to the forces which have tended to hold those clashes in some kind of check; and it bypassed the sterile non-debate between Marxists and New Right theorists as to whether capital or labour was the dominant interest in British politics. But having said that, the explantory utility of corporatist theory was always somewhat less than was promised and the whole perspective has been undermined by the practice of British politics in the 1980s.

Corporatist theory was overwhelmingly geared up to making sense of the way in which governments managed the economy. Moreover, it was geared up to making sense of this process of economic policy-making in the context of a situation where governments chose to manage in a direct, hands-on way that involved their working with trade unions and employers' organisations. Corporatist theory was born of the political practice of the 1970s when governments tried to plan the economy; when governments tried to implement prices and incomes policies; and when governments saw the sense in developing 'social contracts' that would give trade union and business leaders a voice in many domestic policy issues in exchange for their being prepared to deliver their members' compliance with government wage norms and productivity hopes. However, even in the 1970s, tripartite arrangements fell far short of the ideal contained in the corporatist view-point precisely because the peak organisations of business and labour had great difficulty in implementing the agreements they had entered into with the governments of the day. Marsh and Grant have noted how 'both the Confederation of British Industries (CBI) and the Trades Union Congress (TUC) have weaknesses which make it doubtful whether they could function effectively as pillars of a tripartite system . . . [and] it is by no means certain that either group, once it had entered into an agreement, can ensure that its members accept that agreement as authoritative. Neither group is more than a coalition of more or less diverging interests.' Trade union leaders, in particular, may well have entered into 'social contracts' with governments and pledged themselves (and their members!) to wage restraint and productivity agreements in return for social benefits and an extension of trade union powers, but their control over their own members was limited. Rank-and-file revolts and unofficial strikes frequently destroyed cosy deals worked out at the top in a way which made a mockery of the reality of corporatism in practice. But for all that, corporatist theory had a relevance to the seventies, not so much because the tripartite arrangements were successful or stuck, but because the attempt to create such arrangements was central to the policy-making process in that decade. This theory is of less relevance to the eighties precisely because we have witnessed a move away from corporatist practices and the destruction of tripartite arrangements. Since 1979, Conservative governments have chosen not to manage the economy in a hands-on way, and they have chosen not to rely upon a corporatist style of policy-making. In its first two years in office the Thatcher government presided over a major manufacturing recession that involved a sharp rise in unemployment. Recession and unemployment (and a series of 'anti' trade union laws) weakened the power of organised labour. In this state of affairs the government did not need to enter into collaborative arrangements with the unions and it did not need to promise state benefits in return for their support. Not only did the unions have very much less power and potential to disrupt, but the hands-off economic policy of the government and its preparedness to leave matters in the hands of the market meant that it had a narrower range of policies that were far less vulnerable to any challenge which the weakened unions might choose to make. Not surprisingly, therefore, institutions such as the National Economic Development Council (NEDC) have been downgraded; intermediary bodies which played a key role in the 1970s have disappeared altogether; and trade union and business leaders no longer have beer and sandwiches with the Prime Minister in order to resolve tricky industrial disputes and settle social policies. Lord Young, the former trade and industry secretary has even claimed: 'We have rejected the TUC; we have rejected the CBI. We do not see them coming back again. We gave up the corporate state.' All things considered, it is clear that corporatist accounts have been massively challenged by the reorientation of policy *and* policy-making that has taken place since 1979. Indeed, Grant has recognised that 'if there is a criticism which can be made of the corporatist debate, it is that the academic analysts responded too slowly to changes that were taking place in the relationship between the state and interest organisations in a number of West European societies. By the time they had developed a conceptual apparatus to analyse the phenomenon, and had managed to organise large-scale research projects, the object of study was already dwindling in importance.'

Corporatists have bounced back in the face of the practical challenge of national politics. First, they have chosen to argue that corporatism is best regarded, not as a description, but as some kind of 'ideal type'. They argue that only approximations of corporatist type arrangements can be expected to be found in the real world and so some corporatists are prepared to recognise that with respect to certain kinds of issues and at certain levels of the state competitive and pluralist patterns of pressure politics can still be detected. All this is true, but the fact that empirical examples of corporatism are much more difficult to find than has been claimed limits the descriptive and explanatory potential of corporatist theory. Second, the demise of macro-corporatism at the level of the central state, and involving the peak organisations of labour and capital, has not encouraged these theorists to shut up shop but has prompted them to discover corporatism in new forms and new places. The fact that learned tomes now tell us about the importance of meso-corporatism (involving discrete interests in particular sectors and issue areas), micro-corporatism (involving bipartite arrangements with individual firms), local corporatism, and corporatism within the institutions of the European Community probably tells us rather more about the sunk costs which corporatists have in their way of looking at the world than it does about the reality of politics and policy-making.

Corporatism was a child of its time and like a precocious child it has tended to be overambitious in its explanatory reach. It had useful things to say about economic policy-making during the 1960s and 1970s. However, you are on dangerous ground if you want more and if you think that you can generalise out from that field of policy and from that period of time, using corporatism as *the* theory to describe and explain the general role of interest groups in British politics. Corporatist theory continues to be of use, but as an ideal-type embodiment of how interest groups and government *might* well relate, and this notwithstanding the fact that some critics have (wrongly) argued that the theory itself is insufficiently distinguished from, and adds little to, the pluralist theories that corporatists have sought to supplant and supplement. But for all that, if you are overattentive to the politics of incorporated interests then you run the risk of underplaying the troubling significance of the unincorporated politics of protest and disorder at the same time as you might fail to see that a pattern of competitive, or pluralist, politics continues to bubble away with respect to certain issues and at certain levels of the state system.

Conclusion

Students of interest groups lost their way in the 1980s and few political scientists now see groups as the key to making sense of British politics. All the group-based theories have provided us with important insights into aspects of British politics but they have only ever fitted the facts at distinct periods of our history and with respect to particular political issues. Nowadays, it is widely recognised that pluralists were limited more than they were wrong in that they adopted an overly restricted frame of reference and took too much for granted. Moreover, few would now subscribe to the grossness of the Marxist perspective on interests and groups; the New Right critiques of overload were always shallow (although the Public Choice perspective is of more enduring importance); and corporatists developed their distinctive perspective at a time when the phenomenon itself was dwindling in importance. Having said all that, some interest groups do assume an important position within the political system and so they need to be considered. However, once we realise that all groups are but a *part* of the system then we are forced to attend to the significance of other things as well. Moreover, the fact that all the literature on interest groups tends to dwell on strong and powerful groups not only takes us away from the larger and problematic significance of 'interests' in society but also encourages us to see the state system itself as weak in the face of outside pressures–and this quite regardless of *which* groups theorists choose to see as powerful. Pluralists see many groups as influential; Marxists attend to the power of business; New Right theorists see trade unions and 'sectional' groups as key; feminists dwell on the power of male groups; and black theorists argue that the group world is biased in favour of white interests. *All* these perspectives (and regardless of whether they assess interest groups as 'good' or 'bad' for democracy) tend to see the state as weak in the face of strong societal pressures so that they downplay the power and significance of the state itself and see no need to study it as of any importance in its own right. We reject this perspective on the state and so we will return to the British constitution in our next chapter before we move on to consider the power of the secret state in chapter 6. Once we have dealt with these matters then we are better equipped to explore other theories of British politics, theories which are less inclined to take the view that 'when the groups are stated, everything is stated'.

Works Cited and Guide to Further Reading

Beer, S. H. (1982) *Modern British Politics*, 2nd edn, London, Faber.
There are many goods things in this book but in terms of its relevance for this chapter it has to be seen as the classic study of British politics from a pluralist point of view.

Beer, S. H. (1982) *Britain Against Itself*, London, Faber.
The pluralist writer falls into line with the newer orthodoxy and offers us a New Right critique of pressure politics in Britain.

Carling, A. (1986) 'Rational choice Marxism' *New Left Review*, 160, 24–62.
Critical assessment of the work of those Marxists who have used Olson's Public Choice perspective in order to explore problems of group formation and collective action.

Cawson, A. (1986) *Corporation and Political Theory*, Oxford, Blackwell.
Good digest of the literature from one of the leading corporatists but a bit too concerned to find corporatism everywhere.

Dahl, R. A. (1982) *Dilemmas of Pluralist Democracy*, New Haven, CT, Yale University Press.
The leading pluralist theorist reflects on over two decades of his work and nudges towards what some have seen as a corporatist argument.

Danziger, R. (1988) *Political Powerlessness: Agricultural Workers in Post-War England*, Manchester, Manchester University Press.
Powerful reminder that not all interest groups are powerful and worth reading alongside Self and Storing.

Dearlove, J. (1973) *The Politics of Policy in Local Government*, London, Cambridge University Press.
Based on research in the London Borough of Kensington and Chelsea. Chapter 8 challenges the pluralist perspective on interest groups in local politics.

Douglas, J. E. (1976) 'Review article: the overloaded crown', *British Journal of Political Science*, 6, 483–505.
A discussion of the New Right overload and ungovernability theses. Of limited critical worth.

Eckstein H. (1960) *Pressure Group Politics*, London, George Allen and Unwin.
One of the pioneering studies of interest-group politics in Britain. Looks at the British Medical Association and tries to explain the reasons for its 'effectiveness'.

Grant, W. (1989) *Pressure Groups, Politics and Democracry in Britain*, London, Philip Allan.
Short punchy textbook that covers the ground.

Grant W., and Marsh D. (1977) *The CBI*, London, Hodder and Stoughton.
The first major study of the role of the Confederation of British Industry in the British political system. The authors are content to argue that their evidence 'seems to fit happily within a pluralist analysis'.

Jordan, A. G., and Richardson, J. (1987) *Government and Pressure Groups in Britain*, Oxford, Clarendon.
Good basic guide to the subject and the literature on interest groups in Britain.

King, A. (1975) 'Overload: problems of governing in the 1970s', *Political Studies*, 23, 284–96.
New Right perspective that fed into the anti-state politics of Thatcherism with the argument that 'political scientists . . . should be concerned with how the number of tasks that government has come to be expected to perform can be reduced'. Never troubles to say *why* political scientists should have this as their concern.

King, A. (ed.) (1976) *Why is Britain Becoming Harder to Govern?* London, BBC.
Published to accompany three television programmes on the subject. The article by Coates is a good critique of the overload/ungovernability thesis.

Lash, S., and Urry, J. (1984) 'The new Marxism of collective action: a critical analysis', *Sociology*, 18, 33–50.
Another critical assessment of the work of those Marxists who have used Olson's Public Choice perpective in order to explore problems of group formation and collective action.

Marsh, D., and Grant, W. (1977) 'Tripartism: reality or myth?', *Government and Opposition*, 12, 194–211.
Doubts the reality of the extent to which tripartism, or corporatism, has ever been well-entrenched in British political practice.

Middlemas, K. (1979) *Politics in Industrial Society*, London, Deutsch.
Leading contemporary historian, hailed as the new Bagehot, sees 'corporate bias' as the hidden code to explain the experience of the British system of government since 1911.

Miliband, R. (1969) *The State in Capitalist Society*, London, Weidenfeld and Nicolson.
Still the classic account of British politics from the Marxist perspective. Chapter 6 on 'Imperfect competition' provides a critique of pluralism.

Olson, M. (1965) *The Logic of Collective Action*, Cambridge, MA, Harvard University Press.
Powerful Public Choice perspective on the problems of interest-group formation. At one level at the cutting edge of New Right accounts but has also been picked up by Rational Choice Marxists.

Olson, M. (1982) *The Rise and Decline of Nations*, New Haven, CT, Yale University Press.
Very much a New Right account of the problems which 'sectional' interest groups pose for social change and economic growth.

Rose, R. (1979) 'Ungovernability: is there fire behind the smoke?' *Political Studies*, 27, 351–70.
Defines ungovernability 'as the prospect of a fully legitimate government losing its effectiveness, losing popular consent, or both.' Saw signs of fire behind the smoke!

Saunders, P. (1979) *Urban Politics*, London, Hutchinson.
Based on research in the London Borough of Croydon. Chapter 1 contains a critique of pluralist theory and a useful discussion of the concept of 'interests'.

Scarman, Lord (1982) *The Scarman Report*, Harmondsworth, Penguin.
Leading judge's inquiry into the Brixton disorders of 1981. Should serve to remind us that not all interests are organised into groups and that some politics takes place on the streets and not in cosy corporatist arrangements.

Schmitter, P. (1979) 'Still the century of corporatism?' In P. C. Scmitter and G. Lehmbruch (eds), *Trends Towards Corporatist Intermediation*, London, Sage.
Classic article on corporatism looked at from the point of view of a particular system of interest-group representation within capitalism.

Self, P., and Storing, H. J. (1962) *The State and the Farmer*, London, George Allen and Unwin.
Early account of the power of the farmers lobby and worth reading alongside Danziger's study of the powerlessness of the farmworkers.

Chapter 5

The Constitution in Crisis

*A thousand textbooks describe our government as representative and respon-
sible, but in fact it is neither.*
M. Vile (1988), 'Unbuckling Bagehot', *The Times Higher Education
Supplement*, 10 June, p. 17.

*What is being perceived, then, is a crisis in the living constitution, as rules
and principles taken so much for granted in the past are now being ignored,
or subverted by those who claim, or are generally expected, to uphold them.*
J. P. W. B. McAuslan and J. F. McEldowncy (1986), 'The constitution under crisis', *Parliamentary Affairs*, 39, p. 498.

*Britain faces a cruel irony. At a time when constitutional reform is most
needed, it is least likely to occur.*
C. Graham and T. Prosser (1988), *Waiving the Rules: The Constitution under Thatcherism*, Milton Keynes, Open University
Press, p. 193.

Introduction

For most of the twentieth century the British constitution has not been an
issue *in* politics as there has been a rough contentment with the essentials of the liberal-democratic set-up. In consequence, the constitution has
remained outside and *above* political dispute, serving as some kind of
settled context within which the practice of politics was able to take place.
This reality encouraged students of British politics to ignore the constitution. Because it was not disputed it was not noticed. There was the limp
presumption that the constitution was irrelevant and was always going to
stay outside of politics and hence outside of the research concerns of any
serious student of British political practice who was geared up to making
sense of how things *really* worked. Having said that, the constitution was
a central issue in politics in the three decades before the First World War
and it has become an issue again in the period since the 1970s.

Before the First World War, some people (including Dicey) came to

"Principled people poring over a new constitution or sour losers who cannot take a fair beating?'' The 'Charter 88' Programme. (Reproduced by kind permission of Rex Features.)

worry about the dangers of democracy and the related threat of socialism; women (who were without the vote) resented their exclusion from the established system; and disputes revolved around the question of Home Rule for Ireland, proportional representation, the possibility of using referenda and even the survival of the House of Lords itself. The Parliament Act, 1911, the Representation of the People Act, 1918, and the Anglo-Irish Treaty, 1922, served to set many of these matters to rest and did much to remove constitutional issues from British politics for almost fifty years. The Liberal Party – always keen on debating the rules of the political game – fell from power in the inter-war period and so ceased to pose a challenge to the established constitution; the Labour Party held to the view that the central issues in politics were economic and so took no interest in constitutional matters; and the Conservatives were happy to go along with the established set-up and accept a constitution that allowed them to stay in government for most of the time.

For most of the period since the Second World War, the British constitution got taken for granted as the 'best in the world' in providing for a system of representative and responsible government and so there was no call for constitutional changes of any major significance. It is true that in the 1960s there were minor, and seemingly unconnected, grumbles about many of the *parts* of the constitution. Local government was seen as inefficient and lacking in leaders of calibre; the Civil Service was regarded as too amateurish; the House of Commons was said to need more teeth through a strong committee system that would check the executive; the Cabinet was criticised as poorly geared towards long-term planning and strategeic oversight; a question mark hung over the composition of the House of Lords; any many felt that there was scope for reform with respect to the redress of individual grievances against the state. But these grumbles (and the piecemeal reforms and pseudo-changes which they inspired) did not spill over into any generalised sense of unease as to the essence of the *whole* liberal-democratic constitution.

In the 1970s, constitutional fundamentals were opened up with a vengeance in a way that challenged the very guts of the established constitution and brought constitutional issues back into politics and onto the political agenda for debate and even action for the first time in over fifty years. Entry into the European Community in 1973 challenged parliamentary sovereignty; the growth of extra- (and even *anti*-) parliamentary politics in Northern Ireland and on the mainland challenged the rule of law and liberal-democracy itself; the ups and downs of nationalism in Wales and Scotland and the pressure for devolution challenged the unitary state and threatened the breakup of Britain; the use of a referendum in 1975 on whether Britain should stay in Europe revealed the crumbling legitimacy attaching to the indirect democracy of voting for people to Parliament; and the conventions underpinning Cabinet government were buffetted by a series of published memoirs that did much to weaken the notion of collective responsibility and Cabinet solidarity. All of these developments

challenged the established constitution at the same time as they made for
constitutional confusion and uncertainty.

The constitutional authorities – those who do so much to define what *is*
the constitution – were themselves unclear as to the reality of the British
constitution, even though they were very clear that a 'gap' was opening up
between the favourable tone of the established liberal-democratic constitutional *theory* and what they saw as the horrors of day-to-day political *practice* with respect to party and pressure group politics. This awareness that
there was a growing gap between constitutional theory and political practice was nothing less than a statement that the constitution was in crisis
because when politics 'breaks out' two things of constitutional significance
become manifest. First, political practice no longer gets legitimised. When
it falls outside of the framework of the established constitutional theory it
tends to be regarded as improper and unacceptable in a way which weakens
support for the established political system. Second, the fact that politics
takes place outside of the established rules opens up the prospect of a
change in constitutional fundamentals. If the rules of the political game are
being challenged they may even be broken by the brute reality of political
practice and power fashioning an entirely new constitutional set-up better
geared to responding to new needs and interests. In concrete terms, the
experts on the constitution no longer saw a viable limited *liberal*-democracy
but an unrestrained *mass* democracy that pushed for ever more state intervention. Instead of the joy of responsible party government they saw only
the evil practice of adversary party politics and an 'elective dictatorship';
and instead of the happy harmony of pluralist group competition they saw
only the reality of an overload of demands with the trade unions as the
dominating lads on the top.

In the 1970s, then, the constitutional authorities were agreed that British
politics had slipped beyond the explanatory grasp *and* the restraining control of the established liberal-democratic constitutional theory. Instead of
continuing to parrot praise for the British constitution as the best in the
world the experts were agreed that things were very badly wrong and constitutional change was called for as a matter of urgency. Constitutional
change does not, however, spring forth from the pen of constitutional
experts. It is the play of politics and power that is vital and so it is important
to note that sections of the public and elements in the major political parties
seemed to share the unease of the constitutional authorities with the
established set-up. In 1973 the Royal Commission on the Constitution
reported that 'the people of Great Britain have less attachment to their
system of government than in the past', and leading figures in all the
political parties were beginning to take a keener interest in constitutional
issues in a way that threatened to open the system up.

In little over a decade, constitutional clarity was replaced by confusion;
praise was replaced by piercing critique; and support for the system was
replaced by conflicting demands for a new constitutional settlement that
would rechannel the flow of political practice. Simply expressed, the set-up

as it was, as it was said to be, and as it was said it should be, had all pulled apart in a way that called for constitutional change. By the mid-seventies, then, the British constitution was clearly in some kind of crisis. Instead of just being part of the context within which politics occurred and was constrained, it had become an issue in politics on which political parties and social interests were keenly divided.

The Conservative victory in the general election of 1979 seemed to blunt the prospects for constitutional change. Certainly, most of the established constitutional authorities were happy to see a party in office that was committed to strong, but limited, government. Their critique of the constitution was put on hold, with Lord Hailsham ceasing to press the case for a new written constitution because he claimed that there was no longer a danger of an 'elective dictatorship' under Mrs Thatcher's premiership. The Conservative Party as a whole was clearly happy with the established constitution since it had enabled it to secure governmental power with the support of 43.9 per cent of the voters and just 33.3 per cent of the electorate. This being the case, a Conservative government was hardly likely to press for a change in the rules of the political game when it was clear that their Party could win within the established set-up – and this notwithstanding the fact that the New Right had a package of proposals for substantial constitutional change. In a 1981 Commons debate on the British constitution, the minister of state at the Home Office put the case for no constitutional change, arguing that 'this is a time when we should stand up for our great tradition of parliamentary democracy. . . . I think that it is a great and positive system, a marvellous system. . . . There is nothing more important than that we should stick up for the system that we have inherited down the ages, and that still has so much to offer the people of our country.' None of this should surprise us. In the nature of things political pressure for constitutional change tends to come from those who find it difficult to secure state power within the established rules of the game and this is why the centre parties have been at the forefront of the pressure for constitutional change in the contemporary period. Indeed, on the day of its launch in 1981, the leaders of the Social Democratic Party (SDP) took the view that 'Britain needs a reformed and liberated political system'. They argued that 'the present "winner-takes-all" system of electing MPs is unfair' and they stressed the need for 'a sensible system of proportional representation' – although they refrained from adding that such a system would open up the prospect of their own Party securing enhanced representation within the Commons.

The Conservatives won again in the 1983 general election, but the fact that they secured two-thirds of the seats in the Commons with well under half of the popular vote simply encouraged the centre parties to cry still louder for electoral reform.

And the fact that the Conservatives won still again in the 1987 general election may have blocked the likelihood of a change in the system of government but that victory led to many on the Left doubting *their* capacity to win within the established set-up and so they too have come to embrace the cause of electoral reform and the call for a new constitutional settlement. It would be wrong, however, to suggest that the case for constitutional change is made only by political parties and only for reasons of partisan advantage. In the late eighties a new breed of constitutional scholars with rather different political connections from those of the more established constitutional authorities has become increasingly vocal in expressing their concern about liberties, accountability, openness, the centralisation of power, and the fate of the constitution under Thatcherism. They too have provided us with the guts of a new constitutional settlement that we will need to set down and consider in this chapter.

So, the Conservative victories in the elections of 1979, 1983 and 1987 may have done much to damp down the *prospects* for speedy constitutional change, but those victories did everything to boost the *cases* for change. The other political parties were forced to ponder on their own prospects for power within the established system at the same time as there were those who were caught up in making a case for change on the basis of less partisan considerations. The play of party politics at the ballot box may block the easy implementation of any new constitutional settlement but that does not alter the fact that the British constitution is up for grabs, in politics, and on the *agenda* for change.

We are now in a period of decisive constitutional significance every bit as important as those periods when the balanced constitution gave way to the liberal constitution and when that constitution gave way to a liberal-democratic set-up during the closing decades of the last century. This being the case it is important to explore the various proposals for constitutional change at the same time as we assess the prospects of their being implemented in a new constitutional settlement. This is our concern in this chapter.

The Established Constitutional Authorities

In 1976, Lord Hailsham, an elder statesman of the Conservative Party who had been (and was to become again) the Lord Chancellor – the most powerful position in the British legal system – was invited by the BBC to give the annual Richard Dimbleby lecture: he called it 'Elective Dictatorship'. Lord Hailsham carefully unpicked the shreds of legitimacy attaching to the established constitution and called for 'nothing less than a written constitution for the United Kingdom, and by that I mean one which limits the powers of Parliment and provides a means of enforcing those limitations both by political and legal means'. Four years later, Lord Denning, a distinguished judge, delivered the Dimbleby lecture on the 'Misuse of Power'. He recognised that 'in our constitutional theory Parliament is supreme' but he saw the judges as the real 'guardians of our constitution' and he felt that they 'ought to have a power of judicial review' so they could 'set aside statutes which are contrary to our unwritten constitution – in that they are repugnant to reason or to fundamentals'.

It is never easy to say just who are the established constitutional authorities, but people like Hailsham and Denning do much to define what is the British constitution in the absence of a written legal document. They may lack the power to put a new constitution into effect but their notions as to what is 'unconstitutional' can have a certain impact on politics; their views command public attention and the interest of politicians; and so we must attend to their critique of the established constitution and to their proposals for constitutional change.

The critique of the established constitution

The sovereignty of Parliament has long been the linchpin of the British constitution and yet the constitutional authorities came to see this as *the* fundamental constitutional problem needing challenge and change – and they took this view as a result of their pondering on two developments which caused them concern in the 1970s.

1 They were alive to the *presence* of external political challenges to the power of Parliament. Elections (with the auction politics of an adversarial party system) were seen as a challenge because they gave power to electors and party politicians in a way which made it next to impossible for Parliament itself to decide what was best for the nation in the long run; and overbearing pressure groups were seen as a challenge because they made for an overload of demands on Parliament that could not be resisted. Also, the need to secure obedience to the law challenged what Parliament could do because it was pointless Parliament passing laws if they were going to be defied by mass action on the streets or through strikes.

2 They were also alive to the *absence* of legal checks on Parliament. This, when combined with the presence of external political challenges and pressures on Parliament, they saw as leading to a steady increase in state intervention which they regarded as injurious to individual liberties and to the health of the British economy.

In theory, Parliament consists of Crown, Lords and Commons, and the assent of all three parts is needed for a bill to become law. But the concern about the sovereignty of Parliament has to be seen in the context of a political reality in which the sovereignty of Parliament has increasingly become the sovereignty of the Commons, which has itself given way to the sovereignty of the majority party and the government in a situation in which the doctrines of mandate and manifesto were seen as giving power to party activists and extremists outside of Parliament. In hard reality, therefore, the constitutional authorities considered that the sovereignty of Parliament *really* meant the sovereignty of a party leader who was dictated

to by outside interests at the same time as he was allowed a free constitutional rein to wreak political and economic havoc. The constitutional
authorities were critical of the established constitution precisely because it
had not limited the emergence of a pattern of party politics and interest-
group competition which together had led to the extended state intervention which they regarded as so disastrous.

For most of this century the constitutional authorities were pleased with
the set-up: they applauded the demise of parliamentary government and the
decline of Parliament, and they were happy to see the rise of the strong one-
party executive that was responsible to the electorate. In the 1950s and
1960s they painted a picture of responsible party government and saw the
electorate as a perfectly adequate check upon Cabinet (or prime ministerial)
government. In the 1970s, however, the established experts on the constitution were unhappy about the electoral check and were anxious as to the
workings of what they saw as an unfettered mass democracy. They regret-
ted the demise of Parliament as a whole; and they were profoundly uneasy
about the power of party in politics and government. In a word, they were
critical of what the sovereignty of Parliament had become in practice and
what the constitution had allowed to take place in politics.

Proposals for a new constitution

Three proposals were at the core of the new constitution proposed by the
established constitutional authorities in the 1970s. First, they wished to
limit the sovereignty of Parliament by law; second, they were concerned to
bolster a more 'balanced' constitution; and third, they looked to checks on
government that were implicit in the revival of Parliament and parliamentary government.

Limiting the sovereignty of Parliament

This proposal centred on the introduction of a written constitution with
judicial review and the entrenchment of a Bill of Rights as some kind of
'higher' law that would lie beyond easy parliamentary repeal. A written constitution would codify and set down the laws and the unwritten conventions
relating to the main institutions of the state, the relations among them and
between them and the ordinary citizen. In effect, such a constitution would
aim to clarify the confusion which existed around the constitution because
it would set down in law the 'proper' principles for the working of the
British state and would attempt to secure those principles against repeal
or amendment except by some specially prescribed procedure that would
involve more than a simple majority vote in the Commons. For its part, a
Bill of Rights insists that certain rights, privileges and liberties are basic and
must be afforded to all individuals and so governments would be limited
by their having to work within what a Bill of Rights allowed.

Bolstering a more 'balanced' constitution

In order to secure a more balanced constitution that would reduce the power of the Commons, there was a concern to strengthen the position of the House of Lords, the Monarch and the judiciary. There was a grudging recognition that only limited legitimacy (and hence power) could attach to a second chamber whose membership was largely based on heredity and which gave a permanent majority to the Conservative Party and so there was a preparedness to contemplate changes in the composition of the Lords. Britain is said to possess a constitutional monarchy. Put another way, the Queen reigns but does not rule because the independent personal powers of the Monarch have gradually come to be exercised by ministers responsible to Parliament. However, she retains the power to select the Prime Minister in circumstances where there is no obvious candidate at the head of a clear majority party and the power to dissolve Parliament itself. These powers could be of immense and controversial importance were we to find ourselves with a 'hung' Parliament in which no one party had a clear majority over all others. But nowhere are the powers of the British sovereign formally laid down. Bagehot felt that the sovereign had the right to be consulted, to encourage and to warn; Lord Crowther-Hunt considered that the Queen would be perfectly 'justified' in witholding her consent from a bill which sought to abolish the House of Lords even if the government proposing this had secured a mandate through a manifesto set before the people at a general election. It is clear that the Monarch still has a highly 'efficient' role to play in resolving critical constitutional periods – a role that would probably be sustained and defended by the established constitutional authorities who have come to dislike the idea that Britain has nudged towards being some kind of 'disguised republic'. In pressing for a written constitution with judicial review the established constitutional authorities were clearly staking out a position of greater political power for the judges. In the 1970s, as these authorities detached themselves from wholehearted support for our system of government, so they envisaged the judges assuming a role of massive constitutional significance in defending liberty and in checking what they saw as the misuse of power by government and the institutions of the state.

Caught up in this concern to balance the power of the House of Commons was an attempt to recapture elements of the eighteenth-century constitution in a way that would have watered down the power of the democratic side of the state machine.

Reviving parliamentary government and the power of a more independent House of Commons

The situation in which the government, through party discipline, is able to control the House of Commons and absorb its powers unto itself was regarded as undesirable. There was a concern to increase the independence of MPs and to give the Commons a more effective checking, choosing and legislating role of the kind it enjoyed prior to the extension of the franchise and the organising implications of strong and disciplined political parties. Those who have been concerned to revive the powers of the Commons hoped for great things from the system of select committees established in 1979.

Caught up in this concern to secure a more independent House of Commons was an attempt to revive the pre-democratic nineteenth-century liberal constitution.

Prospects for implementing the new constitution

Introducing a written constitution and a Bill of Rights to limit Parliament and restrict state intervention involves mounting a two-pronged attack on the established doctrine of parliamentary sovereignty. If a Bill of Rights is to limit the exercise of political power through the state then it really has to be 'entrenched' beyond the repeal of future Parliaments and yet this hits at the doctrine that Parliament cannot bind, or curtail, the powers of future parliaments. And if a Bill of Rights were to be entrenched as a higher law, then all 'ordinary' legislation would need to be checked against that law. This would involve judicial review through some kind of supreme court. Judges would be charged with the duty of interpreting and protecting the written constitution in a way that would involve them keeping the legislative sovereignty of Parliament within the written, legal limits, and yet this hits at the established constitutional doctrine that the courts recognise no legal limits to Parliament's legislative power.

The constitutional difficulty of this attack on parliamentary sovereignty is clear enough: the proposals to limit parliamentary sovereignty stumble against the sovereignty of Parliament itself. The problem to be solved blocks the solution! If the leadership of the majority party in the Commons were keen to introduce a Bill of Rights and a restraining written constitution then we could have this new system right away. But this would not solve the problem of parliamentary sovereignty as within our constitution no Parliament can bind a future Parliament and so this new system could be repealed by a subsequent vote of yet another simple Commons majority. There are a number of tortured perspectives on how to get around this problem, but they are themselves fraught with problems. The idea of using a Constitutional Commission and a referendum to endow any new constitutional settlement with a special prestige to make it stick in the face of a subsequent Commons majoriy that was keen to reverse the new settlement sounds fine, but it does not alter the fact that within our constitution a referendum is only of an advisory character and none have ever served to limit Parliament's ultimate discretion. From a different tack, constitutional lawyers have written about 'old' Parliaments being able to bind and limit a 'new' Parliament, and have suggested that a 'new judicial attitude' (whereby judges no longer accept that they are subordinate to Parliament) would make for a fresh constitutional start so that 'the doctrine that no Parliament can bind its successors becomes ancient history'. But these tricky *legal* formulations do nothing to alter the fact that constitution-making involves a *political* process and this conditions what is feasible and sets limits on what the constitutional authorities can get away with. But having said that, the fact that the British constitution is in part what the constitutional authorities say it is means that a kind of constitutional change can occur simply as a result of authoritative attacks on the sovereignty of Parliament as a 'dogma' and a 'myth' that needs to be challenged. Although any 'alternative doctrine must be highly speculative', the highly influential *Halsbury's Laws of England* recognises that

> for many constitutional theorists the question of whether parliamentary sovereignty presupposes that Parliament must always remain sovereign and cannot be bound by the legislation of its predecessors, or whether Parliament's sovereignty entitles it to restrict its power to legislate, or deprive itself of the power to legislate, remains open.

Leaving aside the problem of implementing and entrenching a written constitution based on a Bill of Rights there is still the problem of deciding just *what* rights should be included in any Bill and on this there is much dispute. Most of the constitutional authorities who have lent their weight to a Bill of Rights for Britain envisage our incorporating the European Convention for the Protection of Human Rights and Fundamental Freedoms into our domestic law. We ratified the treaty in 1951 but under our constitution this gives no right of action in our domestic courts although since 1965 (when individuals could directly petition the Commission) a large number of cases of British practice with respects to rights have come under European scrutiny. There would be a certain logic to this incorporation as if we were to have a Bill of Rights enforced in Britain then in a situation in which we have ratified the European Convention it would be difficult for us to bypass these rights and draw up a completely new set. Moreover, if we were to attempt to bypass the European Convention and draw up a new set of rights this would open up conflict as to the rights to be included, and if a new code were eventually passed by Parliament then its existence alongside the European Convention would create confusion and cause additional difficulties for the courts. But there are those in British politics who are sceptical as to the value of the European Convention because it only gives expression to traditional liberal and democratic freedoms bearing on such matters as freedom of association, speech, belief, the Press and so on.

These freedoms are clearly of importance (and are of particular importance in the face of the *public* power of the state) but they give small confort to those who would like to see the position of individuals and communities stengthened in relation to the exercise of *private* power in the economy. Although there are disputes as to the rights to be included within any Bill, the perspective of the established constitutional authorities tends to be coloured by the fact that they see the state in 'negative' terms as a threat to individual liberty. They take this view because they define freedom itself negatively and as existing where there is an absence of *public* and legal constraints on individuals. Caught up in this perspective on the problem of rights and liberties is a lack of sympathy for a more 'positive' view of the state and of rights. A lack of sympathy, that is, for a view which sees the democratic state as a vehicle for securing rights against the power of private interests, and a view which embraces a perspective on freedom that is not just about the absence of restraints but requires the provision of real opportunities for individuals if they are to be positively free to develop themselves. In fact, behind the bland constitutional concern to protect freedom through a Bill of Rights there often lurks the reality of a partisan and political concern to restrict the role of the state because of an attachment to a theory of limited, liberal government, born of a desire to use the law to defend the private sphere and capitalism in a way which hits at the possibility of an unfettered democracy working to secure socialism. When we consider the constitutional proposals of the Labour Party we will see how there are those in that Party who are aware of this possibility and their opposition could frustrate the secure and long-term implementation of any proposals to limit the sovereignty of Parliament through a Bill of Rights.

The concern of the constitutional authorities to secure a more balanced constitution which would give greater powers to the Lords, to the Monarch, and to the judges would meet with opposition from those on the Left and centre of British politics who regard those parts of the constitution as too undemocratic and geared to the reactionary defence of the status quo to be given more power. There is wider support for reviving the power of the House of Commons to check the executive, and the investigative Select Committee system introduced in 1979 has done something to increase the accountability of government. But the fact of party in politics tends to make Parliament subordinate to the government of the day and this keeps the committees on the sidelines and blocks the possibility of their serving as vehicles for parliamentary control of the kind envisaged as desirable by the constitutional authorities.

Rival Constitutional Theorists

The established constitutional authorities have not been having it all their own way. In the last decade or so, and in reaction to the process of government under Thatcherism, a new generation of constitutional theorists have sought to knock Dicey off his perch at the same time as they have provided a critical perspective on the established basis of governing Britain and an alternative vision as to how the British constitution should be reformed for the future. Harden and Lewis's study of the British constitution and the rule of law, *The Noble Lie*, is of particular importance because it is the most ambitious attempt by British public lawyers to deal with the theory and practice of governing Britain. It criticises the fragmented, arbitrary, informal and secretive nature of British government and explores the possibility of utilising American experience to try and make our system more open and accountable so rendering it compatible with the ideal implicit in the rule of law.

The critique of the established constitution

Orthodox constitutional theory is founded on the belief – given definitive shape a century ago by A. V. Dicey – that British constitutional aspirations are realised through the institutions and processes of the nineteenth-century liberal state. Harden and Lewis see this as a 'noble lie' that is only preserved because of the secrecy which cloaks all governmental operations in Britain. They note 'the lack of fit between the real location of decision-making functions and the map of such functions implied by the traditional delineation of constitutional authority' and argue that the British constitution does not provide the openness and democratic accountability that is needed for government according to the rule of law to be a reality. Parliament, primarily because of the government control of its business, 'does not govern, but more importantly neither does it fulfil the constitutional promise of accountability implicit in the notion that authority to govern flows through Parliament. It does not ensure that sufficient information is made public, it does not scrutinze the work of government effectively and it does not ensure adequate debate about policy and choices'. With respect to government itself, Harden and Lewis argue that 'the concept of ministerial responsibility to Parliament implies a picture of executive decision-making that is false'. Ministers do not engage in effective planning and policy is not made exclusively by politicians (but by civil servants and pressure groups as well) and yet these realities are rarely translated into constitutional debate. 'British constitutional arrangements lack an "efficient" mechanism for rational prioritisation and strategic planning' with the result that modern government is fragmented and is conducted through informal, secretive, incrementalist and corporatist networks that are anything but open to the kind of public scrutiny that is necessary for a true system of representative and responsible government. For their part, the courts have not done enough to ensure and promote legitimate government. They have done little to respond to the increase in the number and scale of government functions because they have been content to work within Dicey's concept of the rule of law and have lacked a clear understanding of the nature and purposes of judicial review and so have failed to prevent the growth of arbitrary and autonomous public power – power that is left unchecked within the British system of government.

'The British constitution', say Harden and Lewis, 'is in a sorry state, unable to deliver either democratic accountability or effective policy planning.'

Proposals for a new constitution

Harden and Lewis 'are not attempting to provide a blueprint' but they do make a case for a new constitutional settlement that would secure processes of government geared to openness, genuine participation and accountability. In effect, they are concerned to reform out of existence a secretive and inefficient constitution that is at odds with rule of law principles in order to create an institutional framework within which 'rational, informed decision-making could take place' that would be in accord with the cultural claims and expectations of the rule of law. At the heart of their reforms is the view that the constitutional order should be legalised and that legal procedures should confine public decision-making processes within acceptable bounds at the same time as they 'promote critical reconstruction of outmoded or inappropriate policies', encourage 'public discourse, criticism and collective learning', and 'institutionalise participative politics'. They argue that any reform of parliamentary procedures will do little to restore the power of Parliament. Although they do not think that Parliament could carry out the direct scrutiny of government itself, they do suggest that Parliament's role should be to 'ensure that scrutiny takes place'. The courts should transcend the limitations of Dicey's conceptions of the rule of law and act as 'a final quality-control mechanism for open and participative policy-making processes'.

Harden and Lewis are impressed by the American contribution to public law. They argue for a Freedom of Information Act to give the citizen the right of access to information held by the government; they make a case for a Government in the Sunshine Act to establish the general principle of public access to meetings of government bodies; and they suggest that we should legislate for a Bill of Rights to cut into the arbitrary powers of the state. They also argue that we require a British Administrative Procedure Act 'dedicated to producing open discussion, natural justice and rational planning processes' that would formalise procedures in relation to decision-making by public bodies and ensure that we could complain effectively against the decisions of government, and challenge policy-making and planning through institutions that insist decision-makers take a hard look at alternatives. And they say we need a Standing Administrative Conference to oversee the operation of the new institutional framework with a roving brief to exercise a control over all constitutional matters. Above all, they see the need to ensure that alternative bodies of information, professionally sifted, are available to Parliament and to the public so that we do not make choices in the dark or in a narrowly partisan fashion.

Prospects for implementing the new constitution

In certain ways the concerns and reforms of Harden and Lewis parallel those of the established constitutional authorities. Both see the established constitution as deficient in failing to shape political practice; both place an emphasis upon law providing the solution; and both are concerned to create a new constitutional order that will better restrain the political process. But whereas the established authorities are sceptical as to the virtues of (too much) democracy Harden and Lewis are keen to institutionalise a more participatory politics even though they fail to explore whether these reforms would increase their other objective of governmental effectiveness. However, Harden and Lewis place too much faith in legal remedies for political problems and fail to recognise that in a system based on the sovereignty of Parliament what law can do to restrain politics is extremely limited; they are somewhat naive in thinking that elements of American administrative law can be transplanted into a very different constitutional order. So it is not surprising that their package of proposals lacks substantial purchase amongst those in politics whose support would be needed for implementation.

The constitutional concerns of the established authorities (who, almost by definition, are not on the Left of British politics) were at their peak in the 1970s when Labour was in power and seen as a threat. The concerns of constitutional theorists like Harden and Lewis have surfaced during the decade of Thatcherism – at a time when those out of power politically see the need to refashion the constitution in order to restrain those in power at the same time as 'space' is opened up to allow them to secure power more easily in the future. The problem is that no government is likely to legislate to set limits to its power and to provide increased opportunities for political rivals. This not only makes it unlikely that Harden and Lewis's proposals will be put into effect but it also highlights the importance of our attending to the constitutional concerns of those who *are* in a position to put constitutional changes into political effect, namely the established government and the rival political parties waiting in the wings.

Conservatives and the New Right

It has been a persistent theme in British conservative thought that political institutions should not be constructed on abstract principles and over the years the Conservative Party has been hostile to generalised plans for constitutional reform. In displaying a preference for evolutionary political change the Party has been content to work within a changing and developing constitution that has enabled it to stay in government for much of the time and over a long period of history.

During the 1970s, however, Lord Hailsham was not the only Conservative to express anxiety as to the state of the British constitution. In 1974, the electoral system had 'allowed' Labour to form a government with a smaller share of the vote than the Conservatives. Moreover, the sovereignty of Parliament meant that there were no effective constitutional constraints within the system and so a Left-wing Labour government was constitutionally enabled to pass laws that might hasten the transformation of Britain into a detested socialist society. In this kind of situation, many Conservatives saw limited government as under challenge from the brute reality of political power and so they saw the need for coherent constitutional reforms that would institutionalise and secure limited government even though the nature of the conservative tradition meant that they were ill-equipped to devise a blueprint for change. Members of the Party may have become critical of the established set-up (and there was talk of the need to reform the House of Lords, to embrace electoral reform, devolution, the use of referenda, and even a Bill of Rights) but the leadership of the Party has always been reluctant to institutionalise limited government through constitutional change. This reluctance has stemmed from two causes. At the philosophical level, Conservatives may want to see governmental power kept within bounds but they have also seen the need for strong government. This has meant that they have been unwilling to weaken authority through the restrictions of rigid rules but have chosen to hope that those in power would be restrained by their own sense as to the proper limits to their authority as well as by the moral pressures in society which they should respect. And at the more pragmatic level, the party in power has been reluctant to institutionalise changes that would block their own unfettered right to govern as they saw fit.

During the 1980s, Conservative governments under Margaret Thatcher may have been bent on rolling back the frontiers of the state but this has not led to their proposing new constitutional constraints on central government. Pragmatic political considerations have reinforced the Party's natural philosophical reluctance to engage in constitutional engineering and the whole debate about the need for constitutional reform died within Conservative circles. When in opposition, Lord Hailsham discovered an 'elective dictatorship' and proposed 'nothing less than a written constitution for the United Kingdom'. Once in government, he dropped his concern for constitutional change; he was happy that the Prime Minister was at his side in mounting a purely *political* challenge to big government. And when he accepted office he admitted that he was 'given no remit to carry through constitutional changes of any kind, and no proposals for constitutional change formed any part of the election manifesto.' In 1989, the Prime Minister responded to Charter 88's proposals for a new written constitution in the following terms:

> The Government consider that our present constitutional arrangements continue to serve us well. . . . The Government could not consider any constitutional reforms which were not widely understood and supported in Parliament and in the country at large. Furthermore, the Government does not feel that a written constitution in itself changes or guarantees anything.

For a variety of reasons, then, we cannot look to the Conservative Party for any crisp analysis of the deficiencies of the British constitution or for a package of reform proposals to set matters aright. However, neo-liberal theorists of the New Right have been more forthcoming in criticising the set-up and in proposing changes. It is important to attend to their arguments because the New Right has been influential in shaping contemporary conservative thought and if the Conservative Party tumbles back into opposition the Party leadership could well display a keener interest in the New Right's package of constitutional reforms.

The critique of the established constitution

In the 1970s a certain kind of New Right political analysis came to prominence that was critical of the practice of British politics. Political parties were adversarial, they 'bought' votes with unrealistic promises of policies, and they managed the economy with an eye to the next election so that they were responsible for creating political business cycles that were injurious to the health of the economy; pressure groups were unrestrained and contributed to an overload of demands on the system; civil servants and bureaucrats were not geared to the public good but had an interest in trying to maximise their own budgets; and the combined effect of all this was that government grew and the state came to intervene more and more in the economy and into the freedoms of individuals. Much of this analysis was superficial and did little more than massage a cynical commonsense. Although reforms were sometimes advanced to eliminate political business cycles or to stop bureaucrats maximising budgets this work rarely pushed into a critique of the liberal-democratic constitution itself – still less into a prescriptive package for a new constitutional structure.

Professor Friedrich Von Hayek, however, is a radical anti-socialist and an influential neo-liberal theorist of the New Right who has not been shy to voice his criticism of the British constitution before going on to advance a detailed set of proposals for achieving a 'constitution of liberty' and a limited role for the state.

Throughout his long life Hayek has been concerned to make the case for the market and for individual freedom at the same time as he has been eager to make the case against state intervention and central planning precisely because he sees these challenges to the market as leading to a totalitarianism that destroys personal freedom. For Hayek the proper end of politics is the pursuit of individual freedom (defined negatively as the absence of coercion) and the basic duty of government is to provide a secure framework within which freedom can exist and prosper. From this point of view *laissez-faire* liberalism and not democracy is the antithesis of totalitarianism. 'Democracy is not an end, but merely a limitation upon power' and because Hayek sees the practice of democracy as simply one important constitutional safeguard to maintain our liberty against oppressive governments he is prepared to argue that 'a thing is not necessarily good because it is democratic'. It is perfectly possible for an omnipotent and democratic majority to coerce a minority in a way which cuts into their right to freedom. Hayek is supportive of a limited and liberal democracy that is secured by written legal constitutional structures but he is critical of unlimited and majoritarian mass democracies.

Put in constitutional terms, Hayek believes in the rule of law but is critical of parliamentary sovereignty. Dicey argued that parliamentary sovereignty reinforced the rule of law, but Hayek considers that the legal omnipotence of Parliament undermines the rule of law because it gives governments the unrestricted capacity to remove the liberties of British subjects unfettered by any constitutional or legal constraints on their power to legislate. In Hayek's words,

> because the rule of law means that government must never coerce an individual except in the enforcement of a known rule, if constitutues a limitation on the powers of all government, including the powers of the legislature. [So,] when the British Parliament claimed sovereign, that is unlimited, power . . . it proved in the long run the great calamity of modern development that soon after representative government was achieved all those restraints upon the supreme power that had been painfully built up during the evolution of constitutional monarchy were successfully dismantled as no longer necessary . . . this in effect meant the abandonment of constitutionalism which consists in a limitation of all power by permanent principles of government.

Hayek's criticism of the British constitution is not unfamiliar. It picks up on the concerns of the established constitutional authorities and echoes the anxieties of those nineteenth-century liberals who were sceptical as to the virtues of democracy. But his prescriptions for constitutional change are in a league of their own.

Proposals for a new constitution

In Hayek's constitution of liberty there would be two distinct representative assemblies. A new Legislative Assembly, elected on the basis of a once-in-a-lifetime vote by people who (having reached the age of 45) would elect their peers for a period of 15 years, would be entrusted with 'law-making', setting down only those abstract and general rules of just conduct that were equally applicable to everyone. A Governmental Assembly, hopefully composed of just two parties and elected on a universal franchise without the use of proportional representation, would be entrusted with the task of government, would organise the apparatus of the state and would decide about the use of governmental resources. As Hayek states:

> The one important difference between the position of such a representative Governmental Assembly and the existing parliamentary bodies would . . .

be that in all that it decided it would be bound by the rules of just conduct laid down by the Legislative Assembly, and that, in particular, it could not issue any orders to private citizens which did not follow directly and necessarily from the rules laid down by the latter.

Hayek's constitutional proposals aim to limit the sovereignty of Parliament, not through a Bill of Rights (because of the difficulty of singling out the particular rights to be protected), but through a separation of powers and a reliance upon the Legislative Assembly. Hayek hoped that the members of that assembly would be impartial in reviewing new legislation because the manner of their election and the basis of their tenure would free them from party pressures and from challenges to their good sense and independent judgement.

Prospects for implementing the new constitution

There is not the slightest chance that the British constitution will be restructured and assume the form advocated by Hayek: no political party or interest group has displayed an eagerness to press for his proposals and we have already seen that any proposal to limit the sovereignty of Parliament stumbles against that very sovereignty. It is tempting, therefore, to ignore Hayek's proposals because they are too eccentric and distant from the world of practical politics to be of any significance for those of us interested in the future shape of the British constitution. Graham and Prosser take the view that 'this would be a mistake, for his importance lies in his realisation that any fundamental rethinking of the role of the state is essentially a legal or constitutional matter, and that radical political change needs radical legal change for its effectiveness to stick'. Mrs Thatcher has learnt much from Professor Hayek but neither she, nor the Conservative Party, has picked up on this, his most important, lesson.

The Centre Parties

The Liberals formed a government in 1915 but by 1979 there were just 11 Liberals sitting in the House of Commons. In that same year, Roy Jenkins, an ex-Labour Minister and President of the European Commission, was invited by the BBC to give the Richard Dimbleby lecture. In his 'Home Thoughts from Abroad' he chose to talk about the state of British politics and how the 'system' had gone wrong and ought to be changed and improved. In 1981, Roy Jenkins became the leader of the newly formed Social Democratic Party (SDP) and the Alliance between that Party and the Liberals encouraged those in the centre ground of British politics to believe that they could 'go forth and prepare to govern' and break the mould of British politics. In reality, the Alliance secured 25.4 per cent of the vote in the 1983 election (but just 2.8 per cent of the seats in the Commons) and although they did slightly less well in the 1987 election the parties then fell into disarray: the Liberal Party was wound up and the Social and Liberal Democrats was launched as a new party in 1988 but David Owen's Campaign for Social Democracy refused to die and the SDP was relaunched as an independent party in its own right but did eventually die in 1990.

Notwithstanding the cut and thrust of centre party infighting and the ups and downs of their electoral support, these parties have long been in the forefront of the case for constitutional reform perhaps because there has been little prospect of their securing power, or the implementation of their political objectives, within the established rules of the political game.

The critique of the established constitution

The major element of the centre parties critique of the established constitution has dwelt on the electoral system – a system which they consider has entrenched the Conservative and Labour Parties in positions that have enabled them to alternate in government for much of this century against the wishes of the electorate and the best interests of the country. On the day of its launch, the SDP stated that 'Britain needs a reformed and liberated political system without the pointless conflict, the dogma, the violent lurches of policy and the class antagonisms that the two old parties have fostered', and it went on to argue that 'the present "winner-takes-all" system of electing MPs is unfair to the voters and opens the door to extremism, whether of left or right.'

The centre parties critique of the established set-up has, however, gone beyond concern about the failings of the electoral system to embrace anxiety about individual rights as well as the extent of centralisation and secrecy within the system. David Steel, when he was leader of the Liberals, argued that 'the constitution is quite simply outdated, a relic of the nineteenth century, unsuited to our modern society and unable to provide real safeguards against a highly centralised, secretive and authoritarian government' within a system in which the conventions are 'manipulated or avoided', where 'parliamentary sovereignty no longer guarantees accountability to Parliament', and where 'the present structure of government allows mistakes to be covered up, prevents proper accountability, and actually promotes inefficiency.' At the 1987 election, the Alliance leaders were mindful of the importance of social and economic issues but they sought to make constitutional reform the centrepiece of their appeal and aimed 'to convince the country that no matter who is elected it is impossible to tackle our underlying problems with machinery that is antiquated and irrelevant to those problems.' In their manifesto, *Britain United*, it was stated that, 'most of the problems facing our country cannot be solved unless we get better government. That means government which can carry the people with it in its major policies, and it means government which the citizens can call to account. Our system is currently failing in both respects, and it is getting worse.' In a policy declaration at the launch of the Social and Liberal Democrats, the Party argued that,

Britain's democracy has always been incomplete. We have never enjoyed firm guarantees of basic human rights. Our voting system has never been fair. Our system of government has always been highly centralised. Parliament has been far too subservient to the Executive. We live under a political system which, by its nature, produces arrogant and unrepresentative government. Both the old parties are products of that system. Both have maintained it. Neither is willing to change it. It is, in fact, their joint legacy. The central purpose of the Social and Liberal Democrats is to liberate the British people from that legacy.

Proposals for a new constitution

At the 1987 election, the Alliance considered that it was 'time for a new era of reform' and they launched their 'Great Reform Charter' in which they argued that 'if empowered by the British people' they would introduce the following reforms to get 'the structure of our democracy right':

1 Replace the undemocratic 'first-past-the-post' electoral system with proportional representation for all Westminster and local authority elections.
2 Introduce PR for elections to the European Parliament.
3 Repeal the Official Secrets Act and replace it with Freedom of Information legislation providing for a public right of access to all official information.
4 Reform the law of confidentiality to ensure that freedom of expression on matters of public interest is not unnecessarily restricted.
5 Incorporate the European Convention on Human Rights into British law in a Bill of Rights.
6 Remove the right of the Prime Minister to determine the date of general elections and replace it with fixed-term parliaments.
7 Devolve power to a legislative Scottish Assembly, establish a Welsh Senedd and decentralise decision-making to elected regional assemblies throughout England.
8 Extensively reform Whitehall procedures in order to make the governmental system more responsive to the wishes and needs of the people.
9 Reform the House of Commons procedures through making greater use of select committees and giving greater opportunities for private members bills.
10 Reform the House of Lords through phasing out the rights of hereditary peers to vote in that chamber and including members elected from the regions and nations of Britain.

This package of proposals for constitutional change shares with the established constitutional authorities a concern to check government through a Bill of Rights, a more balanced constitution, and a revival of the position of Parliament and parliamentary government. However, the centre parties depart from the perspective of the constitutional authorities in their advocacy of proposals for devolved, decentralised and open government; in their concern to secure opportunities for a wider and more positive conception of individual freedom; in their enthusiasm for democratic politics; and in the case which they make for proportional representation. Indeed, the proposal for PR is at the core of the centre party case for constitutional change – if only because it is a precondition for the parties getting into a position where they have some prospect of taking part in government and so a hope of being able to put the rest of their constitutional proposals into effect. What, then, are the arguments for and against the established electoral system, and how powerful is the case for PR?

The case for the established electoral system

Under the established system for electing MPs, each elector has only one vote; each constituency returns only one MP, and the winner takes all, as the candidate who is first-past-the-post with the most votes becomes the MP whether or not he or she has an overall majority of the votes cast in the constituency. This system has been defended on a number of grounds.

1 It is a simple system as the voter only needs to put an 'X' against the name of the preferred candidate. It is also a well-understood system and so facilitates an easy involvement with the democratic process.

2 Compact single-member constituencies (as opposed to large multi-member constituencies) provide for just one MP in a small area and this facilitates contact between MPs and their constituents and so encourages the redress of individual grievances in a way which fosters support for the system.

3 The established system *does* discriminate against third parties securing seats in proportion to votes, but this disadvantage in representation has to be traded off against an advantage in governmental strength, stability, responsiblity and accountability which would be threatened if the system gave way to PR. Put more directly, the established electoral system helps to maintain the two-party system in the Commons in a way which contributes to the maintenance of responsible party government, with the majority party in the Commons forming the government (without the need for coalition) and being challenged by a single opposition party that is waiting in the wings as an alternative government. In this state of affairs, the electorate is presented with a clear choice between alternative programmes and parties in a way which enables it to choose the government and the broad drift of public policy. At the time of the next election, it is possible for the electorate to hold the government to account, to subject its record to public scrutiny, and to start the whole cycle of responsible government all over again. All of these good things would be less possible with PR because that system would make a multi-party Commons more likely. So, it would be less possible for the electorate to directly choose the government as the government would emerge from the deals done by party leaders in the Commons; it would be less possible for the electorate

to have a say in choosing and determining the drift of government policy because that policy would derive from the same process of deals that created the coalition; and it would be less easy to hold a government to account as with the confusion of coalition each party would try to distance itself from the bad bits of the government record whilst claiming the successes as theirs alone.

4 Whilst it might be 'fair' to have an electoral system which gave seats in the Commons in proportion to votes in the country, this might lead to a situation that was less than 'fair' once the implications for governmental power were considered. The leaders of a centre party with under 20 per cent of the vote, but with 80 or so MPs, could well be in a position to determine whether Labour or the Conservatives were to be the major party to government at the same time as they would be likely to insist on a goodly share of plum ministerial posts for themselves. All of this would give a centre party a position in government and an influence over policy that was out of proportion to the size of their vote and their 'fair' representation in the Commons. Simply expressed, proportional representation in the Commons might translate into quite disporportionate power in government.

5 The established system provides for moderate government in the long run because the two parties in a two-party system must always strive to occupy the middle ground where the votes lie thickest. This means that both parties must be ready to adapt their policies to the wishes of the majority of the voters, and they must also display a willingness to rein in their extremists who might dissaude the middle-of-the-road voters from giving the party their support.

The case against the established electoral system and the case for proportional representation

1 The established system may help to provide 'strong' government in that most post-war governments have been able to count on an absolute majority of seats in the Commons to put their policies into effect. But this strength is a bad thing in the context of a situation when no government has been elected by a majority of the electorate and secured 50 per cent of the vote since 1935. In reality, therefore, strong government has simply meant that a series of 'minority' governments have been able to push their policies through the Commons in a manner more authoritarian than democratic.

2 The established system, in helping to entrench a two-party system, has not made for responsible party government but has rather contributed to the instability of adversary party politics. 'Strong' governments have pushed their policies through the Commons only to find themselves replaced by another strong government which then proceeds to reverse the previous government's policies as a matter of course and party pride. Since the crack-up of the consensus in the 1960s, one doctrinaire and mandated government has been replaced by another with scant regard to the policy aspirations of the moderate majority in the country at large.

3 Under the established system, a small swing in votes tends to produce a major change in party strength in the Commons and this 'exaggerates' a party's lead in a way that further prompts sharp shifts in policy when there are only small shifts in votes and still more limited changes in public opinion. All things

considered, therefore, the alleged stability of government since the post-war period is more apparent than real, with critics of the established system claiming that the period is best characterised as one involving policy change and instability.

4 In the grossest possible sense, the established system does not provide for representative government in that in the elections of 1929, 1951 and February 1974, the party which returned the largest number of MPs actually had a smaller share of the overall vote than the runner-up party. In those elections, the electoral 'winner' was, in fact, the governmental 'loser'!

5 The established electoral system is not 'fair' and is not properly representative in that parties do not secure seats in the Commons in proportion to their votes in the country. This is the main argument in the case for PR. We may have a system of 'one person one vote' but we do not have a system of 'one person one vote one *value*' since some votes are more equal than others depending on the party you choose to vote for and where you happen to live. There are a number of aspects to this. First, we have already pointed out that all British governments tend to be minority governments in that they do not enjoy the support of 50 per cent of the voters and in some cases the party that has formed a government has had less votes than the party pushed into opposition. In February 1974 Labour formed a government on the basis of the votes of 37.2 per cent of the voters; in 1983 the Conservative landslide of seats (their parliamentary majority trebled!) was based on just 42.4 per cent of the vote – less than they got when they lost in 1964, less than they got in 1979, the fifth lowest Conservative vote since the war and the lowest vote for a government with a secure majority since 1922. In 1987 the Conservatives won their third election in a row but on the strength of 42.3 per cent of the vote or just 31.8 per cent of the electorate. Second, the Labour and Conservative parties secure seats in the Commons in numbers far larger than warranted by their voting strength in the country. In 1987, for example, the Conservatives won 57.8 per cent of the seats in the Commons with 42.3 per cent of the vote, and in 1983 the Labour Party won almost a third of the seats with only 27.6 per cent of the votes. Third, and obviously related, there is the position of 'third' parties. A third party whose support is regionally concentrated may do well within the established system, but a third party that lacks a geographical base and whose support is spread across the country may obtain many thousands of votes in the individual constituencies without ever coming top of the poll and so can amass a national vote in millions without winning a single seat. In October 1974 the Liberals with 18.3 per cent of the vote secured 13 seats, whereas the Scottish and Welsh nationalists with 3.5 per cent of the vote were able to secure 14 seats; in 1987, the Alliance polled 22.6 per cent of the vote but only managed to win 3.4 per cent of the seats; and in the 1989 elections for the European Parliament, the Green Party secured 15.0 per cent of the vote but not a single seat. If the election of 1987 had been fought on the basis of PR, then the Conservatives would have won 275 seats (instead of 375); Labour would have won 200 (instead of 229); and the Alliance would have won 147 (instead of 22).

6 If the British persist with the established electoral system and if the public at large come to recognise that many of their votes are being 'wasted'; that their

votes bear little relation to the final distribution of seats; and that parties are able to form governments in spite of the fact that more people voted against that party than for it, then all of this could deter turnout and encourage a cynicism that would threaten the legitimacy of the whole system of government.

Prospects for implementing the new constitution

PR is the linchpin of, and the precondition for, the centre parties entire programme for constitutional change and yet the prospects for achieving this new electoral system do not look good. True, Anthony Wigram founded Conservative Action for Electoral Reform in 1974 and urged the adoption of PR because 'the present electoral system could easily give power to a Socialist Party controlled by an extreme left wing group', but since 1979 few Conservatives have sought to press the case for a change in the electoral system. By 1989, a number of leading figures within the Labour Party had expressed their support for PR but the Party as a whole has chosen to stay with the established winner-takes-all electoral system and has rejected the case for PR. The centre parties are on their own in pressing the case for PR. If they were to gain a clear majority in a future Parliament then they could legislate for PR, but the prospect is unlikely given the way the established electoral system tends to work against a third party with a spread of support. If a future Parliament were to be 'hung' with the centre parties holding the balance of power then they have claimed that they would only support a minority government if there was an agreement to introduce PR. However, it is far from certain that either of the established parties would agree to a change since they could be bidding away the long-term electoral advantage they seem to enjoy within the established system for a short-term in office in a coalition government. Out of office both Labour and the Conservatives have toyed with support for PR as a vehicle for blocking a government by their rivals. Once in office, however, party leaders have seen less of a need for change and yet PR could only come about as a result of a party in power deciding to legislate for such a system.

If the centre parties were ever in a position to implement electoral reform then we would clearly enjoy a 'fairer' electoral system – if fairness is defined as meaning seats in the Commons in proportion to votes in the country. But such a system could give the centre parties disporportionate power in government. And the greater likelihood of coalition government would make the accountability of a single-party government to the people less likely notwithstanding the fact that this responsibility has been the *essence* of our system of parliamentary democracy.

The Labour Party

In the past, the Left has not displayed an interest in the British constitution because two models for socialist transformation, the parliamentary and the insurrectionary, have dominated thinking, debate and political action. More recently, however, a variety of factors have encouraged the Party to display a keener consciousness of constitutional matters and the need to reform the British constitution.

The critique of the established constitution

The parliamentary, or reformist, road to socialism has been the major tradition within Britain where the Labour Party has long been the dominant organisational force on the Left and amongst the traditional working class. Revolutionary struggle and the extra-parliamentary politics of agitation and demonstration have invariably been rejected as undemocratic, undesirable and unnecessary. There has been the view that socialism will come gradually, but inevitably, through a democratic Parliament as a result of the cumulative effect of piecemeal reforms pushed through Parliament consequent upon the Labour Party winning elections and being in a position to organise Parliament and determine the laws of the land. A parliamentary majority and the government based on that majority are seen as at the controlling centre of the state. The state machine as a whole is regarded as neutral and is viewed as available to be used and driven to the Left if Labour is in office and in power. From this perspective, the liberal-democratic British constitution has been taken for granted as a good thing and has not been subjected to extended critique.

The insurrectionary, or revolutionary, road to socialism is associated with Lenin and with third-world struggles for political change. It is not a strategy that is organisationally entrenched within British political experience, but it is intellectually entrenched as a challenge to parliamentary socialism *and* to liberal-democracy. Trying to attain socialism through an established Parliament is seen as doomed to failure because such a strategy places a commitment to the parliamentary means above a commitment to the socialist end. As a result socialism is sacrificed on the alter of the grubby struggle for office and government within the system. Elections to a bourgeois Parliament are not seen as providing a pathway to socialism because elections simply 'incorporate' the working class into the established set-up and Parliament controls nothing since power resides in the rest of the state apparatus and in the ecomony. Revolutionary socialists take the view that meaningful change cannot come through the established constitution because bourgeois democracy provides the best possible political shell for capitalism. The reforms and concessions that have been gradually won by the Labour Party are worthless since they shore up the essentials of the established system whilst creating the illusion that real change is possible at the same time as they cut into the grievances of the working class so turning them away from a commitment to revolutionary action for fundamental change. Socialists can achieve nothing by working within the established political set-up and so no serious socialist should consider trying to reform the British constitution. The system as a whole has to be 'smashed' and set aside by a vanguard party of intellectuals that is prepared to make a revolution and lead the working class to socialism. From this perspective, the liberal-democratic Britain constitution is not seen or taken seriously. It is not regarded as 'really' important and so it is not subjected to any kind of detailed critique but is dismissed as an irrelevant façade that conceals the reality of bourgeois rule behind the smoke screen of democracy.

If this were the extent of constitutional debate within the Labour Party we would have little more to say. However, over the past decade or so elements on the Left have begun to rethink old positions on reform and revolution. This has also forced serious thought on the British constitution and its reform with a view to creating a system of rule and a different kind of democracy that would better facilitate the attainment of socialism. With respect to the case for revolution, socialists have become increasingly critical of the authoritarian role of Communist parties in the Soviet bloc in a way that has challenged any radical chic attachment to the revolutionary road. History rather suggests that vanguard parties linger on as authoritarian rulers *after* the revolution in a way the blocks the attainment of the goal of socialism. With respect to the case for reform, the fact that elements on the Right of British politics were critical of the British constitution in the seventies encouraged those on the Left to think that there might be more life in the parliamentary road to socialism than many had supposed. Moreover, there were good things about the British constitution that needed to be defended – even though the entrenchment of the Conservatives in government in the eighties encouraged the Left to think about the need to change some of the rules of the established political game.

So, a developing tradition within the Labour Party has come to take the British constitution and liberal-democracy seriously. The established constitution is not seen as perfect but neither has it been criticised along the lines advanced by the established constitutional authorities who were crushingly concerned about the *absence* of legal constraints on parliamentary sovereignty. Because the Left has been insensitive to the established debates on the constitution it has not been attentive to the potential for change – and socialism – that has flowed from the constitutional reality of parliamentary sovereignty with all the unlimited authority that gives to a majority party in the Commons. The Left has tended to criticise the established constitution by attending to the *presence* of constraints on the democracy within the system. The constraints are seen as deriving from the reality of unaccountable economic power and from the independent power of those closed and secret parts of the state that are neither popularly elected nor properly controlled by the House of Commons. They are criticised precisely because they are seen as blocking the possibility of radical change and the attainment of socialism through the established system. The Civil Service, the House of Lords, the Monarch, the judges, the police, the military, the security services, the Bank of England, a host of appointed governmental bodies and even the Cabinet and the 'absolute' premiership, are all criticised for enjoying political power that is not properly constrained or held in check by any elected assembly or democratic mechanism. But in addition to emphasising the importance of these 'internal' checks on democracy, stress has also been placed on 'external' factors that have contributed to a loss of powers and to a significant reduction in the scope of our capacity to govern ourselves. Although the new 'realism' within the Labour Party has tended to soften the anti-American, get out of Europe, Little Englander stance that has been so strong, concern is still expressed as to the role of the USA in Britain's domestic policy-making. And elements within the Party worry about the implications of NATO membership for 'our' defence policy in addition to the challenge to a sovereign British Parliament that is seen as having resulted from British entry into the European Community.

Attending to the constraints on democracy within British constitution does not exhaust Labour's critique of the established set-up. The election defeats of 1979, 1983 and 1987, and the strong position enjoyed by the Conservative Party in government have prompted a further rethink that has now encouraged the Labour Party to take on board the more familiar grumbles about 'elective dictatorship' and the absence of 'judicial checks or legislative balances to hold back the sovereignty of Parliment'. Moreover, in its policy review document for the 1990s we find the Party taking more seriously the problem of individual rights within the established constitution. In the past the Left chose to emphasise the importance of community rights, seeing individual rights as a rather bourgeois concern that was best left to the liberals in all parties and none.

Proposals for a new constitution

Labour's latest package of constitutional reform proposals are set out in their policy review document, *Meet the Challenge, Make the Change*, published in May 1989:

1 Altering the established voting system is rejected because it is claimed that the introduction of PR would entail the 'confusion of coalition government'; would give the centre parties 'disproportionate' influence over policy; and would throw out the message that Labour no longer had the confidence to win a general election on its own.

2 In spite of a concern to secure 'a massive extension of individual rights', a Bill of Rights is rejected because it 'would not provide the protection which we regard as necessary. . . . For even if it were enshrined in an Act of Parliament other specific legislation would supercede it and it could be repealed by a government with no concern for individual liberty. . . . A more dependable and more permanent constitutional change is necessary.'

3 The more dependable basis for securing individual rights is seen to lie in the abolition of the House of Lords and its replacement with an elected second

chamber with 'a specific and precisely defined constitutional role' geared to safeguarding human rights legislation from repeal. The new chamber (to be known as the Senate and to be elected on a basis that 'will be a matter for further consideration') would be given power to delay the repeal of legislation affecting fundamental rights for the whole life of a Parliament. It is suggested that this would be enough to safeguard rights because it would provide an opportunity for the electorate to determine whether a government proposing such measures should stay in office.

4 Reforms are proposed to 'increase the powers of the House of Commons' and these centre on 'streamlining' current parliamentary procedure; extending scope for parliamentary scrutiny through changes in the committee system; and giving the Commons power to exercise democratic control over key public appointments.

5 To break down the centralisation and concentration of power and the danger of an elective dictatorship, power should be devolved and government decentralised. Scotland and Wales should be given their own national assemblies; ten elected regional assemblies should be established in England; and local government (based on the existing districts) should be given wider powers and an income from a property tax and an income tax in place of the Poll Tax.

6 To ensure that the public, parliament and the Press know what government is doing, a Freedom of Information Act would be introduced but national security information and personal privacy would be properly safeguarded.

In effect, Labour's current policy review rejects the 'fashionable remedies' of a Bill of Rights combined with electoral reform; gives virtually no attention to the reform of the administration; and sees the key to a better system lying in the constitutional role proposed for a new elected second chamber and in the proposals for the devolution of power to elected governments in Scotland, Wales and the English regions. The fact that Labour is unlikely to be united on these constitutional proposals forces us to give some attention to other proposals that have had an airing and enjoy a certain support within the Party even though most are unlikely to come to prominence.

There is limited sympathy within the Party for a Bill of Rights, but the Party is clearly split on the issue of electoral reform. Publicly, the leadership rejects PR: it says that Labour can win within the established electoral system (but not under PR) and it chooses not to worry anout 'fairness', talking only about the accountability on offer within the established system. But there are a growing number in the Party who doubt that victory is possible within the old rules; who are concerned to create a fair system; and who are critical of the strength which any 'minority' government can enjoy as a result of the established electoral system at the same time as they are not defeatist about Labour's capacity to govern alone under a reformed and fair electoral system.

For many years the Labour Party has been committed to the abolition of the House of Lords but there is likely to be concern whthin the Party about the proposals for a new second chamber. There is the view which suggests that one elected chamber is enough and that a Labour government based on a majority in the Commons should not be checked by a rival assembly. If any new chamber were to be less democratic than the Commons then it should not be able to check and delay legislation, but if it is just as democratic then there is no point in having two chanbers – the more so since there is always the potential for constitutional deadlock.

Republicanism has never been strongly established within the Labour Party. When the position of the Royal Family was last debated at a party conference in 1923 a resolution for abolition was lost by an overwhelming majority. Republicanism may have been exorcised from the arena of 'reponsible public opinion' for over a century but there is constitutional concern as to the Monarch's powers with respect to the selection of the Prime Minister and the dissolution of Parliament. In so far as a quiet republicanism comes to life it will find some kind of uncomfortable expression within the broad church of the labour movement – much to the embarrassment of the Labour Party leadership.

Sections on the Left of the Party have been of the opinion that the Prime Minister is too powerful within the established system. In order to secure a 'constitutional premiership' that is less powerful and more accountable it is suggested that prime ministerial patronage should be limited, and the constitutional convention which gives the Prime Minister the right to choose the Cabinet should be be broken so that Labour MPs elect Ministers to the Cabinet of a Labour government. This particular proposal has to be seen as part and parcel of the concern to create a greater measure of *intra*-party democracy within the Labour Party itself. This movement for delegate democracy was strongly developed in the 1970s and was related to a trend of support for participatory democracy and local socialism. In concrete terms, the movement for delegate democracy found expression in the party reform that ensured that Labour MPs would be reselected by their local parties, and in the reform that required the Labour leader to be elected by a party constituency larger than the parliamentary party. It also found expression in the unfulfilled demand that the election manifesto should be drawn up by the party at large instead of by the leader alone. This concern to foster intra-party democracy involved a challenge to the leadership of the Labour Party *and* to the kind of democracy that was praised within the liberal-democratic British constitution. Within our system of government – within the 'Westminster Model' – only *inter*-party competition has been seen as desirable and there has long been the view that popular participation should be limited, with party leaders left free to devise programmes that would appeal to the electorate as a whole. The Left within the Labour Party was challenging this conception of democracy. Parliamentary democracy and the representation of individual electors by 'strong' party leaders in Parliament was challenged in favour of delegate democracy and the representation of class interests where the wishes of the party activists outside of Parliament would be interposed between the parliamentary leaders and the electorate to restrain the former and provide the party programmes for choice by the latter. Prime ministerial power, and therefore prime ministerial government was challenged; Cabinet government and collective responsibility were challenged because of the claim that Labour Ministers owed their first allegiance to the policies decided by the party conference; parliamentary government and the autonomy of MPs to deliberate as representatives was challenged by the argument that Labour MPs were mandated delegates; and liberal-democracy itself was challenged because of a refusal to accept the limited political participation and representative democracy that was on offer within the established British constitution. Nowadays, three election defeats in a row have given the Labour leadership a firmer grip on the Party – and on the Left within the Party – and so it is unlikely that these demands for a different *kind* of democracy will push to the fore and provide the basis for Labour's constitutional proposals in the next election manifesto. But bursts of intra-party democracy within the Labour Party (reflected in the cry that 'Conference should decide') have a habit of returning and bubbling to the surface of Labour Party policy-making. This being the case, we should not rule out the possibility of future party demands for constitutional changes that tear at the heart of the established British constitution. The Party as a whole has never been united behind the virtues of liberal-domocracy and representative government, and there is a deep hostility to the role and nature of law.

Prospects for implementing the new constitution

Irrespective of the problems Labour faces in getting party backing for their constitutional proposals and in winning an election and forming a government, the prospects for the constitutional changes set out in the Policy Review for the 1990s do not look good. The proposals themelves are ill-thought out and are likely to do little to restrain government or protect individual rights. In ruling out a Bill of Rights and electoral reform (in order to block the rise and entrenchment of the middle ground in British politics) and in rejecting the Left case for a more radical, direct and participatory democracy, the package tends to a constitutional conservatism that embraces support for the essentials of the established system even though an attempt is made to appease potential critics within the Party with talk of abolishing the House of Lords and devolving power to the regions. But the Labour leadership must know that the abolition of the House of Lords is not a simple matter. It would be unlikely to get off the ground if Labour were to find itself in government, just as a Labour government would be reluctant to devote expensive parliamentary time to devolution proposals that would, if implemented, only serve to limit their capacity to govern from the centre.

The Labour Party sees itself as a democratic socialist party. However, democracy is about means whereas socialism is about ends and the two do not necessarily fit together. This being the case, the Party is always going to be ambivalent and divided as to the virtues of any system of rule. Tony Benn, the long-serving Labour MP and guru of the Left, was right to make the point that 'constitutional questions are the key to power in a parliamentary democracy' and that 'socialists need to give at least as much attention to the institutions of the state as to the power structure of the economy'. But the party still has a long way to go in its consideration of constitutional questions.

The Nationalist Parties

The proposals for constitutional change that we have considered so far have all accepted the legitimacy of th United Kingdom. There have been disputes as to how the constitution and system of government should be changed, but there has been an acceptance as to the territory and unity of the established nation state and neither the centre parties nor the Labour or Conservative Parties have sought to opt out of the system. This is not the position of the nationalist parties in Scotland, Wales and Northern Ireland. These parties have no wish to be party to cosy debates about Bills of Rights, electoral reform or the abolition of the House of Lords, since they see the British constitution and the established rules of the political game as stacked against them and the interests they represent. They take the view that they can never 'win' within the system – even if it is reformed – and so they see the only hope of salvation lying in Home Rule, self-government and independence, their own territory and a total opting out of the British system of government *and* of the United Kingdom itself.

The Scottish National Party, formed in 1934, rejects the fact that Scotland is governed by a party which the Scots have not elected and has stated that its principal aim is 'to win support for the establishment of an independent Scottish Parliament'. In their 1987 election manifesto they called on the electorate 'to vote for their national freedom. . . . Scotland needs more than ever to regain her independence. We must win back our Parliament and reclaim the power to make decisions for ourselves.'

Plaid Cymru, the Party of Wales formed in 1925, adopts a similar position. it recognises that 'our votes in Wales cannot determine the outcome of a British general election' and it is concerned to secure 'an independent Welsh government answerable only to the people of Wales', taking the view that 'at present Wales is ruled by a colonial-style government'.

The position of Sinn Fein in Northern Ireland is rather more complex. Because the Party rejects the partition of Ireland into north and south and does not accept the legitimacy of Northern Ireland, it does not seek Home Rule for Northern Ireland but rather 'the unity and independence of Ireland' and an 'end to British interference in Irish affairs'.

The problem for all these parties is how to implement and attain the independence they desire. Almost by definition, they lack votes and can never win enough seats to push their demands through the British Parliament. The limitation of the ballot box has encouraged some to believe that the only way they can secure their goal is through the bullet.

Conclusion

There may be dissatisfaction with the established constitution of Britain and we may be in a period of decisive constitutional significance, but there is no consensus as to what should be the form of a new constitution and there is no objective criterion as to what would make for a 'better' set-up. Conflict revolves around the ills of the established system and around the form of any new settlement precisely because the rules of the political game are not neutral in their implications for the power of interests and parties over the state and even for the likely role and direction of the state itself. The proposal of the established constitutional authorities to limit parliamentary sovereignty by law would increase the political power of the (highly conservative) judges in a way that was intended to block the prospect of Britain becoming socialist via the ballot box. The centre parties concern to secure PR would not only give them more seats in the Commons but it would also heighten the prospect of coalition government and the probability of the kind of moderate and 'sensible' policies which they see as the key to a better Britain. Calculations of party advantage are also caught up in the stance of the Labour Party as it wrestles to come to a settled view on the proper position for a second chamber and on the case against (or should it be for?) electoral reform. And the Conservative Party feels able to stand above these constitutional concerns to change the system precisely because it is (currently) winning within the established rules in a way which is totally denied to the nationalist parties on the fringes of British politics.

The Conservative government's opposition to constitutional change in the 1980s (notwithstanding the case that was made *for* change by Conservative lawyers in the 1970s!) has been matched by pressures for constitutional change from parties that are self-interestedly anxious about their capacity to secure state power within the established constitution in the 1990s. This highlights a problem: those in a position to implement constitutional changes are unlikely to want to do so because they are doing well within the established system, whereas those not in a position to implement constitutional changes are mostly likely to be eager to do so – even though their eagerness may diminish if they themselves win through to power within the established system. Put another way, at a time when constitutional change is most needed it is least likely to come to easy fruition.

But this kind of conclusion is a touch overcynical and 'political' as there is more to constitutional change than simple self-interest alone. At the present time, there is a less partisan and more enduring case against the system and for change that bears on the the absence of constitutional constraints on governmental power and the related problem of safeguarding rights and freedoms within the established system no matter which party is in government. From this broad perspective, it is argued that there is a need to effect constitutional changes that will better secure individual rights in a future system, even though there are disputes both as to the rights to be safeguarded and the methods that will do the trick.

The substance of this chapter highlights the extent to which the constitution is in crisis. Put another way, Britain is in a period of decisive constitutional significance – albeit one where the absence of any consensus as to a better system blocks the prospects for easy constitutional change. The established set-up may hold but maybe a break will be made: no system of rule has lasted forever.

Works Cited and Guide to Further Reading

Benn, T. (1982) *Arguments for Democracy*, Harmondsworth, Penguin.
Ex-Labour Minister who became a leading figure on the Left of the Party attacks 'the power of the establishment' and sets out 'the way ahead'.

Buchanan, J.M. (1975) *The Limits of Liberty: Between Anarchy and Leviathan*, Chicago, University of Chicago Press.
Key American figure on the New Right who is pro-maket and anti-state. Concerned to design a constitution through a social contract that will better reflect individual choice and secure a limited 'protective' state that will enhance his kind of liberty.

Charter 88 (1988) *New Statesman and Society*, 2 December.
A 'reforming alliance of citizens of the libertarian Left and the democratic centre in Britain' that calls for a 'new constitutional settlement' that would include such things as a Bill of Rights, PR, open government and a reformed second chamber.

Conservative Party (1987) *The Next Moves Forward*.
The election manifesto. A pretty detailed statement as to future policies but practically nothing on the need for constitutional reform.

Denning, Lord (1980) 'Misuse of power', *The Listener* 27 November and reprinted in his (1982) *What Next in the Law*, London, Butterworth.
Retired senior judge and constitutional authority attacks the misuse of power by just about everyone within the established set-up – except the judges – and makes a case for the judges having more power within a new written constitution.

Gilmour, Sir I. (1978) *Inside Right*, London, Quartet.
Good 'wet' Conservative stuff that makes the case for a new constitution that would involve a reformed House of Lords and electoral reform.

Graham, C., and Prosser, T. (eds) (1988) *Waiving the Rules: The Constitution Under Thatcherism*, Milton Keynes, Open University Press.
Looks at 'the changes wrought by the Thatcher governments on the the structure and institutions of the British state' and argues that 'on all sides, a major rethinking of our approach to constitutional fundamentals is long overdue'.

Hailsham, Lord (1976) 'Elective dictatorship, *The Listener*, 21 October, and eleaborated in his (1978) *The Dilemna of Democracy*, London Collins.

Senior Conservative, leading lawyer and constitutional authority attacks the established constitution as an elective dictatorship and calls for a new written constitution that would limit Parliament and give more power to the judges. After the electoral victories of his party he ceased to criticise the established constitution.

Hain, P. (1986) *Proportional Misrepresentation*. London, Wildwood House.
Ex-young Liberal, but now on the Left of the Labour Party, puts the case against proportional representation.

Halsbury's Laws of England, Vol. 8, *Constitutional Law*, 4th edn, (1980) London, Butterworth.
The book on the laws of England. Paragraph 811 on the sovereignty of Parliament is worth a very close read because it challenges the 'orthodox doctrine' and eases towards the case for limiting Parliament.

Harden, I. and Lewis, N. (1986) *The Noble Lie: The British Constitution and the Rule of Law*, London, Hutchinson.
They see a gap between constitutional theory and political practice and argue that major constitutional reforms are needed if the rule of law is to be the guiding spirit of the British constitution today.

Heyek, F. (1960) *The Constitution of Liberty*, London, Routledge and Kegan Paul.
Leading New Right thinker who sets out the case for freedom and the case against state provision at the same time as he devises a constitution to secure his objectives.

Hodgson, G. (1981) *Labour at the Crossroads*, Oxford, Martin Robertson.
Left-Labour perspective analysing the failures of parliamentary socialism/Labourism and making a case for a 'third road to socialism': 'an interaction between parliamentary and extra-parliamentary action'. Subsequent election defeats have tended to mean that this kind of perspective is no longer at the cutting edge of Labour Party thinking.

Holme, R., and Elliott, M. (eds) (1988) *1688–1988: Time for a New Constitution*, London, Macmillan.
Published by the Constitutional Reform Centre, which 'provides a focus for those people in all parties and none' (but especially within the centre) who are concerned about the maintenance of rights and freedoms within the established constitution and who 'believe that our constitution needs to be reformed'.

Jenkins, R. (1979) 'Home thoughts from abroad', *The Listener*, 29 November.
The lecture that set the ball rolling for the formation of the SDP. Criticises adversary party politics; concerned to strengthen the political centre; and makes a case for electoral reform.

Johnson, N. (1980) *In Search of the Constitution*, London, Methuen.
Still an excellent (high Tory) critique of the established constitution that makes a plea to 'refashion the rules of the political order' through a written constitution, electoral reform, a revival of Parliament, and so on.

Johnson, N. (1980) 'Constitutional reform: some dilemnas for a Conservative philosophy'. In Z. Layton-Henry, *Conservative Party Politics*, London, Macmillan.
Recognises that some Conservatives have been worried about the established constitution but sees them as ill-equipped to fashion a better system because of the nature of Conservative political thinking.

Labour Party (1987) *Britain Will Win.*
The election manifesto. Talks of the general need to 'strengthen democracy', 'enhance rights' and 'increase freedoms' but weak on *how* to do this.

Labour Party (1989) *Meet the Challenge, Make the Change.* The final (!) report of Labour's policy review for the 1990s. Includes 'A Modern Democracy' (the report of the Policy Review Group on Democracy for the Individual and the Community) that opposes electoral reform and a Bill of Rights whilst making a case for a new second chamber and the decentralisation of power to regional assemblies.

McAuslan, J.P.W.B., and McEldowney, J.F. (1986) 'The constitution under crisis', *Parliamentary Affairs*, 39, 496–516.
Argues that 'there is an incipient crisis in our constitutional arrangements' that bears on the issue of 'legitimacy – the right of the government to excercise power and whether the arrangements governing the exercise of power are still the appropriate ones.'

Maude, Sir A., and Szemery, J. (1982) *Why Electoral Change?*, London, Conservative Political Centre.
Conservative case against proportional representation.

Nairn, T. (1988) *The Enchanted Glass: Britain and its Monarchy*, London, Century Hutchinson.
Zany essay by one of the few people to take the Monarchy seriously as at once the apex and the essence of the British state. Nairn also makes the case for a 'quiet republicanism'.

Norton, P. (1982) *The Constitution in Flux*, Oxford, Martin Robertson.
Best available coverage of the 'challenges' to the established constitution and the 'new dimensions' but could now do with an update.

Phillips, O. Hood (1970) *Reform of the Constitution*, London, Chatto and Windus.
Leading constitutional authority makes an early case for a written constitution.

Royal Commission on the Constitution (1973) *Report*, Cmnd. 5460, London, HMSO.
Set up in response to the nationalist pressures for elected assemblies in Wales and Scotland. Emphasised the need to preserve the unity of the UK, but alive to the problem of maintaining consent for the system.

SDP/Liberal Alliance (1987) *Britain United: The Time Has Come.*
The election manifesto. Under a section on 'Better Government' the Alliance sets down its 'Great Reform Charter' for a new constitution for Britain.

Steel, D. (1985) 'How to restore real power to the people' *The Guardian*, 22 March.
The leader of the Liberal party crticises the established constitution and sets out the Liberal proposals for a better system.

Wigram, A. (n/d) *Constitutional Reform Now*, London, Conservative Action for Editorial Reform.
A brief pamphlet by a Conservative making a case for proportional representation as it would put an end to socialist extremism.

Chapter 6

The Power of the Secret State

For five years we bugged and burgled our way across London at the State's behest, while pompous bowler-hatted civil servants in Whitehall pretended to look the other way.
    Peter Wright (1987) *Spychatcher*, Australia, Heinemann, p. 54.

One of the things which influenced my mind profoundly when I came to the original judgment on how to deal with the 'Crown Jewels' was that it was quite apparent to me that the more information we provided the more it would be argued yet more information was needed.
    Michael Heseltine, Secretary of State for Defence, November 1984,
        on the disclosure of information to Parliament with respect to the
            sinking of the *Belgrano* in the battle for the Falklands.

Democracy is . . . a principle that is unacceptable to the establishment in our society. That establishment, by which I mean leading men in the City, captains of industry, press barons, those at the top of the church hierarchy and the professions, is determined that the government in Britain should remain elitist, oligarchic, bureacratic and secretive. Indeed, government in Britain today is so secretive that even the true nature of our constitution is hidden from the people.
    B. Sedgemore (1980) *The Secret Constitution*, London, Hodder and
                                                        Stoughton, p. 11.

Introduction

So far we have dwelt on the public face of democratic politics in Britain but it is now time for us to break out in order to consider other facts and rival perspectives. Democratic politics, and debates as to the explanatory virtues of various types of democratic theory are not the be-all and end-all of the matter when it comes to describing and making good sense of British politics. To look at British politics as if it were *just* a democracy encourages a very narrow view. It leads to things being ignored and left out of account; it leads to things being written out as irrelevant of consideration; and, when certain things *are* explored, then the presumption that democracy is the

"Will these new recruits to the state be the servants or the masters of our democracy?"
(Reproduced by kind permission of The Hulton Picture Company.)

essential stuff of British politics leads to those things being considered in a way which we think misrepresents and hides their true role in the political system so that understanding is actually blocked. There is more to British politics than meets the eye; there is more than the public and democratic face of elections, parties, pressure groups, government and the huff and puff of parliamentary debate; and – in the context of this chapter – there is more to the state than government and Parliament alone. We do not discount the importance of democracy and we do not deny that the *elected* side of the state machine is of enormous significance but we also need to deal with the political power of the non-elected secret state *and* with the political significance of the fact that the British economy is essentially capitalist.

In chapters 7 and 8 we will be exploring two very different perspectives on the political significance of capitalism, but in this chapter we will deal with the secret state. We will deal, that is, with some of those state institutions which are *non-elected*; which enjoy substantial *autonomy* from the control of the elected side of the state; which tend to be closed and *secret* in their manner of operation; and which exercise very substantial political *power*. In concrete terms, we will be paying particular attention to the Civil Service (the 'the permanent government' of Britain that some see as our very own ruling class) but we will also attend to the role of the Bank of England in economic policy-making; to the role of the judiciary in law-making; to the role of the police in selectively applying the law; to the role of the military in shaping defence policy; and to the role of the highly secretive security services in policing and 'defending' our civil liberties and the whole state system itself. In chapter 12 we will discuss the political system beyond Westminster and Whitehall, paying attention to the local state; regional institutions; national institutions in Scotland, Wales and Northern Ireland; and to the implications which flow from our involvement in a variety of international organisations.

It is easy to say that a decent account of British politics needs to take on board the significance of the secret state but it is another matter to advance understanding given the fact that we lack a strong state tradition in this country. In the last quarter of the nineteenth century and the early years of the twentieth century the idea of the state exercised some influence over the British study of politics. Politics was defined as being about the state– it was sometimes called 'the science of the state' – and there was a rough agreement that in order to deal with the modern nation state it was important to go beyond an easy emphasis on the government of the day because that was but a *part* of a state system. During the course of the twentieth century, however, a variety of factors encouraged political scientists to actually *define* politics as being less about the state and formal institutions and more about political 'systems' and informal behaviour. This meant that a concern to develop theories of the state fell by the wayside and the state itself got written out of the discipline. Moreover, the fact that the British political system was increasingly being defined as a democracy gave a further twist to the demise of an interest in the state because of the democratic presumption that all state institutions are crisply controlled by the elected government and are therefore of no importance in their own right. The weakness of the state tradition in Britain when coupled with this belief in the existence of democracy has encouraged a situation in which the state is not just obscured and seen as dependent and controlled, but actually disappears because it gets dissolved in the government of the day. In a word, government and state are all too easily seen as one and the same thing – as was made perfectly clear by the judge at the trial of Clive Ponting (a civil servant charged under the Official Secrets Act of disclosing information concerning the sinking of the *Belgrano* at the time of the battle for the Falklands) when he argued:

> We have general elections in this country. The majority party in the House of Commons forms the government. If it loses majority support, it ceases to do so, but for the time being, it *is* the government, and its policies are those of the State. It is not a question of the Conservative Party being the State. It is not a political matter at all. The policies of the State were the policies of the government then in power.

In Britain, then, it is now a well-established 'fact' that when a party wins a general election and forms a government it also wins *all* state power. Government is regarded as the motor at the heart of the state machine and the various institutions that make up the state are seen as devoid of any independent political significance and power because they are viewed as tools used by the government in the implementation of policies and laws that have been determined by the government and passed by Parliament. The secret state – the *permanent* side of the state – is scarcely noticed but is seen as obedient and responsible to the government of the day, and the government in its turn is seen as accountable to the people through Parliament. From this kind of perspective on British politics there is *not* the idea that power may flow downwards from the secret state; there is *not* the idea that the secret state may sometimes dominate a democratically elected government; and there is *not* the idea that the secret state may possess unaccountable power so that it needs to be studied in its own right independently of – and even *against* – democratic theories and orthodoxies as to its lack of significance and power.

The fact that a democratic perspective is entrenched which almost certainly obscures and misrepresents the reality of state power; the fact that we lack a genuine state tradition; and the fact – as our next chapter will make clear – that Marxist theory on 'the capitalist state' offers us few insights, all serve to mean that it is difficult for us to find a way to break in to the study of state institutions. Moreover, these problems of perspective and theory are compounded because is is hard to get at even fairly basic 'facts' about state institutions given the secrecy which surrounds the whole of our system of rule. The Cabinet is at the pinnacle of the elected side of the central state and yet the existence, composition and chairmanship of

Cabinet committees are kept secret from the public. The secrecy of the non-elected side of the state machine is even more of a problem. Secrecy is at the heart of the way in which Whitehall works, and constitutional conventions (and the law) exist to prevent us finding out about how decisions are really made in the Civil Service; judges consider that their work should be shrouded in mystery and they are censured if they break rank and talk to the media; the police regard an interest in their work as hostile and politically motivated; much to do with military matters is kept under wraps in order to 'protect national security'; and the security services scarcely even exist officially. The system of official secrecy finds its official counterpart in the deliberate 'leaking' of (mis)information to journalists, many of whom are prepared to be 'good chaps' and work through a lobby system which ensures that they play by the Whitehall rules of responsibility so that we are provided with facts which tell us very much less than the whole story about the system of state power in Britain.

Given the problems that surround any attempt to make sense of the British secret state, our concerns in this chapter are modest. We have no plans to advance a general theory of the secret state because we doubt the utility of such a theory. We are of the opinion that the complexity of the institutions that make up the secret state – the fact that the state is not a single cohesive entity subject to a single compelling logic – means that the state system is likely to be a good deal messier than any single abstract theory about it. So priority has to be given to working from the bottom up in order to discover how the parts of the system actually operate in practice. However, before we can even get down to this work we need to clear the intellectual decks. The prevalence of a democratic perspective on British politics has encouraged the entrenchment of a whole series of orthodoxies as to the position of the various parts of the secret state. These need to be recognised and set down because they occupy positions of academic *and* political importance in that they help to legitimise and sustain a particular system of rule. We regard the orthodoxies that are part of a simple democratic perspective on the secret state as seriously flawed. We intend to challenge the adequacy of these orthodoxies because they do not provide an accurate account of the power and position of the various institutions that make up the secret state.

Challenging established perspectives and orthodoxies is negative and can only get us so far. If we are to be more positive we need to go on to try and open suggestive chinks of light into the behaviour of these secretive state institutions. To this end, we think it is important to set down the functions of the various state institutions and to be aware of the implications which flow from the fact that they are organised in a particular way. At a more detailed level it is important to attend to the backgrounds of the people who are recruited to the commanding positions of power at the same time as we explore the processes of their training and socialisation within the institutions of the state. We do not pretend that social background will *determine* the way that judges or police officers will behave on the job – far from it – but background does *condition* the way the world is viewed. Moreover, if social backgrounds are shared by those in positions of leadership and if those leaders enjoy a certain autonomy, then background (and our knowledge as to background) will provide us with pointers to the way in which power will be used and exercised by the institutions that make up the secret state. None of this will enable us truly to crack the state but it will get us beyond the orthodoxies and it should enable you to start thinking about the state in new and different ways.

The Civil Service

Orthodoxies

The orthodox perspective on the power and position of the Civil Service is clear enough. Civil servants are recruited on merit to a non-political and disciplined career service. They are anonymous, permanent and politically neutral, and serve with equal loyalty the duly elected government of the day, no matter what its political complexion. The Civil Service does not possess political power and it does not control the direction of the state because it does not have the job of making public policy but is geared to the more modest task of administering policy. Put another way, the Civil Service implements the policies determined by the government and passed by Parliament and has to manage and deliver the services for which the government is responsible, although civil servants are also available to advise their ministers on how best to achieve the government's own policy objectives. Underpinning all this is the crucial relationship between ministers (the elected policy-makers) and civil servants (the non-elected administrators and advisors), and the essence of this relationship is seen as captured in the constitutional convention of individual ministerial responsibility. According to this convention, the duty of the civil servant is first and foremost to the Minister of the Crown who is in charge of the Department in which he or she is serving. For their part, ministers make policy and are answerable and responsible to Parliament for the actions of their departmental civil servants who are anonymous and shielded from public criticism. Given the secure position of civil servants, the convention obliges ministers to take the blame and possibly resign if a significant mistake is made within their department. This happened in 1982 when three Foreign Office ministers resigned following the invasion of the Falklands and again in 1986 when the Secretary of State for Trade and Industry resigned consequent upon an official from his department 'leaking' information to the Press in connection with the Westland affair.

Sir Brian Hayes, when he was the permanent secretary at the Ministry of Agriculture, not only expressed the orthodox view as to the position of the Civil Service in its relationship to policy *and* to ministers, but *also* argued that practice was in conformity with this position, suggesting that this was the end to the matter with respect to the power of the Civil Service:

> Civil servants ought not to have power because we're not elected. Power stems from the people and flows through Parliament to the minister responsible to Parliament. The Civil servant has no power of his own, he is there to help a minister and to be the minister's agent. . . . I think the job of the civil servant is to make sure that his minister is informed; that he has all the facts; that he's made aware of all the options and that he is shown all the considerations bearing on those options. It is then for the minister to take the decision. That is how the system, ought to operate and that is how I think, in the vast majority of cases, it does operate.

The January 1985 trial of Clive Ponting (the civil servant charged, but acquitted, under Section 2 of the Official Secrets Act of disclosing official information to a Member of Parliament concerning the sinking of the Argentinian cruiser *General Belgrano* at the time of the battle for the Falklands) opened up issues to do with the responsibility of civil servants and the power of Parliament, and produced a flurry of concern about the constitutional position of civil servants and ministers. In an editorial on 'The Ponting acquittal', *The Times* buttressed the orthodox position arguing:

> It is Ministers who are responsible to Parliament, and civil servants, as such, are responsible to Ministers, not to Parliament (let alone to individual interested MPs) or some less concrete concept of National Interest.

In February 1985, Robert Armstrong, as Head of the Home Civil Service, issued a note on *The Duties and Responsibilities of Civil Servants in Relation to Mninsters* in which he felt obliged to restate the conventional position, arguing that:

> The determination of policy is the responsibility of the Minister (within the convention of collective responsibility of the whole Government for the decisions and actions of every member of it) . . . it is the duty of the civil servant to make available to the Minister all the information and experience at his or her disposal which may have a bearing on the policy decisions to which the Minister is committed . . . . When having been given all the relevant information and advice, the Minister has taken a decision, it is the duty of civil servants loyally to carry out that decision with precisely the same energy and good will, whether they agree with it or not.

Ministers and civil servants

Ministers and civil servants who have been intimately involved in the process of policy making have sometimes been prepared to drop guard and paint a picture of civil service power at odds with the orthodox view. It is, however, another matter to put flesh onto these bones of constitutional dissent. Case studies of policy-making are needed because these are likely to be more disinterested than the memoirs of the great and the good. However, a general understanding of the relationship between ministers and civil servants can be advanced if we are attentive to the limitations of ministers and to the related factors and resources which advantage the position of civil servants in their dealings with their elected masters.

The limitations of ministers

1   The overwhelming majority of ministers are drawn from the House of Commons as some 80-5 ministers and whips are selected from the 326 + MPs in the majority party. Not only is this a tiny pool of talent that must take those of little competence into office, but the skills that an MP must cultivate are different from those that are needed for success in ministerial office.

2   British ministers are amateurs when it comes to their departments. At best they are 'intelligent laymen'. They are unlikely to have been picked for their specialist knowledge and background, and very few will have had experience in managing a large organisation of any kind.

3   Ministers are frequently reshuffled from ministerial post to ministerial post so that they are rarely in a particular position for more than two or three years. From 1979 to 1986 there were four Secretaries of State for Defence and six Ministers of Defence Procurement, and from 1944 to 1986 there were twenty-one Ministers of Education. It is clearly difficult for a temporary intruder who lacks expertise to get a grip on the work, ethos and character of a department, and so it will be an uphill struggle to challenge the 'departmental view' and the 'Civil Service policy' that has developed over a long period.

4   Opposition parties are rarely prepared for government, in part because of the absence of resources for policy formulation in opposition. This lack of planning and preparation and the fact that few ministers seem to come to office with well-defined policy objectives and priorities does little to advantage ministers in their dealings with the permanent government in Whitehall.

5   Convention limits the access of ministers to the papers of previous administrations and this inhibits the possibility of a minister learning from experience – and mistakes. A new minister will be handed the briefing papers written in the pre-election period and a document entitled 'Guidance to Ministers'. Ponting argues that this merely 'emphasises the continuity of British government and . . . enshrines the view that there is an accepted way of conducting the nation's affairs which must be followed by each government.'

6   Ministers tend to be isolated in their departments. They have rivals and bitter opponents among their party 'colleagues' and tend to lack the kind of supportive network enjoyed by top civil servants.

7   Ministers are caught up in a Whitehall and Westminster timetable that

is not of their making and that is beyond their control but within which they are constrained to operate. All of this tends to operate to ministerial disadvantage.

8 Ministers are not just full-time ministers, they are also, and perhaps mainly, senior party politicians with a short political fuse and extra-departmental responsibilities in the Cabinet, the Commons, their constituencies, and the country at large. This limits their perspective and the amount of time and energy which they can devote to running and controlling their department. The sheer burden and pace of work, and the weariness which this must engender, inevitably plays into the hands of the permanent and full-time civil servants.

9 Entry into the European Community has compounded many of the problems facing ministers. It has increased the burden on ministers. It has also resulted in a situation in which British civil servants have had to develop close working relationships with their European colleagues in order to 'prepare the ground' for ministerial discussion and decision. This has probably circumscribed ministerial freedom of action at home and in Europe.

10 The developing idea that ministers should not just be policy-makers-in-chief but managers and chief executives of their departments as well has increased the load of work on ministers and given them a task for which they are ill-equipped. This must increase ministerial dependence on civil service help and guidance.

The resources of civil servants

1 In contrast to the temporary and hard-pressed minister, permanent senior civil servants can devote the whole of their working week to the affairs of the department and so they have more time to spend on policy matters and are not distracted by the need to pursue a political career.

2 Top civil servants have frequently been criticised for being amateurish all-rounders who lack expertise. Compared to their ministers, however, civil servants *are* experts – the more so since many are likely to spend their whole careers in the one department.

3 The fact that civil servants work in departments and the fact that every department in Whitehall has its own character and ethos means that civil servants tend to be socialised into the 'departmental view'. This view confronts and weakens ministers at the same time as it strengthens civil servants and gives them a perspective on policy and policy options that is likely to be a good deal firmer and better worked out than those of their minister.

4 The Civil Service is in a near monopoly position as the supplier of information and advice to ministers. This places ministers in a weak and dependent situation.

5 Civil servants also enjoy a virtual monopoly of the written words that float around the state machine. Indeed, at Cabinet meetings, civil servants not only provide pratically all the papers for discussion, but it is a civil servant who provides the authoritative minute of the meetings. So, the Cabinet decides what the Civil Service says it has decided on the basis of policy papers which civil servants themselves have drafted!

6 Civil servants have to be concerned to protect their ministers from an overload of departmental work. This means that they must limit the information, questions and options that are passed up for ministerial decision in a way that inevitably constrains the room for ministerial manoeuvre and policy-making.

7 The fact that ministers have a limited amount of time to devote to their departments means that they simply cannot deal with all the policy matters that could, and perhaps should, concern them. They have no choice but to delegate (and have delegated for them!) the bulk of departmental decision-making to their civil servants. In this situation, many civil servants are inevitably caught up in the business of making public policy. It is nonsense to suppose that there is a simple distinction between matters of policy and matters of administration, and it is even more nonsensical to suppose that certain people (ministers) can just make policy whilst others (civil servants) can limit their activities to administration alone. Even if it were to be the case that civil servants 'only' took 'less important' policy decisions, it is they who have a capacity to define what is important and so they can come close to defining what is the appropriate field for ministerial action.

8 Even in those areas where ministers do seem to decide policy, it is the civil servants who do a great deal to set up the policy framework and who define what is sensible, realistic, practical, feasible, responsible and possible – and it is always the civil servants who have the job of implementing the policy and working out the details.

9 For the most part, ministers and civil servants identify closely together when they face Parliament with its potential for embarrassing critique. However, the fact that ministers are keenly dependent on their civil servants in order to get a bill properly drafted and through Parliament gives civil servants a role of power and importance in determining the precise shape of legislation.

10 For most of its history the Civil Service has been in a position virtually to control its own internal affairs. This control was given as the price to be paid for formal civil service servitude to ministers. We shall see that this has given the Civil Service a power to resist critique and to block changes in the way in which it conducts the business of the state.

Ministers, civil servants and Thatcherism

The fact that ministers are limited and that civil servants have powerful resources has led some commentators to argue that the Civil Service is really Britain's ruling class. According to this kind of view, civil servants run an essentially negative machine that is geared to continuity. They can obstruct new policies of which they disapprove at the same time as they are able to push ministers into adopting the established policies of the department that have been build-up by the civil servants themselves.

In fact, it is a sterile debate to argue about who has 'real' power because ministers and civil servants are locked together within a *system* of government. This makes it difficult to come to a firm and settled view as to the precise relationship between ministers and civil servants – the more so since much *does* depend on personalities and issues and on the sheer will of a minister and of a government. Having said that, and whilst we shrink from subscribing to a crude 'conspiracy theory' which suggests that the Civil Service runs the show and that the elected side of the state is as of nothing, it is nevertheless clear that civil servants have more influence, and ministers less, than constitutional theory would lead us to believe should be the case. However, it is also clear that none of this is determined and set in stone. Politicians have regularly baulked at the power of the Civil Service and have sought to tilt the balance back towards ministers and the elected side of the state machine.

At the beginning of this century, the prospect of a growing civil service was regarded with alarm because it was seen as a harbinger of collectivism and socialism. In the period since the Second World War, however, much of the criticism of the Civil Service came from those on the Left of British politics who saw the Service as part of an upper-class Establishment that was geared to Conservatism and maintaining the status quo so that it obstructed Labour policies designed to secure socialism. The 1960s was a period of major institutional reappraisal when there was widespread concern that the Civil Service was closed, secretive, amateurish, hierarchical, defensive and overly concerned with precedent and staffed by civil servants who were ill-equipped as managers and out of contact with the outside world. In 1966, the Labour Prime Minister, Harold Wilson, set up a committee on the Civil Service under the chairmanship of John Fulton. This committee eventually came up with a report that included 22 recommendations for change but the report was only half-heartedly implemented and many of the proposals were watered down or abandoned – perhaps because the task of implementation was left to the Civil Service itself. In the 1970s, a New Right perspective came to political prominence that was as supportive of the market as it was critical of the state and of the Civil Service itself. Civil servants were seen as in a powerful monopoly position with an interest in maximising public sector budgets and extending the role of the state because this was the way to increase their own pay and power as well as the number of secure jobs in public employment. Moreover, they were operating in an organisational situation where they could get away with this because there were no incentives for them to increase the efficient supply of services. And the growth of a militant civil service trade unionism was a constant pressure on the government which was supposed to act as a 'model employer' and not just attend to market considerations with respect to pay and conditions. Margaret Thatcher had an intuitive grip on much of this analysis, and she brought a passion to civil service matters when she came to office in 1979. Civil servants were to be distrusted and top civil servants were to be detested. All of them were the 'guilty men' who had helped to entrench the failed consensus at the same time as they constituted an obstacle to the creation of a more dynamic private enterprise culture. Margaret Thatcher was determined to 'de-privilege' the Civil

Service and cut it down to size; she was determined to increase effeciency; and she was determined to reassert effective political control, but just how successful has she been in these three endeavours?

Size

When the Conservatives came to office in 1979 they inherited 732,000 civil servants. They set a target of 630,000 by April 1984 but the total was actually down to 624,000 by that date. The size of the Civil Service in 1986 was down to 594,000, smaller than at any time since the Second World War. A government prepared to cut – to 'hive off' and 'privatize' – the functions of the state is clearly going to need fewer civil servants but one of the basic problems in counting the Civil Service is that there is no agreed definition of what is a civil servant. For example, until the mid-1960s all Post Office employees were civil servants but then their status was changed. In this situation some of the cuts since 1979 are arbitrary and purely cosmetic as certain employees still in the public sector (such as the staff at Kew Gardens) have just ceased to be called civil servants. Moreover, cuts in civil servants do not necessarily lead to cuts in public expenditure. For example, 43 per cent of all the reductions between 1980 and 1984 were made by the Ministry of Defence but none of these has contributed to a saving of public expenditure because the MOD has a single block budget and so all the savings on civilian manpower have been used up elsewhere in the Defence Budget, on such things as buying new equipment. In numerical terms, then, the Thatcher government's programme for civil service cuts has been very successful but much depends on what we mean by the Civil Service and Ponting has argued that 'there is little evidence to show . . . that the reductions have been made in areas where there was over-staffing'.

Efficiency

Immediately after the 1979 election, Margaret Thatcher appointed Sir Derek Rayner, the then joint managing director of Marks & Spencer, to advise her on ways of improving efficiency and eliminating waste in central government. Rayner instigated a series of specific efficiency scrutinies by young 'insider' officials that involved 'radical questioning, direct observation, proposals based firmly on detailed evidence, and a sense of urgency' with the hope that a 'demonstration effect' would lead to lessons being applied so as to change the traditional culture of the entire Civil Service. By the time that Rayner moved back to Marks & Spencer at the end of 1982, 130 scrutinies had produced £170 million savings and economies of 16,000 posts a year, plus £39 million more in once-and-for-all savings with another £104 million worth of possible savings. In 1985 the Efficiency Unit (as it was then called) conducted a scrutiny of scrutinies, *Making Things Happen*, in which it pointed out that there had been 266 scrutinies since 1979 with cumulative savings of around £750 million, but it noted that it took at least two years, and sometimes five, to implement the savings. These savings may be small when compared to the total cost of contemporary government but Ponting is probably wrong when he asserts that 'Whitehall . . . absorbed Raynerism' and failed 'to implement reports that were disliked'. Improving efficiency has been pushed up the agenda of civil service priorities and has changed thinking, even though the implications for the human side of the Civil Service has been anything but a success story.

Political control

Reducing the size of the Civil Service and endeavouring to increase its efficiency involve a general assertion of political control, but what of Margaret Thatcher's ministers in their dealings with departments and civil servants?

Civil servants had long been criticised for lacking skills in management. The New Right was increasingly turning that criticism against ministers who were urged to go beyond their traditional policy-making role in order to take on an additional role as managing directors of their departments. Ministers were to get a grip on management through the Management Information System for Ministers (MINIS), a system that was designed to enable them to explore 'who does what, why and at what cost' so that they could ensure that resources were allocated in accordance with their priorities. In reality, however, there was little ministerial interest in MINIS – and even management – and the Financial Management Initiative (FMI) which emphasised the need for a general and co-ordinated drive to improve financial management in departments left most ministers cold. In part because they did not go into politics in order to be good managers, but also because they lacked time, competence and adequate experience of the details of departmental work where civil servants were able to continue to reign supreme.

Thatcher's ministers may continue to be limited managers of their departments and civil servants. However, in their concern to keep policy-making secret they have asserted a tighter grip on their civil servants and have shown a marked reluctance to allow them to present information to Parliament or to Commons select committees. We know a little about this because of the publicity surrounding the Ponting case and the Westland affair.

The civil servant Clive Ponting defended his action in sending documents to the Labour MP Tam Dalyell on the grounds that he was being required to assist ministers to evade, through deliberate deceit, legitimate parliamentary scrutiny. At his trial, the constitutional expert Professor Henry Wade expressed the view that if a civil servant was convinced that truthful information was not being given by ministers to Parliament then it 'might be in the public interest for him to give his information direct to Parliament.' Notwithstanding this judgement and Ponting's subsequent acquittal, we have already seen that the government reasserted the traditional view which suggested that civil servants were responsible to their ministers alone. From this perspective on the responsibilities of civil servants there was no conception that they had a responsibility to Parliament or the public interest and the notion that civil servants should obey ministerial orders denies that they have an overriding moral responsibility to tell the truth. Such a perspective clearly limits the accountability of the executive at the same time as it restricts the role of Parliament.

Disputes within the Cabinet surrounding the takeover of the Westland helicopter company led the Secretary of State for Defence to resign from the Cabinet in January 1986 on the grounds that there had been a breakdown of collective responsibility. Two weeks later the Secretary of State for Trade and Industry was obliged to assume ministerial responsibility and resign consequent upon the leaking of information from his department to the Press Association. When the Defence Committee of the House of Commons inquired into the Westland affair it was denied the opportunity to question the DTI officials concerned in the leak as the government took the view that 'it is not appropriate for the inquiries of select committees to be extended to the conduct of individual civil servants'. Later on they made it clear that when civil servants do give evidence to select committees they are 'subject to the instructions of ministers and remain bound to observe their duty of confidentiality to ministers'. These judgements as to the position of civil servants and the role of select committees produced outrage in Parliament and in the top civil servants' union, the First Division Association. The furore surrounding Ponting and Westland reveal a government keen to get a grip on civil servants and even keener to keep Parliament out of governmental policy-making.

Recruitment, socialisation and Thatcherism

There are civil servants and civil servants. Any study concerned with policy-making and power in Britain is bound to focus attention on the 650 or so senior civil servants (who occupy the top three grades of permanent secretary, deputy secretary, and under-secretary) because it is these people who run the service and interact with ministers in advising and making policy. Moreover, the fact that the Civil Service is a career service (once in, people stay in and move up the ladder to positions of power) explains why public attention and debate has focused on the recruitment of the small number of graduate generalists. It is these administration trainees (ATs) who will go on to become the senior civil servants of the future.

The Civil Service tends to recruit in its own image. Each generation of civil servants favours the recruitment of ATs much like themselves. The Expenditure Committee of the House of Commons produced a report on the Civil Service in 1977 when they set down evidence with respect to recruitment for the period 1971–5. They painted the familiar picture: there was a preference for applicants from private schools; whilst 21.6 per cent of applicants were from Oxbridge they made up 50 per cent of recruits; and whilst 42.5 per cent of applicants had degrees in arts and humanities, they nevertheless accounted for 56.7 per cent of recruits into the Service. In the 1985 selection procedure for ATs, 14 per cent of Oxbridge applicants eventually passed the Final Selection Board compared with a non-Oxbridge rate of 1.3 per cent, and it was still the case that arts graduates were more likely to apply for this generalists' competition than science graduates and relatively more likely to succeed in it as well. There has been much discussion as to whether statistics of this kind are suggestive of what Ponting calls a 'massive bias towards upper-middle-class male candidates from public schools and Oxbridge who have arts degrees', or whether they simply reflect the fact that the Civil Service is out to recruit the best and most able people who just happen to have come from certain backgrounds and to have enjoyed a particular kind of education.

Social and educational background is not everything and, besides, it will be many years before the graduate recruits will be in senior positions. This being the case, it is important to appreciate the implications of the way in which entrants move up through the Service. New recruits do not so much join *the* Civil Service as join a specific department. This department will be their career and they will be initiated into its values and view of the world. The classic British approach to public administration is that it is 'something that can only be learned by doing' and observing others. There is no real tradition of formal civil service training, and training itself is not taken seriously because emphasis is placed upon new recruits serving a lengthy apprenticeship under more senior colleagues. After two years in the Service, the best ATs are 'fast streamed' and promoted to become Higher Executive Officers (Development). After a year or so they can expect to be promoted to Principal – still a learning grade but one that allows the incumbent to concentrate on a small area of policy even though the role in policy-making is fairly circumscribed. The 'high-flyers' can expect promotion to Assistant Secretary by 35 (but all the time reports and assessments by more senior civil servants are crucial to advancement) and the bulk of Under-Secretaries are promoted from Assistant Secretary between the ages of 43 and 48.

This pattern of new recruitment in the image of the established service, and promotion according to seniority if in conformity with the norms and 'view' of the department, results in a service which has a keen sense of itself and of the need to protect Civil Service interests. More than this, it also produces a contentment with 'the system' as it is; a governing ethos that is cautious and conservative; and a broad belief that continuity and the established pattern of policy commitments that have been built up slowly and pragmatically over the years should be maintained in the face of wild and 'political' demands for ill-considered change. Not surprisingly, senior civil servants find it hard to cope with adversary politics and conviction politicians, and the style of administration works badly for governments bent on implementing a radical programme of change.

We have already suggested that figures on the Left have been critical of the Civil Service because they saw it as Conservative. In the 1970s they argued that ministers should have a larger say in the appointment and transfer of senior departmental officials; that ministers should have their own private political office of specialist political advisers; and that junior ministers should be involved in the work of departmental and interdepartmental committees which were the preserve of officials. In the Labour government of 1974–9 there were some 38 political advisers, but experience rather suggested that the Civil Service could work around them, and senior ministers themselves were none to keen to have advisers since they could limit them as much as they could counter the alleged Conservatism of the Civil Service itself. Notwithstanding the problems of turning the Civil Service around – or perhaps *because* of the problems of turning the Civil Service around and using it as a tool to implement policies that challenged the consensus – once the Conservatives came to office in 1979 it was their turn to express concern about the conservative nature of the Civil Service. Sir John Hoskyns (one-time head of Margaret Thatcher's Policy Unit before becoming Director-General of the Institute of Directors) believed that 'the present system of career politicians served by career officials (was) a failed one' because the Civil Service was too 'passive' and hostile to change. He took the view that politicians needed to challenge the closed career nature of the Civil Service and recruit politically appointed outsiders who would then work on short-term contracts and be really committed to implementing the radical objectives of politicians. What, then, has been the extent of change with respect to the recruitment of senior civil servants under the premiership of Margaret Thatcher?

During the 1970s, between 150 and 250 ATs were appointed every year but in the 1980s this figure was halved and in 1982 just 24 ATs were appointed. In the last eight months of 1986 there were 52 inward secondments at senior level and it was becoming clear that the annual rate of mid-career secondments into the Civil Service was running at roughly the same rate as the number of external candidates recruited as ATs to start a career in the Service. During the period 1979–85, some 70 appointments were made from outside the Civil Service at the grade of under-secretary or above; in 1985 there were over 900 secondments in *and* out of the Service; and over the period 1979–83, 505 senior civil servants left the Service with many going into business appointments. All of this is suggestive of something of a breakdown in the closed nature of the career Civil Service, and the movement of top civil servants into industry on – and sometimes before – retirement has caused particular concern because it may erode and compromise the traditional independence and impartiality of the Civil Service. Just over half of those who were heads of departments in 1982 have since retired, and by 1984 over half of those had taken up business appointments. In fact, the career nature of the Civil Service has led to a situation in which the post-war generation of civil servants that entered in the late forties retired together from senior posts in the early eighties and aside from the issue of their work in retirement there is also the matter of the appointment of their successors in the Service. Between 1979 and 1985, 43 permanent secretaries and 138 deputy secretaries (the two grades where the Prime Minister has a direct say) departed. This gave the Prime Minister an unprecedented opportunity and Margaret Thatcher has taken a keen interest in senior civil service appointments. How people get to the top of the Civil Service and the role of the Prime Minister and the Senior Appointments Selection Committee (SASC) is 'shrouded in secrecy'. It has been claimed that Margaret Thatcher has not been interested in the political views of her officials and whether they are 'one of us' although she has displayed a strong preference for 'the civil servant who embodies the "can do" approach and is willing enthusiastically to implement the minister's policies'. Nowithstanding her precise role in particular appointments, her involvement has encouraged the *impression* of creeping civil service politicisation. There is no doubt that certain officials have flown higher and faster because of her patronage and there is the danger that a promotions culture may get established so that *all* officials will see the need to trim their advice to what ministers want to hear rather than what they need to know.

Margaret Thatcher may have taken an interest in civil service matters but she saw her basic job as turning the economy around. She had no wish 'to muck around with the machinery of government' but in setting her face against major institutional change Hennessy is right to suggest that 'she dominated Whitehall but she did not . . . transform it' and much change has been more a matter of style than of substance. Ministers and elected politicians *do* matter (and they have probably mattered more under Thatcher than they have under many of the less-committed consensus governments of the post-war period) but ministers cannot govern alone and the fact that they have always found it hard to transform the Civil Service and bend it to their will highlights the continuing power of bureaucratic organisation.

Bureaucracy and accountability

The Civil Service is a large and complex series of bureaucratic organisations. For the most part, civil service activity is in the hands of appointed career officials who possess expertise and knowledge, and day-to-day business is conducted on a continuous basis in accordance with a clear body of internal rules where a hierarchy of authority prevails. Such a system is indispensable to government given the range and complexity of the tasks performed by the British state and given the need to reach down to the millions of citizens touched by the state and its services. However, the technical superiority of this form of organisation in tackling problems and marshalling large-scale activity in a purposeful way means that it possesses a permanence and an indispensability that gives it a power so that it tends to transform itself from an implementing tool at the service of elected politicians into a policy-making body in its own right. As the German sociologist, Max Weber, observed at the beginning of the century, any attempt to run a complex society *without* a bureaucracy would result in chaos, and yet running a society *with* a bureaucracy inevitably leads to a loss of control to the bureaucrats themselves. In this situation it is easy to see how it can be argued that the permanent Civil Service controls the state and that the state controls the people – and this in spite of all the claims about democracy and the power of the people and the power of elected politicians. The problem of any civil service taking over the direction of the state is only one of the dangers inherent in bureaucratic organisation. There is also the danger of bureaucracies becoming 'rule bound', with bureaucrats defending themselves from criticism by slavishly following the rules even though this may well work against the attainment of the ends to be secured and at great cost to many of the individuals caught up in the rules.

The combined result of all this is that the Civil Service tends to be a powerful force, also a conservative force, that is often able to exert a 'negative' power so that it can block and frustrate the radical changes pressed on it by its elected 'masters'. Given its permanent and long-standing involvement in the business of the state and given the bureaucratic way it conducts its affairs (and the implications of the established processes of recruitment and socialisation), the Civil Service is almost bound to be sceptical of the case for change at the same time as it will be committed to maintaining the established policies which it helped to build up through advice and implementation as well as a goodly touch of public policy-making. Governments come and go, but no matter who you vote for the Civil Service goes on for ever and stays at the heart of the state machine.

The Bank of England

History

The Bank of England was founded in 1694 so that the government could raise money for a war against the French. For over 250 years the Bank was formally a private bank with a jumble of increasing responsibilities, but it was always more than just a purely 'private' institution because many of its powers and duties were granted by Parliament, as in 1844 when the Bank was given a monopoly to print and issue bank notes. In 1781, when the Prime Minister, Lord North, proposed the renewal of the Bank's charter, he described the Bank as 'to all important purposes the public exchequer' and recognised even then that the Bank was' from long habit and usage of many years . . . part of the constitution.' Notwithstanding the intimate connections which existed between the Bank and the government, once the government took on board responsibility for the health of the economy the Bank found itself in an increasingly strange position. It was at one and the same time both a key part of the state's system of economic management *and* a private corporation accountable to private shareholders. The central position of the Bank in the economy made it an obvious target for public ownership.

The Labour government of 1945 had memories of the Bank's stubborness towards the first Labour government in the 1920s and took the view that 'the Bank of England with its financial powers must be brought under public ownership and the operations of the other banks harmonized with industrial needs' because 'the people of the country . . . have suffered greviously in past years through unwise decisions taken by persons associated in the past with the Bank'. The Bank was nationalised as a publicly-owned corporation in 1946.

Orthodoxies

The Bank of England Act, 1946, was vague as to the precise relationship between the Bank and the government. Moreover, because the government took the Bank's view that a central bank 'must' have autonomy and independence, the Act did not put the Bank under firm and clear political control. In formal terms, the Bank was made an agent of the Treasury as the Act stated that 'the Treasury may from time to time give such directions to the Bank as, after consultation with the Governor, they think necessary in the public interest' but such directions have never been given to the Bank and the Act did not provide for a situation in which the Treasury might give a direction but the Bank might not observe it. Notwithstanding a certain lack of clarity, ultimately (and in theory) the Treasury is boss and the Chancellor of the Exchequer is the Bank's formal master. In this situation, and in the particular context of monetary and economic policy, we are thrust up against the familiar constitutional orthodoxies which assert the importance of ministerial responsibility and the ultimate sovereignty of the people. In effect, the Chancellor is said to be responsible for the work of the Bank to Parliament and through Parliament to the people, and the Bank, although without the power to determine policy, is able (in the words of one Governor) 'to give independent and candid advice based upon experience'. In 1987, *The Economist* noted that 'in Britain, monetary policy is formally in the hands of the Treasury; it is the Bank's duty to carry it out.'

These kind of orthodoxies are much the same as those that have been used to describe the position of the Civil Service. We have already suggested that they are problematic in that context because they downplay the power of the Civil Service, but they are especially fraught in the context of any consideration of the Bank of England. Central banking is a difficult and delicate business that cannot be learned overnight by inexperienced ministers (or even Treasury civil servants) and it is actually recognised that Bank independence is important and so many of the day-to-day operations of the Bank of England are very much a matter for Bank decision alone.

What, then, are the precise functions of the Bank and what are the powers of the Bank in practice *vis-à-vis* the Treasury and the government with respect to the determination of monetary and economic policy?

Functions and powers

On behalf of the government, and acting as its agent, the Bank assumes functions of staggering significance.

1 It designs, prints and issues bank notes.
2 It is the government's banker. The government pays its tax revenues into the Bank and draws cheques on its account to make payments for such things as civil servants' salaries and social security payments.
3 It issues gilt-edged stock (government bonds) on behalf of the government in order to raise income for the government when there is a gap between government tax revenues and government expenditure. More than this, Bank activity in attempting to manage the money markets influences interest rates and so has implications for all facets of monetary and fiscal policy.
4 It is the government's operator in the foreign exchange markets; it has a particular interest in protecting sterling against speculation; and as it intervenes in the markets in order to manage the pound's exchange rate it can seriously affect the domestic economy and the country's international economic standing.
5 It manages Britain's gold and foreign currency reserves.
6 It is the bankers' bank and commercial banks are required to keep a certain percentage of their eligible liabilities in non-interest bearing deposits at the Bank of England in order to provide the Bank with resources and income.
7 It is the supervisor and guardian of the entire banking system. Until the early 1970s, there was little formal supervision of banks in Britain but the secondary banking crisis in the early 1970s led to a more formal system of regulation. Nowadays, the Bank of England supervises and licences anyone wishing to set up in business as a bank in the United Kingdom and so the Bank bears a heavy responsibility in safeguarding individual deposits and in maintaining the stability and integrity of the banking system as a whole.
8 The Bank is the traditional lobbyist for the City and the financial world in Whitehall and Westminster and so occupies a key position in what is a highly informal system of interest representation. On the one hand it represents the views of the City to the government but on the other hand it has the job of communicating the government's 'wishes' to the City often on the basis of nods and winks that have to be taken very seriously.

Taken together, these functions mean that the Bank is at the very centre of the financial system and is involved in almost the whole range of economic policy, even if it has exclusive rights over none of it. But is the Bank controlled by the politicians or is it powerful in its own right so that it is very much more than just an adviser to, and an agent of, the government of the day?

It is important to stress at the very outset that the Bank of England was nationalised in close consultation with the Bank itself and although the Labour government wanted control, it wished to secure the 'confidence' of the financial world and this involved minimising 'political aspects' and emphasising the independence of the Governor and the Directors of the Bank. The Chancellor of the Exchequer at the time of nationalisation, Hugh Dalton, made it perfectly clear that 'no day-to-day interference by the Government or Treasury with the ordinary work of the Bank was intended: that would be left with confidence to the Directors and their efficient and well-trained staff'. The change in the legal status of the Bank left much as before, in part because of governmental caution and ignorance of banking matters but also because so much to do with the politics of banking depends on history, experience, 'confidence', informalities and personalities rather than on the formal realities of what the law does (and does not) lay down.

The very informality of the relations between the Bank, the Treasury and the government makes it hard for us to know the precise power of the Bank over economic policy but much of it hinges on the Bank's central involvement in the management of the money and foreign exchange markets in the context of a situation where maintaining 'confidence' in the currency is seen as an all-important constraint on government policy. Geddes has noted how 'it is an article of faith among Bank staff that outsiders, and particularly politicians, do not understand the markets and how they work. It is also the Bank's ultimate defence against political intereference: when a politician proposes a course of action of which the Bank disapproves, it can be stopped with the simple statement "it will cause problems in the markets".' Lord Bruce-Gardyne, a former Conservative Treasury minister, recalled one visit paid by the Governor to the Treasury: 'He came to say that the market was demanding a rise in interest rates . . . and we argued the point at great length. But in the end the Governor was in a position to insist that he had no option. Now was the market forcing the Governor or the Governor forcing the market? I don't know. It is certainly true that the Treasury does feel at a certain disadvantage in that sort of argument.' In 1964, Labour won the general election, but in the context of crisis of confidence in sterling that pulled the Governor of the Bank into a position of political power. The Prime Minister, Harold Wilson, has described the daily reality of what was involved in dealing with the crisis: 'The Governor of the Bank of England became a frequent visitor . . . we had to listen night after night to demands that there should be immediate cuts in government expenditure. . . . It was not long before we were being asked, almost at pistol point, to cut-back on expenditure.' It was not long, either, before the Governor's 'advice' was formed into the very stuff of government policy itself. More generally, the present Governor of the Bank, Robin Leigh-Pemberton, has made it clear that 'if you have a Treasury that is hellbent on an inflationary programme I think a central bank has to do its best to reduce the implementation of that policy.' In 1979 a Conservative government was elected that was committed to the very antithesis of an inflationary programe and it has been widely assumed that the Bank of England's influence and independence have declined under Margaret Thatcher's governments. In reality, however, Britain's economic performance and policies have come close to fulfilling the Bank's dreams. Monetary policy, the Bank's chief responsibility, has been moved to centre stage; curbing inflation and financial stringency, key concerns of the Bank, have been at the heart of the government's economic policy; and there has been a general preparedness to work with the markets instead of developing policies for public expenditure that would clash with the kind of market imperatives that have always concerned the Bank.

The Bank and accountability

In a situation in which the Bank of England continues to be one of the least known institutions in Britain it is hard for anyone to tease out the precise responsibilities of the Bank, still less to come to a view as to the power which it wields in relation to Parliament, the Treasury, and the elected government of the day. This is itself inevitablity limits the possibility of any effective public or parliamentary scrutiny of – still less control of – the Bank's role in economic policy-making. Until 1971, the Bank did not even publish accounts and its annual report was so 'meagre' that the Select Committee on Nationalised Industries was led to argue that the Bank was effectively 'accountable to nobody'. The Bank may have become somewhat more open in recent years but Moran is right to note that Bank–government relations are continually dominated by the problem of 'how to reconcile the rise of elected governments intent on ambitious programes of economic management with the Bank's desire to keep control of money and banking in its own hands.'

The Judiciary

Basics

Who are the judges?

The most senior judge of all, and the head of the judiciary, is the Lord Chancellor. The top professional judge is the Lord Chief Justice of England, and he mainly presides over the Criminal Division of the Court of Appeal. The Master of the Rolls, next in the judicial hierarchy, sits in the Civil Division of the Court of Appeal with two other appeal judges. The ten Lords of Appeal in Ordinary – commonly known as the Law Lords – sit in the highest court in the land, the House of Lords, and they deal with 50 or so appeals a year. Below them are the 27 judges of the Court of Appeal, the Lords Justices of Appeal. The next tier down are the 80 or so High Court judges who are divided into specialised divisions. The 408 Circuit judges sit in the Crown Court conducting criminal cases and in the county court where they hear civil cases. They dispose of 85 per cent of all criminal and civil cases above magistrates' court level. The ranks of full-time judges also include pre-trial judges and the English system makes use of part-time judges on a massive scale. The system of criminal justice would collapse but for the fact that the judiciary is backed up by about 28,000 magistrates (who are not called jusges) since these unpaid, part-time, ama-teurs handle 98 per cent of all the criminal cases in the country with the help of their clerks who guide them on the law. Behind the judges and magistrates is a legal system of around 50,000 solicitors; 6,000 practicing barristers; 1,000 Citizens' Advice Bureaux (plus 600 or more small advice centres); and a huge tribunal system which handles legal problems and deals with tens of thousands of cases annually.

What do judges do?

They make decisions on the cases that come before them having regard to the law and the 'facts'. In a criminal case at a level above the magistrates' courts, the jury has to decide whether the accused is guilty and, if so, the judge has to decide what is the appropriate penalty. In a civil case, the ques-tion is one of deciding which of the parties wins the case and, if it is the plaintiff, what damages or other remedy is appropriate.

These are very basic and sterile answers to questions of enormous poli-tical importance, but in order to go further and explore what judges actually do and who they 'really' are gets us into a world of orthodoxies and controversies.

Orthodoxies

In our chapters on the British constitution we had occasion to discuss the sovereignty of Parliament. From the point of view of the established theory, Parliament can make and unmake any law whatsoever; there is no higher legislative authority; and no court is in a position to declare properly passed Acts of Parliament invalid or unconstitutional. In this situation, orthodoxy sees judges as independent and apart from politics and law-making. Law is something impersonal and mechanical for which the judge has no real responsibility. The judicial role is passive and uncritical, almost bureaucratic, as judges exist to declare the law and apply it to particular cases and disputes. Moreover, because judges are neutral in their stance to the law, they apply it to cases in an impartial, unbiased and disinterested manner, and they do so notwithstanding the fact that they are bound to have personal views as to the merits of the law in question. In applying the law to do justice in particular cases, judges are said to rely on the three 'rules of statutory interpretation':

1 The 'literal rule' according to which they interpret a statute by giving the words their plain meaning.
2 The 'golden rule' according to which they apply the plain meaning unless that produces an absurdity.
3 And the 'mischief rule' according to which they look to the purpose behind the act.

In those legal areas where Parliament has not spoken at all, judges are said to rely on the 'rules of precedent' which involve their looking to the thrust of past judicial decisions. Going further, there is sometimes the suggestion that judges are caught up in the noble act of securing justice and rights as a result of their capacity to tease out the single right answer that is embedded in the principles which underlie the law.

From this kind of perspective on what judges do there is no suggestion that they are *powerful* (because they are presented as lacking discretion and as bound by laws and rules that are not of their making); there is no suggestion that they are *law-makers* (because they simply declare, find and apply the laws made by Parliament or laid down in the judicial decisions of the past); there is no suggestion that they are *in politics* and are political actors fulfilling a political function (because they are presented as independent of politics and politicians, with an autonomy that derives from the separation of powers); and so there is no suggestion that students of British politics should be interested in finding out exactly who are the judges and what they do in their workaday lives.

A certain mystique needs to attach itself to the law in order that the system can 'work' and secure support, and an *image* is needed to put the judiciary beyond critique. However, we have to face the fact that although the judicial orthodoxies provide a politically useful mystique and image, they are pretty much wrong-headed fairy tales as to the reality of the judicial role. Judges are powerful – after all, over 50,000 people are in prison as a result of judicial decision –; they are law-makers; and they are political actors. This being the case, we need to push beyond the orthodoxies and make the judges the subject of an adequate political science of British politics.

Judges as powerful law-makers in politics

As a variety of developments have served to demystify judges and the law, so the orthodoxies are being opened up. Judges are forced to recognise this even though their position gives them an interest in upholding the myths *and* in hiding reality. Lord Radcliffe thought that 'judges will serve the public interest better if they keep quiet about their legislative function'. Lord Reid (the leading Law Lord of the 1960s and early 1970s) recognised that 'there was a time when it was thought almost indecent to suggest that judges make law – they only declare it. . . . But we do not believe in fairy tales any more. So we must accept the fact that for better or worse judges do make law.' What exactly is meant by this?

In Britain, laws are of two kinds. There is statute law and there is common law, but the former predominates over the latter wherever there is a conflict between the two, and much statute law is made to change and replace parts of the common law. Statute law is made by Parliament – or rather it is passed through Parliament by a government acting on the advice of its civil servants and under pressure from a variety of interests in the country at large. Common law is made by judges. As judges decide the cases that come before them and give the reasons for their decisions so their judgements gradually build up into a body of law because of the power of precedent as a guide to future judgements in similar cases. It has never really been in doubt that judges make law through the development of 'their' common law, but there has been a reluctance to recognise that the interpretation of statute law is a 'creative' function that also involves the judges in making law. Of course, the vast majority of judges do not spend the vast majority of their time making law because the reality is that in easy cases judges make simple 'production-line' decisions which apply settled law to disputed facts. However, as we move up the legal hierarchy the judge will confront 'hard cases' where the settled legal standards from precedent or statute clash or do not provide a clear answer, or where the law itself points to a result which appears to be 'unfair'. In these cases, judges quite simply cannot rely on deductive reasoning from law and precedent; in these cases, according to Bell 'judges have to make important value-judgements in which they create or shape legal standards according to their views as to the best answer they can reach. Inevitably, the judge does not come to a case neutral as to the political values to which he is to give effect, but with a necessary degree of political commitment'; and so in these cases, judges make law. Of course, we should not exaggerate the law-making role of judges in comparison to that of Parliament since Parliament can choose its topics and change the law dramatically whereas judges are more restricted. They have to wait for problems to arise in litigation and can only develop the law incrementally. But, having said that, judges are law-makers none the less at the same time as they also have a political function in that they are in a position to give direction to society.

In reality, then, judges have always played a much larger role in law-making and in deciding issues with a political and policy content than has generally been admitted, but the extent of this involvement is not a settled matter and a number of factors have served to increase the political involvement of the judges:

1 Increased political controversy has led to governments pulling the judiciary out of their courts and into politics so that they can conduct inquiries into events such as Bloody Sunday in Londonderry, the Brixton riots, the Zeebrugge ferry disaster, the Hillsborough football tragedy, the Cleveland child sex abuse cases and so on. In effect, governments have been prepared to use

the judiciary – and above all the *image* of the judiciary – for political purposes but in ways which could tarnish the judiciary and injure its role in the courts.

2 From the 1970s onwards, the British constitution has become an issue in politics. Some judges have argued for a written constitution and a Bill of Rights. If a Bill of Rights were ever to be enacted then judges would have to interpret the Bill and decide on the constitutionality of particular statutes passed by Parliament. In doing this, judges would enjoy a massive increase in overt political power.

3 Over the years the all-important Law Lords have thrown off some of the self-imposed limitations on their role. They have come to regard themselves as less the slaves to precedent and the passive restaters of accepted doctrines, and as more the activist and pragmatic developers of new doctrines. Their Practice Statement in 1966 made the point:

> Their Lordships regard the use of precedent as an indispensable foundation upon which to decide what is the law and its application to individual cases. . . . Their Lordships nevertheless recognise that too rigid adherence to precedent may lead to injustice in a particular case and also unduly restrict the proper development of the law. They propose, therefore to modify their present practice and, while treating former decisions of this House as normally binding, to depart from a previous decision when it appears right to do so.

In giving *themselves* the power to overrule their previous decisions, the Law Lords were prepared to unsettle settled law. Lee is quite right to make the point that 'the power of overruling . . . is judicial law-making at its most powerful.'

4 Judicial review – the means by which the courts can keep public authorities within their remit and review the procedural correctness of administrative actions – has become an increasingly popular way of trying to contest controversial government and local authority decisions. The Divisional Court of the Queen's Bench Division in the High Court has shown that it is not frightened of finding ministerial decisions unlawful, and in the last few years the procedures by which aggrieved citizens can seek such review have been significantly reformed.

5 Entry into Europe and the European Communities Act, 1972, have qualified the scope of parliamentary sovereignty at the same time as the judges have been involved in exploring the implications of the EC directives and regulations that are directly binding in United Kingdom law.

For us to say that judges are always but increasingly involved in politics and law-making does not tell us what laws they make and neither does it tease out the precise policy implications of judicial law-making. In order to deal with these kind of concerns there are those who see it as important to attend to 'judicial bias' – to a bias which they see as explained by the social background and legal socialisation of those who become the senior judges.

Bias and background

Judges may be independent and they may try to be fair and impartial, but they are human with human prejudices. They cannot discard their politics and prejudices when they don their wigs and gowns and sit in judgement in those hard cases where they have to be creative and exercise discretion before coming to a decision.

John Griffith, in an influential and provocative book on *The Politics of the Judiciary*, has looked at the ways in which senior judges have made law and dealt with cases. He was concerned to tease out the bases of decisions and the themes in judicial judgements in order to see whether they displayed a wide spectrum of opinion or a consistency of approach that was located within a fairly narrow part of the spread of political opinion in Britain. Griffith argued that judges undertook their tasks with an eye to securing the 'public interest' but he recognised that what is defined as in the public interest is an intensely political question which admits of a great variety of answers. He argued that:

> The judicial conception of the public interest, seen in the cases discussed in this book, is threefold. It concerns first, the interest of the State (including its moral welfare) and the preservation of law and order, broadly interpreted; secondly, the protection of property rights; and thirdly the promotion of certain political views normally associated with the Conservative Party

It is one thing for Griffith to suggest that judges display a consistent bias in judicial law-making, but it is another matter for him to explain this pattern. In Griffith's view it is important to have regard to the class background of the judges because 'their interpretation of what is in the public interest and therefore politically desirable is *determined* by the kind of people they are'. Put more directly, Griffiths argues that

> the judges define the public interest, inevitably, from the viewpoint of their own class. Judges are the product of a class and have the characteristics of that class. Typically coming from middle-class professional families, independent schools, Oxford and Cambridge, they spend twenty to twenty-five years in successful practice at the bar, mostly in London, earning very considerable incomes by the time they reach their forties. This is not the stuff of which reformers are made, still less radicals.

So, the senior judges are a distinct elite group that comes from a certain class, and by virtue of the job and the pay (in 1988 a High Court judge received £68,500 a year) they stay locked within that class. More than this, the judges are overwhelmingly male (in May 1986, of the 114 most senior judges only three were women); they are old (the average age for the Court of Appeal in autumn 1986 was 65); and they are white (in 1987 only one Asian was a full-time judge and there were no blacks at all). Griffith and those on the Left in British politics have made much of the class bias of judges; feminists have drawn attention to the policy implications of an absence of women judges; and the Society of Black Lawyers has pointed to the problem of racial discrimination in the whole of the legal profession and to the implications of this for justice for black people in Britain.

What are we to make of these arguments about the significance of background and bias? There is little doubt that the class, gender, and ethnicity of judges does have policy implications but we should not exaggerate the extent to which drawing judges from different backgrounds would change things. Lord Devlin was mindful of the criticism of the judges as an out-of-touch upper-class elite and he was aware of the case for change but he did

> not believe that measures of this sort would make a pennyworth of difference. Let the practice of law be opened up by all means and let the judiciary be composed of the best that the practice of law can produce. You will find, I am sure, that judges will still be of the same type whether they come from major or minor public schools, grammar schools, or comprehensives, whether they like to spend their leisure in a library or a club. They will be the type of men. . . . who do not seriously question the status quo . . . You can see this already at the university where students in the law faculties all over the world are nearly always on the right.

Knowledge as to the childhood background of judges, and arguments about the 'type of men' attracted to the law provide us with insights into the performance of the judicial role. But it is also necessary for us to recognise the importance of the judiciary's shared experience and socialisation as barristers. We need to attend to the implications of the appointment process and we should be mindful of the nature of the judicial world itself. Before a lawyer becomes a senior judge, the years of affluence as a successful barrister and the professionally cocooned life in chambers that is part of the closed world of the bar tends to produce a set of attitudes and a conformity to the norms of the legal profession that is likely to transcend the implications that might flow from a long-lost working-class upbringing or from the fact of a particular gender or ethnicity. Moreover, a secretive and informal appointments process does not ensure that decisions are made on adequate information but does ensure (in Zander's words) 'that a person with markedly radical political views, either of the Right or the Left, would be unlikely to be appointed to the bench.' The world of the higher judiciary is a small, tight, inward-looking one. Paterson, in his study of the *Law Lords*, found that they paid little attention to the views of academic lawyers and steered clear of politicians, preferring to lunch together and discuss cases amongst themselves.

Notwithstanding the importance of background, socialisation and so on, we delude ourselves, if we think we can read off the performance of the judicial role from these factors alone. Simon Lee, in *Judging Judges*, has criticised the Griffith thesis because

> it does seem to assume, mistakenly, that judges have homogenous views. It does seem to assume, mistakenly, that judges always agree with one another. It does seem to assume, mistakenly, that they always decide for the Conservative government. It does seem to assume, mistakenly, that the interests of the State, its moral welfare, the preservation of law and order and the protection of property rights are all dangerous values to be associated solely with the Conservatives. It does seem to assume, mistakenly, that cases involve one class against another.

How, then, does Lee make sense of the reality of the judicial role?

Reality and research

Lee rejects the fairy tale that judges do not make law at the same time as he rejects Griffith's nightmare that judges simply make law in accordance with their class interests. Lee is cautious, and concerned to discover 'the reality of judicial law making' in hard cases, taking the view that 'a variety of factors influence judges' and that it is important to make sense of controversial cases and assess the contributions of well-known judges. Lee's 'thesis is that judicial decisions are, and should be, influenced by many factors which can be usefully analysed under three main headings: first, the judges' view of the past law (statutues, precedents and principles); second, the judges' evaluation of the consequences of the options before them; third, the judges' view of their own role.' Lee considers that past law is not the only decisive factor in an appellate judicial decision and that it is wrong that judges fail to acknowledge the importance and influence of the second and third factors in their work. It is, however, of the essence of Lee's approach that he has specific questions more than he has the general answers that come from Griffith's bold-brush approach to the judiciary. Not surprisingly, therefore, Lee highlights the need for a multi-disciplinary army of researchers to track down the attitudes of judges although he recognises the hostility of the judiciary to research into their work – a hostility which we think has implications for accountability and democracy in Britain.

The judiciary and democracy

We have argued that judges are powerful, political figures who make law and give direction to society. However, the fact that Britain is a kind of democracy means that the power and position of the judges is something of a problem.

1 The judges are in no sense representative of the public in that they are drawn from a very narrow slice of the community. This makes it difficult for the judges to rely on common knowledge and to give effect to the range of values in society, rather than to their purely personal (and class- and gender-based?) preferences, as they develop the law. Moreover, the fact that the law is made and administered by a remote group whose attitudes and ideals are sometimes foreign to those of ordinary people makes it difficult for all of us to develop respect for the law. This does much to weaken the rule of law in Britain today.

2 The judges are not responsible, or accountable, to the people through Parliament. It is difficult to question the Lord Chancellor, the head of the judiciary; there is no minister in the House of Commons to answer for him; and there is no select committee for the Lord Chancellor's and the Law Officers Departments.

3 The judges are appointed and promoted through a loose and secretive system that centres on the Lord Chancellor but which in reality gives his unaccountable senior officials enormous power. This system affords no opportunity for interested parties to voice their concerns about a judge before appointment or promotion; barristers wishing to become High Court judges are not permitted to apply; and those passed over do not know why and are not in even in a position to refute damning untruths that may have found there way onto their files. This is all the more alarming given the fact that once a judge has been appointed to the full-time bench he (or very occasionally she) is in practice virtually irremovable and there are no procedures for dealing with complaints about judicial misbehaviour aside from the Lord Chancellor having a private word with the judge concerned.

4 The doctrine of judicial independence has been shamefully used and misrepresented in order to protect the judiciary from any outside scrutiny and criticism so that we know much less about them than is healthy in a democratic polity. Until 1987, judges were not allowed to speak to the Press or television without the permission of the Lord Chancellor (and that permission was rarely given) and judges have continued to block academic research into themselves and their work.

Can a democracy continue to sustain all this, or do we need a Ministry of Justice 'covered' by a select committee on the administration of justice; a Judicial Services Commission to deal with appointments and discipline; a Judicial Ombudsman (responsible to the select committee) to handle complaints about legal services; and a goodly measure of openness that would facilitate the possibility of a dialogue between judges and the judged, the powerful and the powerless?

The Police

Facts and figures

In 1908 there were just 30,376 police in England and Wales but by 1988 there were 124,759 police (and about 100,000 'private police') backed up by 39,209 full-time civilians, 15,788 special constables, 2,088 dogs, 457 horses, 4,644 traffic wardens and a whole host of specialised equipment as befited the new era of the politicised 'technocop'. In 1908 the police were organised into over 250 separate forces but by 1988 there were just 43 forces in England and Wales and the close links between these forces led many to argue that we were nudging towards a centralised national police force. In the year 1987–8 expenditure on the police service in England and Wales stood at £3,512 million, up more than 70 per cent on the 1981–2 figure. In addition to the regular police forces there are (amongst other groupings) the British Transport Police, the Ministry of Defence Police, the UK Atomic Energy Authority Constabulary, and the highly secretive Special Branch. The Special Branch was formed in 1883 to protect the security of the state against 'subversive' Irish organisations. In the 1960s there were only about 200 special branch officers but by the late seventies numbers had increased to over 1,600 and the Branch was working closely with M15.

Facts and figures of this kind give us an impression of the scale of policing but what do the police actually do and how do they go about performing their tasks; do they have power and assume a political role; and who controls the police and holds them to account?

Orthodoxies and revisionism

The orthodox and police point of view portrays the British police as a benign, popular and 'fair' force that works for the benefit of society as a whole and guards the weak against the strong. In more concrete terms, the police are presented as law-enforcers and crime-fighters geared to the prevention and detection of crime and the catching of criminals. They also have the job of maintaining the Queen's peace and are a kind of social service ready to befriend anyone who needs help at the same time as they are available to cope with all manner of emergencies. From this perspective, the police are not political, partisan, powerful and the police of government. They are presented as the police of the public they serve, are neutral and independent, and available to enforce the laws passed by Parliament without fear or favour. More than this, they are seen as subject to the 'control' of the people, partly as a result of the existence of formal channels of legal and democratic accountability but fundamentally as a result of their not being distinct from the people and imbued with the sense that their powers derive from public consent not coercion. This orthodox perspective regards the police as outside of politics and as lacking in power because they are seen as acting on behalf of the people as a whole and as tightly bound by the law of the land.

In the 1970s these rosy orthodoxies came under challenge. A growing turbulence brought the police into the centre of political controversy and encouraged the development of a revisionist perspective on policing. It was suggested that the police were not fair and impartial but were tools and agents of coercion and oppression geared to maintaining the dominance of the ruling class against the interests and opposition of the working class, blacks and women who together constituted the majority of the population. Far from detecting crime and catching criminals, the police were seen as creating crime and criminals through their labelling and stereotyping activities against particular communities. In their concern to preserve the Queen's peace, the police were not seen as neutral law-enforcers but were regarded as assuming a powerful and political role that was geared up to controlling and crushing political behaviour and protest that posed any kind of challenge to the maintenance of the established capitalist order. The orthodox picture of the popular control of the police was challenged as a myth and there were strident calls for greater police accountability to the people through the democratic process.

We are provided with these two sharply conflicting perspectives on the police and policing. Reality is more complex, contradictory and confused than either perspective allows, but it is not easy to analyse the role and function of the police in an era of change and controversy when policing has become thoroughly politicised and subject to partisan dispute. Having said that, we see the orthodox rosy perspective as deficient. Talk of policing by consent means that there is limited recognition that policing inevitably involves (increasing) coercion against some; assurances about fairness and neutrality ignore the reality of partiality; the idea that the police are simple law-enforcers downplays the political role of the police and their ability to exercise very real power because they are not simply bound by the law but must exercise discretion. Moreover, the orthodox perspective minimises the extent to which the police are an unaccountable power unto themselves that lies beyond the reach of effective democratic and popular control. In saying all this it might be thought that we are prepared to locate our understanding of the police within the revisionist perspective. That perspective does constitute an advance on the rosy view because it pushes beyond platitudes. However, in adopting a basically anti-police and anti-capitalist stance it tends to see policing as a simple all-of-a-piece activity that is totally geared to maintaining '*the* system' and advancing the interests of *the* rich ruling class against *the* poor working class and various minority groups. Such a perspective fails to recognise the complex of interests in society and the complexity of police work. Although law and policing do mainly reproduce established social divisions we should not ignore the extent to which much policing does help to preserve the conditions for a civilised and stable social existence that is of benefit to all.

In chapter 11 we will attend to the highly political public order aspect of police work but at this point in our discussion we will do three things that should help to penetrate to the realities of policing in Britain:

1 We will highlight the extent to which it makes little sense to see the police as simple law-bound law-enforcers because police work inevitably involves the exercise of discretion and therefore choice, partiality and power.
2 We will attempt to explain the way in which that discretion is exercised against certain interests by attending to the social background of the police and to their socialisation into the values of 'cop culture'.
3 In view of the politics and power caught up in all policing, it is vitally important for us to see who controls the police so that we can establish the extent of police accountability to the public in a political system that is defined as a democracy.

Police discretion

On joining the police force each new constable takes an oath to carry out the duties 'without favour or affection, malice or ill-will' and the Police Discipline Code restricts the police from taking part in activities which the public might feel conflict with their impartiality. Notwithstanding the police concern to be seen as impartial in enforcing the law it is now a commonplace of the sociological literature on police operations that discretion is the name of the game and that it increases as one moves on to the street where the rank-and-file officer is the primary determinant of law enforcement. Discretion is quite inescapable. At the level of policy-making for the force as a whole there is the necessity for choice about priorities in resource allocation as the police do not have adequate resources for the full enforcement of every law. And with respect to street-level actions the individual police officer has to exercise discretion because even the most precisely worded law needs to be interpreted and applied in concrete situations. Lord Scarman has recognised this. In his enquiry into the Brixton disorders of 1981 he argued that

> the exercise of discretion lies at the heart of the policing function. It is undeniable that there is only one law for all: and it is right that this should be so. But it is equally well recognized that successful policing depends on the exercise of discretion in how the law is enforced. The good reputation of the police as a force depends on the skill and judgement which policemen display in the particular circumstances of the cases and incidents which they are required to handle. Discretion is the art of suiting action to particular circumstances. It is the policeman's daily task.

In Britain, law-breaking is very common among all social classes, all age groups and both genders. An obvious case in point is motoring offences, for most of us who drive probably exceed the speed limit or engage in some manoeuvre which could be construed as 'dangerous driving' almost every time we get out on the road. Our law-breaking does not stop here. 'Self-report' studies have shown that large proportions of the population have engaged in shoplifting or stealing from work as well as other offences against property and people, not least with respect to women and the 'care' of children. However, these studies also show that few of us are ever caught, still less charged and sentenced. Why is this?

In part it is a matter of our crimes not being detected because they are carried out in 'private', but it is also a matter of how our public behaviour is seen and interpreted. Whether a U-turn in the high street constitutes 'dangerous driving' will depend on how the police officer who observes the incident chooses to interpret it. Similarly, the elderly woman who is stopped outside Woolworth's carrying a jumper for which she has not paid may be defined as 'old and confused' and as in need of help or as a 'thief' caught in the act deserving of prosecution. Is the umbrella carried by the football fan on the way to the big match a harmless precaution against the British weather or is it an 'offensive weapon' for use against rival supporters – or the police? And is the black youth on the street corner 'loitering with intent' or simply waiting for a friend?

Police officers are called on to make judgements with respect to these kind of matters every day of the week. The law is little help. The law does not tell them how reckless a U-turn has to be before it is dangerous; how senile old ladies have to be before they cease to be responsible for their actions; what an offensive weapon actually looks like; or what *exactly* constitutes loitering with intent in a specific context. In all these situations the police have to rely on their 'common sense' – they have to use discretion. We all rely on 'common sense' to get us through the day and to help us behave 'properly' in social encounters, and the police do much the same thing. They could not possibly proceed with their work if they were not party to certain shared wisdoms so that they (think they) 'know' the sort of people who engage in specific kinds of illegal behaviour in particular situations. What is involved here is a process of stereotyping: if you 'fit' the 'type' who engages in drunken driving, shoplifting, or hooliganism then the police are likely to show an interest in you but not otherwise – and this almost regardless of whether you are or are not involved in illegal behaviour.

Middle-aged women do not get stopped and searched as they enter a football ground on a Saturday afternoon because the police 'know' that football hooligans are young and male. Middle-aged men in smart suits driving new BMWs are stopped much less often than young men driving Ford Capris because the police 'know' that young people are more likely to steal cars, drive defective cars, drive under the influence of drink and so on. Young blacks on the streets are constantly questioned by the police whereas white adults may go about their lawful (and unlawful!) business for years without ever speaking to a police officer, for here again the police 'know' that young blacks are the types who possess drugs or stolen goods, and who plot muggings and burglaries.

Once stopped by the police, a suspect may still be able to convince an officer that she or he is not the 'type' that she or he appears to be on first blush. Careful manipulation of language, facial expression, humour and demeanour may result in an informal caution ('Make sure you get the tyre seen to, sir') rather than an arrest, for any incongruity in the impression made is likely to sow doubt in the officer's mind. However, the subsequent interaction may confirm the officer's first impressions, in which case the suspect is more likely to be escorted to the police station and charged notwithstanding any pleas of innocence. The police have been known to have been so sure of the guilt of suspects that they have planted evidence and forcibly extracted confessions in order to ensure that their charges stand up in court. More than this, senior officers have repeatedly made it clear that police work could not be done effectively if legal procedures were properly adhered to. This opinion is common among the rank and file as well and so it is not surprising that it is often argued that legal rules and departmental regulations are marginal to an account of how the police work in practice.

The recognition that the police routinely exercise a considerable amount of discretion in the way they enforce the law does not tell us the precise 'pattern' of discretion in practice. Students of policing have been concerned to uncover this and have questioned whether discretion really means unfairness and discrimination, particularly against blacks, although some feminists have also suggested that the police routinely exercise power and discretion against women. The issue is complex. The fact that the young, the lower working class, and blacks are at the sharp end of the use of police powers does not in itself establish discrimination. Radical writers claim this and accuse the police of racism, stereotyping and a bias against the socially disadvantaged and powerless. But against this position, conservative writers argue that the discretionary use of police power does not reflect police discrimination but rather the varying deviance of different social groups in combination with the police response to public demand and information which guides their essentially reactive interventions. Reiner's review of the research evidence leads him to note that 'there is a clear pattern of differentiation in police practice, with young males, especially if they are black and/or unemployed or economically marginal, being disproportionately subject to the exercise of police powers'. He argues that although there is disproportionate involvement in some minor and marginal offences 'there is evidence of police discrimination not explicable by differential offending'.

All of this invites us to identify the determinants of police discretion and so raises the important question of where the police get their stereotypes and common-sense knowledge from in the first place.

Recruitment and socialisation into 'cop culture'

Only limited research data exist about the kind of people who join the police service but the general pattern of recruitment and promotion to the top is somewhat different to the situation with respect to the other institutions of the secret state. Who, then, are the police?

1 The average police officer is recruited from within the skilled manual working class and it has been suggested that the choice of a police career embraces a desire for upward social mobility.

2 The police force is an almost exclusively white organisation. In 1988 there were just 1,197 ethnic minority officers in England and Wales out of a force of 124,759. Lord Scarman and the police have recognised that the service needs to be representative of the people it serves if we are to enjoy policing by consent. But efforts to attract and retain more black officers have been of limited success because of an undercurrent of hostility towards the police among many of West Indian origin, coupled with a fear of being alienated from family and friends, and of being ostracised because of colour prejudice within the police service itself.

3 The police force is very much a male organisation. In 1988 women constituted around 10 per cent of the police force and as we move up through the ranks so the proportion of women officers steadily declines: in 1982 of the 829 top police jobs in England and Wales just 8 were held by women. Female recruitment has not increased dramatically as a result of the Sex Discrimination Act, 1975, and one research study has suggested that there is a 'lack of real commitment and will' to use and promote women.

4 Police recruits have generally been of a poor educational standard and this has been a continuing cause for concern. The 1983 Policy Studies Institute inquiry into the Metropolitan Police suggested that entry standards into the force were too low by international standards. In 1988, 50 per cent of the recruits to the police forces in England and Wales had fewer than four 'O' levels and although there has been a commitment to increase the number of graduates, under 10 per cent of the 1988 recruits possessed a degree.

5 Although the Home Office has blocked research into the political views of the police so that we lack solid evidence, there is some suggestion that the police force attracts conservative and authoritarian personalities. Certainly the Police Federation (the police trade union) has increasingly come to express views at one with the Conservative Party, and Reiner's interviews with British police officers found that they supported a narrow conventional morality on a variety of social issues.

The background and education of police recruits may well have implications for the way they carry out the job. The fact that they tend to be marginal people with status anxieties who are keen to 'get on' encourages them to police in a way that reinforces the expectations of middle-class opinion so that they themselves gain more of a foothold in 'respectable' society. However, the nature of the job and the social distance between the police and the rest of the community makes it difficult for the police to know the views of respectable society and so it is almost inevitable that the police perspective on society, crime and their own role derives from the views of other police officers above all else. Recruits are trained, (and increasing attention is being given to this) but there are still complaints that it is inadequate for the complex needs of a modern and multi-racial society with public order problems. Moreover, formal training can achieve only so much in the context of the on-the-job informal socialisation into a highly pervasive police subculture. The Policy Studies Institute survey into the Metropolitan Police found that 'certain themes tend to be emphasised in conversation in an exaggerated way: the prime examples are male dominance (combined with denigration of women), the glamour (but not the reality) of violence, and racial prejudice.' Of course, the culture of the police is neither monolithic, universal nor unchanging, but certain core characteristics tend to ripple through a number of studies of cop culture. The danger of the job, the authority in the office and the concern to 'maintain order' and 'fight crime' encourage not only a sense of mission and internal solidarity but also a certain cynicism and an attitude of constant suspiciousness that generates a set of discriminating stereotypes and a particular perspective on the divisions within society. For sure, the police are basically conservative and they think in terms of 'them' and 'us', rough and respectable, but finer distinctions are needed to enable them to police a divided society and stay secure. Reiner suggests that the police distinguish seven important groups, 'good class villains'; 'police property' (the low-status groups that the general public are prepared to see policed in a 'hard' manner); 'rubbish' (and this includes domestic disputes); 'challengers' whose job enables them to penetrate the secrecy of police culture; 'disarmers' who can weaken the police; 'do-gooders', such as the National Council for Civil Liberties, who are seen as critical of the police and concerned to limit their autonomy; and 'politicians' who, Reiner tells us, 'are regarded suspiciously'.

Police practice emerges out of this tangle of law, formal rules, the 'type' of people who join the police, the training and the implications of a socialisation into the informal 'cop culture' – and all in the social context of the police needing to respond to different audiences and pressures at different moments in history. The police inevitably reflect wider societal prejudices in their enforcement of the law but because they exercise a coercive authority on the basis of a massive discretion they have power. We need to explore the extent to which they are accountable for the way in which they exercise their power.

Police accountability: who controls the police?

The rosy perspective on policing makes great play of policing by consent. In seeing the police as the servants of the people at one with the public, and in stressing the ancient ideal of communal self-policing, it maintains that the 'people' somehow control the police. The fact that this perspective does not dwell on the mechanisms and channels through which control by the people is achieved in practice means that we are told little of real substance. In theory, the police are accountable in two ways:

1 The prime channel of accountability is supposed to be legal accountability through 'the law'. The police have a duty to enforce the law, but in enforcing the law they must act within the law and this enables the courts to regulate police conduct. In the case of serious complaints alleging criminal misconduct the Director of Public Prosecutions may recommend prosecution; civil actions can be brought for damages in cases of wrongful arrest, assault and so on; a writ of *habeas corpus* can be sought for illegal detention; and judges have discretion to exclude evidence obtained in violation of due process of law.

2 The Police Act, 1964, outlined the respective responsibilities of the various bodies responsible for the police in Britain and sought to clarify and rationalise the situation with respect to the relationship between police authorities, chief constables and the Home Secretary. Notwithstanding the particular position of the Chief Constable it is argued that the police are accountable to their local communities through police authorities (consisting of two-thirds elected county councillors and one-third local magistrates) and to the central government through the Home Secretary.

In practice, despite the theory of the police officer's individual responsibility to the law for the exercise of his or her powers, the courts do not play a major part in the control of police activity. Much of the law relating to police powers is vague; many of the rules governing police behaviour are not statutory at all, but simply guidelines; and the courts have shown themselves reluctant to hold that a police officer has acted unlawfully, particularly where the action, though unlawful, appeared reasonable in the circumstances. The Law Lord, Lord Diplock, has expressed the view that 'it is no part of a judge's function to exercise disciplinary powers over the police'. Even if police officers were accountable to the courts for their individual actions there would still be a problem in that there is no collective accountability to the courts for policing policy or for those areas of police work that fall outside of law enforcement. What, then, of the position of local police authorities and of their capacity to control the police? Police authorities have the duty of securing 'an adequate and efficient' force, but they have few powers of control and almost all of their actions are subject to the approval of the Home Secretary. In London, the Home Secretary alone is the police authority for the Metropolitan Police and so no locally elected representatives have any direct responsibility for policing the metropolis. Outside of London, the local police authorities are empowered to appoint, discipline and retire the senior officers (subject to the Home Secretary's agreement) and to receive an annual report from the Chief Constable. They are also entitled to ask for further reports on 'matters connected with the policing of the area'. However, the Chief Constable can refuse to give such a report and if the police authority does receive a report with which it is dissatisfied, it is given no powers to instruct the chief constable to change any of his operational policing policies or practices. In fact, the framework of police accountability is generally thought to be characterised by ambiguity precisely because it is not possible to state the position with any clarity simply by referring to the relevant legal statutes. Having said that, Reiner argues that 'for all the rhetoric about the democratic accountability of the British police they have become virtually impervious to any control by elected political bodies, and are adamant in remaining so.'

Chief Constables occupy positions of immense power and influence. Each police force is under the 'direction and control' of its chief constable but Chief Constables are not under the control of elected representatives. The autonomy and independence of Chief Constables is unique. In local government itself, the elected councillors determine the policy on such matters as education, housing, planning and so on, and the officials are simply there to advice and implement the policies of the council. In the case of the police, however, these positions are reversed. The police authority can only advise the Chief Constable on general matters connected with the policing of the area; decisions are the responsibility of the Chief Constable alone.

At one time police authorities were prepared to accept this state of affairs and defer to their Chief Constables. In the 1970s, however, the legitimacy of the police crumpled and the recognition by some that Chief Constables were exercising political power led to pressures for change and increased police accountability to locally elected representatives. The control of the police has become a thoroughly political issue: Conservatives and the police defend the established system and the autonomy and independence which it gives to Chief Constables, whereas the Left, centre and many civil libertarians are concerned to call the police to keener account.

The established system is defended on a number of grounds. It is claimed that the police *are* accountable to the 'people', to the law, and to elected representatives, but we have already explored the limited cogency of these arguments. It is also suggested that the police *should* be independent because they have a duty to treat all citizens as equal before the law and to enforce the law impartially in an even-handed and non-partisan manner and this would be prejudiced if they were to be under the political control of local politicians with anti-police axes to grind. Any moves to give stronger powers to police authorities are attacked on the grounds that this would compromise the principle of a strictly impartial and independent police service. More than this, policing is defined as a purely technical matter that involves skilled judgements that can only be acquired through training, experience and operational involvement in police work. By definition, elected representatives can never be in a position to acquire this kind of detailed knowledge and so it is seen as best to leave decisions on policing to the police themselves because it is they, and they alone, who are the professionals with special expertise and an ability to exercise the kind of sound judgements that will secure public order and the impartial enforcement of the law.

Against this position, it has been argued that the police should be responsible to a democratically elected body in much the same way as applies with respect to the various services provided by local government. This view is taken because the police are seen as powerful, political and not tightly bound by the law. In a democracy it is not regarded as acceptable that those who are in a non-elected position should escape being answerable to, and controlled by, those who are elected and who have to face the people at the polls. Advocates of change are proposing a radical transformation of the constitutional position of the police. Democratically elected representatives in reconstructed local police authorities would be given the power to determine police policies, priorities and policing methods (but not the power to direct day-to-day operations), albeit within a framework of national guidelines and standards laid down by Parliament. The claim that proposals of this kind would bring the police into politics and impair police impartiality is rejected. It is argued that the police are already politicised and partial and have to exercise discretion, and it is seen as right and proper that the discretionary use of political power should be under the control of those who have been elected to represent the views of the public.

Nothing substantial has come of these proposals for change but Lord Scarman's recommendation that a statutory framework should be developed to facilitate 'consultation' between the police and the community struck a chord and in June 1982 the Home Office issued a circular to police authorities and chief constables urging them to establish formal community liason procedures. In effect, the Conservative government was forced to respond to the pressures for change whilst defending the established position and opposing moves for the democratic control of the police. It is easy to condemn this, but radical demands for democratic control are unlikely to be a panacea and when they come from those hostile to the police it is doubtful if their implementation would solve the problems of policing a perplexed and divided society.

The Armed Forces

Orthodoxies

Britain is an independent sovereign state and the 320,000 members of the armed forces (backed up by 175,000 civilians in the Ministry of Defence) exist to defend and secure the established territory of the state from external attack. In the past the armed forces were also much involved in the aggressive acquisition of an empire and new territory overseas, and at the present time these forces assist in suppressing disorder and terrorism at home. Also, they are available to maintain essential services should they be disrupted by industrial action or a disaster. The armed forces are at the cutting edge and are 'in' politics in a big way.

'The security of the realm' is perhaps the most fundamental task of government and so the control of the armed forces and the conduct of diplomacy are matters of vital importance. From the formal, constitutional, point of view, the supreme command of all air, sea and land forces, and the power to conduct foreign and external affairs is vested in the Crown. Having said that, ours is a constitutional monarchy and so the Crown 'must' act on the advice of the Secretary of State for Defence and the Foreign Secretary, both of whom are leading members of the Cabinet. Put another way, ministers are said to make the decisions and be in control of defence and diplomacy. More than that, they – and the government of which they are a part – are seen as responsible to Parliament for matters to do with defence and foreign policy. From this point of view, ministerial responsibility is the name of the defence decision-making game. Individual ministers resign if mistakes are made by their cvil servants (as happened when the Foreign Secretary resigned at the time of the Falklands War because of deficiencies with respect to intelligence concerning the intentions of the Argentinians) and key decisions on defence and foreign policy are taken collectively by the Cabinet with the Defence and Overseas Policy Committee (chaired by the Prime Minister) assuming the key decisional role for the matters under consideration in this section. Of course, it is recognised that ministers and Cabinets do not make defence and foreign policy in isolation from civil servants, technical experts and the armed services but the democratic orthodoxies which surround our whole system of rule assert that ministers are the key policy makers. Civil servants in the Foreign and Commonwealth Office (FCO) and the Ministry of Defence (MOD) exist to advise and implement government policies; the Chief Scientific Adviser is exactly that, an adviser only; and the armed services (working through the important Chiefs of the Defence Staff and the less important Service Chiefs of Staff organised into the Chief of Staff Committee) are, like civil servants, simply involved in the task of providing the Cabinet with military advice and information about defence planning and strategic matters.

What are we to make of this perspective on the control of the military and the making of defence policy? Arc ministers the key decision-makers and are they accountable to Parliament or are they subject to powerful pressures that rob them of decisional autonomy; what is the nature of civil–military relations and are the civil powers really in control; what part does the arms industry play in defence decision-making; what impact does the American government have on our defence policy given the fact that we are members of the NATO alliance; and how can those in the whole defence establishment strike the right balance and cope with the economic, technological and political challenges that confront the world at the present time?

Ministers and Parliament

We need not dwell on the part played by ministers and Parliament in defence decision-making. Of course ministers are centrally involved but Smith is right to argue that 'decisions in British defence policy are not the sole prerogative of the Defence Secretary nor of the Cabinet, whatever the formalities, and the policy would hardly be workable if they were. Decisions emerge out of a balance between the elected goverment, civil servants, the uniformed military, military sectors of industry and other influences.' In a very real sense governments have continually struggled to *avoid* making clear and major decisions on defence, choosing instead to muddle through and make an incremental succession of relatively minor decisions that maintain a messy continuity and stability that just about holds together. For its part, Parliament has been kept out of defence matters by secretive governments that have been bent on limiting public debate. Although Parliament has developed machanisms for extracting information about defence issues it is doubtful whether the Select Committee on Defence (established in 1980) has much impact on decision-making.

Civil–military relations

The problem of civil–military relationships is one that concerns all societies. In Britain, although there are those that argue that the relations between political leaders and military leaders are essentially the same as those between ministers and civil servants, there is clearly something special about a relationship in which one side has the potential and the capacity to coerce and take over by force of arms. In fact, except for isolated periods, effective political control of the armed forces has not been a serious problem since Cromwell's day. Britain is regarded as possessing a long history of stable civil–military relations in which the civil power and the elected government has continually prevailed over non-elected military might. This pre-eminence of civilian authority and the related apoliticisation of the military has usually been explained in terms of 'political culture' and the 'professionalisation' of the military. According to Finer, Britain has a 'high' or 'mature' political culture because public attachment to civilian institutions is strong and widespread. In this state of affairs there are few opportunities for military intervention and the military can expect little public support should they choose to intervene. Weak governments and not strong armies are seen as accounting for the prevalence of military coups in other countries. For his part, Huntingdon sees the stability of civil–military relations and the supremacy of civilian governments as hinging upon the degree of professionalisation demonstrated by the officer corps. As the British military became fully professionalised at the turn of this century, so they accepted the nation state as the highest form of political organisation; held that war was the instrument of politics; and saw themselves as obedient servants of statesmen. Other writers have explained the pattern of civil–military relations in Britain by pointing to the absence of both 'opportunity' and 'disposition' for military intervention in the context of a situation where the social backgrounds of political leaders and military officers have been remarkably similar and where there have been easy opportunities for senior military professionals to enter other elite groups, including the political elite itself.

These kind of perspectives, whilst admitting that the military exerts *influence* over British defence policy through officially approved channels, suggest that it lacks *power* because it has been content to limit military purpose to the loyal service of the policies and priorities chosen by the elected government of the day. In a simple sense this may well be true and we may be right to congratulate ourselves on the subordinate position of the military in Britain. Having said that, however, it is not always easy to distinguish influence from power and the similarity of social background between politicians and the military bespeaks more of a *commonality* of interest and viewpoint than it does of any clear-cut subordination at the same time as it is a fragile basis for civil supremacy in a society that is becoming increasingly complex and socially mobile. In fact, the struggle now may be less over power and more over priorities (how much of the national wealth should be devoted to defence; how much should each service secure; and what weapons should be bought; and so on). But, in hard reality, politicians are in a weak position in relation to the military because military advisers come to Whitehall and Westminster with expertise, information and emotion on their side which inevitably serves to give them a role beyond that of simply offering advice. In times of peace it is not surprising that governments have been disinclined to ignore military advice and ride roughshod over the professional and sectional interests of those with the guns. This has been the price to be paid for the loyalty and 'subordination' of the military in times of peace. In times of war when a government has chosen to adopt a military solution to a political problem (be it with respect to the sovereignty of the Falkland Islands or the situation in Northern Ireland), then it is inevitable that the power of the military to decide the course of events will increase relative to the power of the 'controlling' civilian authority. In the mid-1970s informed speculation as to the prospects for a military coup in Britain bruised comfy talk about the subordination of the military. And when the Labour Party was committed to unilateral nuclear disarmament the fact that elements within the military doubted whether they could serve under a Labour government and implement such a policy took the military into an influential position in party politics, shifting them beyond the role of giving quiet and confidential advice to the government of the day.

The arms industry

Britain has a major defence industry and about 720,000 industrial jobs depend upon the production of arms. In 1987–8, £8,270 million of the defence budget was spent on equipment, and the keen commitment to maintaining the domestic arms industry (for reasons to do with national independence and the desire to retain the trappings of Great Power status) has meant that 75 per cent of the equipment budget is spent directly in this country with another 15 per cent benefiting British industry working on collaborative projects. The Ministry of Defence estimates that it has contracts with 10,000 companies. Over 120 defence contractors were paid more than £5 million by the Ministry of Defence in 1987–8 and six contractors were each paid over £250 million in that same year. Many of these companies are chronically dependent on securing military contracts and would collapse without them in a way that would inevitably contribute to unemployment in some of the most depressed parts of the country.

The arms industry as a whole suffers from excess capacity in that the government's domestic demand for military equipment is insufficient to absorb the potential output of the industry. This problem has been getting worse. The accelerating costs of military equipment consequent upon the development of new technologies has meant that *more* money is needed to cover the same output, but this at a time when governmental budget-makers have sought to provide *less* defence expenditure in the hope that a general reduction of public expenditure would contribute to Britain's economic revival.

One way around this problem of excess capacity has been for the arms producers to export their surplus. This has been encouraged by successive British governments at the same time as they have developed what they say are 'strict controls . . . to prevent weapons or other sensitive equipment falling into the wrong hands'. Britain is now the third largest exporter of defence equipment. In 1987 defence exports were valued at £1,233 million (with £351 million of equipment going to the Middle East and North Africa) and in the following year contracts were signed worth £3,500 million.

Another way around the problem has been for the arms industry (and the trade unions involved) to lobby the government for further defence projects. The sheer scale of the arms industry in Britain means that there is a cohesive, politically visible constituency continually pressing for high levels of defence spending. Politicians sceptical of the need for high military spending have had to face a strong military and industrial lobby opposed to them, and hawkish colleagues have recognised that the domestic 'military-industrial complex' adds clout to their case for more. For all that, it is a mistake to see the arms producers as all-powerful in determining military spending. Smith and Smith are surely right when they argue that the military-industrial complex . . . functions not on the basis of conspiracy (though that happens) nor on the basis of bribery and corruption (though they also happen, especially if one recognises that not all bribery is legally corrupt). Rather, it functions on the basis of a structural pairing that inevitably develops into mutual interests. Both the military and the corporations require high military spending. Both are organised around major items of equipment, for use and for production.

In effect, specific ties build up between particular companies and particular parts of the military. In the context of assumptions about the importance of national self-sufficiency in arms production and the virtues of the latest technology it is inevitable that the arms industry is not just a passive supplier of equipment but is a powerful player in the defence decision-making game. The fact that Britain has spent a greater than average proportion of its anual military budget on equipment and that this proportion has been rising in recent years is a testament to the political power of the arms industry.

NATO and Anglo-American relations

The North Atlantic Treaty Organisation, formed in 1949, was largely an American project designed to provide for American influence in Europe and for the collective defence of the West against the perceived threat from the USSR and the Communist countries of Eastern Europe – countries that subsequently formed themselves into the Warsaw Pact in 1954. Britain now devotes 95 per cent of her defence expenditure to the NATO area and so discussing British defence policy really means looking at the context of the alliance in which British military preparations are almost wholly organised. The government's *Statement on the Defence Estimates* of 1989 extolled the importance of Britain's contribution to NATO with respect to nuclear forces, the defence of the United Kingdom, the defence of the European mainland, and the deployment of maritime forces in the Eastern Atlantic and Channel areas.

The United States provides the largest single contribution to NATO but in 1988 Britain devoted 4.3 per cent of GDP to defence and that put her third in the NATO rankings. NATO is, first and foremost, an alliance of 16 member states. It is also a vastly complex organisation which runs 435 committees and any number of working groups, task forces and so on. In theory, NATO decisions are taken on the basis of consensus and the consent of all the member governments. This requires unanimity and therefore compromise and if such a system were left entirely to itself not much would ever get decided. In reality, NATO is not an equal partnership as not all participants are of the same importance and pressures can be applied to get things moving. According to Smith, in *Pressure: How America Runs NATO* 'The USA is consistently able to prevail, to win on policies which are unpopular with allied governments or their electorates, or both. It is neither secret nor surprising. It is part and parcel of the USA being a super power. It wins on such issues because it is a superpower; it is a superpower because it wins.' Of course, the USA does not always get its way but the fact that the security policies of European NATO governments are predicated on the continuing US military commitment to NATO and Europe means that we are dealing with a system of highly dependent partnerships within which Western European governments have been prepared to make concessions on policy and even on sovereignty in order to ensure a continuing US military presence in Europe. Although NATO may be run by the USA ('and if it were not then it would not work') we still have to ask where this leaves Britain, a country with an independent nuclear deterrent and with a 'special relationship' to the USA itself.

Britain is one of five declared nuclear powers – the other four being the USA, USSR, France and China. It could have this status without US assistance, since Britain's nuclear bombs for aircraft are both designed and made in Britain, but the Polaris fleet and the successor fleet of Trident submarines are equipped with missiles bought from the USA. Without the British desire to buy and the American willingness to sell, Britain's nuclear status would be a very modest and pretty obsolete affair. Moreover, when Britain bought Polaris, as with Trident, it was with the explicit understanding that the force would be committed to NATO. Although there is the suggestion that 'our' nuclear weapons could be used independently if Britain's 'supreme national interest' were jeopardised, this would be politically problematic at the same time as it would be technically difficult given the fact that targeting information would have to come from US satellites. It is difficult to think of a situation in which Britain would, or could, use its independent nuclear deterrent independently. The Labour politician Denis Healey (who was himself the defence minister from 1964 to 1970) told the House of Commons on 29 October 1987 that Britain faced

a prolonged and humiliating dependence on the US which will cover the whole of our foreign and defence policy . . . the 'rent-a-rocket' Trident programme – in which the missiles will be exchanged from the US pool every seven or eight years, and British-made warheads had to be tested on a US test-range – made Britain totally dependent on the Americans and totally incapable of standing up to them.

The term 'special relationship' was first used by Churchill in his 'iron curtain' speech at Fulton, Missouri, on 5 March 1946 when he urged the continuation of 'a special relationship between the British Commonwealth and Empire and the United States'. There is no doubt that Britain has continued to be the USA's closest, most trusted and loyal aide, but the British view on the special relationship has emphasised the special influence it provides for Whitehall in Washington and in NATO where we see ourselves as more equal than others within the alliance. There is no doubt that the USA has consistently consulted more closely and fully with successive British governments about NATO affairs and Britain has received US intelligence briefings which are fuller and at a higher level of classification than those provided for the other NATO countries but whether all this has provided Britain with special influence is a moot point. True, the special relationship helped to ensure that the USA provided Britain with intelligence and material aid in connection with the Falklands War but this created a debt to Washington which had to be repaid when we were dragged along behind US ventures in the Middle East which were injurious to larger British interests in the region. The special relationship does provide more opportunities for British influence than are available to other Western European states, but within the tighter context of Anglo-American relations itself influence flows mainly from Washington to London and not vice versa. Moreover, maintaining the relationship has not been without its costs for Britain. It has demanded a loyalty to US policy aspirations that has inhibited British independence in matters of defence and diplomacy so that one is forced to wonder in what sense Britain is in control of its own defence policy and is a truly sovereign state. It has also made it difficult for Britain to forget the past and the world power status which it once had and so has inhibited the development of closer defence collaboration with European allies. Juggling Europe against the special relationship with the USA is just one of many challenges facing Britain in the field of defence.

Defence challenges

Economic

Throughout the post-war period there has always been an imbalance between the economic resources Britain has been willing and able to devote to defence and the sheer scale of the country's overseas defence commitments as defined by successive governments. In this situation all post-war governments have faced the problem of trying to balance defence needs in one area against those in another – and this whilst also trying to create the conditions that would maintain a healthy economy and whilst facing other pressing demands on the public purse for education, health care, housing and so on.

Given Britain's aspirations to be a world power it is not surprising that Britain has occupied fourth or fifth place in the global military league in terms of the percentage of GNP spent on defence but it has been a constant struggle to maintain this level of defence expenditure in the context of a weak economy. There have been those who have argued that military spending is economically necessary and good for the economy, for it generates jobs, technological advance and growth. But it has been increasingly recognised that public expenditure in general and heavy military expenditure in particular has been an economic burden that has burnt up resources in a way that has impeded economic growth. As the problem of the economy has pushed to the top of the political agenda so the sheer scale of defence expenditure has become more and more of a problem, and governments have faced the challenge of trying to achieve an effective defence posture at a cost that would not destabilise the economy.

Over the years, and notwithstanding an all-party commitment to maintaining Britain's defences, the economic constraint has effectively forced successive British governments into making hasty and piecemeal cuts in defence whilst continuing to pretend that defence is provided for on all the established fronts. During the first half of the 1980s the Conservative government gave a high priority to defence, and between 1979 and 1985 defence expenditure rose by 18 per cent in real terms. But this is still not enough to service the scale of British defence commitments and unless there are further increases in defence spending something will have to go as there is 'a funding gap' between what the defence programme on the books would cost and what government documents reveal it intends to spend. Muddling through and spreading the misery might continue to be the way the problem is 'solved' (by being shelved) because such an approach to defence decision-making is in tune with the coarse political reality of powerful defence interests. However, the continuing imbalance between commitments and capabilities, aspirations and resources, suggests the need for a radical review of defence that would establish priorities and cut one of Britain's major defence commitments.

Technological

The sheer pace of technological innovation in weapon technology has been one of the startling features of our time. This has compounded the economic problem because 'better' equipment always costs more and with defence inflation running at six to ten per cent above the general rate of inflation it is not too surprising that an increasing percentage of the defence budget has 'had' to be spent on equipment. In 1950, 30 per cent of the defence budget went on equipment; in 1975 this had risen to 35 per cent; and by 1989 it was 41 per cent. But military technology poses a challenge in its own right quite irrespective of cost. Not only does it crank up the political power of the arms manufacturers and of the military relative to the power of the elected politicians who are supposed to 'make' defence policy, but it also makes for an impersonal self-generating momentum all its own – a momentum that is often unrelated to real military needs and devoid of rational justification or control. What do we mean by this?

The military will always demand the best (that is the latest and most technologically sophisticated) equipment and arms manufacturers will always be happy to supply it. The result will be a rolling programme of development and production that will generate 'solutions' before anybody has identified the defence needs and the 'problems' to be solved. In this state of affairs weapons can be deemed obsolete before they are even completed.

Costly projects may get cancelled mid-course and weapons systems may have to be changed and modified during the procurement process itself. Behind all this lies a philosophy of technology which will always see the need for follow-up projects embodying a 'better' (and more complex and costly) technological solution. Politicians are part of the process of buying defence equipment and they are supposed to be in control but they face problems because they lack any expertise in weapons technology and are dependent on advisers. More than this, they have to operate within the context of a technology in which it can take a decade or more to develop a major weapons system from initial research to final assembly and during that time there may be two or three changes of government and several changes of Defence Secretary. Governments are short-term actors in a long-term defence play which they did not write. Moreover, they come onto the stage of defence policy-making whilst the play is already in progress. In this kind of situation politicians have little choice but to make relatively minor decisions that simply carry on or amend established plans for defence and equipment. In effect, the range of commitments that were built-up in the past are beyond reach. Hence passing politicians lack the easy opportunity of making major decisions that might rock the stability of a technologically driven continuity that is rooted in the defence of a past pattern of commitments, notwithstanding the extent to which these commitments are bought at a draining cost.

Political

Economic constraints and the challenge of military technology have clearly been of importance in shaping British defence policy but such a perspective is tinged with a determinism which downplays the significance of politics and ignores the political challenges that now face the whole military and defence establishment. At home, the parties of the Left and centre have been forced to be 'realistic' in the face of electoral defeat and respond to the challenge of a public opinion that would not accept a non-nuclear defence policy, but this at a time when all parties are challenged to reassess their defence postures consequent upon the pace of developments abroad. The liberalisation and democratisation of the countries in the Warsaw Pact and the improvement in East–West relations since Mr Gorbachev came to office challenge the superpowers to secure a peace without nuclear deterrents and without a pattern of defence expenditure that eats into their capacity to do more useful things with their scarce resources. Britain is not alone in facing a dilemma with respect to these developments and in having to ponder on the implications of increased pluralism within the international community as other nations rise on the world stage. Given these changes and challenges, can NATO continue in its present form; is there anything in the 'special relationship' or should Britain look more to co-operation with Europe; should Britain continue to maintain its 'own' nuclear deterrent and does it need to (and can it afford to) maintain such a wide range of military capabilities; and if politicians and public agree that defences can be cut can we be sure that the armed forces and the arms industry will also agree and allow the democratic process to work as it should?

The Security Services

Orthodoxies

In John Le Carre's thriller, *The Spy Who Came in from the Cold*, 'control' tells Leamas about the nature of British intelligence:

> The ethic of our work, as I understand it, is based on a single assumption. That is, we are never going to be aggressors. Do you think that's fair? Thus we do disagreeable things, but we are defensive. That, I think, is still fair. We do disagreeable things so that ordinary people here and elsewhere can sleep safely in their beds at night. Is that too romantic? Of course we occasionally do very wicked things. . . .

In this section we are in a twilight world of turned-up collars and defensive organisations that operate beneath the threshold of public consciousness and behind walls of silence where little is even visible until a 'leak', a crisis or a spy scandal pushes restricted and secret information up onto the surface of party politics. In a situation in which polite society *and* elected governments have generally felt happiest ignoring the reality of the secret security state within the state, control's observations provide us with a comfortable perspective – a perspective that is important precisely because it has been buttressed by journalists and writers sympathetic to the work of the security services. Moreover, when governments have been forced to pronounce on the work of 'their' – and 'our' – intelligence agencies then they too have been content to present control's view as the official and orthodox line. For example, the Security Service Act, 1989, placed the Security Service, M15, on a statutory basis for the first time and that act stated that:

> The function of the Service shall be the protection of national security and, in particular, its protection against threats from espionage, terrorism and sabotage, from the activities of agents of foreign powers and from actions intended to overthrow or undermine parliamentary democracy by political, industrial or violent means.

This kind of perspective on the security services presents them as keen supporters of democracy and liberty. Individual spies and spycatchers are simply busy collecting intelligence in order to protect our freedoms and way of life from the threats of enemies abroad and from subversives and terrorists here at home. So although enemy spies, terrorists and violent revolutionaries may well have cause to fear the ruthless efficiency of the British security services, ordinary citizens will be left untouched. They will be able to sleep more safely in their beds so that they are free to awake to enjoy their liberties and a democratic system that is protected and defended by the security services themselves.

Views of this kind are of massive political importance precisely because we think that they mystify the reality of much of what the security services are about. For sure, these services are caught up in the quite proper task of dealing with 'the enemies of the state' at home and abroad. But the comfy perspective on their work fails to bring out the extent to which they are also intruding into the civil liberties of quite ordinary people; it fails to attend to the implications of security service activity for what has traditionally been seen as the normal rough and tumble of ordinary politics within a healthy democracy; and it does not dwell on the problems of holding the security services to account for what they do in our name. Having said all that, it is next to impossible for us to prove these kind of assertions and penetrate to the 'reality' of things. Not only does official secrecy (protected by the Official Secrets Act, 1989) limit the information which is available, but most of the writing on the security services is highly politicised. The hard Right sees the security services as in the grip of Soviet moles and the Left sees it as dominated by crypto-fascists who are bent on using the power of the security services to weaken Left-wing dissent within British politics. True, there is a small academic literature, but this too is limited because it tends to play by the official rules and so is content to devote itself to the ancient and laundered history of security. Most of the available literature is based on security service leaks and misinformation. There is, however, a useful and developing tradition of critical investigative journalism that provides us with insights even though journalists of this persuasion have had to work from outside of the system whilst clinging to the gossip and the memoirs of insiders who have chosen to spill the beans.

Let us try to get at the basics, set down the institutions that make up the British security system; assess their role in protecting national security and combating subversion; and comment on the problems which they pose for a liberal-democracy.

The institutions of the security services

Britain has several intelligence agencies but the organisation of British intelligence is a state secret. Sir Robert Armstrong, the head of the Civil Service, told the New South Wales Supreme Court during the British Government's civil action to prevent the publication of the book, *Spycatcher*, by Peter Wright, a former counter-espionage officer in M15, that:

It is not the policy of the British government that no information about the work of the security services should ever be released. The practice and policy is that that, when in the view of the government information may be disclosed without risk of damage to national security, it should be done by way of official publication, based on official records with a view to giving a comprehensive and accurate account.

In reality, the concern for 'national security' has blocked the release of full information and led to the provision of official misinformation; no records of the main intelligence services have ever been officially released; the Official Secrets Act hovers over everything; and the D notice system of voluntary co-operation between the media and the government to keep sensitive matters of defence and national security out of the public eye may have lost its hold but it has still not been officially abolished.

Notwithstanding these restrictions on our right to know, the most secret arm of the secret state consists of a number of organisations. M16 and M15 emerged from the division of the Secret Service Bureau in 1910. Nowadays, foreign intelligence and spying outside of Britain is the responsibility of M16, also known as the Secret Intelligence Service, SIS. SIS is a part of the Foreign and Commonwealth Office and reports to the Foreign Secretary and is tasked by the Joint Intelligence Committee which also prepares the intelligence assessments in accordance with government policy. Domestic and colonial intelligence is the responsibility of M15, also known as the Security Service, and the Director enjoys the right of direct access to the Prime Minister. After the trial and conviction in spring 1984 of Michael Bettany, an M15 officer who had passed secrets to the Soviets, the Security Commission began a review of M15 that led to its reorganisation in mid-1985. In addition to these two organisations, there is the Government Communications Headquarters, GCHQ, at Cheltenham which is officially responsible for government codes and cyphers but also intercepts the communications of others; there is the Special Branch of the police force which acts as the official investigating and arrest agency for activities defined as subversive although it also has to deal with issues of nationality and the activities of aliens; the three armed services each have their own intelligence bodies co-ordinated by the Defence Intelligence Staff of the Ministry of Defence; each Ministry has its own security force responsible for the security of personnel and documents; and the Overseas Information Department works closely with the intelligence services in releasing certain kinds of information to selected journalists, politicians and opinion leaders.

The cost of all these intelligence organisations is a state secret. The 'secret vote' – as the intelligence budget officially presented to Parliament is known – shows spending of only £76 million for 1984–5. The real level has been put at nearer £1,000 million because the secret vote only covers the salaries of M15 and M16 staff and further cash for the security services is 'laundered' through departmental budgets in a variety of ways. In reality it has been estimated that M16 has a budget of about £140 million and 3,000 personnel; M15 costs about £160 million, has 2,000 personnel and files on over a million British citizens; GCHQ costs almost £600 million a year and has a staff of 11,500; and, according to a 1985 report of the Home Affairs Committee of the House of Commons, the more modest Special Branch operates on a budget of £15.5 million with around 1,247 officers.

Security and subversion

It is one thing to say that the security services protect national security and parliamentary democracy from subversion but it is another matter to say what this involves and how the agencies define their role. Over the years, the interpretation of national security and the common enemy has changed its ground. During the Second World War, the Germans and their allies were the threat and a few British fascists were put in prison. After the war and with the onset of the Cold War between East and West, the countries of the Communist bloc were the enemies and Soviet spies and British communists were seen as the threat. More recently, the Irish situation, the growth of student militancy in the 1960s and the industrial militancy of the early 1970s shifted M15 toward domestic concerns but in the context of a situation when it was very much less clear just who should be targeted as subversive threats to the system. Should the security services see the National Union of Students, the Workers Revolutionary Party, the Socialist Workers Party, the Campaign for Nuclear Disarmament and the National Council for Civil Liberties as serious threats, or should they continue to see the Russian KGB as the threat and spend their time attending to communist subversion in industry, looking for Soviet spies in the Labour Party, the Civil Service and the intelligence services themselves? The Cold War warriors found it hard to adjust. The security services were divided.

Alongside this changing focus of security concern has come a broader definition of 'subversion' – a term which still has no legal definition. The term 'subversive' was traditionally taken to mean a link, direct or indirect, with communist or fascist groups. Lord Denning in his 1963 report on the security implications of the relationship between John Profumo, the Secretary of State for War, and Christine Keeler who was also having a relationship with a Russian spy, defined a subversive as someone who 'would contemplate the overthrow of government by *unlawful* means'. In 1985, the Prime Minister announced revised security vetting procedures to cover over half a million civil servants and many thousands of people working in the nuclear industry, British Telecom, the police forces and defence contractors. She stated:

It is the policy of Her Majesty's Government that no one should be employed in connection with work the nature of which is vital to the security of the state who:

1 Is, or has recently been, a member of a communist or fascist organisation, or of a subversive group, acknowledged to be such by the Minister, whose

aims are to undermine or overthrow Parliamentary democracy in the United Kingdom of Great Britain and Northern Ireland by political, industrial or violent means.

2 Is, or has recently been, sympathetic to or associated with members or sympathisers of such organisations or groups, in such a way as to raise reasonable doubts about his reliability.

3 Is susceptible to pressure from such organisations or groups.

Elements of this statement were anticipated in a 1975 speech by a junior Home Office minister and in a report by the Security Commission in 1982. We have, however, shifted way beyond Lord Denning's point about 'unlawful means' and the second and third parts of the Prime Minister's definition of subversion are new and place a huge number of people in the subversive ranks. M15 and the Special Branch have been given a blank cheque. They have the power to collect intelligence and then blacklist individuals who are engaged in perfectly lawful, non-violent political acitivity be they in the Civil Service, the nuclear industry, defence companies or the BBC. Hollingsworth and Norton-Taylor are surely correct to argue that 'the current definition of "subversive" is now so wide and vague that it is dangerously open to abuse'.

Who, then, are the targets of security service surveillance? And how do the security services go about their task of keeping tabs on those they choose to call 'subversive'?

There are no easy answers to these questions because so much is secret, but the autonomy enjoyed by the security services means that much hinges on the personnel and traditions within the agencies themselves. In a debate on official secrecy in 1988, Edward Heath, the Prime Minister from 1970 to 1974, recognised 'we are dealing with people, and it is the choice of people that matters. In the inner control of the security services, the first point to remember is the selection of people. . . . I . . . met people in the security services who talked the most ridiculous nonsense and whose whole philosophy was ridiculous nonsense. If some of them were on a tube and saw someone reading the *Daily Mirror*, they would say "Get after him, that is dangerous. We must find out where he bought it".' Miranda Ingram, an M15 officer from 1981 to 1983, would have recognised the sense in this observation since she has pointed out that some M15 officers 'thought that people who wore jeans were potentially subversive' and she explained this by noting that 'some officers live a very sheltered life and never work in the real world and it often means they become conservative . . . and probably Conservative.' Lord Carver, a retired Chief of British Staff and a self-confessed 'customer of the security services for many years', told the House of Lords that 'I have unfortunately come across some of these people who seem to be a little amateurish . . . the people concerned seem to live in a completely closed world whereby what really went on and what people actually thought and did, they just did not understand.'

In a situation in which the security services do not advertise for recruits they have little choice but to rely on old-boy networks of recruitment from the police and the army, and on the nods and winks from well-placed 'friends' in touch with the younger generation at certain universities. The security services recruit in their own image and although a Right-wing tone may be endemic in the nature of much security work, in the context of the British security services we are dealing with people from particular backgrounds who operate in closed institutions that have a history – and files – which suggest that the threats to the system come almost exclusively from the Left in British politics even though the 'Left' and 'subversives' are no longer seen as confined to members of the Communist Party alone. For the security services, securing Britain and the national interest can come to mean holding back the tide of a particular kind of social and political change, and even trying to reverse it, so that they can recover *their* image of what Britain *should* be like for all decent and god-fearing British folk. In a quite literal sense, the security services are a reactionary element in British politics.

In early 1985, Cathy Massiter, an M15 officer from 1970 to 1984, told the banned '20/20 Vision' television programme how the National Council for Civil Liberties and the Campaign for Nuclear Disarmament were targeted by M15 as subversive organisations. Files were opened up on those active within the organisations and telephones were tapped. In that same year the government responded to an adverse ruling against it in the European Court of Human Rights in August 1984 by introducing the Interception of Communications Bill. This Act clarified the legal basis of post and telephone surveillance but it did the bare minimum necessary to comply with the European judgement. In 1988 the Home Secretary approved warrants for 412 telephone taps covering an undisclosed number of individual lines, but unofficial estimates have set the figure far higher at between 2,000 and 4,000 a year. In 1983, the Defence Secretary, Michael Heseltine, set up a special unit inside the Ministry of Defence to 'publicise the Government's nuclear weapons policy' and to counter the CND message. It has been alleged that this unit used M15 and Special Branch files to smear the leadership of CND for what amounted to party political propaganda. It might comfort 'ordinary' members of the public if we could suggest that the security services were only interested in the leading activists in the 'subversive' organisations but this can hardly be the case given the sheer scale of security operations. John Alderson, the Chief Constable of Devon and Cornwall from 1973 to 1982, told a hearing of the House of Commons Home Affairs Committee inquiry into the Special Branch that 40 per cent of the people on the files of the Special Branch in his force were there because they had outspoken views. The Police National Computer (PNC) is not without its significance for the political surveillance of quite ordinary people. The computer fulfills a number of functions but the largest involves maintaining a file of registered owners and keepers of vehicles. In 1977 it was revealed that the PNC record on a particular vehicle included that fact that its owner 'was a prominent member of the Anti-Blood Sports League', and the following year a member of the Gay Activists Alliance found that details of his association were recorded on his vehicle file.

All of the above involves the surveillance and monitoring of many, many quite ordinary people, but the security services have also taken a keen interest in industrial action and have often been egged on in their concerns by elected politicians. During the controversy over the decision to ban trade unions at GCHQ in 1984 the Prime Minister argued that 'there is an inherent conflict between the membership of a trade union and the defence of national security' so suggesting that many trade unionists could be legitimately scrutinised by M15 as potential subversives. Having said that, it would be quite wrong to suggest that security service interest in trade unions is simply related to the period of Conservative government since 1979. M15 was involved in the 1929 General Strike, and in 1966, the Labour Prime Minister, Harold Wilson, used M15 to bug the leaders of the seamen's strike in the hope of exposing a 'Red plot' which could be used against the strikers so as to end the strike. More recently, the Special Branch was almost certainly involved in the miners' strike of 1984–5, and allegations of phone tapping and claims that some police officers were acting as *agents provocateurs* were widely made though hard to substantiate.

The security services have also displayed a keen interest in the loyalty of elected politicians and so have chosen to investigate those who are their nominal masters within our system of democratic rule. M15 opens a file on every new MP, but there has always been particular interest in Left-wing Labour MPs – sometimes at the behest of the Labour leadership them-selves. For example, in 1961, after losing three general elections in a row and convinced that a return to power was only possible if the party was purged of 'extremists', the Labour leader, Hugh Gaitskell, established a committee of three MPs to investigate those MPs who were thought to be communist supporters. A meeting was arranged with M15 and the names of fifteen Labour MPs were handed over for investigation. The investi-gation involved telephone tapping, shadowing, the opening of mail, the examination of bank accounts, and other 'routine' methods used by the intelligence services. The inquiries proved negative, but it is probable that the security surveillance of certain Labour MPs goes back long before the initiative of Hugh Gaitskell just as it certainly extends forward beyond the 1960s.

Security service interest in the Labour Party is not confined to the activities of individual MPs since it focuses particularly sharply on Labour when it is in government or when it displays a dangerous potential for government. In 1924, during Ramsay MacDonald's election campaign, both M15 and M16 were involved in leaking the notorious Zinoviev letter to the *Daily Mail* as part of a plot to weaken Labour's re-election prospects. Leigh has argued that 'the electoral plot against the 1929 Labour govern-ment was just as sordid' since it 'involved turning M15 into a branch of Conservative Central Office (or possibly vice versa)' in order that agents could be placed in key centres and in the Labour Party headquarters itself. The relationship between M15 and the Labour Government of 1945–51 was intricate and involved a kind of sulky tension, but the fact that Labour lost the three elections of the 1950s encouraged many in the security services to see Labour as a dead electoral force and so as an increasingly limited security problem. This obituary was premature. Under the leadership of Harold Wilson, Labour won the elections of 1964 and 1966 as well as the two elections of 1974. In the 1960s, there were those in the security services who feared that Labour was becoming too much the natural party of government.

Peter Wright, a counter-espionage officer in M15 from 1955 to 1976, was not a man who was prepared to accept the verdict of the electorate. He regarded Harold Wilson as a Soviet agent and was concerned to use the security services against him and his Labour governments. Led by Wright, 30 like-minded officers in British intelligence mounted an extensive and 'official' surveillance operation against Harold Wilson, his government, and his circle of friends that was to come to a head in the mid-1970s. In *Spycatcher*, the book the British Government tried to ban, Wright recalls that

> the plan was simple. In the run-up the [1974] election . . . M15 would arrange for selective details of the intelligence about leading Labour Party figures, but especially Wilson, to be leaked to sympathetic pressmen. . . . It was a carbon copy of the Zinoviev letter, which had done so much to destroy the first Ramsay MacDonald Government in 1924. . . . Although the full Wilson story never emerged, it was obvious to me that the boys had been actively pushing their plan as much as they could. No wonder Wilson was later to claim that he was the victim of a plot!

Notwithstanding the best efforts of the security services, Wilson won the elections of 1974 but he did resign suddenly in 1976 even though Leigh has suggested that Wilson 'actually decided to organise his resignation immediately after a blazing confrontation with Michael Hanley, the head of M15, in early August 1975. He accused members of Hanley's M15 of plotting against him. This accusation the evidence shows to have been perfectly true.' In 1987, the Prime Minister told the Commons that she had been advised by the head of M15 'that all the Security Service officers who have been interviewed have categorically denied that they were involved in, or were aware of, any activities or plans to undermine or discredit Lord Wilson and his government when he was Prime Minister'. Such a denial is to be expected but would not be accepted by Chapman Pincher who argued as long ago as 1978 that 'the undermining activities which Wilson complained of were not only genuine but far more menacing then he revealed. Certain officers inside M15, assisted by others who had retired from the service, were actually trying to bring the Labour Government down and, in my opinion, they could at one point have succeeded.'

All this information about security service efforts to destabilise properly elected Labour governments is staggering. It constitutes a body blow to those who cling to the simple belief that the security services are only involved in defending British democracy against subversive threats. The security services seem to be a law unto themselves and as they go about their task of political surveillance through phone taps, burglaries and raids on the files of other government departments they are often involved in operating outside of the law and even against the law. Moreover, on those rare occasions when the security services have been shown to have broken the law the courts have displayed a marked reluctance to intervene and challenge such action when they have been confronted with the claim that illegality was necessary 'in the interests of national security'. During the *Spycatcher* case, Lord Donaldson said, 'It is silly for us to sit here and say that the Security Service is obliged to follow the letter of the law, it isn't real.' He recognised that it was sometimes essential for M15 officers to break the law and for such breaches not to be prosecuted but he sought to set limits on this saying that 'murder is an entirely different matter'. The language of Lord Diplock in his judgement on the government ban on trade unions at GCHQ suggests that a claim by a government that action is necessary in the interests of national security is not open to challenge in the courts. This knowledge that there is little judicial control over decisions taken by a government or the security services in the interests of national security can only intensify the present disquiet that exists about the absence of control over the intelligence services of the state.

The security services, accountability and civil liberties

Few would deny that there is a place for the security services within a liberal-democracy but disputes abound on a number of issues:

Secrecy

Intelligence is an ill-defined activity which has secrecy at its core and yet secrecy is a troublesome notion in the context of a democratic polity where government is supposed to be open and where information should be freely available to enable citizens to make informed judgements. More than this, it is clear that the efficiency of the security services can be harmed by too much secrecy every bit as much as by too little. If too much information is made secret then security safeguards are bound to be weakened and whistle-blowing and leaking will become more of a problem. In a similar way if too many people are targeted as subversive then it is difficult to sort out the substantial threats from the background 'noise'. Excessive secrecy can discredit the case for any secrecy and for the security services themselves in a way that may well inhibit public understanding and support for security-service work at the same time as it can also exacerbate the problem of recruiting security-service staff and force to the fore the issue of the public's 'right to know' about everything to do with security matters.

Secrecy and the freedom of information divide the parties in Britain. The Conservatives oppose greater openness and freedom, but their rivals are committed to freedom of information in ways that have profound implications for the work of the security services.

Accountability

It is clear that Parliament has no effective means of scrutinizing the security services. Ministers refuse to answer questions falling within the realm of 'national security' and select committees seeking testimony from members of the intelligence community have been refused access. In practice, the security services enjoy an autonomy that has been unchecked by the democratic side of the state machine. If any checks exist, then they are internal to the services. In the case of MI5, a Security Commission (chaired by a senior judge) was created after the Profumo scandal to investigate important leaks and to advise generally on security arrangements. The Commission reports to the Prime Minister and the public reports reveal nothing of consequence. Such a situation is anomalous among the Western democracies where most legislatures have some limited scrutiny over their intelligence communities. In the past, Parliament 'accepted' this state of affairs. An all-party consensus existed on security matters. It was recognised that acountability should be to ministers (rather than to Parliament) and most MPs trusted ministers to discharge that responsibility faithfully – even though ministers themselves may well have had difficulty keeping tabs on the security services. By the 1980s, however, the consensus broke down. The accountability of the security services became a political issue. Many claimed that the security services were outside of political and legal control and beyond the authority of ministers as well. Nothing has changed. During the passage of the Security Service Bill through Parliament in 1989, rebel Tories proposed scrutiny by a body of Privy Counsellors. Labour and the centre parties urged the establishment of proper parliamentary accountability through a Select Committee on the security services, but most Conservatives were happy to defend the established position and so the Act itself did not provide for any form of parliamentary oversight over MI5. No matter what the established constitutional position, it is clear that blind trust in the intelligence services does not easily 'fit' within the ethos of a democracy. Even if the issue of security service accountability is eventually resolved in favour of greater parliamentary control this does not mean that such accountability will become a reality: Peter Wright is right to remind us that 'politicians may come and go, but the Security Service goes on forever.'

Civil liberties

We live within what has been defined as a liberal-democracy where we enjoy rights and liberties that take us beyond the simple act of voting once every five years. In theory, we can organise ourselves into pressure groups and trade unions to criticise the powerful and press for change; we can assemble and protest on the streets at the injustices caught up within the established system; and we can dissent from prevailing orthodoxies in the struggle for a better tomorrow. However, the practice of these rights seems to be under pressure and scrutiny in the name of national security. If we cannot make a phone call, attend a public meeting, be active in a trade union, or apply for a certain kind of job without fear of surveillance from the security services then just how free are we and how healthy is our system of democracy?

Conclusion

We have attempted to do a number of things in our consideration of the role and significance of the secret state in British politics.

1 We set down the well-established orthodoxies that have dealt with the non-elected parts of the state. These orthodoxies are grounded in liberal-democratic constitutional theory. Not surprisingly, therefore, they assert that the non-elected parts of the state lack real political power because they are either controlled by the elected government of the day or else they are held in check by the law of the land passed by Parliament.

2 We argued that these orthodoxies were of limited utility in enabling us to understand the role of the non-elected parts of the state machine. Moreover, in some cases these orthodoxies were misleading and just plain wrong so that they actually served to block an adequate understanding of the power and significance of the institutions that comprise the secret state.

3 At a more positive level, we were concerned to demonstrate a number of things:

(a) A distinction needs to be made between the elected government of the day and the state itself. The government is but a *part* of a complex of distinctive, impersonal state institutions that also include the Civil Service, the judiciary, the armed forces, the police, and the security services, as well as a host of institutions that operate below the level of the central state in the regions and localities of the country.

(b) Contrary to the presumptions of liberal-democratic constitutional theory the government is not firmly in control of the various institutions that make up the non-elected side of the state machine and some of the institutions are clearly out of control.

(c) Precisely because the institutions that make up the non-elected side of the state are not simply accountable to and controlled by the elected side, and because they all enjoy a goodly measure of independence and autonomy and are able to exercise discretion, so we are dealing with institutions that enjoy political power in their own right. It is because the institutions of the secret state are powerful and in politics that they demand the attention of political scientists who are concerned to map out the patterns of politics and power within Britain.

(d) Information about the workings of the non-elected side of the state is restricted by the prevalence of liberal-democratic myths and by the cult of an official secrecy that is enshrined in a host of laws and conventions. This secrecy makes it difficult for anyone to penetrate to an adequate understanding of the closed institutions that comprise the secret state.

(e) We do not have a 'theory' to make sense of the institutions of the secret state. Moreover, we doubt whether one perspective could ever capture the reality of a complex of different institutions even if they did become more open so that we were provided with more information to weave into an explanatory framework.

(f) Notwithstanding the implications of secrecy and the problems of developing explanatory theory we argued that understanding could be advanced if we set aside the liberal-democratic orthodoxies and set down concrete information on the social backgrounds and institutional socialisation of those influential in the institutions of the secret state; if we dealt with the implications of the organisational structure of those institutions; and if we attended to the role and functions of the various institutions within society as a whole.

(g) For the most part we found that those influential in the secret state were in no sense representative of the population at large in terms of social background, education, gender, race or income. The fact that the institutions of the secret state are led by similar 'types' and the fact that connections exist between the various institutions has led some to assert that Britain is run by a self-perpetuating 'Establishment'. There is something in this view, but we feel that it attaches too much importance to social background at the same time as it exaggerates the extent to which the institutions of the state hang together as a whole.

(h) The institutions of the secret state tend to be organised on bureaucratic or even authoritarian lines. New recruits are expected to assume a quiet, learning, apprenticeship role, and power tends to go to those with service and seniority within the institutions. These forms of organisation tend to inhibit innovation and change at the same time as they encourage continuity and stability in a way that can frustrate the aspirations of governments that are keen to implement the radical programmes that they put before the electorate.

(i) For the most part the institutions of the secret state assume a conservative (but probably not a Conservative) role in society in that they maintain the broad essentials of the status quo and the established patterns of policy and power relations. The Civil Service can hardly throw away all its files and start afresh; much law (and therefore the activities of the police and the judges) does involve the defence of established patterns of power, privilege and authority; the armed services are unlikely to want to give up their stocks of weapons; and in our kind of society it is practically inevitable that the security services will see 'subversion' as coming from the Left in British politics.

The orthodoxies surrounding the secret state may block understanding but they are slowly crumbling as aspects of the reality of their practice have come into view. The institutions of the secret state have become an issue in politics. On the one hand, there are those who see the secret state as a problem and who press for freedom of information, for an end to official secrecy, for more open government and for closer controls on the non-elected side of the state so that the institutions are made more accountable to the democratic and elected side of the state system. On the other hand, proposals of this kind for greater openness and accountability have met with opposition from the secret state itself and from those who are keenly attuned to the need to preserve the established set-up. There is, then, something of a conflict between those who seek to create a more truly democratic state and those who are bent on maintaining a strong state where huge chunks of political power are left beyond the reach of the rough intrusions of the ballot box. Notwithstanding the outcome of this conflict, it is clear that much of what we have set down in this chapter is disturbing of the simple view which suggests that Britain is a democracy where the holders of political power are responsible and held to account for their actions to elected politicians and ultimately to the public at large.

Works Cited and Guide to Further Reading

Andrew, C. (1986) *Secret Service*, London, Sceptre.
By far the best account of the making of the British intelligence community but has very little to say about the situation since the Second World War.

Andrew, C. and Dilks, D. (eds) (1984) *The Missing Dimension*, London, Macmillan.
Useful series of academic essays on the intelligence services in a number of countries that tries to offer insight instead of leaks and self-serving gossip.

Aubrey, C. (1981) *Who's Watching You?*, Harmondsworth, Penguin.
Discussion and critique of Britain's security services and the Official Secrets Act from a man who was arrested under the Act in 1977.

Baylis, J. (1989) *British Defence Policy*, London, Macmillan.
Good basic presentation. Particularly useful in dealing with the various challenges and dilemmas facing defence decision-makers.

Bell, J. (1983) *Policy Arguments in Judicial Decisions*, Oxford, Clarendon.
Analyses the judicial function in contemporary government; argues that judges are in politics because they exercise discretion and give direction to society; and worries about the unaccountable political power of judges in a democracy.

Berlins, M. and Dyer, C. (1989) *The Law Machine*, 3rd edn, Harmondsworth, Penguin.
Short, punchy book that is concerned to make sense of how the machinery of justice – the law machine – actually works in practice.

Committee to Review the Functioning of Financial Institutions (Chair, Sir Harold Wilson) (1980) *Report*, Cmnd 1937, London, HMSO.
Somewhat dated in the light of Big Bang, but chapter 25 contains a good discussion of the position of the Bank of England.

Devlin, Lord (1981) *The Judge*, Oxford, Oxford University Press.
Distinguished judge recognises that judges do make law but worries about this and does not want them to do it too much.

Dockrill, M. (1988) *British Defence Since 1945*, Oxford, Blackwell.
Brief general history that also includes a useful chapter on the Thatcher government and defence.

Drewry, G. and Butcher, T. (1988) *The Civil Service Today*, Oxford, Basil Blackwell.
Good basic study of the Civil Service. Covers all the familiar ground on such matters as 'recruitment and training', 'ministers and civil servants' and so on, but also deals with such *causes célèbres* as the banning of trade unions at GCHQ, the Ponting affair, the Westland crisis, and the government's efforts to prevent the publication of Peter Wright's *Spycatcher*.

Dunhill, C. (ed.) (1989) *The Boys in Blue: Women's Challenge to the Police*, London, Virago.
Feminist perspective that focuses on 'the very real abuses of police power towards us and the shortcomings of the way in which the police deal with issues against us, within the context of a . . . Right-wing ideology.'

The Economist (22.9.84) 'Flexible old Lady'; (14.11.87) 'Where the Treasury rules'; (11.6.88) 'Bank of England: right turn at Threadneedle Street'.
Three useful articles that bear on the functions and power of the Bank of England.

Efficiency Unit, Report to the Prime Minister by K. Jenkins et al. (1985) *Making Things Happen*, London, HMSO.
A report on the implementation of the Conservative government's efficiency scrutinies – scrutinies that identified opportunities to save £600 million per annum.

Estimates Committee (1965) *Recruitment to the Civil Service*, London, HMSO.
Highlights the public school, upper-class background of recruits to the higher ranks of the Civil Service.

Expenditure Committee (1977) *The Civil Service*, London, HMSO.
Critical of the pattern of recruitment into the higher ranks of the Civil Service and of the power of civil servants *vis-à-vis* ministers and Parliament.

Finer, S. E. (1970) *The Man on Horseback*, London, Allen Lane.
Classic but general discussion of the role of the military in politics.

Fry, G. K. (1985) *The Changing Civil Service*, London, George Allen and Unwin.
An 'interpretative essay of assessment' that considers the Civil Service as it has developed since the Fulton report of 1968. Evaluates the Thatcher government's attempts to cut down the size and the influence of the Civil Service.

Geddes, P. (1987) *Inside the Bank of England*, London, Boxtree Books.
This book arose out of a documentary made about the Bank by Television South. Chapter 4 'Excuse me, Chancellor . . .' is a useful discussion of the Bank in relation to the Treasury and the government.

Gerth, H. and Mills, C. Wright (1948) *From Max Weber*, London, Routledge and Kegan Paul.
Chapter 8 provides the classic discussion of bureaucracy from one of the founding fathers of modern sociology.

Gordon P. (1983) *Whitelaw*, London, Pluto.
Argues that racism is institutionalised in the police, the courts and the prisons – a view rejected by Scarman.

Graef, R. (1989) *Talking Blues*, London, Collins Harvill.
The author lets hundreds of policeman and women talk about their lives and their work in a way which disturbs cosy cliches about the good old British bobby. Important chapters on public order, community policing, race and complaints.

Griffith, J. A. G. (1985) *The Politics of the Judiciary*, 3rd edn, London, Fontana.
Asserts that judges act politically (not neutrally) and tend to promote 'certain political views normally associated with the Conservative Party'. Been much criticised but still a good read and provides a political perspective on the judiciary that you can get your teeth into.

Heclo, H. and Wildavsky, A. (1981) *The Private Government of Public Money*, 2nd edn, London, Macmillan.
A study which gets inside the 'culture' of the Civil Service in general and the Treasury in particular.

Hennessy, P. (1989) *Whitehall*, London, Secker and Warburg.
851 pages on the Civil Service! Not particularly analytic but strong on personalities and contains an interesting section on 'Mrs Thatcher's Whitehall' as well as an 'assessment of performance' and his own 'personal ideas for reform'.

Hollingsworth, M. and Norton-Taylor, R. (1988) *Blacklist*, London, Hogarth Press.
Explores the extent of political vetting by the security services within the Civil Service, defence companies, British Telecom and the BBC, and by the Economic League within the engineering and construction industries.

Home Affairs Committee (1985) *Special Branch*, London, HMSO.
Discreet and fairly uncritical inquiry into the Special Branch. Enlivened by David Winnick's minority report and by some sharp questioning at the hearings.

Hoskyns, Sir J. (1983) 'Whitehall and Westminster: an outsider's view', *Parliamentary Affairs*, 36, 137–47.
Former head of Mrs Thatcher's Policy Unit makes a case for a fundamental overhaul of the machinery of government and calls for more politically appointed officials.

Hunt, A. (1981) 'The politics of law and justice', *Politics and Power*, 4, 3–26.
Criticises Left positions on law, and argues that the Left have failed to take law seriously. Makes a plea for a 'socialist politics of law' and a more rigorous approach to questions of rights and justice.

Huntington, S. P. (1957) *The Soldier and the State*, Cambridge, MA., Harvard University Press.
General discussion of the theory and practice of civil–military relations. Dated the uncritical of the situation in the West but still a classic in the field.

Jones, S. (1986) *Policewomen and Equality*, London, Macmillan.
Careful but laboured study that describes and tries to explain the reasons why so few women are recruited to the police and promoted up through the ranks.

Judges on Trial, (January 1987) *Labour Research*, Vol. 76, no. 1, 9–11.

Hard, simple, Left view. Recognises that judges come from a very narrow section of society but thinks that you can explain what judges do by simply attending to their 'background' alone.

Lee, S. (1988) *Judging Judges*, London, Faber and Faber.
Witty book. Criticises the orthodox fairy tale that judges do not make law and criticises Griffith's nightmare that judges use their discretion to further their own class interests. Seeks to move 'towards reality' through an exploration of cases and judges in order to examine 'what does, and should, happen when judges are required to decide a disputed point of law'.

Leigh, D. (1988) *The Wilson Plot*, London, Heinemann.
Detailed and careful study that documents the MI5 plot to discredit the Labour Prime Minister, Harold Wilson.

Leigh, D. and Lashmar, P. (1985) 'Secret service cash soars in secret', *The Observer*, 3 March.
Argues that the government plans to spend almost £1,000 on the intelligence services in the coming year – more than ten times the publicly acknowledged sum.

Marshall, G. (1965) *Police and Government*, London, Methuen.
Puts the orthodox, rosy view of the accountability of police to the law.

Moran, M. (1980) 'Parliamentary control of the Bank of England', *Parliamentary Affairs*, 33 67–78.
Highlights the *lack* of any parliamentary control.

Moran, M. (1986) *The Politics of Banking*, 2nd edn., London, Macmillan.
A book 'about money, power and policy' that also deals with the Bank of England in relation to the government.

Paterson, A. (1982) *The Law Lords*, London, Macmillan.
Closely rersearched study of the Law Lords which argues that they have room for choice and discretion and so 'cannot avoid making law'.

Pattullo, P. (1983) *Judging Women*, London, National Council for Civil Liberties.
A feminist study of the attitudes that rule the British legal system. Argues that 'our laws are administered by predominantly white, middle-class, middle-aged males who, in their professional lives, often express stereotype notions about women and show little understanding of the nature of women's lives'.

Pincher, C. (1978) *Inside Story*, London, Sidgwick and Jackson.
Journalist's insights into the workings of the security services that points to the existence of a plot against the Labour Prime Minister Harold Wilson.

Policy Studies Institute (1983) *Police and People in London*, London, PSI.
A four-volume study of the Metropolitan Police based on a survey of Londoners; a survey of 1770 police officers; a study of young black people in a self-help hostel; and lengthy observations of police practices over two years in eleven divisions. Volumes 3 and 4 of particular importance. Very much a warts-and-all picture.

Ponting, C. (1986) *Whitehall: Tragedy and Farce*, London, Sphere.
Presented as 'the inside story of how Whitehall really works'. Ponting advances 'the thesis . . . that Britain is appallingly badly governed and that the blame for this state of affairs has to be shared by the political class of both major parties and the top mandarins of the Civil Service.' Argues that the Civil Service is always able to

defeat the reformers but this does not stop him setting down his own proposals for 'transforming Whitehall'.

Radcliffe, Lord (1968) 'The lawyer and his times'. In A. E. Sutherland, (ed.), *The Path of Law from 1967*, Cambridge, MA., Harvard University Press.
Another judge who recognises that judges make law but who wants them to keep quiet about it.

Reid, Lord (1972) 'The judge as lawmaker', *The Journal of the Society of Public Teachers of Law*, 12, 22–9.
The title is self-explanatory. Yet another judge prepared to explode the myth that judges only 'declare' the law with the assertion that they 'make' it as well.

Reiner, R. (1985) *The Politics of the Police*, Brighton, Wheatsheaf.
Full and balanced discussion of the history, sociology and politics of policing in Britain that gets beyond the myths, orthodoxies and easy slogans for change. Includes interesting chapters on 'cop culture' and police accountability.

Robertson, K. G. (ed) (1987) *British and American Approaches to Intelligence*, London, Macmillan.
For the most part the essays dwell on safe historical matters, but chapters 10 and 11 deal with the contemporary situation with respect to the law and the politics of the security services in Britain.

Roshier, B. and Teff, H. (1980) *Law and Society in England*, London, Tavistock.
Excellent discussion of the reality of the law in action. Chapter 3 contains important material on police discretion and police power.

Royal Commission on the Police (1962) *Report* Cmnd 1728, London, HMSO.
Set up in the wake of anxieties surrounding the police. The report considered the case for a national police force, the roles of chief constables, local police authorities and the Home Secretary, the relationship between police and public, the complaints system and police pay. Recommendations did not really disturb the established system of police accountability, and the report was complacent as to police–public relations and the problem of complaints.

Scarman, Lord (1982) *The Scarman Report*, Harmondsworth, Penguin.
The liberal judge's sensitive inquiry into the 1981 Brixton disorders. Scarman was critical of the police and 'heavy' police tactics, and he argued that police priority should be given to maintaining public tranquility over strict law enforcement. The report was stuffed with recommendations for improvements (many of which were criticised from the Right and the Left, and some of which have been put into effect) but Scarman rejected the case for the control of the police by locally elected police authorities.

Select Committee on Nationalised Industries (1970) *The Bank of England*, London, HMSO.
Good, hard-hitting, account that focuses on the lack of accountability of the Bank to the democratic side of the state.

Smith, D. (1980) *The Defence of the Realm in the 1980s*, London, Croom Helm.
Good critical account of defence in the eighties.

Smith, D. (1989) *Pressure: How America Runs NATO*, London, Bloomsbury.
Argues that 'NATO is run by the USA; if it were not, it would not work.'

Smith, D. and Smith, R. (1983) *The Economics of Militarism*, London, Pluto.

Powerful analysis and critique of militarism that also includes a careful assessment of the economic consequences of military spending.

Spencer, S. (1985) *Called to Account*, London, National Council for Civil Liberties.
Makes the case for police accountability to locally elected representatives but prepared to set down the case for the status quo as well.

Statement on the Defence Estimates 1989, (1989) Cm 675, I and II, London, HMSO.
Glossy government publication justifying the range of our defence commitments and presenting them in a particular light, but volume II is a useful presentation of up-to-date defence statistics.

Stevens, R. (1970) *Law and Politics*, London, Weidenfeld and Nicolson.
Massive and important study of the House of Lords as a judicial body since 1800. Points out that the Law Lords have an important 'creative' function in making law.

Thompson, E.P. (1980) 'The secret state'. In E.P. Thompson (ed.), *Writing by Candlelight*, London, Merlin, pp. 149–80.
Powerful critique of the security services and their lack of accountability

Treasury and Civil Service Committee (1986) Seventh Report *Civil Servants and Ministers: Duties and Responsibilities*, HC 92, London, HMSO.
The Committee considered the position of ministers and civil servants in the light of the Ponting case. It was mindful of changes in the relationship between civil servants and ministers but wanted 'guidelines for ministers which would set out their duties to Parliament and responsibilities for the Civil Service.' The Government in its response to the Report (Cmnd 9841) saw no need to further define the responsibilities and duties of ministers and was reluctant to see Parliament questioning civil servants.

Treasury and Civil Service Committee (1988) Eighth Report *Acceptance of Outside Appointments by Crown Servants*, HC 302, London, HMSO.
The Committee was anxious about civil servants retiring to take up jobs in industry. It recognised the principle of 'free movement' but wanted to avoid any appearance of 'impropriety' and so advocated a redrafting of the rules. The Government in its response to the Report (Cmnd 9465) saw no need to change the rules to prevent impropriety.

Wright, P. (1987) *Spycatcher*, Australia, Heinemann.
Retired and bitter MI5 counter-espionage officer grumbles about his pension and worries about Soviet spies in the security services but also tells us about 'the Wilson plot' and his own role within it. A harmless enough book but in trying to ban it the government only succeeded in boosting its sales.

Young, H. and Sloman, A. (1982) *No Minister: an Inquiry into the Civil Service*, London, BBC.
Ministers and civil servants talked about the role of the civil service in a number of radio programes. The series concluded that the civil servants were 'the masters' because they were 'the guardians of what they're pleased to call reality', but this begs the question of who defines reality today?

Zander, M. (1989) *A Matter of Justice*, Oxford, Oxford University Press.
Excellent discussion and assessment of the great range of recent developments in the different parts of the legal system. Useful chapter on 'The Judges', and also considers perspectives on the reform of the legal system.

"Down with Marxism and the Communist State!" (Reproduced by kind permission of Rex Features.)

Chapter 7

Capitalism, Marxism and Labourism

The capitalist class rules but does not govern.
> Karl Kautsky (1902) *The Social Revolution*, London, Twentieth
> Century Press, p. 13.

Taken together, as they need to be, these three modes of explanation of the nature of the state – the character of its leading personnel, the pressures exercised by the economically dominant class, and the structural constraints imposed by the mode of production – constitute the Marxist answer to the question why the state should be considered as the 'instrument' of the 'ruling class'.
> Ralph Miliband (1977) *Marxism and Politics*, Oxford, Oxford
> University Press, pp. 73–4.

State power is not a machine or an instrument, a simple object coveted by the various classes; nor is it divided into parts which, if not in the hands of some, must automatically be in the hands of others: rather it is an ensemble of structures.
> Nicos Poulantzas (1973) *Political Power and Social Classes*,
> London, New Left Books, p. 288.

Introduction

Paragraph four of Clause Four of the Labour Party Constitution is printed on the card issued to every member of the Party. Drafted at the Party's 1918 Conference, and reaffirmed by various conferences since, this paragraph states that it is the object of the Party 'To secure for the workers by hand or by brain the full fruits of their industry and the most equitable distribution thereof that may be possible upon the basis of the common ownership of the means of production, distribution, and exchange, and the best obtainable system of popular administration and control of each industry or service.' It is this paragraph which marks the British Labour Party unambiguously as a *socialist* party.

There are, of course, many varieties of socialism, both in theory and in practice. The socialism practiced by bloody tyrants such as Stalin, Mao or

Pol Pot has little in common with the democratic socialism pursued, for example, in Sweden, and the kind of socialism to which Labour's leadership (though not necessarily all of its members) has always been committed – one which emphasises its democratic character. Nevertheless, what all forms of socialism have in common is an antipathy to capitalism and a belief in collective forms of social and economic organisation. It is this position which is reaffirmed by Clause Four of the Party's constitution.

Clause Four commits the Labour Party to bringing about a fundamental change in British society. It does not (as is often imagined) commit the Party to nationalising key productive assets such as land, factories, offices and banks, but it does commit it to socialising them. In other words, these assets are to be seized or compulsorily purchased from their existing owners and placed in some form of 'common ownership' which may, presumably, take the form of worker co-operatives rather than nationalised corporations. Nor does Clause Four commit the Party to bringing about a totally egalitarian society, but it does proclaim the need to achieve the most egalitarian distribution that is possible, and it does assert that all workers should receive in wages and salaries the full value of the goods or services which they produce through their labour (which implies that employers should not be allowed to make profit out of employing them). Finally, Clause Four does not suggest that the Party should pursue a centralised planning strategy, but it does indicate a commitment to planning as the principal means of organising economic activity, and it does believe that such planning should be accountable and democratic. In short, the Labour Party stands for the replacement of capitalism by a system of social ownership, social justice and democratic planning.

In practice, of course, the Party stands for no such thing. Although it has always contained within it a rump of committed socialists who actually believe in the principles of Clause Four, it has always been led by people who have been more or less happy to accommodate themselves to a capitalist economic order and who have sought simply to ameliorate its social effects. There has been (and still is) a commitment to *limited* social ownership (normally through nationalisation), to *limited* redistribution of wealth and income (normally through progressive taxation and welfare provisions), and to *limited* planning (normally by means of national agencies which have been more corporatist than democratic). Today, the British Labour Party is socialist in its formal objectives but social democratic in its practice.

In this chapter, we shall consider why and how the Labour Party has for most of this century been committed in theory to socialism yet has failed to implement this commitment and has today ended up as little more than a pro-capitalist party with a human face. Our way into this analysis is through a discussion of Marxist political theory. There are three reasons for linking a discussion of British Labourism with a discussion of Marxist theory. The first is that Marxism has been one main source of socialist thinking within the Labour Party, and there are still several Marxist groups operating within the Party's constituency and trade union sections. To understand what socialism means, it is essential to understand the basic elements of Marx's theory. The second reason is that debates within British Marxism have for long been dominated by the problem (as they see it) of the Labour Party. Elsewhere in Europe (for example, in Italy, France or Greece), Marxists have addressed themselves to questions of Communist Party strategy, but in Britain the Communist Party has always been very weak and the only conceivable vehicle for achieving a socialist transformation of British society is the Labour Party. The third reason is that Marxist writing represents a major strand of social scientific thinking about the state and political power. This is a perspective which should be considered and evaluated against both liberal-democratic perspectives (discussed in chapters 2 and 4) and so-called 'New Right' perspectives (discussed in chapter 8).

A reading of the Marxist literature on British politics thus fulfills three objectives. It provides us with a statement of what socialism is; it offers an explanation of why the Labour Party has in practice shied away from it; and it represents one of the major academic perspectives on the question of the state and political power.

Marxist Theory: Economics, Politics and Class Struggle

Marxism is both a claim to knowledge and a recipe for action. This is not to deny that the various social sciences may also reflect a desire for change on the part of those who research, write and teach within them, for most social scientists hold strong personal views about the sort of society they would wish to live in and the various ways in which this might be brought about. What is distinctive about Marxism is, however, that it is both a mode of scientific analysis of society and a political movement to change it. From Marx onwards, Marxist intellectuals have consistently sought to relate their theories and ideas to the current practices and strategies of working-class (generally Communist Party) movements. As Marx himself put it: 'The philosophers have only *interpreted* the world, in various ways; the point, however is to *change* it.' In this commitment to what Marxists themselves term 'praxis' (i.e the fusion of theory and practice, and hence of intellectuals and workers), Marxism is distinctive, for none of the social sciences share this belief that a scientific analysis of society only has point in the context of a political struggle to transcend it.

Another feature which is also distinctive about Marxism is that, notwithstanding the many different varieties and nuances of contemporary Marxist thought, it holds to the fundamental assertion that the way in which any society is organised and operates must reflect in some sense the way in which it organises its productive activities. If we are to understand contemporary Marxist analyses of British politics, we must begin by considering what is entailed in this basic axiom of Marx's theory.

Marx arrived at his conclusion that an understanding of the social organisation of production is the key to understanding the organisation of the rest of society by means of a two-step argument. First, he made the 'obvious' point that production is a prerequisite of social organisations. In other words, before a group of people can develop a means of governing themselves, systems of law by which to regulate themselves, religous practices, artistic forms or any other aspect of social organisation, they must organise themselves to produce from their environment the basic necessities of life – the food, clothing, shelter and so on, which are necessary if they are to reproduce themselves. Indeed, Marx argued that what makes human beings unique in the animal world is their capacity consciously to work upon and change their environment. Beavers may build dams and birds their nests, but these activities are simply repeated across the generations. Human beings, by contrast, develop and change their world through their labour, as is evident in the fact that we no longer live in caves, eat our meat raw or rely on clubs and stones as our tools.

The second stage of the argument is that the way in which a group of people organises production will leave its imprint on the way in which they organise other aspects of their collective existence. Production, that is, is not simply prior to other activities but is fundamental in shaping these other activities. This idea has sometimes been expressed by means of an architectural metaphor, for just as the foundation of a building limits and affects the style and dimensions of the construction which is developed upon it, so too the organisation of production in a society constitutes a 'base' which limits and affects the 'superstructure' of government, law, religion, arts and so on which can develop from it.

The organisation of production in any society will, of course, depend to a great extent on the materials which are available in the environment and on the tools, skills and know-how which the members of that society have developed over the generations. It is hardly possible for a society to develop a factory system of production, for example, if it has not developed the tools and knowledge necessary for mining coal, smelting iron, generating power and so on. Marx's argument goes much further than this, however, for he suggests that the productive forces which are available in any society at any one time will tend to shape the way in which productive activity is socially organised. In virtually all human societies up to the present, this organisation has involved a basic division between two classes of people: those who own the means of production and those who provide labour. The nature of the relationship between these two classes has, however, changed as the productive forces have been developed. On the great estates of ancient Rome, for example, the relationship was that of master and slave; in feudal Europe it was that between lord and serf; in contemporary capitalist societies it is that between capitalist and wage-labourer. As the productive forces have developed, so new relations of production have arisen.

Taken together, the 'productive forces' (i.e the technology and materials used in production) and the 'relations of production' (i.e the way in which productive activity is organised through a division between those who own the technology and materials and those who provide the labour) constitute the foundation or 'base' of any society. The 'superstructure' of law, politics and so on which then arises in that society will, in essence, reflect the character of this base. The argument is summarised in a famous passage written by Marx in 1859:

> In the social production of their life, men [*sic*] enter into definite relations of production which . . . correspond to a definite stage of development of the material productive forces. The sum total of these relations of production constitutes the economic structure of society, the real foundation on which rises a legal and political superstructure and to which correspond definite forms of social consciousness.

Marx is, of course, aware that societies with a similar material base may develop different forms of government, different types of law, different cultural characteristics, and so on. Societies organised on the basis of capitalist relations of production, for example, have often varied in their forms of government – Britain has retained a constitutional monarchy, the USA has a Federal republic, Sweden exhibits an advanced form of social democracy, Germany under the Third Reich was dominated by a fascist dictatorship, and so on. What is entailed in this claim, however, is first, that certain forms of government are not possible given a capitalist system of production, and second, that those forms that are possible are, in essence, variations on the same theme.

The argument that certain forms of government are ruled out by a particular system of production is based on the claim that no political system can survive for very long which fundamentally contradicts the essential requirements of the economic system on which it is based. For example, the feudal system of politics and law is essentially incompatible with a developed capitalist economy since capitalism is organised around a contractual relationship between employer and worker, in which both sides are in principle 'free' to seek alternatives in the market, while feudalism sought to bind lord and serf together through a legally enforceable system of mutual obligation. Neither capitalists nor workers would for long put up with a political system which denied the right of the former to lay off workers or the right of the latter to change their source of employment.

The argument that the forms of government which are possible in any mode of production all represent different variations on the same basic pattern, is based on the claim that the political system must reflect and sustain the prevailing relations of production in society. Thus, in a capitalist society, the role of the state – whether it takes the form of a constitutional monarchy, a Federal republic, a social democracy or a fascist dictatorship – must always be the same; namely, to safeguard and promote capitalist production. If, over the long term, the state does not do this, then the economy itself will collapse and the state will collapse with it to be replaced by a new political system which better reflects the requirements of the economy at that time. It therefore follows that, in a capitalist society, the state must attempt to maintain the conditions in which capitalists can make profits, for without profits they cannot invest and without investment they cannot produce. So it is that, whether they be fascists, democrats or monarchists, those who run the machinery of government will in different ways (for example, by shooting trade union leaders or by coming to agreements with them) be obliged to pursue policies which are in the long-term interests of the capitalist class.

The political system (and, indeed, the rest of the 'superstructure') of any society thus reflects the character of its economic organisation. Yet this economic organisation itself undergoes change over time. The mainspring of this change is the development of the productive forces. In feudal Europe, for example, the mode of production was based primarily on a labour-intensive system of agriculture which was organised through the system of serfdom by which those who owned the land allowed those who did not to farm a strip of land for their own subsistence in return for which they were obliged to render a specified amount of labour on the land retained by their overlord. This system was reinforced by a political system through which the landed nobility ruled the country in conjunction with the monarch, by a legal system through which the landed class was able to enforce the obligations owed them by the serfs, by a religious system which taught that such a mode of social organisation had been ordained by God, and so on. All of this was, however, gradually undermined from within by the development of new productive forces. New machines enabled the gradual development of a manufacturing sector. New forms of transport enabled the growth of markets for manufacturers. Innovations in agricultural techniques reduced the reliance on human labour-power in the fields. These and other developments slowly brought about a new system of production based, not on the relation between lord and serf, but on that between industrial capitalist and wage-labourer. A new pattern of capitalist-production relations thus grew up side by side with the old system of feudal-production relations.

As the new capitalist mode of production matured within feudal society, so the old feudal relations of production, expressed through the feudal state, came to represent an intolerable blockage to its further development. The rising capitalist class required a free labour force but this was hindered by feudal relations of serfdom; they required venture capital yet usury was prohibited under feudal law and religion; they demanded a say in running the country but found their paths blocked by an hereditary system of government. Thus, a system which had at one time reinforced the old system of production was now holding the new one back, and revolution became inevitable. In country after country, whether peacefully or by violent means, the old rulling class of feudal landowners was overthrown to be replaced by a new political system which better reflected the requirements of the new dominant class of capitalists.

According to Marx, much the same process is now under way in capitalist societies. Indeed, the process has speeded up because capitalism has developed the productive forces much faster than in any previous period. This is because capitalism is based on competition for markets between different producers, each of whom is keen to undercut his or her competitors by investing in the newest labour-saving technology, and this provides an enormous stimulus to technological innovation. Yet, as in the feudal era, the more the productive forces are developed, the more they encounter the limits of the existing relations of production, and the more quickly they bring into existence the class (in this case, the proletariat) which will eventually lead the revolution against the dominant class. Thus today, our productive capacity is truly staggering yet a system of production in which nothing can be produced unless a profit can be realised from it has created a situation in which much of this capacity lies idle while basic human needs remain unfulfilled. Over a million of workers in Britain are unemployed at the same time as desperate housing need goes unmet, the hospital service is crippled by lack of staff and factories containing millions of pounds worth of machinery are left to rot. For present-day Marxists, such evidence is indicative of the growing contradiction between the productive forces (which, they suggest, have developed to a point where we could meet the basic needs of everybody in society) and capitalist social relations (which prevent this technology from being used to bring about such a result), and this contradiction will, it is felt, eventually result in the revolutionary overthrow of the entire capitalist system by the proletariat.

The role of the state in all this is to attempt to safeguard the interests of the capitalist class (the 'bourgeoisie') as a whole, just as the feudal state represented the interests of the feudal landowners right up to the point at which it was overthrown. This does not mean that the state is simply manipulated by capitalists. Indeed, this would not be possible since the capitalist class is internally fragmented (individual producers compete with each other and there are fundamental conflicts of interest between different types of capitalists such as industrialists and financiers). The state, therefore, must act as the representative of the capitalist class as a whole, even if this means that at times it follows a course of action of which particular sections of the capitalist class strongly disapprove. The state is in this sense, 'a committee for managing the *common* affairs of the *whole* bourgeoisie'.

As for the proletariat, it follows from this analysis that little can be achieved through the pursuit of political demands within the existing state system. Both Marx and Engels recognised that concessions could be won by the working class within a capitalist system of parliamentary democracy, and Engels even went so far as to suggest that an eventual socialist revolution in Britain could possibly come about through the electoral process, but in general both writers were adamant that the very nature of the capitalist state was such as to render parliamentary action largely ineffective. However it comes about, a proletarian revolution must involve the abolition of the state in its present form and its replacement by a form of political organisation, such as that of the ill-fated Paris Commune in 1871, which will be consistent with the development of socialist relations of production in which all producers own in common the productive resources of their society. Just as the capitalist class had to replace the feudal state apparatus with a 'bourgeois' system of representative government which would safeguard its class interests, so the proletariat must replace the capitalist state with a form of political organisation which expresses and reinforces the new socialised mode of production.

Capitalist Domination of the British State

The obvious question to arise out of Marx's theory is how the state in a society such as that of Britain manages to safeguard the interests of the capitalist class. What is the mechanism by which this is achieved (assuming, of course, that it is achieved)? There is, in fact, considerable dispute within Marxism about how to answer this question, and there has been an unfortunate tendency for theoretical innovation to race ahead of our empirical knowledge about how the political system actually operates.

Most Marxist analyses begin by drawing two important distinctions. The first (which we have already noted in earlier chapters) is that between the 'state' and the 'government'. The second is that between the 'state' and 'civil society'.

In his, by now, classic study of the British state (*The State in Capitalist Society*), Ralph Miliband warns against any confusion between the terms 'state' and 'government'. The government, he says, is just one among several institutions which together make up the system of state power, and while the government is the public face and official voice of the state, it is not necessarily its most powerful or significant element. To gain control of the government (for example, by winning a general election) is no guarantee of gaining control of the state. Thus, in addition to government, the state system also comprises what we have termed the 'secret state': a vast system of administration (including the Civil Service the public corporations and nationalised industries, the Bank of England etc.), the military and the police force, and the judiciary, as well as the system of local and regional authorities, and the representative assemblies such as the Houses of Parliament. Any analysis of the operation of the British state must, therefore, encompass all of these interrelated institutions.

What such an analysis must also accomplish, however, is the identification of the relationship between these state institutions and the wider society from which they are, in a sense, 'set apart'. There is no necessary and direct relationship in capitalist societies between economic power and state power. In earlier societies such as those of feudal Europe or ancient Rome, those who owned the means of production also 'owned' the state in that there was a direct relationship between one's social position (for example, as a member of the landed aristocracy) and one's political position. In these societies, the state was in the hands of just one class whose members alone enjoyed the right to develop policies and make laws. The relation between economic and political domination was thus clear and unambiguous, for the two were synonymous. This is not the case, however, in modern capitalist societies such as Britain where there is a formal separation between state power and 'civil society' and where political representation is organised, not on the basis of one's class membership, but according to a principle of one citizen, one vote.

Taken together, these distinctions between 'government', 'state' and 'society' help to define the basic problem to which all Marxist analyses of British politics have been addressed: how does the capitalist class in Britain ensure that the state operates in its collective long-term interests when the state itself is made up of a number of different and partially autonomous institutions, and when these institutions are formally set apart from any exclusive control by those who own the means of production? How can a single class, the members of which represent only a small minority of the total population, ensure that popularly-elected governments pursue policies which favour it, that appointed 'independent' judges interpret laws in its favour, that administrators adopt practices which take account of it, that the police and armed forces are used to protect it, and so on?

Some of the 'classical' statements of Marxist political theory suggest that the capitalist class in some way directly controls the various arms of the state in just the same way as earlier ruling classes have controlled earlier forms of states. There are traces of such an argument in Engels' view that: 'The state is nothing but a machine for the oppression of one class by another.' And in Lenin's assertion that: 'The state is a particular form of organization of force; it is the organization of violence for the purpose of holding down some class.' Such stark statements are, however, less common in the contemporary Marxist literature where it is recognised that the state is not simply a tool to be manipulated at will by those who own the means of production, but rather operates to some extent autonomously while at the same time safeguarding the fundamental interests of the capitalist class.

Perhaps the clearest exposition of this rather more subtle position is that provided by Miliband who suggests: 'While the state does act, in Marxist terms, *on behalf* of the ruling class, it does not for the most part act *at its behest*.' He identifies three basic mechanisms by which this comes about.

The occupancy of key state positions

Miliband argues that one reason why a formally autonomous state generally operates on behalf of the capitalist class is that its key positions are held by members of that class or by others whose outlooks are broadly compatible with the interests of capitalists.

This argument is perhaps at its weakest when applied to the elected institutions of the state – Parliament, government and local councils – for the growth of the Labour Party during the twentieth century has brought into leading political positions men and women who, if not fully representative of the mass of the population in terms of their backgrounds, are hardly drawn from traditional capitalist families either. Miliband, of course, is aware of this, but argues that at least three factors can be identified which suggest that representation of non-capitalist interests in elected agencies of the state has done little to undermine capitalist interests.

The first is that Parliament, and elected assemblies at the local level, are weak and have become progressively weaker as time has gone on such that very little power is vested in ordinary elected members. The second is that radicals have successfully been held in check within these assemblies and within government – the radical MP at Westminster finds herself or himself cut off from the support of rank-and-file activists and subject to the intense pressures towards conforming with established parliamentary procedures and ways of thinking, while Left-wing socialists in local authorities are more in touch with radical activists but find themselves at the mercy of central government dictates and financing (see chapter 12). The third is that one major political party (the Conservatives) is generally predisposed to favour the interests of capital while the other (the Labour Party) has been reluctant to confront them and has preferred to pursue a mildly reformist strategy in which the continuation of capitalism is never seriously questioned. The result has been that the alternation of governments between different parties has had little fundamental impact on capitalist relations of production.

Nevertheless, Miliband does recognise that the elected agencies of the state do sometimes respond to popular pressures and aspirations expressed through the ballot box or through lobbying and other organised activities. Indeed, he suggests that the stability of the system as a whole depends upon this ability of governments to make concessions to groups other than the capitalist class in that this helps to contain pressure from below and to keep it within manageable limits. The other institutions of the state, of course, are not subject to these diverse and competing pressures, and he suggests that it is their task to ensure that elected governments do not stray too far from an orthodox pro-capitalist line: 'Universal suffrage brings a government to office: the rest of the state system sees to it that the consequences are not so drastic as to affect conservative continuity.'

Drawing on various sociological studies of elite recruitment, he shows that the top civil servants, the police and military leaders, the judiciary and other groups such as those in control of the media who are in a position to influence public opinion all are drawn from bourgeois backgrounds or else are socialised into bourgeois values through their schooling and their advancement up the career hierarchies. His argument here, of course, is only as strong as the data on which he relies, yet these studies are severely limited in that they have rarely provided evidence to show what Miliband claims they show – namely, that all these people subscribe to a 'narrow' range of political values from 'moderate Labour' at one extreme to 'reactionary Conservative' at the other. Nevertheless, we can probably safely assume that for most of them this is indeed the case, if only because most people in the country as a whole fit into much the same continuum, which is perhaps not as 'narrow' as Miliband tries to make out.

Miliband's first argument, then, is that governments generally seek to support capitalist interests and that, when there is the slightest danger that popular pressure might blow them off course, the remainder of the state apparatus, staffed by solidly conservative individuals, will bring them back into line. Disappointingly, he gives little actual evidence for such assertions, but this perhaps does not matter too much since this first argument is probably the least significant of the three he develops to support his thesis.

The political power of business interests

We saw in chapter 4 that pluralist interpretations of British politics emphasise the range of diverse pressures, organised through shifting alliances and coalitions of interests, to which the government and other elected agencies, such as local authorities, are constantly subject. Miliband does not deny this. Nor, indeed, does he deny that organised labour is often prominent among pressure groups in Britain, for he notes that no government can afford simply to ignore organisations such as the trade unions and the TUC which claim to represent the interests of millions of workers. What he does deny, however, is the assumption which is often implicit in pluralist theories that the different interests which pressure government and other state agencies are of comparable power, and the assertion in such theories that no one interest routinely prevails over a range of policy issues. There is, he suggests, a competition for the ear of government, but it is a one-sided competition in which the rules are biased, the referee is biased and the favoured side – big business – enjoys a goal start. Big business, in other words, is a uniquely influential pressure group in Britain.

The arguments and evidence which Miliband puts forward to support this view are mostly familiar. Business, he points out, is the wealthiest of all organised interests in society, and this has at times enabled it to mount very expensive campaigns such as those in the 1950s against steel nationalisation and in the 1970s against rather half-hearted Labour Party proposals to take the major banks into public ownership. It is also a major source of funding for the Conservative Party and can generally rely on the strong support of many MPs, a substantial majority in the House of Lords, most of the national and provincial press and even the Royal Family whose members have increasingly taken to making pronouncements in favour of private enterprise. Business also exerts a pervasive yet virtually invisible influence over state institutions by virtue of its strategic importance in controlling production, for all governments know that their programmes and their survival depends on continued investment and growth in the private sector. No government can single-mindedly pursue policies which result in a loss of business confidence; a run on the pound, a shift in the balance of payments and a quite word of advice from the Governor of the Bank of England will normally suffice to encourage governments to drop those policies which threaten to undermine capitalist profitability. Where this is not enough, British capitalists can always rely on pressures from overseas to bring British governments to heel; the International Monetary Fund effectively buried the Labour government's social programme in 1976 by imposing conditions of financial orthodoxy on a loan which it granted at that time, and together with other international agencies such as the European Community (discussed in chapter 12), pressures from other governments, and the impact of decisions taken by international currency speculators, multi-national corporations and the like, such external influence and control works strongly against any moves which are liable to threaten levels of profitability or the sanctity of private property.

Such arguments are indeed strong ones and, paradoxically perhaps, they appear all the stronger at times of economic recession when the power of organised labour is weakened by unemployment (as unemployment grew through 1981, for example, male trade union membership fell by a staggering 8 per cent) and the pressure to 'revitalise the economy' by adopting policies favourable to big business is almost irresistible. As the influential Marxist and Labour Party activist Harold Laski noted during the Great Depression of the 1930s, popular pressures for social reform and improved living standards can often be accommodated during periods of economic growth, but at times of economic contraction, governments' responsiveness to democratically articulated demands must take second place to the need to increase private-sector profits.

For many Marxists, however, the clearest evidence for the continued and highly successful pressure brought to bear by big business upon the state concerns the fiscal policies of successive British governments. In a book published in 1961, Sam Aaronovitch argued that 'finance capital' (by which he meant the major banking and industrial companies which he saw as fused through their interlocking directorships) constituted the British 'ruling class', and as evidence for this he pointed to the long-standing commitment of both Conservative and Labour administrations to maintaining the overseas value of the pound sterling and keeping a strong overall balance of payments. Finance capital, he suggested, seeks to invest in areas of highest potential return, and these have often been overseas in countries where labour is cheaper and pickings are richer. In order to pursue such investments, big business desires first, full convertibility of currencies to allow it to change its pounds into whatever local currency is needed for its overseas investments; second, a liberal system of exchange controls to allow it to export as much money as it wishes; third, a strong pound so that its profits do not decrease in value when it converts its overseas earnings back into sterling; and fourth, an equilibrium or surplus on the balance of payments to cover the drain of money going overseas and thereby avoid any devaluation of the currency. 'In all this', he concludes, 'it has been evident that the state apparatus has been occupied with furthering the aims of finance capital. The Treasury, the Board of Trade and Cabinet have shared the same views as "the City".'

Subsequent events and later analyses have both supported Aaronovitch's basic argument. As we shall see in chapter 9, for example, the Labour government elected in 1964 was so committed to maintaining the value of the pound that it struggled for three years to avoid the devaluation which had to come given the declining competitiveness of British industry in overseas markets, and during this time most of its social and economic programme was sacrificed to this end. Throughout the post-war period, governments have confronted balance of payments crises which have been caused by massive outflows of money to finance overseas investments, and invariably they have responded by cutting domestic demand in an attempt to reduce imports rather than by cutting overseas spending.

This predisposition on the part of British governments to support major financial interests has never been clearer than under the Conservative governments from 1979 onwards. One of the government's first acts following its election in 1979 was to abolish all exchange controls, and this resulted in a flood of money overseas (overseas investment increased ten fold in four years). Indeed, so much money went overseas during the 1980s that by 1990 Britain recorded a deficit on its 'invisible' balance of payments account for the first time since the Industrial Revolution. The government also relied throughout the eighties on a policy of high interest rates to curb inflation, and while this helped maintain a (relatively) strong pound, it did so by making borrowing prohibitively expensive for many industrial firms.

Those who have benefited from such policies have been the big companies which can seize overseas investment opportunities and which do not need to borrow on the British market. Those who have lost have been the smaller companies whose products have been priced out of world markets by an over-valued pound and who rely on domestic borrowing to finance their expansion. Such evidence points strongly to the validity of Miliband's assertion that big business has generally been able to secure from government commitments which support its financial interest, even at the cost of further weakening an already crippled home economy.

The constraints of a capitalist system

The third and final factor cited by Miliband to explain why and how the state in Britain comes to be subordinated to the requirements of major capitalist interests is also the most significant. Even if the people who occupy the key positions in the state system were radicalised overnight and big-business pressure were to cease, this third factor alone would ensure a continuing bias towards capital, for the main reason that the interests of big capital are safeguarded by the state is simply that the state is charged with administering a system which itself generates a continuing advantage to those who own the means of production. For as long as those who control the state take as given the continuation of a system based on the capitalist organisation of production, capitalist interests will continue to be the main beneficiaries.

Miliband notes that political leaders, media commentators and others often tacitly equate business interests with the 'national interest', assuming that what is good for business is also good for Britain as a whole. This, he suggests, is no simple delusion, for, given a capitalist system, the whole society does indeed depend on the vitality of the private sector. If capital does not continue to make profit, then investment will fall away, unemployment will rise and government will lose the tax revenue on which it depends in order to finance schools, hospitals, defence and all other policies. When politicans and others tell the electorate that we must 'tighten our belts', accept cuts in public services, see our wages reduced and curb the tendency to strike in order that business may increase its profits, they are simply expressing the logic of a system of production in which profits must be sustained if economic activity is to continue. When Mrs Thatcher repeated time and again to the unemployed, and to those reliant on declining public services and provisions, that there was no alternative to her policies, she was appealing to this same logic, for if business must make profit before it will produce, and if profits are being eroded by 'high' wages, 'high' taxes and a surplus of 'inefficient' labour, then it does indeed follow that wages must be driven down, government spending must be reduced and workers must be made redundant – if the system itself is taken as given.

Clearly, the question of who is in control of the state and of which groups are most able to pressurise them will make some difference to how governments respond to the requirements of capital. Labour and Conservative administrations for example, may be expected to respond more or less enthusiastically and with lesser or greater coercion to the dictates of capitalist profitability. At the end of the day, however, it seems that the values, wishes and concerns of those who run the state count for very little: as Miliband concludes: 'The trouble does not lie in the wishes and intentions of power-holders, but in the fact that the reformers . . . are the prisoners, and usually the willing prisoners, of an economic and social framework which necessarily turns their reforming proclamations, however sincerely meant, into verbiage.'

It is in the analysis of this system of constraints that Marxist work is most distinctive. Miliband's first two factors – the identity of those who run the system and the relative power of different organised interests which influence it from the outside – have also been examined in work which is by no means Marxist in its orientation. One does not have to accept any of Marx's arguments concerning the inevitability of class struggle and the primacy of the economy to recognise the significance of the narrowness of recruitment into key state positions or of the wealth and contacts enjoyed by business organisations. Where Marxist political analysis makes its major contribution is in the recognition that the major explanation for what happens in the political system may lie, not in what individuals in that system do, but in the economic constraints which a capitalist system of production places on their actions. In this way, the focus of analysis shifts from politics to the economy and from individual actions to system constraints – a shift which reflects Marx's argument that the political 'superstructure' is in some way dependent upon the economic 'base' which sustains it and from which it derives.

Such a shift of focus raises again the problem concerning the point at which the power of individuals ends and the constraints of the system begin. How much scope for action does a Prime Minister, a top civil servant or the head of a nationalised industry have in shaping the future course of events? How much difference does it really make whether the country is governed by a Right-wing Conservative or a reforming Labour administration? Do the requirements of a capitalist economic system effectively preclude any but the most minor of political changes? Such questions go to the very heart of Marxist analysis in that they refer to the nature of the relationship between economic and political organisation. Just how determinate is the 'determinate' relationship between economics and politics? Can the political system operate to some extent autonomously of the economic system and if so, what degree of discretion do political leaders enjoy when it comes to shaping policies?

Miliband himself is rather unclear on all this. He insists that the state is not totally constrained by the capitalist system in which it operates, that individuals in key positions do have some power to shape events independently of the compelling logic of the system in which they find themselves, and that the state cannot simply therefore be seen as the instrument of those who own the means of production. Those who control the state enjoy some degree of freedom in deciding how best to serve the interests of the capitalist class, and their decisions may not always meet with the approval of that class. They may, furthermore, sometimes pay attention to groups other than the capitalist class and make concessions to their demands even where this runs counter to the immediate interests of capital (for example, by increasing trade union rights or by providing services which involve increased taxation on profits):

The state and those who were acting on its behalf did not always intervene for the specific purpose of helping capitalism, much less of helping capitalists for whom power-holders . . . have often had much contempt and dislike. The question is not one of purpose or attitude but of 'structural constraints'; or rather that purposes and attitudes, which can make *some* difference, and in special circumstances a considerable difference, must nevertheless take careful account of the socio-economic system which forms the context of the political system and of state action.

What remains unclear in this passage, however, is how much is 'some' difference, and what are the 'special circumstances' in which 'some' difference becomes 'considerable'? How are we to recognise a situation in which power-holders may be deemed responsible for the outcomes of the policies they have pursued?

In part, the problem here reflects a confusion over the notion of 'constraints', for it is important to distinguish 'structural constraints', (about which we can literally do nothing) and 'rational constraints' (which prevent us from doing anything given the values and beliefs we hold). Rational constraints clearly do not absolve the individual of responsibility for his or her actions, for in this case a choice of action is available even though the individual concerned may consider only one alternative acceptable. The distinction between the two notions of 'constraints' is never clear in Miliband's work, however, for although he talks of political leaders as 'willing prisoners' of the capitalist system, he shrinks away from analysing the extent to which they are willing and the extent to which they are prisoners.

In part too, the problem reflects a lack of good empirical research by Marxists on what the British state actually does. Thus one way of deciding whether those who run the state are responsible for any given outcome is to investigate instances where they have attempted to fly in the face of system constraints. It may, of course, be difficult to find such instances given Miliband's assertion that no Labour government has ever been totally committed to carrying through a socialist programme – i.e. the constraints have never been fully tested. Be this as it may, there have been governments, in Britain and abroad, which have changed capitalist societies in rather important ways – the post-war Attlee government is one example, and (albeit in a very different sense) the 1979 Thatcher government is another. The Attlee administration nationalised large sectors of the economy while the Thatcher administration privatised others; the former created a network of welfare provisions which the latter either dismantled or reformed; and so on. The question is whether and to what extent the condition of the British economy in 1945 and in the early 1980s necessitated such changes, and Miliband's analysis makes it almost impossible to provide an answer.

There is, in all of Miliband's work, a failure to grapple with the relationship between power and constraint, autonomy and determinism, active choices and imperatives. The result, when he does consider what particular governments have done, is that he shifts inconsistently and unpredictably between blaming the individuals and blaming the system, at one point attributing the failings of socialist governments to the 'ideological dispositions' of those who ran them, and at another denying that people's beliefs and values are of any great significance. This also means that we are left with few indications as to whether a socialist transformation of British society is possible on the basis of a parliamentary strategy. In his book on *Capitalist Democracy in Britain*, for example, he recognises that no extra-parliamentary revolutionary strategy is open, asserts that a parliamentary road to socialism is 'a very unlikely prospect', yet concludes that 'a strong and unambiguous political force on the Left is . . . indispensible for the achievement of great economic and social changes'. How such change is to be brought about remains a mystery, not least to Miliband himself. Marxist 'praxis', it seems, has here ground to a halt.

The Relative Autonomy of the State

One response to such problems from within recent Marxist theory has been to deny altogether the significance of individuals in politics. According to this view, which was most fully elaborated from the late 1960s onwards by a Greek Marxist, Nicos Poulantzas, the personalities of Prime Ministers, the club memberships of Cabinet ministers, the prejudices of judges and the maze of informal contacts between business and political leaders cannot explain the inherent class bias in the operation of the capitalist state. It is to the system, and not the individuals within it, that we should look if we seek to understand why the state operates in the long-term interests of big corporate capital. Put another way, the constraints on individuals are over-whelmingly 'structural' in character such that they can do little other than fall in line with the logic of the system.

In an intermittent, but protracted, debate with Miliband in the pages of the Marxist journal, *New Left Review*, Poulantzas suggested that the evidence cited by Miliband concerning the class backgrounds of those who run the state should be seen, not as the cause but as the effect of class bias in the state's mode of operation. It is because it is a capitalist state that it tends to be staffed by people sympathetic to the capitalist class, not vice versa. In this way, Poulantzas echoed Marx himself when he wrote in the preface to the first volume of *Capital*:

> I do not by any means depict the capitalist and the landowner in rosy colours. But individuals are dealt with here only in so far as they are the personifications of economic categories, the bearers of particular class relations and interests. My standpoint . . . can less than any other make the individual responsible for relations whose creature he [*sic*] remains.

Individuals, in other words, are 'slotted into' already existing sets of social relations which they can do little to change. Capitalists, whether they be altruistic Quakers or grasping tycoons, must still act as capitalists, for they are part of a system of production which demands that they keep their labour costs down by cutting wages if they can and by investing in machines that throw their employees out of work, no matter how unhappy they may be about doing these things. Similarly, those who occupy positions within the state are also part of this same system and, whether they be tories or socialists, this means that they are obliged to follow the logic of that system in what they do.

For Poulantzas, therefore, individuals are merely agents of the system in which they find themselves. They 'personify' this system in that they are the means through which the system operates. To understand why they do what they do, it follows that we should not investigate their personal motives for action, but rather the nature of the system of which their actions are merely the expression.

Poulantzas begins his analysis of the system by distinguishing between capitalist societies as they actually exist (what he terms 'social formations') and a theoretical abstract model of a 'pure' capitalist system (which he terms a 'capitalist mode of production'). He suggests that a pure capitalist mode of production would consist of three interrelated subsystems or 'levels' – an economic system, a political system and a system of ideology. In a purely capitalist economy there would be only two classes, capitalists and workers, for capitalism is a system of wage labour in which those who own the factories, banks, shops and offices make profits through the direct or indirect exploitation of those who sell their labour-power in return for a wage. In a capitalist political system, the role of the state would be to regulate the system as a whole in order to maintain the conditions in which this system of wage labour could function, and in the ideological system, institutions such as schools, churches and the mass media would function in order to legitimate this system of wage labour.

Now Poulantzas recognises that actual societies are more messy and confused than this model suggests. This is because different countries with different histories all represent a mixture of different 'modes of production' – no country is purely capitalist. In France, for example, there is still a substantial independent peasantry, a legacy from an earlier pre-capitalist period. Similarly in Britain there is still a landed aristocracy and a monarchy which became established during the feudal era. All countries also contain people such as independent craft workers and the self-employed – groups which arose out of the transition from feudalism to capitalism and which are neither purely capitalist nor purely proletarian. Nowhere, therefore, is the economy organised on purely capitalist lines, and this is reflected in the political and ideological systems of these countries (an obvious example in Britain being the continued existence of the House of Lords and the persistence of aristocratic festivals such as Henley and Ascot).

Although a country like Britain contains elements and traces of several different 'modes of production', Poulantzas nevertheless argues that it is predominantly capitalist in which case the abstract model of a pure capitalist mode of production is the best way of analysing how the system works.

According to this model, the three 'levels' of the system – the economic, the political and the ideological – are related in such a way that what happens in one will affect what happens in the other two. Poulantzas is keen to escape from the traditional and, in his view, over-simplistic notion in Marxist theory that the organisation of the 'economic base' determines what goes on in the 'superstructure' of the state and ideology. He recognises that the organisation of the economy will influence the way in which the three levels operate and relate to each other – in a feudal system, for example, the ideological level will have a particularly important part to play because the economic organisation of serfdom is so blatantly biased towards the landowners that institutions such as the church will be crucial in justifying this to those who suffer from it. But having said this, he insists that each of the three levels has its own autonomy. Thus, what the state does in a capitalist society will certainly be influenced by economic factors, but developments at the level of the economy will not lead directly to political responses. Furthermore, political developments themselves may to some extent take on their own momentum and this will, in turn, influence the organisation of the economy.

All of this sounds very complex, but the basic idea is simple enough. In Britain, for example, the state has, in recent years, obviously been affected by the decline of profitability in the economy, but the economic problems faced by capitalist firms have not led directly to the adoption of particular policies demanded by capitalists. From the mid-1960s onwards, British governments have tackled economic problems in a variety of ways. We have had controls on incomes and prices, both compulsory and voluntary, and the abandonment of such controls. Firms have been nationalised and privatised, company profits have been bolstered by grants and weakened by taxation, the state has bought shares in some companies and sold shares in others, interest rates have been held down or pushed up, and so on. What all this shows is first, that the actions of the state cannot simply be deduced from the nature of the economy; second, that the state is clearly influenced by factors other than the demands of capitalists; third, that different sections of the capitalist class will be more or less pleased or displeased with what the state does at any one time; and fourth, that the actions of the state are not simply a response to economic developments but themselves influence the future course of those developments. The political system is, in other words, *relatively autonomous* of the economy and hence of the dominant economic class.

According to Poulantzas, a relationship of 'relative autonomy' between the economic and political levels, and hence between big capital and the state, is a necessary feature of capitalist societies if the state is to perform the function required of it by the system of which it forms a part. As we have already seen, the function of the political level in the capitalist mode of production is to regulate the system as a whole, to smooth out problems which may arise to threaten future profitability. The major problem, of course, arises out of the perpetual conflict betweeen capitalists and workers. These two classes are tied together in an inherently antagonistic relationship. They need each other, for capitalists need workers to supply the labour-power to run their machines, and workers need capitalists to supply the means of production for them to work with. Yet this mutual dependency is founded on a relationship of exploitation in which capitalists try to keep wages down so as to maximise the profit which they can extract from their employees' labour, while workers will constantly seek to retain in wages as much as they can of the value which they have created for their employers through their labour. Class struggle between the two is thus inscribed in the very fabric of capitalist societies and is reflected all the time in all areas of life – in wage negotiations and strikes, in worker absenteeism and 'skiving', in political elections, in the pages of the Press and the studios of the television companies, in pulpits, in classrooms, in supermarkets, in leisure pursuits.

It is the state's role, not to eliminate class struggle (for this is impossible), but to regulate it, to keep it within manageable proportions and to head off any direct challenge to the system of production. Such regulation is only possible if the state has some degree of autonomy from the dominant class, for it needs room for manoeuvre, scope for flexibility. Given this relative autonomy, the state is then able to do two things.

1 It can work in a coherent way on behalf of capitalist interests which are themselves fragmented and lacking in cohesion, and in this way ensure that the long-term interests of the class are safeguarded even if in the short term certain members of that class are unhappy about the decisions being taken.
2 It can work to disorganise the working class, to bring about divisions where none previously existed and to wrong-foot working-class demands for change by making short-term concessions which defuse conflict and buy off those whose complaints are loudest. And precisely because the state does sometimes act against the short-term interests of one or other section of the capitalist class and does sometimes make concessions to working-class demands, it is able to represent itself as neutral, as the voice of the people as a whole – in short, as a responsive liberal-democratic state in a pluralist society.

The question which all this raises, of course, is, how does it do it? We have already seen that Poulantzas dismisses as insignificant any analysis which focuses on individuals as the causes of state action, so where is the mechanism by which the state acts to ensure that the long-term conditions of capitalist profitability are safeguarded? It is one thing to identify the 'function' which the state 'must' perform in a capitalist system, but quite another to identify the mechanism which ensures that this function will in fact be discharged.

For Poulantzas, the mechanism is class struggle. Indeed, he argues, in a way which may initially seem puzzling, that the state is not a 'thing' which can be controlled by individuals, but is rather the expression of the relation between classes at any one time. In saying this, he is not of course denying that state institutions – the Civil Service, Parliament and the rest – exist, but is simply suggesting that what these institutions do will reflect the relative strengths of workers and capitalists in the society as a whole at any given time. Thus, at times when the working class is relatively strong and its demands cannot be ignored, state policies will reflect this strength (for example, through the introduction of social reforms, a liberalisation of trade union law, improvements in the quality of welfare services, action to curb some of the worst excesses of landlords or employers and so on). At times when the working class is relatively weak, however, such measures will be reversed or diluted in order to bolster capitalist profitability. By responding in this way, fundamental challenges to the capitalist system itself are headed off and the long-term security of that system is safeguarded at the cost of short-term concessions on the part of the capitalist class, or sections of it.

This argument can be illustrated with reference to the years between 1974 and 1980 in Britain. Despite a deepening recession, the working class in Britain was still relatively strong in 1974 and groups of workers (notably the miners) were able to resist government attempts to hold down wages. This resistance came to a head in the miners' strike of that year when coal deliveries to power stations were successfully disrupted to a point where the rest of industry was forced onto a 3-day working week. The Prime Minister at that time, Edward Heath, called an election and was defeated, and for two years after that, the Labour administration which replaced him presided over a 'wages explosion' coupled with a spate of reforms in favour of workers in general and organised labour in particular. By 1979, however, the crisis of profitability (which was exacerbated by these reforms) had reached a point at which, pressured by the International Monetary Fund, the Labour government began to reduce public spending and introduced a new supposedly 'voluntary' incomes policy. By this time, worker militancy had successfully been bought off, and by 1978/9, when various groups of low-paid workers attempted to force an improvement in wages through strike action, rising unemployment had severely weakened the unions to a point at which they could no longer force concessions. With the return of a Conservative government in 1979, the resurgence of the capitalist class took on a new impetus as wages were further reduced and unemployment rose in an attempt to restore profitability while the state reduced taxation on companies by dismantling large areas of welfare provision.

This example, while illustrating Poulantzas's argument that the state is an expression of class relations rather than of the motives of those who control it, also serves to point to some of the major difficulties in applying his analysis. Four points in particular may be noted.

1 The argument is circular. If the ralative power of the two main classes is held to be the cause of state actions, then we clearly need to be able to assess when the working class is strong and when it is weak. The only way in which we can do this, however, is by looking at what the state does. Thus, for example, the judgement that the working class was strong in 1974–6 depends entirely on the fact that concessions were being made to it during this period, but it could presumably equally be argued that the working class was weak and that a Labour government chose to protect and strengthen it! It seems difficult if not impossible to find evidence to support the view that class struggle causes state outcomes rather than the other way round.

2 The argument is tautologous. To argue that the state is 'relatively auto-nomous' of the dominant economic class is to have your cake and eat it since such an argument can never be disproved. Evidence that the state has acted in the interests of the working class can be 'explained' in terms of the 'autonomy' which it enjoys, while evidence that the capitalist class has benefited can be 'explained' by the fact that this autonomy is only 'relative'. Poulantzas fails to provide any criteria by means of which his theory can be tested empirically; it is true by definition and therefore of limited use in trying to understand any given example of state action.

3 The argument is incomplete. We have seen that Poulantzas argues that the function of the state in a capitalist system must be to safeguard the interests of the dominant economic class in the long run. The mechanism by which this function comes to be carried out is class struggle. But on what ground are we to believe that class struggle (the cause) will always lead in the end to the reassertion of capitalist interests (the effect)? It is plausible, as the example of the 1974–80 period shows, to suggest that working-class strength may lead to reforms which reduce working-class militancy and thus pave the way for the reassertion of capitalist interests. But surely it is equally plausible to suggest that working-class strength may lead to reforms which strengthen that class's resolve to go for even more reforms leading eventually to the transcendence of capitalism itself. Poulantzas fails to show any necessary connection between the cause and the effect posited by his theory. This, we would suggest, is an inevitable failing of any theory which refuses to take account of individuals' actions, for 'the system' simply does not work mechanically, and the way in which the state responds to a shifting balance of class relations will depend crucially on the values and beliefs of those taking the decisions. To deny that it will make any significant difference whether John Major or Neil Kinnock is Prime Minister or whether the Cabinet and the back-benches are filled with old Etonians or Trotskyist members of the Militant Tendency is as absurd as the opposite argument that such people can do exactly what they want without tak-ing into account the economic context in which they make their decisions. The problem with Miliband's analysis, it will be recalled, was not that he asserted the importance of both people and the system but that he failed to give any clue about how their relative importance might be assessed. To respond to this pro-blem by denying that people have any importance is to duck the issue rather than resolve it.

4 The argument is too narrow. The causal element in political analysis is, for Poulantzas, class struggle. When we consider any particular period in British politics, however, it is immediately obvious that many other groups, apart from capital and labour, are involved in struggle and that many issues other than questions of wages or union reform or taxation, come to dominate political argument. Poulantzas himself recognises this and attempts to argue that all political movements in some way 'represent' the major class interests in society even though they are not organised directly on class lines. Such an argument is, however, unsupportable. From the 1970s onwards in Britain, many issues have surfaced in the political system which simply cannot be analysed through the categories of Marxist class theory. The civil war in Nor-thern Ireland has involved, not capitalists and workers, but Catholics and Pro-

testants, Republicans and Loyalists. The emergence of green issues in the late eighties cannot be understood through an analysis of the conflict between capital and labour, nor can many issues concerning the rights of women or blacks or youth. One response by Marxists to this problem has been to assert that the state or the capitalist class has in some way engineered such divisions in order to set worker against worker,and thus blind the working class as a whole to its shared interests and common political aims. Such an argument is, however, arrogant and involves a surprisingly derogatory view of working-class people who, it is assumed, are too dulled by ruling-class ideological manipulation to see where their true interests lie. Class *is* a crucially important factor in British politics, but this does not allow us to represent all political conflicts as in some way class-based.

The major problem in Poulantzas's work stems from his refusal to accept that individuals do make a difference to the way in which the system works. Miliband is right: we cannot understand why the state does what it does unless we take account of both the system of which it forms a part and the individuals who run it and influence its decisions and day-to-day operations. The problem in Miliband's work is that he gives no indication of the extent to which 'power-holders' are constrained by the system, but this is a problem which can only be overcome through detailed analysis of different examples of state activity (such as those discussed in the chapters that follow). It is no solution at all to emphasise the constraints to such an extent that 'power-holders' disappear out of the analysis altogether as is the case in Poulantzas's writings.

Capitalism, Socialism and Liberal Democracy

The ideas and arguments developed by Marxist theorists such as Poulantzas are often very dense and very abstract – sometimes to the point where they defy understanding altogether. Clearly, work like this is unlikely to be read much outside of a small circle of like-minded intellectuals. Nevertheless, despite its opacity, such work has been important in shaping or influencing political movements, for as we saw earlier, Marxists generally claim to marry together a scientific analysis of how capitalist society operates with a political guide to transcending it. Poulantzas himself, for example, was a member of the French Communist Party and much of his writing was addressed implicitly or explicitly to debates within the Party during the 1970s concerning electoral strategy, the need to build alliances, the nature of the support base for the Party and so on.

Seen in this light, the arguments we have been discussing in this chapter have been crucial in informing socialist and communist thinking and strategy in continental Europe and, to some extent, in Britain as well. Of particular significance here has been the issue of whether the actions of the state are best explained with reference to the individuals who run it or the wider capitalist system of which it forms a part. If you believe that the state benefits the capitalist class mainly because it is controlled on the whole by members of that class then it is perfectly plausible to suggest that the state can be used to benefit other groups once these key individuals are replaced (for example, through elections). If, on the other hand, you believe that the state simply reflects the logic of the system of which it forms a part, then it follows that a change of personnel will achieve nothing until the wider system itself is overthrown.

These, in essence, are the two polar positions around which much of the political argument within Marxism over the last hundred years has taken place. On the one hand, there have been those (sometimes disparagingly referred to by their opponents as 'revisionists') who have argued that it is possible to change capitalism from within by using the democratic institutions of the capitalist state to bring about a socialist transformation of the society as a whole. On the other, there have been those (such as Lenin, for example) who have argued that the capitalist state is inherently structured in such a way as to ensure domination by the capitalist class, that the institutions of liberal democracy are little more than a sham, and that effective working class power can only be achieved by smashing the 'bourgeois state' and replacing it with an altogether different kind of apparatus which will ensure domination by the proletariat (organised through the Communist Party).

As is so often the case in arguments like this, the truth of the matter probably lies somewhere between the two extremes, and most Marxists today tend to adopt a position which is rather more subtle or complex than either of these two polar opposites. Indeed, Marx himself was never entirely clear in his writings on whether or not liberal democracy could effectively be used to bring about a socialist transformation.

Marxist theory and parliamentary socialism

There are many points in Marx's works where he appears to reject the possibility of using existing state institutions to bring into being a socialist society. Such a rejection would seem to follow from his argument that the economic 'base' (i.e. the organisation of the forces and relations of production) determines the political 'superstructure' rather than the other way round, for, although he recognised that the superstructure could and did react back upon the base, it is clear from his writings that he saw the economy as the prime mover in bringing about social change, in which case the state will always tend to follow change rather than instigate it.

Overall, Marx's position appears to have been that any system of state power is a system of class power, that the state in a capitalist society will be an instrument of bourgeois domination and that in a future socialist society a socialist state form would need to be organised as a means of institutionalising working-class domination.

There is, however, another side to Marx's writings in which he appeared to recognise at least a limited role for 'bourgeois democracy'. According to his collaborator, Engels, Marx believed that in England (the country which at that time had the most developed capitalist economy and the most established system of parliamentary democracy) it may be possible to bring about a revolutionary transformation 'entirely by peaceful and legal means'. Engels elaborated on this theme on a number of occasions, arguing that 'bourgeois' political freedoms such as the right of assembly and the freedom of the Press could be used to good effect by workers' movements, and that elections were themselves an important aspect of the class struggle in that they provided an opportunity to develop workers' consciousness of themselves as a strong and united political force.

This second strand in Marx's theory was never developed as forcibly as the first, however, and following the Russian Revolution, most Marxists for most of this century have tended to argue that a parliamentary socialist strategy of 'reformism' is unlikely to get very far, and that sooner or later, bourgeois domination will have to be directly confronted outside Parliament through, for example, the organisation of a general strike and the mobilisation of workers on the streets. The example of Chile, where the first elected Marxist government in the world was swiftly deposed by an American-backed military coup, has often been cited in defence of such a position and as evidence that a seizure of power that stops with an electoral victory will always turn out to be hollow and precarious.

In Britain there are still a few Marxists who subscribe to this insurrectionary strategy, but the influence of this sort of thinking has declined since the sixties in response to two major developments overseas.

1 The move, in the 1970s in many European Communist Parties towards what became known as 'Eurocommunism'. In the major Western European Marxist parties in Greece, Italy, Spain and (to some extent) France, leaders began to weaken or sever their links with Moscow, to renounce the doctrine of the 'dictatorship of the proletariat', and to endorse both liberal parliamentary democracy and certain key elements of the bourgeois legal and economic system (for example, the recognition of private property rights). In Britain too the Communist Party adopted its own version of Eurocommunism in the early 1970s, although this was not especially significant given that the Party had no MPs and could muster only around 15,000 members.

2 The collapse of Communist regimes in Eastern Europe in 1989. The impact on West European Marxists of the popular revolutions in East Germany, Poland, Hungary, Czechoslovakia, Rumania and Bulgaria was devastating, for these events finally demonstrated the bankruptcy of socialist central planning. In France the General Secretary of the once-powerful Communist Party went on national television to complain that he and his comrades had been 'duped' by East European leaders about the supposed successes of their regimes, and like many other communist politicians and academics he concluded that the system had 'clearly not succeeded'. These dramatic events did not, of course, lead Marxists to abandon socialism, but they did generate

a search for a 'third way' which would be both democratic and egalitarian. The idea of imposing socialism through violent revolution effectively disappeared from Europe the night the Berlin Wall was breached.

Today, therefore, the old debate within Marxism between revolutionaries and revisionists has finally been settled. Who today could harbour dreams of storming the Winter Palace when television has relayed throughout the world the evident desire of millions of people in Eastern Europe to embrace both Western-style democracy and Western-style consumerism? If socialism is to be achieved in Britain, it must be achieved through popular democratic consent and it must safeguard both the freedoms and the prosperity which people in Britain have come to take for granted. This leads us back to the Labour Party as the only possible means of bringing about such a change. Whether they like it or not, Marxists and other socialists in Britain today must look to the Labour Party to realise their dreams and aspirations, for there is no other route open to them.

Labourism and Marxism in Britain

Most British Marxists, despite their many differences with each other, are probably agreed that a parliamentary strategy based on getting a radical Labour Party elected into Parliament is not itself enough to bring about a socialist transformation of British society. Where the arguments begin, however, is over the question of whether the Labour Party can play any effective part at all in such a transformation. Those who believe it can have become involved in the Party and have attempted to change it into an effective revolutionary political force despite the evidence of the last 80 years that such attempts have never previously succeeded. Those who believe it cannot become involved instead in a bewildering variety of fringe Left parties despite the evidence that such parties have never been able to build up a mass working-class membership. The dilemma for British Marxists, in other words, has been that the Labour Party is the only Left Party with any chance of gaining any significant political power, yet it also appears to be unshakeable in its commitment to parliamentary reformism which Marxist analysis believes to be inadequate for the task it has set itself.

At the heart of the problem as seen by Marxists is the Labour Party's longstanding commitment to the constitutional practices of parliamentarianism; i.e. to what was set out in the first three chapters of this book as a liberal-democratic or pluralist theory of the state. Labour's first ever Prime Minister, Ramsay MacDonald, spelt out this commitment clearly when he suggested that: 'The modern state in most civilised communities is democratic, and in spite of remaining anomalies and imperfections, if the mass of the ordinary people are agreed upon any policy neither electors, privileged peers nor reigning houses could stand in their way.'

As we have seen, however, Marxist theories of the way in which the state operates suggest this view is quite simply wrong! The historic commitment of the Labour Party to constitutional propriety is founded on a basic misconception of where power in British society lies. The power of the Civil Service, the military chiefs, the press barons, the bankers and the boards of directors or multinational companies simply cannot be dimissed as, in MacDonald's words, 'anomalies and imperfections', for it can and does prevail, even against the wishes of 'the mass of the ordinary people'.

This has long been argued by Marxists in the Labour Party. In the 1930s, for example, Harold Laski argued in his *The State in Theory and Practice* that capitalism and democracy were fundamentally incompatible and that at times of crisis, the capitalist class would, if necessary, suppress democratic institutions rather than see its interests subordinated to those of the majority of electors. For Laski, constitutional methods could and should be followed until they are exhausted, but at that point violent revolutionary action would be necessary in order to counter the power and privilege of capital. Nowhere, he suggested, have peaceful methods successfully brought about a transfer of power and wealth from one class to another, for 'the owners of property rarely yield save what they must'.

The legacy of Laski lives on in the Left of the Labour Party today, and much of the turmoil that followed the 1979 election defeat and which culminated in 1981 in the breakaway of the 'social democrats' to form a new party revolved precisely around the battle between those (including the then leader, Michael Foot) who remained wedded to MacDonald's vision of the sovereignty of the British people in Parliament, and those (concentrated mainly among the Constituency Party activists) who sought to reduce the autonomy of parliamentary members and to develop a challenge to the government outside the Palace of Westminster as well as within it.

For a time in the early and mid-eighties, the Marxist Left seized the initiative within the Party. Trotskyist groups like *Militant* thrived in the constituency section and two *Militant* supporters were elected to Parliament as Labour candidates. The Left took over many constituency parties and made itself felt in forcing through a number of crucial organisational changes (notably the establishment of an electoral college to choose the leader and deputy leader, and the mandatory reselection of MPs). The acknowledged leader of the 'hard Left', Tony Benn, ran under the new electoral college system for the deputy leadership of the Party and was only defeated by the narrowest of margins. Policies dear to the Left – notably an extension of public ownership, unilateral nuclear disarmament and withdrawal from the European Community – were adopted and reaffirmed as Party policy, and in town halls up and down the country, Marxists and Left-wing socialists pursued radical policies in respect of employment, public transport and gender issues in an attempt to build new electoral alliances (see chapter 12).

And then, in 1983, the wheel came off. At the general election of that year, Labour fought on its most avowedly socialist manifesto ever, and went down to the most resounding defeat in its history. Labour's share of the vote fell in absolute terms to its lowest level since 1918 and in proportional terms (i.e. votes cast per Labour candidate) to its lowest level ever. The Social Democratic Party (which had been formed when some Right-wing Labour MPs broke away from the Party in 1981), in alliance with the Liberals, came within two per cent of Labour's vote. Pundits began to suggest that the Labour Party was on the point of final collapse.

It took another five years to get the Party back into electoral shape. A new leader – Neil Kinnock – set out explicitly to crush the Left and as part of this strategy he launched a series of expulsions of *Militant* supporters. Gradually too he weaned his party away from the policies which they held so dearly yet which had cost them so dear. Labour became pro-Europe, so much so that by 1990 it was the Labour Party which was criticising the Conservative government for its tardiness in joining the European Exchange Rate Mechanism. It dropped its plans for future nationalisations and even accepted that at least some of the companies which had been privatised during the Thatcher years could remain in the private sector. Opposition to the sale of council houses was quietly dropped, and most of the trade union reforms introduced by the Conservatives in the teeth of bitter Labour opposition were now endorsed. Even unilateral nuclear disarmament was dumped. Symbolically, the red flag was replaced by a red rose. By the end of the 1980s, Labour had arguably returned to the pale-pink Fabian tradition which was dominant through most of its history.

Tony Benn has suggested that the Labour Party has its roots in a wide range of historical movements which include Marxist socialism but which also include (arguably more significantly) Christianity (especially non-conformist religions), the arguments of the Levellers during the Civil War period, the programme of the Chartists during the 1840s, and the writings of radicals of various shades of opinion including Robert Owen, Tom Paine and Sydney and Beatrice Webb. Most crucially of all, of course, the Labour Party sprang from the organisation of workers in trade unions, for it was set up in 1900 as the Labour Representation League by trade union leaders who sought to gain expression for the voice of organised labour in Parliament. Two crucial points follow from all of this.

1 The diversity of intellectual origins of Labourism gave rise to two main strands of Labour Party thinking. One, reflecting above all the Fabian influence of the Webbs, was rationalistic and pragmatic in that it saw in the Labour party an electoral instrument for improving the lot of ordinary working people through reform and legislative change within the context of an existing capitalist system of production. The other was more emotional and utopian in that it absorbed from the religious teachings of non-conformism a moral zeal to crusade against perceived injustice. The rationalistic element soon prevailed over the utopian one but what is most important from a Marxist point of view is that neither of these strands could alone provide a clear theoretical and philosophical basis for the development of a socialist strategy. As a result, the history of the Labour Party has been a history of muddling through based on

good intentions and high ideals but precious little analysis. There has arguably never been a Labour Government which has assumed office with a clear idea of how it was going to implement its programme. The catalogue of defeats from the debacle of MacDonald's National Government in 1931, through the half-hearted nationalisation programme of the Attlee government after the war and the collapse of the Wilson government's National Plan in 1965, to the bitter conflicts over the Callaghan government's Social Contract in 1978/9 (all of which is discussed in chapter 9) is indicative of the failure of all Labour administrations to understand the relation between parliamentary democracy and power in a capitalist society. Similarly, wherever a crisis has developed – the outbreak of war in 1914, the General Strike of 1926, the collapse of the Gold Standard in 1931, the appeasement of Hitler in the late 1930s, the devaluation of the pound in 1947 and 1967, the miners' strike of 1974 and the International Monetary fund loan of 1976 to cite just a few examples – Labour's parliamentary leadership has been caught wrong-footed. Labourism, in short, has been conspicuously lacking in theoretical understanding of its own position (indeed, there is a strong anti-intellectualist current within the labour movement as a whole which has militated against the fusion of political theory and political action which is entailed in the Marxist notion of 'praxis').

2 The second important legacy of the history of Labourism in Britain lies in the relationship between the Labour Party and the trade unions. Ever since 1918, the labour movement has been split between the industrial and the political wings, and this division has been crucial in preventing the development of a coherent socialist strategy. In part this is because the unions (or, to be more accurate, the union bosses) have always commanded a massive majority of conference votes by virtue of the block-vote system, and although some union bosses are more radical than others, this has generally operated as a brake upon Left activists in the constituency parties. The problem, however, goes deeper than this for the division between industrial issues (handled by the unions) and wider social and political issues (handled by the Labour party in Parliament) has simply reflected and institutionalised a division which is characteristic of liberal capitalism but which is entirely inconsistent with what most Marxists would see as socialist democracy. This is because socialist democracy, unlike liberal democracy, sees as artificial any separation between the political sphere (where government makes decisions) and the economic sphere (where owners of capital make decisions). Socialist democracy, if it means anything at all, means that working people share in making *all* decisions which affect their lives, and this is a far cry from voting once every five years in parliamentary elections!

What we are suggesting, therefore, is that the division of the labour movement into a Labour Party and trade unions has set up artificial barriers between the two and has fostered the limited parliamentarianism of the Party which we identified earlier. The Labour Party, to put it another way, is by its very nature the voice of organised labour *within* capitalism; it exists to represent in Parliament workers' interests as wage labourers rather than to transcend the system of wage labour itself, and for as long as it remains the political head of the trade union body, it will continue to be limited to such a role.

As the political mouthpiece of organised labour, the Labour Party exists to get the best it can for workers within the context of a capitalist system. Its job in Parliament is to express the aspirations of working-class people and of their organisations, the trade unions. As such, it has never really been interested in leading the working class, only in representing it. Political education within the Labour Party has never been a high priority, for the Party's task has always been defined in such a way that it takes peoples's desires as it finds them and tries to translate them into legislation. As the party's line on immigration controls demonstrates, Labour governments have generally ducked out of giving a principled lead where this conflicts with popular opinion and prejudice, and have preferred instead to adjust their conception of socialism to the non-socialist and often anti-socialist sentiments of the mass of the population. It is for this reason more than any other that socialism has never really been placed on the political agenda in Britain.

Today the Labour Party is effectively a 'Left-centre' party. Its major policy review, completed in 1989, recognises that the market has 'a vital role' in Britain's economy and that there can be no return to 'old-fashioned nationalisation'. This explicit move back towards the centre ground of British politics succeeded in seeing off the threat from the centre parties (the SDP was wound up in 1990 and the Liberal Democrats were achieving no better support than had the liberals on their own prior to 1981) and in reestablishing Labour's popular support base (opinion polls gave the Party a record lead over the Conservatives of some 25 per cent in the spring of 1990). But was all this really necessary? Is it the case that, to win office, Labour must shed its socialist principles?

The Left believes this is not the case. They believe that there are millions of people in Britain ready and willing to vote for a full-blooded socialist programme. Even the 1983 election debacle is seen as evidence for this proposition, for Tony Benn argued that for the first time, electors had been offered a genuine socialist manifesto and that seven million people had supported it. At local level too, evidence is cited of Left-wing councils improving their vote while more pragmatic Labour administrations are deserted by electors. All that is needed, according to the Left, is more resolution and more commitment (the very qualities which Margaret Thatcher is thought to have brought to the Conservative Party in the eighties).

The question, then, is simple. Are Marxists and others on the Left justified in their belief that millions of ordinary working people constitute a potential support base for socialism? Is it really the case that, if the socialist message is spelled out loud enough and long enough it will touch a nerve in the working-class collective consciousness which will spark off an irresistable popular surge for change? Or are the pragmatists correct when they calculate that Labour can only win power when it jettisons its socialist credentials and puts itself forward as a party determined to manage capitalism rather than transcend it?

The Labour Party and the working class

Most Marxist political analysis – and most Left political activism for that matter – assumes that there is in a country like Britain a potential mass base for socialism, a natural in-built majority which is lying dormant and which only needs to be roused by the correct socialist strategy in order for its power to be unleashed and for capitalism to crumble. Given this assumption, the problem for the Left is simply one of strategy and organisation. The world is there to be won if only a way can be found to 'raise the workers from their slumbers'.

This mode of thinking rests on four crucial and generally unexamined premises. First, it is taken as axiomatic that all significant political struggles are in one way or another class struggles. Second, it is argued that the working class constitutes a majority of the population, which means it must be the most potent political force in the society. Third, it is taken as given that socialism is the natural political home of the working class, and that when workers embrace other ideologies they are in some way misguided as to where their true interests lie. Fourth, it is asserted that such misguidedness can be countered by socialists taking a bold lead which eventually will strike a chord in workers' consciousness as the scales fall from their eyes. All four of these basic Left assumptions are in our view highly questionable.

'All significant political struggles are class struggles'

This is patently not the case, for class is only one dimension of inequality and domination in British society. Divisions based on gender, ethnicity and sectoral cleavages cut through and across class divisions and are clearly revealed in political struggles.

This has to some extent been recognised by some sections of the Left in Britain which have made conscious efforts to support, say, women's groups or black organisations. However, there is inherent in Marxist thinking an assumption that, even if such groups cannot be seen simply as part of the class struggle, they can be seen as secondary to it or as reinforcing it, for the 'real' struggle remains that between capital and labour. Non-class divisions, in other words, may be recognised but their significance is not, for there is generally a failure on the Left in Britain to understand or accept the *inherent* heterogeneity of the working class which follows from the fragmentation by gender, race, age, religion, income, type of employment, housing tenure, area of residence and many other factors besides.

The first problem which the Left faces but does not recognise is, therefore, that the homogeneous working class of its theory does not and cannot correspond to the working class as it exists in British society. Put another way, people have many interests other than their interests as workers and these often conflict with each other with the result that actual political alignments and struggles will always escape from the narrow confines of a class analysis and a class movement.

'The working class constitutes a majority interest'

Again, this is questionable for the working class can only be seen as a majority force in British society if class divisions are identified in a very simplistic and unhelpful fashion.

We have seen that for Marx, the basic class division in a capitalist society is that between the owners of capital and those who have to sell their labour-power in order to live. However, this 'basic' division has become very confused, for not only are there important divisions between different groups of workers (for example, between professional and manual workers, state-sector and private-sector workers and so on), but ownership of capital has changed as well with the growth of financial institutions such as pension funds and insurance companies, and with the division between ownership and management of capital.

Recent Marxist class theory has tried to take account of these changes. In particular, there have been various attempts to develop Marx's original theory in order to take account of the existence of a 'middle class' which is distinct from both capitalists and proletariat. Some writers, for example, suggest that only private-sector workers employed by capitalist firms can be said to be 'working class'. Others suggest that the 'real' working class be limited to those engaged in industrial production as opposed to the growing service sector. Still others suggest that the working class should be defined in such a way as to exclude employees such as managers and foremen who carry out supervisory functions on behalf of capital.

Most of these formulations remain unconvincing (even to other Marxist theorists), but what they all have in common is a recognition that the working class cannot simply be defined as all those who work, for this is to ignore the crucial economic and political differences between, say, hospital consultants and hospital porters, or university lecturers and university cleaners, or middle-level management and the shop floor. There is, in other words, an uneasy recognition that the working class – that group to which socialism is addressed and in which the hopes and aspirations of socialists are vested – may not be very big after all. Indeed, in some formulations, such as that of Poulantzas who limits the working class to non-supervisory manual workers employed in industry, this class turns out to be disconcertingly small (around one-quarter of the total employed population in this case).

The second problem for the Left, therefore, is that the belief that socialism must eventually prevail given the size of the working class appears to rest on an outdated and redundant understanding of what the shape of the British class structure actually looks like.

'Socialism is the natural political home of the working class'

There are real problems with this argument, historically and theoretically.

The historical problem is quite simply that in all countries at all times, the working class divides fairly evenly in its support for the Left, Right and centre parties. There is no evidence here to suggest that the working class naturally inclines towards socialism

Theoretically too, there is no reason to suppose that this should be the case. The Left's assumption that one's economic position should in some way determine one's political position derives, of course, from Marx's arguments regarding the primacy of the economic 'base' over the political 'superstructure'. However, when we consider the issue more carefully, it is obvious that there is no necessary reason for assuming that the fact of being a worker should generate a socialist commitment as opposed to any other. Different people may, and do, experience and interpret the same situation in different ways, and the way in which people align themselves politically will be a product, not of some automatic connection with their economic location in society, but with the way they respond to political and moral arguments. There is nothing in your class situation which will necessarily lead you to favour unilateral as opposed to multilateral disarmament, trade union autonomy as opposed to legal regulation, public ownership as opposed to privatisation of industry. People's views on these and similar issues, and their willingness to support one or other party, will reflect a host of factors, and it is a mistake, therefore, to assume any automatic pre-disposition on the part of one class or another towards any particular political ideology.

The third problem for the Left, then, is that its commitment to socialism has no prior claims on the sympathies of the working class. The socialist message is one among several competing philosophies, and it has no head start in this competition. Indeed, given the character of key institutions such as the mass media and the schools (discussed in chapter 11), it may even start at a distinct disadvantage, for it is always likely to be easier to win popular acquiescence for keeping things much as they are than to generate support for changing them in dramatic and perhaps unpredictable ways.

'A bold socialist lead will eventually strike a chord in working-class consciousness'

As we have already seen, the failure of socialism in Britain is generally explained by the Left as a failure of strategy and in particular as a product of the faint hearts of Labour leadership over the years. It follows from this that the working class can be mobilised through a concerted and single-minded commitment by the Party to move towards full-blooded socialism with no concessions, and to drag the working class along behind it.

Any evaluation of this argument can only be tentative. However, it should be noted that in June 1983, an explicitly 'Left' manifesto which generally enjoyed the support of many constituency and trade union activists in the Labour Party failed to inspire mass support at the polls despite the dismal economic performance of the Conservative government over the previous four years. As we noted earlier, Labour's total vote in 1983 was the lowest since 1918, and its average vote per candidate was the lowest ever.

This crushing rejection of a socialist programme by the great majority of British people did not, however, lead to much – if any – reassessment by the Left of its policies and its basic assumptions. Rather, it was argued that the policies were right but that the working class, misled by a 'false consciousness' fostered by the media, had yet again got it wrong. The lesson which the Left learned from 1983 was not that its strategy had failed or that its message was out of tune, but that the same strategy must be followed in future with even more zeal, and that the same message must be repeated, only louder, in order to drown the propaganda emanating from 20 million televison sets.

Conclusion

The resurgence of interest in Marxist political theory since the 1960s has provided a valuable corrective to some of the more orthodox approaches within mainstream political science. In particular, Marxist work on the capitalist state has pointed to the inadequacies of liberal-democratic theories which seek to analyse power through an almost exclusive focus on political institutions, for Marxists have emphasised that political processes cannot be understood except in relation to the organisation of the economy.

The problem, however, is that neither traditional nor recent Marxist work has been able to demonstrate the nature of this relation. What is distinctive to Marxist political theory is the view that politics are in some way determined by economic forces, but the question of how this occurs remains unanswered.

In this chapter, we have considered two major theorists, both of whom recognise that there is some degree of autonomy between the political system and the economic system, but who differ markedly between themselves over how this autonomy is to be explained.

On the one hand, we have Miliband's position which is that, although those who run the state apparatus are generally drawn from the capitalist class, are sympathetic to its interests, are strongly pressured by big business and are constrained by the requirements of the economic system, they do retain some autonomy in deciding how best they can serve the long-term interests of capital. In this view the 'relative autonomy' of the state is a reflection of the limited autonomy enjoyed by those who run it.

There are two problems with this 'explanation', however. First, as we saw earlier in his chapter, Miliband gives no indication of the degree to which those who run the state are able to make up their own minds about the actions they deem necessary. How much scope do they have? How far can they go? How relative is 'relative' autonomy? Clearly, the 'concessions' which the British state has made over the years are by no means trifling, and their cost in terms of taxation on profits has been considerable. Indeed, as we shall see in chapter 9, some Marxists (and non-Marxists) have argued that one major factor in the continuing slump in British capitalism has been the size of the state's budget as it has expanded its provisions for working-class people, thereby eating into capitalist profits. Such evidence would seem to suggest that the autonomy of the state may at times be considerable, but there is no way of judging this from Miliband's analysis.

This leads us into the second problem with Miliband's explanation of the relative autonomy of the state, and this is that it seems to assume a degree of canniness and foresight on the part of those who run the state which is historically highly dubious. The notion that Cabinets, civil servants and others carefully and correctly calculate how many concessions will need to be made in order to contain pressure from below seems faintly ludicrous in the light of what we know about the haphazard way in which British governments have responded to crises and problems, yet Miliband's argument rests on the view that these people are endowed with such a degree of political intelligence and sophistication that their actions always turn out in the end to have been exactly what capitalism as a whole required. What else, other than their supposed political acumen, can explain why they may not make disastrous decisions from the point of view of capital? To suggest that the constraints of the system prevent this from happening is to give no answer at all, for the argument that the system must be supported if it is to continue does not explain why the system is in fact supported and does continue. What is lacking in Miliband's analysis, in other words, is any explanation of what it is that has prevented the 'relatively autonomous' state leaders from using their autonomy in such a way that the system itself is fouled up or collapses.

On the other hand, there is Poulantzas's position which is that the 'relative autonomy' of the state reflects not the scope for action on the part of those who run it, but rather the shifting fortunes of class struggle such that, when the working class is in the ascendant, the state will respond with reforms. As we saw earlier, however, this is an inadequate formulation, for not only does it neglect altogether the motives of key individuals and the significance of political struggles which are not class-based, but it also fails to demonstrate why class struggle (the cause of state policies) should always result in the maintenace of the long-term interests of big capital (the necessary function of such policies). As in Miliband's formulation, so too in that of Poulantzas, there is a basic failure to identify the necessary mechanism by means of which the state responds to one class while safeguarding the interests of another.

In these, as in other Marxist approaches, the basic problem stems from the commitment of any Marxist theory to some view of politics as determined by economic organisation. That the economy influences political processes is undeniable; that it determines them, however, seems insupportable.

It is the failure of Marxist theory to resolve this problem which has led to the tangled debate within Marxism in particular, and within the Left in Britain in general, over whether or not parliamentary socialism represents a viable strategy for transforming capitalism. Clearly, if politics are simply 'determined' by economic forces, then there is no possibility of a capitalist state being used as an instrument of socialist change. But if some degree of 'autonomy' is accorded to the political system, then this self-evident 'truth' becomes rather less compelling.

In the final section of this chapter, we saw that most Marxists in Britain see a parliamentary strategy as a necessary but not sufficient condition for achieving far-reaching social change. However, it is also commonplace in the Marxist literature to express considerable doubt regarding the capacity of the Labour Party to carry off such a strategy, and many writers (including Miliband) see little hope of transforming Labourism into socialism. The prognostication, therefore, seems gloomy, for Marxists doubt both the possibility of transforming capitalism though electoral victories and the possibility of transforming the Labour Party into a vehicle of socialist change.

The conclusion to be drawn from all of this is that, while Marxist political theory has been important in demonstrating the inadequacies of alternative approaches, it has itself been found wanting in certain important respects as well. The basic question of the relationship between politics and economics remains unresolved, and despite their claims to provide an overall 'total' explanation, it turns out that Marxist theories can no more provide all the answers than liberal theories can.

As regards Marxist practice, the conclusion must surely be that the replacement of capitalism by socialism is no longer a viable objective. Margaret Thatcher claimed as one of her goals the desire to remove socialism from the political agenda in Britain. She has probably succeeded. The Labour Party has been pulled back to the centre ground after a brief and deeply-damaging flirtation with radical socialist policies, and many of the changes introduced in the 1980s – the sale of council houses, the reigning in of the welfare state, the sale of nationalised industries, the reform of trade union law – are unlikely to be reversed by any future Labour government. Political prediction is a hazardous business, but the best guess we can make about how British politics will develop over the next ten or fifteen years is that we shall see the emergence of a new fundamental consensus based in acceptance by all parties of the value of private enterprise and the importance of individual liberties. It could, after all, have been Margaret Thatcher who wrote of the need to create 'a genuinely free society in which the protection and extension of individual liberty is the primary duty of the state'. In fact, this was how the Deputy Leader of the Labour

Party chose to begin his new book on socialism in 1987. The name of the book made no mention of equality or common ownership. It was called *Choose Freedom*.

Works Cited and Guide to Further Reading

Aaronovitch, S. (1961) *The Ruling Class*, London, Lawrence and Wishart, especially chapter 5.
In many ways a forerunner of Miliband's more influential work. Argues stridently, but not always convincingly, that the British state is dominated by large industrial-financial interests

Anderson, P. and Blackburn R. (eds) (1965) *Towards Socialism*, London, Fontana.
A collection of essays bemoaning the past and looking to the future in the wake of Labour's 1964 general election victory. See especially Nairn on 'The nature of the Labour Party' and Anderson on 'Problems of socialist strategy'.

Coates, D. (1980) *Labour in Power*, London, Longman.
One of many commentaries which sees the Labour Party as a means by which the working class has been politically incorporated into the capitalist system.

Gold, D., Lo, C. and Wright, E. (1979) 'Recent developments in Marxist theories of the capitalist state,' *Monthly Review*, 27, pp. 37–51.
A useful introductory guide to the work of Miliband and Poulantzas.

Hattersley, R. (1987) *Choose Freedom*, London, Michael Joseph.
In which the Deputy Leader of the Labour Party attempts to reclaim the language of Thatcherism for the socialist cause. 'What we stand for is freedom,' writes Hattersley – but what he means by freedom is not necessarily the same as what the New Right means by it.

Hindess, B. (1983) *Parliamentary Democracy and Socialist Politics*, London, Routledge and Kegan Paul.
A stimulating critique by a Marxist of Marxist orthodoxies. In particular, Hindess takes issue with the view that 'the real working class is out there somewhere, patiently awaiting the socialist call'.

Jacques, M., and Mulhern, F. (eds) (1981) *The Forward March of Labour Halted?*, London, Verso.
The Marxist Left agonises about the implications of Labour's electoral decline and seeks all manner of solutions. See especially the essay by Eric Hobsbawn.

Laski, H. (1935) *The State in Theory and Practice*, London, Allen and Unwin.
In which one of the key figures of the British Left this century drives home his message (made all the more urgent by the rise of Nazism in Germany at that time) that capitalism and democracy are fundamentally irreconcilable at times of economic recession.

Lukes, S. (1971) 'Power and structure'. In S. Lukes (ed.) *Essays in Social Theory*, London, Macmillan.
An interesting discussion of the constraints on the powerful. Lukes draws the distinction between 'structural' and 'rational' constraints, and then uses this to

criticise Poulantzas for his over-deterministic and over-structuralist analysis of state power.

Marx, K. and Engels, F. (1968) *Selected Works in one Volume*, Moscow, Progress Publishers.
Contains many of the key political essays including the Communist Manifesto and 'The Civil War in France'.

Miliband, R. (1969) *The State in Capitalist Society*, London, Weidenfeld & Nicolson.
Now becoming something of a classic. Despite its lack of theoretical subtlety and good empirical evidence, it remains the best single Marxist analysis of politics and the state in Britain.

Miliband, R. (1982) *Capitalist Democracy in Britain*, London, Oxford University Press.
Overall, a disappointing work. Thirteen years and umpteen debates after 'The state in capitalist society', it demostrates that Miliband still lacks theoretical subtlety and good empirical evidence.

Poulantzas, N. (1973) *Political Power and Social Classes*, London, New Left Books.
Appallingly written and virtually impossible to read. Those who wish to get to grips with Poulantzas might do better to approach him via his debate with Miliband in the journal *New Left Review*. This began in 1969 (no. 58) when Poulantzas reviewed Miliband's book, and continued through no. 59 (1970) when Miliband replied; number 82 (1973) in which Miliband reviewed Poulantzas's book; and no. 95 (1976) when Poulantzas replied to this and to a later critique from Laclau. A good (but again difficult) critical review of Poulantzas's theory can be found in S. Clarke (1977) 'Marxism, sociology and Poulantzas's theory of the state', *Capital and Class*, 2, pp. 1–31.

Chapter 8

Liberalism, Conservatism and the 'New Right'

We have progressively abandoned that freedom in economic affairs without which personal and political freedom has never existed in the past.
Friedrich Hayek (1944) *The Road to Serfdom*, London,
Routledge, p. 10.

In spite of appearances, in spite of the rhetoric of freedom, in spite of being a 'liberal', Hayek has a conception of order having much in common with the authoritarian tradition in social theory, and is therefore no stranger to the authoritarian New Right.
Andrew Belsey (1986) 'The new right, social order and civil liberties'. In Ruth Levitas (ed.), *The Ideology of the New Right*, Cambridge, Polity Press, pp. 180–1.

The basic premises of socialism (even with a Croslandite gloss) and conservatism are unjust because they demand altruism, the former from the community as a whole and the latter from the least advantaged, and when, inevitably, this is not forthcoming, both philosophies must fall back on the power of the state.
R. Carey (ed.) (1986) *Unveiling the Right*, London, The Tawney Society, p. 9.

Introduction

Towards the end of the 1979 general election campaign, the Labour Prime Minister, James Callaghan, was told by his senior policy adviser that the opinion polls were improving and that Labour might just snatch victory. Callaghan was less optimistic. 'There are times,' he replied, 'perhaps once every thirty years, when there is a sea-change in politics. It then does not matter what you say or do. There is a shift in what the public wants and what it approves of. I suspect there is now such a sea-change – and it is for Mrs Thatcher.' James Callaghan was right. Margaret Thatcher's Conservatives won a majority of 43 seats in 1979 and she went on to become Britain's longest-serving Prime Minister this century. The impact of this victory on the pattern of British politics has been profound.

". . . but are some *more* 'Free to Choose' than others in the Britain of today?"
(Reproduced by kind permission of The Hulton Picture Company.)

The previous 'sea change' had been in 1945 when the Labour Party had unexpectedly and resoundingly defeated the Conservatives under the leadership of Winston Churchill. As we shall see in chapters 9 and 10, that post-war Labour government fundamentally reorganised the relationship between state and society in Britain. It introduced a battery of social reforms in the areas of education, health care, social security and housing; it took into 'public ownership' a swathe of industries including coal, the railways, iron and steel and the utilities; it embarked upon an economic policy in which government played a pivotal role in managing demand and boosting employment; and in foreign policy it presided over the end of the Empire while linking the country's defence firmly to a nuclear-based Western military alliance. Although later governments were to fiddle with the details of this post-war settlement, the broad outlines of social and economic strategy which were laid down in the late forties remained more or less in tact for the next thirty years.

The Conservative victory on 3 May 1979 broke radically with this strategy. Through the 1980s the Conservatives remodelled social policy in a wave of radical reforms of education, health and housing; they sold off most state-owned industries thereby reducing the size of the public sector workforce by forty per cent; and they abandoned attempts at managing the economy in favour of a policy of reducing direct taxes and controlling inflation through restrictions on the creation of money and (later) through manipulation of interest rates. Just as the post-war Labour government set the agenda of British politics for all parties for the next thirty years, so too the Conservative governments of the 1980s succeeded in shifting the terms of political debate. Although politics in this latter period were highly contested and there was no sign of the emergence of a bipartisan consensus such as characterised the 1950s, the opposition parties were nevertheless obliged to rethink many of their most fundamental beliefs and assumptions. As we saw in chapter 7, the Labour Party had, by 1990, backed away from its earlier commitments to central controls and state ownership and regulation. Rather than seeking to return to the policies and ideals of the 1970s, most Labour leaders were now looking for ways to outflank or 'leap-frog' Thatcherism by developing innovative forms of consumer-oriented market socialism.

That Conservative governments should have had such a dramatic impact on the future direction of British politics is remarkable, for British Conservatism has traditionally been pragmatic rather than ideological. Conservatives have generally been committed to slow 'evolutionary' social development rather than to rapid 'revolutionary' social change. They have generally distrusted legislative innovation, have scorned appeals to populism in favour of an appeal to values of elitism, and have taken care to safeguard the privileges of entrenched economic and professional interests. As their name suggests, they have been 'conservative' rather than 'radical' in outlook and sentiment. Yet all this changed after Margaret Thatcher won the leadership of the Party in 1975. Since then, Conservatism has looked more like a crusade than a holding operation. Parliament has creaked under the weight of new legislation, appeal has been made directly to a working-class and lower-middle-class constituency, and assaults have been launched against the protected privileges of a variety of vested interests including lawyers, doctors, manufacturers, financial institutions and school and university teachers as well as the massed battalions of organised labour. For the Conservative Party to have been in the vanguard of such changes, leaving the Labour Party to emerge as an uneasy defender of the status quo, represents a dramatic inversion of the relationship between the two parties as it had developed since the First World War.

To understand British Conservatism today it is therefore necessary to understand the theories and ideologies which inform its practice. Just as in chapter 7 we traced the theories of the Left in order to analyse the practice of Labourism, so now we have to address the theories of the Right in order to understand the practice of Conservatism.

Capitalism, the Free Market and the State

We saw in chapter 7 that Marxist theories are premissed on a view of the capitalist system as one which is exploitative, repressive and chronically unstable. The system is seen as *exploitative* because those who own property can profit by employing the labour of those who do not. Thus, while the working class creates new wealth through its labours, it is the capitalist class which creams off the proceeds. The system is *repressive* because the maintenance of exploitation requires some way of suppressing opposition and dissent. The working class will not willingly and forever tolerate dehumanised conditions of life and work and must therefore be held in check, either by direct use of force by the state or by more subtle ideological control (see chapter 11). And the system is chronically *unstable* because the capitalist free-market economy involves competing individuals pursuing their own short-term interests in ignorance of the deleterious longer-term implications for them all. Gluts are followed by shortages, mass unemployment alternates with periods of labour famine, inflation supercedes recession, and all of this testifies to the endemic anarchy of the capitalist free-market system.

Traditionally, Marxists and socialists have believed that the only solution to these problems lay in abolishing capitalism itself and replacing it with a different economic, social and political order in which property is owned in common and where exploitation and all the evils that flow from it cannot therefore arise. Today this belief in a fundamental root and branch transition from one system to another is less widespread following the spectacular collapse of the Eastern European socialist regimes in 1989. In its place, most socialists now emphasise the need to use state power to moderate what they see as the excesses of a capitalist market system.

Private ownership of land, factories, offices and banks is accepted, and the operation of free markets in labour, land and capital is endorsed – up to a point. But the state still has a crucial role to play in curbing exploitation and in regulating markets so as to bring about less inequality and more stability in economic affairs. As one of Labour's economic advisers has recently explained, markets are like donkeys – very useful for getting things done, but also very stupid and therefore in need of clear and strong guidance.

In contrast to all of this, there is a very different view of capitalism – one which derives from the liberal rather than the socialist tradition of political philosophy. According to this view, capitalist market systems entail competition and free choice rather than exploitation; they maximise individual liberty rather than leading to repression; and if left alone, they exhibit a tendency to economic equilibrium and collapse into chronic economic instability only when politicians and bureaucrats start fiddling with them. According to this classical liberal view, capitalism is a system which was planned by no one and which works because rather than in spite of the lack of deliberate and conscious political control or planning. In contrast to the socialist belief in the use of state power to achieve desirable objectives, this liberal standpoint is deeply distrustful of state power, even where it is used by people with honest and benevolent motives. While socialists believe that the state must be used to counter exploitation and to extend freedom, liberals argue that in practice the state itself comes to be used as a means of exploitation and as a way of limiting liberty.

If the nightmare for socialists is that of working people being mercilessly repressed by voracious capitalist enterprises operating without check from governments, then the nightmare for classical lliberals is that of the mass of citizens being enslaved by an omnipotent state machine operating without check from civil society. It was this nightmare which inspired the growth of so-called 'New Right' thinking in Britain through the 1960s and 1970s when state activity was expanding at a startling rate, and it was the concern to reduce the escalating role of the state in British life which lay at the heart of the political project which became known through the 1980s as 'Thatcherism'.

The political practice which we have come to know as 'Thatcherism' had its roots in a set of ideas which has generally been referred to as 'the New Right'. The basic principles of the New Right can be traced back through the eighteenth- and nineteenth-century liberal tradition to the ideas of political economists such as Adam Smith who published his *The Wealth of Nations* in 1776. In the twentieth century, however, most of these ideas and principles disappeared from the mainstream of British politics as the Liberal Party itself came to embrace strategies of state intervention in economic and social affairs. Through the long years of the post-war political consensus with its emphasis on centralised planning and universal state welfare there was no political party in Britain willing to express traditional liberal principles of governance, and like a flickering flame in a cold wind, these principles were only kept alive by a handful of economists and political philosophers working and publishing through tiny independent organisations such as the London-based Institute of Economic Affairs.

For most of the post-war period, groups like the IEA were either ignored by politicians and academics or were derided as hopelessly out of date and reactionary. By the mid-1970s, however, the political climate was changing. Conservative Party intellectuals and activists were bitterly disillusioned by what they saw as the failure of the Heath government of 1970–4 which they believed had ended up no less socialist than the Labour governments of the sixties. Leading figures in the Party such as Sir Keith Joseph began to search for a new philosophy on which to base a fundamental shift in Conservative thinking. They found it in the work being produced by groups like the IEA.

The label New Right, which came to be associated with groups like the IEA, is perhaps somewhat misleading, partly because the ideas are not new. The Austrian economist and social philosopher, Friedrich Hayek, who is probably the leading exponent of these ideas, has been writing since the 1930s, and the IEA, which has played a key role in disseminating them, was founded in the mid-fifties. All that is new is that people have begun to pay attention to what they are saying (Hayek, for example, was awarded the Nobel Prize for economics in 1974).

More than this, however, it is apparent that many of the core ideas of the New Right have been around for two hundred years or more! As already noted, one major source for these ideas is Adam Smith who wrote *The Wealth of Nations* as an attack on 'mercantilist' state controls on trade back in the eighteenth century. In Smith's view, such controls tended to benefit rich producers to the detriment of ordinary consumers, for they inhibited international competition in domestic markets and thus maintained artificially high prices. He argued that the general good is best served not by state controls and restrictions (which normally end up benefitting small vested interests at the expense of everybody else), but by enabling free-market exchanges to take place. Indeed, in his famous comment on the 'hidden hand' of market systems, he argued that the best way to further the public interest is to allow individuals to pursue their own self-interest through free exchanges. Co-operation, in other words, arises out of the pursuit of economic self interest:

Man has almost constant occasion for the help of his brethren, and it is in vain for him to expect it from their benevolence only. He will be more likely to prevail if he can interest their self-love in his favour, and show them that it is for their advantage to do for him what he requires of them. . . . It is not from the benevolence of the butcher, the brewer or the baker that we expect our dinner, but from their regard to their own interest. We address ourselves, not to their humanity but to their self-love, and never talk to them of our own necessities but of their advantages. Nobody but a beggar chooses to depend chiefly upon the benevolence of his fellow citizens.

Of course, Smith recognised that the pursuit of self-interest had to be limited by law (for example, I must agree a price with the butcher and cannot be allowed to steal the meat which I want). He also recognised that there were cases where the pursuit of self-interest by individuals could not be relied upon to maximise the common good (for example, we may all benefit by the provision of a public good or service which no individual would freely choose to provide). In cases like these, he readily accepted that the state has a role to play. In particular, he believed that the state should provide a system of justice (so that disputes between individuals could be resolved), a system of common defence (from which all benefit but which cannot be left to individuals to provide), and a system of public works (which promote economic efficiency even though they are themselves inherently unprofitable). Beyond this, however, it was in everybody's interest that the state keep out of everyday life.

Many of these ideas were developed and elaborated by liberal political philosophers in the nineteenth century. For example, in his book *On Liberty*, published in 1859, John Stuart Mill took up the question of the extent to which it was legitimate for the state to curtail the liberties of individuals. He argued that interference in the affairs of individuals could only be justified in order to prevent them from harming others, and like Smith he suggested that the general good was best furthered by allowing individuals the freedom to think and act as they saw fit. Social development and improvement come about as a result of individual diversity, for only by allowing people the right to be different can a society encourage and benefit from innovation. Mill was concerned that the balance between the state and the individual had shifted too far in favour of the former. He was opposed, for example, to state licensing of the professions since this enables those who control the state to determine who may practice and how. He was hostile to state provision of schooling since 'A general state education is a mere contrivance for moulding people to be exactly like one another.' And he resisted calls for the state to provide benefits for its citizens since this undermined self-reliance, substituted the preferences of the state for the preferences of the individual and added enormously to the power of centralised bureaucracies.

The arguments advanced by writers such as Adam Smith and J.S. Mill are today central to the thinking of the New Right. The arguments were developed by writers who were concerned to push back (in the case of Smith) or resist (in the case of Mill) the intrusions of state power into the affairs of individuals. Since the mid-nineteenth century, these arguments have been flattened by the seemingly inexorable advance of the state juggernaut. It was not until the 1970s (by which time the British state was processing half of the Gross National Product) that they began to resurface in mainstream political argument.

Liberalism and Conservatism

As is obvious from our discussion of Smith and Mill, the liberal tradition is in principle distrustful of state power. This certainly identifies it as anti-socialist, but it also suggests that it is just as strongly anti-conservative! Both socialism and conservatism believe in using state power to bring about certain ends. Socialists seek to use the state to foster greater social equality and to attack the privileges of those with property in the name of the mass of the people; conservatives seek to use state power to maintain the existing social order and to defend the privileges of those with property while 'looking after' less fortunate groups so as to maintain a national unity of all the people. Neither approach seems to have much in common with a body of thought which seeks to limit the powers of the state and to leave people alone to lead their lives as they see fit.

One of the problems with our political terminology of 'Left wing' and 'Right wing' is that it implies a continuum of political beliefs between two diametrically opposed poles. This is, however, an incomplete 'map' of politics, for in Britain political thinking and argument has ever since the nineenth century been structured around *three* positions – conservatism (support for the status quo), socialism (support for a new, egalitarian social order) and liberalism (support for individual liberties). Sometimes liberals and conservatives can be found on the same side opposing socialists, but on other issues socialists and conservatives align with each other against liberals. If conservatism is taken to be 'Right-wing', then there seems no more reason to apply the same label to liberals than to socialists!

Liberals and conservatives tend to take up a common position against socialists on issues to do with private property and wealth redistribution. Liberals strongly oppose socialist prescriptions for achieving a more egalitarian society since they believe that individuals have the right to enjoy their property provided only that they have come by it legitimately. The socialist belief in taking from the rich to give to the poor is seen as an unjustifiable intrusion into the rights of the individual.

Socialists and conservatives tend to take up a common position against liberals on issues to do with the rights of the collectivity. Despite its rhetoric, socialism is often strongly nationalistic in its practice since, like conservatism, it defines its goal as the defence of the common interest of 'the people'. Conservatives and socialists alike talk of the duties and responsibilities which individuals owe to the collectivity and they justify policies on the grounds that they contribute to the common good even if some individuals lose. Liberals, on the other hand, place the rights of the individual above those of the collectivity and are sceptical of any claim (whether by conservatives or socialists) to know better than individuals themselves what is and is not in their best interests.

As we have seen, liberal ideas gradually lost their influence in British politics after the mid-nineteenth century. Indeed, in the twentieth century the term 'liberal' has become virtually synonymous with collectivism and 'democratic socialism' (so much so that in 1987 the Liberal and Social Democratic Parties in Britain merged their identities). In the classical sense used here, however, there is no 'liberal' party in Britain and there has not been one since, at the very latest, 1906. Inevitably, therefore, if liberal ideas were to resurface, it had to be through one of the non-liberal parties. As things turned out, this was the Conservative Party under the leadership of Margaret Thatcher.

Given the deep divisions between liberalism and conservatism, we should not be surprised that the phenomenon which became 'Thatcherism' reveals an uneasy tension between these two traditions. There is much in the philosophy and practice of the Conservative governments of the 1980s which owes little or nothing to the ideas of liberalism, for despite the dramatic changes in the Party since the mid-seventies it is still the Tory Party and it still maintains many of its old loyalties and sentiments. On many social questions, in particular, these governments proved most 'illiberal' – for example, in laying down a new national curriculum to be followed in every school, in seeking to tighten censorship over the Press, television and publishing, in strengthening the powers of central government relative to local authorities and 'intermediate institutions' such as the universities and the professions, in increasing official secrecy, in legislating against the 'promotion' of homosexuality, and so on. Liberal ideas have regained a toehold in British politics through the Conservative government, but as with the relation of Marxist thought to the Labour movement, they have been diluted and much compromised in the process.

The Value of Freedom

Freedom, equality and democracy

The liberal tradition, and the 'New Right' as its contemporary expression, has always held as central its belief in individual freedom. Most political philosophies, of course, claim to support freedom – as we saw in chapter 7, the deputy-leader of the Labour Party, Roy Hattersley, has recently published a book under the title *Choose Freedom* in which he equates socialism with 'true liberty'. The question, therefore, is not whether this or that political doctrine supports freedom, but what it means by it and where it places it on a hierarchy of desirable principles.

New Right liberals place freedom at the top of their scale of values, and what they mean by the term is simply 'absence of coercion'. Freedom, in other words, is defined negatively – you are free if nobody is forcing you to do what you do not want to do. This is very different from socialist conceptions of freedom. For a start, socialists embrace other values which are inevitably placed higher on their scale of priorities. Liberalism is more concerned with freedom than with anything else because liberty is precisely its objective. Socialism, however, exists primarily to bring about a new social order in which means of production are owned (or at least organised) collectively and in which human behaviour will necessarily be different from how it is under capitalism. Most socialists hope that this objective can be realised without intruding too much on individual liberties, but all socialists accept that some freedoms will have to be curtailed if the goal is to be achieved. For liberals, freedom is the goal; for socialists it is a value which has to be safeguarded as far as possible while pursuing their goal.

Socialists and liberals also mean different things when they talk of 'freedom'. Socialists often use freedom in a positive rather than a negative sense – I am free if I can do something. This enables them to claim that individuals are often 'unfree' in market systems (since they may not be able to afford to buy what they want) and that freedom may be enlarged rather than diminished by state intervention (since individuals can then be provided with resources and may be able to vote for what they want).

Liberals like Hayek totally dismiss these arguments. Freedom, they say, does not depend upon the existence of a wide range of alternative choices. I may not have the skill or intelligence or motivation to become a brain surgeon, for example, but this does not mean that I am less free than somebody else who does. Sombody who is born crippled is no less free than someone who is born able-bodied. Similarly, an individual with one pound is no less free than an individual who owns a million. The point, in other words, is that freedom is not the same as capacity – provided we are not forced to do something, we are free no matter how much innate ability or money we may have.

Similarly, Hayek disputes the notion that democratic government is a means of extending freedom. All legislation reduces freedom irrespective of whether it is enacted by elected assemblies or military dictatorships. To revert to an earlier example, a law which imposes a national curriculum on all schools prevents parents and pupils from selecting a different syllabus. The fact that this law was introduced by an elected government makes no difference to its effect in limiting individual liberties. Hayek warns that democratic government is often a means by which majorities can impose their will on minorities. As we shall see in chapter 12, Protestants systematically discriminated against Catholics in Northern Ireland through a democratically-elected Parliament at Stormont prior to 1969, and many Scots today object that they did not vote for and do not wish to be ruled by the government in Westminster. At local level too, thousands of electors are obliged to finance and accept councils which pursue policies which they do not favour.

From the point of view of the minority, therefore, democratic procedures are little consolation for the loss of individual liberties. Hayek accepts that when collective decisions have to be made, they are best made by means of democratic majority decision, but he insists that *all* forms of government destroy liberties and that democracy is no justification for increasing government control where it is not absolutely necessary:

'Liberalism . . . is concerned mainly with limiting the coercive powers of all government, whether democratic or not, whereas the dogmatic democrat knows only one limit to government – current majority opinion.'

It follows from all this that freedom and equality are, to some extent, incompatible objectives. To make people equal is to prevent some of them from doing what they want since this would benefit them more than others. Conversely, to make people free is to allow them to pursue their own interests as they see them even if others do not benefit. Given that, for many of us, both liberty and equality seem desirable and appealing objectives, the argument that we cannot have both represents a major moral dilemma. It is for precisely this reason, of course, that conflict and argument has always been endemic to political systems, for it seems inevitable that some people will always place equality above liberty while others will always, and just as passionately, place liberty above equality.

Freedom and the minimal state

The central concern with individual freedom above all other values sets New Right liberals apart from conservatives as well as socialists, for it has long been a feature of conservative thought that individuals' desires and actions need to be constrained and regulated as much for their own good as for the good of others. Conservatives emphasise the crucial importance of moral training, in order to regulate the passions from within, and of law and punishment, in order to control them from without (see chapter 11). Liberals, or libertarians as they sometimes now call themselves, tend to be just as suspicious of these arguments as they are of socialist dreams of remoulding humanity in a new egalitarian social order.

In some ways, then, the New Right seems to have more in common with anarchism than with either conservatism or socialism. Indeed, there used to be a 'libertarian bookshop' in London's Covent Garden where New Right and anarchist tracts nestled side by side on the bookshelves. Yet again we see here the difficulty in maintaining a conventional 'Left–Right' map of politics, for most observers would place New Right liberals and anarchist libertarians at opposite ends of the political spectrum! Despite the similarities between them, however, the new liberals are not anarchists. While anarchists believe in a social order without a state, liberals believe in a social order with a *minimal state*. Robert Nozick, himself a former libertarian anarchist, explains why in his book *Anarchy, State and Utopia*.

Nozick accepts the anarchists' claim that a state with a monopoly over the legitimate use of force in a territory represents a violation of individual rights and freedoms, but argues that a state invested with minimal powers would arise anyway in an anarchist society. The reason is that individuals would come together to form associations for mutual protection and these associations would in turn eventually co-operate and fuse so as to create a single-umbrella system of rules and enforcement. For this reason he (like all New Right liberals) accepts the existence of a minimal state with powers to protect and defend individuals from other individuals and from other states. He accepts, in other words, that the state has legitimate law and order and defence functions. Beyond this, different writers disagree on how far the liberal state may go, although most agree with Adam Smith that provision of unprofitable public works is also legitimate, and many are also prepared to accept other functions such as the relief of distress and poverty, care for those (like children or the mentally ill) who cannot take responsibility for themselves, provision of a stable and sound monetary system, and enforcement of strong anti-trust (i.e. anti-monopoly) rules so as to ensure competition in commodity markets.

We need not dwell here on the arguments for and against inclusion or exclusion of specific functions in the state's role. The point is simply that, wherever possible, the presumption is made that individuals should be left to do things for themselves rather than allowing the state to take responsibility.

The Case for the Free Market

Why are new liberals so determined to keep the role of the state to an absolute minimum (however defined)? And why do they believe that market systems are in general preferable to state control and regulation? There are at least six reasons.

Individual freedom as a moral imperative

Liberals believe that no person has the right to force another to do what he or she does not wish to do. It follows from this that (with a few exceptions) the state does not have this right either, for the state is nothing more than a collectivity of individuals. Even if its intention is to act benevolently towards its subjects, increases in state power beyond what is strictly necessary for social life to continue (as in the enforcement of certain rules of conduct) must be resisted. Individuals must be left free to make their own choices for they are the best judges of their own interests.

Equally, the duties which individuals owe to the state are circumscribed. In his inaugural address, President Kennedy told the American people to think not of what their country could do for them, but of what they could do for their country. In the eyes of New Right liberals, neither of these attitudes is healthy, for the first is a sign of paternalism and dependency while the second is a sign of authoritarian government and individual subjugation. As the American neo-liberal economist Milton Friedman puts it, 'Neither half of the statement expresses a relation between the citizen and his government that is worthy of the ideals of free men in a free society.'

Of course, enjoyment of liberties also entails responsibility for the consequences which follow when we exercise these liberties. We cannot demand freedom from government interference in our lives and then expect other people (through the government) to bail us out when things do not work out as we had hoped. A free society must allow people the freedom to make bad or even disastrous choices, but this also entails that they must be prepared to suffer the consequences. Equally, if things go well, free individuals can enjoy the benefits and are under no ethical obligation to share them out (for example, through high tax payments) among those who chose other, less beneficial, courses of action. Liberalism takes its biblical cue from the parable of the three talents rather than from the story of the prodigal son.

Freedom as a spur to innovation and progress

We cannot predict the future, for we are all ignorant of many of the millions of factors which will come together to shape our destinies. As individuals, however, we each try to achieve various objectives, and the motivation for this is the prospect of improving our own lives or the lives of those close to us. In a free society, some will innovate and fail, and they must bear the costs of this failure themselves. Others, however, innovate and succeed. They may then achieve spectacular gains as they market a new good or service which thousands of other people are willing to buy. As a result of their success, however, everybody else benefits, for new knowledge has been created and new possibilities for human action have been opened up. Consider, for example, the case of the British inventor and entrepreneur Sir Clive Sinclair. In the 1970s he marketed the first cheap personal computer and he made a fortune. In the early eighties, however, he tried to open up another new market by producing the C5 battery-operated moped. People failed to buy his invention and he lost a fortune. As a result of his first innovation, millions of households now own personal computers (made by Sinclair or by his competitors) and thousands of people have found employment in manufacturing hardware, creating new software and retailing computer products. As a result of his second innovation, Sir Clive and those who risked their capital in backing his judgement lost a lot of money but nobody else is any worse off and we have all gained by learning from his mistake. The next battery-operated vehicle may succeed where Sinclair failed.

According to the New Right, innovations like this simply would not occur in a society where the state owns or controls the means of production or where high rewards are prohibited in the name of social justice. A state monopoly has no spur to innovate. Indeed, those employed in it are most likely to be cautious and conservative lest things go wrong and they get blamed by their political masters. Similarly, without adequate incentives individuals are unlikely to have the motivation to innovate, in which case high taxation is counter-productive since it ends up suffocating the geese that lay the golden eggs.

In recent years, the Soviet Union, China and many other state socialist countries have begun to liberalise their command economies while elsewhere in Eastern Europe, central planning has been abandoned altogether. Markets are being encouraged where previously they were banned. Free enterprise is beginning to surface in forms which a few years ago would have been punishable as crimes against communism. Individual incentives are being reintroduced in an attempt to break through the bureaucratic paralysis which has settled upon so many of these economies. There can be no more eloquent testimony to the power of liberal ideas than that erstwhile socialist countries are now struggling to rediscover them in a desperate attempt to stimulate economic growth.

Free markets as essential means of social co-ordination

According to the American neo-liberal, Milton Friedman:

> Fundamentally there are only two ways of coordinating the economic activities of millions. One is central direction involving the use of coercion – the technique of the army and of the modern totalitarian state. The other is voluntary cooperation of individuals – the technique of the market place.

Consider how you came to be reading this book. Thousands, if not millions, of people were involved in enabling this to happen yet few of them knew each other and virtually none of them knew that you would want to read it. We, of course, had to write it in the hope that we could attract people like you to buy or borrow it, and Polity Press had to employ people to commission it, edit it, print it, bind it, market it and run the accounts. A bookseller had to be found to retail it, and transport had to be arranged to get it (and you) to the bookstore or the library. This in turn entailed people assembling a van which depended upon yet others manufacturing the tyres, the window glass and the steel . . . which itself meant that people had to dig the iron ore, build and operate the blast furnace (which required others to provide the coke or gas), plant the rubber trees and so on. The paper for the book could not have been created unless someone in Canada or Scandinavia or Scotland had planted the trees some years before, and they could not have cut down the trees without help from the people who manufacture chain saws. And so it goes on. The scale of interdependence is staggering, yet all of this was achieved in the absence of any overall co-ordinator or grand economic planning strategy.

According to New Right economic theories, a market economy is an unconsciously evolved device by which millions of individuals respond all the time to price signals and choose on the basis of the information available to them whether to spend their time in one way or another. A book by Dearlove and Saunders fails to attract much interest. Retailers are left with unsold stock and cut back their orders. Polity Press receives less income and reduces its demand for paper and possibly lowers the wages it pays to its staff (who then decide whether to stay or seek employment with a more successful publisher). The paper mill transmits the fall in demand to its suppliers who in turn reduce their orders for new sapplings. Everybody adjusts minutely to each change in the market, up or down. The market, in other words, is an information system which needs relatively little conscious co-ordination, and the trigger which shifts people's behaviour is change in patterns of consumer demand.

According to Hayek, it is impossible to devise a collective system of planned production which could come anywhere near this level of co-ordination and responsiveness to changes in people's wants. The reason for this is that no planning agency could possibly monitor and direct all the millions of different actions and decisions which feed off and depend upon each other. We simply cannot have the requisite degree of knowledge, foresight and information to make such a system work. This is why, according to New Right theories, shortages, queues, delays and frustration of consumer preferences are endemic to planned systems of production.

There is a further point about all this which is that, in the absence of price signals and market incentives, people would have to be forced to do the things on which other people depend. Going back to Adam Smith's example, we do not have to coerce the butcher to get out of bed before dawn and go to buy meat at the market because it is in his or her own economic interest to do so. Remove the system of free-market exchanges and there is no other way of getting everybody to do what is required of them short of threatening them. Withdraw the carrot and we are only left with the stick. It is for this reason that Hayek, Friedman and others believe that a free-market economy is a necessary (though not sufficient) condition of political freedom. In most places at most times, human beings have lived under brutal and coercive political regimes. Political freedoms – the right to vote out a government, to speak and publish freely, to travel freely and meet whomever one chooses – were engendered by the development of capitalism, and in Hayek's view they are threatened by any attempt to move away from a capitalist system towards a more planned or equal society.

The inherent tendency to totalitarianism in planned societies

The market was never invented, it evolved. Liberals share with conservatives a distrust of attempts at social engineering through which new institutions are created in order to serve a particular purpose. Institutions which work are those which have stood the test of time rather than those which have been created overnight. Of course, although the market system was never consciously created by anyone, participants in markets do try to plan their own activities. Markets are not anarchistic, for firms plan to meet anticipated demand, workers plan career moves to enhance their prospects and so on. There are, however, two major differences between a market system in which thousands of people develop their own plans, and a state-run system where there is only one plan.

1 A state-planned system puts all its eggs in one basket. In the late fifties and early sixties, for example, British governments decided that high-rise, system-built flats could provide the solution to the country's housing problem and local authorities up and down the country were encouraged to invest millions of pounds bulldozing streets of Victorian terraces to make way for new blocks of flats. The policy proved a disaster for the blocks were often badly designed and poorly constructed and many of those obliged to live in them found them totally unsuited to their needs. It is possible, of course, that in a free market *some* developers would have experimented with these blocks, but they would soon have gone out of business as consumer preferences made themselves felt. The state, however, is immune to such salutory market disciplines. Big state plans carry inherent risks of big and costly mistakes on a grand scale.

2 Different people will always want different things. We may all agree that we would like a properly planned society, but we will most certainly disagree over what form the plan should take.

It is this second problem which, according to Hayek, carries the potential for the emergence of totalitarian government. In his *The Road to Serfdom*, published in 1944, he argued that the incessant squabbling and eventual stalemate which follows from attempts at genuine democratic planning is likely to result in a shift of power away from democratic forums towards bodies of 'experts' and bureaucrats. At the same time it is also likely to stimulate a popular demand for strong leaders who can get things done. The result, as in the German Weimar Republic, is a drift into fascism and the imposition of collective goals in the name of 'the people' or 'the masses'.

Effective planning on a national scale necessitates strong leadership. It also requires the concentration of power and resources in a few hands, for given the interdependency of economic life it is simply not possible to plan production in one area unless you can control the flow of resources in many others. It is for this reason that enlightened and progressive social planners who start out with the aim of improving people's lives often end up seeking ever-increasing powers which erode personal liberties. Hayek who, like so many other writers in this tradition, began life as a socialist, and who witnessed the rise of the Nazis before fleeing to Britain, wrote *The Road to Serfdom* because he believed that the socialist reforms in Britain in the 1940s were paving the way to ever-increasing state powers and the eventual rise of totalitarian government. Britain, in other words, was taking the very route which Germany had taken in the years before the Nazi take-over.

The inherent tendency for state power to be hi-jacked by special interests

In a market system resources are widely dispersed among different suppliers, but state planning concentrates resources at one centre. This then encourages different sectional interests to exert pressure upon the state for favourable treatment. Big capitalist firms begin to demand protected markets or special subsidies. Organised labour mobilises to achieve income and employment guarantees and to gain legal immunities. Farmers push for special protection and price supports, professional groups seek state licensing so as to stop non-approved competitors from setting up in business, and even state employees themselves seize the chance to press for more spending on their departments so as to expand their salaries and enhance their status and prospects for advancement. As each new demand is made, the tendency is to give way to it, for the benefits to the group in question are considerable while the costs can be spread out thinly across the whole population. But as each demand is met, so it stimulates new ones. Like the multi-headed hydra, special interest groups multiply the more they are satisfied. If one firm is granted special treatment, why not others? If one group of workers or professionals gain special protected status, what is to stop others seeking it?

One consequence of this is that state spending spirals upwards while market freedoms become more and more eroded. The only group which cannot pressurise the state for special treatment is consumers, for they are generally fragmented whereas producers are organised and unified. Rather like the mercantilist system in Smith's day, ordinary people end up paying more and getting less. There is a particular body of thought in political science which has developed specifically to analyse this process. Variously termed 'Public Choice theory' or 'the economics of politics', it seeks to show how state agencies come to be 'captured' by special interests, either from within or without, and it sounds a particular warning about the perils in democratic systems where votes can easily be won by targeting benefits at particular interests while spreading the cost across the whole population.

The result is that agencies designed to provide a service to consumers often end up being run in the interests of producers. The welfare state, for example, comes to be run, not for the poor, but for social workers, housing professionals, doctors, teachers and a vast army of managers who administer these services. Expenditure rises year after year yet the quality of the service does not seem to get much better. Not that consumers can do much about it, for while state agencies are captured by service producers, consumers often find that they have in turn been trapped by state agencies. They have no choice but to pay for these services, for they are financed out of taxes compulsorily levied upon everybody whether or not they wish or would choose to use them. Everybody pays for state schools, for the state health care system, and so on and few can afford to pay again in order to 'exit' to an alternative private supplier (assuming one exists). But because they cannot take their money elsewhere, they are taken for granted. Users become dependent clients rather than discerning customers, and they have little choice but to take what they are given.

The injustice of the pursuit of social justice

Socialists seek to use the power of the state to bring about what they call 'social justice'. The term 'social justice' implies that some people have advantages which they do not deserve and that others deserve more than they have got. It is a fundamental aim of socialism and of social democracy to bring about 'social justice', either by redistributing resources in a 'fairer' kind of capitalist society, or by establishing a new socialist order in which resources are allocated according to need rather than by the ability to pay. New Right critics have at least three objections to all this.

One is that it is impossible to determine just deserts. Short of complete equality (which even Marx did not demand) it is difficult to think of any set of principles of distribution which are self-evidently fair. Should people with children receive more than those without? Should lazy people receive as much as those who are industrious? Should people who care for the sick receive more than those who hew coal? Should people who study receive more than those who do not want or are not capable of undertaking training? Should people who take responsibility for making decisions receive more than those who simply do what they are told? Should fat people with large appetites receive more than thin people with small ones? Should people whose services are wanted by many receive more than people who provide services which nobody wants? Should people who have to travel a long distance to work receive more than those who do not? And who is to decide on all these claims and counter-claims?

A second problem with the pursuit of social justice is that it is by no means obvious that the fairest distribution is one where everybody receives roughly equal shares according to their needs. To ask how resources should be distributed is to ignore the fact that they have been produced by somebody and that they therefore already have claims attached to them. This point has been developed most forcibly by Robert Nozick who puts forward what he calls an 'entitlement theory' of justice. The difference between this and the 'distributional theory' advocated by socialists can be illustrated by means of a trite but pertinent example.

Imagine a group of people who come together to play a game of *Monopoly*. They will doubtless all agree at the outset with the socialist who suggests that the only fair and just way of allocating money between them is to give everybody the same amount. Now let the game commence. Nobody cheats, nobody forces anyone else to do what they do not choose to do, and all rules are meticulously observed. Through astute play and not a little luck, some players begin to accumulate substantial wealth and property holdings while others begin to lose. At this point the socialist demands that it is only fair to redistribute all the money and property so that everybody again has equal shares. But at this stage, many of the players are likely to object that this would be extremely unfair and unjust. They have come by their wealth legitimately and they therefore have a right to keep it. They have established an entitlement to what they own and nobody has the right to take it away from them to give to somebody else. As in games of *Monopoly*, so in real life, resources do not belong to the collectivity for it to share out as it sees fit, and attempts to use state power to reallocate personal wealth thus undermine rather than promote social justice and fair treatment.

The third problem with the socialist desire to use the state to bring about more equal shares is that it undermines the Rule of Law on which all civilised social life depends. The basic principle of the Rule of Law dictates that everybody must be subject to the same rules, that these rules must be clearly understood and stated in advance, and that rules should not be framed so that any one group can expect to benefit from them more than any other (i.e. justice must be 'blind' to its effects).

The pursuit of 'social justice' is, however, concerned not with means but with ends. Rules are developed which are deliberately intended to produce certain results which will benefit one group more than another. Rather than treating people in exactly the same way irrespective of who they are, it entails different treatment for different people. Once this is allowed to happen, the Rule of Law disappears, and with it goes the most basic safeguard for citizens against the arbitrary use of state power. A government which is no longer bound to the Rule of Law can pass whatever legislation it pleases in an attempt to benefit one group or deprive another. Laws which allow property to be confiscated from the rich are in principle no different from the laws in Nazi Germany which allowed property to be confiscated from Jews or other non-Aryans. Laws which give trade unionists immunity from prosecution are in principle no different from those in feudal Europe which gave landowners or aristocrats such immunities. Laws which allow certain jobs to be reserved for women or ethnic minorities are in principle no different from laws in South Africa which prohibit blacks from doing certain types of work in certain specified areas.

For New Right liberals, then, any attempt to use legislation to bring about certain social objectives is perilously dangerous irrespective of whom the legislation is designed to favour. Perhaps the most fundamental reason for advocating a minimal state strictly bound by the Rule of Law is that anything more destroys the only barrier that exists to defend individual citizens against the whims of their rulers.

Prescriptions for Change

The six arguments outlined above lead contemporary liberals to the conclusion that state power in Britain has grown too vast. The power of the state must be broken and replaced by free-market exchanges between individuals except in limited cases where it can be demonstrated that the state's role is indispensible. This conclusion has implications in three main areas of policy – the economy, the welfare system and the constitution.

Economic policy

New Right prescriptions as regards the role of the state in economic affairs fall broadly into the three categories of monetary policy, competition policy and fiscal policy.

Monetary policy

In the early years of the Thatcher governments in Britain it was liberal *monetary policy* which received most public attention. In the mid 1970s inflation had risen to over 20 per cent before the Labour government was obliged to accept a loan from the International Monetary Fund in 1976 to cover a damaging balance of payments crisis and to boost the flagging overseas value of the pound sterling. The conditions attached to the IMF loan demanded a sharp reduction in inflation to be achieved through control of the money supply (notably through reductions in the government's own spending). As Prime Minister Callaghan told the delegates at his party conference later that year, 'the party's over'.

When the Conservatives won power in 1979, they sought to strengthen this monetary discipline. Following abolition of exchange controls, the government set out a 'Medium Term Financial Strategy' in which it committed itself to meeting published targets for state expenditure and growth in the money supply. As we shall see in chapter 9, this strategy succeeded in reducing inflation from 15 per cent in 1979 to 2.4 per cent in 1986, although this was achieved at the cost of the worst recession since the 1930s – and inflation crept back up again in the years that followed. The system of setting strict monetary targets was eventually abandoned in 1985 as it became increasingly difficult even to measure the money supply, still less to control it, in an era of financial deregulation and instant credit. By the late eighties the government had come to rely almost entirely on manipulation of interest rates to control borrowing, and thus to control inflation. Although Thatcherism ceased to be associated with monetarism from the mid-eighties onwards, most New Right liberals still insist on the crucial importance of imposing monetary discipline on governments. Their concern is not only with inflation but also has to do with the principles of 'Public Choice theory' outlined above. If this theory is right in its view that democratic pressures tend to encourage governments constantly to raise expenditure to favour particular vociferous groups, then it follows that any attempt to reduce state activity must involve some way of preventing government from increasing its borrowing in order to finance these expenditures.

One writer who has developed these arguments, and who was an early influence on Margaret Thatcher's enthusiasm for controlling the money supply, is Milton Friedman. He argues that inflation is simply a result of an over-supply of money. If a government increases the amount of money in circulation faster than the rate at which the number of goods being bought and sold increases, then prices inevitably will rise as each purchaser will be able to bid more money for the same number of goods. It follows from this that the money supply should be fixed and only allowed to rise to keep pace with the expansion of the economy. Friedman's recipe for achieving this is that governments should each year publish a money supply target and should not waver from it. This, to all intents and purposes, was what the Conservatives tried to do in their Medium Term Financial Strategy.

Why have neo-liberals been so concerned about inflation? There are basically four reasons:

1 It produces unfair redistributive effects – people who save for their old age, for example, find the value of their savings is eroded, people who buy houses make windfall capital gains when house prices suddenly lurch upwards, and so on.
2 It undermines confidence in the value of the currency and this is fatal to a free-market system in which sound money is a condition of any long-term economic activity. Indeed, when inflation turns into hyperinflation, as in Germany in the 1920s, it effectively paralyses economic life and poses a threat to the existence of the whole social and political order of a free society.
3 It enhances the power of the state, partly because governments can print or borrow money to finance increasing levels of activity, and partly because inflation is an easy means of allowing the tax yield to increase and the real value of government debt to fall.
4 Inflation distorts the role of prices as information signals.

The fourth point, which has been emphasised in particular in Hayek's work, requires more detailed explanation.

As we shall see in chapter 9, for thirty years after the Second World War governments of both parties tried to manage the economy by stimulating increases in spending whenever the economy began to slump. This was sometimes achieved by cutting interest rates (so that consumers could borrow more to finance their purchases) or easing credit restrictions or reducing taxes (so that workers had more in their pockets to spend), but the principal strategy was to increase government spending by running a budget deficit (for higher public spending allowed government to soak up unemployment by increasing the size of the public-sector workforce and by stimulating demand for goods and services supplied by private firms). It was recognised that all of this could be inflationary, but the assumption was that all these measures could be reversed once the economy had begun to pick up.

As we saw in the discussion of 'political business cycles' in chapter 2, this ability to stimulate demand artificially proved an attractive proposition for politicians, but having squeezed the toothpaste out of the tube in times of slump it proved much more difficult to get it back in again when the economy began to boom. Furthermore, according to Hayek, such injections of demand built up something akin to a drug dependency, for once the initial effects had worn off governments found it necessary to administer another, larger dose in order to restimulate an equivalent rise in output. The policy thus locked governments into an inflationary spiral from which it became increasingly difficult to escape without bringing about a massive recession.

In Hayek's view, the most damaging effect of all this was that it prevented the market system from operating as a system of information. As we saw earlier, price movements in a free market are the means by which changes in consumer demand come to be transmitted to those who supply goods and services. If demand for a particular good falls (for example, because technical change has created a better or cheaper alternative), the price will drop and suppliers will be obliged either to increase their efficiency or to move into another area of production where demand is rising. Demand management by governments prevents this from happening since it artificially props up flagging consumer demand and therefore encourages suppliers to believe, falsely, that there is still a strong market for their products. Capital and labour both therefore stay put in declining sectors of the economy when they should be moving. The result is massive inefficiency, for the society's resources get stuck producing goods which fewer people want while new and expanding areas of production are starved of the capital and labour which they need to attract in order to expand. This cannot go on indefinitely, especially when other countries are modernising and can flood British markets with the newer goods which home-based industries have failed to provide. In Britain it came to an abrupt halt in the early eighties when the government refused to inflate the economy any further and precipitated a major recession. Many firms went bankrupt and many workers lost their jobs. According to the New Right, this was a long-overdue adjustment to market trends and it could all have been achieved much more gradually and much less painfully had governments over the previous thirty years resisted the temptation to fiddle with the economy and left the market system to operate on its own logic.

For the future, Hayek has argued that the best way of preventing governments from inflating the money supply is to strip them of the monopoly power to print money. He believes that private-sector banks should be allowed to issue their own bank notes. We could then buy goods and services using Midland Bank money, Barclays Bank money or whatever. If any bank succumbed to the temptation to print more notes than were required to finance transactions on the part of its customers, it would soon find that the value of these notes would fall relative to that of money issued by other banks. Its customers would then have to pay, say, sixty Midland pounds for a good priced at fifty Barclay pounds, and they would swiftly transfer their accounts to a rival where their money retained its value. This proposal provides a good example of the faith which neo-liberals place in market competition to achieve what governments conspicuously fail to achieve.

Competition policy

The concern with *competition* is the second distinctive aspect of New Right economic policy. Free markets can only operate if producer cartels and monopolies are (as far as possible) outlawed. A monopoly supplier can exploit consumers by forcing up the price of a good and extracting super profits. Similarly cartels can agree not to compete on price so that all producers are able to extract higher profits than would have been possible had there been free competition between them. It is for this reason that virtually all neo-liberals agree that the state has a crucial role to play in breaking up existing monopolies and preventing the creation of new ones. In Britain, this task falls to the Monopolies and Mergers Commission which investigates any proposed company merger or takeover which might result in an undesirable reduction in competition, although the Commission has often in practice allowed mergers to take place which in the view of many represent a major reduction in market competition.

The attack on monopolies embraces labour as well as capital. A trade union closed shop, for example, restrains free competition in the labour market just as, say a price fixing cartel among the oil companies would represent a restraint on free competition in commodity markets. Neo-liberals accept the right of workers freely to join trade unions if they so choose, but they oppose any attempt to force workers to join unions (as in the closed shop) and they seek abolition of all trade union legal privileges and immunities (since these are inconsistent with the principle of the Rule of Law). In a series of Acts passed in the 1980s the government stripped unions in Britain of some of their immunities (for example, the immunity from prosecution when calling secondary action against an employer not directly involved in a dispute), but a number of special dispensations still remain (for example, a union which organises a 'legal' picket cannot be sued by an employer for restraint on trade).

The anti-monopoly stance also extends to the professions. Many professional associations seek to control entry and stifle competition by state licensing of the right to practice. The government has in recent years begun to erode some of these privileges in line with neo-liberal thinking. The solititors have lost their legal monopoly over house conveyancing, barristers' exclusive right to appear as advocates in a court of law has been attacked, opticians have lost their monopoly over provision of spectacles, and teachers are threatened by attempts to introduce unqualified helpers into classrooms. In every case, predictably, the profession concerned has mobilised against these changes, and many professional enclaves remain virtually unchallenged.

Finally, the attack on monopoly powers extends to the state itself. In the case of 'natural monopolies' (i.e. goods or services which can only realistically be provided by one supplier) neo-liberals often accept state provision or regulation, but the general principle is that government should provide as little as possible. Neo-liberals are enthusiastic privatisers although they tend to be critical of the way the British government has gone about selling off public-sector industries such as British Gas (which was sold as a single company rather than being broken up into a number of smaller competing units). The aim is to reverse over one hundred years of creeping nationalisation by selling off all state-owned industries, deregulating the private sector and contracting out as many as possible of the state-run services so as to open up these areas of the economy to the cleansing blast of market competition.

Fiscal policy

The third strand to New Right economic thinking concerns *fiscal policy*. The argument here is simple: taxation must be kept to a minimum so as to maximise individual incentives and entrepreneurship. People must be allowed to keep the benefits which accrue to them from hard work or successful risk-taking. High taxes which are designed to take from the rich in order to help the poor end up disadvantaging everybody since they discourage people from creating the wealth from which everybody benefits.

Neo-liberals like Friedman and Hayek believe that, left to itself, a capitalist market system will do more to raise living standards and eradicate poverty than any amount of fiscal redistribution. Capitalism is a growth machine. At any one time there will be a large gap in income and wealth between those at the top and those at the bottom, but both groups become increasingly prosperous over time. The luxuries of one generation (car ownership, foreign holidays, home ownership, central heating, colour television) become the taken-for-granted possessions of the majority in the next generation. Hayek likens this to a 'moving column' with the rich at the front and the 'poor' at the back. The column keeps marching forward so that, although those at the back never catch up, they do achieve at time B the standard of living achieved by those at the front at time A. High taxation, however, will stall the growth machine and halt the moving column in its tracks. Nobody gains, everybody loses.

The New Right sees taxes as a necessary evil. Because the state has to discharge certain minimal functions, it has to raise money in order to finance its activities. It is altogether wrong, however, to use taxation as an instrument of policy as opposed to a means for raising revenue. When the Labour Chancellor of the Exchequer, Dennis Healey, promised in the 1970s to increase taxes on the rich until the pips squeak, he was using the power to tax as an instrument of class warfare rather than as a way of raising money. Under the 1974–9 Labour government, the top rate of tax on earned incomes was increased to 83 per cent and that on unearned income was levied at a staggering 98 per cent. Little was achieved by this in terms of revenue-raising, for the small numbers of high earners emigrated, or arranged to be paid in kind rather than in cash (for example, by accepting a company car or free private health insurance or shares), or simply stopped working so hard. Indeed, it has been found in the United States that a reduction in tax rates can actually increase revenue since it encourages people to earn more and makes it less worth their while to devise accountancy tax dodges. The socialist commitment to high taxes on high earners has always had more to do with emotional reactions against privilege than with rational concerns to find new sources of revenue.

Because of his aversion to using taxation policy as a means of redistribution, Hayek argues against 'progressive' taxation and in favour of a single tax rate. The Thatcher governments in the 1980s moved some way towards this by replacing local authority domestic rates with a flat-rate per capita community charge, and by simplifying income tax into just two bands (25 per cent and 40 per cent at the time of writing). However, the fiscal record of the Thatcher years makes dismal reading for neo-liberals, for despite reductions in direct tax rates, the overall tax burden (including national insurance contributions and indirect taxes such as VAT) actually rose from 35 per cent of total output in 1979 to 37.5 per cent in 1989 demonstrating yet again how difficult it can be for any government of Left or Right to effect dramatic and radical changes in core areas of policy.

Welfare policy

The state's role in providing for the welfare of its citizens divides into two areas – social security and welfare services. In Britain the social security system is based notionally on an insurance principle (although this has been eroded since the war and many benefits are now financed through taxation). Workers pay for a weekly national insurance stamp through a compulsory deduction from their wages, and in return they are entitled to claim payments if they become unemployed or sick and to claim a pension when they retire. The system of welfare services, by contrast, is financed wholly through general taxation and, with a few exceptions such as council housing and targeted cash benefits, is available on demand. Apart from housing, the principal welfare services in Britain take the form of 'free' (and compulsory) education, a 'free' National Health Service, and various social services such as care for the elderly. The New Right would like to see major changes in both of these areas of the welfare state.

Social security

In respect of *social security*, some writers see no case for compulsory insurance of any kind while others accept that people must be obliged to insure themselves against sickness, unemployment and loss of earnings in old age but would like to see the compulsory system of national insurance replaced or complemented by systems of private insurance so that people can choose the type of policies which suit them best.

More generally, most neo-liberals accept that the state has a role to play in alleviating the plight of those in dire need although all emphasise that much can be achieved through voluntary effort – for example, charitable work and support within the family unit. Any attempt by the state to support the incomes of the poor must take care not to erode the incentive to work, not to create a culture of dependency among recipients and not to undermine voluntary effort. This usually means that any state aid will need to be rigorously means-tested and set at quite a low level.

Perhaps the most carefully-considered proposal is that by Milton Friedman for a system of 'negative income tax' (NIT). Under such a system, people earning above a certain level of income would pay tax while those below it would receive cash supplements at a fixed percentage rate. If, for example, the threshold taxable income level were set at £80 per week and the rate of NIT were fixed at 50 per cent, then someone with a taxable income of £60 would receive a supplement of 50 per cent of the difference between this and the threshold – i.e. £10. Such a system would, says Friedman, provide a minimum floor below which nobody could fall, it would maintain incentives by avoiding the problems of the poverty trap, and it would substitute a single and easily-understood system of income support for the battery of special benefits and payments which currently clog up the social security system.

Welfare services

Equally radical measures have been proposed for the reform of *welfare services*. In general, the New Right believes that consumers should be left alone to choose their health care, education and so on by paying for it in the market. When the state determines the kind of service that people should be given, consumer demands are likely to go unmet and there is no mechanism for innovating or improving the quality of service delivery. Consumers are trapped because they are forced to pay taxes for state services which they may not want. However, most neo-liberals also recognise that some people would not be able to afford to pay for private health care or private schooling if these services were left entirely to the market to provide.

One solution to this dilemma, again developed by Friedman, is the introduction of voucher schemes. In education, for example, all parents of school-aged children could be given a voucher which they could spend however they saw fit in purchasing education for their children. The recipients of these vouchers (schools, private tutors or whatever) would then cash them with the government. This would effectively create a market in schooling, and as in any other market, those schools which succeeded in attracting most custom would flourish while popular schools would go to the wall. The power relationship between producers and consumers (in this case, schools and parents) would in this way be reversed, for teachers' livelihoods would depend upon their ability to provide parents with what they wanted, and parents would in turn be able to shop around and change between schools to find the best service on offer.

These ideas have found little favour with Britain's Conservative government. People have been allowed to contract out of the State Earnings Related Pension Scheme in order to buy into private pension schemes of their choice, but the system of national insurance remains in tact. Similarly, reforms of health and education have allowed state hospitals and schools to become self-governing and have increased the right of parents to choose between different state schools, but these reforms have stopped a long way short of empowering consumers in the way that Friedman envisages. Government funding for health and education is still channelled to the producer agencies (hospitals and schools) rather than to the consumers of these services. Consumers, that is, still find themselves in the role of dependent clients rather than independent customers.

Constitutional reform

The fundamental constitutional problem from the point of view of the New Right is how to devise a system which will prevent governments from expanding their powers whenever it suits them to do so. As we saw in chapter 4, this is a question which has begun to exercise the minds of representatives of many other shades of political opinion as well and it has given rise to various demands for a written constitution or a Bill of Rights.

It is notable, however, that many New Right theorists are American and they are still concerned about the encroachment of government powers despite the existence in the USA of written constitutional safeguards (such as the balance of powers between the President, Congress and the judiciary) and of the Bill of Rights guaranteeing a range of individual freedoms. In their view, none of this has been adequate, for American governments have still been able to run up huge budget deficits and increase taxes to fund major federal programmes, while special pleading by vested interests – 'pork barrel' politics, lobbying and 'logrolling' – has successfully been developed to a fine art in the American political system with disastrous consequences for ordinary tax payers and consumers who cannot win the ear of government.

Hayek's response to all of this is to call for a radical constitutional reform which would ensure that government remains bound by the principles of the Rule of Law. The essence of his proposal is that there should be a lower house, or governmental assembly, elected on a universal franchise and responsible for devising legislation, but that this would be limited in its powers by a new upper house whose sole responsibility would be to set down general rules of just conduct (freedom of contract, inviolability of property, compensation for damage done to others) and to ensure that all new legislation complied with them. Hayek suggests that elections to this upper house should be held annually among all citizens who reach the age of 45 in that year, and that candidates would similarly be drawn each year from this age group. Each year, therefore, a cohort of 45-year-old men and women would enter the upper house where they would retain their seats until retirement at sixty. The logic behind this seemingly bizarre proposal is that once elected, these representatives would be free from party pressures since they would never again have to seek re-election, and they could therefore act impartially when reviewing new legislation. Any proposed legislation which flouted the principles of the Rule of Law (for example, by deliberately attempting to benefit one group over others) would be ruled invalid.

Other writers have other proposals. Some argue that any new law should require a 75 per cent majority before it could be passed so as to make it more difficult to cobble together alliances of self-interested parties. Others have suggested that it should be made illegal for any government to plan to spend more than it receives in the taxes it levies since this would stop governments expanding their activities through printing money or extending borrowing. In all these cases, the objective is the same – to find a constitutional means for limiting the power of the state so as to safeguard the liberties of the individual and the unfettered operation of the free market.

The New Right and its Critics

Not surprisingly, socialists and conservatives alike have been swift to respond to many of the arguments and assertions developed as a result of the resurgence of liberal thought since the 1970s. Some of these criticisms are more easily countered than others.

The Rule of Law and authoritarianism

The fact that the New Right places so much emphasis on the duty of the state to enforce the Rule of Law while insisting that its social and economic functions should be cut back leads many critics to argue that these ideas are no more than a thinly-disguised apologia for oppression in defence of the status quo. Marxists like Ruth Levitas argue that New Right ideas represent the ideology of the capitalist class and are designed to justify and defend the interests of dominant social strata by strengthening law and order while cutting back on social provisions: 'Private capital has always defended itself against socialism and organised labour in this way . . . the electorate has been persuaded to give sufficient support to a set of extremely damaging policies which are not in their interests.' A number of points can be made about this type of criticism. One is simply to note that many New Right intellectuals in Britain are former socialists from working-class backgrounds and have little or no connection with 'big capital'. Their sympathies lie with 'ordinary people', not with 'privileged classes'. The difference between socialist intellectuals and liberal intellectuals is not that one defends the workers while the other defends capitalists, but is that they identify different 'enemies'. Socialists believe that power and privilege are monopolised by capitalist corporations. Liberals believe that power and privilege are monopolised by those who control the state and shelter under its patronage. The result is that socialists put their trust in the state to liberate working people from capitalist exploitation, while liberals put their faith in the market to liberate working people from political exploitation. Neither group should be accused of bad faith, for it makes no more sense to dismiss neo-liberalism as the self-interested ideology of the bourgeoisie than it does to dismiss socialism as the self-interested ideology of privileged academics employed in the public sector.

It is also a mistake to confuse the New Right's advocacy of the Rule of Law with support for authoritarianism. Support for the Rule of Law has nothing to do with a desire to increase the size or powers of the police and is in some ways its reverse. The Rule of Law is a principle intended to limit the coercive powers of government, not extend them. The more legislation which a government introduces, the greater is the need for coercive measures to enforce it, especially where it is designed to benefit one group at the expenses of another. The Rule of Law, incorporating Hayek's principles of just conduct, is designed to limit powers of legislation and thus reduce the scope for state coercion. But, say the critics, rules are never neutral in their effects. Hayek's principles of just conduct, such as the defence of the inviolability of property rights, clearly benefit some people more than others because some people have more to defend than others. The Rule of Law insists in principle that everybody must be treated in exactly the same way, but in practice this means that the wealthy have their privileges safeguarded while the poor get nothing.

The liberal response to this is twofold. First, the Rule of Law does protect everybody's liberties – it defends your right to keep your bicycle just as it defends my right to keep my Rolls-Royce. Second, in a genuinely free-market system all individuals are free to engage in whatever lawful activity they choose and all individuals therefore have the opportunity to make a fortune if they are clever enough, lucky enough and sufficiently motivated. A law which protects private property does not therefore defend any one social group, for the people with money today will not be the same as the people with money tomorrow.

These arguments are important yet they leave a lingering doubt unresolved. The problem is that not everybody does or could enjoy an equal opportunity to accumulate wealth, for property shares have already been distributed long before we were born. Reverting to our example of a game of *Monopoly*, it is as if a new player were to join the game late on when others already have hotels on Park Lane and Mayfair. The newcomer will still benefit from rules which apply to all (for example, that each player must take it in turn to move), and may still be able to win the game, but the odds are stacked against him or her. In fact, the situation in real life is even more disturbing than this. In the game of *Monopoly* we can at least take comfort in the thought that the owner of Mayfair came by it fairly. In the game of real life, however, many people own property because their ancestors grabbed it (for example, as a result of the Enclosures), swindled for it (for example, as in some of the former colonies) or even killed for it (for example, through conquest). Given that robbery, fraud and murder all contravene the Rule of Law, it is surely incumbent on the New Right seriously to consider how to implement what Nozick has called a 'principle of rectification'.

The limits to competition

The advocacy of the free-market system rests upon the existence of open competition. As we saw in chapter 7, however, Marx and Marxists have argued that competition actually declines as capitalism evolves, and it is certainly true that major sectors of the economy are today dominated by a smaller number of larger firms than ever before. Liberal principles may or may not have been appropriate in the nineteenth century but they have become irrelevant to the late twentieth century where effective competition has all but disappeared with the growth of megacorporations and huge multinational companies.

The New Right hotly disputes the basic assumptions behind this frequently-articulated argument. It is true, of course, that many sectors of the economy are now dominated by fewer, larger companies than in the past, but this does not mean that competition has declined, nor that barriers to entry into these markets have become insuperable. The self-made entrepreneur has not disappeared – in Britain, people like Robert Maxwell (publishing and newspapers), Richard Branson (leisure, retailing and transport), Alan Sugar (consumer electronics) and Terence Conran (retailing) have all established new business empires in recent years, and competition in most areas of the economy has arguably intensified with the spread of world markets and the emergence of Japan, Germany and south-east Asia as strong industrial economies. Indeed, many on the Left favour measures such as import controls and currency restrictions designed to *reduce* competition in home markets, so it hardly makes sense for these same people also to assert that competition has declined.

A further point is that, although this may be the age of the large corporation, big companies still rise and fall over time. Of the 200 largest manufacturers in the USA in 1967, one-third were not in the list just twenty years earlier. Many small and medium-size firms still operate, even in competition with the giants, and rapid technological change constantly opens up new market opportunities which can be (and often are) exploited more profitably by small companies than by large ones (the revolution in personal computing and home electronics is a good example). Even where big companies dominate (for example, in motor vehicles), competition for markets is still intense and specialist niches are still available for smaller firms to fill. Indeed, for all the talk on the Left of 'monopoly capitalism', it is surprisingly difficult to find many examples of monopolistic control of markets outside of the state sector. All of this is true, but two problems with the theory of market competition and consumer sovereignty still remain.

1 There is clearly a massive imbalance in many markets between the power of consumers and the power of producers. Individuals can find it just as difficult to achieve satisfaction from a big company as from a government department – both often appear remote and effectively immune to consumer complaints, and both can find it easy to ride roughshod over the interests of individuals. As a casual viewing of television consumer watchdog programmes readily confirms, the consumer experience of private-sector companies can be no less disturbing than that of bureaucratic departments of state.

2 What consumers want may itself be shaped by powerful producer interests. In books like Vance Packard's *The Hidden Persuaders* and Herbert Marcuse's *One-Dimensional Man*, critics of modern capitalism have often argued that huge corporations can effectively mould popular wants and preferences. Rather than responding to expressed demand, big companies create and stimulate it through a barrage of advertising and by more subtle manipulation of popular culture and fashion. Defenders of capitalism tend to deny this. Advertising, they say, influences choices between competing products but cannot create a preference where none exists, and they are sharply criticial of what they see as the arrogance in a view of ordinary people as the passive receptacles of bourgeois propoganda. We consider this issue in more depth in our discussion of dominant ideologies in chapter 11. Here we may simply observe that people's wants are likely to reflect many influences and experiences, and while capitalist interests cannot realistically be said to dominate and control popular preferences, it would nevertheless be surprising if they were totally without significance in affecting them.

The limits to market choice

There is no better way of meeting the diverse preferences of millions of individual consumers than by allowing them to exercise free choice in a market system. The New Right critique of central planning is well-founded, for no plan, no matter how democratically determined or expertly managed, can hope to cater for individual idiosyncracies in the way that a market system can.

The problem, however, is that markets only enable you to get what you want if you have money in your pocket or your purse to purchase the goods and services on offer. What use is the right to buy what I want if I lack the means to exercise it? Would it not be better for the state to provide the basic necessities of life free to everyone who needs them, even though this limits the choices available, rather than to allow the affluent the right to choose while the poor go without altogether? Two points can be made in response to this powerful plea in favour of collectivism.

1 Most people in modern Britain could afford to buy housing, education, health care, pensions and other necessities if they were not already paying taxes to enable the state to purchase them on their behalf. Times have changed dramatically since the nineteenth century when many people could not afford these things. Yet even a hundred years ago, those working-class households with a breadwinner in reasonably secure employment could often afford to buy or rent modest yet adequate housing, many belonged to mutual aid associations such as the friendly societies which offered reasonable medical care in return for a subscription of a few pence a week, and many received free or cheap education for their children through church schools or charitable foundations. As we shall see in chapter 10, compulsory state insurance schemes met with considerable hostility from working-class people when they were first introduced precisely because many of those affected were already making their own provisions and wanted to be allowed to continue doing so rather than being forced into a government scheme. Given that the 'respectable' stratum of the Victorian working class could apparently afford to buy many of these services without the intervention of the state, it is clear that today many more people could certainly afford to exercise this option if we returned to the principles of a minimal state and a free market. Living standards and real incomes have risen dramatically over the last century and we should not assume that a move to a free market in health or education would plunge the mass of the population into a Dickensian plight of disease, ignorance and squalor.

2 It is also obviously the case that some people would not be able to afford to purchase essential services. As we have seen, many New Right thinkers propose not that the state relinquishes all responsibility for welfare, but rather that it redirects funds away from provision in kind into various forms of income support such as NIT or education vouchers. In Britain, for example, the Liverpool University economist Patrick Minford has devised a scheme for NIT plus child allowances which would enable families on low incomes to purchase health insurance (calculated at £473 p.a. in 1981), schooling (£700 per child p.a.) and a private pension (£93 p.a.) and still be better off than they are under existing arrangements. It is possible, in other words, to construct systems of income support which enable the poor as well as the rich to enjoy the freedom to participate in the market as effective consumers.

The need for state paternalism

Many critics of New Right ideas react with horror to the suggestion that ordinary people should be left to judge for themselves the kind of health care they should buy or the kind of schooling which is best for their children. State provision, they say, is necessary in order to ensure that everybody gets the right sort of services. This is because many people are ignorant and do not have the means to gather the information which is required in order to make an informed choice.

Let us suppose that after the Second World War the government had established a National Food Service (the NFS). Everybody was obliged to pay taxes which were then spent by the government on paying farmers to grow foodstuffs which experts deemed appropriate to the population's dietary needs. In the 1940s this would presumably have meant a national diet crammed full of animal fats, but we let that pass. All supermarkets and grocery stores were nationalised and each week food was distributed to each household, this process being managed and monitored by a vast bureaucratic machinery. Because food is expensive, supplies for each household were strictly limited and rationed, and non-essential foodstuffs like table wine or asparagus were allocated by a queuing principle. Then, forty or fifty years on, a group of academics began to suggest that all of this could better be organised through a market system. People could then choose the food they want rather than having to accept what they are given, and competition would improve quality and reduce costs. The response would doubtless be that people do not know what food is good for them. The argument would be advanced that a market system would allow shops and food manufacturers to profiteer by exploitaing people's ignorance. Many would go hungry since they would not be able to afford a loaf of bread and children would be malnourished as a result of the stupidity and neglect of their parents.

The point is that consumers are generally capable of making rational choices provided they are allowed the responsibility of doing so. When the state decides what we need, we lose the habit of making such decisions for ourselves. Of course it is true that many parents know precious little about the schools their children attend, but this ignorance is more a product of a state system of education than a reason for continuing with it. Give parents the means for purchasing education and they will swiftly find out what is on offer. Schools will advertise their wares and parents will seek out the best buy. Under existing arrangements there is no reason for parents to inform themselves since the government decides for them what type of education their children should have.

Many socialists claim to believe that 'the working class' is quite capable of running factories and even planning and managing a whole complex economy, yet this same 'working class' is apparently incapable of choosing between different health insurance policies and cannot be trusted to select an adequate education for its children. People cannot be empowered if you refuse to let them take responsibility for their own lives. New Right libertarians are quite happy to see this happen. For all their talk of transferring power to the working class, socialist intellectuals seem much more hesitant.

The moral obligations of collective life

Socialists and conservatives alike criticise New Right ideas on moral grounds. There are two elements to this.

The first is that the strong advocacy of individualism against collectivism seems to make a virtue out of self-interest and to encourage selfishness while disparaging altruism. Surely, say the critics, there must be more to social life than simply looking after number one. Do we not as human beings owe each other certain obligations and are there not times when we should be expected to put the interests of others before the interests of ourselves? In fact most (though not all) New Right thinkers agree with much of this. Like Adam Smith, they reply that self-interest is not incompatible with the common good. They also point out that market systems enable communalism just as much as they enable individualism. If workers wish to get together to form a co-operative, nobody in a free society will stop them. If young people want to 'drop out' and form a hippy commune where all possessions are pooled, they are free do so. If parents want to come together to organise an alternative school for the children, that is up to them.

The New Right also recognises and applauds spontaneous and voluntary acts of altruism in which individuals make sacrifices to help others. This happens all the time within families, for example, where parents may go without in order to help their children. It also happens between strangers, for many people support charities and engage in voluntary work to help those less fortunate than themselves. The point is, however, that all such acts of altruism are *voluntary*. The New Right insists that we should not be coerced into being good, virtuous, Christian or socialist. To be forcibly taxed in order to help others is to be deprived not only of liberty but of the right to make moral choices. In this view there is nothing ethically commendable about a collectivistic society in which everybody looks after everybody else because they are forced to by the government. Virtue must be allowed to express itself from below and cannot be enforced from above.

The second aspect to this issue concerns collective morality and permissiveness. Again, conservatives and socialists tend to take much the same view, although they often disagree on the details of what the common set of morals should actually be. Both groups seek a society with a common value system in which individuals reign in their passions and regulate their behaviour in accordance with certain core beliefs and prescriptions. For conservatives these beliefs tend to centre on national solidarity and religion; for socialists they revolve around issues of class solidarity and collectivism.

A truly libertarian ethos rejects all attempts at imposing a collective morality. Individuals must be free to worship any god or none; to travel across borders irrespective of nationality; to abuse themselves with drugs or to debase themselves with pornography; to have sex with anyone they choose provided their partner freely consents, and so on. It is at this point, of course, that the link between the new liberalism and the Conservative Party falls apart at the seams, for while many Conservatives have been prepared to take on board the economic implications of libertarian thinking, few have been willing to adopt an equally permissive attitude towards personal behaviour. As Andrew Gamble notes:

> New right economists love to parade as 'libertarians', but the libertarianism of most of them is meagre. They apply it as a remedy to the ills of contemporary society only in miniscule doses. Few are libertarian about life-styles, or gender relations, or race, or defence issues, or crime and punishment. There is a libertarian wing in the New Right but it is not dominant. The few genuine libertarians stand out among the rest.

This criticism is pertinent and is arguably the most telling of all those we have outlined. Thatcherism in Britain in the 1980s was a hybrid which ran together two sets of ideas and principles which were often contradictory. In its liberal guise it emphasised freedoms which in its conservative guise it sought to restrict. It proclaimed the rights of the individual and the importance of free choice while at the same time legislating against the free expression of homosexual ideas, enforcing a single curriculum throughout the nation's schools, preventing the free movement of people across national boundaries by means of a new Nationality Act, prosecuting those who dared to transgress norms governing official secrecy, controlling broadcasting by banning programmes and outlawing interviews with prescribed organisations, putting more of its citizens in prison than ever before, severely weakening the powers and autonomy of alternative centres of authority such as the local councils and so on. After three terms in office, it is fair to ask of this radical Right government whether its initial liberal instincts did not get eclipsed by its more traditional conservative gut feelings.

Conclusion

The ultimate test of any set of political ideas is what happens when they are put into practice. One reason why the New Right has been so critical of socialism, for example, is that socialist ideas have so often proved disastrous when put into effect. A set of beliefs which emphasises equality and fraternity has produced the *gulag*, the secret police, the privileges of the *nomenclatura*, the filthy pollution, the queues and shortages and black markets, the bloody terror of Stalin's purges, the killing fields of Kampuchea and the tanks in Tiananmen Square. The ideas cannot be absolved from their consequences.

The New Right must itself, however, be judged as it judges others. In various countries of the world (Israel is one example), its emphasis on monetary discipline has fanned hyperinflation and its preoccupation with returning public services to the market place has resulted in increased poverty and illiteracy (as in Chile's privatisation of state schools). Advocates of New Right ideas may argue that these outcomes are not necessary consequences of these policies, or that the ideas were not properly followed in these countries, but such protestations sound rather like the apologies offered by socialist intellectuals who complain that communist revolutions in the Soviet Union, China or Kampuchea went wrong and that the next attempt at operationalising Marxism will get it right. In the messy world of real politics, political ideologies never survive in their pure form, for practical considerations always intervene and compromises have always to be made.

In Britain, as we have seen, the liberal tradition was revived during the 1980s under a series of Conservative governments. The Thatcher years do not represent a perfect test of New Right principles, for these governments were constantly torn betweeen the flirtation with neo-liberalism (particularly in economic and social policy) and the commitment to conservatism (particularly with regard to questions of nationalism and collective morality). Immigration controls are tightened when neo-liberals call for free movement of people and goods across national borders. Law is used to impose increased central controls and censorship when neo-liberals call for limits on the power of government to interfere in people's personal lives. Nevertheless, these governments did take on board a number of neo-liberal ideas, and to this extent Britain in the 1980s can provide a reasonable test-bed against which to evaluate the New Right agenda.

We leave to the next three chapters a detailed review and evaluation of how these policies have fared. At this point, however, it is possible to draw four tentative conclusions regarding the impact and degree of success achieved by New Right ideologies in British politics in the eighties.

1 New Right ideas often proved very difficult to apply in practice. An obvious example is the attempt to maintain tight controls over the supply of money. Monetary targets were published each year to 1985, and each year they were exceeded. Furthermore, it proved almost impossible to measure money supply. So it was that, despite Margaret Thatcher's defiant claim that 'The lady's not for turning', the government did in fact execute a U-turn in the mid-eighties as it quietly dumped monetarism in favour of a policy of controlling interest rates. It is not only socialist governments which find that the economic system cannot easily be moulded to accommodate political principles.

2 New Right ideas have often had to be watered down in order to court political popularity or to avoid damaging confrontations with vested interests. Margaret Thatcher herself swiftly built a reputation as a strong leader who did not cave in under pressure, and this image was sustained by her prosecution of the Falklands War and her resolution in the face of a year-long strike in the coal mining industry. Yet she was always pragmatic and always realistic, and she was reluctant to enter a battle if the odds were stacked against her. When the government privatised industries like British Gas and British Telecom, for

example, it gave in to management demands that the companies should be sold off as single units and resisted calls from liberals to break them up so as to foster genuine competition. Similarly in its social reforms, it shied away from education vouchers (which it decided were 'unworkable') and it made no attempt to break up the monolithic system of state health care, even insisting during the 1987 election campaign that 'The National Health Service is safe in our hands.' The 1980s were indeed years of reform, but the changes which were made fell a long way short of the revolutionary prescriptions favoured by the new libertarians.

3 Many policies or attempted policies quite simply failed to have the effect which they were intended to have. The most glaring failure was in the area of public spending and taxation. Indeed, the Thatcher governments found themselves in the unenviable position of presiding over increased public spending while popular perceptions were that it had introduced swingeing cuts in state provision. It chopped new council house building but spending on housing benefits rose dramatically. It refused to support ailing industries but the social security budget soared as those who lost their jobs signed on for unemployment benefit. Total taxation actually *rose* in the ten years from 1979 despite reductions in rates of income tax. Total public spending did fall, from 43 per cent of Gross Domestic Product in 1979 to 39 per cent in 1989, but this was hardly a dramatic turn around, and New Right theorists would surely have expected much more to show from ten years of a radical-Right government with strong parliamentary majorities.

4 These governments conspicuously failed to transform the popular culture of Britain. The aim was always to undermine what was seen as a 'dependency culture' and to replace it with a new entrepreneurial spirit of 'popular capitalism'. Collectivism and corporatism were to be swept away in an attempt to make British attitudes more like those in the USA where there is a popular distrust of big government and a deeply-felt instinct of individualism and free enterprise. But it never happened. The *British Social Attitudes Survey* for 1988 revealed that popular attitudes had changed remarkably little through the decade. Two-thirds of people still believed that the distribution of wealth is unfair (only 17 per cent disagree). Three-quarters believed that reducing unemployment is a more important priority than reducing inflation. Only one-third of the population believed that state welfare undermines self-reliance, and a tiny 3 per cent said they favoured cutting state services in order to reduce taxes. The unpopularity of replacing student grants with a loans system hardened the more the government talked about it (65 per cent opposed the idea) and only one-quarter of the population supported a move towards private health insurance. Other opinion polls confirm many of these results and also show considerable public unease over liberalisation in economic policy – the bill to privatise the water industry, for example, had only 15 per cent public support as it went through the House of Commons.

Many of the failures and set-backs would, paradoxically, have been predicted by New Right intellectuals. As public choice theorists have always argued, it is a lot easier for governments to expand than to contract, for expansion always pleases somebody while spreading the costs so thinly that nobody really notices. Cut backs, on the other hand, provoke squeals of protest from those who are directly affected yet cannot galvanise mass support because their benefits are diffused and anyway only become apparent (if at all) in the longer term. Seen in this way, neo-liberalism is almost self-defeating. Unlike Marxism, which has always believed that history is on its side, liberalism is inherently pessimistic about the chances of its own success. The failures of Thatcherism are, in a peculiar way, a vindication of New Right theories of the state, for they show just how strong is the drift towards ever-enhanced central state power in a democracy like Britain.

Having said all this, however, it is important not to lose sight of the advances which have been made by the New Right. A quarter of a century ago, liberalism was dead and hardly anybody took its ideas seriously. By the end of the 1980s, the ideas were firmly back on the political agenda, and no party could any longer afford simply to ignore them. Socialists within Britain, as well as those in the socialist countries, have been alerted to the importance of markets as means for the efficient organisation of economic activity, and they have had to take note of the threat which increasing state control poses to individual liberties. Whatever succeeds Thatcherism in the 1990s, it is most unlikely to entail a return to the policies which prevailed prior to 1979. The era of nationalisation, corporatism and universal welfare provision has passed. The New Right may not have achieved what it wanted, but it has succeeded in shifting the future direction of British politics. The 1980s did indeed witness a sea change, just as James Callaghan suspected they would.

Works Cited and Guide to Further Reading

Bosanquet, N. (1983) *After the New Right* London, Heinemann.
One of the earliest, and still one of the best, critiques of New Right ideas. Bosanquet insists that the New Right deserves more careful consideration than it has often received from Left critics, and the chapters in Part One (on monetarism, Hayek, Friedman, Public Choice theory and the work of the IEA) are particularly good critical accounts of what these ideas are.

Buchanon, J. et al. (1978) *The Economics of Politics*, London, Institute of Economic Affairs.
A collection of essays and comments from a seminar on public choice theory convened by the IEA. Useful for Buchanon's pithy summary of his own thinking.

Butler, E. (1983) *Hayek: His Contribution to the Political and Economic Thought of our Time*, London, Temple Smith.
One of the best secondary sources on Hayek, though certainly one-sided. Recommended for those who want to know what Hayek is saying rather than for those who want guidance on how to criticise it.

Butler, E. and Pirie, M., (eds) (1987) *Hayek on the Fabric of Human Society*, London, Adam Smith Institute.
A collection of essays on aspects of Hayek's work edited by two leading figures

associated with the New Right Adam Smith Institute. Includes essays by Sam Brittan (in which Hayek's economic libertarianism is contrasted with his moral authoritarianism), Anthony Flew (a philosophical critique of the concept of social justice) and Pirie himself (who argues that Hayek's commitment to tradition and evolutionary change make him more of a conservative than he cares to admit).

Carey, K. (ed.) (1985) *Unveiling the Right*, London, The Tawney Society.
In which a group of academics connected with the Social Democratic Party wrestle with the problem of how to reconcile individual liberty with state policies of redistribution.

Friedman, M. (1962) *Capitalism and Freedom*, London, University of Chicago Press.
Friedman's classic statement of the case for free markets. Contains an outline of his argument for tight control of the money supply and his proposals for a system of Negative Income Tax.

Friedman, M. and Friedman, R. (1980) *Free to Choose*, London, Martin Secker and Warburg.
Probably the most accessible source for Friedman's ideas – presents all the key arguments in a readable and entertaining style. Based on a ten-part television series, this is a good starting point for those who wish to read further in this area.

Graham, D. and Clarke, P. (1986) *The New Enlightenment*, London, Macmillan.
A popularised discussion of key issues in the neo-liberal agenda by two passionate advocates. Based on a Channel 4 TV series. Uncritical but entertaining reading.

Green, D. (1987) *The New Right*, Brighton, Wheatsheaf Books.
A good introduction to neo-liberal ideas and their implications for social and economic policy. Could usefully be read in conjunction with Bosanquet's less positive analysis.

Harris, R. and Seldon, A. (1987) *Welfare without the State*, London, Institute of Economic Affairs.
Sets out the case for vouchers in health and education and tries to find support for such a move from the results of a rather poorly-conducted opinion survey. More useful for its arguments than for its evidence.

Hayek, F. (1944) *The Road to Serfdom*, London, Routledge.
Hayek's classic statement of the perils likely to befall well-intentioned socialists. Dedicated 'to the socialists of all parties', this is the fountainhead of all New Right critiques of collectivism.

Hayek, F. (1960) *The Constitution of Liberty*, London, Routledge.
A much thicker and more elaborate book than *The Road to Serfdom*, this sets out in detail the arguments for freedom and the case against state provision. Ends with a postscript in which Hayek explains why his ideas should not be confused with Conservatism.

Jewkes, J. (1977) *Delusions of Dominance*, London, Institute of Economic Affairs.
A short pamphlet which takes issue with Marxists and economists like Galbraith who argue that capitalism inevitably produces monopolistic domination of market opportunities.

Jowell, R., Witherspoon, S. and Brook, L., (eds) (1988) *British Social Attitudes: The Fifth Report*, Aldershot, Gower.

Shows that neo-liberal ideas have made precious little impact on popular opinion in Britain. Also shows just how conservative and authoritarian many people in Britain are when it comes to moral questions such as law and order, homosexuality and defence.

King, D. (1987) *The New Right: Politics, Markets and Citizenship*, Basingstoke, Macmillan.
Outlines liberal and conservative thinking on the economy, welfare and the role of the state and speculates on the legacy of Thatcherism. Written from a critical and largely unsympathetic socialist position.

Krieger, J. (1986) *Reagan, Thatcher and the Politics of Decline*, Cambridge, Polity Press.
Explains the rise of the New Right in Britain and the USA as a response to economic decline and the erosion of national influence. Concludes that the Thatcher and Reagan governments centralised state power and marginalised key sections of the population, all of which leads the author to speculate that unbridled capitalism and democratic freedoms may not be able as compatible as writers like Friedman have suggested.

Levitas, R. (ed.) (1986) *The Ideology of the New Right*, Cambridge, Polity Press.
A collection of essays on the New Right by socialists who are resolutely critical of almost everything it stands for. An uneven collection, but Andrew Gamble's essay is helpful.

Mill, J. S. (1982) *On Liberty*, Harmondsworth, Penguin.
Quite readable essay by a leading nineteenth-century liberal. Also contains a helpful introduction by Gertrude Himmelfarb.

Nozick, R. (1974) *Anarchy, State and Utopia*, Oxford, Basil Blackwell.
A lively discussion of why anarchism will always give rise to a minimal state, and of why nothing more than a minimal state can be seen as 'just'. Important for its critique of distributional theories of social justice, but not recommended for beginners.

Seldon, A. (1986) *The Riddle of the Voucher*, London, Instutute of Economic Affairs
A clear outline of the arguments for (and against) education vouchers, together with an analysis of why the Thatcher government refused to have anything to do with them.

Smith, A. (1982) *The Wealth of Nations*, Harmondsworth, Penguin.
Like Marx's *Capital*, few of those who refer to this classic have actually read it. The beauty of the Penguin Classics edition is that it contains a useful seventy page introduction by Andrew Skinner which allows those with a weaker constitution to get away without reading the text itself.

Smith, D. (1987) *The Rise and Fall of Monetarism*, Harmondsworth, Penguin.
Outlines the economic theory behind monetarism, charts its adoption by British governments from 1976 through to the mid-eighties, and analyses what the author sees as the disastrous effects of this short-lived policy.

Tullock, G. (1976) *The Vote Motive*, London, Institute of Economic Affairs.
A clear statement of Public Choice theory – see especially chapters 2 and 4 as well as chapter 3 of Morris Perlman's British commentary, which is appended.

Chapter 9

Managing the Economy

In the future, the Government will have to take on many duties which it has avoided in the past.
John Maynard Keynes (1952) *Essays in Persuasion*, New York, Harcourt Brace, orginally published 1926, p. 331.

What we urgently need, for both economic stability and growth, is a reduction of government intervention, not an increase.
Milton Friedman (1962) *Capitalism and Freedom*, Chicago, University of Chicago Press, p. 38.

If capitalism is to be maintained, the state has to expand and contract at one and the same time.
Andrew Gamble and Paul Walton (1976) *Capitalism in Crisis*, London, Macmillan, p. 189.

Introduction

The British economy has been in decline, relative to other industrial countries, for over 100 years. Sometimes the decline has been gradual and has gone virtually unnoticed, while at others the economy has lurched into slumps of alarming proportions. For much of this period, of course, living standards have risen in absolute terms – this was true during the twenty years following the end of the Second World War, and was also the case through most of the 1980s. But even in these periods, Britain's rate of growth has generally lagged behind that achieved by its major international competitors. At other times – such as the late twenties and early thirties, or the late seventies and early eighties – the economy has slumped absolutely as well as relatively, and at times like these millions of people have been affected by falling real wages and rising unemployment.

As the decline of the British economy has become more marked, so the management of the economy has become an issue increasingly central to British politics. It is of course the case that Britain's fortunes are to some extent determined by factors beyond her shores and out of reach of any government, for as a trading nation the country has long been vulnerable

"Privatisation: towards a share-owning democracy or more profits for the big boys?"
(Reproduced by kind permission of Rex Features.)

to world-market trends. Nevertheless, it is also the case that, when the world economy is booming Britain lags behind, and that when it enters into recession Britain suffers more than most other countries and takes longer to recover. It does seem, therefore, that there is something peculiar to the British economy and to British society which accounts for the country's specific problems; something which successive governments have attempted to isolate and thus to remedy.

There has been no shortage of theories purporting to identify the nature of the problem and to prescribe appropriate solutions. As the country's economic decline has become more obvious and more serious, so successive governments have grasped at different theories and have pursued different strategies aimed at reversing the decline. As each theory has failed and each strategy has been found wanting, so a fresh attempt has been made to grapple with the problem until that too has been found to be inadequate and has in turn been replaced by a new orthodoxy. Indeed, it became obvious by the 1980s that governmental initiatives had gone full circle – from a strategy of minimal state intervention, through attempts to manage demand and to plan production and supply, and back again to a market strategy under the Thatcher regime. The tragedy is that throughout this period, the decline has got worse, and each new strategy has succeeded only in building up yet more problems for the next one to confront.

This record of failure of successive governments trying out different remedies suggests that the problem that they have been grappling with is fundamental and deep-rooted. Whatever the immediate causes of Britain's economic plight, and the specific mistakes made by particular governments, it seems that we can only begin to understand the problem through an historical perspective which takes us back, not simply to the last government or the one before that, but to the beginnings of the decline mid-way through the nineteenth century. In 1850, Britain was the single most powerful country on Earth. Somewhere in the 140 years or so since then lies the explanation for the country's present economic difficulties.

The Retreat from *Laissez-faire*: from the Great Exhibition to the Great Depression

In 1851, Imperial Britain celebrated her domination of the world, militarily and economically, with a Great Exhibition of industrial products and innovations which was held in a magnificent structure of steel and glass erected in London's Hyde Park. At that time, Queen Victoria reigned over a quarter of the world's total population, and her Empire, which had been built on the success of British manufacturing and the supremacy of her navy, was the largest in the world's history. Furthermore, British industry produced one-third of the world's manufactured goods and accounted for a quarter of total world trade. Although, as we shall see in chapter 11, the living conditions endured by many of Victoria's subjects in industrial towns and cities throughout Britain were appalling, the wealth of the country as a whole increased dramatically through the nineteenth century. In the 70 years from 1811, national income trebled while prices halved; in other words, national wealth increased six times in real terms.

From the mid-nineteenth century on, however, the picture began to change dramatically. By the eve of the First World War, the output of British industry had been overtaken by both Germany and the United States with the result that Britain's share of total manufactured goods had fallen from one-third to less than one-seventh. While the country retained the trappings of Empire, it was clear by 1914 that it was fast losing its role as world leader.

One factor which may have contributed to this spectacular loss of industrial advantage was the commitment of British governments throughout this period to a policy of free trade, for this commitment was not shared by other countries. Britain's enthusiasm for a free-trade policy was understandable given her head start in the industrialisation process, for it could be seen as a recipe for maintaining her domination of world markets in manufactures; if every other country allowed British goods free entry into their domestic markets, then their own infant industries could hardly hope to compete against the already-established British industries. It was for precisely this reason, of course, that other countries did not allow free access for British manufactured goods, but instead preferred to erect high tariff walls while nurturing their own manufactures behind them.

By the outbreak of the First World War (which was itself in large part a product of the intensified rivalries between the major industrial countries), Britain's unilateral commitment to free trade had resulted, not only in the stimulation of foreign competition, but also in a marked decline in investment in home-based industries. Net investment in British industry fell from over 8 per cent of total national income in 1870 to around 5 per cent in the first decade of the twentieth century, and the amount of capital equipment per worker in British industry remained virtually constant throughout this period at a time when it was rising quickly in America and Germany. The result was that the productivity of British industry remained stagnant in marked contrast to the situation overseas where industrialists were investing in new machinery which could produce more goods more cheaply than in Britain.

The money which could have gone into re-tooling British industry went abroad instead. In the years 1905 to 1914, 7 per cent of the national income was invested overseas (compared with just 5 per cent invested at home). Foreign earnings from these investments escalated to £200 million by 1913 compared with £35 million in 1870. Put another way, at the start of the war, one-third of total profits came from abroad compared with one-eighth in 1870. These overseas earnings augmented the wealth of the country (or more accurately, they augmented the wealth of those who owned most of the country's financial assets), but at the cost of weakening the country's industrial base. British industry became less and less competitive as British financiers became more and more wealthy, for the capital needed to modernise British factories if they were to hold their own against the newer German and American industries was not being invested here. All of this raises the question of why successive British governments failed to intervene to protect home industry from foreign competition and to encourage greater investment. There were at least three reasons for this.

1 Powerful sections of British society were benefiting from free trade and from governments' commitments to *laissez-faire*; these included exporters and financial institutions such as the banks.
2 The working class, whose votes were assiduously sought following the extensions of the male franchise in 1868 and 1884, were benefiting from cheap food imports, and proposals for tariff reform in the 1900s met with fierce popular resistance since they were seen as an attempt to tax workers' food.
3 The liberal ideology, of which free trade was a major feature, was deeply embedded in both British society and the British state. The economic orthodoxy and political philosophy of the time both underpinned a largely unquestioned commitment to a minimal state role in economic and social affairs.

As we saw in the discussion of liberalism in chapter 8, this economic orthodoxy derived in large part from the theories of political economists such as Adam Smith. Smith had argued in *The Wealth of Nations* that the pursuit by individuals of their own economic self-interest was the best way of ensuring continued growth and affluence for all. The free market was in this view the best available mechanism for co-ordinating the activities of millions of atomised individuals, for the price mechanism ensured that demand would always be balanced by supply and that goods and services would be provided at an optimal level of economic efficiency. Any 'interference' by the state could only upset the delicate equilibrium of the 'naturally' self-regulating market and any attempt to limit free trade with other nations would result in higher prices and lower efficiency of home-based industries. In Smith's view, therefore, the economic role of the state should be limited to ensuring a stable monetary and legal framework within which the free market could operate nationally and internationally.

This argument was then reinforced by political theories of the time. Jeremy Bentham's philosophy of *utilitarianism*, for example, held that the role of public policy was to promote the greatest happiness for the greatest number of people. In Bentham's view, this could normally best be achieved by leaving individuals to enjoy their property and liberty as they saw fit, for a state policy which tried to take from the rich to give to the poor would generate more pain than pleasure (for the misery of losing what we already have outweighs the pleasure of gaining something new). Not everybody agreed with Bentham's reasoning, but most political philosophers of the time concurred with his conclusion that the best form of state is one which is strictly limited. John Stuart Mill, for example, believed that the state should only get involved in people's lives at the point where they begin to hurt others (see chapter 8), and the nineteenth-century liberal theory of the constitution was primarily concerned with the question of how to limit state power as opposed to the different question of how to use it (see chapter 1).

This potent combination of economic liberalism, utilitarian philosophy and constitutional theorising, meant that, in nineteenth-century Britain, state power was widely regarded with deep suspicion. Unlike Germany, where there was a long and strong tradition which saw the state as the expression and embodiment of the people, the Fatherland and the national spirit and identity, in England the state had, ever since the Civil War, been seen as something set apart from the society and as something to be held at arm's length. The prospect of the state actively intervening in economic life, such as occurred in Germany from the time of Bismark, was one which industrialists and financiers alike regarded in total horror, and most political leaders shared this reaction. The state neither wished to, nor was allowed to, intervene.

As time went by, however, the force of these anti-statist sentiments in British political culture came inevitably to be mediated by the practical problems posed by the erosion of British supremacy in the world economy. Following the First World War, the problem confronted by British governments was no longer that of how to maintain Britain's lead over her industrial competitors, but was rather how to revive the country's flagging economic fortunes in order to stay in the race. Following a brief economic boom after the war, whch was stimulated by the explosion of pent-up demand for capital and consumer goods, the economy slumped in 1920/1 and never really recovered again throughout the inter-war period. Although this long period of recession was in part due to external factors (notably, of course, the onset of the Great Depression triggered off by the American stock market collapse of 1929), it was also a reflection of Britain's weakened economic position in the world economy. This relative weakness was undoubtedly exacerbated by the government's decision in 1925 to return to the Gold Standard in order to preserve the value of sterling and hence the value of investors' earnings from overseas.

If free trade was one major pillar of liberal economic thought at this time, then the Gold Standard was the other. Under this system, every national currency was given a fixed price in gold, which meant that every currency exchanged with every other currency at a fixed rate, and that the domestic issue of coins and paper money within each country could not exceed its holdings of gold and other currencies. Individual governments were thus prevented from increasing the money supply in their economies unless they also increased their holdings of gold, since every note they issued had to be backed by the equivalent amount in gold.

If a country was not paying its way, and was importing more than it was exporting, then under this system it had to make good the deficit by transferring gold to its creditors. This then depleted its reserves and forced it to reduce the amount of money circulating in the economy. This then had the effect of lowering domestic demand (and hence cutting the import bill) while at the same time increasing unemployment and reducing wages until such time as its industries again became competitive in world markets. Or such was the theory.

When Britain returned to the Gold Standard after the war, the government fixed the price of sterling at its pre-war level. The reduced competitiveness of British industry, however, meant that the pound was now vastly overvalued, with the result that British exports were priced much higher in overseas markets than goods from other countries. British industry had continued to fall behind that of other countries; between 1913 and 1925, manufacturing output fell 14 per cent at a time when the United States increased its output by 40 per cent and total world manufacturing output rose by 20 per cent. Pegging the value of sterling at its 1913 level was, in this context, a recipe for massive deflation. To compete at all, British industry had to reduce its costs dramatically, and this meant cutting wages and abandoning all but the most efficient sectors of production. The immediate result was the General Strike of 1926 provoked by a wage cut imposed in the mining industry. In the longer term, the result was a stagnant economy with high rates of unemployment, low wages, low prices and falling profits. In 1931, the government was forced to abandon both free trade and the Gold Standard, but by then the world economy as a whole was in the midst of a massive recession from which there seemed little prospect of recovery.

The Great Depression of the 1930s hit all Western capitalist countries. In the United States, industrial production fell by more than half between 1929 and 1932 and unemployment climbed to 14 million as profit rates slumped into negative figures. In Germany the picture was much the same with a 40 per cent fall in industrial production and 6 million unemployed. Compared with these statistics, the British recession was relatively mild, partly because the British economy did not have so far to fall. Industrial production fell by 17 per cent and unemployment reached 3 million (representing 22 per cent of the workforce), although these gross figures are somewhat misleading in that the impact of the recession was variable across different regions and in some areas such as South Wales and the north-east of England, unemployment was much more widespread. One reason why the famous 'hunger march' from Jarrow to London made such an impression was precisely that in areas such as London and the south-east, the full horrors of the economic callapse had never been that apparent.

The British government's response to the Great Depression was as limited as it was predictable. As we have already seen, Britain came off the Gold Standard, and this relieved pressure on exporting industries by reducing the artificially high value of sterling, although the relief was short-lived as other countries also devalued their currencies. The government also belatedly abandoned its long-standing commitment to free trade and began to enter into bi-lateral trading agreements with other countries. While this undoubtedly helped to protect the new fledgling industries (such as cars and electronics) which were then being established in the Midlands and elsewhere, it too had little lasting effect since other countries were pursuing much the same policy with the result that world markets for Britain's exports were shrinking. Finally Ramsay MacDonald's National Government, elected in 1931, drastically cut back government spending by reducing unemployment and other benefits, thus exacerbating the plight of those out of work in an attempt to reduce taxes and stimulate investment.

The basic problem for the government at this time was that, even if it had been inclined to do more (and more positive intervention would of course have flown in the face of the long tradition of antipathy towards state involvement in the economy), it was far from clear what else it could do. Put bluntly, orthodox economic thinking at this time held that a recession on this sort of scale simply could not happen!

As Adam Smith had argued, and as most economists continued to argue, an unfettered capitalist market system should be self-regulating. Put simply, the liberal economic theory of the time suggested that supply would always generate its own demand so that prices would stabilise at the point of full employment. This theory was based on the simple argument that the prices paid by entrepreneurs to the three factors of production (rent payment to owners of land, interest payments to owners of capital and wage payments to those who sell their labour) would reappear in the economy in the form of new demand for the goods which entrepreneurs subsequently produced. Thus workers would spend their wages, landowners their rent and investors their interest on the coal, cars, clothing and other goods which industry was producing, and this would then enable industrialists to plough back their profits into a new cycle of production. The economy, in short, was self-sustaining.

Under the influence of the Treasury, British governments of the 1930s thus sought simply to balance their budgets in the hopes that eventually the mysterious and benign operation of market forces would lead to recovery. What actually happened, however, was that high unemployment and low wages depressed domestic demand such that entrepreneurs could not find markets for their products. The economy therefore became locked into a downward spiral of falling investment, falling levels of demand and falling prices while governments looked on apparently powerless to do anything about it. It was only the onset of war which dragged the economy out of this vicious circle.

Nationalisation and National Planning: the War and the Post-war Labour Government

Rearmament and the mobilisation of the labour force into the military and into industry in order to support the war effort provided the stimulus to new investment which had been lacking throughout the inter-war years. Measures which had been inconceivable in peacetime were seen as necessary in time of war and the niceties of liberal economic and political theory were cast aside as the British state erected a system of economic controls and directives unprecendented in the nation's history.

By the end of the war in 1945, a staggering 60 per cent of the total national product was being consumed by the government while over one-third of national income was accounted for by taxation. Both capital and labour had been made subject to a battery of controls imposed by the coalition wartime government in its attempt to direct all available spare capacity into the war effort. Imports were regulated in order to save precious foreign currency and to release shipping for essential supplies, and this in turn necessitated rationing of consumer goods (notably foodstuffs). Labour was subjected to a system of industrial, as well as military, conscription and the right to strike was curtailed. Capital too became subject to a variety of controls involving restrictions on the use of raw materials, controls on dividends and overseas investments, a wide-ranging system of price controls covering over half of all consumer purchases, and a comprehensive system of licensing which governed virtually all new investment in building and machinery. It was almost as if the government realised that to defeat a centralised and authoritarian Nazi state, it would itself have to construct an authoritarian and centralised system of its own.

When the system of democratic elections was restored following the eventual victory of 1945, the Labour Party won a large parliamentary majority for the first time in its history, this reflecting a popular mood for change among the millions of men and women who had been drafted into the services and into industry during the previous 6 years. The Labour Party was committed to the continuation of a system of state economic planning not simply as a short-term practical expediency following the rigours of war, but as a principle by which the peacetime economy was to be managed and controlled. The old liberal orthodoxies had had their day and were to be replaced by a rational system of economic planning through which the nation's resources were to be harnessed and directed according to democratically-expressed social objectives. In 1945, in other words, the new Labour government set out to do precisely that which nineteenth-century liberal constitutional theorists had feared: namely, to use the state as an instrument of social change by shifting power and resources away from those who had traditionally owned and enjoyed them towards those who had lived by their labour.

This restructuring of the British economy and of British society was to be accomplished partly by retaining wartime controls such as those governing imports, prices and new investment, partly by the introduction of new controls such as a comprehensive land-use planning system, and partly by the adoption of an interventionist economic planning strategy involving the nationalisation of key sectors of the economy and the use of fiscal policy to maintain full employment.

Between 1945 and 1950, the Labour government changed the face of the British economy by taking into public ownership a number of key basic industries which together employed some 2 million people and accounted for some 10 per cent of the country's total productive capacity. Most of these industries were, however, relatively unprofitable and their average rates of return on investment were just one-third of those in industry as a whole. Most of them – such as the coal mines and the railways – were also in desperate need of new investment which their dispossessed owners had long been unable or unwilling to finance. The cost of nationalisation to the public purse was therefore considerable, for not only were the former owners compensated at what, in retrospect, seem often to have been over-generous terms, but the government assumed responsibility for some of the least efficient, least profitable and most undercapitalised sectors of what was already a severely weakened economy.

As we saw in chapter 6, the nationalised industries were generally run as public corporations with little or no opportunity for democratic accoun-tability or workers control. They did not, therefore, represent as dramatic a change in the capitalist organisation of the economy as might at first be imagined. Furthermore, as we shall see in the next section, it does seem that to a large extent public-sector industries have been run since the war to the direct or indirect advantage of many private-sector firms and that limited nationalisation was by no means incompatible with an economy which was still organised predominantly on capitalist lines. Even the sober and some-what conservative weekly journal, *The Economist*, noted in one of its editorials at the time of nationalisation that the government had probably done the least that was necessary if Britain's basic industries were to be nur-tured back to health following the war.

A further point to remember is that, even following the wave of nationalisation by the post-war Labour government, the vast majority of industries and services remained in private hands. It was therefore obvious that a coherent economic planning strategy aimed at achieving growth and full employment would have to entail, in addition to direct ownership, the pursuit of a fiscal policy which would influence investment outside the public sector. The post-war Labour government found such a policy in the *General Theory* of Maynard Keynes which had been published in 1936.

Keynes had basically argued that orthodox economic theory needed to be inverted. It was not true, as economists at that time generally believed, that savings would generate new investment. Rather, new investment needed to be stimulated by rising demand which meant that far from encouraging saving at times of recession, governments would be better advised to encourage people to spend.

The conclusion to be drawn from this analysis was that, in order to regenerate the economy, it was necessary to stimulate new demand, and this was a task which must inevitably fall in the lap of government to perform, for no other agency could be used in such a way as to raise aggregate demand as a deliberate policy. Government alone could stimulate demand through its control of fiscal policy and its role as a major spender.

As we saw earlier, the British Government in 1931 actually cut its spending by reducing benefits. For Keynes, however, this was precisely the wrong policy to adopt, for he argued that public expenditure should be increased at times of recession, even though this would mean running a deliberate budget deficit. Government, in other words, should spend more than it receives (obviously there would be no point in raising government spending and financing this through increased taxation, since this would simply increase public-sector demand by reducing private-sector demand; the task was to raise demand overall, and this meant leaving money in people's pockets while at the same time raising the level of state expenditure). By pumping additional money into the economy, government could stimulate new production both directly and indirectly. A new schools building programme, for example, would lead directly to increased demand for building workers to put up the schools, teachers to instruct in them and administrators to run them. It would also stimulate production of building materials, desks and chairs, textbooks, sports equipment and so on, all of which would be produced by bringing idle industrial capacity into use. Such a programme would also have further indirect effects, for the teachers, bricklayers, carpenters and other who had been brought back into employment would now have more money to spend, which means that the initial increase in demand brought about by increased public spending would be multiplied up by increased private spending. The teachers and others would begin to spend more on food, clothing, holidays and the like, and this would then stimulate new investment in agriculture, textiles and the leisure industries which would then further raise the level of employment. Before long, the economy could be pulled out of recession and a level of output could then be maintained which guaranteed full employment.

In Britain, Keynesian theory was generally resisted through the 1930s by orthodox politicians and Treasury mandarins who saw little to commend itself in a theory which criticised the traditional value of thriftiness, advocated deliberate public overspending and asserted the need for government intervention to make the market system work. Liberal economic orthodoxy was at that time still too strongly entrenched in Whitehall and Westminster to countenance a move away from a balanced budget.

By 1945, however, things had changed, for the war had in a sense been the test of Keynesian theory (Keynes himself had been recruited into the Treasury in 1941). At the end of the war, both major political parties were openly committed to the pursuit of a Keynesian demand-management strategy for maintaining full employment – a strategy which replaced the old liberal orthodoxies of *laissez-faire* and which itself became the new orthodoxy which was to underpin state fiscal policy for the next 30 years.

Demand-Management: the Mixed Economy and the Post-war Boom

The Labour administration which had achieved office in 1945 with such high hopes and extensive aspirations eventually vacated office 6 exhausting years later. It had presided over post-war demobilisation, over the beginnings of the end of the Empire (notably with Indian independence in 1947), and over the establishment of the welfare state and the mixed economy. Its (partially successful) attempt to restructure British society had come at a time when the weakness of the British economy had never been more clear, for the war had proved immensely costly in the winning and had exacerbated the problems which had been building up in the decades before. The diversion of investment into the war effort had left much of British industry vastly undercapitalized; export industries in particular had been badly run down and new investment had been below that required even to replace worn out plant. Massive debts of £3.5 billion had been incurred to finance the war effort, and new loans had had to be negotiated from the United States after the war which had carried the condition that Empire markets be opened up to American companies thus removing one further crutch upon which the ailing British economy had come to depend.

Yet despite all this, the government did succeed in laying the basis for a sustained period of economic growth and full employment during the 1950s – a boom which many economists (including Keynes himself) had believed would never materialise. Real incomes of British workers rose by 50 per cent through the 1950s, while unemployment remained low. The new light industries which had taken root before the war flourished after it, and although economic growth in Britain lagged behind that in most of her competitors, it was at least sustained, leading Harold Macmillan to make his famous pronouncement towards the end of the decade that the British people had never had it so good. For 20 years after the war, Britain shared, albeit less than fully, in an unprecedented period of growth and affluence throughout the Western capitalist world, and this long boom helped to disguise the fact that the basic problems of the economy remained unresolved.

A number of different factors together explain the long post-war boom, of which four seem to have been paramount.

1 There was a plentiful supply of cheap imports required by Western industries. Of particular significance there was cheap oil from the Middle East, and world consumption of oil rose by a staggering 7.5 per cent per year between 1950 and 1970. Other products from the Third World, such as goods and raw materials, were also bought cheaply by the industrialised nations, and the poorer countries contributed cheap labour too, either in the form of European 'guest workers' or as permanent migrants into the former Imperial centres, such as the UK which set out to attract immigrants from the former colonies.

2 The world monetary system was stabilised following the Bretton Woods conference of 1944. By the end of the war, it was clear to all that Britain had been replaced by the USA as the foremost Western nation, and at Bretton Woods it was agreed to establish a new system of international currencies to fill the void left by the collapse of the Gold Standard. This system was based on the convertibility of the American dollar whose price was in turn fixed in terms of gold. All currencies, in other words, were given a fixed exchange rate

against the dollar and this, together with the establishment of the International Monetary Fund, the World Bank and the General Agreement on Tariffs and Trade, laid the foundation for a new era of expanding multilateral world trade.

3 The end of the war opened up massive new investment opportunities. This had, of course, been the case after the First World War as well, but then the boom fuelled by post-war reconstruction had been all too short-lived. What was different after 1945 was that new investment was possible, not only in reconstructing and replacing assets damaged by the war, but also in whole new areas of production. Throughout the depression years, new discoveries and inventions had in a sense 'piled up' without being fully exploited because capital could not be invested at a time of falling prices and low profits. The stimulus given to the Western economies by rearmament, post-war reconstruction and (in the ex-fascist countries where the organised labour movement had been destroyed) low wages and a docile workforce, brought about an expansion of the economy which then promoted investment in these new areas of production. The post-war boom was thus built on the development of new techniques of production (automation, nuclear fission, computerisation, etc.), which unleashed onto the British public an avalanche of new consumer goods such as cars, televisions, domestic labour-saving devices and so on. Throughout the 1950s, industry cashed in on a new technology which offered high productivity and high rates of profit. All of these products had, of course, to be sold if profits were to be realised, and this is where the fourth factor became crucial, for perhaps the major difference between the pre-war and post-war years lay in Western governments' commitment to an inteventionist role in the economy based on the principles of Keynesian economics.

4 Following the end of the war, the long tradition of liberal economic orthodoxy which sought to limit the role of the state in economic affairs to facilitating the operation of the free market was re-established in external affairs (for example, through the return to free trade and the support of a strong pound as an international currency), but was replaced domestically by an interventionist stance adopted by Labour and Conservative governments alike. This new interventionism formed the basis for what has often been referred to as the post-war 'compromise' or 'consensus' through which all main parties agreed on certain fundamental principles of policy – a consensus which gave rise to the term 'Butskellism' (an amalgam of the names of the Conservative Chancellor, Butler, and the Labour leader, Gaitskell).

At the heart of Butskellism were three core principles. First, both parties were committed to the maintenance of a comprehensive system of welfare support which encompassed free health care, universal education, social security, the right to a house (whether private or public), and so on. We discuss this in chapter 10 and shall not discuss it here except to note that, as the years have gone by, so the cost of the welfare state has increased substantially in real terms, thus increasing the pressure on public expenditure.

Second, both parties were committed to the maintenance of the so-called 'mixed economy'. As we have seen, the post-war Labour government nationalised a number of key industries and although the Conservative

administration which won office in 1951 subsequently denationalised steel
(which was then nationalised again in 1967 and denationalised still again
in 1989), it never made any attempt to return other industries such as the
coal mines and the railways to private ownership. Indeed, in later years,
both Labour and Conservative governments were instrumental in extending the size of the public sector (Rolls-Royce aeroengines, for example,
was nationalised by the Heath government in 1971 when it was on the brink
of collapse), and it is only since 1979 that any serious attempt has been
made to sell off core public-sector industries.

There were a number of different reasons why governments of both main
parties were prepared to support the mixed economy through the 1950s. In
some cases it was recognised that the employment prospects of thousands
of workers could only be safeguarded by public ownership since many of
the old staple industries had become too unprofitable and uncompetitive
to survive in private hands. In other cases, nationalisation was seen as a
strategy for maintaining cheap energy supplies for private industry (coal,
gas, electricity), or for providing cheap raw-material inputs (steel), or for
servicing the transportation requirements of the private sector (railways).
Harold Macmillan summed up the thinking of both Conservative and
Labour governments when he argued:

> The socialist remedy should be accepted in regard to industries and services
> where it is obvious that private enterprise has exhausted its social
> usefullness, or where the general welfare of the economy requires that cer-
> tain basic industries and services need now to be conducted in the light of
> broader social considerations than the profit motive provides.

Put another way, public ownership was seen as a necessary cost which
government would have to bear in order to sustain a profitable private
sector. Nationalisation was a strategy for maintaining production in
those areas of the economy on which much of the private sector
depended but which were insufficiently profitable to attract new private-
sector investment.

The third main plank of Butskellism was the commitment to maintaining
full employment and economic growth through the adoption of Keynesian
demand-management policies. If support for the nationalised industries
was primarily an attempt to maintain the supply of relatively cheap energy
and raw material inputs to the private sector, then fiscal policy and
increased public expenditure was oriented towards stimulating demands for
the products of the private sector.

As we saw earlier, the Keynesian economic management strategy rests on
the attempt by government to keep demand in the economy sufficiently
buoyant so as to soak up all that industry can produce when working at full
capacity. This is achieved partly through increased public spending and
partly through encouragement of private spending by easing the supply of
money and credit. The problem with both strategies, as Keynes him-

self recognised, is that they are inflationary, for if more money is made available to buy the same number of goods, then prices inevitably will rise. Keynes argued that a mild inflationary trend was the price that would have to be paid to maintain full employment, and post-war governments in Britain and elsewhere readily accepted this price, with the result that unemployment during the 1950s was generally kept at or below 2 per cent while retail prices and wages rose by a few per cent each year.

The use of this strategy rested on at least three important conditions. The first was the assumption that, when the government stimulated demand in the economy, this would increase domestic investment and raise the output of home-based industries. This did occur to some extent, but such a response was increasingly hindered by the continuing haemorrhaging of British capital into overseas investments once currency controls were relaxed after the war (private investment abroad rose from an average of £180 million in the early fifties to 320 million 10 years later). This, together with the greater competitiveness of German, Japanese and other overseas manufacturers, meant that stimulation of demand was met increasingly by rising imports and a deterioration in the balance of payments. A rising deficit on the balance of payments, which was exacerbated by continued government spending overseas (particularly military expenditure in Aden, Cyprus, Germany and elsewhere), then inevitably led governments to reverse their policies and cut demand by imposing a credit squeeze designed to reduce domestic demand for imported goods. Thus developed the familiar 'stop-go' cycles of the later 1950s and 1960s in which spending would be encouraged by a relaxation of credit controls at one point, only to be squeezed as soon as it led to a balance-of-payments crisis. The uncertainty that this caused further contributed in no small way to the country's economic problems since it discouraged long-term investment, leading industrialists to hesitate before investing in response to a government-induced boom and financiers to look overseas for more stable and profitable places to invest their money.

These consequences could perhaps have been avoided had governments chosen to react to inflationary pressures and balance of payments deficits with measures such as devaluation or import controls. For 20 years, the pound sterling was pegged at a rate of $2.80, and it was not until 1967 that the government eventually devalued, this reflecting the customary concern with maintaining a strong currency, even at the expense of home-based industry whose products were overpriced in overseas markets and undercut by imports in the domestic market. By making British exports cheaper and foreign imports more expensive, devaluation could have eased balance-of-payments problems, but this was strongly resisted by financial interests seeking to maintain the sterling value of their overseas earnings. So it was that a relatively weak industrial base was made even weaker by a commitment to a strong pound and hence to a policy of domestic deflation whenever the balance of payments ran into deficit.

The second assumption on which a Keynesian strategy necessarily rested was that governments would resist the temptation to stimulate the economy at the 'wrong time'. Demand-management appeared as a useful tool for manipulating the economy for electoral purposes, for it enabled a government to induce a mini-boom prior to an election in the knowledge that the inflationary effects would not work through until some time after the election had been won. As we saw in chapter 2, some commentators believe that governments generally did not resist this temptation, with the result that a series of 'political business cycles' came to be overlaid upon the existing stop-go cycles, with the economy being primed during the lead up to an electiion and then slammed into reverse gear immediately afterwards. To the extent that this occurred, it not only exacerbated the decline in business confidence, fuelled wage demands and sent even more investors scurrying overseas with their cash, but it also built up a long-term inflationary pressure, for each politically-engineered boom built on the last and made it that much more difficult to bring the money supply back under control.

This leads us to consider the third assumption of a Keynesian strategy which was that, all that was required to maintain full employment and avert a serious recession was periodic 'fine-tuning' of the economy, raising demand at one point, dampening it down at another. This assumption has been challenged by both Marxist and liberal critics of Keynesianism.

The Marxist challenge came with the publication in 1966 of *Monopoly Capital* by Paul Baran and Paul Sweezy. They accepted Keynes's argument that the basic problem in advanced capitalist economies was that of engineering sufficient demand to enable private firms to operate at full capacity, but they argued that, in the long term, this could not be achieved. The reason for this lay in a tendency in modern capitalist societies for effective demand to fall short of a rising productive capacity. The basic problem as they saw it was that the economy was increasingly dominated by a small number of large firms which have effectively reached a tacit agreement not to cut each others' throats by aggressive price competition. With the virtual eclipse of price competition in this 'monopoly sector' of the economy, each firm is able to fix prices at a level which guarantees an acceptable level of profit, provided that it can sell its goods. In order to raise this level of profit, each firm also seeks to reduce its costs by investing in new technology which raises productivity and hence increases the amount of goods that can be produced by each worker. The result is that more and more can be produced, and even greater profits can be achieved, but this expansion depends upon an ever increasing market. Monopoly capitalism, in other words, finds itself in a perpetual spiral of increasing capacity which demands that more and more goods be sold at a fixed price if the system as a whole is not to collapse into recession. The problem confronting monopoly capitalism is the problem of how to absorb an ever-expanding surplus.

Baran and Sweezy discussed various strategies which have been adopted in an attempt to increase the markets for the goods produced in the monopoly sector, and they stressed the importance of state expenditure (particularly military expenditure) as the major source of new demand. In their

view, however, even massive military budgets are unlikely to prove sufficient to absorb this continually rising surplus. The long post-war boom was
fuelled by enormous military spending, plus private spending on new consumer goods (cars) which was for example, underpinned by a vast expansion of credit, but such a boom could not continue indefinitely. Neither the
state nor private individuals could perpetually increase their purchasing of
goods, for the expansion of credit and the growth of indebtedness would
eventually reach its limits.

Seen in this light, recession was being postponed, not averted. Liberal
critics of Keynesianism agreed with this, though for different reasons.
Friedrich Hayek, for example, believed that Keynesian measures work in
the short run by storing up greater problems in the long term. Keynesianism
is like a drug, providing immediate relief but increasing dependency. And
like a drug, each new fix has to be bigger than the last to achieve the same
effect. For Hayek, market prices are crucial information signals. We adjust
our behaviour as prices change. If governments inflate demand artificially,
then businesses and workers will interpret this new demand (expressed
through increased prices) by assuming that the goods or services which they
are selling must be what the public wants to buy. The initial effect is,
as Keynes suggests, that economic activity is stimulated. Businesses are
encouraged to invest and to take on more workers. The trouble is that some
of these businesses are not economically viable. Artificial stimulation of
demand not only encourages strong businesses to invest, it also encourages
weak ones. Thus, inefficient or out-of-date businesses keep trading, and
perhaps even increase investment, while workers employed in declining
industries stay in their jobs rather than seeking out new ones. Eventually,
of course, the effects of the government's policy begin to wear off, but now
the situation is worse than it was in the first place. Confronted with the prospect of an even deeper recession, government goes for even stronger
remedies and pumps still more demand into the economy. This then per-
petuates the misleading price signals and exacerbates the problem of
economic inefficiency and market rigidity. Before long, government
is locked into a vicious inflationary spiral of its own making as ever-
increasing amounts of non-existent money have to be generated in order to
keep ever-expanding numbers of inefficient enterprises in business.

Keynesian demand-management was an important factor underlying the
continued growth of all Western economies for the 20 years after the war,
but in retrospect it can be seen as having stored up problems for later. Certainly in Britain, it was becoming clear, even by the late fifties, that certain
fundamental problems remained unresolved and that Keynesian fine-
tuning was not going to be enough to overcome them. Particularly worrying was the evidence that Britain was still falling further behind her main
competitors; throughout the boom years, wages increased much faster than
productivity with the result that British industry became less and less competitive on world markets. From a share of world trade of 21 per cent in
1953, Britain experienced a dramatic fall to under 14 per cent in 1964. The

British people may never have had it so good, but the British economy was evidently sick and becoming sicker. Something new had to be tried.

Corporatist Planning: 1962–79

We have seen that during the long period of British economic decline up to the outbreak of the Second World War, governments remained committed to liberal orthodoxies of minimal state intervention. During this period, the role of the state *vis-à-vis* the private sector may be termed 'facilitative'. Following the war, however, we have seen that domestic economic policy became more interventionist as a result of the adoption of demand-management strategies aimed at maintaining full employment. The relation between the state and the private sector in these years may therefore be more accurately described as 'supportive'. From the early 1960s onwards, governments took a further step away from liberal orthodoxy by attempting to plan economic growth. In this sense, the years between 1961 and 1979 may be seen in terms of an increasingly 'directive' role of the state in economic affairs.

It is important to note that this progressive shift away from a facilitative towards a directive role occurred primarily in respect of domestic economic intervention. Throughout this period, British governments remained reluctant to extend planning and direction to Britain's relations with other countries. Some attempt was made during the 1960s to restrict imports through the imposition of a temporary system of selective surcharges, and the commitment to free trade was modified through the eventually successful attempt to join the European Common Market which permitted free trade within its boundaries while erecting a high tariff wall against non-members. The commitment of successive governments to the principle of free trade nevertheless remained strong, as did their commitment to the balance of payments and a strong pound. The new interventionism of the 1960s had much more to do with the planning of investment, incomes and industrial relations than it did with the planning of trade.

The move towards economic planning began under a Conservative government with the establishment of the National Economic Development Council ('Neddy') in 1962. This represented the first formal attempt to establish an institution for economic planning which would bring together the state and the two sides of industry on a regular basis in an attempt to monitor the country's economic performance and to develop government initiatives which would stimulate growth. It was also hoped that formal trade union involvement on the National Economic Development Committee would win the support of organised labour for some form of wage regulation or restraint and thus avoid the need for dramatic measures such as the 6-month pay freeze which the government had imposed in 1961 following the latest in a series of sterling crises.

It was with the election of the Wilson Labour government in 1964,

however, that the marked shift towards a planning strategy occurred. At
the 1964 election, Labour projected itself as a modern technocratic party.
Harold Wilson himself bemoaned the 'thirteen wasted years' of Tory rule
and spoke of regenerating British industry through the planned introduction of new technology. The image of the Labour Party which fought and
won the 1964 election was more that of the white coat than the cloth cap,
while the image of defeated Conservatives under the leadership of Lord
Home was that of the deerstalker hat.

The new Labour government retained the NEDC as part of a new
ministry – the Department of Economic Affairs – which was run by the
party's deputy leader, George Brown. The principal task of the new department was to develop Britain's first National Plan which was published in
1965. This envisaged a growth rate in the economy as a whole of nearly 4
per cent per year until 1970, to be achieved on the basis of a 3.4 per cent
annual growth in productivity and a substantial rise in rates of investment
(this required rate of productivity increase was by no means unrealistic, for
productivity in British industry actually rose by more than 4 per cent
per year between 1962 and 1975). As part of its planning strategy, the
government also established a National Prices and Incomes Board which
scrutinised all wage and price increases before they came into effect and put
considerable pressure on trade unions to enter into productivity agreements
as the means for raising real wages, and this helped to create the conditions
in which growth could be fostered.

The increased investment which was necessary was left to the private sector. Growth targets were published for each industry in the hope that
investment would increase in a new climate of long-term predictability. In
fact, investment did begin to pick up, but not for long. In the summer
of 1966, the government was rocked by another balance-of-payments
crisis accompanied by the familiar run on sterling. George Brown and his
Department argued for a devaluation but they were overruled. Instead, the
government abandoned its National Plan and its growth targets by
introducing severe cuts in public expenditure and a statutory 6-month pay
freeze. The familiar stop-go pattern had returned and Britain's first attempt
at national economic planning had been jettisoned in favour of a massive
deflation. Those businesses which had stepped up investment in response
to the government's assurances of sustained growth were left to contemplate the prospects of a dramatically reduced market for their goods.
Business confidence, never strong, had received another bad knock.

The 1966 deflation had an immediate impact on unemployment which
rose in just 6 months from 250,000 to 600,000; a new post-war high. This
trend to rising unemployment continued through the remainder of the
government's term of office and marks the first decisive break with the
post-war commitment to a Keynesian policy of using public spending to
maintain full employment.

With its National Plan in tatters, the government came increasingly to
rely on pay controls as its major lever of economic management. Statutory

controls on income were renewed following the 1966 pay freeze, but although ministers were still able to count on the support or acquiesence of most union leaders, it was evident that large sections of the rank-and-file union members were becoming restive. The growth of power of shop stewards became manifest in the rise in the proportion of unofficial to official disputes, and government attempts to restrain incomes were increasingly challenged by the growth of shop-floor militancy. Eventually, in 1969, the government responded to these challenges by issuing a White Paper designed to reduce official stoppages by enforcing strike ballots and a 28-day delay on unofficial strikes. The proposals sparked off a storm of protest in both the industrial and political wings of the labour movement, and the government was eventually obliged to back down.

In June 1970, Labour lost a general election which it had been widely expected to win. The government had succeeded in at last bringing the balance of payments into surplus (in this it had been aided by a long-overdue devaluation of the pound later in 1967), but this had been achieved at the cost of rising unemployment, slow growth, accelerating inflation and falling rates of industrial investment.

The evident failure of Labour's attempt at economic planning had had its impact on Conservative thinking, and the Heath government that came to office in 1970 was determined to have no more to do with either Keynesian demand-management or state planning. Government was to return to its traditional facilitative role and economic growth was to be fostered through minimal interference with market processes. The trappings of state planning such as the National Board for Prices and Incomes and the Industrial Reorganisation Corporation (which Labour had established in 1966 to aid company mergers in the hope that this would increase industrial efficiency) were scrapped. The NEDC survived but the government effectively ended any close consultation with the unions. Indeed, one of its first priorities was to introduce the Industrial Relations Act, 1971, which outlawed the closed shop, made provision for legally-enforceable agreements in industry, introduced Labour's earlier proposals for strike ballots and 'cooling-off periods', and established a register of trade unions, all of which was interpreted by the unions themselves as an unprecedented attack on their power. The government also insisted that there would be no more state aid for ailing industries ('lame ducks'), no more legislation on prices and incomes (although state employees were made subject to tight government controls on public-sector wage rises), and no more increases in public expenditure to maintain full employment. Public spending was to be cut back, taxes were to be reduced and the economy was to boom under the influence of pure market forces and a return of the entrepreneurial spirit.

By 1972, the government had executed a famous 'U-turn'. Confronted by rapidly rising unemployment, increasing closures, escalating industrial unrest and spiralling inflation, the government abandoned its free-market strategy and returned to large-scale intervention. In 1972, it nationalised that symbol of British free enterprise, Rolls-Royce, in order to avert its imminent closure. In the same year it introduced a new and highly interventionist Industry Act which allowed the Secretary of State for Industry to purchase shares in companies in order to improve output and efficiency. A new Pay Board and Price Commission was established as the government introduced statutory incomes regulation, and negotiations were opened with the CBI and TUC as union leaders were brought back in from the cold. This remarkable turnaround was completed by a 'dash for growth' on the part of the Chancellor, Anthony Barber, who abandoned the earlier tight monetary controls in favour of a swift and huge injection of money into the economy designed to stimulate new investment. The effect of this last policy was to suck in imports at an unprecedented rate (imports rose by 44 per cent in volume between 1971 and 1973) thereby turning Labour's hard-won balance-of-payments surplus into a resounding deficit, and to raise public spending by nearly 20 per cent in a year. Unemployment continued to climb and passed the million mark while inflation climbed with it, thereby demonstrating that the Keynesian trade-off between inflation and employment was no longer operative in a situation where both were rising simultaneously. And on top of all this, oil prices quadrupled as a result of the 1973 Middle East war, the Gold Exchange Standard worked out at Bretton Woods collapsed following the devaluation of the dollar in 1971 and the subsequent floating of all the world's major currencies, and the whole of the Western capitalist world slumped into recession in 1974 as world trade contracted on a scale not seen since before the war. In Britain, a miners' strike against the government's pay policy put most of industry on a 3-day week as electricity supplies from coal-powered generating stations dwindled. The government called an election on the specific issue of the miners' strike and the unions, and in February 1974, Harold Wilson was back in Downing Street as leader of a minority Labour government.

By now, the crisis of the British economy was becoming acute. Industrial output in Britain had risen by 18 per cent in eight years compared with increases of 40 and 50 per cent by Britain's major European trading partners. Profit rates were falling steeply; returns on capital invested had fallen from 12 per cent in 1960 to under 4 per cent by 1975. This, not surprisingly, was deterring new investment. The proportion of earnings reinvested had fallen from 78 per cent in 1967 to 63 per cent in 1974 as companies attempted to maintain the level of dividend paid to their shareholders, yet dividends continued to fall and the value of shares fell with them. In desperate need of new investment, most companies found that their low profitability made it impossible for them to attract funds. The proportion of new investment funded by shares fell from 12 per cent in the late fifties to just 4 per cent in 1972. This meant that companies were forced to finance new investment through borrowing, yet the financial institutions were increasingly reluctant to lend except at crippling high rates of interest over very short periods. The result of all this was that investment was drying up, even in the more viable firms. British manufacturing industry had become vastly undercapitalized with investment per worker amounting to just one-third of that in West Germany and one-quarter of that in Japan. Given these disparities, it is hardly surprising that goods from Germany, Japan and elsewhere were flooding the British market, undercutting British producers, and laying waste large sectors of British industry including both the old staples such as textiles and the newer light industries such as cars, motor cycles and television tubes.

Faced with such dramatic evidence of Britain's economic decline, the newly-elected Labour government resorted once again to state planning. This time, however, it attempted to intervene directly in the investment policy of key companies rather than simply trying to create a climate in which the companies themselves could choose to invest. It also tried to target its interventions on specific companies and specified industries rather than developing policies designed to stimulate growth in the economy as a whole as had been the case in the 1965 National Plan. The instrument for this fresh attempt at planning economic growth was the Industry Act, 1975.

Labour's Industry Act introduced two major innovations. The first was a system of 'planning agreements'. By the mid-1970s, a series of mergers and take-overs had produced a situation where just 100 firms accounted for half of Britain's manufacturing output. Given that most other firms depended directly or indirectly on these 100 giants (for example, by supplying them with components or raw materials), it seemed that it would be possible to plan the overall course of the British economy by influencing the future investment plans of these biggest companies. This did not require wholesale nationalisation which was unpopular and extremely expensive. Rather, the big firms could be left in private hands but could be encouraged to co-operate with government, pooling information and expertise and drawing on public funds where necessary in order to develop a future growth strategy which would secure both the profitability of the company and a planned growth of the economy as a whole.

As things turned out, however, the system of planning agreements was virtually stillborn. Only one company – Chrysler in 1977 – ever entered into such an agreement with the government, and this was in return for a massive injection of public funds which was necessary to avert imminent closure. The idea of planning agreements as a principal tool of economic management is still alive in parts of the Labour Party today despite this failure, although many advocates of such agreements now argue that they cannot operate successfully on a voluntary basis, and that only some form of state compulsion will ensure the involvement of most large companies.

The second major innovation of the 1975 act was the establishment of the National Enterprise Board. This was more successful, though more limited; indeed, it even managed to survive the election of the Thatcher government in 1979 although its holdings were later sold off.

The purpose of the NEB was to provide investment funds to viable firms which were struggling to survive due to lack of liquidity. As we have seen, by the mid-seventies, many companies were finding it impossible to invest since they could not attract new shareholders and the terms imposed by the banks for new loans were prohibitive. The NEB (which inherited government shareholdings in various companies which had been bought as a result of the Heath government's Industry Act) sought to overcome this problem by buying shares in such companies as well as advancing grants and low-cost loans.

State shareholding through the NEB obviously increased the ability of the government to influence decision-making in the private sector, but it was far from the 'creeping nationalisation' which some Conservative critics saw in it. The state often only took a minority holding, and when and as companies were restored to economic health, even these holdings could be sold off. The NEB was, therefore, a flexible instrument of economic planning, buying and selling shares whenever it seemed appropriate with little direct control from Paliament. And, in a limited way, it worked; firms such as Sinclair Elcctronics, for example, were undoubtedly saved, later to prosper, as a result of its interventions. Together with various regional bodies such as the Scottish, Welsh and Northern Ireland Development Agencies, which were also established in 1975 with power to buy shares in potentially viable firms, it represented an important innovation aimed directly at the major problem confronting British industry for the last 100 years – lack of investment. However, its impact was incvitably limited given the failure of the planning agreements system, for it was bailing out medium-sized firms while the investment decisions of the largest and most crucial companies remained virtually unaffected by government influence.

The Industry Act, 1975 was one leg of the government's economic strategy. The other related not to capital but to labour and involved the attempt to regulate incomes. Wary after its own experiences of statutory incomes controls during the sixties and the Heath government's downfall in 1974, the government applied the voluntary principle to incomes just as it did on the other side of industry to planning agreements. Following a spate of legislation in the early years of the government designed to shift the balance of power in industry back towards organised labour(for example, through repeal of the Industrial Relations Act, 1971, introduction of new rights of unions to gain recognition, run a closed shop and secure immunities from certain common law actions, and introduction of new rights for individual workers pertaining to redundancy pay, protection against arbitrary dismissal and maternity leave), the TUC entered into an agreement with the government in 1975 whereby its member unions would accept a flat-rate pay rise in return for price controls and improvements in the 'social wage' (i.e. welfare and social security provisions). This agreement (which was also endorsed by the employers' organisation, the CBI), formed the basis for what became known as the 'Social Contract' by which, each year, union leaders agreed to voluntary limits on wage rises in return for social provisions or tax reductions from government.

For two years, this voluntary system of pay restraint operated very successfully in that wage increases generally conformed to those that had been agreed while the number and duration of strikes fell considerably. The unions had effectively been co-opted as junior partners in government, being directly involved in the development of policy and carrying the responsibility themselves for implementing agreements on wages. The government's broader economic policy was operating rather less successfully, however, and the inflation which had been stoked up by the Heath government's dash for growth was now spiralling beyond 20 per cent per year, fuelled by the government's commitment to increased industrial and welfare spending. The result, predictably, was a sterling crisis in the autumn of 1976 which was triggered off by a continuing balance-of-payments deficit and the falling value of the pound. As investors scrambled to exchange their sterling holdings into other currencies, the government turned to the International Monetary Fund for assistance. The Fund granted credit to pay off foreign debts and stabilise the currency, but it imposed severe conditions on this loan which effectively undermined the whole basis of the government's economic strategy by insisting on tight monetary controls which inevitably meant substantial cuts in public spending and a massive reduction of demand in the economy. As in 1966, so in 1976, a Labour government was blown off course by international pressure on sterling which in turn reflected the weakness of the country's industrial base.

The 'Social Contract' remained only in name as living standards were reduced and unemployment rose in an attempt to bring inflation under control. In 1977, the government imposed a 10 per cent ceiling on wage rises without the consent of the TUC, since this represented a real cut in wages at a time when prices were increasing by more than twice that figure. In 1978, the government chanced its arm on a fourth round of pay restraint, this time insisting on a norm of just 5 per cent. Through the winter of 1978/9, strikes among low-paid public-sector workers caused massive disruption throughout the public services, and in May 1979, the Conservative Party was swept back into office on a wave of popular anti-union and anti-government sentiment.

Reviewing the years from 1962 to 1979, it is apparent that an important change took place in the relation between the state and the private sector. With the exception of just two years (during the period 1970–2) when the Heath government attempted to revert to a market strategy, governments of both main parties presided over a growth in state involvement which entailed increased planning together with increased participation in policy-making by the representatives of capital (the CBI) and organised labour (the TUC). The fact that Heath had tried and failed to break this trend lent credence to the view that direct state involvement in the economy was becoming established and in some way necessary as a feature of economic life in the last quarter of the twentieth century in Britain. The theory which developed to identify and explain this change was the theory of corporatism (see chapter 4).

For some observers writing in the 1970s, corporatism was to be understood as a new type of social and economic system, distinct from both capitalism and socialism but containing within it elements of both. The clearest example of such a view is found in the work of Jack Winkler who detected a trend towards ever-increasing state direction of the economy and who argued that the state was gradually replacing the owners and managers of capitalist firms as the driving force in the economy. Thus he suggested that, under the new corporatist system which he believed was emerging, those who owned capital would continue to pocket their (strictly-controlled) profits, but they would have less and less say over how their productive resources were to be used. Just as in the war the state had subordinated traditional capitalist concerns with profit maximisation and free enterprise to its own greater objectives, so 30 years further on, the state was once again, in Winkler's view, directing the economy in accordance with its own concerns to ensure unity, order, efficiency and the 'national interest'. Winkler argued that the way in which the state sought to impose these principles was by means of flexible, relatively informal and non-bureaucratic modes of organisation such as the 'Quangos' which enabled technical experts to come together with company and union leaders away from the public gaze and relatively insulated from the political battleground of the parliamentary system. The deals which were worked out there were then administered, not by the state itself, but by the participating organisations. Agreements reached with the TUC over wages, for example, were to be implemented by the TUC itself, while agreements reached with big companies over future investment strategies were carried through by the companies working co-operatively with the government on the basis of planning agreements, price codes and the like. Corporatism thus entailed a flexible and hierarchical system of state economic control characterised above all by the co-option of the organised interests of capital and labour into the heart of the policy-making and implementation process.

The main problem with Winkler's thesis, of course, is that even in the context of the mid-1970s, it does not stand up to empirical examination. For a start, the state's control over capital is overemphasised. Winkler placed considerable weight on the development of planning agreements and the use of price controls, yet as we have seen, only one planning agreement was ever signed (and even this proved toothless), while price controls have rarely been effective for more than a short period precisely because they actually undermine the profitability of companies which the state is supposed to be sustaining. State control over organised labour is also overemphasised in Winkler's model, for although there is no doubt that union leaders have successfully been incorporated into government as junior partners, there is considerable evidence to suggest that their rank-and-file members have remained wilfully antagonistic to many of the deals struck on their behalf. The period identified by Winkler as an era of growing corporatism was in fact a period characterised by the continual breakdown of wages policies and by various efforts by governments and union bureaucracies to control unofficial action at the level of the shop floor.

None of this necessarily means that the concept of corporatism is without value in understanding recent economic policy in Britain, but it does mean that the concept needs to be narrowed down from Winkler's sweepingly broad application of it in ways we suggest in chapter 4. In particular, it makes little sense to argue that, during the sixties and seventies, Britain was changing from a capitalist to a corporatist society for as many critics have pointed out, the country remained capitalist in the sense that those who owned and managed the means of production continued to direct their use and that the economy continued to function according to the overriding principle of the search for profitability. What happened during these years was not that the state took over control the economy and began to run it according to its own objectives, but that it searched in a somewhat haphazard way for new solutions to Britain's long-term economic decline. This search led it to develop new modes of operation, new strategies for attaining its long-standing objective of maintaining the profitability of private sector firms.

Essentially, what happened from the 1960s onwards was that governments tried to involve key economic interests directly in economic policy-making. They did this by developing a form of political representation based not on geographical constituencies but on functional interests. In other words, side by side with the elected parliamentary system of representation there grew up a non-elected corporatist system of representation in which the leaders of particular sections of the population were invited to participate according to their role in the division of labour. Seen in this way, corporatism involved the selective incorporation of particular producer interests within the political system with the aim of developing policies and managing economic growth according to the specific requirements of these groups.

The principal interests represented in this corporatist strategy were, of course, industrial firms (represented by the CBI and other industrial employer groups such as the Engineering Employers' Federation and the National Federation of Building Trades Employers) and organised labour (represented by the TUC). These two blocks remained in regular and close contact with government through their participation in private political forums such as the NEDC, and in return for the opportunity to help shape government policy, they undertook the responsibility for ensuring that the agreed policies were actually implemented (for example, as in the case of the TUC policing government incomes policies). In this way, big capital and organised labour evolved as appendages of the state, as new 'governing institutions' collaborating with the state rather than simply pressuring it from outside.

Now, it is important to emphasise that such a corporatist system of interest representation was not new in Britain in that governments have been more or less willing to share their power with capital and organised labour, and to include these groups within the policy-making process, since the 1930s. What happened from the 1960s onwards was simply that consultation and participation became institutionalised through the establishment of formal organs of economic planning. It is also important to recognise that corporatism was not limited exclusively to governments' relations with industry and the unions; in agriculture, for example, the National Farmers' Union has long enjoyed the fruits of a close and exclusive partnership with government through which farm prices, farm workers' wages and many aspects of investment and marketing policy are determined away from the public gaze, while various professional bodies such as the British Medical Association have similarly developed close consultative relations with the relevant departments of state.

What is common to all these cases is that corporatism can be seen as a strategy of exclusion. While certain key producer groups – major industrial employers, the principal unions, the farmers, the doctors and so on – became integrated and incorporated into the process of state policy-making, other interests in British society – consumers, small business people, the self-employed, non-unionised labour, old age pensioners, single parents etc. – were left out and unincorporated. There developed from the 1960s on a bifurcation of British politics between, on the one hand, the traditional arena of competitive electoral politics as represented by Parliament and local authorities, and on the other, a corporatist system of interest representation wherein participation was selective and exclusive. While a wide variety of different groups could attempt to get their views heard in the electoral arena, this was not the case in the corporatist sector where participation was limited to particular economic interests. Seen in this way, corporatism developed as the antithesis to pluralism. Indeed, corporatism may be understood as a response to the problems of pluralism in that it enables governments to insulate themselves from the clutter of competing opinions and diverging demands and to concentrate instead on responding to those groups which are most strategically important as regards the future development of the economy.

By the late 1970s, however, it had become apparent that this corporatist strategy for managing the economy was not working. The so-called 'winter of discontent' in 1978/9, when millions of low-paid public-sector workers rebelled against continued income restraint, demonstrated that the close co-operative relationship between government and unions had broken down and that union leaders could no longer deliver on their side of the bargain. Furthermore, the continuing rise in unemployment and fall in the profitability of large sections of British industry showed that the economic policies developed within the corporatist sector of the economy were failing to resolve the country's basic economic difficulties. There was a growing and festering resentment among large sections of the population against what was seen as the privileged position of organised labour and the remoteness and non-responsiveness of big government. In 1964, Harold Wilson had been able to rally support with his call for a new technocratic politics involving an extension of state planning, and in 1974, when the country was on its knees as a result of the miners' strike, he had still been able to win an election on the basis of his promise that Labour could work with the unions to manage the economy. By 1979, however, the electorate had evidently had enough, and voters turned in their millions to Margaret Thatcher's new Tory Party which held out the promise of an end to government 'interference' and a return to the principles of the free market. Twenty years of corporatist economic planning had come to an end, and the wheel was about to come full circle.

The Return to a Market Strategy: Thatcherism and Economic Policy in the 1980s

The Conservative government elected in 1979 has a claim to be regarded as the most radical administration since the 1945–50 Labour government in that it challenged all the orthodoxies which had been accepted with lesser or greater enthusiasm by all post-war governments. The three main planks of Butskellism – the mixed economy, the welfare state and the use of Keynesian demand-management to ensure full employment – all came under sustained attack. It is true that the outgoing Labour government had itself eroded welfare spending and abandoned any pretence at achieving full employment following the 1976 International Monetary Fund loan, but the Thatcher administration went much further and attacked such policies as a matter of principle.

It is impossible to understand what happened after 1979 without first understanding what was entailed in 'Thatcherism'. Thatcherism was not simply an economic policy, although the commitment to a free-market strategy was certainly a key component of it. The important point is that the market was supported as a principle in its own right rather than as merely a means for overcoming Britain's economic problems. Thus in the years following 1979, the government aggressively pursued a market strategy even where this entailed increased economic costs: profitable state industries were privatised, for example, thereby reducing public revenues, just as council houses were sold off at large discounts thereby increasing the burdens on the public purse (see chapter 10). Thatcherism in this sense represented a return to the nineteenth-century emphasis on the liberal aspects of liberal-democracy.

This principled support of the free market reflected an individualistic philosophy which held that economic freedom was a condition of political freedom. Milton Friedman, an American economist whose ideas played a crucial role in the development of Thatcherite philosophy, expressed this argument clearly when we wrote:

Fundamentally, there are only two ways of co-ordinating the economic activities of millions. One is central direction involving the use of coercion – the technique of the army and of the modern totalitarian state. The other is voluntary co-operation of individuals – the technique of the market place.

The government's promotion of the market was thus a function of its commitment to a classical liberal philosophy (resurrected in the work of writers like Friedman and F. A. Hayek) in which individuals should be left to make their own choices while the state's role is to be limited to ensuring that the conditions under which free choice can be exercised are maintained. This is a philosophy which has a long pedigree in Britain, going back to the nineteenth-century utilitarians and beyond, yet it is a philosophy which represents a fundamental break with the paternalism of the traditional Tory Party. It is also probably true to say that Thatcher's original appeal was to the 'small people' – the self-employed, the independent professionals, the skilled artisans – rather than to big business. As she often reminded her audiences, she was herself a humble grocer's daughter made good.

This appeal to the very people who had felt themselves excluded from the corporatist planning of the previous two decades was reinforced by a potent mixture of political nationalism, populism and authoritarianism. The nationalism, which had been nurtured by Enoch Powell and others on the extreme right of the Conservative Party through the 1960s and 1970s, took the form of a latent racism (Thatcher, for example, spoke of Britain as having been 'swamped' by black immigrants), a single-minded pursuit of British interests within the European Community, an uncompromising stand against Irish republicanism and Scottish and Welsh separatism (discussed in cahpter 12), and a general reassertion of patriotic sentiment which swelled to a peak in 1982 during the successful war waged to recapture the Falkland Islands from Argentina. This was then combined with the populist campaign against 'big unions' and 'big government', and with a new authoritarian ideology which stressed the need for a strong state which would stand up to Britain's enemies abroad (by a massive increase in spending on conventional and nuclear forces) and at home (by strengthening the police force, imposing stiffer sentences through the courts, and confronting the power of 'anti-social' elements in British society – notably the trade unions).

All of this was the context within which the government's economic strategy was pursued – a strategy which was designed to bury neo-Keynesianism and break up old-style corporatism. It was a strategy which deliberately removed the props and crutches on which so much of British industry had come to lean over the previous 20 or 30 years, and which sought instead to expose British firms to the full cleansing blast of international competition. It was, in a sense, a Darwinian strategy of survival of the fittest; companies would either adapt to these changed circumstances by reducing their costs and improving efficiency, or they would die. As we shall see, many died.

The strategy itself was based on an analysis of the ills of the British economy which emphasised the deleterious effects of at least five main factors: powerful trade unions, weak governments, an anti-enterprise culture, an over-burdened private sector and weak monetary policies.

The argument that *strong unions* have been one important factor in Britain's more recent economic difficulties is by no means peculiar to Right-wing theorists, for some Marxist theorists too have suggested that private-sector profits have been squeezed over the years by a combination of intense foreign competition (which has prevented companies from increasing prices) and a strong union movement (which has forced them to increase wages). This is, however, a view which is more often heard on the Right where there is, in any case, a marked antipathy towards the principle of unionism in so far as it is seen as intruding on individuals' rights (for example, through the imposition of closed shops) and as undermining the operation of a free market. For the New Right, trade unions are the modern equivalent of the feudal barons and they have used their monopolistic control over the supply of labour and their coercive powers such as the right to picket in order to force up wages beyond their 'natural' market level, thereby crippling the profitability of British industry.

Seen in this light, trade union power represents an obstacle to any attempt to force companies to become more competitive since it prevents firms from reducing their costs by cutting wages and shedding surplus labour. From the point of view of the Thatcher government, successive post-war administrations in Britiain had exacerbated this problem through the pursuit of Keynesian full-employment policies, which had strengthened the bargaining power of the unions, and through the adoption of corporatist management strategies which included union leaders within the policy-making process. Just as the old nineteenth-century liberals were concerned that the extension of the franchise would subordinate state power to the sectional demands of the working class, so their new twentieth-century counterparts now argued that this had indeed occurred and that Keynesianism and corporatism had been the instruments of this unwarranted increase in the power of organised labour.

What was required therefore was a weakening of union power rather than compromises with it, and from 1979 onwards, the government set out to do just this by allowing unemployment to rise, by legislating on issues such as the right to picket, by reducing union involvement in policy-making bodies, and by standing firm against workers in the public sector who attempted to breach the government's 'cash limits' on public sector pay. To a large extent the policy worked. Through the early years of the 1980s, the government legislated to enforce secret ballots in union leadership elections, to give individuals the right not to belong to a union (thus breaking the 'closed shop'), to outlaw secondary action (for example, sympathy strikes or picketing of businesses not involved in the dispute) and to regulate picketing. Opinion polls showed clear public support for all of these measures, and most of the legislation introduced in the 1980s seems likely to survive even the return of a Labour government in the 1990s.

Whether this legislation has helped strengthen the economy is less certain. Undoubtedly employers have been freed to develop fresh initiatives which had for years been blocked by powerful and conservative unions such as those in the newspaper printing industry. It is also clear that wage militancy virtually disappeared in the mid-eighties, and the defeat of the National Union of Mineworkers, who lost a long and bitter battle over pit closures in 1986, was in many ways symbolic of the end of an era in which powerful union bosses could confront an elected government and win. Nevertheless, the push for higher wages was arguably dampened more by escalating unemployment than by reduced union power. It was the massive rise in unemployment rates (to 14 per cent in the early eighties) which best explains the slowdown in wages, for by the late eighties (when unemployment fell back to around 7 per cent), real wages were again spiralling and union action in pursuit of high wage claims had once more become a common feature of Britain's industrial relations despite all the government's legislation in this field. The attack on union might was important and in the view of many commentators represented a necessary and overdue move to modernise the law governing labour relations, but it could only ever be one element of an overall strategy for economic renewal.

A second element in the government's strategy rested on the view that *weak government* had been a further factor in Britain's economic decline. This view derived from the thesis, discussed in chapter 4, which held that government had become 'overloaded', and that there had developed a 'bias of excessive expectation in democracy', which had been fuelled by the continuing expansion of state spending from the 1950s onwards. A whole postwar generation had been reared in the belief that it had a right to expect comprehensive welfare support in housing, health care, education and so on, and no government had been strong enough to stand up against the escalating demands from various different sections of the population for more spending on more and improved services. The result had been an ever-widening gap between the level of state spending and the total revenues collected in taxation, even though taxes had increased. This gap had been filled by government borrowing and by 'printing money' – hence the inflation spiral of the 1970s.

This analysis rests on the argument that various groups have been able to use the state for their own selfish ends in that they have been able to push successfully for expensive programmes whose cost must be shared by everybody else. Industrialists, for example, have pushed for increased aids to industry, professional groups such as teachers, social workers and doctors have pushed for more spending on education, welfare and health, trade unions have pushed for increases in the 'social wage', and so on. While there is undoubtedly some truth in this analysis, the question which it fails to address is why the government has generally caved in to such pressures. To explain this simply in terms of governmental 'weakness' is hardly adequate since it involves a tautology; after all, governments that 'give in' to pressures are by definition weak. What we need to know is why governments have apparently been so 'weak' in the face of demands for increased spending for which there are no additional sources of revenue.

One answer, found in the neo-liberal theory of 'Public Choice' (reviewed in chapter 3), is that the benefits to a government of caving in to sectional interests will always outweigh those to be achieved by standing up to them. If, for example, the farmers want an increase in price supports, the cost to everybody else is likely to be minimal, a few pence a week, but the benefits enjoyed by the farmers (and hence their political gratitude) will be considerably greater. It therefore makes political sense for a government to give the farmers what they want. The same logic applies to any other group, especially where they have the ability to cause a public nuisance by going on strike and inconveniencing millions of voters. So it is that, down the years, various and different groups have been bought off with public money and the economy has become increasingly weakened as a result.

An alternative analysis of the problem of weak government was developed in the Marxist literature of the 1970s. According to this work, governments have had little choice but to give in, for a refusal to increase spending would have led to a massive fall in company profts and to an erosion of working people's living standards to a point at which they began to question the very legitimacy of the capitalist system. Such is the argument developed in a very influential book by the American political scientist, James O'Connor, who suggested in the early seventies that Western governments were running up frighteningly large fiscal crises precisely because they were obliged at one and the same time to increase direct and indirect subsidies to the private sector and to supplement people's incomes through expanded social security provisions, while they were unable to meet these escalating costs through increased taxation. Government borrowing was spiralling out of control as a result.

Both the Right-wing view, that governments find that it pays to follow the line of least resistance, and the Left-wing view, that governments have no choice but to try to prop up an ailing capitalist system, agree that pressures on governments to increase spending have been a major factor fuelling Britain's post-war economic problems. The Thatcher government elected in 1979 was determined to resist these pressures in its drive to halt and reverse the decline. Aid to industry was cut despite pleas from the CBI and the TUC. Cash limits were imposed on the public sector and the government showed itself willing to sit out the ensuing strikes rather than give in to them. Welfare spending was cut back despite the campaigns from the poverty lobby. When pressures on the government for a change in policy were intensifying in the early eighties, Margaret Thatcher delivered a defiant speech at the Conservative Party conference in which she announced that 'The lady's not for turning!' Commentators began to refer to her as the 'Iron Lady', and she seemed pleased to embrace the epithet. After years of weak governments, this one was determined to be strong and firm, and even critics were to be heard speaking reverentially of Thatcher's 'resolution'.

As with the reform of the trade unions, so with their attempts to resist special pleading, the Thatcher administrations met with mixed success. Through the 1980s, the government stood firm against some interests (for example, the miners' union) but caved in to others (for example, the legal profession which successfully resisted proposed reforms intended to open up competition). It also gave the impression of cutting back on public spending while actually presiding over an increase. Partly because the dramatic increase in unemployment in the early eighties pushed up government spending on social security, and partly because cuts in spending in one area (for example, council house building) were often balanced by increases in spending in another area (for example, housing benefit), levels of public spending rose by 11 per cent in real terms between 1979 and 1989 (although expressed as a proportion of national output, government spending did fall slightly, from 43 per cent in 1979 to 39 per cent ten years later). Furthermore, although the government slashed personal rates of income tax (from 83 per cent to 40 per cent in the top band, and from 33 per cent to 25 per cent on basic rate), its total tax take as a percentage of Gross Domestic Product actually increased from 33 per cent in 1978/9 to 38 per cent ten years later. The fact that a government committed to cutting spending and reducing taxation ended up increasing both suggests that those Public Choice analysts and Marxist theorists may be right when they suggest that all governments face endemic pressures to increase expenditure which may be extremely difficult to resist.

The third element in Britain's decline which the Conservative governments of the 1980s set out to reverse was the persistence of what has variously been termed an *'anti-enterprise'* or *'dependency' culture*. The thinking here was that forty years of growing state regulation and intervention in many different aspects of life had undermined people's spirit of self-reliance and initiative. The prevailing culture of the nation valued caution over risk, stability over change, bureaucratic rules over buccaneering money-making. In the early nineteenth century, Napoleon had referred to the English as a 'nation of shop-keepers'. By the late twentieth century, the British had become a nation of supplicants. Industry expected state handouts when profits declined; workers expected a decent standard of living to be provided irrespective of whether they worked hard to achieve it; and throughout the country, the knee-jerk reaction whenever anything went wrong was to look to government to put it right. The Thatcher governments set out to change all this by asserting that government not only should not, but could not, act as the nation's 'nanny'.

Where previous generations of politicians had, whether out of conviction or political pragmatism, proclaimed a commitment to values such as 'compassion' and 'citizenship rights', the new message from the Thatcherites was one extolling the virtues of 'individual success' and 'self-help'. In this way, the government deliberately tried to emphasise the responsibility of people to solve their own problems rather than to look to government to help them. The role of the state was to enable rather than to provide, and there could be no long-term economic regeneration until this lesson had been learned.

To some extent, this cultural revolution was successful. The heroes of the Thatcher years were the self-made men and women who made fortunes by establishing new companies or by exploiting new opportunities opened up by the deregulation of the City financial institutions. The epitome of the Thatcher years was the 'Yuppy' – the young, upwardly-mobile professional who made lots of money and who was not embarrassed to display it. In a book published in 1981, Martin Wiener argued that the roots of the British malaise lay in a disdain for new money, an attitude which he traced to the snobbbishness of the aristocracy and gentry of the nineteenth century who had sneered at the bourgeois values of the manufacturers and traders who had elbowed their way into wealth during the Industrial Revolution. Unlike old-style Toryism, which had for long been associated with precisely these same elitist sentiments, Thatcherism proclaimed the virtues of the capitalist entrepreneur and was scathing towards those, such as landowners, church leaders and university dons, who emphasised caution about acquisitiveness and who elevated 'compassion' or 'culture' above the rough and tumble of the market-place.

In retrospect, however, it seems doubtful whether the governments of the 1980s really did make much of a dent in popular culture and attitudes. A series of surveys on *British Social Attitudes* has shown that there is still strong popular support for high levels of spending on socialised services such as the NHS and state schooling. There is also some two-thirds of the population who believe that income and wealth distribution is unfair, and nearly half who believe that government should redistribute income from the better-off to the less well-off. More people in Britain react favourably to the image of socialism than to that of capitalism. Following more than ten years of Thatcherism, the prevailing mood in the British electorate still seemed to favour a positive social and economic role for government, and there was little sign of a new 'enterprise culture' blooming among ordinary working people.

The fourth strand in the Thatcher government's strategy for reversing Britain's economic decline entailed an attack on public sector bureaucracies which were widely seen as inefficient and overpaid. British industry, it was believed, had been held back by the growth of this unproductive and parasitic workforce. Put another way, a burgeoning public sctor had *overburdened the private sector*.

The intellectual rationale for this belief came in the form of a book written by two economists which summarised the country's problems as due to 'too few producers'. What the authors, Robert Bacon and Walter Eltis, meant by this was not simply that the private sector had shrunk in comparison with the public (although it had), nor that industry had shrunk in comparison with services (although this again was true), but most crucially that the proportion of marketed to non-marketed output of goods and services had fallen. Through the 1960s and 1970s, the number of workers employed in producing profitable goods and services, whether in the private or public sector, had fallen while the numbers employed by the state and engaged in non-profitable activities such as administration, teaching or production of loss-making outputs such as coal or Concorde, had correspondingly risen. The consequence of this was that a declining marketed sector was increasingly called upon to finance an expanding non-marketed sector.

One obvious solution to this problem of too few producers having to sustain too many non-producers was to cut back the size of the non-marketed sector by cutting public spending and by ending state subsidies to loss-making public-sector industries such as Rover Cars and the National Coal Board. This is precisely what the Thatcher government set out to do by selling off public assets, closing down 'inefficient' pits, ending subsidies on council houses and selling houses wherever tenants expressed a desire to buy, laying off thousands of steel workers, teachers and other public-sector employees, cutting financial grants to local authorities, and so on.

Undoubtedly the most significant of these measures was the drive to privatise large sections of public-sector industry. In the view of the government, the state should be responsible for providing only those goods and services which the private sector could not provide. Public ownership was criticised as inefficient and monopolistic. Unlike private firms, which are forced by competition to improve their efficiency, reduce their costs and stay responsive to their customers, nationalised industries were seen as bureaucratic, non-innovative and as a burden on the public purse. Immune from the threat of bankruptcy and sheltered from the blast of competition, they had no incentive to economise, for funds could always be raised through government's unique power to increase revenue through taxation.

The privatisation programme began modestly with sales of shares in small companies such as Cable and Wireless and Amersham International which had been acquired by Labour's National Enterprise Board in the 1970s. Then, in 1984, the government launced its first big flotation when it announced the sale of 51 per cent of its shares in British Telecom. Backed by an aggressive advertising campaign, the sale was a resounding success. Five times oversubscribed, the shares attracted an 86 per cent premium on their first day of trading, and this then set a snowball in motion as each successive privatisation attracted widespread public interest. British Gas was oversubscribed by one hundred per cent and generated an immediate 20 per cent premium for those who purchased shares; the Trustee Savings Bank was oversubscribed sevenfold with a first-day premium of 72 per cent; and this was followed by British Airways (nine times oversubscribed with a 68 per cent premium), Rolls-Royce (ten times and a 50 per cent premium) and the British Airports Authority (BAA). The stock market crash of October 1987 caused a hiccup when BP suffered losses on its privatisation, and British Steel showed no premium when it came to the market, but the momentum was regained by the sale of the ten water authorities in 1989 and of the electricity supply companies in 1990. The effect of these sales was twofold.

1 They massively reduced the size of the public sector. Between 1979 and 1989, nineteen industries were sold raising revenue of over twenty-two billion pounds and reducing the size of the state-owned industrial sector by 40 per cent. Three-quarters of a million jobs were transferred from the state to the private sector as a result. The privatisation programme thus represented a major restructuring of the balance of the so-called 'mixed economy' in Britain.

2 The major privatisations resulted in a substantial increase in personal share-holding in Britain, from around 4 per cent of adults in the early 1980s to nearly one quarter of adults (eleven million people) in 1990. In its 1987 election manifesto, the Conservative Party claimed to have brought about an 'historic transformation' in British society as a result of the spread of small-scale share ownership, although the majority of these new owners held shares in only one company and had a portfolio with a value of less than one thousand pounds.

On balance, the privatisation programme has been a success. Some companies (NFC is the clearest example) have witnessed staggering increases in productivity and profitability following their sale, and most have succeeded in attracting new investment which would previously have had to come from public funds. The programme has, however, proved politically contentious, especially in the case of the former public utilities such as gas, water, electricity and telecommunications, and in these cases the Labour Party has remained committed to restoring them to some form of 'social ownership' (but has stated that it is no longer in favour of what its 1989 policy review termed 'old-fashioned nationalisation').

The fifth and most central element in the Thatcher government's economic strategy was the commitment to monetarism, and this reflected the view that the major cause of Britain's economic ills lay in *irresponsible monetary policy*. It is this, of course, that lies behind the other four factors, for the pursuit of full employment to appease the unions, the weakness in the face of demands for greater expenditure, and the growing size of the public-sector workforce have all been possible only because governments have been willing to increase the supply of money. It was here, above all else, that the Thatcher government sought to break with the past. Influenced by its economic guru, Professor Milton Friedman, it published monetary targets (which referred to the amount of money in circulation, plus bank deposits, plus money 'created' through credit) which sought to reduce the amount of money in the economy so as to reduce price inflation. In this way, the government tried to return to the old monetary discipline of the pre-Keynesian years before the war when the money supply had automatically been held in check through the operation of the Gold Standard. In the 1980s, with no such external controls on spendthrift governments, this meant self-imposed monetary discipline.

This doctrine of sound money had first been imposed during the Labour government's term of office in 1976 as a condition of the International Monetary Fund loan, but from 1979 it was adopted freely and enthusiastically, almost as a matter of faith. Monetarism represented the antithesis of Keynesianism in that it stressed the need to control the money supply in order to avoid inflation rather than the manipulation of the money supply in order to avoid unemployment. Thus, for monetarists such as Friedman, the main (and in some views the only) economic responsibility of government is to ensure price stability.

When the government came to power in 1979, inflation was running at 15 per cent. Reduction of the rate of inflation became the government's overwhelming priority. There were a number of reasons for this. The principal one was that Britain's inflation rate was higher than that of most of her competitors with the result that British goods were being undercut on world markets. The government was also concerned that inflation was undermining the value of savings (and was therefore encouraging immediate consumption and penalising those who were thrifty), and was distorting price signals (for businesses were unable to distinguish the effects of inflation from those of real shifts in the pattern of demand).

Following Milton Friedman, the causes of inflation were thought to lie primarily in governmental failure to control the supply of money. Monetarist theory holds that the price of goods will increase as the amount of money in circulation increases. Put simply, inflation is the result of too much money chasing too few goods, in which case it can be checked by slowing the rate of increase of money. So it was that the first Thatcher government imposed a tight monetary squeeze on the economy by raising interest rates and by publishing its own targets for the growth of money supply.

Pre-war policies brought about pre-war consequences, and the country soon crashed into a recession of 1930s proportions. Between 1979 and 1983, industrial output fell by a staggering 13 per cent as viable and non-viable firms alike went to the wall. Manufacturing output fell even further, by 19 per cent, thus more than wiping out the previous ten years hesitant growth. Unemployment rose at an unprecedented rate reaching 14 per cent (3.25 million) on the official figures by 1983. Investment stagnated, for the high interest rates which had been designed to control the growth of credit also had the effect of rendering loans too expensive for companies to contemplate. The removal of exchange controls resulted, predictably, in a flood of money going abroad – overseas investment increased tenfold in just four years. Only the happy accident of North Sea oil kept the economy afloat and the balance of payments within bounds, but even the oil revenues could not disguise the fact that, for the first time in British industrial history, the import of manufactured goods outweighed manufacturing exports. Britain's share of world trade fell from eight to six and a half per cent.

At the cost of considerable disruption, the policy did nevertheless seem to work. The inflation rate fell to 2.4 per cent in the summer of 1986 – something which Britain had not known since the 1950s – and following the spectacular collapse of 1981, economic growth began to pick up and was running as high as 4 per cent per annum through much of the decade. Cautiously, newspapers and commentators began to refer to the 'end of decline' and to compare Britain's economic performance favourably with that of other industrial countries.

It was not to last, however. In 1985 the government effectively abandoned monetarism, claiming that it was impossible to measure money supply with any degree of accuracy (there was some truth in this given the deregulation of the money markets and the explosion of personal credit). In its place, the Chancellor chose to tie the value of the pound as closely as possible to the strongest currency in Europe – the German mark. His thinking was that the low German inflation rate could be reproduced in Britain by shadowing the German currency. Unfortunately, the pound began to look very attractive to speculators and the government lowered interest rates significantly in order to maintain parity with the falling mark. The result was that borrowing became cheap and credit expanded rapidly as people used their plastic cards to fuel the biggest consumer spending boom in the country's history. By 1990, inflation was back over eight per cent, interest rates had been raised to record levels in an attempt to dampen spending, and the rate of economic growth had fallen back to around 2 per cent. The bouyancy of the mid-eighties began to look increasingly like a false dawn as once again the country's fundamental economic weakness was revealed in all the familiar indicators – pressure on the pound, high inflation, rising unemployment and a growing balance-of-payments deficit (including, for the first time since the Napoleonic wars, a deficit on so-called 'invisible trade' – insurance, tourism and the like – as well as on manufactured goods).

Conclusion

We have noted several times in this and earlier chapters that a key function of the state must be to maintain the conditions in which production can continue and expand. It is, however, one thing to say what the state 'must' do, and quite another to say what it actually achieves. It is clear from the evidence reviewed in this chapter that the British state over the last 100 years or so has failed to discharge this key function adequately, for the economy has been in a long and steady decline relative to other industrial countries, and this decline shows no sign of coming to an end. Clearly, we need to ask why the state has failed to reverse this trend. There are two main answers. One is that the scope for effective action is restricted and is becoming ever narrower. The other is that it is by no means clear what should be done, even within these constraints on action.

First, the state has not been an autonomous agent; policy choices have been hemmed in by economic constraints. Economic factors have not, of course, determined political strategy – government leaders, Treasury mandarins, Bank of England chiefs and the rest have always enjoyed some discretion in determining their policies. Indeed, as the radicalism of the Thatcher government makes clear, governments may enjoy considerable leeway and are certainly not all constrained to follow the same path. The constraints under which they operate are as much rational as structural: the Wilson government did not have to abandon the National Plan in 1966 (it could have devalued instead); the Heath government did not have to execute its famous U-turn in 1972 (it could have let unemployment rise and companies go to the wall as Thatcher did 10 years later); and so on.

Nevertheless, the discretion which governments have enjoyed has been a discretion within limits imposed by factors beyond their control – governments are not free agents. One major source of constraint upon their actions has been the operation of world markets, for ever since the abolition of the Corn Laws, the British economy has been dependent upon, and thus vulnerable to, the international economy, and this dependency and vulnerability has increased as the cushion of the colonies has been lost. When Harold Wilson blamed the faceless 'gnomes of Zurich' for the eventual devaluation of the pound in 1967, there was some truth in the charge, just as Edward Heath's complaint about the impact of a quadrupling of oil prices in 1973, or James Callaghan's plea of impotence in relation to the International Monetary Fund in 1976, or Margaret Thatcher's identification of the world slump as a major factor in Britain's recession in the 1980s, all contained more than a germ of truth.

Furthermore, developments in recent years have exacerbated the British economy's dependency on world market forces and have correspondingly weakened the capacity of governments to pursue their own remedies. One such development has been the growing integration of the UK economy within the European Community with its insistence on the removal of all trade barriers from 1992 and its increasing domination by the powerful German mark within the European Exchange Rate Mechanism (the significance of the EC is considered in more detail in chapter 12). Another equally important development has been the abolition of currency controls and the growing internationalisation of the world's financial markets, for not only does this enable institutions to move funds in seconds between London, New York, Tokyo or Frankfurt, but it also makes it nigh on impossible for a national government effectively to control and keep tabs on the creation of credit. The British economy today is one small outpost of a European system which is itself increasingly bound in with the huge American and Japanese economies. When even the Soviet Union has abandoned the attempt to remain insulated from world markets, it is clear that the days of effective British economic sovereignty have long since passed.

The second factor in the explanation of the apparent failure of the state to halt Britain's economic decline is that it is by no means clear what policies should have been adopted. The history of British economic policy through the twentieth century has been one of muddled and incoherent responses to seemingly intractable problems. Since the end of the First World War, British governments have, without much success, embraced a minimalist strategy (in the inter-war years), central planning (in the 1940s), Keynesianism and the mixed economy (from the fifties to the mid-seventies), and a return to monetary policy and a free-market strategy (since 1976). None of this seems to have worked. By 1990 the situation had been reached where neither of the two principal parties in Britain had any clear strategy for economic regeneration, for both monetarism and socialist planning collapsed in the mid-eighties. All that the Conservatives could offer was a reliance on interest-rate policy to try to control inflation, while Labour's ill-defined alternative rested on the need to encourage investment (a chronic problem in British manufacturing throughout this period) but with little evidence that it knew how this could be achieved. Both parties, it seems, were trapped on the horns of a dilemma. On the one hand, it is clear that high levels of state intervention and regulation in the economy have created as many problems as they have resolved down the years, and in an increasingly open world economic system, any attempt to 'buck the market' seems destined to result in a flood of capital overseas and an immediate and crushing balance-of-payments crisis. On the other, the evidence of the Thatcher years suggests that liberalisation leaves much of British industry dangerously exposed to competition from overseas which it cannot meet and exacerbates problems such as the growing division between north and south and the failure to invest in long-term manufacturing projects.

Faced with this uncomfortable dilemma, commentators have often looked overseas for inspiration. What they ask, have the Japanese and Germans done that the British could profitably copy? The answer is that, in their different ways, both Japan and German have evolved economic strategies in which the state and capital have operated in tandem. Yet Britain tried this strategy in the corporatist years from 1962 to 1976, and it all ended in dismal failure. Whether the problem lies in the British electoral system, with its sharp polarisation between a 'party of capital' and a 'party of organised labour', or in the deep class culture of British society, which seems to breed distrust and antagonism and to preclude consensus and co-operation, is difficult to judge, but it is clear that the problems of British economic policy down the years cannot simply be explained by governmental incompetence. Over the last fifty years, virtually all the feasible strategies have been tried, yet none have worked.

As for the future, it seems that British governments will become less and less significant in shaping the fate of the British economy. Many commentators are worried by this loss of national sovereignty, yet it may represent the one ray of hope in an otherwise gloomy outlook. Harnessed ever more tightly to Europe, it is possible that the British economy will be carried along on the coat tails of Brussels and the Bundesbank. Similarly, a rising tide of Japanese investment in Britain is beginning to resuscitate manufacturing to the point where a surplus on the balance of trade could once again be achieved during the 1990s. As we shall argue in chapter 12, a focus on the British state and British domestic politics is likely to become increasingly irrelevant to an understanding of the forces shaping life in this country in the years to come. Nowhere is this more obviously the case than in economic policy.

Works Cited and Guide to Further Reading

Bacon, R. and Eltis, W. (1978) *Britain's Economic Problem: Too Few Producers*, 2nd edn, London, Macmillan.
An influential analysis which traces the post-war decline of the British economy to the growing imbalance between marketed and non-marketed production of goods and services, and which documents the sadly missed opportunities in the 1960s and 1970s to put this right.

Baran, P. and Sweezy, P. (1968) *Monopoly Capital*, Harmondwoth, Penguin.
From a broadly Marxist position, the authors seek to argue that American capitalism in particular, and the world capitalist system in general, faces a mounting problem of absorbing a growing surplus capacity generated by the small number of large multinational companies which now dominate the market. In identifying the problem as one of 'underconsumption', Baran and Sweezy were clearly influenced by Keynes as well as by Marx, and their book has often been criticised by other Marxist economists who suggest that the problem is not so much how to absorb a surplus as how to generate it in the first place.

Cawson, A. (1986) *Corporatism and Political Theory*, Oxford, Basil Blackwell.
A useful review of theories of corporatism which ends up arguing that corporatist strategies have tended to develop most fully in areas of economic policy-making. Interesting for its analysis of the conditions which enabled 'macrocorporatism' to flourish in countries like West Germany, Austria and Sweden while it collapsed in Britain.

Friedman, M. and Friedman, R. (1984) *The Tyranny of the Status Quo*, London, Secker and Warburg.
An analysis of government economic policies under Reagan in the USA and Thatcher in Britain. Bemoans the failure of these supposedly 'New Right' governments to reduce state spending and bring inflation under control. Finds the explanation in the power of an 'iron triangle' of vested interests consisting of sectional interests, vote-seeking politicians and self-interested state bureaucracies.

Gamble, A. (1985) *Britain in Decline*, 2nd edn. London, Macmillan.
A stimulating analysis by a Marxist political economist of Britain's long-term economic decline. This is explained in terms of the international role of the British state and of British finance capital, the peculiar relationship between the state and society which has prevented any effective direction of the economy by governments, and the incomplete incorporation of the working class into the institutions of British society. The book also considers the extent to which the Thatcherite social market strategy and a socialist 'alternative economic strategy' may be expected to reverse the decline. A gloomy yet largely persuasive analysis.

Neuberger, J. (1987) *Privatisation*, London, Macmillan.
Contains combative articles both in favour of and against the privatisation policies of the 1980s.

O'Connor, J. (1972) *The Fiscal Crisis of the State*, New York, St Martin's Press.
An influential book by a radical American political scientist who argues that Western states have been obliged to run up dauntingly-large debts in order to support private-sector profitability. According to O'Connor, this support has taken the form of both 'social capital' expenditures, through which governments have reduced the price paid by private-sector firms for raw materials and infrastructure, and 'social consumption' expenditures, such as housing and health care which have reduced the level of wages which firms have had to pay. In addition to all this, governments have also had to increase spending on social control items such as police and social security, and such 'social expenses' have represented a massive drain on the public purse. These three categories of state spending have all increased in ever more desperate attempts to stave off recession with the result that expenditure has far out-run revenue. Hence the onset of 'fiscal crisis' in the 1970s.

Sked, A. (1987) *Britain's Decline: Problems and Perspectives*, Oxford, Basil Blackwell.
A little book of just 83 pages which nails the fallacy of a 'moral decline' in Britain but which accepts the evidence for a long-term relative economic decline. The latter is explained as the result of early industrialisation, the absence of a growth culture, a burdensome world role and an archaic system of industrial relations. Retains an open mind on the likely long-term success of Thatcherism in rectifying all this.

Stewart, M. (1972) *Keynes and After*, 2nd edn, Harmondsworth, Penguin.
A standard and readable work which outlines the major elements of Keynes's ideas, sets them in the context of their time, and considers the success of their application over the first 25 years after the war. Chapter 4 is a particularly useful exposition of Keynes's theory of how savings and investment determine the level of employment. The book also contains a timely chapter on monetarist economics.

Veljanovski, C. (1987) *Selling the State*, London, Weidenfeld and Nicolson.
Arguably one of the best and most comprehensive treatments of privatisation which outlines the history of the policy, its objectives, the mechanisms for regulating the newly privatised companies, and the likely economic and social effects of the sales. Veljanovski is a supporter of privatisation, but the book successfully avoids shrill polemic.

Wiener, M. (1981) *English Culture and the Decline of the Industrial Spirit 1950–1980*, Cambridge University Press.
Explains Britain's long-term economic decline as the product of an elite culture which views capitalism and money-making with disdain. Sees the main challenge facing Thatcher as the need to change this culture.

Winkler, J. (1975) 'Corporatism', *European Journal of Sociology*, 17, pp. 100–136.
In which Winkler most clearly sets out his argument that, by the end of the 1980s, Britain will have developed into a fully fledged corporatist society based on private ownership and state control. An object lesson in the perils of social science prediction!

Chapter 10

Providing for Social Need

It is clear that, in the twentieth century, citizenship and the capitalist class system have been at war.
  T. H. Marshall (1950) *Citizenship and Social Class*, London,
  Cambridge University Press, p. 29.

The translation of a want or need into a right is one of the most widespread and dangerous of modern heresies.
  Enoch Powell (1972) *Still to Decide*, London, Elliot Right Way
  Books, p. 12.

The embarrassing secret of the welfare state is that, while its impact upon capitalist accumulation may well become destructive (as the conservative analysis so emphatically demonstrates), its abolition would be plainly disruptive (a fact that is systematically ignored by the conservative critics). The contradiction is that while capitalism cannot coexist with the welfare state, neither can it exist without the welfare state.
  Claus Offe (1982) 'Some contradictions of the modern welfare
  state', *Critical Social Policy*, 2, p. 11.

Introduction

Social policy is probably the most politicised area of state activity in the contemporary period. To most of us, questions of economic policy seem remote, but this is not the case with social policy. Most of us are directly affected in personal ways by the state's role in organising social welfare. The vast majority of people in Britain rely on state provision for their medical care and for the education of their children, and they experience changes in the quality of service firsthand. Every family in the land regularly visits the Post Office to draw family allowance and every one of us who lives to retirement age will draw a state pension.

Given this personal interest in the welfare state, it is not surprising that myths abound in popular consciousness concerning the way in which welfare policy operates. Some of these myths are positive in their

"Born into a lifetime of poverty beyond the reach of the welfare state and the market?" (Reproduced by kind permission of Format Partners. Photograph: Brenda Prince.)

evaluation – for example, that the British welfare state is the 'envy of the world', that it has succeeded in abolishing poverty, and so on. Others – such as the myth that there exists a veritable legion of welfare 'scroungers', that life is easier on the dole than it is for those in work, that the council estates are creaking under the weight of Jaguar cars and colour television sets – are negative and reflect the fear and indignation which stem from the sense that one is being taken for a ride by an anonymous and parasitical bunch of freeloaders.

Most myths are not entirely without foundation. There was a time, for a few years after the war, when welfare provisions in Britain were probably in advance of those in many other Western countries, and it is true that welfare benefits are subject to some abuse by a small minority of claimants (although it is impossible accurately to assess its scale or extent). Yet by and large, these are myths, or at best half-truths. The problem of poverty, for example, has clearly not been overcome, although the extent of poverty in Britain depends on the definitions which we adopt. Nobody today receives so little income that they cannot feed or clothe themselves, but around a quarter of the population enjoys insufficient income to enable them to participate in social activities which most people regard as 'normal'. Nor is it true that welfare provision in Britain is more extensive than in other comparable countries, for even in the early 1970s (i.e. after a considerable expansion of state welfare provision and before the cuts which began in 1976), spending on pensions, child allowances and unemployment and sickness benefits amounted to just 7.7 per cent of Gross Domestic Product in Britain (less even than in the United States and nearly 5 per cent below that of France and Germany), while total welfare expenditure at 12.6 per cent of GDP was lower than the average of eighteen Western countries and was surpassed by ten of them. As for 'dole scroungers' the facts are that a married man's unemployment benefit in Britain in 1983 stood at just 29 per cent of average earnings, compared with 70 per cent in West Germany and 80 per cent in France. In recent years, welfare spending in Britain has been systematically cut back, partly as a response to the worsening economic plight of the country discussed in chapter 9, and partly as a function of the resurgence of an individualist and anti-statist ideology in the form of Thatcherism.

In this two-part chapter we shall first attempt to explain why and how the state came to be increasingly involved in the provision of welfare from the nineteenth century onwards. We will then explore two contemporary critiques of state welfare provision. Both the Left critique and the Right critique challenge the rosy perspective on the welfare state, and they both have a bearing on the current reversal of the trend to increased state involvement in this field of public policy and provision.

The Development of State Welfare Provisions

Laissez-faire: self-help and provision by the market in the nineteenth century

The provision of welfare services by the national state is a comparatively recent phenomenon. In 1860 there was no system of income security, no state medical care apart from lunatic asylums, vaccination and environmental health regulations, no state education apart from grants to religious schools, and no system of state housing. A century later, the state was operating a battery of income support schemes (old age and invalidity pensions, sickness, maternity, work injury and unemployment benefits, family allowances and national assistance), a comprehensive and largely free health service, free and compulsory primary and secondary education and grant-aided higher education, and was landlord to over a quarter of all the nation's households. Over the same period, welfare spending as a proportion of GNP increased seventeen times. Over 7 million people are today employed by the state, many of them in administering or providing welfare and social services.

The relative lack of state welfare provision in the mid-nineteenth century did not of course mean that there was no system of social support. In the main, however, this was a period when people's basic consumption requirements – the need for accommodation, for medical treatment and so on – were met, to the extent that they were met at all, through the market rather than by the state. Private landlords provided housing in return for rents, private tutors provided education in return for fees, private doctors charged for elementary medical treatment. Those who could not afford to pay went without, or relied on private charity and the benevolence of a hard-nosed Victorian middle class, or banded together into friendly societies to provide mutual aid in times of unemployment or sickness.

Not surprisingly, the quality of provision for most people was patchy and in many respects inadequate: Engels, for example, painted a vivid picture of the squalor, overcrowding, disease and ignorance which afflicted the English working class in town and country alike in the 1840s, and more rigorous poverty surveys at the turn of the century, by Booth in London and Rowntree in York, confirmed that even on the strictest criteria of need and deprivation, poverty in Britain was widespread. Indeed, as army recruitment at the time of the Boer War demonstrated, many young working-class males were not even fit and healthy enough to offer their lives in the service of their country, for thousands had to be turned away on grounds of ill-health. The prosperity of Victorian Britain was built to a large extent on a combination of exploitation of the colonies abroad and through the pitiful poverty of millions of working-class people at home. The profits of the new industrial bourgeoisie were achieved at the cost of wages which were often too low to provide for the basic physical necessities of life and conditions of work which themselves gave rise to disease and crippling disablement.

Government thinking about the relief of poverty and distress during the nineteenth century was shaped by the Poor Law reforms of 1834 which sought to distinguish the 'deserving' and 'undeserving' poor. The former category included those, such as widows, orphans and the chronically sick, who had fallen upon hard times which made it difficult or impossible for them to work. The latter encompassed the able-bodied who, it was assumed, were idle and feckless and were happy, given half the chance, to subsist on the charity and pity of others. In both cases, poverty was seen as an individual problem rather than as the product of the way in which society was organised. The problem, therefore, was how to aid the genuinely deserving without at the same time giving comfort to the work-shy and the shiftless.

The solution to this problem was found in the extension of the work-house system. This entailed a deliberate policy of deterrence in the provision of aid; the conditions of poor relief were to be made so bad that only those who were in genuine and desperate need would turn to the state for help. This was achieved by fixing the level of relief at a point lower than the lowest wage, and by curtailing 'outdoor relief' in favour of the work-house where families were split up and conditions of life and work were kept intentionally harsh. As the 1833 Report of the Poor Law Commissioners explained; 'Into such a house none will enter voluntarily; work confinement and discipline will deter the indolent and vicious; and nothing but extreme necessity will induce any to accept the comfort which must be obtained by the surrender of their free agency.' The British state has inflicted many horrors on its people over the centuries, but the barbarism of the workhouse system must rank as among the least forgiveable.

Forgiveable or not, this cold-comfort policy was remarkably effective, for the workhouse represented a symbol of popular dread and hatred throughout the nineteenth century. Its deterrent value was undoubtedly high. Yet in another respect, the policy was an obvious failure in that thousands of people continued to rely on poor relief despite the conditions which were attached to it. Every downturn in the economy brought more destitute people to the workhouse door and served to demonstrate that widespread poverty had less to do with individual pathology than with the evident failings of a free-market economy. Within ten years of the introduction of the new Poor Law, the workhouses were crammed with nearly 200,000 people.

The basic problem with leaving provision for people's needs to the operation of the market was, quite simply, that at that time large numbers of people could not afford to buy what even then was generally considered to be the basic necessities of life. The problem was particularly acute, of course, for those who could not find work or were not capable of working, but it did not end there, for many of those in employment similarly suffered immense deprivation.

The inability to pay for crucial items of consumption was due above all else to low wages. In the nineteenth century, labour represented a major cost of production in most industries – not only in the primary sectors such as agriculture and mining, but in manufacturing as well. This meant that labour costs had to be kept to a minimum if profits were to be maintained, yet low wages meant that workers could not provide for themselves and their families by buying the services which they so desperately required. The problem is clearly illustrated with reference to the housing question in nineteenth-century Britain.

Working-class housing at this time was built as an investment. Landlords bought whole streets of houses in order to rent them out to working-class tenants, and they did so in the expectation that they would be able to receive a level of rent which, after deductions for repairs, interest payments and running costs, would at least be comparable to the rate of return they could achieve by investing their capital elsewhere. The working-class tenants themselves, however, were in receipt of very low wages which prevented landlords from charging high rents. The result was that housing was built as cheaply as possible, maintenance was kept to a minimum and tenants were crowded into insanitary rooms and cellars in order to raise the total rental income to an acceptable market level. This in turn led to disease which spread virtually unchecked because the tenants could not afford to pay for medical treatment either. The problems and deprivations were thus compounded, and for as long as consumption was organised primarily through the market, there was no way out of the vicious circle.

From this example, it can be seen that the basic problem which lay behind the efforts of governments, philanthropists and working-class people themselves to improve conditions during the nineteenth century was the contradiction between the operation of the market for labour, which led to low wages, and the operation of the market for consumption goods and services, which led to high rents and other living costs. It was the evidence of this contradiction which gradually led government to temper their principled commitment to *laissez-faire* with a pragmatic acceptance of the need to do something to alleviate the worst and most unpalatable aspects of working-class living conditions, even if this meant treading on the toes of those with property. Nobody planned it, but gradually the extreme self-help philosophy of the early Victorian period was eroded by piecemeal social reform.

At first, governments restricted themselves to regulating conditions at work and at home. As early as 1833, for example, Parliament legislated to limit the length of the working day and to restrict the use of child labour in certain industries, and further Factory Acts in the 1840s and 1850s imposed tighter restrictions, closed loopholes and increased surveillance by factory inspectors. From the 1850s onwards, locally elected Boards of Health began to regulate Britain's towns and cities in an attempt to eradicate the insanitary conditions, and middle-class concern about the spread of diseases from working-class slum areas led to a programme of compulsory vaccination (which was fiercely resisted by the advocates of old-style liberalism).

Later in the century, however, state intervention was stepped up from mere regulation. A succession of Housing Acts, for example, permitted local authorities to purchase and clear slum areas and to provide alternative rental housing for the tenants who were made homeless as a result. Because this legislation was permissive rather than mandatory, its effectiveness remained limited, but from 1890, local authorities did begin to build new dwellings as well as to demolish old ones. This was also the period when the state began to take on responsibility for educating the children of the working class. A series of Education Acts, in 1870, 1880 and 1891, culminated in the provision of free, universal and compulsory elementary education designed, in the words of Matthew Arnold (the headmaster of Rugby school) to spread 'sweetness and light' and to counter the 'barbarism' of the newly-enfranchised proletariat. By the turn of the century, therefore, the commitment to *laissez-faire* and to Benthamite principles of utilitarianism had been undermined in practice by 50 or 60 years of hesitant and sometimes grudging social reform. The question, of course, is why did it happen?

There is no doubt that the potential threat to capitalist social order posed by the concentration of millions of working-class families in the slums of the new industrial cities loomed large in the consciousness of many reformers and many politicians throughout the nineteenth century. The spectre of the 1789 revolution in France and of later upheavals in Europe in 1830 and 1848, coupled with the agitation at home during the Chartist years and the later growth of trade unions among skilled artisans and unskilled workers, was clearly one factor which helped focus political attention on the question of reform and social policy. The extension of the franchise to the working class also led to increased political concern with working class living conditions (Disraeli, for example, saw the provision of elementary education as crucial in 'gentling' the new political majority), and middle-class philanthropists did much to publicise the squalor, ignorance and disease which existed at the very heart of the Empire. Yet having said all this, it does not seem to have been the case that the working class *itself* was instrumental in pressuring the state for reforms in this period, but policy was made in the *presence* of that class and there was a consciousness of its *potential* for disruption and disorder that prompted action if only to block the threat of more fundamental changes coming from below.

There is considerable controversy among nineteenth-century historians on these points and it may be that certain sections of the working class did press for certain types of reform. In general terms, however, it seems that the hostility towards the state, fostered by the operation of the Poor Law, and sustained by a widespread view of the state as the preserve of a wealthy few, led many working-class people and their leaders (for example, in the trade union movement) to suspect and distrust most attempts to extend state regulation through new welfare provisions. The Housing Acts, for example, resulted all too often in the displacement of working-class people from their homes rather than in the provision in new housing, and over-crowding actually increased as a result. The early Education Acts made it compulsory for working-class people to send their children to school yet levied fees which many could not afford or were unwilling to pay. Even the various Factory Acts were often unpopular since they prevented working-class families from increasing their income through the extensive use of the labour of their children. Much of the nineteenth-century legislation, there-fore, was unpopular not only among those with property, but also among those without, and it is notable that the extension of the franchise in 1886 did not thrust social reform into the mainstream of political argument, for none of the elections between then and the turn of the century were fought on issues of social policy.

Such evidence suggests caution is necessary in explaining the nineteenth-century origins of the centralised, interventionist welfare state. Indeed, it raises something of a puzzle, for if reform was far from popular, then it is difficult to understand why it ever came about. In retrospect, we may be justified in arguing that social policy in this period was introduced in a rather paternalistic way on behalf of the working class, and was certainly pursued out of a concern with the working class and a fear of the threat which it represented, but most of this legislation cannot be said to have been achieved through working-class agitation or struggle.

The welfare state: cradle to grave and provision by the state in the twentieth century

Much the same point may be made of the period up to the outbreak of the First World War despite the fact that the 1906–14 Liberal government is often seen as having laid the basis of the modern welfare state. For a start, this government was not elected, as was the Labour government follow-ing the Second World War, on a popular programme of social reform (the general election of 1906 turned more on the issue of free trade than on domestic social policy). Furthermore, with just one exception, the govern-ment introduced precious little social reform until Asquith replaced Campbell-Bannerman in 1908 (the one exception being the introduction of school meals in 1906 which was largely a response to the horrifying evidence of working-class malnutrition thrown up by recruitment for the Boer War).

The two major items of social legislation introduced under Asquith were the provision of old age pensions in 1908 and the introduction of selective compulsory sickness and unemployment insurance in 1911. The first of these was undeniably popular, although even here it seems that the govern-ment was responding as much to the demands of middle-class and bour-geois reformers, such as Charles Booth and the Cadbury family, as it was to working-class pressure through the trade unions and the sprinkling of newly-elected Labour MPs. As with so much of the nineteenth-century legislation, the introduction of pensions seems almost to have been in advance of popular aspirations.

As for the National Insurance Act, 1911, the popular response seems at best to have been muted. The scope of the legislation was in any case limited; unemployment insurance, for example, covered only 2.25 million workers in industries where jobs were thought to be reasonably secure and provided benefit for only 15 weeks, while the health insurance scheme was whittled down following pressure from the big insurance companies (widows and orphans, for example were removed from the scope of the Act) and the British Medical Association (which succeeded in bringing the operation of the scheme more under the control of doctors and in raising charges for medical treatment under the Act to nearly double those prevailing in 1906). Furthermore, compulsory insurance was financed by regressive flat-rate contributions, the level of sickness benefit was little better than that provided by the voluntary friendly societies to which many workers already belonged, and the creation of a virtual state monopoly on health insurance represented a defeat for the various agencies of mutual aid (such as the friendly societies and medical clubs) which had developed among skilled workers in the nineteenth century and which had offered their members a greater degree of control over their doctors than could be offered under the new scheme. The Act did, however, represent a positive step away from the ethos of the Poor Law, in that it established a right to benefit, and it did cover groups of workers who had not previously been able to afford medical treatment. It was, in short, a mixed blessing, and it brought forth an equally mixed reaction.

Taken together, reforms such as the introduction of school meals, the provision of old age pensions and the enforcement of a state-run system of health and unemployment insurance have to be seen as the product of a number of different factors. These include: the influence of pressure groups, top civil servants and middle-class reformers (for example, as in the case of old age pensions); the concern of leading Liberals such as Lloyd-George, Churchill and Asquith himself with alleviating poverty and improving the efficiency of the workforce (for example, by providing school meals to counter malnutrition); a desire to head off the possibility of socialism by incorporating the working class within the capitalist system (for example, a major motive behind the introduction of national insurance in 1911 was to emulate Bismark's example in Germany where such a scheme had deliberately been introduced in order to counter the appeal of socialist propoganda), and, in virtually every case, the consideration of short-term tactical electoral advantage in response to the emergence of what was to become the Labour Party. Whatever the particular explanation for particular reforms, however, it is noticeable that in most cases, the government was in advance of popular opinion and aspirations; in the period to 1914, changes in social policy originated more from above than from below.

The four years of war which followed did much to change this. The First

World War was the first war in British history in which millions of working-class people were conscripted to fight for their country, and the government was well aware that the massive tragedy of their sacrifices demanded some reward. The war had also seen a massive mobilisation of the country's economic resources by the state – the size of the budget in 1918 was five times that of 1914 – and this effectively countered any argument that the country could not afford to expand social provisions. But on top of all this, the war years had been politically traumatic, both at home, where labour militancy had produced a wave of industrial unrest, which continued after hostilities had ended, and even spread to groups such as the police and the troops, and abroad, where revolutionary movements had succeeded in toppling the Tsar in Russia and threatened to sweep through Germany as well.

There was an air of popular expectation, if not militancy, in the immediate post-war years in Britain, and unrest was fueled by the sudden slump which trebled unemployment within just six months in 1920. The government was haunted by the spectre of the Bolsheviks in Russia; the Cabinet received weekly intelligence reports on 'revolutionary organisations' such as the National Unemployed Workers' Movement (founded by the Communist Party in 1921) and these seem to have convinced most leading politicians and civil servants that concessions would have to be made if the security of the realm was to be guaranteed.

The major issue which dominated social policy at this time and throughout the inter-war years was, of course, unemployment. The problem for the government was that neither the system of Poor Law relief, nor that of unemployment insurance, established in 1911, were adequate in making provision for mass unemployment, for both were premissed on the assumption that, for most people, lack of work was a temporary problem. An insurance-based scheme, for example, could only work if most of those contributing to it did not need to draw benefit from it. From 1920 onwards, however, this proved not to be the case, and gradually successive governments were obliged to resort increasingly to state funding in order to support the unemployed. In 1920, state contributions to the unemployment insurance fund amounted to just over £3 million at 3.4 per cent of total social services expenditure; by 1930, this had risen to £37 million (37 per cent of total spending on social provisions).

This break with the strict insurance principle resuscitated the fears expressed by thinkers a century earlier that state aid to the unemployed would deter people from working and would thus encourage malingering. In order to avoid this, the government introduced the infamous 'means test' and enforced a 'genuinely seeking work' condition.

The means test was widely seen by those who were subjected to it as a return to the methods of the nineteenth-century Poor Law. Applied to all those who were claiming benefits to which their contributions did not fully entitle them, it entailed a thorough investigation of the assets and income of both the individual concerned and the household. Benefit could be, and was, witheld where a spouse or children were found to be earning or where the household still owned assets which could be sold to realise income. This pernicious and despised system was eventually ended in 1927.

The 'genuinely seeking work' condition was, as its name implies, intended to ensure that those in receipt of benefit were actively searching for employment. In many ways, the effect of this condition was even harsher than that of the means test, for the burden of proof lay on the claimant who had to provide evidence to show that each day of the previous week had been spent walking the streets in search of non-existent jobs. Unlike the means test, this condition was not the subject of any great political opposition; indeed, in 1924, it was extended to all claimants, irrespective of whether or not they had full entitlement to benefit.

The use of the means test and the genuinely seeking work condition reveal the way in which, during the 1920s, governments were obliged to extend unemployment relief yet at the same time attempted to avoid the erosion of individual responsibility which this seemed to entail. Throughout this period, unemployment-relief policies emerged in a haphazard, trial-and-error fashion as pragmatic responses to a worsening situation which demanded actions which governments were reluctant to take. Eventually, in 1934, Ramsay MacDonald's National Government did at last come to terms with the fact of long-term structural unemployment by establishing the Unemployment Assistance Board which provided benefits as of right to those without work and without entitlement by virtue of contributions paid. The stigma of the dole still remained, but at least the philosophy of the Poor Law had finally been abandoned.

These changes, together with various other piecemeal reforms affecting state provision of housing, education and pension benefits, meant that, by the outbreak of the Second World War, Britain had a *de facto* welfare state in the sense that the state was committed to providing a 'safety net' and a minimum level of support as of right to all those in need. The unemployed, the elderly and the sick were covered by state-administered insurance schemes. All children were entitled to free state education up to the age of 14. Those in desperate housing need were entitled to rent a house built and subsidised by the state. None of this, of course, had in any final sense overcome the problem of poverty, for the provisions were in most cases minimal and largely inadequate. It was a 'sticking plaster' system of welfare aid in which the state attempted to bandage up the worst wounds inflicted by a capitalist economy in long-term recession. Nevertheless, the nature and scale of state intervention was such that the Poor Law had been buried as governments accepted responsibility for alleviating need and recognised the principle of free provision.

Between 1942 and 1948, this system of social support and provision was extended and overhauled as war again revolutionised popular aspirations and overturned conventional thinking about the acceptable and tolerable limits to state activity. In 1942, Beveridge published his report on the future organisation of social security schemes in which he outlined a system of national insurance which would provide protection 'from the cradle to the grave' in return for a weekly compulsory payment by all workers. In fact, these proposals, which formed the basis of the National Insurance Act 1946, did not represent any radical departure from the situation pertaining before the war, but rather brought unemployment, sickness, retirement and maternity benefits together under a single system while retaining the National Assistance Board with its means-tested benefits as an additional resource of last resort for those whose incomes still fell below a minimal subsistence line. This unified system of national insurance was still to be financed out of insurance payments rather than taxation; as Beveridge himself emphasised: 'The plan for Britain is based on the contributory principle of giving not free allowances to all from the state, but giving benefits as of right in virtue of contributions made by the insured persons themselves.' Like all previous insurance schemes since 1911, it involved a regressive system of flat-rate payments in which all workers paid the same premiums irrespective of their income; and because the level of payments had to be fixed at a point which the lowest-paid workers could afford, the scheme necessarily provided only subsistence levels of benefit. It was never intended that national insurance should provide anything more than a minimal 'safety net' for those in need; the main achievement of the National Insurance Act was simply to weave such a 'net' more tightly.

Other social reforms introduced during and immediately after the war did, however, represent a more radical break from the 1930s. In 1944, for example, Parliament passed a Town and Country Planning Act, later consolidated in 1947, which enabled local authorities to acquire land for housing at a price reflecting current use rather than future speculative value, and this was followed in 1949 by a Housing Act which empowered local authorities to build housing for all members of the community and not simply for those in proven housing need (this reflecting the assumption of the Labour Government at that time that public renting would gradually become the main form of housing provision). Throughout the late forties and early fifties, local authority house building far outstripped that in the private sector, and it was only from 1958 onwards that this pattern began to be reversed.

Also in 1944, Parliament passed the Butler Education Act which not only raised the school leaving age to 15, but also introduced the tripartite system of grammar, technical and 'modern' schools, which was designed to increase working-class educational opportunity. As things turned out, many working-class and lower-middle-class children did benefit from this system, but research through the 1950s and 1960s also demonstrated that many others were falling foul of the class discrimination which was implicit in the system, and gradually, from the mid-sixties onwards, selective secondary schooling came to be replaced in most parts of the country by comprehensive systems.

Perhaps the most important piece of social legislation introduced during this period, however, was the National Health Service Act, 1946. This established the principle of free and universal medical care and treatment, although the effective veto power of the British Medical Association forced considerable concessions (for example, to permit pay beds in NHS hospitals) in favour of the doctors just as it had when health insurance had first been introduced back in 1911. The principle of free treatment was also eroded soon after the Act was passed when prescription charges were introduced in an attempt to reduce the high cost of the service by dampening down popular demand for medicines and appliances such as spectacles.

In 1948, the modern welfare state had been fully established. It stood on two pillars. The first was the system of national insurance which guaranteed a minimum income in the event of sickness, accident, unemployment and old age and was financed out of individual contributions. The second was the system of assistance and services financed wholly or partly out of taxation and including free and universal health and school systems, income assistance through family allowances and doles, and specific provisions such as rental housing and child welfare clinics. Although the pre-war insurance principle was retained as part of the new welfare state, the major part of the system entailed free services paid for out of general taxation. Indeed, as time went on, the 'insurance' component became increasingly fictitious as the cost of pensions and other benefits far outstripped revenues collected from insurance contributions. Today, the two parts of the welfare system have effectively fused although the notional separation between national insurance and income tax payments has been retained.

Through the 1950s and 1960s, governments of both major parties administered and developed this comprehensive system of welfare with little basic disagreement between them. On some issues, they did diverge in their relative emphases; the Conservatives, for example, were always somewhat less enthusiastic about the spread of public-rented housing than was the Labour Party, although by the early sixties, both parties were committed to encouraging owner-occupation while at the same time continuing to subsidise public rental for those who could not afford or did not wish to buy. In general then, there was a broad degree of consensus between them, and changes introduced in these years (for example, the development of earnings-related contributions and benefits) met with the tacit support of both parties. As in economic policy, so too in social policy, the years of post-war affluence underpinned a remarkable degree of bi-partisanship in British politics.

The mixed economy of welfare: attacking the welfare state

There are two main reasons why this bi-partisan consensus on welfare was eventually undermined during the 1970s.

1 As the years went by, it became increasingly apparent that the state welfare system had not achieved the greater degree of equality which those on

the Left had sought from it. There have been only slight shifts in the distribution of income since 1945; taking tax and benefit payments into account, the top 20 per cent still receive 40 per cent of the nation's income while the bottom 20 per cent receive just 7 per cent. Indeed, Beveridge's fond hope that the need for national assistance (which later became supplementary benefit) would gradually disappear proved totally unfounded, for the number of people reliant on non-contributory cash benefits to raise their total income to the minimum deemed necessary for subsistence actually rose from 1 million in 1948 to 2 million in 1965 and reached 3 million by 1978. Groups such as pensioners, one-parent families and the low-paid were clearly slipping through the national insurance net in alarming proportions, and this led to increasingly vociferous demands within the Labour Party and the new crop of welfare pressure groups (for example, the Child Poverty Action Group and Age Concern) for more radical redistributive measures financed out of increased progressive taxation. This was a prospect regarded with deep suspicion by many Conservatives, and those on the Right of the Party (notably Enoch Powell and later Keith Joseph and Margaret Thatcher) began to express their sense of unease at the continuing increases in personal taxation levied to finance welfare measures.

2 The welfare state became more and more expensive at a time when the British economy was again revealing its fundamental weaknesses. Government spending on social security, personal social services, health care, education and housing increased dramatically from the 1960s onwards – from 16 per cent of the country's Gross National Product in 1951, to 24 per cent in 1971 and to 29 per cent in 1975 when it was accounting for half of all public expenditure. By 1977, a staggering 14 million people were in receipt of benefits (nearly double the figure for 1951), while the public-sector services had grown much faster than any other sector of the workforce. Gradually, the New Right of the Tory Party began to question whether the country could afford to underwrite this increasingly heavy financial burden, and familiar arguments about the need to re-establish work incentives and to discourage 'scrounging' and indolence began once more to find a voice.

During the 1970s, therefore, both Left and Right began to reappraise their support for the welfare state. On the Left, it was increasingly argued that the welfare state, as it had evolved in Britain, was an inadequate response to the problems generated by capitalism, and even that it was of greater benefit to dominant groups than to ordinary working people and their families. On the Right, by contrast, the welfare state came increasingly to be seen as a major source of the problems which were once again besetting British capitalism, for provision as a right was seen to be undermining individual initiative and the work ethic while the cost of universal provision was identified as a crippling drain on private-sector profitability. The Right was concerned to roll back the state in this field of policy and saw a place for private and voluntary provision in a mixed economy of welfare approach which challenged the cradle-to-grave ethic of the welfare state. If we are to understand contemporary changes in and arguments over the question of social welfare, it is necessary to consider each of these two positions in turn.

Critiques of the Welfare State

The Left critique of social welfare

What is distinctive to the Left critique of social welfare as it developed through the 1970s is the view that, despite appearances, the British welfare state has functioned as much, if not more, in the interests of dominant groups as of the working class. At first sight, of course, this seems paradoxical, for bankers and industrial magnates are not generally found living in council houses or drawing social security benefits, yet they have had to pay increased taxes to finance the ever-increasing welfare budget. How, then, can they be said to have been the principal beneficiaries of increased state welfare spending? Many Marxist analysts have suggested that the capitalist class in general has benefited from such spending in three main ways.

The first and most indirect benefit has come from the increased markets which the welfare state has created for many private-sector producers. This is a point which was fully discussed in chapter 9 where we saw that state spending has been used in part to raise the level of effective demand in the economy, and thus to help private companies to find a market for their products. Building firms have often relied on government contracts for their very survival; drugs companies have made super-profits by supplying the NHS; and many enterprises, large and small, have benefited from the custom of the 7 million people employed by the state to administer or carry out its various services. Such benefits have often been important for private firms (and they are perhaps now becoming more important as various welfare-related services such as school and hospital cleaning are put out to private tender), but they are not themselves enough to warrant the conclusion that the welfare state aids capitalists more than it does their workers.

A second and more important benefit for capital has, according to many writers, derived from the way in which social provisions have helped to co-opt the working class into the capitalist system by legitimating that system in the eyes of those who benefit least from it. Seen in this way, the welfare state represents the 'human face' of capitalism, for it has succeeded in overcoming the most brutal effects of the capitalist industrial system and therefore tends to reduce levels of popular discontent and to stifle revolutionary fervour. Slums still exist in Britain, but housing conditions for most of the population are undeniably far superior to those of, say, a century ago. Old people still die of hyperthermia as a result of inadequate heating and poor nutrition, but such cases do not represent the norm. Some parents still cannot afford to feed and clothe their children properly, but we no longer see children begging on street corners or wending their way to school with no shoes on their feet. Council housing, old age pensions, child allowances and all the other paraphernalia of the modern welfare state can thus be said to represent the 'necessary overhead expenses' of running a capitalist system; they are, in a sense, an alternative to further expenditure on more formal agencies of social control such as the police and the army, for they help to dampen down unrest. In this sense, welfare policies have sometimes been seen as an insurance policy for the privileged, as a way of smoothing out the conflict-laden relationship between capital and labour (an argument which we consider in more detail in chapter 11).

Such a motive for supporting reform has often been openly and surprisingly acknowledged by politicians over the years. During the nineteenth century in particular, political philosophers such as John Stuart Mill, educationalists such as Matthew Arnold and political leaders such as Benjamin Disraeli all argued openly about the therapeutic effects of social policy for the 'health' of a capitalist society. As we saw earlier, the introduction of unemployment insurance by the Liberals in 1911 represented a deliberate application of Bismark's thinking in Germany to the effect that the working class could be incorporated within capitalist society through such measures, and this strategy was endorsed by the Conservative Prime Minister at the turn of the century (Balfour) who argued that: 'Social legislation . . . is not merely to be distinguished from socialist legislation, but is its most direct opposite and its most effective antidote.' Socialists and revolutionaries of the time also agreed with this, and their argument with the Fabians was largely based on the view that support of reform within a capitalist framework would make a future transition to socialism all the more difficult to bring about (an argument which continues to this day on the Left of British politics). What all of these people were arguing, therefore, was that social policy represented a most effective instrument for 'buying off' the working class; exploitation of wage labour in the world of work could be maintained by ameliorating the worst effects of such exploitation in the world beyond the factory gates. Or, to put it another way, concessions in the sphere of consumption (housing, health, education, etc.) were the price to pay to avoid more fundamental changes in the sphere of production.

Such arguments carried particular force during and immediately after the two world wars. War has often been a forcing agent of radical change, for the widespread disruption of 'ordinary life' which it causes brings about a considerable upheaval in people's taken-for-granted expectations about what their world has to offer. The desire for a 'new start', a fundamental break with the past, was widespread and pervasive in Britain in 1918 (when the fledgling revolution in Russia seemed to offer new hope to many working-class people) and in 1945 (when the Labour Party was swept into office in a wave of popular support for radical change). In both cases, this appetite for far-reaching social change was sated by welfare reform. Following the First World War, this took the form mainly of housing legislation (reports to cabinet at this time stressed the significance of poor housing conditions in fermenting popular unrest) although subsequent reforms of the unemployment insurance system can also, to a large extent, be explained in terms of governmental fear of the prospect of millions of poverty-stricken unemployed workers turning to a revolutionary solution to their problems. Following the Second World War, it took the form of a comprehensive reshaping of welfare policies under the Labour government, although most of these changes had been planned during the war years by Churchill's National Government which was well aware of the importance of the promise of a 'new Britain' in maintaining wartime morale and damping down unrest.

There is no doubt that fear of unrest and a desire to incorporate the working class within the capitalist system have been crucially important motives behind the growth of the welfare state in Britain. Indeed, they have clearly continued to be so; the 'social contract' of the 1974–9 Labour government represented a deliberate attempt to reduce working-class militancy in the face of real wage cuts by promising improvements in welfare services. Yet such arguments can be overemphasised. In particular, those who seek to explain the development of social reform purely or even primarily in these terms run the twin dangers of exaggerating the conspiratorial canniness of ruling groups while ignoring the active role of the working class in forcing concessions. While it is true that political leaders have often consciously used welfare policies in an attempt to control the working class, it is also true that they have often been most reluctant to extend state provision and have attempted to resist popular demands for improved support and better services. The 'ruling class' has never been so clever as to manipulate social policy on its own initiative to further its own ends without at least some degree of prompting from below. Similarly, the working class has never been so inert as to have merely played the role of meek recipient without also flexing its political muscle. To explain the growth of the welfare state purely in terms of the desire of powerful groups to co-opt the working class is to exaggerate the foresight of the powerful and to strip the working class itself of its history.

The third and perhaps most crucial way in which the welfare state is said to have aided the capitalist class is that it has lowered the production and reproduction costs of human labour-power and has thereby raised the rate of profit. In other words, the state has assumed responsibility for providing many of the resources which workers need to consume if they are to provide labour-power for the factories and offices of capitalist firms. This has meant that employers have been able to pay lower wages than would otherwise have to be paid.

The logic of this argument is fairly simple (although the detailed theoretical arguments which it throws up are often highly complex). Basically, it is argued that human labour-power, whether that of muscles or of brains, gets used up in the process of production. This is true in two senses. First, it is used up during the course of the working day – people return home tired and weakened by their expenditure of labour-power in factory or office. Secondly, it is used up over the years – each generation of workers gradually gets worn out as it gets older, just as machines do. This means that, in the absence of state intervention, employers must pay sufficient wages to enable workers first to replenish their energies on a day-to-day basis (i.e. by consuming food, housing, leisure, and so on), and second, to raise a new generation of workers which will eventually replace them (i.e. by feeding and clothing their children, paying others to educate them up to the standard required by employers, and so on).

If, however, the state steps in and begins to provide some of the items which workers need to reproduce their labour-power and to raise a new generation of workers, then employers will no longer have to cover all these expenses in the wage packet. Provision of council housing at subsidised rents, for example, means that workers no longer have to spend so much on their housing, and, other things being equal, this will enable wages to fall. Similarly, free state schooling removes the burden of school fees, free medical care removes the costs of 'repairing' labour-power when it is sick or damaged, and so on. In this way, provisions which appear to be in the interests of workers actually turn out to be in the interests of their employers.

Indeed, this argument can be carried further, for it can be suggested that state provision of welfare services not only lowers the cost of reproducing labour-power, but also increases the efficiency of that labour-power. Workers who live in slum housing will often fall ill, those who are poorly educated will be slow in adapting to the rigours of work, those who cannot afford decent medical treatment will have to take a lot of time off from work. Furthermore, as Marx himself suggested in his discussion of the nineteenth-century Factory Acts, workers become less efficient if they are overworked and overexploited. Thus, social provision (for example, of health and housing) and state regulation (for example, of hours of work or of safety standards at work) both function in the long-term interests of the capitalist class by raising the productivity of labour and thereby increasing profitability.

One obvious objection to this suspiciously neat argument is that all these provisions still have to be paid for in some way. If capitalists are no longer paying for the reproduction of their workforce through the wage-packet, are they not, nevertheless, still paying for it through their taxes?

The response to this objection from those who argue for this explanation of the welfare state is that it all depends on the relative power of the two main classes at any point in time. If the working class is strong, then it will usually be able to shift the burden of paying for the welfare state onto capitalists – this seems to have happened during the 1960s. But if the working class is weak, then attempts will be made to reduce the tax burden on capital and to finance welfare spending through taxes on wages. If neither of these options is politically or economically feasible – as in Britain from the late sixties onwards when organised labour was still strong enough to resist any erosion of real wages but the profitability of capital was too low to support additional taxation – then such provisions are likely to be

financed by mounting deficits (i.e. increased public borrowing and inflation). This is a point to which we shall return in the next section of this
chapter.

There are, however, other objections to this attempt to explain the
growth of the welfare state in terms of the requirements of the capitalist
class. Three in particular deserve comment.

1 It is important to distinguish between the question of who benefits from
welfare provision and that of who causes it to be provided in the first place.
In other words, even if we accept that the welfare state has aided capital by
reproducing labour-power more cheaply and efficiently than before, this does
not explain its origins. Policies which are brought into existence through the
actions of one group may turn out to benefit another; the fact that the capitalist
class may have benefited from welfare policies does not therefore justify the
conclusion that it was this class, acting in its own interests, which generated
such policies. Furthermore, the simple identification of a functional 'need' tells
us nothing of whether or how this need comes to be met (for example, to say
that capital 'needs' labour-power to be reproduced as cheaply and efficiently
as possible is undoubtedly true, but whether this has actually happened or not
remains an open question). The first objection to this sort of argument,
therefore, is that it focuses on outcomes, not causes, and we cannot deduce a
cause from an effect.

2 The argument would seem to be grossly over-stated. It may be, for example, that capitalists 'need' their workers to be housed in reasonable accommodation, and 'need' future generations of workers to be schooled to a
resonable standard, but the post-war welfare state in Britain would seem in
many respects to have exceeded these 'requirements'. It simply makes no sense,
for example, to suggest that capital 'requires' its workers to be housed in
centrally-heated council houses with garages, or 'needs' future generations of
workers to be educated for at least 11 years in subjects such as the geography
of Africa, the literature of France, the history of Greece or even the political
science of modern Britain. There is an enormous gap between the level of provision which capitalists may deem 'necessary' for reproducing labour-power or
ensuring legitimacy, and that which has actually been provided over the years.

3 The argument has to some extent been overtaken by events, for since the
mid- to late seventies, welfare provisions in Britain have been cut back quite
dramatically to a point where we may validly begin to question whether such
provisions are as important to capital as many Marxist writers during the 1970s
assumed. Widespread provision of council housing, for example, has often
been cited as crucial in ensuring the reproduction of labour-power, yet in the
period following 1979, the Thatcher government virtually put an end to new
building, sold off as much housing as it could to existing tenants, and raised
the rents of the remainder by around 160 per cent in just three years. It may
be responded to this that such a policy is doomed in the long run, and that state
subsidies to housing provision were in any case retained in respect of owner-
occupied stock (where tax relief on mortgage interest repayments now far
exceed subsidies on public-sector rents), but the fact remains that a key area

of provision has been the subject of unprecedented cuts and that employers do not seem that worried about it.

There is an additional point to be made about the period from the late seventies onwards, and that concerns the rising level of unemployment. Unemployment in the 1980s never fell below 6 per cent and at one point reached 14 per cent. This would seem to suggest that the need to reproduce labour-power is rather less pressing than may have been the case in times of labour shortages in the fifties and sixties. The standard response to this is to suggest that welfare provisions are still necessary, not so much to reproduce labour power, but to maintain legitimacy and social order. Even this argument, however, seems weak in the context of the 1980s, for there was no generalised breakdown in legitimacy, nor any coherent threat to social order, despite the apparently potent combination of high unemployment and reduced welfare spending (much the same observation, incidentally, may be made of the 1930s).

None of this is to deny that certain types of welfare provision at certain times in Britain's recent history have probably benefited certain sections of the capitalist class as much if not more than the direct recipients. The important point which is made forcibly in this literature is that welfare expenditure is not necessarily a 'drain' on capitalist profitability, for it may aid the pursuit of profits by helping to relieve capital of some of the costs of investing in labour-power. It is also doubtless the case that certain pieces of legislation have at particular times been supported or even sponsored by capitalist interests, in which case we should be wary of interpreting the development of the welfare state in terms of a glorious history of working-class struggle.

Yet when all of this has been said, we are still left with the fact that the welfare state has been, and continues to be, an arena of political conflict in which dominant groups in British society have more often been concerned to limit than to extend the scope of state provision. In our view, the welfare state is first and foremost a manifestation of the growing power of labour in British politics in the twentieth century.

One obvious way in which the working class in Britain has actively contributed to the growth of the welfare state is through its electoral influence over governments. The extension of the franchise to working-class men in 1868 and in 1884 obliged the Liberal and Conservative Parties to court the working-class vote, and led eventually to the emergence of the Labour Party during the first 20 years of this century. Working-class aspirations were thus to some extent transmitted to government through the electoral process in the way in which liberal-democratic theories of politics and the constitution suggest (see chapters 1 and 2), although the representation of working-class interests by the various political parties was by no means always obvious or direct. Indeed, beginning with Ramsay MacDonald (who cut unemployment benefit by 10 per cent in 1931 and precipitated a disastrous split in the Labour Party in the process), Labour leaders have not shown themselves averse to subordinating working-class interests to the pursuit of capitalist profitability by enforcing wage reductions (for example, through incomes policies) and trimming welfare expenditure.

Despite the set backs, however, it is undeniable that the extension of political rights to the working class in the nineteenth and early twentieth centuries (women were given the vote after the First World War) has been a major factor in the subsequent extension of 'social rights'. The development of such social rights has not brought about social equality, but they have made inroads into the traditional rights of private property and they do represent a constant threat and challenge to the continuing system of class inequality. Put another way, the welfare state is a real gain by the working class and the principle of free social provision as of right does represent (as various Right-wing politicians have warned) a real challenge to the basic principles on which a capitalist society is founded.

This is a crucial point and one which is often overlooked in Left critiques of the welfare state which tend to emphasise the usefulness of social policy to the capitalist class while ignoring the challenge which it represents to that class. It is not in our view any exaggeration to suggest that the existence of a comprehensive system of universal welfare provision within a capitalist society represents an element of socialism in the very heart of capitalism, for it breaks the link, on which capitalism depends, between work and material sustenance and establishes the right to enjoy services on the basis of need rather than ability to pay. This is not to deny that the principle of the work ethic has often been reasserted by governments, just as the notion of social rights has often been eroded, for ever since 1834, governments have been concerned to make welfare beneficiaries work for their benefits (for example, through the workhouse system of the nineteenth century, the 'genuinely seeking work' condition of 1920s unemployment relief, and the 'Youth Opportunities Programme' and 'Youth Training Scheme' of the 1980s) and welfare services are to this day linked to the importance of wage labour (for example, in the condition that the unemployed must be 'available for work', in the definition of sickness as 'inability to work', in the concern to orient schooling to the 'demands of work', and so on). Nevertheless, the welfare state still represents a 'Trojan horse' within the citadels of capitalism in that it rests firmly on a set of values which are fundamentally opposed to those of capitalism. If capitalism entails a system of allocating power and resources according to the ownership of private property, welfare services entail a system of allocating society's resources according to the right of all citizens to share in the common wealth of the society according to their need. There is, therefore, a fundamental ideological contradiction – that between property rights and citizenship or social rights – built into the very foundations of any advanced welfare-capitalist society.

This is a contradiction which can be, and has been, exploited by those who do not benefit from ownership of the means of production. During the 1960s and early 1970s, for example, there is little doubt that one reason

why the profitability of capitalist industry fell so dramatically was precisely because non-owners of capital – ordinary workers, the professional
middle classes, old age pensioners, claimants of supplementary benefit and
others – were able to lay claim to a greater proportion of the country's
wealth through an extension of welfare provisions, and it was this that
led to a 'fiscal crisis' of the state as governments attempted to expand
social spending while defending the private sector against crippling rises in
taxation.

Seen in this way, it is clear that social reforms have not simply been
'ceeded' by dominant groups as a way of maintaining order and legitimacy,
but have been struggled over. Sometimes – as in the two periods of war and
again in the 1960s – these struggles have resulted in real gains for working-
class people. At other times – as in the inter-war years and the period from
the mid-1970s – they have resulted in real losses as wages have been cut
back and welfare provisions curtailed. It is only in certain historical situations, therefore, that the less-privileged strata in British society have been
able to 'usurp' resources controlled by the more-privileged strata.

The first type of situation in which real gains have been secured relates
to periods of war. This is because government and other powerful groups
in society have been obliged at times of war to subordinate all other concerns to the pursuit of victory over the external enemy, and this has enabled
working-class people, organised through trade unions, tenants associations
and other such organisations to secure concessions in return for their
continued co-operation in the war effort. Furthermore, with the economy operating at full capacity, the industrial strength of workers
(especially those employed in strategic sectors such as the production of
munitions) has been maximised, and this has been reflected not only in
increased wages, but also in social reforms which might otherwise have
been unthinkable in peacetime.

The second situation in which working people have been able to secure
real gains in their standard of living through improved state provision of
services is at times of economic growth. In a thriving economy such as
that of Britain in the 1950s, full employment and even labour shortages
strengthen the hand of organised labour in bargaining with both employers
and governments. Indeed, government may itself take the lead in developing social provisions, for at times of economic prosperity it is possible to
extend provisions to the working class without eroding to any great extent
the existing material privileges of the wealthier sections of the population.
To revert to an analogy much beloved by politicians, if the national 'cake'
is getting larger, then it is possible to give working people larger and larger
slices without necessarily changing the proportionate shares going to different social groups. Put another way, it is possible in such situations for
the working class to win without anybody else actually losing. As the
statistics on the distribution of income and wealth reveal, this does seem
to have been largely the case over the years in Britain.

This being the case, the end of a period of economic boom clearly marks a crucial point in the development of social provisions, for as the boom turns into recession, organised labour becomes weakened as unemployment rises, and the scramble to maintain existing shares of a dwindling cake may be expected to intensify. As Harold Laski observed some 50 years ago:

> The concessions that the government can offer in times of prosperity do not seriously invade the established expectations of those who control the means of production. They are prepared to pay the price . . . But the situation is wholly different when capitalism is in a phase of contraction. The price of concessions expected by democracy then appears too high. The assumptions of capitalism then contradict the implications of democracy. If the phase of contraction is prolonged, it becomes necessary either to abrogate the democratic process or to change the economic assumptions upon which the society rests.

The Right critique of social welfare and the privatisation of the welfare state

The critique of the welfare state which emerged from the New Right of the Conservative Party during the latter half of the 1970s was in part a response to the growing problems of the British economy and in part a product of the neo-liberal theories and philosophies which were beginning to spread through the Party at that time. When the Conservatives returned to power in 1979 and set about cutting social expenditure, they did so not only because they saw this as necessary in order to regenerate private-sector profitability (something which the Labour government had itself reluctantly come to accept during the last years of its tenure of office), but also because they believed in reducing public reliance on state provision as a matter of principle. As in its economic strategy (discussed in chapter 9), so too in its social policy, the Thatcher government was thus inspired both by what it saw as a pragmatic necessity, and by what it believed to be its moral duty. By cutting welfare provisions, in other words, it was also intent on liberating the British people from what it saw as the stifling yoke of years of social-democratic paternalism.

Paradoxically, perhaps, this libertarian strand of New Right philosophy tended to agree with many of those on the Left who were arguing that the welfare state was not benefiting those whom it had orginally been intended to benefit, although different explanations were advanced for why this was the case. In particular, Friedman and others who provided much of the inspiration for the resurgent Right-wing of the Tory Party argued that such a failing was inherent to any attempt to use the state to bring about social objectives, no matter how laudable such objectives may at first appear.

The dramatic increase in state expenditure on welfare in the post-war years has not eliminated poverty and hardship. Indeed, the more that has been spent, the more intractable the problems seem to have become. New Right analysts offer two principal explanations for this.

1 State welfare creates and reproduces the very problems it is designed to rectify. Unemployment benefit is intended to relieve the distress of being jobless, but in doing this it reduces the incentive to find work and therefore increases the number of people on the unemployment register. A statutory duty on local authorities to house the homeless aims to ensure that everybody has a roof over their heads, but the knowledge that accommodation will be provided can result in more people presenting themselves at the offices of local housing departments demanding shelter. Free provisions are particularly susceptible to this problem. A free General Practitioner service, for example, means that doctors' surgeries become overcrowded as patients with trivial ailments avail themselves of the opportunity for a consultation. As the post-war Labour government found when it introduced free spectacles on the NHS, the potential demand for free provisions is almost limitless. Thus, the more the state takes it upon itself to relieve a social problem, the greater the size of the problem becomes. The result is that increasing numbers of people become dependent upon state delivery systems. In the view of the New Right, state welfare actually creates widespread state dependency.

2 Much of the money directed at the system is syphoned off by those who least need it. This tendency, sometimes referred to as Director's Law, suggests that the welfare state is primarily a system which taxes *the rich and the poor* to the benefit of those in the middle. One indication of this is that the middle class tends to make greatest use of the most expensive services: education is an obvious example, for students from middle-class backgrounds are greatly over-represented in further and higher education, but the same is also true of the health services where the greatest provision is centred on the most affluent parts of the country. Furthermore, there has developed alongside the visible welfare state an 'invisible' one in the form of tax allowances to the better off; those who can afford to take out a mortgage for house purchase, to contribute to private pension schemes or to purchase private life assurance have been able to claim tax relief on their payments, and the cost of this (which amounts to something like twice that of all state cash benefits) has been met through higher taxes on those with lower incomes.

As things have turned out, therefore, the welfare state has tended to benefit the middle class at least as much as the poor, and it has been paid for largely out of the pockets of ordinary working people. This was probably never intended by the legislators and reformers of the last 150 years, so why has it happened?

According to Friedman, Hayek, and other Right-wing critics of the welfare state, such an outcome may be seen as almost the inevitable result of the pursuit of social objectives through the use of state power. In their view, such a strategy inevitably ends up by sacrificing the general interest to the particular interests of relatively small groups which are able to direct the use of the monopoly coercive power of the state to their own ends. In other words, once the principle of forcing individuals to make provisions which they would not otherwise freely make is accepted, it becomes possible for sectional interests to mobilise to force others to subsidise them. This, according to the New Right, is precisely what has happened with the development of welfare policies.

A further related point can be made about this, and that concerns the people who administer or service the welfare state. The doctors, organised through the BMA, have for example been major beneficiaries of the extension of state power in the area of health care, for, as we saw earlier, they have been able (in 1911 and again after the Second World War) to exact considerable concessions from governments as the price of their co-operation. The same has been true, to a greater or lesser extent, of various groups of public-sector workers whose numbers have swollen over the years and who, through their unions, have sought to secure their own interests as producers of services without necessarily improving the quality or quantity of service provision to consumers. Thus it is argued that those who are direcely employed by the state in the administration and delivery of welfare services have been able to direct state expenditures in their own interests; much of the additional spending on welfare during the 1960s, for example, went on building up the bureaucracy and extending the career prospects of social workers, teachers and others rather than on materially improving the services received by the clients of welfare bureacracies.

For the New Right, then, a major explanation for the spiralling cost of the welfare state could be found in the power of certain groups who saw that it was in their interests to perpetually expand spending on public services. The task, therefore, was to reduce the power of these groups by cutting state spending, thereby reducing taxation and enabling consumers to make their own choices based on the money in their own pockets. The liberty of the individual was thus to be extended through a reduction of state compulsion.

The problem with such a strategy, as the more perceptive analysts recognised, was that, as in the nineteenth century, many people could not afford to pay for their basic consumption requirements. True, wages have increased enormously in real terms in the last 100 years, but it remains the case that millions of people still cannot possibly afford to pay market rates for their housing, or their medical needs, or their children's education. As we saw earlier in this chapter, there was, and to a considerable extent still is, a fundamental contradiction between the need to keep wages down in order to ensure profitability and the need on the other hand to ensure that people can gain access to necessary, yet inherently costly, means of subsistence.

The development of the welfare state through the twentieth century was one response to this problem. For all its faults – the spiralling costs, the lengthening waiting lists, the lack of consumer choice and the unresponsive public bureaucracies which it brought into being – the socialisation of consumption through state welfare provisions did at least succeed in improving the living standards of working-class people. The housing built for rent by local authorities far surpassed that offered by the private landlords; medical treatment was brought within reach of millions of people who had not previously been able to afford it; working-class children received at least a basic education and some were able to seize this opportunity to move out of the working class altogether.

It is also evident, however, that the basic contradiction was displaced, not resolved, by increasing state welfare provision, for the houses, hospitals, schools and home helps which the state now provided itself, still had to be paid for. If ordinary working people could not afford to pay, then somebody else would have to. The state, in short, had to pick up the bill. This meant that the contradiction, far from being resolved, was simply shifted from the market-place to the public sector.

The problem is well illustrated by the development of unemployment relief between 1911 and 1934. We saw that, in 1911, the government tried to provide some measure of benefit for the unemployed, but that this was limited to workers who represented a good risk in actuarial terms and was to be financed strictly out of contributions rather than taxation. During the inter-war years, however, the scheme came under pressure as a result of mass unemployment, and this led both to its extension to workers who represented a greater risk, and to the eventual establishment of the Unemployment Assistance Board which paid benefits as of right even in those cases where there was no entitlement on the basis of contributions. By 1934, in other words, it had been recognised that workers could not pay for their own benefits and that unemployment relief would have to be financed out of taxation. Despite the attempt to retain an insurance system, financed out of contributions, after the war, benefits have continued to be paid increasingly out of taxation, and the burden on the central exchequer has correspondingly risen.

This financial 'burden' on the state has increased in similar fashion as a result of the expansion of other welfare services. Once established, the scale of the provisions has grown, and the real cost has grown with it. The problem has therefore arisen of how to finance these increasing commitments.

Throughout the 1960s and 1970s, this massive expansion in state spending was paid for to some extent by wage-earners – mainly through direct taxation and national insurance contributions – and the number of people liable to pay income tax increased in the 30 years after 1948 from 15 to 21 million. There was, however, a limit to how far the working class could be called upon to finance welfare provisions – after all, it was their inability to pay the full cost of such services which had led the state to take over responsibility in the first place. Capital too, therefore, had to contribute, and by 1975, companies were paying 18 per cent of the state's total tax revenue (not including local authority rates). Yet there was a limit here as well, for rising taxes represented a drain on profitability which threatened future levels of investment.

The original contradiction, therefore, reappeared, but in a new guise. By the 1970s, the problem was no longer that the working class could not afford to pay for its key consumption requirements, but was rather that the state could not afford to pay for them. If it continued to increase taxation on workers, then this would either drive large sections of the working class back into poverty or would result in higher wage claims to compensate. But if it continued to raise taxes on capital, this would reduce profits, drive many companies out of business, and further increase demand for social security and other benefits as unemployment rose.

Until the late 1970s, government's response to this dilemma was to attempt to maintain the level of provision and to finance this through increased borrowing. Between 1971 and 1975, the gap between state revenues and state expenditures widened to 11 per cent of GNP and government borrowing increased to £11 billion per year. Such a policy could not be pursued for long, and in 1976 the mounting 'fiscal crisis', which was most clearly manifest in an inflation rate in excess of 20 per cent, led the then Labour government to accept an International Monetary Fund loan which stipulated that public expenditure had to be cut back.

When the Conservatives were returned to power in 1979, they were determined to embark on an entirely different strategy. Rather than providing a wide range of services free or at low subsidised prices, they would attempt to increase the ability of people to pay for services provided from within the private sector. Whereas before, governments had acted to reduce the cost of social provisions, now the government was to pursue the logical alternative strategy of enhancing people's ability to pay while leaving the supply of services to the market. The problem to be addressed was thus how to put more money back into people's pockets.

In principle, this could be done first of all by reducing personal taxation consequent upon a radical reduction in the scale of state spending. This, however, would probably be insufficient and would not in any case help those people who were not in work and were not therefore paying tax on incomes. Something else was therefore required. According to writers such as Friedman, for example, the problem could in principle be overcome through the introduction of a system of negative income tax (in which those in receipt of income below a specified level would receive a 'top-up' cash supplement from the state) and by the development of various voucher schemes (through which people would receive vouchers which they could spend in whichever way they chose on education, or medical treatment, or whatever other service was covered by the scheme).

It was this radical 'libertarian' thinking, as much as the pressing need to cut public expenditure in the face of a fiscal crisis, which lay behind the Thatcher Government's assault on the welfare state. The government never got so far as to introduce negative income tax, and its support for education vouchers proved impossible to put into practice. Nevertheless, the aim was to return as much as possible state provision to the private market (for example, by selling council houses, encouraging private health insurance, and so on) while supporting people's incomes by reducing direct taxation, increasing tax relief on items such as mortgages and private pension contributions, and continuing to pay cash benefits such as family allowances. This was not a return to the nineteenth-century market mode (as many of the government's critics made out) because it involved considerable state subsidisation. The point was, however, that the subsidies were to be directed to incomes rather than to providing services.

Now it may be suggested at this point that such a strategy was unlikely to prove any more successful than had the socialised mode of consumption, for both involved high levels of state expenditure but on different things. Surely, if government could no longer afford to subsidise the provision of education, housing and so on, nor could it afford to subsidise people's incomes to a point where they could themselves afford to buy such services? Was not the shift from a socialised to a privatised mode merely a shift from the swings to the roundabouts?

In one sense, this was indeed the case, for the Thatcher government found that it simply could not afford to reduce its demands for revenue. Personal taxation, for example, actually increased by 9 per cent between 1979 and 1983, and the real value of cash benefits such as pensions and family allowances (i.e. benefits which needed to increase substantially if people were to be able to buy housing, health care and so on) failed to rise. Over the decade as a whole, the rich and middle income groups prospered, but the poorest strata got no better off in real terms.

The failure of the government to support people's incomes did not, however, mean the total failure of its privatisation strategy, for unlike the situation in the nineteenth century or even that between the wars, many people could now afford to begin to buy at least some of the basic items of consumption. This was due to the fact that the old contradiction between low wages and high consumption costs had to some extent resolved itself without any help from government, for over the preceeding 30 years, the real incomes of most households in Britain had risen substantially. Real wages rose continually through the long post-war boom and through most of the 1960s and 1970s, and the increased participation of women in the labour market meant that many households were in receipt of two incomes. By the time the Thatcher government came to office in 1979, many people in Britain could already afford at least some of the services which their parents or grandparents could never have paid for and private provision in areas such as personal transportation (through car ownership) and housing (through owner-occupation subsidised in most cases by mortgage-related tax relief) had already become widespread, even among the working class (over half of all households, for example, were buying or owned their homes, and 40 per cent of manual workers were home-owners).

What the Thatcher government did was to encourage this existing trend towards private-sector provision. It did this by first raising various welfare user charges in order to reduce or eliminate the element of subsidy, and then by encouraging private producers to take over responsibility from the state for provision of these services. Prices of school meals, for example, were raised to a point at which private catering firms could be invited to tender to provide them. Health service charges were raised and, together with the continuing deterioration of NHS health care, this led to a considerable increase in the use of private health insurance (even some trade unions such as the Electricians' took out health insurance subscriptions for their members). Higher education fees were raised at the same time as the 'independent' university at Buckingham was awarded a Royal Charter, and the government began to consider ways of replacing student grants with bank loans and reintroducing scholarships. Most dramatically of all, council-house rents were pushed up to notional 'market levels' at the same time as council tenants were offered the right to buy their homes at discounts of up to 50 per cent.

This drive to restructure the welfare state encountered its major obstacles in those services from which the great majority of the population benefited. It was a relatively easy matter to force up council house rents, for most voters are owner-occupiers and are not adversely affected by such a change. Much more problematic was the reform of state schooling (accounting for around 93 per cent of all pupils) and of the National Health Service. Changes to these two key pillars of the post-war welfare state were not attempted until the late 1980s, and when they were introduced they fell a long way short of a full-scale privatisation.

In education, New Right thinkers had long been pushing for the introduction of a voucher scheme (see chapter 7). Instead of government spending money to provide state schooling, the logic of this proposal was that it should direct the cash (in the form of vouchers) into parents' pockets instead, leaving them to decide which schools to patronise. Naturally, this sort of thinking was abhorrent to most teachers and educational administrators who believed that they rather than parents were the best people to judge how schools should be organised. A pilot voucher scheme was planned for 26 schools in Kent but was abandoned following opposition from teacher unions, and in 1983 the government announced that it was no longer interested in pursuing a voucher policy.

What emerged instead was a reform which seemed to pull in several different directions at once. In an attempt to increase parental choice over schooling, parents were given the right to sent their children to any state school provided it was not already full. The governing bodies of schools were also reformed to allow elected 'parent governors' one-third of the seats, and control over spending was devolved to school governing bodies. Schools were, in addition, given the right to 'opt out' of local authority control if a majority of parents voted for such a course of action. Schools which opted out were then funded directly by the Department of Education in London on a simple per capita basis (i.e. the more pupils they enrolled, the more money they were given). In addition to all this, the government imposed a 'national curriculum' on all state schools specifying which subjects should be taught and laying down criteria of achievement at various ages.

This package of reforms fell a long way short of the New Right's advocacy of a market system in education. It did strengthen parental choice, but (predictably) the new system of elected parent governors did little to empower ordinary parents since most of those who put themselves forward for election were drawn from the ranks of middle-class activists who were already the most vociferous section of the community under the old system. Furthermore, the national curriculum represented a fundamental move towards centralising control. Whereas a voucher scheme is designed to allow parents to choose between competing types of schooling, the reforms of the late eighties ended up imposing an unprecedented degree of uniformity across the entire state system.

The changes to the National Health Service were similarly mixed and rather modest. The most fundamental change was one which allowed hospitals and general practitioners to 'opt out' of control by their District Health Authority and to take responsibility for their own budgets. This was coupled with the introduction of an 'internal market' in the NHS which allowed patients waiting for operations to be referred to a hospital outside their home area, the cost of the operation being recouped from the patient's own health authority. As with the education reforms, the changes stimulated considerable political controversy. They may have gone some way to enhancing consumer choice, but they fell a long way short of a full-blooded privatisation strategy for they left Britain's socialised system of medical care virtually in tact. Compared with most of the countries in Europe, which operate with insurance-based systems, the system of health delivery in Britain after a decade of a radical Right government remained remarkably state-controlled and state-directed. Nor did the government even succeed in reducing NHS spending, for notwithstanding recurrent complaints about 'cuts', spending in real terms was higher at the end of the eighties than it had been when Margaret Thatcher first assumed office.

There are some important lessons in all this as regards our understanding of the forces shaping contemporary British politics.

1 As in its management of the economy so too in its social policy, government seems to be quite tightly constrained in the range of realistic options it can follow. The Thatcher government elected in 1979 made no secret of its desire to break with the post-war consensus and to usher in a period of fundamental change, yet British society in the nineties does not look that different from British society in the seventies. Even the much-heralded policy of selling council houses has only succeeded in privatising one-fifth of the total stock, and Britain still has the largest state-rental housing sector in the western world. It still has a socialised medical system, and the schooling system has become more tightly controlled by the central state than has ever been the case in the past. The value of some state benefits has been trimmed, and various detailed changes have been made in rules of eligibility for benefits, but the social

security system remains much as it was before this government came to office. When the history of social policy during the Thatcher years comes to be written, it is more likely to emphasise the remarkable degree of continuity with the past than it is to dwell on the specific changes which were introduced. The fundamental conservatism of British public opinion proved too strong to allow for radical change, and the power of welfare professionals and pressure groups proved sufficient to block more fundamental reforms.

2 Another lesson to be drawn concerns the kinds of interests which are mobilised around social policy and welfare issues. It is clear that powerful forces are ranged on each side of the socialised versus privatised division, and the future of the welfare state remains to be determined (just as its origins were) by the outcome of political struggles. What is crucially important about all this as regards an analysis of contemporary British politics is that consumption issues – housing, health, education, pensions and so on – have increasingly come to the forefront of political argument and conflict as the welfare state has come under attack from government cuts and the move to privatisation. The question of how vital areas of consumption are to be socially organised and managed has become a highly charged and highly politicised one, and it has thrown up new patterns of political alignment and conflict which do not correspond to the conventional lines of class cleavage on which so much of British politics has traditionally been fought out.

The essential point here is that political struggles around issues of consumption cut across class lines. Sometimes, this results in the formation of new and strange alliances between people who more often find themselves on opposing sides. Middle-class teachers join with working-class parents to fight school closures; local 'anti-cuts' movements are formed which bring together members of public-sector unions threatened by job losses, welfare state clients threatened by an erosion of services, radical intellectuals committed to an extension of socialism, and so on; community activism draws together members of the women's movement, of ethnic groups, of gay rights campaigns and of the Labour movement in a common cause of, say, campaigning for a community centre.

At other times, however, this redrawing of political alignments results in a hopeless fragmentation among people who more often find themselves on the same side. Council-house rent rises, for example, may be fought by working-class tenants, yet may be welcomed by working-class owner-occupiers who see such a policy in positive terms as reducing the burden on their rates. Low-wage earners may ally themselves with prosperous professional and business interests in demanding tighter restrictions on welfare benefits claimed by the unemployed, one-parent families and others who are popularly seen as parasitical and 'scroungers'. The politics of consumption, in other words, are often divisive and entail struggles and conflicts between sectors of the population which cut across social classes.

The conventional wisdom in the Conservative Party and elsewhere that an extension of private-property rights to the working class is a sure way of undermining the appeal of socialism is not without foundation. If the extension of state provision in the early part of this century was seen by politicians at the time as a way of maintaining political stability and social order, then the erosion of state provision in the later part of the century has, paradoxically, also come to be seen in the same way.

Despite the relative modesty of the changes introduced by government in the 1980s, it is clear that there is in Britain a long-term tendency for increasing numbers of people to purchase basic services rather than rely on state provision. As we have seen, private housing has been growing at the expense of council housing, private pension schemes have been expanding, private medical insurance has grown to cover over five million people by 1989 and so on. Should these trends continue, then it may be that not only private housing and private pension schemes, but also private medicine and perhaps even private education may eventually come to represent the majority form of consumption provision (subsidised, where necessary, through state support by means of tax relief and other income-support measures). If this should come about, then the implications for British politics – and for British society as a whole – would be enormous.

Sociologists have become accustomed to representing the social structure of modern Britain in the form of a pyramid with a small upper class at the pinnacle and a large working class at the base. This has, for some time now, been a less than perfect metaphor – the growth of the middle class, for example, has led to a considerable 'bulge' mid-way up the pyramid, and the breakdown in the relation between social class and voting (discussed in chapter 2) has made such a model increasingly useless for political scientists interested in explaining patterns of political alignment. A major problem with this pyramidal model, however, is that it relates solely to social class – to the question of how production is socially organised. It therefore ignores the equally important question of other sources of inequality and other bases of political alignment – notably those concerning the social organisation of consumption.

If the question of consumption is taken into account, then we may have to end up inverting our pyramid model. As more and more people find themselves able to buy vital services, so those who cannot will become an increasingly marginalised minority reliant on a dwindling and deteriorating state sector. The signs are already present in housing and, to some extent, in health care. The initial responses of this marginalised minority are also present, and they range from violent explosions of unrest (such as the 1981 and 1985 inner-city riots) to a return to mutual aid strategies in some more stable working-class communities. Just as, in chapter 9, we saw that the decline of the British economy was creating a division between a majority of people in reasonably secure and well-paid employment and a minority of unemployed and low-paid insecure workers, so now we see that much the same division is emerging with the decline of the welfare state. The time is coming when we may need to re-examine our traditional 'them-and-us' conceptions of British society, for the tendency in relation to both produc- tion (the world of work) and consumption (the world outside the factory gates) is towards an increasingly large 'them' and an increasingly marginalised and desperate 'us' (though still, of course, with a tiny 'them' at the very top of the heap!)

Conclusion

We have seen in this chapter that the determinants or causes of social policy over the years have been many and varied. Sometimes governments have acted on their own initiative in response to some perceived problem. At other times, policies have been introduced as a result of pressure from particular interest groups or individual reformers. The organised working class has loomed large as a factor in social reform, but much of the earlier legislation was introduced despite working-class antipathy and resistance, and sometimes social policy has represented an attempt to head-off anticipated working-class militancy rather than as a response to working-class pressure itself. Middle-class and professional groups have also played an important part in shaping the development of the welfare state, and policies initially designed to benefit one group have sometimes been re-moulded to suit the interests of another. Even today, struggles continue over the issue of welfare, and the groups engaged in these struggles are as disparate and varied as ever. Clearly, there is no one group or class which has dominated or controlled social policy, and different alliances of different interest groups tend to form around different specific issues.

All of this lends support, not to a simple Marxist theory of the state, but to some kind of pluralist theory, for it is in the work of pluralist theorists (discussed in chapters 2–4) that we find the emphasis on political competition between shifting groups of alliances and it is this pattern of politics which seems to characterise the history of the development of social policy in Britain. Having said that, 3 qualifying points must quickly be made.

1 The build up of the welfare state has carried within itself the fact that it is now a substantial employer of labour. The professionals employed in health and social service provision have enjoyed an inside track with respect to their influence over policy-making and this is suggestive of a corporatist, closed style of policy-making rather than the open, pluralist pattern.

2 As we have already made clear, it is important to make a distinction between who causes welfare provision and who benefits from that provision. To say that welfare policy is made in response to a variety of pressures from many interests does not lead us to say that everyone in society benefits equally from the provision that results: the Left argues that welfare provision is to the ultimate benefit of the capitalist class, and the Right is not unmindful of the benefits which the welfare state brings to the middle class. In many ways identifying who benefits from welfare policy is more fundamental than identifying who makes that policy although it has to be recognised that reform is necessarily ambiguous in terms of whom it advantages.

3 On the policy-making front, it is important to recognise that the responsiveness of government to pressures is constrained, and, in the context of economic recession, it is constrained by the need to take account of the implications of different policies for future private-sector profitability. In other words, political competition has been imperfect and unbalanced and the government and the state has not been the neutral referee between competing interests but an active and involved participant.

When we look at the evidence on welfare policy-making as compared to the evidence on economic policy-making set down in the last chapter, then we see it as reasonable to suggest that certain areas of state activity seem to be more open to pressure and influence by competing groups than others. Economic policy-making is a relatively exclusive business in a way which is less evident with respect to policy-making in the field of welfare provision. Indeed, the determination of social policy cannot be achieved exclusively given its direct and obvious impact on a wide range of people and the popular concern and political activity which it arouses. Furthermore, social policy is developed and implemented at many different levels and in many different agencies of the state which would make it difficult to insulate if from popular pressure – elected local authorities, for example, play a key role in the organisation of public housing, schooling and personal social services, and the fierce battles which developed from 1979 onwards, between Labour-controlled authorities intent on defending the welfare state and a central government intent on weakening it, bear eloquent testimony to the diversity of interests which come to be represented in the struggles over such policies (the relation between different agencies of the state is discussed in chapter 12).

It is precisely because so many groups now have a vested interest in so many different areas of the welfare state that the Thatcher governments of the 1980s found it so very difficult to effect fundamental changes. Core areas of the welfare state – in particular the National Health Service – seem to have become almost sacrosanct, and even modest attempts at reform can provoke intense opposition from vociferous organisations like the British Medical Association, the health service unions and a battery of pressure groups. So it was that the most radical government of the last forty years failed to break down some of the most important pillars of statism and collectivism in Britain, and even ended up boasting that it was spending *more* on state schools and *more* on NHS hospitals than the Labour governments of the 1970s had done!

If it is correct that certain core segments of the welfare system have effectively become political 'no-go areas', then the implications could be serious. As we saw in chapter 9, the British economy is fundamentally weak and is unlikely to reverse its relative decline in the foreseeable future. The resources which are available to fund expensive universal provisions such as the National Health Service are therefore strictly limited. The demands on these provisions are, however, growing all the time. In the case of the NHS in particular, an ageing population and the spiralling cost of new drugs and innovative treatments seem certain to overload demand as the years go by. The system currently rations health care through queuing (which means that two- or three-year waiting lists for minor surgery are already common) and through professional selectivity (for example, expensive operations such as heart by-passes or kidney transplants may not be offered to older patients). If fundamental reforms of the financing of the NHS cannot even be debated for fear of the electoral repercussions and political fallout, as now seems to be the case, then the queues will simply get longer and the selectivity more capricious.

The simple truth appears to be that Britain cannot afford to run a first-class welfare state system on the strength of a third-rate economy. The problem, however, is that no political party seems willing or able to tell this to the electorate.

Works Cited and Guide to Further Reading

Barratt Brown, M. (1971) 'The welfare state in Britain', *Socialist Register* London, Merlin Press. Or reprinted in his (1972) *From Labourism to Socialism*, Nottingham, Spokesman Books.
Quite a good example of New Left analysis of the welfare state at a time when the cuts and Thatcherism were still some way off. Concludes, unlike most Marxist approaches, that free welfare services represent 'a bastion of socialist conception' within capitalist Britain.

Fraser, D. (1973) *The Evolution of the British Welfare State*, London, Macmillan. Has become a standard text on the development of welfare policy in Britain – perhaps a bit weak on explanation, but strong on detail.

George, V. and Wilding, P. (1976) *Ideology and Social Welfare*, London, Routledge and Kegan Paul.
A useful if slightly superficial account of four contrasting ideological approaches to the questions of welfare – those of the 'anti-collectivists', the 'reluctant collectivists', the 'Fabian socialists' and the 'Marxists'.

Goodin, R. and LeGrand, J., (eds) (1987) *Not only the Poor*, London, Allen and Unwin.
Contains various articles on Britain, the USA and Australia, all of which document the ways in which the middle classes have come to benefit from welfare services originally established for the poor. See especially the authors' concluding chapter which suggests that this is probably inevitable and which goes on to consider the implications for future social policy.

Gough, I. (1979) *The Political Economy of the Welfare State*, London, Macmillan. Probably still the best of what has become a very large literature analysing the question of welfare from a Marxist perspective. Gough's analysis is careful and coherent in showing how social expenditure has benefited capital as well as labour, and he shows himself adept at distinguishing the causes of particular policies from the functions which they have come to perform.

Green, D. (1982) *The Welfare State: For Rich or For Poor?* Institute of Economic Affairs, Occasional Paper, number 63.
A nice example of an application of the ideas of Hayek and Friedman to historical analysis; in this case, to an analysis of how the medical profession was able to secure its own position through the introduction of compulsory state health insurance in 1911.

Hay, J. (1975) *The Origins of the Liberal Welfare Reforms, 1906–14*, London, Macmillan.
A slim but useful volume which traces the diverse pressures – from within and outside the state – which resulted in the spate of welfare reforms before the First World War. Hay argues that different pieces of legislation had different origins, and his book is therefore a useful corrective to those – on the Right and the Left – who seek to explain the growth of state intervention through monocausal theories.

Hayek, F. (1960) *The Constitution of Liberty*, London, Routledge and Kegan Paul.
In many ways the most comprehensive and compelling development of the neo-liberal position including its relevance to contemporary problems of welfare provision. In a very readable way, Hayek traces the dangers for individual liberties which he sees as emanating from the growth of state intervention, and thus poses a series of uncomfortable problems which defenders of the welfare state will ignore at their peril.

Laski, H. (1935) *The State in Theory and Practice*, London, Allen and Unwin.
See guide to further reading at the end of chapter 8.

Marshall, T.H. (1950) 'Citizenship and social class'. In T.H. Marshall (ed.), *Citizenship and Social Class, and Other Essays*, London, Cambridge University Press.
A classic essay in which it is argued that the development of legal rights in the eighteenth century led inexorably to the extension of political rights in the nineteenth and thence to the establishment of social rights of citizenship in the twentieth. Particularly insightful in pointing to the growing tension between rights of private property and rights of citizenship – i.e. to the conflict between a capitalist system of production and a collective system of welfare provision.

Marx, K. (1976) *Capital, Volume I*, Harmondsworth, Penguin, chapters 10 and 15.
In which Marx analyses the nineteenth-century Factory Acts in the context of his theory of exploitation. The analysis is more subtle than is sometimes imagined, for while state regulation is seen as a product of class struggle, it is also seen as having aided capital by safeguarding the quality of labour-power and stimulating investment in new capital-intensive means of production. A standard reference for later Marxist analysis of social policy.

Murray, C. (1988) *In Pursuit of Happiness and Good Government*, New York, Simon and Schuster.
Argues that much social policy has been counter-productive, undermining self-reliance and self-esteem and fostering a crippling dependency culture. Finds the alternative in a strengthening of the 'little platoons' of family and neighbourhood.

Murray, C. (1990) *The Emerging British Underclass*, London, IEA.
Murray's short essay argues that an underclass has developed in Britain despite (and to some extent because of) extensive welfare provision. The book also contains critical responses from Frank Field and others.

Offe, C. (1984) *Contradictions of the Welfare State*, London, Hutchinson.
A collection of essays by an important contemporary Left writer. Argues forcefully that capitalism can live neither with nor without the welfare state, and that the state itself thus confronts recurring problems which it cannot resolve.

Pelling, H. (1968) *Popular Politics and Society in Late Victorian Britain*, London Macmillan, chapter 1.
An important analysis of the growth of state intervention in the nineteenth century which suggest that, far from being a response to working-class demands, many policies were introduced in the face of working-class antipathy or even opposition.

Savage, S. and Robins, L. (1990) *Public Policy under Thatcher*, London, Macmillan.
Chapters 7 to 11 outline and evaluate major policy initiatives introduced through the 1980s in health, housing, education, personal social services and social security.

Segalman, R. and Marsland, D. (1989) *Cradle to Grave*, London Macmillan.
Hard-nosed right-wing critique of the welfare system. Argues that much of what the state now does would be better left to families and local communities to organise.

"A powerful challenge to the law and good order of the state?" (Reproduced by kind permission of Rex Features.)

Chapter 11

Maintaining the Social Order

Quite clearly, the greatest of all dangers to the capitalist system is that more and more people . . . should come to think as both possible and desirable an entirely different social order.
Ralph Miliband (1969) *The State in Capitalist Society*, London, Weidenfeld and Nicolson, pp. 260–2.

We are surely heading for a situation in which stricter measures of social control may have to be applied to stabilise society and secure our democratic system.
James Anderton, Chief Constable of Greater Manchester (1977), *Annual Report.*

Introduction

One of the most fundamental propositions of modern political philosophy is that, irrespective of what other duties it assumes, the primary task of the state is to maintain social order by enforcing the Rule of Law.

One of the most fundamental propositions of modern political sociology is that this task cannot successfully be discharged simply through use of force. The maintenance of social order requires consent as well as coercion, legitimation as well as force.

Every modern society is bound together partly by the threat or use of force and partly by the reproduction of a basic consensus embracing most of its members for most of the time. Without some element of popular legitimacy and basic consensus, even the most repressive regime cannot be expected to last for long. The sudden collapse in 1989 of a succession of Eastern European Communist states revealed just how precarious are those systems of power which enforce obedience yet which fail to induce consent.

The use of coercion and, where necessary, of physical violence is a characteristic feature of all modern states. Indeed, coercion – whether it take the form of physical incarceration, corporal punishment, fines, community service orders or electronic tagging – is not only a necessary feature of the modern state, but is also its defining feature. As the

German sociologist, Max Weber, recognised early this century, the state is unique in that it alone of all modern institutions claims for itself a mono- poly over the legitimate right to use force to back up orders and commands within a given territory. No other organisation has the right, enshrined in law and endorsed by custom, to use force to make us do what we do not wish to do. The Ford Motor Company cannot force me to buy one of its cars, the school which my children attend cannot force them to wear a uniform, my employer cannot force me to perform a given task, my landlord cannot force me to pay the rent and I cannot force my children to do the washing up. Multinational companies, schools, employers, land- lords and heads of families are all powerful in their different ways, but they cannot use force to achieve what they want unless the state explicitly grants them the right to do so (for example by authorising schools or parents to inflict corporal punishment on children). The state, then, is the only organisation in modern society with the right to coerce.

As we have seen, however, coercion is never a sufficient guarantee of order, for the maintenance of social order must also entail the planting, nurturing and propogation of a spirit of consensus in society. This need not involve the state, but increasingly it does. As we shall see, there are institu- tions beyond the state in 'civil society' which have traditionally played a crucial role in transmitting and developing the core values of our culture. However, these institutions – one thinks immediately of the family and the church – have become weaker as time has gone by, and the messages which they relay to their members have also become more confused. It is for this reason that the state has come to extend its activities. Today, state agencies are centrally involved in both coercion *and* legitimation. On the one hand, the state organises the police force, the law courts and the prisons; and on the other it organises the schools, the social workers and the broadcasters. Seen in this way, the division between 'state' and 'civil society' has become blurred. Today, the people who teach us are paid by the same institution – government – as the people who police us. Legitimation has been twinned with coercion, for both are today organised and managed primarily by state agencies.

The 'Velvet Glove': Managing Consent

Over the years, it has often been suggested by observers of British politics and society that the country exhibits a peculiarly 'deferential' political cul- ture. Probably the best known statement of this view came in the nineteenth century with the publication of Walter Bagehot's influential study of the English constitution (see chapter 1), but the idea has persisted in various guises through twentieth-century political sociology as well. As we saw in chapter 3, for example, many analyses of voting behaviour have suggested that deferential attitudes may explain the apparently puzzling phenomenon of working-class Conservatism, and sociologists too have devoted considerable time and energy to studies of groups such as farm workers or employees in small, family-owned companies whose behaviour and attitudes seem to result in a rather passive endorsement of their own subordination and relative powerlessness.

Such views of British political culture and of large sections of the British working class as deferential must be treated with some caution. The society has never been as calm and well-ordered as these accounts seem to assume, and there are obvious dangers in taking behaviour which appears to be deferential as indicative of genuine belief in the right of social and political elites to rule. Often we may find, for example, that the farm workers tugging their forelocks with one hand may be giving a 'V'-sign behind their backs with the other, and workers who vote Conservative may do so for a variety of reasons which have nothing to do with a belief in the political wisdom of their social superiors.

While rejecting the concept of a deferential political culture, we would nevertheless emphasise that, notwithstanding the various explosions of unrest and rumblings of discontent which from time to time have threatened political order, Britain does seem to have been peculiarly stable when compared with many other Western capitalist nations. Even when we take account of such manifestations of popular unrest as the Peterloo massacre, the great Chartist demonstrations, the Captain Swing riots, or the 1926 General Strike, it does seem that ever since the upheavals of the Civil War in the seventeenth century, the political order has never come under the sustained and real threat of revolution. Britain in the nineteenth century was shielded from the waves of revolutionary change which ebbed and flowed across much of continental Europe, and in the twentieth century it has stood relatively immune from communist uprisings and fascist coups alike. In short, those who tell us that liberal-democracy is as deeply embedded and as secure in Britain as in any other country on this globe may be guilty of chauvinism but should not lightly be accused of hyperbole.

Explanation of this relatively enduring stability of the political and social order in Britain is no simple task, and there are obviously many different factors which would need to be taken into account. Britain's geographical location as an island off the coast of mainland Europe is undoubtedly one factor, for the Channel has, on more than one occasion, provided a physical barrier against the wars of conquest which have done so much to shape the present character of other major European countries. The legacy of the Civil War is a second important factor, for the restoration of the monarchy in 1688 effectively sealed a truce between the old ruling class of landowners and the new rising class of industrialists and financiers and thereby avoided the bloody turmoils and struggles for power which took place between these classes in France, Germany and elsewhere through the nineteenth century. Britain's history as the world's first industrial capitalist country is a further element in the explanation, for the working class reached maturity here long before the development of socialist and Marxist ideology on a world scale with the result that revolutionary Marxist ideas have never really taken root in the Labour movement. Add to all this the impact on British society of an Empire which was systematically exploited to the advantage of (among others) the working class at home, and which unleashed a jingoistic and nationalistic strand of popular sentiment which resonates throughout the class structure to this day, and we have identified some of the major factors which any explanation of British political stability would need to address.

Whatever the explanation, it is apparent that this relative stability has meant that the balance between coercion and consensus, the iron fist and the velvet glove, has tended over most of this period to emphasise the latter more than the former. It has, in other words, been the 'soft' agencies of social control rather than the 'hard' ones which seem to have played the major role in maintaining order over the last 300 years.

By 'soft' agencies of control, we mean those institutions which have contributed to social and political order by supplying, maintaining or reinforcing particular beliefs, values, standards of behaviour and understandings of the world which are consistent with the contemporary organisation of the society. According to which theory you read, or which ideology you subscribe to, their function may be identified as that of 'socialisation' or 'legitimation'. The term 'legitimation' is one which is more often found in radical and Marxist literature (but which is not exclusive to left political positions) and which refers to the process whereby a particular organisation of state, economy and society comes to be seen by the members of that society, including those in subordinate positions, as morally correct or legitimate. For our purposes, socialisation and legitimation may be taken to refer to essentially the same thing–the direct or indirect control over people's ways of thinking and acting other than through the use of physical force.

Traditionally in Britain, the three most important institutions involved in socialising individuals, and in legitimating the existing social and political order were the family, the church and the local community. While all three retain some significance today, it is clear that each of them has declined in importance and has to some extent been replaced by other agencies, among which welfare institutions, the educational system and the mass media are probably the most important. As we shall see, these more 'modern' agencies have not generally achieved the same degree of cohesion and power which the more traditional agencies once enjoyed, and this has led in recent years to an attempt by Conservative governments in particular to reinforce the moral bind of family, church and community as a response to what has been seen as a growing crisis of social control and of morality in the contemporary period. Before considering all this in more detail, it is important to stress one point at the outset. Socialisation into particular norms, values and beliefs never has been and never can be total, and legitimation is thus always more or less but never completely successfully achieved. Human beings are not empty receptacles into which can be poured those ways of thinking and action which dominant groups or their agents in the pulpits, the classrooms and the editorial offices of Fleet Street wish people to accept. Both Marxism and political sociology have often forgotten or ignored this. Much of the sociological theory of the 1950s, for example, was guilty of assuming an 'oversocialised' conception of human beings in which individuals came to be seen as little more than puppets reacting to situations according to preprogrammed internalised role responses. Similarly, Marxist thinking has long been bedevilled by the concept of 'false class consciousness' bequeathed by Engels as a label to be applied whenever working-class people failed to embrace a Marxist revolutionary ideology. Neither Right nor Left should assume that the 'soft' agencies of social control are, or ever could be, all-pervasive in their impact on our customary ways of thinking and modes of understanding the world in which we live, for we are all conscious, acting subjects, and we all reflect on the world not only through the cognitive tools handed to us by schools, the church or whatever, but also through our immediate, everyday-life experiences. As we shall see, these experiences may often conflict with the images handed down through soft control agencies, and in cases like this received ideologies may well be questioned or even rejected.

Traditional 'soft' control agencies

The family

Of the three traditional soft agencies of social control, the family was – and remains – the most important. This is because the family is the principal agency by means of which newly born members of the society come to learn what their world is like and how they are expected to behave within it. Even today (and even more so in the past) the first and most crucial years of childhood are spent almost exclusively within the family unit with the result that the family enjoys extensive control over how infants develop. It is in these years that the child learns what its parents expect as 'normal' and 'correct' behaviour in various situations; 'normal' ways of thinking and 'normal' assumptions about the way the social world works are taken in with the mother's milk. It is similarly in these early formative years that the child will learn, from those with whom it is in closest and most regular contact, the difference between 'good' and 'bad', the distinction between what it is in its power to control and what is controlled by others, the differentiation of the world into 'people like us' and 'people like them', and so on. It is, and has long been, overwhelmingly the task of the family to equip the new members of our society with the basic social skills and 'cookbook recipes' by which they will go on to live their lives, and it is for this reason that the family was, and is, a crucial agency in the transmission of social values and normative standards across the generations.

Having said that, however, it has also immediately to be recognised that the family in Britain no longer plays so central a role in the maintenance of order as once it did. The shape and nature of the family has changed and is still changing. Although the historical evidence is to some extent debated in details, it is the case that in pre-industrial Britain, before the dawn of capitalism had transformed the country and its people in the most dramatic and far-reaching of social changes the world has witnessed, the family unit was typically based on a close network of extended kinship ties. Especially where they were living off the land (where the family functioned as much as a unit of production as anything else), families often consisted not simply of the nuclear unit (comprising husband, wife and immature offspring) but also of grandparents, siblings, aunts, uncles, nephews, nieces and cousins, all living in close proximity and all contributing in one way or another to the many different tasks which the family as a whole was called upon to perform. Thus, in addition to working the land, it was typically the responsibility of this extended family unit to rear and educate its young, to tend to its sick, to care for its aged, to protect its members and so on. It was, in short, the basic and most crucial unit of social organisation at that time, for it was in the family that the individual found a role and identity, and it was through the family that the individual was integrated into the wider society.

With the onset of capitalist industrialisation, all this changed. As people were displaced from the land and propelled into the squalid housing and bleak factories of the new industrial cities, so it became increasingly difficult for households based on extended kinship to stay together. Young people left their families to find work and the basis of employment in the factories and the mines was the individual rather than the family unit. Although wives and children were often recruited into the labour force, more extended kin ties were progressively broken or weakened. Today, most sociologists suggest that the 'typical' family form has changed from the extended to the nuclear (or in some views, 'modified-extended') type whose members rely only occasionally and tangentially, for aid on more distant kin (for example, for services such a child-minding or for financial support in the case of more affluent families).

Even this nuclear family type is, moreover, still changing. In a shifting moral climate, for example, the number of single-parent families is increasing quite rapidly. Improved financial autonomy for women has meant that increasing numbers of women today enjoy a real choice as to whether to marry and whether to raise children themselves or with a partner. Liberalised divorce laws mean that marriage is less and less a contract for life, and some observers have detected a phenomenon of 'serial marriage' in which individuals move from one relatively stable monogamous relationship to another, taking some or all of their children with them as they go. What is clear, therefore, is that literally millions of children in Britain today are being brought up either by a single parent or by at least one adult who is not their natural parent.

Not only has the form of the family changed over the last two or three hundred years, but so too have the functions which it is called upon to perform. With the exception of the small family firm, the family is no longer a significant producer unit, and its consumption functions too have been whittled down. Where once the extended family educated its young, there now exist state schools, nurseries and colleges. Where once the extended family catered for its sick and its elderly, there now exist state hospitals, state nursing homes and state-employed home helps. There is, however, still one key area where the state has not, as yet, assumed responsibility from the family, and that is in the socialisation of the infant.

The importance of this continuing socialisation function is recognised by government in the battery of supports it provides for the nuclear family with young children. These include family allowances, tax concessions, family income supplements, child clinics, home nursing services, family casework and so on. Yet despite such supports, it has become increasingly clear that the family is not discharging its socialisation function in such a way as to contribute to social order as it once did. Over recent years, it has become commonplace among many commentators and politicians to attribute manifestations of social malaise such as vandalism, street crime, soccer hooliganism and other forms of anti-social behaviour to the weakness of the family. Family discipline, it is suggested, has been eroded, the emotional security of children has been weakened by mothers working, and there has been a general laxity in moral standards.

The Thatcher governments of the 1980s set themselves the task of reversing this decline in the traditional family. In a drive to disinter what Thatcher herself referred to as 'Victorian values', an attempt was made to increase the responsibility of families in caring for their own members while reducing reliance on state agencies. Families (normally married daughters) were encouraged to look after elderly or disabled relatives at home rather than leaving them in the care of state-run institutions. Errant fathers were traced so as to enforce their financial responsibility to their deserted partners and children who would otherwise be totally dependent on state benefits. The government even considered ways of making parents liable for crimes committed by their children in the hope that this would strengthen parental responsibility and authority. The net effect of all this was minimal. For all its rhetoric and its claims to be the 'party of the family', the Thatcher administration actually presided over a continued weakening of the traditional family structure. Many on the 'moral right', for example, argued that mothers should be encouraged to stay at home with their children rather than going out to work, yet in the Thatcher years, more women than ever before found full- or part-time employment. Between 1981 and 1987, when male economic activity rates fell from 76.5 per cent to 73.7 per cent, the female rate rose from 47.6 per cent to 50.0 per cent – one of the highest figures in western Europe.

Other indicators tell a similar story. The divorce rate rose from 11.9 per thousand married people in 1981 to 12.6 in 1987 – or putting it another way, a staggering one in three of all marriages now end in divorce (again, one of the highest figures in western Europe). The illegitimacy rate soared in the 1980s. In 1981, 13 per cent of live births were to unmarried mothers.

By 1987 this figure had risen to 23 per cent. Some of this increase, of course, is accounted for by couples living together but choosing not to get married (two-thirds of illegitimate births are registered in the names of both parents). Nevertheless, the number of single-parent families in Britain rose from just over half a million at the start of the seventies to around a million by the late eighties and they now account for some five per cent of all households in the country. Abortion too has been increasing. One hundred and thirty-nine thousand unwanted foetuses were aborted in 1981; by 1987 this had risen to 166,000.

All of this strongly supports the contention that the traditional family is in decline in Britain. Whether this is producing deliterious social and psychological consequences is arguable, although there is evidence that children raised by only one parent are more likely to become involved in criminal or delinquent behaviour (due, it is assumed, to the inadequate socialisation following from the absence of the second adult). The decline of the traditional family seems to be part of a more widespread social and moral upheaval in which individuals (and particularly women) are less willing than they once were to embrace conventional role behaviour. We expect more freedom to choose how to lead our lives, and inevitably this means that we show less respect for the social rules emphasising our obligations and responsibilities. The old certainties have vapourised in an age of individualism and ethical pluralism.

Old-style conservatives have been appalled by these developments. Paul Johnson, writing in the *Daily Telegraph* in 1987, described the lack of a positive family policy as 'a devastating hole' in the heart of Thatcherism, and in 1986 a group of disaffected Conservatives formed the Conservative Party Family Campaign in an attempt to bring greater pressure on the government to fulfil its moral agenda. Clearly the 'moral right' failed to achieve much of an impact in the eighties despite the existence of a strong and apparently sympathetic government, and its various campaigns aimed at permissiveness, abortion and other such emotive issues generally came to nothing. Calls to extend censorship were generally resisted, moves to restrict legal abortions were defeated, and a lengthy campaign to prevent GPs from giving contraceptives to girls under sixteen without the consent of their parents was similarly unsuccessful. Even the government's own propoganda came to undermine traditional family values as the AIDS panic of the late eighties led to millions of pounds being spent on advertising which depicted promiscuity as normal and which simply advised us all to carry condoms around in our pockets or handbags.

As in its economic and welfare policies, so too in its family policy, it seems the Thatcher governments bit off more than they could chew. The changing role and structure of the family reflects a strong undercurrent of cultural change in British society since the war, and there is probably little that any government can do to influence this. There is no longer (if indeed there ever was) a core value system which is transmitted through the family to successive generations. Governments cannot recreate such a value system, and state policy cannot be expected to strengthen the family when its decline is directly related to the decline in traditional morality in the society as a whole. Government may be able to encourage and reinforce cultural trends, but it cannot change or redirect them.

The Church

The significance of the Church as a 'soft' agency of control in pre-industrial England lay in the virtual monopoly which it enjoyed as the source of authoritative explanations and justifications of the world as people experienced it in their everyday lives. Religion was, in other words, integrated into everyday life as a taken-for-granted reality, and there was little dispute or even conscious reflection over its moral content. The Church thus played a crucial legitimating role in that it provided explanations for the harsh conditions in which most people lived and worked, and these explanations usually stressed the role of divine will such that mere mortals could and should do very little to change them;

> *The rich man in his castle*
> *the poor man at his gate*
> *God made them high and lowly*
> *and ordered their estate.*

It was precisely this legitimatory role of religion which led Marx to his well-known formulation of religion as 'the sigh of the oppressed creature, the soul of soulless conditions . . . the opium of the people', for in his view, organised religion served the interest of the ruling class by obscuring people's understanding of the 'real' causes of their misery and by providing a social safety valve through which ordinary people could be offered the compensation of salvation in the next world in return for material damnation in this one.

This view of organised religion as the mouthpiece of a ruling class should not be accepted too readily, however. The Church has sometimes acted as a compliant partner of the state, but at others it has challenged state power. In the noncomformist sects, for example, preachers have as often railed against capitalism as rallying to its defence, and as Labour's veteran Left-winger Tony Benn has observed, an important strand in the history of British socialism can be traced through the importance of non-conformist religions in the Celtic fringe of Wales, Scotland and the south-west of England. The Church of England too has increasingly come to challenge government and the ethics of unbridled capitalism. In 1985, for example, the Archbishop of Canterbury's Commission on Urban Priority Areas clashed publicly with the Thatcher government when it published its report, *Faith in the City*. The report criticised 'the evident and apparently increasing inequality in our society', it attacked what it called the government's 'dogmatic and inflexible macroeconomic stance', and it called into question the 'alleged benign social consequences of individual self-interest and competition'. Calling for increased public spending on jobs, housing, urban infrastructure and family support, the report deliberately set a collision course with the government and claimed Christian morality and theology as its justification. By the 1980s, the old jibe that the Church of England represents the Tory Party at prayer seemed to have lost much of its pertinence.

The Church of England is, nevertheless, the established Church, and its organic links with the state are still symbolised by the role of the Monarch as the titular head of both. The Monarch (on the advice of the Prime Minister) appoints the bishops and archbishops and is in turn crowned in Westminster Abbey by the Archbishop of Canterbury. The bishops occupy seats specially reserved for them in the House of Lords, and changes proposed by the General Synod of the Church (for example, the ordination of women or of homosexual men) must be approved by the Crown and by Parliament. Under the 1944 and 1986 Education Acts, religious instruction is a compulsory subject on every state school curriculum. The law of the land still recognises the offence of blasphemy against the Christian God. Yet for all this, the significance of the Church as an agency of socialisation or legitimation seems very weak today. The reason is simply that British society has to a large degree become secularised.

One obvious indicator of secularisation is formal participation in the activities of the Church – the number of christenings and baptisms, the rate of attendance at key services such as Easter communion, the number of church weddings, and so on. On all such indicators, the Church has declined in significance since the mid-nineteenth century. However, secularisation goes much deeper than this, for statistics on christenings, weddings and the like are to some extent misleading. This is because for most people, most of these religious rituals retain importance for their form rather than their content. The church wedding is important not so much for the solemn sanctification of the marriage vows in the eyes of God as for the display of the wedding dress, the carnations and the confetti in the eyes of friends and relatives. Religious ceremonies for many people play a secular role as what anthropologists term 'rites de passage'; i.e. as rituals designed to mark a change in status. We thus use the Church to mark important stages of our lives – notably, to mark our entry into this world, our transition from single to married status and our exit from the world – but for little else.

Britain is today without any doubt a secular society, and the fact that the schools set aside a particular period for religious instruction and that the broadcasting media isolate a special 'God slot' within their weekly programming is, paradoxically, strong evidence in support of this view. It is precisely the hallmark of a secular society that religion is marginalised and compartmentalised in this way, for the Church has lost its monopolistic position as the all-embracing source of moral influence and knowledge. There are of course sections of our society for whom religious teaching and

faith remains crucial. The uproar in 1989 in the Muslem communit
Salman Rushdie published a book which many Muslems considered
cal bore testimony to the deeply-held religious sentiments of many *A*
for example. For most people, however, religion has lost its preem
and influence. In Britain today, the voice of the Church is simply one point
of view being expressed among a cacophony of other points of view, many
of which conflict with it. Few people today look to the Church for moral
guidance, and fewer still rely on the Church for explanations of world
events. The Church, then, is of only marginal significance as an agency of
social order, and the vacuum which has been created by the loss of its
'general presidency' has been filled by a plurality of groups and institutions
expressing different values, different beliefs and different orientations
to the world. Social order has thus been problematised precisely because
there is no longer any one powerful institution through which a set of 'core
values' can consistently be expressed and reinforced.

Community

This 'problem' has simply been exacerbated by the erosion of the third
traditional agency of social cohesion and control, the local community. In
pre-industrial Britain, most people lived in settlements of such a size that
personal relationships based on face-to-face interaction could be sustained
between most or all inhabitants. Furthermore, the difficulties entailed in
travel, together with the lack of opportunities outside of the home village
or town meant that most people spent most of their lives in the same place,
thus reinforcing the strength of neighbourhood ties. None of this should
be taken to imply that, because people tended to know each other, they
therefore necessarily liked each other, but it does mean that they were constantly aware of each other's actions across virtually all aspects of their
lives. Precisely because there was little or no opportunity for the individual
to carve out a separate and private existence, overall behaviour could easily
be monitored and any deviation from the shared expected norms would
swiftly incur sanctions in the form of gossip, ostracism, family shame, and
so on. Because the individual was known, the scope for individualism was
limited and pressures of collective standards and conformity was intense.

Just as capitalist industrialisation undermined the traditional strength
of the extended family, so too it disrupted these moral ties of localism.
Urbanisation broke down face-to-face modes of social control, for in the
relative anonymity of the large industrial city, individuals could carve out
discrete areas of their lives and could move through a series of different and
unrelated social worlds in which associates in one area of activity had little
or no contact with those in another. In such a setting, the old informal sanctions of gossip, ostracism and dishonour lost their grip, and the symbolic
and material significance of neigbourhood was weakened.

As in our earlier discussions of the family and the Church, these changes
should not be exaggerated. Relatively cohesive neighbourhoods can still be

found even in the heart of the large metropolises, and for many of us, the place in which we live still retains some significance. Furthermore, even though community based on residence and locality has been weakened, it has to some extent been replaced by communities formed around other axes – for example, the sense of community which we experience as members of an occupational group, or a voluntary organisation or a trade union or political party. Informal social control has not, therefore, collapsed entirely, for, to the extent that the people we mix with are important to us (irrespective of whether or not they live near us), we are likely to take their expectations into account in the way in which we think and behave.

Nevertheless, the significance of informal norms and expectations does seem to have weakened, and our recognition of responsibilities owed to others has correspondingly declined. In the late eighties, Margaret Thatcher seemed to recognise this when she called for a renewed sense of 'citizenship' in which people should care for their neighbours and look out for those less fortunate than themselves. Those who had benefited materially from the Thatcher years were called upon to 'put something back'. But unlike the old paternalist upper class which was always keenly aware of its social obligations, the new yuppy class seemed much less keen to observe such moralities. Notwithstanding some impressive charity drives such as the 'Live Aid' Wembley rock concert prompted by a famine in Ethiopia and the launch of a televised 'Comic Relief' day which saw thousands of otherwise sane citizens walking the streets wearing red noses, donations to charity in the 1980s remained virtually constant. The introduction of a payroll charity donation scheme was a flop, raising only around one million pounds in the first full year of its operation. Most people in Britain still held to the view that the relief of want was the duty of the state rather than of the individual citizen, and in this sense they were happy for the government to discharge the obligations of 'community' on their behalf.

Not only have social expectations weakened, but they have also become partial and fragmented. In a small-scale cohesive community it may be possible to enforce one set of social norms, but this is virtually impossible in modern mass societies. Peer group pressure among adolescents, for example, can undoubtedly be every bit as strong as ever the old traditional village pressures to conformity were, but they may well result in the development of 'deviant' subcultures which confront rather than reinforce the norms and values of mainstream society. Furthermore, the pressures we experience in one area of our lives (for example, among workmates) may to a greater or lesser extent be inconsistent with those we experience in another (for example, among fellow members of the bowls club).

What this means is that the cohesion of the traditional agencies of control has been lost even where the extent of their influence remains strong. Traditionally, the individual stood at the centre of a series of concentric circles of control, each of which reinforced the other. Thus, the individual was a member of a family, which was itself part of a wider local community which was integrated through the Church into the society beyond. Today, however, the individual stands at a point where many different circles of control intersect but do not overlap. As such, the individual is still subject to what we have termed 'soft' agencies of control, but each one impacts on her or him only partially, and taken together they may well pull in different directions. The erosion of the three key traditional agencies of social control has thus resulted in a situation where there is no longer any single set of values or any single institution which can be relied upon to guide people's thoughts and actions. In the modern period, there is only one institution which could possibly fulfil such a central and co-ordinating role, and that is the state. Increasingly, therefore, the state in Britain has been sucked into the vacuum left by the erosion of the family, the Church and the local community in an attempt to reassert conformity in the face of diversity.

Modern 'soft' control agencies

The educational system

Without doubt, the most important of the state's activities as regards socialisation and legitimation is its responsibility for providing and managing the educational system. Education is, of course, about much more than social control, but maintenance of the social order is one important aspect of mass schooling in the twentieth century. There are two aspects to this. One is that schools are the means by which individuals are selected to fill different positions in society. The other is that schools are the principal agencies through which core stocks of knowledge and sets of values come to be transmitted to new generations. We shall consider each of these aspects in turn.

While family connections and inherited wealth can still be important in determining entry to certain favoured positions in British society, educational qualifications have for most people become the key criterion by which individuals are judged for entry into the occupational system. Schools thus perform a sifting and sorting function by issuing certificates and diplomas which serve to discriminate between people on the basis of their abilities and aptitudes. While it is still often possible for people to 'work their way up' within a job, initial qualifications gained at school or at college have become increasingly significant in shaping subsequent career progress.

Now there is much debate and argument over the extent to which educational success is skewed by existing patterns of privilege and inequality. There is no doubt that children from middle-class backgrounds tend to achieve higher rates of success than those from working-class backgrounds. Similarly, white pupils do much better on average than Afro-Caribbeans (though both are out-performed by Asian pupils). The arguments begin when we try to explain these patterns. Some researchers claim that they are the fault of the schools themselves – that an implicit and sometimes explicit white-middle-class culture pervades the educational system, and that this clearly favours white-middle-class pupils while alienating others. Other analysts suggest that the problem lies more in the home – middle-class parents may be more supportive of their children's education, they can offer more help when their children need it, the facilities in the home like books and quiet rooms for study are more conducive to learning. Still others find the explanation in the peer group and its support for anti-school values (especially marked, it seems, among certain groups of adolescent working-class boys for whom manual labour has a strong symbolic value as against the perceived non-virility of brainwork). And some academics claim that to some extent these differences may reflect differences of natural ability – intelligent parents tend to get middle-class jobs *and* tend to give birth to intelligent children, which is why children from the middle class tend to perform better in school than those from the working class.

Whatever the relative truth and plausibility of these competing explanations, the key point is that schools not only select and sort out those deemed 'bright', 'dull' and 'average', but they also get these labels to stick with the pupils themselves. Although the old eleven-plus examination has disappeared in most parts of Britain, academic selection by means of streaming and setting still takes place from a relatively early age, and from 1989 onwards all state school pupils have also been tested on national assessment criteria at the ages of seven, eleven and fourteen. Experiments down the years have shown that pupils and teachers alike tend to internalise the labels which come to be applied as a result of academic selection. In other words, children who come to be designated as 'gifted', or 'slow', or whatever tend to go on to behave accordingly. By the time they reach their teens, most pupils have a pretty good idea of their academic standing and of their anticipated performance. Those who are not going to make it into prestigious and well-paid positions already know this several years before they come to leave school, and this gives them plenty of time to dispense with childhood dreams of piloting a Boeing or running a veterinary practice, and to replace these fantasies with images of shop work or clerical tasks. Britain is full of people who will happily tell you that they are 'not bright enough' to do a more challenging job than the one they have. Whether or not such self-evaluations are correct is hardly important; what matters is that people *believe* it.

Of course, not everyone accepts that they have received their just deserts. School-leavers who cannot find work are unlikely to be convinced that this is either fair or fitting, and it was precisely this problem of soaring youth unemployment which prompted the government to introduce the Youth Training Scheme which guaranteed every school-leaver a trainee placement with a local employer. By 1987, 59 per cent of those leaving school at age 16 or 17 were enrolled on YTS schemes. Another even more difficult problem arises where there is a mismatch between people's level of education and the jobs which may be open to them. Legitimation is seriously threatened when young people are encouraged to spend years chasing qualifications which do not produce the anticipated benefits. A dissatisfied and well-educated population is much more threatening to the social order than a dissatisfied and poorly-educated one. As one senior official in the Department of Education told an academic researcher: 'When young people drop off the education production line and cannot find work at all, or work which meets their abilities and expectations, then we are only creating frustration with perhaps disturbing social consequences. . . . There may be social unrest but we can cope with the Toxteths [an area of Liverpool hit by rioting in 1985]. But if we have a highly educated and idle population we may possibly anticipate more serious social conflict. People must be educated once more to know their place, (quoted in Brian Simon's *Bending the Rules*, pp. 42–3). Clearly legitimation through the selectivity of schooling is far from unproblematic.

The second aspect of schooling which we need to consider relates to the content of education. This became a crucial political issue from the mid-seventies onwards. Traditionally in Britain, schools have been left to teach what they want and they have also enjoyed considerable discretion over teaching methods. This liberal tradition was challenged in a famous speech by the then Labour Prime Minister, James Callaghan, in 1976. Initiating what he hoped would be a 'Great Debate' over education, Callaghan expressed his concern at standards of basic numeracy and literacy among school-leavers and voiced his worries about the apparent aversion to industry of many of the most able students. Much of his speech echoed the complaints of the educational 'New Right' whose *Black Papers* had been attacking progressivism and the falling standards which it was thought to have produced. The result of all this was that much more attention came to be paid by governments to the relationship between schooling and the needs of the economy. Among the responses of government during the 1980s were the launching of a new Training and Vocational Education Initiative by the Manpower Services Commission, the introduction of centrally-run City Technology Colleges, and the establishment of a new national curriculum under the 1988 Education Reform Act.

Schooling came increasingly under central government control during the eighties, for not only did Whitehall set curriculum content, but it also set down national attainment standards for each subject. Central government also undermined the power base of the local education authorities by giving school governors greater responsibility for detailed decision-making and by enabling schools to opt out of local government control altogether if they wished to do so (see chapter 10). One critic of all this, Oxfordshire's Chief Education Officer, claimed to see in it the sinister seeds of fascism – 'I cannot rid myself of images of shirts of black and brown', he wrote in the *Observer*.

Schools are, however, rather cumbersome instruments of central state control. As places of learning and inquiry, schools and colleges have to some extent to open themselves up to competing ideas and differing definitions of reality. Furthermore, many teachers do not themselves sub-scribe to the values cherished by government – or, for that matter, by big business. The two big teacher unions have become among the most militant in Britain and staff noticeboards and teachers' lapel badges are today more likely to display Left-wing sentiments than a commitment to establishment values. Marxists like the French philosopher, Louis Althusser, may claim that schools are part of the ideological state apparatus', but the reality seems somewhat less dramatic.

This is not to deny that schools are nevertheless crucial agencies of socialisation. This can be seen not only in the formal content of what is taught, but also in what has been termed the 'hidden currriculum'. What we learn in school – though are rarely taught – is how to sit still, to speak when addressed, to stand in rows, to divide our time into 'work' and 'play' or 'free time', to be punctual, to treat learning as a means to an end (i.e. passing an examination), to control our exuberance and channel our aggres-sion, to respect authority, to be passive, to be subordinate. When most of us at 16 come to exchange our school uniform for blue overalls or a grey suit, and to exchange our school desk for an office desk or a factory bench, we are already well equipped with all the unwritten yet crucial knowledge which we are required to have if the economic system and the social order which rests upon it are not to crumble under the strain of an undisciplined workforce and an active citizenry. The school, in other words, is an agency of socialisation second in importance only to the family itself.

It is important not to exaggerate the significance of schooling as a soft control institution. Nevertheless, it is apparent that schools are as close as we have come in the contemporary period to finding a functional equi-valent of and replacement for the traditional role of the Church. They are, in other words, the major source of knowledge and moral guidance in modern society, and although the teacher's word will never carry the power and conviction that the priest's once did, we should not forget that, unlike the Church of old, schools today are compulsory institutions which enjoy the right to control the flow of ideas to young people as they grow from infancy to adulthood. Seen in this way, their potential power to shape our understanding of the world is staggering.

The Press

The educational system is to some extent aided in this respect by the various organs of the mass media. This is because socialisation – and, for that mat-ter, legitimation – is a continuous process. The beliefs, norms, values and taken-for-granted assumptions which we develop in childhood through the family and the school do not remain rigid and fixed for all time, for in a rapidly changing world we constantly encounter new situations and com-peting interpretations of reality which may throw some of our most basic assumptions into question. In modern Britain, the media – notably the newspapers which we read and the television programmes which are channelled into virtually every household in the country every night in the week – have come to play an important role in informing us about our world and in providing ready-made frameworks through which to understand and evaluate it.

Two points should be made at the outset in relation to both the Press and the broadcasting media. One is that they are overwhelmingly national institutions, for most people in Britain who read a newspaper (and newspaper readership per head of population is the highest in the world) read a national paper produced from London, while both the BBC and Independent Television, although organised through a regional structure, are also overwhelmingly nationally oriented and centrally controlled. Although recent developments such as local radio and satellite and cable television may represent some challenge and alternative to this London-dominated focus, it remains the case that our media are remarkably centralised and homogenous when compared with most other countries.

The second point is that both press and broadcasting are formally free of government control. The state is, of course, involved in broadcasting through its funding of the BBC and its responsibility for licensing independent television operators but both the BBC and the commercial stations are legally and constitutionally independent of government and are required by statute to ensure 'balance' in their output as between different views and opinions. As for the Press, all newspapers are privately owned and there are no legal restrictions on the rights of any individual to publish a newspaper.

In recent years, the development of new computer-based technologies, coupled with the successful attack on trade union power and the exodus of newspapers from Fleet Street, has reduced the costs of starting up new newspapers, and several new titles have been launched. Some, like *Today*, *The Independent*, and *The Independent on Sunday*, have survived and even flourished. Others, like *The Sunday Correspondent*, the *News on Sunday* (a Left-wing popular paper funded largely by trade union investments) and the *London Daily News* (a 24-hour newspaper for the capital) have rapidly failed. The net result, however, is that the long-term tendency for the number of titles to decline has been halted and even reversed, and the national press now looks healthier and more pluralistic than for many years. At the time of writing there are some 11 national dailies, 16 provincial morning papers, 64 provincial evening papers and 359 provincial weeklies.

Ownership of the Press is, of course, still remarkably concentrated, particularly among the popular tabloids. Rupert Murdoch's News International accounts for 35 per cent of the daily tabloid readers and 33 per cent of the popular Sundays (and its ownership of *The Times* and the *Sunday Times* also gives it 12 per cent of the quality market and 45 per cent of the quality Sunday market). Robert Maxwell's Mirror Group takes 26 per cent of the daily tabloid readership and 40 per cent of the popular Sunday market. The rest of the popular press is owned by just two further groups – United Newspapers (25 per cent) and Associated (14 per cent). Between them, these four giants also own most of the provincial press as well as having significant stakes in other media interests such as satellite broadcasting. Ownership of the quality press is more fragmented, however, for *The Guardian*, the *Independent* and the *Daily Telegraph* are all owned by different individuals or trusts.

Politically, the British Press is slanted in favour of the Right. The *Morning Star* is the ailing mouthpiece of the Communist Party and has been badly shaken by a split in the party and by the termination of a bulk standing order from Moscow. The *Mirror* is a consistent supporter of the Labour Party, and the *Guardian* adopts a left-of-centre line and is the favoured reading of the intellectual Left. Both *Today* (which favoured the alliance of the Liberals and Social Democrats at the 1987 General Election) and the *Independent* seem to occupy a space somewhere in the centre, although the latter in particular seems strongly committed to the sort of free-market principles more often advocated by the Right (soon after its launch in 1986, for example, it ran an editorial calling for the introduction of a system of education vouchers). The rest of the dailies are more or less strongly pro-Conservative in their sympathies. This is made explicit in their editorials, and it is often at least implicit in their choice of stories, the headlines which they give them and the way in which they choose to report them. The key question, however, is not who owns the Press, nor even the extent of its political bias, but rather whether any of this makes an impact on popular opinion. Do newspapers shape our political views and influence the way we think about events and policies?

Research suggests that, while television is the most important source of information about politics and current affairs, newspapers are still significant. Twenty-nine per cent of people in one survey claimed that newspapers were their primary source of information on politics (this compares with 63 per cent who cited television and 4 per cent who relied more on radio). As Ralph Negrine (who reports these findings) argues, we live in a 'second-hand world' and therefore rely heavily on the media both to select and to present information to us. Few of us attend political meetings, or go on rallies and marches, or sit in the Strangers' Gallery in the Palace of Westminster. Fewer still get inside the corridors of Whitehall, or sit in offices in Brussels, or rub shoulders with union leaders and business tycoons. And even the best-informed and most interested of us are unlikely to be able to grasp unaided the intricacies of many contemporary policy issues. Most of us rely almost totally on the media to explain many of the most crucial political issues – British membership of the European Exchange Rate Mechanism, criteria for assessing what local authorities need to spend each year, and the likely effects of introducing an internal market in the NHS were, for example, all pressing issues in 1990 yet their technical complexity was such that even full-time politicians were likely to be left baffled. What the newspapers tell us about what is going on, and how they present their information, is therefore likely to be crucial in shaping both our knowledge and opinions.

It is notoriously difficult to assess the impact which years of exposure to, say, the *Daily Mail* has on people's beliefs and ways of thinking. A number of points may, however, be noted. First, people freely choose which newspaper to buy; they are not forced or constrained to read a Right-wing paper, for although most papers are Right-wing, there is in principle no reason why they should not choose to read the *Mirror*, the *Morning Star* or even *Newsline* (the daily paper produced by the Workers Revolutionary Party). Second, most people are probably aware of the bias of the paper they read (although there is evidence that some readers of papers such as the *Sun* and the *Express* believe them to be Labour papers; this could suggest either that the bias is insidious and has become routinised to the point where readers do not notice it, or that the bias is ineffecive and that readers are immune to it). Third, people tend to read newspapers selectively; there is a healthy scepticism which holds that 'you cannot believe everything you read in the papers', and it seems that readers tend to ignore or shrug off opinions which do not accord with their own position. Finally, there is in much of Britain's press precious little news anyway, for in the so-called 'popular papers', presentation and analysis of domestic economic and political affairs tends to be brief while treatment of foreign affairs is generally derisory. Readers of newspapers such as the *Sun* and the *Daily Star* are likely to learn far more about the sacking of football managers, their latest bingo numbers, the week's special offers at Tescos and the bust measurements of 19-year-old beauties from Bognor than they are about parliamentary exchanges or the latest diplomatic moves in the Middle East. As a former head of the *Mirror* group once candidly observed: 'You have got to give the public what it wants . . . it is only the people who conduct newspapers and similar organisations who have any idea quite how indifferent, quite how stupid, quite how uninterested in education of any kind the great bulk of the British public are.'

In our view, the significance of the Press as an agency of social control lies not so much in what it says as in how it says it and what it does not say. Put another way, its importance derives, first from its selection as to what is to count as 'news', and second from the assumptions about the world which are reinforced (often unconsciously) through the way in which the 'news' which has been selected is presented and interpreted.

The selection of news is obviously crucial and reflects both tacit journalistic criteria of what constitutes a 'good story' and external constraints on the gathering of information. Criteria of a good story are, among other things, that it should be personalised (thus much of the treatment of politics, for example, revolves around what key political leaders say or do rather than around questions of policy), that it should be near to home (hence the remarkable lack of foreign news coverage in most papers), that it should be readily understandable in terms of familiar stereotypes and categories of thought (the machinations of city financial institutions are, for example, much less newsworthy than strikes in the car industry) and that it should be dramatic (such that unusual events of little significance tend to achieve greater prominence than recurring events of considerable significance – the 'man bites dog' syndrome). The emphasis on news as drama is particularly important since it tends to rule out reporting on 'everyday' aspects of economic and political life – another factory closure in the north-east, another sectarian murder in Northern Ireland – which may have a crucial bearing on people's lives but which do not readily lend themselves to the banner headlines which sell popular papers.

Reinforcing these selective tendencies are pressures from the environment in which the news media operate. The popular image of news gathering as investigative journalism is largely a myth, for all papers rely to a great extent on 'feeding' from agencies and from official sources. Much of the political news which appears in the papers, for example, is little more than repetition (sometimes word for word) of government press releases, official briefings, press conferences and carefully-managed 'leaks' from Whitehall. Of particular significance is the 'lobby system' which works on a 'you scratch my back and I'll scratch yours' principle. Ministers and their senior advisers issue non-attributable statements to lobby journalists who then write them up as if they were inside information achieved through diligent journalistic probing. Some journalists and editors have become worried about participation in the lobby briefings, for newspapers can easily become uncritical mouthpieces of government if they come to rely upon such a close and secretive relationship to fill their political pages. Two papers – the *Independent* and the *Guardian* – have boycotted the lobby for this reason.

When journalists do take a more active role than that of the government's ventriloquist's dummy, they find that material is difficult to dig up, that there are enormous constraints on what they are allowed to write (libel laws, contempt of court, D-notices, etc.), and even that transmission of copy may be hindered (as during the 1982 Falklands war when correspondents were often kept away from the fighting, had their dispatches censored and delayed and were sometimes unable even to get to a transmitter). 'All the news that's fit to print' thus all too often turns out to be very little news at all.

What is also crucial is the way in which this 'news' is reported. Just as there is a 'hidden curriculum' in the schools, so there is a 'hidden agenda' in the newspapers. News is presented through the use of a language which derives from a particular interpretive framework in which certain 'obvious' 'facts' about the world are taken as given. One example is the use of words such as 'militant' and 'moderate' to describe trade unionists and politicians. We are never explicitly told what these words mean (moderate by whose standards?), nor are we ever told that 'militancy' is a bad thing and that moderation is to be commended. We do not have to be told, for these are inherently evaluative words which are used in a matter-of-fact way in order to structure our reading of particular reports. When we are told that 'the militant miners' leader' has said one thing, or that a 'leading moderate in the Labour Party' has done another, we are being presented with 'facts' which are inextricably tied up with opinion. Nor is this solely a problem for the Left, for in 1989 leading Conservatives complained about the way the reactionary communist factions in Eastern Europe were being referred to as 'conservatives'. Some Conservatives were also unhappy about the way in which the new 'Community Charge' system for financing local government spending swiftly came to be referred to as a 'Poll Tax'. The words we use to describe the world – 'terrorist' or 'freedom fighter', 'invasion' or liberation', 'revolution' or 'coup', 'riot' or 'struggle' – themselves inform us about how to evaluate events. They function as cues which prompt us to classify new information as an example of this, or as typical of that, and in this way they make things intelligible and order our responses to them.

It is too crude to suggest that the papers tell us what to think, but they can be important in furnsihing us with the framework through which to make sense of what is going on. Men like Rupert Murdoch and Robert Maxwell do not impose their values on us, but they do have enormous power to influence the way we see things. It is in this sense that the Press can be seen as one of the 'soft' media of social control, for in presenting us with an image of social reality which is inevitably partial and one-sided, newspapers can effectively help reproduce a mainstream world-view while marginalising other perspectives.

The broadcasting media

The same is true of the broadcasing media. Television, in particular, is almost certainly more significant than the Press in this respect, for the degree of exposure to television is for most people greater than that to the newspapers, the impact of this exposure is also greater due to the power of visual images, and – most significantly of all – television and radio are seen as more 'trustworthy' and 'reliable' sources of news given the legal requirement that they maintain balance and impartiality. This faith is particulary marked in popular attitudes towards the BBC.

Ever since 1927, the BBC has been run as a public corporation by a Board of Governors who are appointed as 'trustees of the public interest' to shield public-service broadcasting from both commercial and political pressures. In theory, the Board of Governors *is* the BBC. They take responsibility for policy and for the oversight of management, and they assume a position of special significance in that they make the senior appointments to the permanent professional staff. By Royal Charter, the Board is accountable to Parliament, not to government or to a particular department of state, although it has faced the problem of trying to work out independently (as the Charter enjoins it to do) how it can best establish the accountability of the corporation. Inevitably, the Board has to display trust in the people who plan and make programmes, and the government has an interest in the material produced by the BBC. The relations between the Board of Governors, the professional and creative staff, and the government of the day are potentially fraught with problems. For the most part, however, conflict tends not to occur for reasons that bear on the nature of the Board and the organisation of programme making.

The Board itself, in spite of its independence, tends to be drawn from the ranks of the 'great and the good' and to mirror the predominance of the upper middle classes in the ranks of political life in elected and non-elected positions of power. Of the eighty-five governors who have served during the first 50 years of the BBC's history, fifty-six had a university education (forty at Oxford or Cambridge), and twenty were products of Eton, Harrow or Winchester. The political experience of Board members has come mainly from the House of Lords, although there have been nineteen former MPs, of whom eight were Labour. By convention, from 1956 one governor has had a trade union background, but in no sense can the Board be said to be representative of the population at large.

For their part, programme makers, in spite of the fact that they do enjoy an independence in that the government does not tell them what to do, nevertheless tend to produce programmes that do not seriously offend the views, still less the interests, of the Board or the government. This tends to be the case because what is acceptable is internalised, and potentially hostile reactions are anticipated and avoided in the interests of personal and organisational survival. Programme makers are socialised into an awareness of what will and will not 'go', and if they wish to get on the air (and stay on the air) then they 'choose' to operate within the confines of acceptability.

The Home Secretary has a power of veto over the output of both the BBC and independent television companies, but this has never been exercised. What happens instead is gentle (and sometimes not-so-gentle) pressure from politicians coupled with an acute awareness by producers themselves of the limits within which they are expected to work. During the 1980s, the Conservative Party and government became increasingly convinced that the BBC in particular was biased against them, and this led to a series of squabbles and put the relationship between the state and the broadcasters under considerable strain. In 1982 the government made clear its objections to BBC reporting of the Falklands conflict and admonished the *Newsnight* programme in particular for referring to 'British troops' rather than 'our troops'. In 1985, a programme profiling the lives of leaders of Sinn Fein and an extreme Unionist group was pulled from the schedules following government pressure on the BBC governors, and although the programme was later broadcast, ministers ended up banning the transmission of any interviews with Sinn Fein or IRA leaders on British television. In 1986 a programme dealing with official secrecy – the Zircon Affair – was stopped when Special Branch raided the television studios and took away the tapes. In the same year, the government complained bitterly about the BBC reporter, Kate Adie, when she covered the American bombing of Libya (the bombers had taken off from USAF bases in England with the backing of the British government). In 1989, a programme *Death on the Rock* ran into a storm of government protest when it claimed that three IRA bombers in

Gibraltar had been shot in cold blood by SAS men sent to track them down. And so it has gone on.

As with the Press, we are not suggesting that the broadcasting media directly shape people's beliefs, values and opinions, but rather that they help to establish one set of views as 'normal' and others as marginal. Paradoxically, perhaps, this tendency is reinforced by the legal need to ensure 'balance', for this has led the BBC and ITV to equate 'impartiality' with majority or middle-of-the-road opinion and to seek 'balance' in the safe middle ground of consensus politics. The broadcasting authorities could, of course, reply to this charge (and with some justification) that to provide equal air time for the views of communists (or indeed fascists) as for mainstream political party orthodoxy would be the epitome of imbalance since it would distort the balance of opinion in the country as a whole. In one sense this is true, but it raises familiar 'chicken and egg' problems, for it is at least plausible to suggest that one reason why mainstream opinion remains mainstream is precisely because it is treated as such in the nightly output of the broadcasting media.

This immediately raises a further related issue, and that is whether there is a discernible 'mainstream' political culture in Britain any more. As we have suggested throughout this chapter so far, the old certainties have been eroded and it is difficult to argue that in Britain today there is a single 'core' value system to which virtually everybody is committed. On most major issues, the nation often turns out to be deeply divided, in which case the search for balance in the middle ground is a recipe for bias. There is, to put it another way, an obvious danger that in seeking to express 'mainstream' values, the media actually express merely establishment values (a danger which is clearly exacerbated given the nature of recruitment into such bodies as the BBC). Be that as it may, it should be obvious that the political 'centre' (however that is identified) is no less a political and partial position than what the media themselves tend to designate as the political 'extremes'.

The question of bias and partiality goes deeper than this, however, for as with the Press, it is as much the form as the explicit content of output which has given rise to concern. Of particular importance here has been a series of studies of television news carried out by the Glasgow University Media Group since the mid-1970s. This, together with other similar research, has shown that television news is a remarkably homogeneous product across all channels and that its treatment of events such as industrial disputes consistently rests upon take-for-granted assumptions which turn out to be the assumptions of dominant groups in our society. Strikes, for example, are treated as irrational acts, usually provoked by a small number of 'militant' leaders, which disturb what is taken to be the 'normal' state of 'harmonious' joint endeavour by capital and labour. Their negative impact on customers and on the ailing British economy is emphasised, and this is brought out in the way in which representatives of the two sides to the dispute are interviewed. Strikers' leaders are invariably interviewed in the street or on the picket line and the tone of questioning is aggressive, while managers are sat in the calm of the television studio and are subjected to a passive line of interviewing in which they are invited and encouraged to spell out in eminently 'reasonable' language the negative implications of this latest stoppage for the future of the company and of the workers' jobs. Add to this the systematic message that strikes lie at the heart of Britain's economic problems, that wage rises are the cause of inflation, that workers have priced British industry our of world markets, together with the equally systematic exclusion of other items of economic news from any meaningful coveage all (for example the massive flow of capital overseas, the 'stoppages' caused by machine failure or by shortage of parts due to management miscalculation, and so on), and it is little wonder that so many workers in this country are prepared to believe that trade unions are the cause of the country's economic ills even though they go on to argue in the same breath that their own union has done precious little to safeguard their own living standards and working conditions.

To some extent, of course, bias is in the eye of the beholder. The series of books published by the Glasgow University Group has itself been questioned and criticised, and a new monitoring group has recently been set up by Right-wingers who are convinced that media bias operates in precisely the opposite direction to that identified in the Glasgow studies. This group's first target was the Radio Four *Today* programme whose presenter, Brian Redhead, was shown to have been more aggressive when interviewing Right-wingers than when interviewing those on the Left. The group also analysed BBC job advertisements and found that most are clustered in Left-wing newspapers (notably the *Guardian*) with the result that recruitment is likely to be skewed in favour of those with socialist sympathies.

Developments in the 1990s and beyond are set fundamentally to transform broadcasting in Britain. Following a special report on the financing of the BBC by the Peacock Committee in 1986, the government embarked on a legislative overhaul of the BBC, ITV and other broadcasting agencies with the intention of loosening state regulation and encouraging competition. While the BBC was to retain its licence fee, it was also encouraged to develop subscription as a long-term replacement basis of funding. A new authority was established to issue licenses for ITV and cable franchises, a fifth terrestial channel was authorised, and various cable and satellite broadcasting systems were recognised. This major shake-up of British broadcasting alarmed many in the industry, for while BBC buffs claimed that the Corporation would be driven 'down-market', the ITV companies anticipated that there would be insufficient advertising revenue to keep all the new independents afloat. Whatever else happens as a result of these reforms, however, it seems clear that the BBC/ITV duopoly has now been broken and that media output will be more diverse and less tightly regulated by government than before. Indeed, given that satellite channels like Rupert Murdoch's *Sky* are international in their content and their audience, it will be increasingly difficult for any goverment to specify what may or may not be shown on the nation's television screens. Most of the concern so far has been about European soft-porn being beamed at Britain, but more significant in the long run is likely to be European and American news and current affairs programmes which will almost certainly challenge some of the orthodoxies and preconceptions which tend to be reproduced uncritically by Britain's own broadcasters.

Like the Press, therefore, the broadcasting media are important in confirming certain values and beliefs as the norm and in relegating others to the sidelines. Precisely because socialisation is not a once and for all process which ends when we reach adulthood, socially accepted ways of thinking and acting have constantly to be reinforced through 'secondary' agencies of socialisation if they are to maintain their hold in a world which is in perpetual change. The media are today the most important institutions by means of which this process of reaffirmation may be accomplished. In this sense, the nine o'clock news has replaced the confessional as the major source of guidance on what to believe and how to live in the increasingly confused and confusing world of the late twentieth century.

Social work agencies

There is one final soft agency of control which must be mentioned before closing this section, and that is social work. Understood through the concerns of this chapter, social work stands on the borderline between 'soft' and 'hard' control agencies, for it is the first line of defence against those who in one way or another step out of line. The social worker, that is, steps in when the family, the schools and the media have failed.

In chapter 10, we discussed the view, common on the Left, that the welfare state can be understood as an agency of control and class domination. This is a view which in general we reject, for the historical causes of the growth in state welfare provision are too varied, and the beneficiaries of such provision too diverse, to permit of such a singular interpretation of the welfare state's role and function. However, there is one aspect of the welfare state where it useful to interpret state intervention in such terms, and that is the casework undertaken by various types of social workers and, of course, probation officers.

Now it is true that social work as a profession has undoubtedly been radicalised over the last 20 years, and more than any of the other agencies discussed in this chapter, local authority social-work departments contain many employees whose values run counter to those of dominant groups in our society. Nevertheless, it is also true that the *nature* of social work is such that, notwithstanding the views and opinions of those engaged in it, it identifies as 'deviant' those whose way of life fails to conform in some ways to standards laid down by the state, and then goes on to explain such deviancy as the outcome of individual pathology which must be 'treated'. In this way, it functions as an important control agency by identifying those who are not conforming in various ways and by prescribing methods of changing their behaviour.

One clear example of this is in the designation of 'problem families'. They are said to be those who, for reasons of personal inadequacy, cannot manage their money properly or cannot look after their homes properly, or cannot raise their children properly. Once identified by a social worker, a problem family may lose many of the social rights which most of us take for granted. Problem families find themselves re-housed in 'dumping' estates along with other problem cases; their privacy is invaded by social workers who come to look through their rent books, to inspect their children or to counsel them on how to spend their money; their children may forcibly be taken from them and placed in the 'care' of a state-run children's home or of state-approved foster parents who can manage their money properly, look after their homes properly and raise children properly.

Similar points have been made from time to time about other social-work client groups. It has been suggested, for example, that psychiatric social work similarly identifies non-conforming people, sticks a negative label onto them (in this case that of 'mental illness') and then uses this label to justify various state-enforced measures such as therapy or electric-shock treatment in an attempt to bring their behaviour more into line.

The power granted to social workers can be considerable, and the rights of their clients are all too easily ignored. This became clear in 1988 when the appointment of a new paedeatrician in Cleveland, Dr Marietta Higgs, resulted in a major upturn in the diagnosis of child sexual abuse. Using the controversial method of anal dilation to check for abuse, Dr Higgs found evidence of sexual malpractice in hundreds of children who had been referred to her for various unconnected reasons. Social workers and the police then removed these children from their parents, causing considerable upset and anguish on all sides, and it was only following tortuous legal proceedings that most of those involved were able to reclaim their children from the clutches of the state and to clear their names of the gross charges which had been made against them. Neither Dr Higgs nor Cleveland Social Services ever issued an apology, still less compensation, to those who had fallen foul of their sweeping powers.

As with other 'soft' agencies discussed above, social work has been criticised from both the Left and the Right. In the Right-wing view, social workers are attacked for their tendency to blame 'society' for the problems which clients have really brought upon themselves. In a speech in 1988, for example, Margaret Thatcher complained of the 'professional progressives among broadcasters, social workers and politicians who have created a fog of excuses in which the mugger and the burglar operate'. Seen in this way, social work rationalises and thereby excuses the bad behaviour of individuals.

In contrast, the Left tends to attack social work on precisely the opposite grounds! Left critics complain that social work is premissed on the assumption that problems experienced by individuals are individual problems and can thus be treated as such. Put another way, the essence of social work is that it individualises social problems and privatises public issues. The social problem of unemployment, poor housing and low pay thus becomes translated into the individual or family problem of an inability to manage money or a failure to bring up the children properly. Not only does this encourage the individual to look to his or her own personal character as the cause of his or her problem (in much the same way as selection in schools teaches children that failure is a result of their own intellectual disabilities), but it also casts the social worker in the role as helper, the client's friend. Children are forcibly placed into the care of the local authority for their own good and for the good of the family, even if the parents and children concerned 'cannot' see it that way; depressed housewives are incarcerated in mental institutions and subjected to psychiatric treatment for their own good even if they may suspect that the 'problem' has more to do with the domestic role which they are expected to play; and so on.

Both the Right-wing and Left-wing critiques of social work have some pertinence. The training of social workers can lead to an excessive emphasis on social causation to the neglect of individual responsibility, but equally the practice of social work does often entail the treatment of socially-generated problems at an individual level. Critics from both Left and Right may also be justified in expressing fears about the power invested in social workers, for the power to take children away from their parents or to commit adults to mental institutions is one which could be chilling if not very carefully exercised and regulated. None of this is to deny that children may sometimes 'objectively' benefit by being removed from their home environment (especially where domestic violence is rife), nor that people may respond to anti-depressant drugs or psychoanalysis, nor even that social workers may genuinely have the best interests (as they define them) of their clients at heart. What we are suggesting, however, is that social work also functions as an agency of social control which uses the power of the state to intervene in people's lives where behaviour is deemed to fall short of, and thus in some way to threaten, certain standards which the state itself identifies as acceptable. Seen in this light, social work represents the soft face of the coercive state.

The 'Iron Fist': Organising Coercion

Law and order has often figured centrally as an issue in British politics. Whether or not their beliefs are justified by the evidence, significant sections of the electorate seem to be convinced that crime is on the increase, that too many offenders are getting away with their crimes, that those who are apprehended often receive laughably lenient punishments, and that government should 'do something about it'.

Doing something about it normally entails some strengthening of police numbers, police powers, or both, and both strategies were explicitly pursued by the Thatcher governments of the 1980s. There is, however, more to 'law and order' than simply policing, for behind the police stand the courts, the judges, the probation officers, the prisons and, ultimately, the military and the security services, all of which represent the coercive instruments available to the modern state as the means for maintaining order and enforcing law.

From old to new policing

The rules of eighteenth-century England cherished the death sentence and supported a system of criminal law crudely but effectively based on terror. The number of capital statutes grew from about 50 to over 200 between years 1688 and 1820 and almost all of them concerned offences against the established division of property. In these times the suppression of crime was still a simple community affair. 'Civic responsibility' was a sufficient spur to action for the apprehension and punishment of offenders. There was little call for specialised agents and facilities. True, the office of constable was established in the late thirteenth century, but officials went without pay and their duties were to be discharged out of civic rather than pecuniary motives.

With the decline of feudalism, so the informal and voluntary system of social control through family, church, and community became increasingly problematic. Public spirit was no longer enough. Private interests came to replace social obligations as the mainspring of the control system. Fear and greed went hand in hand. The fear of capital punishment and transportation was designed to hold potential wrongdoers in check, whilst greed was appealed to through a network of incentives and rewards in a way which called into being a privately organised system of crime control. Policing was conducted for profit. Constables were able to demand rewards and portions of recovered goods in exchange for their services, and imprisonment provided an opportunity for private gain as fees were paid to those who provided a crude lock-up. The wealthy paid gamekeepers to protect their property and middle-class traders formed voluntary protection societies. These private and ill-organised solutions were always of limited effectiveness unless solidly buttressed by the soft agencies of control. The system was poorly co-ordinated, irrational and inefficient, and because those enforcing the law were paid by results there was every incentive for them to instigate crime just as it made good sense for them to sell to prisoners the chance to escape.

As the market system developed and as trade grew so a stable public order became a crucial prerequisite for further development and yet private solutions were of limited value in securing this. The use of the army was inevitable at moments of major unrest. However, this too was problematic. The army was not popular in the late eighteenth century and neither the officers nor the men liked riot duty; it took time to get a detachment of troops to a riot area and once there they had very limited local knowledge; and, more fundamentally, the fact that army training was mechanistic and geared to the fighting of set-piece battles meant that the military lacked any capacity to develop a flexible response geared to the control of unarmed protesters but instead engaged in an unlimited offensive. The vicious military control of crowds reached a climax in August 1819 when local yeomanry on horseback killed eleven people and injured several hundred more in the Peterloo massacre. It was some kind of turning point in the control of public order. The moral consensus of the nation outlawed the riding down of an unarmed crowd and so there was the need to create a system of 'new policing' that would secure public order and hold down the 'dangerous classes', *and* solve the related problem of crime and criminality all of which was increasingly beyond the capacity of the soft agencies of family, church and community and the informality of the 'old policing' system based on parish constables and justices of the peace.

The country's first public professional police force was founded in 1829 when Sir Robert Peel persuaded the unreformed House of Commons to set up the Metropolitan Police for London. The County and Borough Police Act, 1856 made the recruitment of a regular police force obligatory, and by 1860 there were some 259 separate forces in England and Wales. So, instead of the old combination of low-profile policing in ordinary times mixed with brutal suppression by the military in extraordinary ones, the police were to establish a regime of permanent surveillance attempting to win consent and public acceptance for their controlling work through tact, discretion, benevolent prevention, and the minimum use of unarmed force.

Establishing the police as bureaucratic organisations of permanently employed professionals relieved the ordinary citizen of the need to perform police duties (and the urban middle classes were never keen on this); made the all-or-nothing use of the military in internal peace-keeping less necessary; and drew attacks onto the police so that they served as buffers insulating the wealthy from the more direct threats of popular violence for change. Professional policing and the Rule of Law together created a situation in which constitutional authority and law were seemingly separated from the reality of social and economic dominance. Ideas developed (and came to assume a position of dominating orthodoxy) suggesting that the law was neutral and in the public interest, and that the police were simple servants of the community as a whole.

In Chapter 6 we pointed out that the police have the task of preserving peace and public order, and the task of preventing crime and trying to catch those who break the criminal law. In that chapter we only dealt with the role of the police with respect to crime, but when we turn to the public order role of the police then the social and political aspect of their work is more keenly revealed – at least in times of political unrest. In periods of relative economic prosperity, when societal consensus and cohesion may more easily be attained, the need for the rough exercise of the public order function does not push to the fore and it is hard even to 'see' the police preserving the peace. However, when the consensus cracks; when the soft agencies of control fail to mobilise support and control behaviour; and when interests and groups are pushing for social change against established interests, then politics quickly burst outside of Parliament and onto the streets. In this kind of situation the police's public order role pushes to the fore (and crime prevention takes a backseat) and preserving the peace has a hard political edge to it that involves the police in containing group pressures from below. The more privileged sections of society rarely, if ever, take to the politics of the streets; they do not pose a threat to the prevailing social order (why on earth should they when they benefit from it?); and so they just do not come up against the police in their public order role. But where there is a strike, there are also the police and behind the police are laws to assist them in their work. Where blacks and youth gather on street corners, there are also the police backed up by laws giving them the right to 'stop and search'. And where there are demonstrations against nuclear weapons, there are also the police, police photographers, and the special branch who have a brief to combat 'subversion' which takes them way beyond the policing of the unlawful alone since the Home Secretary defined subversion in 1978 as 'activities which threatened the safety and well-being of the state, and are intended to undermine or overthrow parliamentary democracy by political, industrial or violent means'. Far from the police being outside of politics, the exercise of their public order function means that they are always at the sharp end constraining social and political change. Indeed, the ex-Commissioner of the Metropolitan Police, in his book *Policing a Perplexed Society*, firmly placed the role of the police in the context of opposing socialism: 'the police are very much on their own in attempting to preserve order in an increasingly turbulent society in which socialist philosophy has changed from raising standards of the poor and deprived to reducing the standards of the wealthy, the skilled and the deserving to the lowest common denominator.' The Chief Constable of Greater Manchester, James Anderton, put the purely criminal aspect of police work firmly in its place when he told a *Question Time* audience in 1979:

I think that from a police point of view . . . the basic crimes such as theft, burglary, even violent crime, will not be the predominant police feature. What will be the matter of the greatest concern to me will be the covert, and ultimately overt, attempts to overthrow democracy, to subvert the authority of the state and, in fact, to involve themselves in acts of sedition designed to destroy our parliamentary system and the democratic government of this country.

The police, then, are not just a thin blue line against (and occasionally in) crime, since they are also against a different kind of political order as well: they are at the hard front line acting as guardians of the social order as a whole. We will attend to the problem of policing the eighties and the drift into a law-and-order society shortly, but for the moment we need to attend to the significance of law itself. Law is central to the work of the police (even though they may break it) and it is also central to the maintenance of particular patterns of 'proper' behaviour since the law defines certain types of acts as illegal and prescribes the penalties which will be exacted against those found guilty of such acts.

The law

Law is important, but it is not equally important in all societies. In simple societies, where custom and traditional norms are well-established, there is little need for a systematised and officially enforced code of law to order relations and regulate behaviour in predictable ways. As societies become more complex and subject to change and conflict, and as custom and tradition decline in importance, so law comes to assume a place of central significance offering a kind of social regulation distinct from that provided by religious taboos, established conventions, or naked violence and arbitrary power. Social regulation under capitalism is typically conducted through law and it is not difficult to see that the law of property and the law of contract are basic to the effective and smooth functioning of this particular economic system.

1 Law, then, guarantees and protects existing productive relationships and ways of distributing resources and serves as some kind of guarantor of 'business as usual'. Law also fulfils other functions.
2 In seeking to establish certain simple fundamental rules for living together it assumes a peace-keeping and social harmonising function.
3 In providing principles and procedures for settling conflicts between individuals and groups its fulfils a conflict resolution function.
4 Law also criminalises certain kinds of social action and although it is invariably presented as neutral and remote from particular interests, in reality it bears very unevenly on different interests. The law may forbid rich and poor alike from stealing bread, and it may forbid both employers and workers from engaging in certain kinds of picketing in the furtherance of an industrial dispute, but in reality it is not difficult to appreciate the true significance of laws of this kind.
5 Law is also important because it mobilises symbols and encourages the formation of popular views about, for example, the 'necessity' for private property and the problem of mugging (and its connection to black youth), and this is crucial because all day-to-day politics occurs within the constraining context of these views.
6 Law is a crucial arena for political struggle because politics often revolve around the claim for rights, and because rights really need to be entrenched

in law to be secure. Indeed, much statute law 'made' by parliament is developed in response to organised pressures and is designed to change and replace the judge-made common law that is often just the embellished codification of old customs and traditional ways of doing things.
7 Finally, and of particular importance in this chapter, we should not forget that law is increasingly becoming a primary mechanism of social control or social order.

The role of law is analysed very differently in different political traditions. As we saw in chapter 8, the liberal tradition is wary of arbitrary power and has therefore come to insist on the principle of 'The Rule of Law'. This principle asserts that all citizens are subject to the same laws without exceptions or favours, and that no law in a liberal order should draw distinctions between different categories of people. When the state upholds the law, it is therefore acting on behalf of all of us, for without clear and universal rules governing the relations between us, there could be no social order and no individual security.

The Marxist tradition has seen things very differently. In chapter 7 we saw that Marxists tend to view law in capitalist society as but an instrument of the needs and will of the capitalist class. Law and state are run together, and both are tied down to the all-determining economic base and to the power of the capitalist class in the economy. The capitalist class is seen as in control of the state; the state makes laws; and so laws inevitably reflect the interest of the economically dominant class. From this kind of pessimistic determinism there is no possibility of a progressive politics of law and little significance is attached to struggle in the legal field because the nature of the law is crisply determined by the need to maintain the system.

Although this perspective is too general to enable us to analyse the nature of law in Britain, it does at least thrust to the fore the need for us to see law in the context of the larger society and in the context of competing interests struggling for advantage through the entrenchment of political victories in the solidity of law itself. In fact, we do not see it as possible to provide a general theory of law, but we can say that law needs to be seen as an arena of struggle and that the nature of particular laws is not predetermined according to the narrow controlling interests of dominant classes but is some kind of register of the balance of competing interests around issues in question. Gains and losses can, therefore, be made by all contending interests, and legislation consolidating the rights of workers to combine in unions or reducing the length of the working day represents a positive gain for labour. Some laws, then, favour specific classes; some laws cut across class boundaries and protect the basic conditions of existence for all individuals; and some laws have little or nothing to do with class and class struggles. We cannot escape the fact that law is a complex, contradictory, and ambiguous phenomenon.

E.P. Thompson is an English Marxist historian who has attempted to tease out the ambiguities surrounding law and policing. In his analysis of law in eighteenth-century England he recognised that law did organise class relations to the advantage of the rulers, but at the same time the law *also* mediated those relations through the legal forms and the entrenchment of civil liberties which imposed, again and again, inhibitions upon the actions of the rulers. In this sense, Thompson argues that the Rule of Law does matter; is not just a legitimating ideology and a mask for class power; and does actually inhibit, curb, and check the exercise of arbitrary power and direct unmediated force to the advantage of those subject to rule. More than this, any realistic account of law needs to recognise that there is a world of difference between law in the books and law in action. Law needs to be enforced to impact on behaviour and as we saw in chapter 6 the police exercise discretion and discriminate in the way in which particular laws are enforced over particular groups and individuals. Indeed, police discretion has been widened in recent years. Following the 1984 Police and Criminal Evidence Act and the 1986 Public Order Act, police officers can stop and search pedestrians, permit or prohibit public speeches, newspaper selling, money collecting or busking, move pickets, redirect or prohibit marches and disperse gatherings, all at their own discretion. In 1984, during the miners' strike, a group of Kent miners driving to Nottingham was intercepted and turned back at the Blackwall Tunnel east of London by police who feared a possible breach of the peace. In Britain we enjoy the crucial civil rights of free speech, freedom of assembly, freedom to travel and freedom to publish, but all of these liberties are exercised at the discretion of the Chief Constables.

Although it is important to see law as a political battleground fought over by different interests, it is also necessary to recognise that the *context* of struggle has an impact on the outcome. The extension of the franchise mattered and did something to change the context of law-making. After the Second World War the commitment to full employment reflected the wishes of ordinary people *and* further strengthened the economic and political hand of the trade unions in law-making. Much legislation through to the 1970s has to be regarded as some kind of grudging gain for many disadvantaged and discriminated groups in society. Landlord-and-tenant law challenged the private landlords' freedom to dictate the terms on which property was let, and set rent levels, provided for security of tenure, and made it a criminal offence for a landlord to evict a tenant unlawfully; Race Relations law sought to protect racial minorities from discrimination in the fields of housing and employment; women secured the right to legal abortions and the establishment of the Equal Opportunities Commission sought to counter discrimination against them in the field of employment; the law came to allow consenting adults to engage in their preferred sexual behaviour in private so freeing homosexuals over the age of 21 from the restraint of the law; the legislative floor of rights for the individual worker was radically extended by the Employment Protection Act 1975; and so on and so on across a swathe of concerns.

Through the sixties and seventies, these and other changes in the law expressed and reinforced a changed balance of power in British society together with a new spirit of 'permissiveness' in British culture. Organised labour made advances at the expense of capital, just as tenants made gains at the expense of landlords. At the same time, special interests such as the ethnic minorities and gays mobilised the law to defend themselves against the tyranny of the majority. Put another way, the moral pluralism to which we referred earlier in this chapter not only chipped away at the homogeneity of the 'soft' agencies like the schools, but also came to be represented in the enactment of new laws. In the eighties, however, the balance of power in British society shifted again, and there was something of a traditionalist backlash against permissiveness and moral pluralism. This, coupled with a dramatic rise in unemployment in the early part of the decade and evidence of growing inequality throughout these years, seemed to create new fissures and a deepening sense of social polarisation. And as trade unionists, young west Indians, disaffected white youths and others with real or imagined grievances came out onto the streets, so there they confronted an increasingly militarised police force wielding new discretionery powers and displaying a new weaponry of riot shields, video cameras and water cannon. In the 1980s, policing emerged as a problem.

Policing in the Thatcher years

In theory, we have a system of policing by consent by an unarmed force that is close to the people. The police are seen as bound by law and as outside of politics. When people talk of Britain as having the best police in the world then this is the image in their minds backed up by a smiling bobby on his beat. In fact, this characterisation has always been somewhat at odds with the reality of policing for, as we saw in chapter 6, the police are only partly bound by law and they are in politics. Moreover, a steady trend to an increasingly centralised force backed up by sophisticated hardware had taken police officers off the streets and made them more remote. In the more recent past, however, a series of developments has made for a crisis in policing, and practice has moved in ways very sharply at odds with the traditional picture.

The crisis of policing in terms of their success, image, the relationship to the public, has been made up of a number of components. First, there has been the running sore of police corruption. Between 1969 and 1972, a score of London detectives went to prison, hundreds more left the force in disgrace, and the old CID hierarchy was savagely restructured. We are not just dealing with a few cases of individual police malpractice, but with an ethic of detective work that prevailed among wide sections of the London CID. The issue, then, was about more than rotten apples, and the problem was not confined to London alone.

Second, there is the problem of police complaints (discussed in chapter 6) and the related problem of police violence. For example, over the period

1970–9, 143 of the 245 deaths in police custody were from other than natural causes. A growing chorus of complaint about police violence came to a head in 1990 when four Irish people who had been convicted of bombing a pub in Guildford in 1974 had their convictions quashed when Appeal judges accepted that evidence against them had been fabricated and that their confessions had been beaten out of them following their arrest. By the end of the eighties, public confidence in the integrity and reliability of the police was lower than it had been for many years. The British Social Attitudes Survey of 1988 found that only 11 per cent of the population always trusts the police not to 'bend the rules' in order to secure a conviction (the same proportion as those saying they never trust them). One-third of the public only trusts the police 'some of the time' – and these results were reported *before* the Guildford case came to light.

Third, the police have not been conspicuously successful in dealing with crime. Any strategy of deterrence would seem to have failed given that the crime rate has grown consistently since the war. In the 1930s, around 350 notifiable offences were recorded per one hundred thousand population; in 1957 this figure had risen to 1,283 per hundred thousand; and by 1986 it stood at a staggering 7,650. Nor do the statistics on detection read any better, for the overall 'clear-up rate' stood at 32 per cent of all crimes reported in 1986, as compared with 45 per cent just twelve years earlier. The likelihood of the police apprehending someone who burgles your house is just 22 per cent, and the probability that you will get your property back is even lower than that.

Fourth, the police have increasingly been drawn into physical confrontation with demonstrators and rioters and this has only exacerbated public unease about their role. Bloody rioting in inner-city areas like Brixton and Toxteth in 1981 and again in 1985; a mob murder of a police officer in Tottenham in 1985; pitched battles with striking miners during the 1984/5 strike (for example, at the Orgreave Colliery in 1984 when 1,700 police officers fought hand-to-hand with an equivalent number of pickets) and with print workers at Grunwick in 1977 and at Wapping in 1986/7; running battles with football hooligans in football grounds (as in the televised battle at Millwall in 1985) and in the streets outside them; the desperate attempt to contain widespread disorder and looting in central London during a mass anti-Poll Tax demonstration in 1990; these are the images of contemporary policing, and they bear little in common with the comforting and consensual picture painted by the familiar 1950s television series *Dixon of Dock Green*. Sometimes – as at St Paul's in Bristol in 1980 – they have been unable to contain situations and have withdrawn, effectively ceeding 'victory' to rioters, looters and law-breakers. At other times – the attack on the hippy convoy at Stonehenge in 1985, for example – they have been accused of overreacting, of using excessive force, and of fanning trouble rather than averting it. But at all times, engagement in such bloody and violent clashes has only served to frighten respectable society while alienating the disaffected fringes.

These four factors – corruption, dishonesty, failure to clear up crime and growing involvement in military-style public order operations – have combined to change the image and pattern of policing in Britain. To some extent at least, policing by consent has given way to policing by coercion and confrontation. Preventive policing by the patrolling bobby has been replaced by reactive, 'fire brigade', policing – by a system of quick co-ordinated response to reported incidents that relies on the technological cop in which the car, the radio, the computer dominate the police scene. The use of computerised command and control systems dates from 1972 with the Home Office assuming a co-ordinating role of great importance. During the 1970s, the police brought the application of scientific knowledge to many different aspects of their work. This included the use of closed-circuit television; the creation of specialist Technical Support Units; the use of helicopters for surveillance; and the back-up provided by the Police National Computer at Hendon that in addition to filing away the 23.25 million adults registered as keepers and owners of vehicles also contains an undisclosed amount of political intelligence. At a centre in London, the facility exists to tap one thousand different telephones all at the same time, and the NCCL believes that there is strong evidence that phones are tapped for political as well as criminal intelligence purposes (for example, during the 1984/5 miners' strike).

As back-up to the 'quick response' system provided by computerised command and control, most police forces now have specialist units dealing with specific categories of crime. These include special squads for drugs, robberies, fraud, obscene publications, terrorism, firearms, and public order. As regards the last of these, 30 out of the 43 forces in England and Wales now have special public order squads consisting of specially-trained officers equipped with shields, helmets and para-military uniforms who can be transported swiftly whenever trouble breaks out. The best-known squad was probably the Metropolitan Police's Special Patrol Group which saw action at a series of celebrated clashes including the 1974 Red Lion Square demonstration (when a student died), the Grunwick picketing in 1977, the Southall anti-National Front march in 1979 (when another demonstrator died) and the Brixton riots of 1981. The Scarman report on the 1981 riots was critical of the role played by the SPG, and it was eventually disbanded in 1987 but it was replaced by eight 'Territorial Support Groups'. Politicians may debate whether or not Britain should have a 'third force' standing between the army and the regular police, but in practice this has already happened. As long ago as 1981 it was estimated that there were at least 11,000 specially-trained riot police in Britain.

Nor can the British police any longer be viewed as an unarmed force. First, some 12,000 rank-and-file officers are now trained in the use of firearms, and all newly recruited police officers receive firearms 'familiarisation' training. Second, many forces have formed Firearms Support Units as specialist firearms squads. The police are reluctant to talk about guns, but to put this development of practice into perspective we should remember that between 1980 and 1985 the police in England and Wales only fired their guns on 40 occasions resulting in two deaths and fourteen injuries (although this was a marked increase in the number of shooting incidents – shots were only fired on 20 occasions between 1970 and 1979.) The weapons held by the police go beyond truncheons and guns, however, as since the mid-1960s every police force has maintained stocks of CS gas. This gas has been used extensively in Northern Ireland since 1969 (over the period 1970–5 some 5,359 cartridges and 22,602 grenades were fired) and was used to control the Toxteth riots in Liverpool in 1981 in defiance of manufacturers instructions and at a cost of four serious injuries. In the immediate aftermath of the summer of riots in 1981, the government made the provision of new anti-riot weapons a top priority including the provision of CS gas, rubber bullets, and water cannon wherever the police wished to employ them. Merseyside's Chief Constable, Ken Oxford, said that he would be reluctant to use water cannon but he would like armoured personnel carriers.

In addition to these developments with respect to the public police, we also need to attend to the developing role of the private police and to the role of the military in matters of internal security.

In chapter 6 we pointed out that in 1971 there were some 105,000 private police in the whole of the United Kingdom. Securicor by itself accounted for more than 20,000 of these. In effect, boring tasks, like enforcing parking restrictions or searching hand baggage at airports have been hived off to traffic wardens and private firms, and dangerous jobs like guarding bank shipments have been hived off to private security firms. An old-boy network ensures 'co-operation' between the public police and ex-colleagues in the private sector with the exchange of information and the leakage of confidential official records to those prepared to pay the going rate.

The role of the army in matters of internal order and security is a complicated matter that has been subject to change over the years *and* to mystification as to the true extent of its involvement. Earlier in this chapter, when we dealt with the development of the police force, we saw that prior to the formation of modern forces in the nineteenth century the army was regularly called in to quell mob disorders. Since that time, however, the police have supposedly been in sole control. In fact, between 1910 and 1914, and 1918 and 1926, military interest and involvement in civil order generally and industrial unrest in particular grew steadily in intensity. To a large extent the military came not only to supplement but almost to supersede the role of the police in these matters. Having said that, between 1926 and 1970, the police reasserted themselves and regained overall control – thanks partly to the process of militarisation and professionalisation within the regular police force instigated in 1919. Of course, the military were not entirely absent from the domestic scene in this period (some 10,000 troops were used to discharge ships during the 1945 dock strike), but after the Second World War the army was preoccupied with anti-colonialist struggles overseas and the long post-war boom of the fifties and sixties did not push public order questions to the fore at home. The demise of Britain as a world power and the loss of Empire, and the problem of disorder at home (manifested most forcefully in the onset of the 'troubles' in Northern Ireland in 1969) encouraged the military to see a new role for themselves geared to subversion and insurgency in Britain. Brigadier Frank Kitson wrote *Low Intensity Operations* in 1971 specifically to draw attention to the steps that needed to be taken 'in order to make the army ready to deal with subversion, insurrection, and peace-keeping operations during the second half of the 1970s'. Moreover, Kitson made it clear that he did not see the army's role in these matters confined to Northern Ireland alone since 'there are other potential trouble spots within the UK which might involve the army in operations of a sort against political extremists who are prepared to resort to a considerable degree of violence to achieve their ends'. In a speech in 1980, 'The place of the British army in public order', General Sir Edwin Bramall, the head of the army, made it clear that 'the police will never have to turn in vain to us for help'. By now most infantry units have served for a tour of duty in Northern Ireland. In 1974, the army *and* the police jointly occupied London airport and the surroundings areas in four successive exercises, and in August 1978 they carried out a similar operation. The army has also come to assume a substantial and significant role in industrial disputes: in 1970 they were used in the Tower Hamlets refuse collection strike; in 1973 they were used in a fire service strike in Glasgow and in that city again in 1975 to cope with a refuse collection strike; they provided fire-fighting facilities during the fire service strike of 1977–8; they have guarded prisoners during industrial action by prison warders in 1980; and they have staffed ambulances during a period of industrial action by ambulance crews in 1989/90. Given these developments in military strike breaking it was hardly surprising that the Ministry of Defence sought to change the Queen's Regulations in 1978 so as to legitimate the use of troops in national strikes in a way that gave the military powers beyond those intended by Parliament when it passed the Emergency Powers Act, 1964. In fact, the increasing centrality of the military and the private police in matters of order and security today takes us back to the situation of the eighteenth century when the forces of the public police were backed up by these agencies precisely because the public police could not cope.

Many of these 'hard' policing developments have occurred beneath the skin of public debate in response to the 'need' for an iron fist in troubled times. They have, however, been buttressed in law by the Police and Criminal Evidence Act, 1984 which extended police powers in such matters as stop and search; arrest; searches of bodies, houses, and workplaces; detention; fingerprinting; and so on. Now, many of these developments do little to respond to that aspect of the police crisis that bears on the problem of public confidence and support, and so it is no real surprise that much publicity has been given to the virtues of reinvigorating traditional 'community policing – of putting bobbies back onto the beat in a preventive role.

One aspect of this move to community policing was the launch in 1983 of the Neighbourhood Watch schemes of which there are now around 30,000 nationwide. Some Chief Constables and police committees have also tried to divert extra resources into foot patrols and local involvement in school visits and the like. Community policing, though, is generally unexciting and very often unrewarding work, and any small advances that it does achieve can swiftly be reversed by just one well-publicised incident of a police 'frame-up' or an over-zealous drugs squad raid.

For Marxist writers like Stuart Hall, the changes in policing over recent years add up to a drift into what he calls a 'law-and-order' society. He believes that the economic liberalism of the Thatcher years in some senses *required* a toughening up of the repressive aspects of the state's role in order to manage the social fall-out of rising unemployment and growing class polarisation. The state may well be doing *less* in the 'modern' fields of economic management and welfare provision but it is being forced to do *more* in the 'traditional' areas of state activity. It is no coincidence that attempts are being made to cut back on welfare spending at the same time as funding is willingly increased for the police and for the building of prisons. If the market is to be free then the people need to be disciplined in its support, not just through the rigours of unemployment in the market itself, but through the full force of the law as well.

For Conservatives, by contrast, the growing signs of disorder and social breakdown during the 1980s were to be explained as the products of the per- missiveness and social deregulation of earlier years. They saw the riots and violence as evidence of the weakness of the family and the lack of tradi- tional discipline in the home and the school. In a speech in 1979, Margaret Thatcher equated the 'vandals on the picket lines' with 'the muggers in our streets', arguing that both were expressing the same sentiments – 'We want our demands met or else.' The refashioning of public morality would take a long time, and in the meanwhile it would fall to the police to hold the line against the anti-social fringe elements who were willing to challenge the law in pursuit of selfish gain.

Conclusion: a Crisis of Legitimation?

We have seen that the traditional soft agencies of social control – the family, the Church and the local community – have to some extent been weakened over the years while the newer agencies which have developed to replace or complement them are generally not as powerful in their influence over the way people think and behave. Nor does their combined influence necessarily always run in the same direction. And internally, the existence of radical teachers, socialist social workers and left-wing journalists means that these newer agencies are never fully reliable in the way that the Church of old was, for the growing numbers of people who are 'in and against the state' poses a constant potential threat of subversion on a small or a grand scale.

When an economy is growing, legitimation by means of soft control agencies is unlikely to be a major problem because in a situation of expansion and rising general levels of affluence, a capitalist system will, in a sense, look after its own legitimation with little help from government, for it will be *seen* to be working. People have more money in their pockets, the shops are full of the latest consumer goods which many people can realistically aspire to buy, home ownership (which is often thought to have a conservatising influence) is expanded, and although people may feel that there is something missing in their lives, and that a new car, a dishwasher and home video do not entirely compensate for this, they are unlikely to begin fundamentally questioning whether the system in which they live is the most appropriate to their needs.

When the economy slumps, as it did in Britain in the late seventies and early eighties, all this changes. Rising popular material aspirations can no longer be met which means that some attempt has to be made to justify the system, even though it is no longer producing the goods. In this situation, the state's role in securing legitimation becomes central, and if the soft agencies begin to fail, then the more coercive agencies such as the police and the army will come into prominence.

The argument that economic problems exacerbate legitimation problems is one that became familiar in both New Left and New Right thinking from the 1970s onwards. While the Left saw the worsening recession as a potential trigger for a radical break from the status quo, the Right saw in it a dangerous threat requiring a firm and steadfast response.

The reasoning of the Left was best revealed in a book written in the mid-1970s by a German Marxist, Jürgen Habermas, and entitled *Legitimation Crisis*. The book is a dense and complex piece of writing, but the essence of its argument is that advanced capitalist societies such as Britain suffer from four related tendencies towards crisis and breakdown.

1 A tendency towards economic crisis – a tendency which became ever more apparent in Britain from the mid-1970s onwards.

2 The tendency to what Habermas termed a 'rationality crisis', or an inability to find the means for bringing about desired objectives. What he meant by this was that governments in capitalist societies seek to support economic growth yet do not control the means for achieving this goal since control over investment is generally in private hands. As we saw in chapter 9, worsening economic problems thus tend to provoke ever-more frantic political responses, none of which succeeds in turning the economy around.

3 This tendency, which emerges as a result of such governmental failures, is the development of a 'legitimation crisis'. Thus Habermas argues that intervention in the economy by the state politicises the operation of the market and raises popular expectations. Whereas in the nineteenth century people tended to accept slumps and recessions as in some way natural and unavoid-

able, today they look to government to manage the economy in such a way that dramatic economic downturns are avoided, or at least to make provision through welfare support, job creation and so on for those who are hit by them. If, however, government lacks the tools to manage the economy, then it will fail to fulfil the expectations which people have of it. This then creates a situation in which mass loyalty to the state, the government and the capitalist system itself may easily be undermined.

4 The final tendency to crisis involves the development of a 'crisis of motivation' in which the erosion of legitimacy leads people to question traditional values, re-examine conventional ideologies and reject ways of life which have hitherto been taken as 'normal'. When and if crisis reaches this fourth level, then consensus in society has finally broken down and all that remains for securing the future of the state and the capitalist system is the explicit use of force.

There is much in Habermas's thesis which makes sense and which strikes a familiar chord in the context of recent British government and society. Certainly we would agree with him that the root cause of legitimation problems is economic, and that the deeper the economic difficulties, the more strain we should expect to be placed on both traditional and newer agencies of socialization and legitimation.

Yet having said that, it does not seem to have been the case that the country's recurring economic weaknesses and successive governments' failures to rectify them has resulted in a real crisis of legitimation or motivation. In order to understand why this is, we need to consider the response of the New Right to the growing threat of social breakdown from the mid-1970s onwards.

We saw in the previous two chapters that Thatcherism was much more than simply an economic doctrine. Viewed against Habermas's four crisis tendencies, it is now apparent that Thatcherism was in effect a fresh assault, not only on economic problems, but on rationality, legitimation and motivation problems as well.

The New Right tackled the problem of motivation by attempting to reassert traditional 'Victorian' values. Of particular importance here was the Falklands war in 1982, for this provided the opportunity for mobilising all the nationalistic and jingoistic sentiments which had been laid down in the popular consciousness during the age of Empire but which had to some extent lain dormant during the post-war years when the Empire had been lost, military expeditions (notably Suez in 1956) had ended in farce and Britain had been consigned to a walk-on-role in the theatre of world affairs. Coupled with the Falklands hysteria (ably whipped up by most of the popular press) went a new emphasis on traditional values stressing the family, individual self-help and self-reliance and discipline, all of which was contrasted with the shallow trendiness of permissiveness and the sloppy and easy assumption that the world owed you a living. Tendencies to motivation crisis, in other words, were countered by dusting off the well-worn and trusted values of a by-gone age in the hope that the classes which had embraced them once would readily embrace them again.

The assault on the tendency to legitimation crisis followed from this. Habermas, it will be recalled, saw a crisis of legitimation as the product of a situation in which people have been led to expect effective resolution of problems by government at a time when government actually fails to carry this off. The Thatcher governments' answer to this was to tell people that the problems from which they were suffering were problems of their own making and that they should look to themselves rather than to government for their solution. Government, we were told time and again, could actually do very little. If people were losing their jobs, this was because they had driven up wages to such a point that they had priced themselves out of a job. If British manufacturing was collapsing, this was because people were not working hard enough to compete with the industrious Germans, Japanese, South Koreans and the rest. If the welfare state was crumbling, this was because for years the country had been taking more out of the economy than it had been putting in and the day of reckoning had to come sooner or later. The same message was proclaimed loud and long: there is no point in blaming government (still less capitalism), the answer lay in the people themselves.

This denial of responsibility was then carried over into the New Right's response to tendencies to rationality crisis, for rather than trying to find new ways in which the economy could be managed, the government claimed that it had been precisely these attempts in the past which had prevented the capitalist system from functioning properly. From now on, government would step aside and let market forces do the job which they are so good at. There was, we were told, no alternative to this, for, as every housewife knows, you cannot spend more than you earn; thus a government cannot spend its way out of slump.

The problem with all this, of course, was that sooner or later the economy would have to show some signs of recovery and unemployment would have to start going down. As we saw in chapter 9, it did seem for a brief period in the mid-eighties that the government had achieved such a recovery, for both unemployment and inflation fell quite dramatically while growth rates rose to four per cent, outstripping all of Britain's major industrial competitors. By 1990, however, the economy was back into deep problems with record interest rates, a massive deficit on the balance of payments and rising unemployment. This being the case, the government's juggling of motivation, legitimation and rationality problems could not be expected to continue indefinitely, for the fundamental economic problems which lay at the heart of the other three crisis tendencies would eventually re-emerge. The unemployed person, can after all, get on a bike to look for work (as the unemployed were recommended to do by the Employment Secretary in 1982) only so many times before coming to the conclusion that it is the economic system rather than his or her own character which is at fault. You can try to 'pull yourself up by your bootstraps' only so many times before recognising that you are not actually getting any higher. You can turn out to wave flags welcoming home the victorious Falklands fleet only so many times before you begin to ask why these ships are then turning round again to be refitted in overseas dockyards. The Thatcherite solution to the problem of legitimation was, in other words, only ever a temporary solution, a holding operation whose success, like all legitimation strategies, still depended ultimately on the performance of the economy.

It was for this reason that the coercive apparatus of the state had to be strengthened, for the soft agencies could not be expected to hold up for ever under increasing pressures. People are not simply passive receivers of wisdom transmitted from above, and no matter how persuasive the ideology, there will eventually come a time when it will lose its power if it fails to relate to people's everyday-life experiences. As we have suggested at a number of points in this chapter, there is no single, all-embracing value system, no one, cohesive and authoritative view of the world which is endorsed across all classes and all regions at all times. In an age of compulsory universal education and pervasive instruments of mass communication, we may all be subject to much the same ideological pressures from above, but our different life situations – the sorts of work we do, the types of areas we live in, the kind of people we interact with on a day-to-day basis – mean that there are other influences which help to shape our values, beliefs and assumptions, and that these may not be consistent with the messages which we hear from school teachers, newsreaders and social workers.

What this means is that what may be termed a 'dominant value system' is unlikely to have things all its own way, for it must compete with other sets of values and other understandings of how the world works which arise out of people's life experiences and which may be reinforced by what we hear from, for example, shop stewards on the factory floor, radical local councillors or even disaffected teachers and journalists. Legitimation and the construction of a social consensus is, in short, always a precarious business and always a contested terrain. Where ideological messages transmitted from above come constantly into conflict with commonsense wisdoms generated through the process of living one's everyday life, social control becomes problematic. In such a situation, people are likely to become at best (from the point of view of system order) ambivalent in their attachment to dominant norms and values, and at worst they may come to reject these norms and values altogether and turn to an alternative ideology which seems to make more sense in accounting for their everyday experiences.

In Britain in the 1990s, we would suggest that few people have become totally detached from the dominant value system, but that many have become more or less ambivalent towards it. Such a mood of ambivalence and fatalism is an unsure foundation on which to base an aggressively capitalist economic and social order, and the government itself seems to have recognised this. Increasingly over recent years, it has become clear that the government has recognised the dangers of an over-reliance on legitimation strategies as the major means of ensuring social control. It is for this reason that, within the velvet glove, the iron fist has been re-cast.

Works Cited and Guide to Further Reading

Anderson, P. (1965) 'The origins of the present crisis'. In P. Anderson and R. Blackburn (eds) *Towards Socialism*, London, Fontana.
Argues that capitalist hegemony is more secure in Britain than in any other Western country and explains this in terms of various peculiarities of British history – its early and incomplete bourgeois revolution, its early industrialization, its huge nineteenth-century Empire and its escape from conquest for a thousand years. Interesting.

Brown, P. and Sparks, R., (eds) (1989) *Beyond Thatcherism*, Milton Keynes, Open University Press.
A collection of generally rather silly articles by Left-wing academics who do not like what has happened to social policy under Thatcher but do not really know what else might be done instead. Contains chapters on education, the media, the family, social work and law and order, so useful for its breadth of coverage. Shame about the content.

Critchley, T. A. (1978) *A History of Police in England and Wales*, 2nd edn, London, Constable.
Thorough, standard, but fairly uncritical account by the former head of the Home Office Police Department.

Gamble, A. (1979) 'The free economy and the strong state: the rise of the social market economy'. In Ralph Miliband and J. Saville (eds) *The Socialist Register, 1979*, London, Merlin, pp. 1–24.
Explores the connections between the moves to a free economy and the trend to a stronger state through a particular emphasis on the writings of F. A. Hayek.

Glasgow University Media Group (1983) *Really Bad News*, London, Routledge and Kegan Paul.
The third in the series of 'bad news' studies monitoring and analysing the news output of the BBC and ITN and demonstrating a systematic bias of presentation and interpretation. These studies have attracted considerable criticism from government and the broadcasting agencies, but the evidence they contain is impressive.

Habermas, J. (1976) *Legitimation Crisis*, London, Heinemann.
An important but exceedingly difficult book. Somewhat easier to digest is Habermas's short paper on 'Legitimation problems in late capitalism' which is included in P. Connerton, (ed.) (1976) *Critical Sociology*, Harmondsworth, Penguin.

Hall, S. (1980) Drifting into a law and order society, London, Cobden Trust.
Powerful analysis, and critique, of the trend to a more disciplinary society based on an 'authoritative populism'.

Harris, R. (1983) *Gotcha!: The Media, the Government and the Falklands Crisis*, London, Faber and Faber.

The disturbing story of how journalists were effectively prevented from informing the British public about what was going on in the military campaign to reclaim the Falkland Islands from the illegal Argentian occupation.

Kitson, F. (1971) *Low Intensity Operations*, London, Faber.
Frank statement by a leading army officer urging the army to prepare itself for a role in keeping the lid on domestic disorder.

McCabe, S. and Wallington, P. (1988) *The Police, Public Order and Civil Liberties*, London, Routledge.
The 1984/5 miners' strike gave rise to a mountain of books discussing the way it was policed. Most are shrill, polemical and virtually worthless for any purposes other than those of the propogandist. This is a pity, for the issue is an important one. McCabe and Wallington offer a much more measured discussion which arises out of an inquiry sponsored by the National Council for Civil Liberties. The authors see the policing of the strike as 'a major watershed in the development of the way Britain is policed'. Particularly worrying is the way Chief Constables allowed their neutrality to be compromised by pressure from the government.

McLennan, G., Held, D. and Hall, S., (eds) (1984) *State and Society in Contemporary Britain*, Cambridge, Polity Press.
A collection of predominantly Marxist essays. See especially David Held's concluding piece on power and legitimacy in which he sees post-war mass 'acquiescence' as instrumentally-based and explains the maintenance of order since the end of the post-war boom as the product of economic compulsion, policing, surveillance, media manipulation, a working class divided by ethnic and gender rivalries, and much else besides. A good example of the characteristic Marxist approach to questions of coercion and legitimation.

Maclure, S. (1989) *Education Reformed*, London, Hodder and Stoughton.
A detailed guide to the 1988 Education Act by the editor of the Times Educational Supplement. Useful not only for explaining the changes but also for a short final chapter which traces their origins through the black papers of the New Right, the 'Great Debate' launched by James Callaghan in the mid-seventies, and the abandonment of the voucher proposals by thc Thatcher government.

Mark, R. (1977) *Policing a Perplexed Society*. London, Allen and Unwin.
Ex-Chief Commissioner of the Metropolitan Police agonises about the problems of maintaining law and order in difficult times.

Negrine, R. (1989) *Politics and the Mass Media in Britain*, London, Routledge.
A very useful review of the evidence and the arguments concerning the political significance of the press and broadcasting. Discusses both the influence of the media on politics, and the influence of government over the media, and includes a chapter on the likely impact of new technologies (cable and satellite).

Piven, F. and Cloward, R. (1972) *Regulating the Poor*, London, Tavistock.
An American study of how social welfare functions as a method of maintaining social control.

Scarman, Lord (1986) *The Scarman Report: The Brixton Disorders 10–12 April 1981*, Harmondsworth, Penguin.
The report on why young Afro-Caribbeans rioted in Brixton. Discusses social conditions and policing policy. Recommended a new complaints procedure and action

against prejudiced police officers. Also suggested the long-term need for a black middle class – 'Young black Britons must show a much greater determination to help themselves'.

Thompson, E. P. (1980) 'The secret state'. In E. P. Thompson (ed.) *Writing by Candlelight*, London, Merlin.
See chapter six.

Uglow, S. (1988) *Policing Liberal Society*, Oxford, Oxford University Press.
A clearly-written and balanced discussion of the changing pattern of policing in Britain. Includes material on problems of public order, rising crime rates, innovations in police organisation and the question of accountability.

Westergaard, J. & Resler, H. (1975) *Class in a Capitalist Society*, London, Heinemann.
The chapters in Part IV deal with the inequalities of opportunity in Britain and focus specifically on the ways in which the education system operates selectively on social-class lines.

Willis, P. (1977) *Learning to Labour*, Farnborough, Hants., Saxon House.
An influential study of how working-class children rub up against the culture of school and end up desiring working-class jobs.

Chapter 12

Government and Politics Beyond Westminster and Whitehall

The public in any area, or those members of the public who are local govern-
ment electors, choose their representatives who collectivity undertake the . . .
host of . . . local government functions. If the electors do not like what their
representatives do, they have the right to change them periodically.
> Town Planning Institute (1968). Memoranda submitted to the
> Committee on Public Participation in Planning, *Journal of the*
> *Town Planning Institute*, 54, July/August, pp. 343–4.

For over a decade the party has been considering the case for regional
authorities in England. Britain now stands alone in Western Europe as the
only large country which does not have any system of regional government.
> Labour Party (1989). *Meet the Challenge. Make the Change: Final*
> *Report of Labour's Policy Review for the 1990s*, London, Labour
> Party, p. 57.

Historically, the United Kingdom is a composite of nations. . . . Most
studies of 'British' politics concentrate on the politics of the largest single
nation, England.
> Peter Madgwick and Richard Rose (eds) (1982) *The Territorial*
> *Dimension in United Kingdom Politics*, London, Macmillan, pp. 1, 3.

The idea that Europe can be nothing more than an economic entity without
political power is absurd. Transfer of sovereignty will become increasingly
necessary.
> Ciriaco de Mita, Prime Minister of Italy (1988). *Speech at Lake*
> *Maggiore*, October.

Introduction

The orthodox study of British politics is all too often the study of the
central government at Westminster, together with its administrative arm
in Whitehall. Modern political scientists may have pushed beyond these

"Beyond the power of the local state and towards the power of the European super-state?" (ECU reproduced by kind permission of The World Gold Council: GLC Abolition poster reproduced by kind permission of The Greater London Record Office Modern Records Section.)

formal institutions in order to consider the impact of parties and pressures on the centre, and Marxists and theorists of the New Right may be mindful of the significance of the larger economic context within which the central state 'must', or is constrained, to operate, but to attend to these differences of emphases ignores a larger agreement on basics which exists within the bulk of the literature on British politics. In bald terms, students of all political persuasions have tended to underplay, if not ignore, the territorial dimension of British politics because there has long been a tacit agreement that it is enough to study government, politics, pressures, power and the machinations of economic relationships as they work themselves out at the very centre of the state machine. The argument that we need only to focus on the central state (and not on the politics above and below that centre) surely derives from the shared view that Britain is both a unitary state and a sovereign nation state. However, before we accept the virtues of the dominant centralist perspective we need to be sure that the reality of the British state is actually in accord with the unitary and sovereignty viewpoints because if this is not the case then we need to push our analysis beyond Westminster and Whitehall in order to take account of government and politics above and below the centre.

In a formal but narrow sense, Britain *is* a unitary state in that the constitutional reality of parliamentary sovereignty does mean that only the Parliament at Westminster is in a position to make laws. Within such unitary systems of rule, subcentral governments are established by the central authority which can abolish them at will; the powers of local governments are delegated or devolved from the centre which can revoke them at will; and local governments play no role in the constitutional amending process, and the centre's actions towards them cannot easily be declared unconstitutional by any court. Put another way, unlike the USA, Britain does not possess a written constitution that establishes a federal system of rule. Within that kind of system, both the central state and the constituent states are established and guaranteed by the constitution; both the states and the central state receive their powers from the constitution and sovereignty is divided so that both the states and the central authority enjoy supreme powers within specified spheres of concern. These powers are not delegated, and may not be taken away, by the other level of government; and neither the states nor the central authority can unilaterally amend the constitution because a Supreme Court exists to referee, according to the constitution, disputes between states and the central authority. Having said all this (and whilst being mindful as to the importance of constitutions) we should not exaggerate the distinction between federal states and unitary states in so far as the power of the central state is concerned. First, no matter what a constitution decrees, a central state can never do everything, be all-powerful and cope alone without help and assistance from state institutions outside of the centre and this plays into the hands of those institutions. Second, interests are bound to exist within the localities and regions of a country and so administrative or governmental institutions based on those interests are likely to press for powers in ways which are going to impinge on the authority of the central state – and this regardless of what a constitution says 'should' be the case. In other words, the extent to which political power and authority is centralised or decentralised is a matter of degree rather than of absolutes and it is always going to be contingent on the play of practical politics within a country. In Britain, the supposedly directive and all-powerful central government may pass a law, provide money, inspect and, on occasion, directly provide a service but, for the most part, it needs the active co-operation of other bodies if it is to implement its policies and it is not always easy for the centre to secure the necessary degree of support and compliance from the messy system of sub-central government. In reality, then, the unitary character of the British state is practically and politically restricted by the existence of power outside of the centre and by various forms of devolution and decentralisation to local governments, to regional authorities, and to governmental and administrative institutions within Scotland, Wales and Northern Ireland.

The most extended system of decentralisation concerns the situation in Northern Ireland. From 1920 to 1972, Northern Ireland possessed its own separately elected Parliament at Stormont, an executive responsible to it, a local government structure and a system of courts. In this period, Northern Ireland was governed partly from Stormont and partly from London, the division of powers being laid down in the Government of Ireland Act of 1920 and subsequent statutes. The situation between the government of the United Kingdom and that of Northern Ireland was quite clearly a kind of federal relationship. In 1972, the Stormont system was suspended by the British government and replaced by 'direct rule' pending the establishment of a new constitution. Federalism has been less a feature of the situation with respect to Wales and Scotland, but Wales does possess various administrative bodies exclusive to itself. Although Scotland possesses neither a government nor a Parliament of its own, it does have a strong constitutional identity and a large number of political and social institutions as well as its own legal system which means that the people of Scotland are subject to many laws exclusive to Scotland alone. Attending to the situation in Northern Ireland, Wales and Scotland and attending to the rise and fall of nationalist movements may involve our studying the political geography of power in its grossest and most constitutionally pressing form. However, we should not assume that this exhausts the consideration which we must give to the importance of the territorial distribution of state power in Britain since we need, at a minimum, to recognise the part played by state institutions at the local and the regional levels as well.

Britain may be seen as a simple and integrated unitary state – a United Kingdom; power and authority may be seen as concentrated so that the state is regarded as a kind of monolith that possesses a 'oneness' and unity that is all based at the centre; and there may be no real recognition that there are elements of federalism and currents of nationalism within our system. However, this kind of unitary and centralist perspective is partial and misleading. Because the central state is fragmented and not all-powerful should surely force all students of British politics to recognise that we need to attend to the power of state institutions outside of the centre at the same time as we take on board the problem of political integration and centre-periphery relations as well as the importance of intergovernmental relations between different levels of the state system.

What of the sovereignty of the British state; can we study British politics without attending to the play of politics in the international arena above Westminster and Whitehall? There is no doubt that the fact that Britain once had an Empire and ruled the waves has encouraged the view that Britain is an independent sovereign state of power and substance that can be studied as a closed political system in isolation from international considerations and the impact of external events. Students of British politics have rarely troubled to think hard about the extent to which we may lack real sovereignty and the very capacity to govern ourselves as we would wish. However, the fact that we are an open political system and are members of a variety of international organisations, which have varying degrees of significance for our domestic politics and policy-making, should surely force us to question the concrete and practical reality of sovereignty and the notion of Britain as a self-contained, self-governing nation state. If we do this, then we need to look above the central state in order to try and bring the study of international relations and power politics into the very heart of the analysis of British politics itself. This is not something that normally features in texts on British politics which tend to be narrowly nationalistic.

In chapter 6, we got away from democratic orthodoxies and the elected side of the state system in order to assess the power of some of the institutions that made up the non-elected secret state. We did this because we recognised that British politics embraced more than just democracy alone and was a good deal messier than many of the established theories would have us believe. In this chapter, we are concerned to get away from the fixation on Westminster and Whitehall and the whole centralist perspective in order to attend to the territorial dimension of the organisation of the British state and to the fragmented and disaggregated nature of state power. We want to do this because, here again, we recognise that the reality of British politics is messier than the theories and so we need to push beyond what happens at the centre of the state. Space precludes our dealing with all the organisations that are part of our system of subcentral government (the territorial ministries, such as the Northern Ireland Office; the decentralised structures of the central departments, such as the regional offices of the Department of the Environment; the enormous range of non-departmental public bodies, public corporations, and fringe bodies such as the National Health Service and the Manpower Services Commission; other types of *ad hoc* bodies, otherwise known as 'quangos'; and so on), but we will be exploring some of the institutions of subcentral government that operate 'below' the centre, be they at the local, the regional, or the national level. More than this, we will not only be considering government 'below' the centre since we will also attend to the significance of our membership of international organisations that are somehow 'above' the level of the central government precisely because organisations such as the International Monetary Fund, the North Atlantic Treaty Organisation, and the European Community have done much to restrict British sovereignty and our capacity to govern ourselves through a democratically elected Parliament. Let us, then, look at government and politics beyond Westminster and Whitehall and begin at the bottom by attending to the significance of the local level.

The Local Level

In our discussion of the secret state we made it clear that the central state contained many institutions run by people whose name has never appeared on any ballot paper. This is also the reality at the local level of the state, since we cannot elect the Chief Constables who control the police; the local magistrates who administer justice; the administrators at the local offices of central departments who are involved in providing such things as social security payments; the various local authority implementation agencies and inter-governmental forums; and the whole bureaucratic and official side of the local government system itself. Not surprisingly, then, many of the decisions which are taken locally by those in state institutions and which impact directly on our everyday lives are not taken by elected local councillors at all. There is, in short, much more to the local state than simply local government and so no account of the local level of the state is complete which does not attend to the central government's 'arms length' agencies; to local authority implementation agencies; to public/private partnership organisations; to user organisations; to inter-governmental forums; and to various joint boards and joint committees. Having said that, the system of local government does warrant particular attention precisely because it is elected (and this gives it a legitimacy to challenge the centre); it is multipurpose, with every local authority having many jobs to do and a variety of services to provide; it does account for about a quarter of all public expenditure and is in a position where it can raise some of its own revenue through the Community Charge, or Poll Tax; and it does employ nearly three million people. All of this means that local councils are in a unique position to challenge the centre and the policies of the central government, and the whole system of local self-government also provides a medium through which groups excluded from effective representation at the centre can try and flex their political muscles in order to secure what they want fron the local public purse. This is exactly what has been happening in Britain. As local government has become increasingly strident and politicised so it has become more of a problem for the central state. However, before we deal with the developing field of central–local relations and with the problem of local government itself, it would be as well to set down the essentials of the local government system, making sense of it by attending to its nineteenth-century origins and to twentieth-century developments. Once we have a grip on the system and the background then we are in a better position to appreciate some of the factors which have prompted the central state to try and assert a keener control over local government at the same time as we can understand the problems of effecting that control and the reasoning behind the local authority fightback and struggle for autonomy from the centre.

The local government system

There is no single United Kingdom local government system, but several distinct systems: three in England, together with separate arrangements in Wales, Scotland and Northern Ireland. The Local Government Act, 1972, provided for a two-tier system throughout England with the addition of a third tier of parish councils in some places. Outside of the conurbations, local government consists of a top tier of 39 non-metropolitan, or 'shire', county councils and a bottom tier of 296 district authorities, beneath which there are nearly 8,000 parishes with but limited powers and responsibilities. Within the major conurbations such as Greater Manchester, Merseyside, and Tyne and Wear, and following the abolition of the metropolitan counties in 1985, local government now consists of a single tier of 36 metropolitan districts. In London, although the London Government Act, 1963, provided for a two-tier system consisting of the Greater London Council and 32 London Boroughs (plus the City of London), the abolition of the GLC has left the capital with a single tier of local government, albeit one that is supported by various joint boards and new *ad hoc* bodies. The 1972 Act that reorganised the local government system in England also reorganised the system in Wales, creating 8 counties (from the existing 13), 37 districts (from the existing 164) and a large number of community councils but no metropolitan authorities. The Local Government (Scotland) Act, 1973, created regional councils, 53 district councils, 3 islands councils, and over 1,200 community councils that were quite different in character to those in Wales. In Northern Ireland, local government consists of 26 unitary district councils elected under a system of proportional representation, but many services that are provided by local government on the mainland are provided at the provincial level in Northern Ireland although the district councils are limply associated with some of these services through a system of regional boards.

Nineteenth-century origins and twentieth-century developments

The roots of today's local government system lie in the nineteenth century and in the political developments which followed on from the messy process of industrialisation and urbanisation. In chapter 1 we explored the growth of the liberal-democratic constitution and the extension of the franchise to embrace the working class. But during the nineteenth century Parliament also set up a system of locally elected multipurpose local authorities to replace the jumble of established *ad hoc* bodies that were run on undemocratic and inefficient lines. Not surprisingly, Parliament was prepared to heap additional functions on these new authorities and, because the functions falling on local authorities were of manifest importance, the central state took an increasing interest in what these bodies were doing – and spending – in a way that has involved a gradual extension of central control over the affairs of local government. The case for autonomous local self-government – for local democracy – and the somewhat conflicting case for the extensive central control of local authorities were both crucial aspects of the nineteenth-century political debate about what should be the form and scope of a modern local government system. Moreover, these concerns have continued to dog the twentieth-century political agenda at the same time as much of the academic literature about local government has revolved around the 'reality' of local democracy as against the 'true' extent of central control. Let us, then, explore some of these developments before we flesh out the concerns about local democracy and central control, concerns which are the warp and woof of the situation of local government in Britain.

The Municipal Corporations Act, 1835, created elected councils for the boroughs; the Local Government Act, 1888, created directly elected county councils; and in 1894 and 1899, further reforms established a range of directly elected multipurpose authorities below the county councils. In effect, a two-tier system of local self-government was adopted consisting of county councils as the top tier and borough, urban district and rural district councils as the bottom tier, although in the major towns and cities county borough councils were established as all-purpose authorities able to operate on their own outside of the county council framework. All of these bodies were democratically elected on the basis of a franchise which embraced the bulk of the working class and this had inevitable implications for the class control of local government. In the early years of the nineteenth century, local government was in the hands of a traditional elite of landowners and the gentry. With industrialisation a rising class of local businessmen came to the fore in many of the major urban areas; but the selfsame developments which created a business class also helped to make a working class which, through the ballot box and the Labour Party, was able to get a purchase on the local level of the state through the newly democratised system of local government. True, it was possible for the established elites to retain control in the more rural counties and districts, but in the urban areas these men of substance were increasingly replaced by men drawn from the ranks of the working class – men who have continually been defined as of 'low calibre' and as not up to the job of running the affairs of a local government system that has increasingly been seen as akin to big business. Notwithstanding this hostility to working-class involvement in local government, in the 1919 local elections Labour secured control of half the metropolitan borough councils and by 1934 had captured the London County Council itself. The history of most large urban local authorities in the period 1880–1920 would be a history of 'the "gentlemen" being crowded out and the working men coming in' aided and abetted by the rise of the Labour Party.

In the early decades of the nineteenth century, local government, in trying to cope with law and order, paving, cleansing, street lighting, and aspects of public health, was caught up in providing a simple basic infrastructure of services and 'public goods' which were of fairly general interest. These services were of benefit to *all* those living within a particular locality. The creation of a new system meant that some responsibilities could be transferred from existing *ad hoc* authorities (for example, school boards were abolished and local authorities took on the provision of education). As new responsibilities were taken on by the central state, so many of these were devolved down to local authorities that were often eager to extend the range of their responsibilities, particularly if they were Labour controlled and took the view that the state should help those in need. By 1929, when the Boards of Guardians were at last disbanded and control of poor relief and the provision of hospitals was transferred to local councils, local government had become wholly or partly responsible for a wide variety of functions. These included town planning, the building of low-cost housing, education, the provision of a range of health and welfare services, municipal enterprises, and the development of public utilities such as water supply, town gas, electricity distribution and, in the case of Hull, a telephone system. Local government might still have been providing some kind of general infrastructure for all, but it was also increasingly involved in the provision of services that conferred *particular* benefits on *sections* of the local community. Moreover, the cost of providing these services fell on the more wealthy elements within the community who paid domestic and non-domestic rates direct to local government as well as taxes to the central state which was itself having to help fund local government through a complex system of central government grants. Between 1900 and 1938 total local authority expenditure increased nearly fourfold in real terms.

A central government that created the local government system; that has been bent on giving local authorities more to do; that has been prepared to help fund the local system; and that has taken a keen interest in the standards of local services across the country, could hardly be expected to be indifferent to what local authorities were doing and spending. And the more so since local government was increasingly in the hands of people who were using it to provide services that were seen by many as controversial and injurious to their interests. Moreover, the fact that local authorities were becoming increasingly big spenders and big employers meant that their activities had a major economic impact in ways which intruded into, and had implications for, the central state's sphere of concern for the health and management of the British economy. It should not surprise us, therefore, that 'central control', or rather the attempt to *assert* central control, has long been a feature of the local government system and of the relations between the central state and the local authorities. Indeed, a dominant tradition of writing on local government has argued that during this century, and particularly since the Second World War, local authorities have gradually been robbed of any autonomy. They have become the mere 'agents' of the central government charged with the task, not of local policy-making, but of simply administering and implementing the policies laid down by the all-powerful central government. The most popular explanation accounting for the increasing extent of central control is based upon the fact that local authorities have become ever more dependent on the finance provided by the central government. There is the simple idea that 'he who pays the piper calls the tune'. Writers assert that central control has increased, note that central funding has also increased, and weld these two observations together to form a causal explanation suggesting that control has increased because central funding has increased. We need not form a view as to the cogency of this explanation (and we should be wary of the whole central control/local government as agent argument because the demise of local government has been forecast so many times over the years) but it is clear that the central state has long been concerned to control local government precisely because elected local government has often proved to be a thorn in its side. This is a key part of the problem of local government in this country and it needs to be looked at alongside the reality of local democracy; the changes that have occurred with respect to the class control of local government; and the development of local authority services and responsibilities.

The problem of local government

For the most part, writers on local government have been critical of central control and of the 'trend' to centralisation precisely because they have been attached to the whole system of local self-government, seeing it as a check on the central state; as a way of providing services that are attuned to local needs; and as a vehicle for civic education and training in a way enhancing of the democratic climate of opinion within a country. Having said that, there has been a long-standing undercurrent of concern about the 'declining' calibre of local councillors at the same time as commissions and committees have worried about the 'inefficiency' of the whole local government system. These concerns are not trivial; they are a coded way of referring to the problem of local self-government itself.

Talk about the declining calibre of councillors consequent upon the rise of local democracy constitutes a lament about changes in the class and party composition of local councils in the major urban centres. In effect, we are being told that a democratised local government system has gradually slipped beyond the reach of business. Moreover, this has proved to be a particular problem precisely because the system has also been beyond the easy and compensating control of the central state. In part because of the practical difficulties of controlling hundreds of local authorities but also because the widespread attachment to the ideology of local democracy has itself inhibited the political feasibility of such control. Put a slightly different way, concern about councillor calibre involves a keen recognition that it does matter what kind of people and political parties run a relatively autonomous system of local government precisely because this has a bearing on the nature and efficiency of local services, on the sheer scope of local government, and on the scale of local public expenditure. Local public expenditure has tended to outpace expenditure at the central level and this in itself has been seen as a problem. However, the fact that many of the services provided by local government have been regarded as expendable because they merely meet social needs that could be provided for privately through the market has encouraged the belief that much local service provision could be cut back at the same time as the rest is made more efficient.

In our chapter on 'Managing the economy' we made it clear that state intervention and public expenditure came to be seen as general problems for the health of the British economy. It is important to stress that although these problems have long been focused at the local government level (for the reasons we have given about changes with respect to the control of local government going back to the beginning of this century), the rise of a 'new urban Left' in the 1970s that was bent on the implementation of 'local socialism' did much to crank up local state intervention and public expenditure in a way that posed a major challenge to the centre's right to govern.

Solving the problem of local government, that is reducing the scale of local public expenditure and changing the thrust of local government activity, has embraced a number of related strategies. One of these has involved restructuring the entire local government system. There was the hope that this would increase councillor calibre and reduce the vulnerability of local government to other local pressures at the same time as it would produce a system that was rather more efficient and cost-effective in providing services. What, then, have been the guts of this strategy and how successful has it been?

Restructuring local government in the twentieth century

Notwithstanding a constant stream of grumbles about local government, the system established in the nineteenth century remained largely undisturbed until the 1960s. In that decade, serious moves were made to tackle the boundary problem: the problem of small and supposedly inefficient local authorities. Later on, the central government grappled with the management problem: the problem of 'outdated' administrative arrangements which needed to be swept away through the wholesale internal reorganisation of decision-making procedures within local authorities. It was hoped that this dual restructuring strategy would 'improve' the calibre of councillors so that the local government system could then set *itself* back on the right and efficient track of limited service provision.

The boundary problem in London was tackled as a result of the Local Government Act, 1963, and this was followed by further reforms for the rest of Britain consequent upon the passing of the Local Government Act, 1972, the Local Government (Northern Ireland) Act, 1972, and the Local Government (Scotland) Act, 1973. The established system was seen as democratic, but as inefficient and lacking in councillors of real calibre. The view was taken that if the system were rationalised through the creation of a smaller number of larger authorities then this would increase efficiency and secure the services of councillors of calibre. Efficiency would be increased because it was argued that larger local authorities would be better able to reap economies of scale in the provision of services (and this notwithstanding the failure of research to demonstrate a clear link between size and efficiency). It was hoped that councillor calibre would also be increased through the creation of larger authorities. First, it was argued that an increase in the size of local authorities would expand the scope of local government in a way which would make the position of councillor more attractive to businessmen used to making big and strategic decisions. Second, it was felt that removing outdated boundaries and throwing the suburbs in with the central cities would come to terms with the fact that the middle classes who lived in the suburbs were disenfranchised from formal and direct participation in the politics of the small local authorities that covered the economically active city centres. In effect, it was hoped that larger local authorities embracing city and suburb would reduce the unfettered control which working-class voters and Labour-dominated councils had over the affairs of the central city. Yet it was recognised that there was a risk in this whole strategy in that the Conservative voters in the rural and suburban areas could just as easily be swamped by urban-based Labour voters.

The Conservative government of 1970–4 was mindful of this risk, and of the pressure from the Tory-dominated shire counties which bitterly opposed any move to legislate them out of existence, and so the government rejected the idea of a unitary system based on city-regions. Instead, the Local Government Act, 1972, retained the shire counties and created new district counties under them, but in the large English conurbations six new metropolitan counties were created presiding over 36 metropolitan district councils. Given the geography of electoral support, the Conservatives were confident that the shire counties and many of the district councils under them would remain overwhelmingly Conservative, but it was less clear which party would control the new metropolitan counties and the GLC precisely because they straddled the city and the suburbs. In practice, some of the metropolitan counties have been won by the Conservatives in some election years. By 1981, however, the GLC and all six metropolitan counties were Left-Labour controlled and they were pursuing interventionist policies with respect to fares for public transport, planning, economic development and industry, policing, the arts, and for positive discrimination for women and 'minorities', which were all contrary to the philosophy and policies of the Thatcher government at the centre.

A Conservative government was re-elected in 1983 on a manifesto that included a commitment to abolish the GLC and the metropolitan county councils. Publicly, this was presented as a reform to 'streamline the cities' and to bring local government closer to local communities on the grounds that there was no 'practical' or 'strategic' role for this tier of government at the same time as there was a need for an economy and efficiency in local government that was not being practiced by these authorities. Privately, however, it had become increasingly clear that these authorities were beyond Conservative control through the local ballot box, and the fact that they were controlled by Labour meant that they were a thorn in the side of the Conservative government at the centre. The GLC and the metropolitan counties ceased to exist after 1 April 1986. Some of their functions were transferred to the metropolitan districts and London boroughs but a system of non-elected special purpose authorities, joint boards and joint committees was also established so contributing to the reassertion of officer influence and to the build-up of the local secret state that lies beyond the reach of the local ballot box.

Concomitant with the 1972 reorganisation of local government boundaries, the central government issued comprehensive guidelines (the Bains report) advising the new authorities on how to set up their internal administrative arrangements so as to solve the management problem. In bald terms, the established system of 'traditional administration' based on committees and departments working in tandem was seen as deficient because it fragmented the effort of local authorities; it entrenched an incremental style of decision-making; it failed to co-ordinate local services in an innovative way; and it was just not up to the task of managing the whole range of local government responsibilities. It was also argued that the time-consuming and unbusinesslike nature of decision-making within this system deterred 'employers, managers, professionals, and farmers' from becoming councillors.

To solve all this, the Bains report recommended the establishment of a 'corporate management team' of chief officers under the leadership of a chief executive that would then liaise closely with an 'inner cabinet' of elected members drawn from the majority group on the council and headed by the group leader. Bains hoped that concentrating strategic policy-making within the hands of a joint elite of councillors and officers working away from the glare of the full council meeting would be more businesslike. At the same time it would facilitate co-operation between departments and increase the efficiency and 'effectiveness' of local authority operations.

Virtually all the new authorities adopted the Bains proposals but they did so with varying degrees of enthusiasm, partly because no one was quite sure what was really meant by the 'corporate approach' to local government. Notwithstanding this lack of certainty, there is little doubt that the logic of Bains' recommendations reflected a technical rather than a political view of the future role of local government because it was rather assumed that the 'ends' of local government were given by the central government or by common sense itself. This being the case, policy-making was construed as being all about the apolitical choosing of the most cost-effective means to solve given problems. And this in spite of the fact that such a view rather ignores the extent to which local government *is* political, just as democracy is bound to involve argument and debate about the appropriate ends of government action. During the 1970s there was little doubt that the adoption of corporate management in British local government did do much to limit this debate because it was effective in empowering the officers and in holding most councillors (and the public) at arms length from the effective centres of power within the town halls. During the 1980s, however, the heightened politicisation of local government and the growth of a more assertive party politics has increased the likelihood of tension within the joint elite of councillors and officers in a way that has opened up debate as to what should be the ends of local government action. Management may be all about containing the play of politics, but when it sits on top of an open system of local democracy it may not always succeed in keeping the lid on things.

To what extent have changes with respect to local authority boundaries and management processes achieved their objective and brought men of calibre back into local government? Or, put more directly, has the class composition of local councils changed so as to increase the representation of business and the professionals because through this change reformers hoped to be able to secure a better 'fit' between local government and the needs of business and the concerns of the central state?

Contrary to many of the expectations integral to the declining councillor calibre thesis, a survey of councillors back in 1964 found that employers, managers, farmers and professionals occupied 'a larger proportion of seats in the councils than their proportion in the general adult male population', just as the converse was true of skilled and unskilled manual workers. The picture of councillors as overwhelmingly male, middle-aged and middle class – and of course, white, had changed relatively little more than ten years later by the time of the 1976 survey carried out for the Robinson Committee on the Remuneration of Councillors. Since then, images of local government in the popular press have rather suggested that many of the larger urban authorities were increasingly being run by groups of relatively younger members, from different kinds of social and occupational backgrounds from their predecessors, and among whom both women and blacks were considerably more strongly represented than previously. This was scarcely what those bent on increasing councillor calibre were hoping for, so what are the facts of the situation as revealed in the 1985 survey undertaken for the Widdicombe Committee of Inquiry into the Conduct of

Local Authority Business? Councillors are getting younger (but only significantly so in the London boroughs and the other metropolitan areas) and there are more women being elected (but much less noticeably in Wales and Scotland than in the major English authorities) but councillors in professional and managerial employment continue to be overrepresented compared to the situation with respect to manual workers. Only one-fifth of currently employed councillors are in manual jobs (compared with nearly half of their constituents) although over a third of Labour councillors had manual working-class backgrounds and one in twelve was unemployed – hardly the stuff of 'high calibre'.

The basic stability with respect to the kinds of people who become councillors contains litle joy for those who hoped to engineer a change in the class composition of local councils, but data with respect to employment sectors has caused real concern to those anxious about the problem of local government and empire building at the town hall. A MORI survey carried out in 1982 showed that out of a sample of 176 councillors on 6 councils in England, 39 per cent of the total (and 48 per cent of Labour members) were employed in the public sector. The larger survey for the Widdicombe committee confirmed this picture, showing that 36 per cent of employed councillors worked in the public sector, with this figure rising to 47 per cent among London councillors and 55 per cent among members of the since abolished metropolitan county councils. The fact that many (Labour) councillors depended for their livelihood on local government employment led to the suggestion that these 'twin tracking' councillors had a material interest in increasing public sector jobs and local government expenditure in a way that was bound to exacerbate the whole problem of local government itself. The Local Government and Housing Act, 1989, sought to get around this particular problem by banning all council employees earning above a specified salary level from political activity, including the right to stand as a councillor.

Solving the problem of local government through restructuring the system has scarcely been a success, but the history of British local government in the twentieth century provides us with examples of other strategies that have been adopted to get round the problem of local democracy.

The loss of local government services

From the 1930s onwards, the central government has legislated to strip local authorities of many of their most significant functions.

The process began in 1934 when local councils lost control over local poor relief, thus clearing the way for central government to impose cuts in the level of relief without encountering the sort of local resistance which had occurred a few years earlier in Poplar where the socialist-controlled Board of Guardians, backed by the unemployed themselves, had raised the level of payments in the face of central demands that they should be reduced. In fact, the success of persons ideologically committed to a policy of generous poor relief in first securing election as Guardians and then in fulfilling their election pledges at the expense of local manufacturers and the more conservative and wealthy unions had actually brought the question of the local franchise to the forefront of British politics in the 1920s. The government came within a hair's breadth of disenfranchising hundreds of thousands of its citizens and each time it only drew back for fear of the political repercussions, eventually choosing to solve the problem by taking the control of relief out of local hands altogether.

Once the problem of poor relief was out of the way and in the hands of central officials, there then followed a flurry of legislation removing local government responsibility for trunk roads (1936), administration of supplementary benefits (1940), hospitals (1946), electricity supply (1947) and gas (1948). The Heath government of 1970–4, through the Local Government Act, 1972, transferred the remaining local authority health responsibilities to the National Health Service at the same time as local water and sewage responsibilities were transferred to new regional authorities. The Thatcher governments from 1979, through their privatisation policy, reduced the effective scope of local government service provision in a number of new and sometimes subtle ways. First they encouraged the sale of local authority assets, such as council houses. Second, local authorities had to face the discipline of market competition: bus services were 'de-regulated' in a way which challenged the dominance of public sector operators and opened up space for private operators. The development of competitive tendering forced public sector providers to compete with private contractors in a way which meant that services such as refuse collection and street cleaning were often 'contracted out' to more efficient private businesses that put in lower bids. Third, there has been a susbtantial growth in initiatives aimed at encouraging the private sector to provide services that have traditionally been provided by local government (and this has been the case with respect to schools, homes for disturbed adolescents, the mentally ill, the handicapped and the elderly) and various schemes have sought to substitute private-sector for public-sector resources with respect to urban renewal.

Whilst it is easy to point to the loss of local authority services and to bemoan the extent to which centralisation and privatisation have 'robbed' local authorities of their powers, it is nevertheless important to qualify this picture.

1 The loss of local authority services has not just been a Conservative Party attack upon (Labour) local authorities, since Labour governments have been party to much of the legislation which which has attempted to centralise (and nationalise!) local authority services. In the post-war period the Labour Party was increasingly confident of its capacity to secure a long-term grip on the central government and this made it want to expand the power of the central state at the expense of local government. Moreover, it chose to do this notwith-

standing the fact that the Party had enjoyed its first taste of governmental power at the local level and notwithstanding the extent to which local government continued to provide opportunities for ordinary working people to secure control of a part of the state. As the Labour Party grew less confident about its capacity to win control of the central government so it came to regret its concern to reduce the powers of local government but by then the damage had been done. The Party talked about the need to build socialism from the bottom through local government but this was less than easy when local authorities had fewer powers and were up against a Conservative central government that was bent on ridding the whole system of socialism.

2 Accounts which attest to the undoubted loss of local authority services do not always draw up an accurate balance sheet since they frequently fail to recognise the expansion which occurred within local government over the period 1955–75 when there was an intensification of local performance within certain established and traditional spheres of concern, be it with respect to housing and planning, or welfare and schooling. This was reflected in the growth of local expenditure and in the growing number of local authority employees and professional staff. The centre might have wished to provide many services itself, but it was less than easy to bypass local government in the absence of there being other bodies to do the job. Moreover, since local government was employing more and more professionals, the central government was increasingly having to work through people who had their own interest in asserting an autonomy to decide in a way which could block the initiatives of the centre.

The growth of the non-elected local state

The operation of non-elected agencies within the local arena is not a new phenomenon. For example, after the Second World War, the central government created a number of New Town Development Corporations to launch a ring of satellite towns around the metropolitan areas of the country. The Corporations took over planning and housing powers from the existing local authorities in their areas. The fact that the members were appointed by the central government helped to ensure that the Corporations were far more responsive to the central government and to local private-sector firms than would have been the case with elected local authorities that were relatively autonomous from, and often hostile to, the central government and to the whole private enterprise system itself.

The range and scope of the non-elected local state grew from the mid-1970s (for example, the Labour government created economic development agencies in Scotland and Wales, as well as various 'partnership' schemes for the declining city centres), but the pace of innovation has accelerated since 1979 when the Conservative central government attempted to bypass local authorities that were hostile to the aims and concerns of the Thatcher agenda. Examples which illustrate this strategy in operation include the creation of Urban Development Corporations to take over planning and development control functions in a number of urban areas; the expanded role given to the Manpower Services Commission to promote training and new education initiatives; and the establishment of 'task force' teams of civil servants in a number of inner-city areas. The Conservatives have seen these single-purpose agencies as more amenable to their policy influence, and their use has helped the central government to maintain a general constraint on local government spending whilst ensuring that resources are targeted according to the specific priorities of the centre. The Thatcher governments also encouraged the growth of non-elected local agencies as a result of their attempts to change the practice and performance of elected local authorities themselves. For example, legislation in 1985 forced local authorities to create companies to manage their participation in bus and airport operations with a view to securing a more efficient and business-like service; laws to enable public sector tenants to 'opt out' of the local authority system have expanded the range of non-elected local agencies in the form of Housing Trusts; and the greater use of non-elected joint boards, committees and quasi-governmental agencies has been an inevitable outcome of the abolition of the GLC and the six metropolitan county councils.

The (Conservative) centre might have used non-elected agencies to bypass local government, but (Labour) local authorities have played much the same game, setting up non-elected 'arms length' agencies as a way of bypassing the central government and reducing the extent of central control at the same time as they have also sought to involve service users in local provision. For example, in economic development, extensive use has been made of enterprise boards, community business and co-operative development agencies precisely because these bodies can operate in ways not open to local authorities given the constraints contained in the law.

Central control and the finance of local government

Our discussion of the 'place' of local government within the British system of rule has highlighted the extent to which local self-government has long proved to be something of a problem for the central government – and for business. Having said that, it has to be admitted that the pattern of central–local relations has changed substantially in the Thatcher years as the central government has increased the intensity and strength of its interventions through the development of a number of strategies of control. First, legislation has increasingly been used to direct local government in a way which has reduced the scope for local authority discretion. This contrasts with the enabling and empowering legislation of earlier years. It has also led to the courts becoming massively involved in defining the relationship between centre and locality, but in a situation in which the centre has always been able to nullify local authority victories in the courts through the passage of still more legislation. Second, the established networks of

consultation between centre and locality based upon negotiation and compromise have been shunned in favour of the central government setting
goals and targets for local authorities on the basis of minimal consultation.
Third, we have already seen that there has been a heightened readiness both
to bypass elected local government and to reduce the range of the services
which it provides. Fourth, central governments have long recognised the
importance of restructuring and reorganising local authorities as a way
of ensuring a better 'fit' between what the localities 'choose' to do and
what the centre wishes of them. Here again, we have already highlighted
the extent to which the Conservative governments of the eighties have
continued to see the value of this strategy. Finally, and perhaps because the
other strategies of control have all proved to be so problematic, the
Thatcher governments were especially ferocious in trying to control local
authority income and expenditure.

Local authorities have traditionally relied upon four sources of income:
user charges (such as rents paid by council tenants); rates (a local tax levied
on domestic and commercial property); central government grants; and
loans for major investments (such as school buildings). Over the years local
authorities have come to depend more and more on central government
grants (and this has long been a key part of the problem of local government) but until the 1980s the central government was content to influence
the spending plans of local authorities simply by altering their level of grant
and by changing the controls over loans for investments. In effect, and in
a very general way, the central government felt able to 'control' and reduce
the spending of local authorities by cutting back central grants and by denying loans, confident in the belief that councils would be reluctant to make
good the shortfall by increasing rates because of the unpopularity of rate
increases amongst local electorates. This relatively simple and partial control was deemed quite inadequate by Conservative governments after 1979
because there was a keen concern to sharply reduce local public expenditure
and to redirect it. The government has succeeded in reducing capital expenditure – indeed this was already happening by the mid-1970s as a result
of the workings of 'loan sanction' in combination with high interest
rates – but controlling current expenditure has proved to be much more of
a problem. Acts were passed in 1980, 1982, 1985, 1986 and 1987 with a view
to increasing the centre's financial control of local expenditure. This pro-
cession of legislation stands as a testament, not to the power of central
government, but to the sheer problem of control when the centre faces local
authorities that are bent on fulfilling their own policy mandates against the
policy position of the centre itself.

The Conservative attack upon local spending since 1979 has come in a
number of waves.

In its first term, the government pursued a strategy of tightening general
financial controls on all councils through the introduction of a new 'block
grant' system for allocating central government financial support to local
authorities. Under the old 'rate support grant' the centre increased its grant

to match increases in local spending as determined by the local authorities themselves. Under the 'block grant' the centre decides how much a local council needs to spend; how much of this it can be expected to raise for itself from rates and charges; and how much therefore remains to be provided from central funds. These calculations are, of course, shaped by the government's own desire to cut local public expenditure and so each year the Department of the Environment (DOE) has tended to reduce the level of expenditure deemed 'necessary' for each local authority in a way that has led to a reduction in the amount of grant paid to local authorities. Under the old system the central grant went *up* as local expenditure increased, but under the new system the amount of grant has gone *down* as local expenditure has increased.

In a second wave of concern about local expenditure the central government grafted a series of targets and penalties onto the block grant scheme so that councils which overspent the DOE targets were penalised by a loss of grant equivalent to between two and four times the amount overspent.

In practice, these initial attempts to cut local expenditure did not work as intended. First, many local authorities were adept at engaging in 'creative accounting' schemes to protect themselves from the uncertainties of block grant targets and penalties, and these schemes were not outlawed until the government passed legislation in 1986 and 1988. Second, some local authorities were quite prepared to increase their rates and raise supplementary rates in order to fulfill their own policy programmes. Left-Labour councils were in the forefront of these moves. Sheffield put its rate up by 41 per cent in 1980 and 37 per cent in 1981 and was still supported at the polls, and the GLC overspent by so much that it no longer qualified for any central government grant and so was liberated from the need to even worry about further central government grant penalties. Other local authorities (including some Conservative shire counties) also overspent their targets, taking the (quite correct) view that if they kept within them then this would simply produce a decrease in their permitted targets in future years. Contrary to all the old orthodoxies about rate increases and electoral success, opinion polls suggested that the public blamed the central government for rate increases and so few high-spending councils were actually voted out of office.

The government reacted to these moves of local defiance with an Act which banned local authorities from issuing supplementary rates (having failed to pass an earlier bill which had proposed that local authorities should hold a referendum if they wished to raise a supplementary rate) and they also established an Audit Commission to oversee local authority finances and encourage 'value for money' from local spending. Neither of these measures was up to the task at hand. Councils intent on maintaining services simply set a higher rate each April in a way which obviated their need to set a supplementary rate later in the year. Although the Audit Commission has tended to support Conservative government claims about 'waste' in local government it has also been critical of the arbitrary and complex nature of central interventions into local government in a way that has done little to advance the cause of central control.

Controlling local government expenditure was proving to be a hard nut to crack, but by the time of the 1983 election, the Conservatives came up with two new ideas. They proposed the abolition of the 'high spending' GLC and the metropolitan counties, and they also proposed to introduce legislation which would 'cap' the rates of overspending local councils. The GLC and the six metropolitan counties were duly abolished under the Local Government Act, 1985. The Rates Act, 1984, gave the Secretary of State for the Environment the power to set the rate for named authorities that were deemed to be overspenders in a way which has involved the central government intruding into the taxation powers of local authorities to a quite unprecedented extent. All but one of the first eighteen councils to be rate-capped were Labour controlled and this has continued to be the pattern. Not surprisingly, the rate-capped Labour authorities launched a major campaign against rate-capping and the policies of the Conservative central government. Although the campaign ended in disarray and failure it nevertheless exhausted the energies of the ministers and officials in the central departments most concerned and encouraged them to rethink their strategy of control.

After almost a decade in office the government itself was grudgingly forced to recognise that it had only achieved a modest success in holding back local spending. Moreover, the extent of central intervention required to achieve even these results had worsened the whole pattern of central–local relations. Central attacks had been repeatedly followed by substantial local counter-attacks in a way that had proved to be time-consuming and self-defeating for all concerned. The centre was forced to recognise that strategies to cut local authority expenditure based upon intrusive central control were of limited value. It was time to change tack and encourage a strategy where the initiative was to be placed firmly in the hands of local people working through the ballot box.

Domestic rates had long been criticised (often by those on the Left who felt that they did not adequately reflect people's ability to pay) but the system itself was resilient; was cheap and easy to collect; the public was used to paying; and those who had looked into the matter invariably failed to come up with any 'better' system. The Conservative Party's October 1974 manifesto promised the abolition of domestic rates, but by 1979 the commitment had been weakened with the promise that domestic rates would go only after other direct taxation had been reduced. It was reported that the Prime Minister favoured replacing domestic rates with a local sales tax but this was dropped once it was realised that this system might offend European Community rules. The 1985 domestic rates revaluation in Scotland made the Conservative government extremely unpopular up there (they performed disastrously in the local elections) and this was the final straw which prompted the government to commit itself to the abolition of domestic rates and to the wholesale reorganisation of local government finance.

A 1986 Green Paper, *Paying for Local Government*, proposed to replace both domestic rates and non-domestic rates; to change the system of central grant; and to introduce a new system of capital finance. Domestic rates would be replaced by a flat rate poll tax, to be known as a community charge, that would be set by each local authority and levied on practically all adults within the authority irrespective of their income, wealth or housing situation. And non-domestic rates would be replaced by a national non-domestic rate that would be set by the central government, collected into a national pool, and then distributed to local authorities as a payment per adult. Initially, the new business rate would be set so as to yield the same amount as the old non-domestic rate, but any future increases would have to be fixed at, or below, the rate of inflation and so industry would gradually come to contribute less to local spending.

Most attention has centred on the Community Charge, or Poll Tax, precisely because all adults will have to pay it. Critics have argued that the Community Charge is 'unfair' because it is a regressive tax that bears no relation to an individual's ability to pay; and they have also suggested that it is costly to collect and easy to evade at the same time as it has adverse implications for people's willingness to register to vote. The Conservative government has rejected these criticisms, claiming that the Community Charge is simple (because everyone pays equal amounts for equal services); fair (because all adults benefiting from local services have to pay something towards their cost instead of just the 50 per cent who previously paid domestic rates); and enhancing of local democracy and accountability (because all adults, in having a direct direct stake in services *and* local authority expenditure, will be more likely to watch their councils and hold them to account for what they are doing and spending). It is this latter argument about the Poll Tax and accountability which embodies the government's new localist strategy for controlling local authority expenditure because the government is returning to basic arguments about the case for local self-government. In effect, the government is rather assuming that because the Poll Tax falls on everyone it will lead to everyone taking a general interest in local politics and a particular interest in local expenditure and the setting of a low poll tax in their own area. The government quite clearly expects profligate (Labour) councils setting high poll taxes to be held to account and voted out of office, at the same time as moderate and prudent (Conservative) councils setting low poll taxes will not only retain office but take over from Labour and the Liberal Democrats as the dominant party in control of local government.

As with so much that the Conservatives have attempted with respect to the control of local authority expenditure, the theory behind the Poll Tax is sound (albeit simple) whereas the practice has proved to be massively problematic for the Conservative government itself. The Poll Tax was introduced into Scotland in 1989 and into the rest of England and Wales in 1990. Right from the start the tax has been opposed. Predictably, the tax has been opposed by the Labour Party, by Labour councils, and by Left-wing 'troublemakers' who have done much to embarrass the new look Labour Party. Less predictably, the tax has also been opposed by Conservative councils (many of which found they were having to set a poll tax up to a third higher than DOE guidelines and this in spite of the fact that they saw themselves as prudent and efficient in the management of the council budget) and by 'ordinary' members of the general public (two-thirds of whom were losers under the new system in a way that seemed to make a mockery of Conservative claims about 'fairness'). Contrary to the theory behind the Poll Tax, the majority of the public did not blame their local councils and hold them to account since they took the view that it was an unfair tax that had been imposed onto local government by a central government that was seen as out of touch with the views of the ordinary man or woman in the street. The Poll Tax became *the* issue in British politics in 1990. It worked for the popularity of Labour and dramatically against the popularity and the electoral fortunes of the Conservative Party which lost a safe seat in a by-election in March 1990 before going on to do badly in the local elections in May. Controlling local government expenditure from the centre may have been a problem, but trying to engineer a situation of control through the local ballot box had simply rebounded against the Conservative government in a way which weakened its capacity to govern the centre at the same time as it worsened the prospect of victory at the next general election.

Conclusion

It is tempting to see the problem of local government and the clash between the central government and local government in purely party political terms. Since 1979, Britain has been governed centrally by a radical Conservative government which has abandoned the post-war consensus and pressed the case for private provision through the market as against public and collective provision through state institutions. During this same period, the trade union movement has been weak; parliamentary opposition has been toothless; but Labour, and Left Labour at that, has secured a grip on local government and has used this as a base from which to challenge Thatcherism, practically through battles over local public expenditure and ideologically through providing services in ways which suggest that there is a viable alternative to the whole ethos of market provision for individuals.

This party political perspective on central–local relations does deal with a crucial facet of the contemporary situation, but it does rather ignore deeper constitutional considerations and the more enduring problem of local self-government. Britain is a unitary state in which the position of local government is not guaranteed by a written constitution and so the central government is always going to be able to claim the *right* to control local government, and this notwithstanding the practical political difficulties of making that control effective. Moreover, even if Britain were not a unitary state and even if Labour were to form the central government, the centre would still want to try and assert a measure of control over local government. We say this because whilst the centre is caught up in the task of governing the country and managing the economy it has to form a view at the appropriate levels of public expenditure, taxation, and service provision, in a way which must have profound implications for the autonomy of local government and the viability of local democracy itself. Put another way, all central governments always have an interest in trying to reduce local authorities to agents of the centre, but all of them also face the problem of confronting interests outside of the centre that see in the tradition of local democracy a basis for autonomy and challenge. Rest assured, the actors may change but the central control/local democracy show will continue to run and run.

Between Centre and Locality

The United Kingdom comprises one state made up of four historic nations – England, Scotland, Wales and (part of) Ireland. With the possible exception of Northern Ireland, which enjoyed its own Parliament until 1972, these four nations ceased to govern themselves when they joined the Union. Their sovereignty was merged (or in the view of some, submerged) within a unitary state governed through a single Parliament.

These national differences have not been eclipsed, however. Culturally, they remain very much alive and can be traced in language, dialect, law, religion, the arts and mundane aspects of everyday life such as diet or leisure activities. The tartan, the *Eistedfodd* and the Roman Catholic church all speak in their various ways to the persistence of cultural traditions associated with the different peoples who today make up the United Kingdom. Nor have these differences disappeared entirely from our politics. The Welsh and the Scots, for example, both enjoy their own civil service department and their own minister whose job it is to look after their specific interests. They are deliberately overrepresented in the national Parliament (an arrangement which tends to inflate Labour Party representation at Westminster) and special days are set aside in the Parliamentary timetable for discussing Scottish and Welsh affairs. The Scots also retain their own distinctive legal and educational systems, and both Wales and Scotland boast their own nationalist parties which can command substantial electoral support.

In Northern Ireland, of course, the differences are even more marked, for here there is still a sizeable proportion of the population which does not identify with the UK state at all but which sees itself as part of a different ethno-national group based on the dream of a united and independent Ireland.

The persistence of distinct national identities within the UK points to one aspect of government and politics operating between the local level and the centre. Another, which is less romantic but arguably just as significant, is represented in the bureaucratic division of the country into various administrative regions. There is a range of state activities and services which are today organised through a regional network, bigger in scale than the district and county councils, but smaller than central departments of state. Sometimes these regions have been drawn to coincide with national boundaries – Scotland, Wales and Northern Ireland are often treated as three 'regions' for administrative purposes while England is then divided into perhaps another five or six. Where regional boundaries do coincide with cultural and historic national entities, the institutions operating at this level may achieve a relatively high degree of political visibility. Where (as is normally the case in England) these boundaries represent little more than lines of administrative convenience drawn on a map, then the institutions operating at this level may achieve little political prominence. The people of Wales may well be aware of the existence of bodies such as the Welsh Office or the Welsh Development Agency, but it seems unlikely that many of the citizens of Kent are aware that they are served by the South–East Thames Regional Health Authority (one of fourteen such bodies responsible for administering the National Health Service in England and Wales).

In this part of this chapter, then, we shall be concerned to look at two types of political institutions operating at a scale somewhere between that of local authorities and that of the central government. One, which generally attracts little comment or attention, comprises the various regional administrative bodies. The other, which can attract strong political passions and attachments, comprises organisations based on the historic claims to nationhood of the component parts of the Union.

The regional state

The development of a distinct regional level of state administration dates from the 1930s. It peaked in the sixties, when Britain came close to establishing a new tier of multipurpose elected authorities in the regions, and it declined significantly in the eighties when the Thatcher government set out to cut back on state bureaucracy and embarked on a large-scale programme of privatising nationalised industries, many of which (for example, the Gas and Electricity Boards) had been organised on a regional basis. It is by no means unlikely that the regional level could be revived in the future, for both Labour and the Liberal Democrats harbour plans for resuscitating it, and the European Community also often organises its interventions in Britain on a regional basis (for example, through regional aid for declining regions, and through large territorial constituencies for elections to the European Parliament).

It is no coincidence that the regional level should have begun to grow in the 1930s at the same time as local councils began to lose some of their powers, for many of the responsibilities which were taken away from local authorities were transferred to newly-created regional offices. When local government lost control of trunk roads in 1936, for example, the Ministry of Transport set up a new regional organisation of offices to adminster them. When gas and electricity were nationalised after the war, new regional boards were appointed to run them. When hospitals were taken out of municipal hands in 1948, they were passed to new Regional Hospital Boards, and the removal of water services from local government in 1974 led to the creation of ten new Regional Water Authorities to take over responsibility for water supply and sewage treatment and disposal. One major factor in the growth of the regional level of the state between the 1930s and the 1970s was, therefore, the movement of services away from the local level.

A second factor was the onset of the Great Depression in the inter-war years, for this highlighted the plight of those regions, such as southern Scotland, south Wales and the north-east of England, which depended on the sorts of traditional heavy industry which were particularly badly hit by the recession. It was in response to this that the government passed the Special Areas (Development and Improvement) Act in 1934 which enabled the appointment of two Regional Commissioners with the task of stimulating economic recovery in four 'Special Areas'. This extremely modest intervention marked the beginning of a long (and arguably rather unsuccessful) history of selective government support for declining regions – a policy which, like so many others, continued to expand until it was abruptly ended in the early years of the Thatcher decade.

A third factor which explains the development of a regional level of state administration from the 1930s onwards was the government's growing concern at that time with threats to social order from within, and to national security from without. In 1925, as part of its preparations in anticipation of a general strike, the government divided England and Wales into ten regions and appointed to each a Civil Commissioner charged with the task of maintaining communications, food supplies, power and public health services in the event of strike action or the outbreak of civil unrest. Similarly, in 1938 the government appointed ten Regional Commissioners for Civil Defence in response to the growing threat of war and invasion, and they stayed in their posts until 1945 despite complaints from local authorities which felt that their responsibilities and powers had been bypassed.

During the war, most government departments set up regional offices based on the 1938 Civil Defence boundaries so that a devolved system of administration could continue even if the centre came under attack. These offices were then co-ordinated from 1940 onwards through ten Area

Boards, each consisting of the heads of the various government departments in each region together with representatives of employers and trade unions. At the end of the war these Area Boards became Regional Boards for Industry on which civil servants continued to sit with industrialists and union leaders. This functional or 'corporatist' mode of interest representation is one which remained characteristic of many regional bodies through the post-war period.

By 1945, then, there was a well-established regional framework for administration in Britain. This was strengthened by the post-war Labour government which adopted a regional structure for many of its newly-nationalised industries and services including British Rail, the gas and electricity industries, physical planning and the health service. For Labour, a regional strategy was fundamental to post-war reconstruction. Through the 1950s, however, this emphasis on regional administration faded as Conservative governments set about deregulating the battery of controls and regulations which the war and the Attlee government had nurtured. Between 1953 and 1958, most government departments closed down or cut back their regional offices and many of the special regional agencies (for example, the Regional Physical Planning Committees set up in 1947) were wound up. With the economy growing everywhere, there seemed little justification for maintaining regional bodies to sort out problems which seemed to have resolved themselves.

The Regional Boards for Industry did survive, however, and in the early sixties the government once again became concerned about 'regional problems' as the long post-war boom began to peter out. The National Economic Development Council, which was established in 1962 (see Chapter 9), pressed for regional development as an integral component of any national growth strategy, and in 1965, when the new Labour government published its ill-fated National Plan, eleven economic planning regions were created (eight in England plus one each in Scotland, Wales and Northern Ireland) in an attempt to ensure a geographically balanced and co-ordinated national economic strategy.

The establishment of these economic planning regions is the closest the United Kingdom has yet come to developing a regional tier of government. Each region had its own Economic Planning Board consisting of civil servants employed in the various regional departmental offices. This board then advised its Regional Economic Planning Council which consisted of employers, trade union leaders, academics and local councillors from across the region. The Planning Boards were often referred to as 'regional Whitehalls' and the Planning Councils as 'regional cabinets', but this latter designation was obviously inappropriate given that the members were all appointed (by central government) rather than elected. Just like the Regional Boards for Industry, which they replaced, these new Planning Councils were essentially corporatist agencies which served to bring together representatives of capital, organised labour and the state undisturbed by the glare of electoral politics. With no electoral mechanism

established at the regional level, it was to be expected that the democratic vacuum thus created would be filled by corporatist forms of
representation.

This system of regional economic planning boards and councils survived
in name for fourteen years, but its political significance and effectiveness
lasted for barely more than two. In 1966, the National Plan was abandoned. This left the fourteen regional boards and councils in the curious
position of having to plan their regional economies in the absence of any
national plan or strategy. They pressed on with drawing up regional plans
in the hope that local authorities would pay them some attention, but this
was always unlikely given that most local councils were suspicious of and
hostile to the whole concept of a regional planning machinery which
seemed to threaten their traditional powers and responsibilities. In 1969 the
Department of Economic Affairs was closed down and this marked the
beginning of the end for the regional councils and boards. They struggled on through the 1970s attempting to influence both Whitehall and
the town halls but achieving little headway with either, and in 1979 the
newly-elected Thatcher government abolished the Planning Councils
altogether.

As in the 1950s, so in the 1980s, the regional level declined in importance
as the national government set its face against further state planning and
intervention. Not only was the Thatcher government ill-disposed towards
bureaucratic and corporatist proliferation (which seemed to be associated with the extension of regional administration), but it also sought to
undermine regional economic policies by drastically reducing the size and
significance of grants, incentives and controls designed to induce or force
new investment into declining areas. The regional planning machinery did
not entirely disappear – agencies like the Highlands and Islands Development Board and the Welsh Development Agency survived and achieved
some success in attracting new investment into their areas. These, however,
are one-off bodies, and they no longer form part of a larger regional tier
of planning.

The demise of the Economic Planning Boards and Councils has not
meant the collapse of the regional level of the state, but it has left it looking
much more ragged and fragmented. Indeed, the subsequent privatisation
of the gas, water and electricity industries has further eroded the scale and
significance of regional administration, for not only has economic planning disappeared as a regional activity, but so too has provision of these
basic utilities which are now organised by public limited companies. In
England the key state activity which is still organised at the regional level
is health care.

The fourteen Regional Health Authorities (RHAs) employ or are responsible for around one million people (4 per cent of the nation's workforce)
and account for over 10 per cent of all public expenditure. They enjoy a
major responsibility for making policy (within guidelines established at
the centre) and for allocating resources. The lower level District Health

Authorities, of which there are over two hundred, work within the context of decisions laid down by the fourteen RHAs.

Who controls the regional state?

When we compare bodies like the RHAs with local government bodies, two crucial points are immediately apparent. The first is that they are far fewer in number and much larger in size. The second is that their members are unelected. The principal political effects of these two simple features of regional level organisations are that:

1 central government is likely to find it much easier to control regional authorities;
2 ordinary members of the public are likely to find it much more difficult to have a say in what regional authorities do; and
3 special interests may achieve a relatively high degree of influence in the administration of services organised at regional level.

These three points may be illustrated with reference to the way the National Health Service is administered through the RHAs.

Central control

Ever since it was set up in 1948, the NHS has consisted of three elements – the hospital sector, general practice and dentistry, and community health care. Until 1974 these were run by different agencies. Regional Hospital Boards and Hospital Management Committees ran the hospitals; Executive Councils managed general practitioners; and local government was responsible for community health (for example, clinics, family planning, school dental services, etc). The 1974 reorganisation brought all three branches under the single umbrella of the new RHAs. As with the reorganisation of local government in the same year, the aim was to raise efficiency and improve managerial coordination.

The result, predictably, was an emphasis on managerialism. In principle, the RHAs are run by their members who are appointed by the Secretary of State. In practice, the initiative clearly lies with the full-time officers. The so-called 'Grey Book', issued at the time of the reorganisation, recommended the establishment of corporate management teams of officers who were expected to arrive at a consensus on the basis of apolitical judgements of the technically-defined best solutions to specific problems. This system changed somewhat in the early eighties when general managers were introduced to head each Regional and District Authority. Since then, the RHAs have been run much as any private organisation might be run – by a single chief executive backed up by a specialist management team.

With responsibility concentrated in just fourteen regional managers, it has been relatively easy for central government to pursue its objectives without encountering major resistance from lower level bodies. Unlike the local councils, where the centre is confronted by over four hundred different authorities each claiming legitimacy through an electoral 'mandate', the regional tier of the state can be and usually is controlled fairly successfully. In the case of the RHAs, for example, government cash limits have been imposed with little resistance or opposition from below. Where local councils claim accountability in a 'downward' direction, to local electorates, bodies like RHAs trace accountability 'upwards', to the Secretary of State.

Consumer weakness

The corollary of strong central control at the regional level is a corresponding political weakness of ordinary members of the public. Whereas central government finds it easier to deal with a small number of large bodies, the public experiences regional bodies as remote and inaccessible. Similarly, while the centre can extend its power and influence over bodies whose members are appointed rather than elected, members of the public are likely to find it more difficult to get a voice when those they are addressing do not have to compete for their votes and support.

These points can again usefully be illustrated with reference to the Regional Health Authorities. Following the 1974 reorganisation of the health service, consumer interests have ostensibly been safeguarded in two principal ways. First, lay members (including representatives of local councils) serve on both Regional and District Authorities. Their role, however, is limited, partly because they are not appointed as representatives of any group or interest, partly because they are part-time 'amateurs' up against full-time medical 'experts', and partly because they are in any case most unrepresentative of the population as a whole (of the 210 appointments made to the newly-established RHAs in 1974, for example, 56 were members of the medical profession, 79 were company directors, managers or professional and business people, 12 were trade union officials and just 3 were ordinary manual workers).

The second conduit of consumer influence is through the Community Health Councils. These function at the District level and are intended to act as 'watchdogs', transmitting complaints and suggestions from the public to the District Authorities and, if the matter is not satisfactorily resolved, from there to the RHA. Like the consumer councils operating elsewhere in the state system (for example, in British Rail), the CHCs are in reality pathetically weak. They have no executive powers, they operate on tiny budgets, and most of the people who use the NHS seem blissfully unaware of their very existence.

Special interests

The regional level of the state offers ideal breeding conditions for corporatist-style administrative arrangements. Corporatism flourishes where electoral competition and pluralism are weakest, for in this situation specific functional interests can forge close and mutually advantageous links with state managers and bureaucrats. In the case of the health service, this has resulted in close liaison and co-operation between NHS management and representatives of the medical profession.

The doctors can exert special influence in three ways. First, they enjoy strong and effective representation through the Medical Advisory Committees which are consulted at both regional and district level. Second, NHS managers are themselves often doctors, with the result that doctors on the advisory committees may find themselves advising doctors on the management boards. And third, decisions at all levels from the DHSS downwards are informed by a rarely-questioned assumption that health care is about curing diseases rather than preventing people from falling ill in the first place. This curative orientation to health care is one which reflects and reinforces the interests of consultants and GPs who make their livings by performing operations or prescribing drugs. As we saw in chapter 10, policy-making in the welfare state is susceptible to the influence of professional groups. This tendency is especially marked in the health service where elected local control has been abolished and where decision-making and administration is concentrated in regional structures which are inaccessible and unaccountable to the populations they serve.

The future of the regional state

On both the Left and Right of British politics there is a recognition of the need to 'do something' about this regional level of the state. The choice, it seems, is between democratising it and abolishing or privatising it.

The argument for democratisation has long been put by the Liberal Democrats and is today also supported by the Labour Party. Both parties link the question of regional assemblies with the issue of Scottish and Welsh nationality, as well as with the need for further reform of the local government system. The desire to devolve at least some powers to new Scottish and Welsh assemblies raises the problem of what to do about England, and the response has been to argue for new elected regional assemblies in England as well. This then has a 'knock-on' effect on local government, for the creation of regional councils opens up the prospect of a bureaucratic tangle of three levels of sub-central elected government (the districts, the counties and the regions). Labour's answer to this is to abolish the county councils and to transfer their education and social services functions to the districts.

Democratising the regional tier of state administration would presumably open up this level to public pressure and influence to a greater extent than is currently possible. There are three problems, however. One is that in England regional identities are often weak and new regional assemblies might excite little interest or enthusiasm from the electorate.

Furthermore, whether elected or not, such authorities will still be operating at a scale which can make it difficult for people to achieve effective access to them, or to mobilise themselves across such large areas. The second problem is that regional boundaries are somewhat artificial and that different bodies operating at the regional level often cover different territories. Bringing different regional functions together under one authority would therefore necessitate considerable upheavel in reorganising boundaries. The third and perhaps most serious problem is that it is by no means clear that there is enough activity still going on at the regional level to warrant the creation of new elected assemblies. Obviously health could be brought under the control of new regional assemblies, but what else? As we have seen, the regional planning machinery has fallen into disuse and many of the functions which used to be located in regional offices – water supply and sewage disposal, electricity distribution, gas supply – have now been privatised. Obviously some central government departments still maintain regional offices, and some of the functions of, say, the Department of the Environment or the Department of Industry could therefore perhaps be carved out for new regional assemblies, but the impression remains that such assemblies would be big bodies with a rather small remit.

The alternative to democratisation is abolition, or privatisation. This was effectively the Conservative government's policy through the 1980s. Thatcherism's antipathy to big government, bureaucracy and corporatism was bound to become focused on the regional tier of the state which displayed all three in profusion. The result, as we have seen, was a massive reduction in the extent of government activity at this level. The Regional Economic Planning Councils were the first to go – they were abolished. The British Gas regions were parcelled up in one huge monopoly company and sold off. The ten Regional Water Authorities were privatised in 1989 as ten seperate companies. The regional Electricity boards were similarly privatised the following year. As for the Regional Health Authorities, the government sought a solution not in privatisation (a recipe for electoral suicide) but in the introduction of a package of NHS reforms designed to introduce an 'internal market' and to allow hospitals to become self-governing. The thinking behind the idea of the internal market was that consumers of health services can be empowered by allowing them to seek treatment outside their own districts thereby short-cutting queues and waiting lists and introducing an element of competitive efficiency into the system. At the same time, hospitals could 'opt out' of RHA control and compete for patients. Not surprisingly given the influence of the medical profession in the NHS, the government's proposals led to a major campaign of opposition from the doctors.

The future of the regional tier of the state is, therefore, uncertain and it depends crucially on the electoral fortunes of the major parties in the 1990s and beyond. Some degree of decentralisation of responsibility is necessary in most areas of public policy-making in order to take account of the varying circumstances of different areas and to monitor the implementation of

central policies on the ground. But as the battles between central government and local authorities over recent years demonstrate, such decentralisation can be dangerous since it opens up the possibility of resistance
from below. Regional agencies have offered a solution to this dilemma, for
their size enables the centre to control them while putting them beyond the
reach of potentially troublesome opponents. In addition, as non-elected
bodies they lack public visibility and accountability, and this too helps the
centre to direct them in accordance with its purposes. The result has been
a regional tier characterised by central control, managerial autonomy and
corporatist closure. Most of us have little knowledge of, and even less
influence over, what goes on at this level of the state. Like the institutions
discussed in chapter 6, the regional state seems best described as part of Britain's 'secret' state apparatus

Four nations, one state

Thus far we have considered the organisation of the state at the regional
level. A *region*, in the sense used here, is simply an administrative subdivi-
sion of a larger territorial unit, something larger than a 'locality' or 'district'
but smaller than a 'state'. Although regions may coincide with nations, the
two concepts are obviously distinct, for a *nation* is a sociological entity
which is territorially bounded and whose members share in common certain
sentiments by which they recognise in each other a common identity and
share with each other a desire to live under the same authority. Nations are
often co-terminous with states, but again this is not necessarily the case. A
state is simply that political unit which reserves for itself the right to use
force within a given territory. A state may govern a territory consisting of
one nation, or (as in the case of the USSR, for example) of many. In
the case of the United Kingdom, we see one state, four nations and an
indefinite number of regions.

The dominant nation within the United Kingdom state is and always has
been England. It is by far the largest of the four nations, and historically
it has been the most powerful, so much so that foreigners (as well as the
English themselves) frequently equate 'England' with 'Britain' or even with
the 'United Kingdom'.

The nation which became England was first unified as a colony of Rome,
fifty-five years before the birth of Christ. The Romans never managed to
conquer the rest of the British Isles, however, and when the Empire collapsed, the unity imposed upon England swiftly disappeared as well. Over
the next five hundred years, this unity was gradually recreated as Wessex
fused with the south of England, East Anglia and the Midlands and eventually grew to encompass Cornwall and the north. By the time of the Nor-
man conquest, England was recognisably one nation under one Crown,
although central authority tended to be weak in outlying regions where
powerful lords retained a high degree of autonomy.

Wales came under English domination in 1277. Up until then Wales had been ruled by various warring chiefs – it had never been a single, unified state. In 1277, the English Crown claimed half of the land in that country for itself while leaving the other half to powerful lords who ruled as semi-sovereign magnates. It was not until 1536, however, that Wales was formally absorbed into the English state and made subject to English parliamentary laws. Prompted by fears of a possible foreign invasion along the Welsh coastline, Acts were passed in 1536 and 1542 which granted Wales representation in the Westminster Parliament, made the country subject to English law, and imposed the Anglican Church as the established Church of Wales (disestablishment did not come until 1920).

Unlike Wales, Scotland did develop as an independent, sovereign state prior to its unification with England in 1707, although the authority of the Scottish Crown in parts of the Highlands was always limited. Also unlike Wales, union with England came, not as a result of conquest and annexation, but as a result of free negotiation and a voluntary treaty. The union was facilitated by the fact that the two countries had shared a common monarchy since the accession to the English throne of James VI of Scotland in 1603, but the principal reason for it was economic. Powerful Scottish interests reasoned that they could do better as junior partners in the emerging imperial state south of the border than as a small independent state shut out of English imperial markets. While the 1707 Act of Union put an end to the separate Scottish state, it recognised and institutionalised the continuation of a distinct Scottish nation. The Scots, for example, were never subjected to the imposition of an established Anglican Church in the way that the Welsh had been, for the Act safeguarded the position of the Presbyterian Kirk for all time. Similarly, Scotland retained its own courts and its own distinctive legal system which remains separate from English law to this day.

The fourth nation to enter the union was Ireland. Notwithstanding late twentieth-century political rhetoric, Ireland (like Wales) had never been a unified state prior to its subjugation by England, for traditional Gaelic society was tribal. It is also important to emphasise the close historic links between the north of Ireland and the Scottish Lowlands, for people had migrated in both directions across the twelve miles of sea for many centuries before English and Scottish colonisation of Ulster began in the seventeenth century. Having said that, however, it is also crucial to recognise the religious distinctiveness of the Irish. While England, Scotland and Wales were predominantly Protestant countries (albeit with different denominations – Anglicanism, Presbyterianism and Nonconformism), the indigenous Irish peasants and lords were Roman Catholic.

It was in 1607 that the leaders of the two big Catholic Ulster clans fled the country following their defeat by the English. The land they vacated was held to have reverted to the English Crown and was swiftly settled by Protestant colonists, mainly from Scotland. In 1641 Irish Catholics rebelled against the immigrant landlords and set in motion a series of bloody conflicts which culminated in the arrival of Cromwell's army in

1649 which ruthlessly crushed Catholic peasant resistance. There then followed a second wave of colonization as more land throughout Ireland was confiscated and settled by Cromwell's soldiers and backers. By 1690, when William of Orange defeated the deposed Catholic King, James II, at the Battle of the Boyne, thereby securing the Protestant ascendency in both Britain and Ireland, nearly 80 per cent of all Irish land was owned by English and Scottish migrants. Following the military victory of 1690, a parliament was established in Dublin from which all Roman Catholics were excluded. This parliament exercised widespread domestic authority but was subject to the Westminster parliament in matters regarding foreign policy and affairs of state. It effectively ran Ireland on behalf of the Protestant landowners until 1800, and throughout the eighteenth century it further weakened the Catholic property-owning class, depriving it of the right to vote in 1727, preventing it from buying or leasing new land, and enforcing a system of inheritance through which Catholic lands had to be divided up among all the sons of the deceased. Towards the end of the century, this militant Protestant rule came under increasing strain, partly as a result of the enfranchisement of Catholics in 1793 following pressure from Westminster, and partly because of a French-backed rebellion in 1798. The result was the incorporation of Ireland into the United Kingdom through an Act of Union passed in 1800. For the next 120 years, the whole of Ireland was governed directly from Westminster to which it elected its own representatives.

Throughout the nineteenth century and into the twentieth, the Union brought considerable benefits to south Wales, the Lowlands of Scotland, and the north-eastern counties of Ireland, for all three areas developed large-scale industries which reaped the harvest of the Empire. The Scottish Highlands (where people were driven from their crofts by the Enclosures), north and central Wales (where the population dwindled as labour was attracted to the south and to the English Midlands), and the southern counties of Ireland (where a backward peasantry was left to scrape a living and where a million died in the potato famine of the 1840s) were, however, left behind in this wave of industrial expansion, and all three areas experienced dramatic depopulation during this period.

It was in Ireland that popular resistance developed most strongly. A history of forcible sequestration of land, bloody suppression of people, religious persecution of Catholics and extreme rural deprivation and poverty resulted in a nationalist challenge being mounted on the basis of the popular religion. Because the domination of the Irish had been organised culturally (through exclusion of Catholics) as well as politically and economically, the reaction against it was structured along similar lines. So it was that, throughout the nineteenth century, Irish nationalism became intertwined with Catholicism, just as in the north, loyalty to the Union became the hallmark of Protestantism.

The rising tide of Irish resistance to British rule forced itself onto the agenda of Westminster politics in 1885 when, following the extension of the franchise to all adult males, eighty-five Irish members were elected on a 'Home Rule' (or what might today be termed a 'devolution') ticket. The Liberal Prime Minister, Gladstone, was willing to cede a limited degree of Irish Home Rule, but neither Parliament nor the Protestants in the north of Ireland agreed with him. The Liberal Party split on the issue and the bill was defeated in the Commons. A second Home Rule bill was introduced in 1893 but was defeated in the Lords. In 1912 a third attempt was made, and this one eventually became law in 1914. In the north of Ireland the Protestants began to prepare for an armed struggle against what they saw as the inevitability of an eventual move to full Irish independence, and civil war was only averted by the outbreak of the First World War and the suspension of the Home Rule Act. While this placated the Irish unionists, it enraged the nationalists, and in 1916 they led an uprising in Dublin which was soon quelled by British forces. Fifteen of the ringleaders were tried for treason and executed. In the post-war general election, Sinn Fein candidates swept the board in most Catholic constituencies, winning 70 per cent of the Irish seats (though rather less than 50 per cent of the vote). The successful candidates proceeded to boycott Westminster and set up their own assembly (the Dail) in Dublin, while on the streets the IRA stepped up its campaign of violence against what it saw as the occupying power.

The British government responded to all this with the Government of Ireland Act of 1920. Recognising the irreconcilable aspirations of the Protestants in the north and the Catholic majority in the rest of the country, this Act established separate parliaments in Dublin (to adminster 26 counties) and in Belfast (to administer the remaining six). This partition was welcomed in the north where the establishment of a devolved assembly in Stormont Castle was seen as a way of guaranteeing the continuing link with Britain and separation from the south. It was rejected by Sinn Fein, however, and the nationalists demanded that the whole of Ireland be recognised as a dominion within the British Commonwealth. Following an escalation of political violence, this demand was partially met when the 26 counties were allowed to secede and become the Irish Free State. Eire's emergence as a separate state was finally completed in 1949 when it left the Commonwealth and declared itself an independent republic.

The Republic of Ireland has ever since its birth maintained a claim to sovereignty over the whole island. In reality, of course, the six counties carved out of the province of Ulster under the 1920 Act have continued to be part of the United Kingdom, and successive British governments have made clear their commitment to maintaining this union for as long as a majority of the people in the six counties desire it. With nearly two-thirds of the population Protestant, majority support for the union has never been in doubt. So it is that, from 1921 until 1972, Northern Ireland ran its own internal affairs through the devolved assembly at Stormont while foreign affairs, external trade and responsibility for the armed forces lay with Westminster.

The fracturing of the United Kingdom by the secession of Eire in 1922 had little impact on the strength of the union in Great Britain. Although demands for Irish Home Rule did help stimulate nationalist consciousness in Scotland, and no fewer than thirteen Scottish devolution bills were presented to Parliament between 1885 and 1914, this had little lasting significance beyond the establishment of the Scottish Office in 1885 and the creation of a post within the cabinet for a Secretary of State for Scotland in 1926. As for Wales, the nationalist party, Plaid Cymru, was formed in 1925 more in an attempt to salvage the Welsh language than as a genuine movement for secession.

As the United Kingdom emerged victorious from the Second World War and embarked on the long period of post-war economic growth, so the question of the union ceased to be an issue. Even the Irish question seemed to have been settled if not resolved. As with so many other aspects of British politics, however, it was only with the end of the boom years in the 1960s that old problems began to resurface.

The re-emergence of nationalism – Scotland and Wales

We have seen that Scotland and Wales are very different countries with very different histories. Wales was effectively annexed by England over seven hundred years ago, and there never has been an independent, unified and sovereign Welsh nation state. Scotland, on the other hand, joined with England in a voluntary union less than three hundred years ago. It was once a sovereign state and it still retains a distinctive set of national institutions including an autonomous legal system, a separate educational system and its own church (the Scottish Presbyterian Church). Scotland is an historic nation in a sense in which Wales never was.

These historic differences are fundamental to the explanation of the very different patterns of nationalism which developed in the two countries from the 1960s onwards. Welsh nationalism had no institutional structure or legacy of nationhood on which to build and its appeal was therefore founded almost entirely in the mobilisation of cultural nostalgia. Born of a despair among Welsh intellectuals who saw the language, the Chapel and the rural way of life disappearing fast, nationalism in Wales was essentially backward-looking. Plaid Cymru, the Welsh nationalist party, never really succeeded in winning and holding the alleigance of the industrial, English-speaking population whose radicalism has traditionally been expressed through the mainstream parties (first the Liberals and later Labour).

Scottish nationalism, by contrast, did not have to create and foster a sense of Scottish nationhood for it was already present. The problem faced by the Scottish National Party (SNP) was rather how to wean Scottish voters away from nearly two and a half centuries of economic dependence on England and to convince them that Scottish independence could actually benefit them materially. This task was facilitated by the happy accident of the discovery of substantial gas and oil reserves in the North Sea. This enabled the nationalists to claim that revenue from 'Scottish oil' was being diverted to prop up the English economy when it could have been used to fund new investment to replace Scotland's declining heavy industries. However, it was not the oil itself which fuelled the growth of Scottish nationalism in the sixties and seventies so much as the recognition that the British economy as a whole was weakening, that Scotland was being hit particularly hard and that the balance of economic advantage might therefore be shifting away from the union and towards independence.

We saw earlier that Scotland's entry into the Union in 1707 was prompted by economic considerations. England was at that time emerging as a major imperial power in Europe, and following the time-honoured dictum that you should join 'em if you can't beat 'em, the Scots tagged themselves onto London's imperial coat tails thereby claiming a share in the advantages of imperial free trade and circumventing the English Navigation Acts. By the 1960s, however, the economic winds had changed. The Empire had gone and with it shrivelled the economic logic of Scottish union with England. If there is advantage now for the Scots in merging their national sovereignty in a larger whole, it points not to union with England but to confederation with the stronger economies of the European Community.

In both Scotland and Wales, nationalism prospered as the post-war economic boom petered out. In both countries industry was hit harder and earlier than in most parts of England. The political fallout began to show in opinion polls and by-elections between 1964 and 1970 with the nationalist vote rising dramatically. This new trend represented a major electoral threat to the Labour Party which has always depended upon strong support in Scotland and Wales to offset the strength of the Conservatives in England. Only twice in its history (in the landslides of 1945 and 1966) has Labour ever managed to win a majority of seats in England. The rise of the nationalists worried English Tories, for the Conservative Party has always been staunchly committed to the principle of the Union, but it shook the Labour government of the time given its electoral as well as constitutional implications.

The answer, predictably perhaps, was sought in the establishment of a Royal Commission on the constitution under the chairmanship of Lord Kilbrandon. Appointed in 1969, the commission eventually reported four years later, but its message was confused. While the commission was unanimous in rejecting any break-up of the Union or move to federation, it split three ways over devolution. Some wanted to restrict any change to Scotland; others wanted to include Wales; and some wanted to extend decentralization to England as well by establishing elected assemblies in the English regions. The Heath Conservative government ignored all three recommendations.

In the February 1974 general election the SNP won seven seats with 22 per cent of the Scottish vote, and together with Plaid Cymru and the Liberals (who have remained advocates of some measure of Home Rule ever since Gladstone's time) held the balance of power in the Westminster

Parliament. Eight months later when another election was called, the SNP increased its share of the Scottish vote to 30 per cent, and its eleven seats made it the second largest party in Scotland behind Labour (Plaid Cymru's vote in both of these elections stayed steady at around 10 per cent). Forced to govern with a precarious majority, the Labour administration sought to woo the nationalists with a devolution bill in 1976 only to see it defeated by an alliance of Conservatives and Labour rebels. The government then published separate bills for Scotland and Wales but, in order to placate enough opponents to get the bills through Parliament, it agreed to a provision that each should only be ratified following a referendum in which at least 40 per cent of the total electorate in each of the two countries supported the change. In the event, 52 per cent of those voting in Scotland supported the proposed Scottish Assembly, but this represented only 33 per cent of the total Scottish electorate and thus failed to clear to 40 per cent hurdle. In Wales only 20 per cent voted for an Assembly representing just 12 per cent of the electorate. Back at Westminster, both bills fell. The nationalists were furious and they joined with the Ulster MPs, the Liberals and the Conservatives to defeat the government on a vote of confidence by just one vote. An election was held and in May 1979 Margaret Thatcher entered Downing Street.

The national question in Wales was effectively killed off by these events, and in Scotland the nationalist case suffered a severe setback. At the 1979 election Plaid Cymru and the SNP won just two seats each, and throughout the 1980s Conservative governments set their face firmly against any suggestion of a move to Home Rule. Despite this, however, the national question in Scotland has not gone away, for two political factors have kept it alive. One is Labour's continuing need to spike the guns of the SNP, and to this end the Labour Party has committed itself to introducing a Scottish Assembly with legislative and revenue-raising powers within a year of taking office. The other is the declining fortunes of the Conservatives north of the border. In 1987, when the Conservatives won a handsome 100 seat majority nationally, they took only ten of the 72 seats in Scotland polling just 24 per cent of the Scottish vote, and this has enabled the nationalists to argue with some justification that Scotland is being subjected to policies which have little electoral support in that country.

None of the main UK parties favours splitting the Union, but only the Conservatives stand out against a Scottish Assembly. Were Labour to come to power at Westminster and introduce such an assembly, the consequences could be considerable in the years to come. In Scotland itself an Assembly would be dominated by Labour and the SNP and would therefore pose a major challenge to any subsequent Conservative government. The demand for independence is as likely to be stimulated as it is subdued by such an innovation. Furthermore, the logical corollary of a devolved Scottish Assembly is presumably that Scottish representation in Westminster should be reduced and that Scottish MPs should be denied the right to vote on matters of concern only to England. At present Scotland is overrepresented at

Westminster (relative to the size of its population it should have 55 seats rather than 72) and Scottish members can speak and vote on English bills for example, those to do with education. If following devolution, the size and scope of Scottish representation in the Westminster Parliament were reduced, this could severely weaken the Labour Party's ability to win an overall majority.

The Scottish question, therefore, continues to pose uncomfortable problems for both main UK parties. For the Conservatives, a strong commitment to the integrity of the Union is fundamentally challenged by the inability to muster votes north of the border. Future Conservative administrations must ask how long they can ignore Scottish demands for Home Rule when their own support in Scotland is so pitifully thin. For Labour, on the other hand, a pragmatic acceptance of devolution threatens to open a Pandora's box by encouraging demands for full independence and by raising the question of reduced Scottish representation at Westminster. Future Labour administrations must ask whether short-term concessions to the nationalist cause do not threaten in the long term to undermine Labour's own electoral prospects. The nationalist advance was repelled in 1979, but the national question is still haunting British politics and it would be foolhardy to believe that it can swiftly or easily be settled.

The re-emergence of the Irish question

The people of Scotland and Wales have never known devolved government within the United Kingdom. The people of Northern Ireland, by contrast, experienced it for fifty years following the establishment of the province, for the Northern Ireland Parliament in Stormont was responsible for a wide range of domestic policy until its demise in 1972. The problem with this arrangement was that Stormont functioned effectively as an instrument of Protestant hegemony, and it was the systematic use of state power to favour one community over another which led eventually to the outbreak of civil war in the province.

Ever since the settlement of 1920-2, the northern Protestants had used their majority position to maintain the exclusion of Catholics from the civil and political rights which are taken for granted elsewhere in the Kingdom. Their power was secured by abolishing proportional representation in 1929 and by retaining a property qualification which disenfranchised one-quarter of the population, most of whom were Catholics. The Protestant ascendancy was further reinforced by blatant gerrymandering of electoral boundaries. In the county of Fermanagh, for example, ward boundaries were drawn in such a way that the half of the electorate who were Catholics was represented by just one-third of the council seats. In the city of Londonderry (known to Catholics as Derry), 14,000 Catholics elected six borough councillors while 9,000 Protestants elected a further twelve. The results of this Protestant stranglehold over the levers of political power were apparent in evidence on employment and housing. The unemployment rate among Catholics, for example, was never less than twice that among Protestants, and while this can partly be explained by non-religious factors such as social class, geographical location and family size, it was also a product of discrimination by both public- and private-sector employers (in Fermanagh, for example, 332 out of 370 council employees were Protestant, and in Belfast the Harland and Wolf shipyard employed no Catholics). In housing too, Protestant councils tended to build houses in Protestant neighbourhoods for Protestant families (although it must also be said that where Catholics were in control of councils the same pattern was repeated in reverse). Discrimination against Catholics was often openly acknowledged and even defended on the grounds that Catholics owed allegiance to the Republic in the south, that the Republic still claimed sovereignty over the north, and that northern Catholics therefore represented an 'enemy within'.

Under the terms of the 1920 and 1949 Acts, there was little that the Westminster Parliament could do to halt or ameliorate this systematic discrimination against the minority population, but in 1967 a group of predominantly middle-class Catholics determined to do something about it themselves. The Northern Ireland Civil Rights Association was formed to campaign against discrimination in housing and employment. Many Protestants regarded the Association as a thinly-veiled challenge to the union itself, but there is little evidence to support such an interpretation. Following the collapse of the IRA offensive in the north between 1956 and 1962, most northern Catholics seem to have been reconciled to the continuing link with Britain. Be that as it may, Protestant resistance to the new civil rights movement swiftly intensified, and in 1968 civil rights marches were attacked by loyalists and rioting broke out in several cities as Catholic neighbourhoods came under attack from Protestant gangs. The province's police force, the Royal Ulster Constabulary, proved unable (or possibly, given its overwhelmingly Protestant character, unwilling) to control these disturbances and the deployment of the reservist B-Specials only inflamed the situation further. Eventually, in 1969, British troops were put on the streets to restore order following two nights of rioting in which one hundred Catholic homes were burned and nine people were killed. The Westminster government also took responsibility for housing away from local councils in the province in an attempt to meet some of the objections raised by the civil rights movement. But it was all too little too late.

The troops, who were at first welcomed by most Catholics, soon became identified in the eyes of the minority population as yet another instrument for maintaining Protestant power and privileges, and following 'Bloody Sunday' in 1972, when thirteen demonstrators in Londonderry were shot by soldiers, they were never again to win Catholic trust. The IRA, virtually defunct just a few years earlier, swiftly attracted support and recruits in the Catholic areas, and as its strength grew, so too did that of the various Protestant para-military groups. The conflict swiftly intensified (467 deaths were recorded in 1972 compared with 174 in 1971 and just 25 in 1970) to a point where the British government felt obliged to take over direct responsibility for security. The Stormont government was outraged and resigned with the result that London imposed 'direct rule' over the province for the first time in its history. Since 1972 the British government has launched two major initiatives (as well as many other minor ones) aimed at trying to defuse the conflict and move towards a long-term constitutional settlement.

1 The reestablishment, in 1973/4, of a Northern Ireland Assembly together with the setting up of a Council of Ireland consisting of representatives from both the north and the south. The Northern Ireland Assembly was to be elected by a system of proportional representation for both the legislature and the executive. Under the terms of this agreement, Protestant and Catholic leaders agreed to establish a system of 'power-sharing' in which the Stormont Assembly would elect an Eecutive consisting of six unionists, four members of the (mainly Catholic) SDLP and one representative of the non-sectarian Alliance Party. The elections duly took place, the Executive was set up, and the province was then brought to a halt for two weeks in May 1974 by a general strike called by the (Protestant) Ulster Workers Council. Eventually the Unionist representatives resigned from the Executive, thus bringing it, and the Assembly and the Council of Ireland, to an ignominious end. London resumed direct rule and the deaths continued.

2 The 1985 Anglo-Irish Agreement. Recognising that previous attempts to find a way out of the impasse had foundered on loyalist resistance, the British government simply ignored the voice of the unionists altogether and imposed a deal worked out with the Irish Republic which allowed for regular ministerial meetings between London and Dublin. In return for giving the Republic a voice in influencing affairs in the north (and hence in theory safeguarding the interests of the Catholic population there), the British government achieved agreement to co-operate on cross-border security as well as a rather limp recognition by the south of the right of self-determination of the people in the north. Predictably the Protestants were outraged, but this time there was little they could do. Mass demonstrations, strikes and even resignation en bloc of all the Unionist MPs at Westminster did nothing to end the agreement, but equally the agreement itself achieved little by way of any significant move towards a settlement.

Northern Ireland is a political stalemate. The Protestant majority continues to emphasise the historic union with Britain because it fears being subordinated within a highly conservative Catholic dominated state (in the 1980s the Irish have voted in referenda to maintain prohibition of both abortion and divorce). It has developed a frontier mentality in which it sees itself threatened from the south and betrayed by London. The Catholic minority continues to emphasise its loyalty to and identity with the south because it deeply distrusts both the Protestant majority and the British state. It has developed a seige mentality in which it sees its interests safeguarded only by politicians in the south or by IRA gunmen in the north. To pretend that any consensus is possible in such a situation is utopian, for Northern Ireland consists of two peoples with different aspirations for the same territory.

An attitude survey conducted in Northern Ireland by Edward Moxon-Browne in 1978 demonstrates the extent and depth of this fundamental schism. While 69 per cent of Catholics in Northern Ireland think of themselves as Irish and just 15 per cent as British, 67 per cent of Protestants think of themselves as British and only 8 per cent as Irish. There is a fundamental division, therefore, in that most basic of issues, namely national identity. Aspirations for the future similarly diverge. Eighty-three per cent of Catholics favour a united Ireland achieved by peaceful means, but this is supported by only 29 per cent of Protestants. This clear split between Protestants and Catholics, loyalists and republicans, structures all other aspects of life and politics in the province. Support for the various political parties, for example, is almost entirely governed by religion: 99 per cent of those voting for the Unionist parties are Protestant; 98 per cent of those voting SDLP are Catholic.

In a society bifurcated as Northern Ireland is, there are no consensual solutions, no compromise middle paths, and no obviously just outcomes. In such a situation, the British government has been able to do little more than attempt to keep the violence within bounds. Armoured cars trundle through council estates, armed soldiers peer nervously from barbed wire enclaves on street corners, shopping centres are fenced off and patrolled by sentries, suspects are interrogated in army barracks and tried in courts without juries , seven hundred thousand vehicles are stopped and over a thousand homes are searched each year, targets on the British mainland and in countries such as Germany and Holland are bombed and ambushed while in Belfast and Londonderry ordinary people are shot in broad daylight, and still the conflict grinds on with no apparent prospect of final victory or capitulation on either side.

Conclusions

We have seen in this section that we should be cautious when generalising about *British* politics, for Britain is not an homogenous entity and the British state does not necessarily operate as a single unit. Different parts of the country have different problems, different cultures and different histories, and some form of devolved administration is therefore necessary in order to take account of this diversity.

The diversity within the United Kingdom is most acutely expressed in the historic divisions between the four nations which comprise it. Analysts and commentators often try to explain political conflicts as an expression of, say, different class interests or as a clash between generations, or ethnic groups or employees in different sectors of the economy. All of these sources of pressure and conflict can, of course, be very important, but underpinning all of them is the more fundamental question of national identity. Struggles around national identities within the United Kingdom are often dismissed by (mainly English) 'progressive' opinion as anachronistic, and many critics on the Left tend to dismiss nationalist sentiment as in some way a displaced or 'deformed' expression of more important and fundamental class loyalties. For these critics, nationalist ideology has in some way been manufactured and sustained as a cunning ploy by the 'ruling class' to divide and confuse the masses.

Such arguments are in our view completely misconceived. If any one interest is more 'basic' than any other, then surely this is the interest which people have in living in a state which corresponds with their national identity and aspirations. The pursuit of the other interests which they may have as members of a particular class, occupational group or whatever is entirely dependent upon this. The Scots cannot defend their industries, nor the Welsh their culture, nor the Catholics in Northern Ireland their religion if they feel themselves to be a minority within a wider state system with which they do not identify. All the political institutions and processes discussed so far in this book – government, the courts, the police, the media and the rest – are organised on the basis of the territorial integrity of the United Kingdom state. If this unity is itself disputed, however, then it follows that the national question will cast its shadow over every other aspect of politics.

The International Level

Introduction

Most analyses of British politics treat it as though it were a self-contained political system untouched by the implications of our being part of an international political and economic order. This is a manifest nonsense. Britain may be a sovereign state but our economy and polity are open to the world and this forces us to go beyond the nation state if we are to make good sense of the politics that affects Britain. No account of British politics is complete which does not attend to our international relations and to the fact that we are members of a host of international organisations – organisations which constrain and sometimes even determine the course of governmental action. Many of the external constraints on the actions of British governments have their contemporary origins in the international settlement effected at the end of the Second World War.

The Second World War confronted its survivors with both a challenge and an opportunity. A challenge because it had been allowed to happen, and an opportunity because it had demolished the old international order and thereby created space for a new one, hopefully built upon more stable principles. On the economic front, world trade was devastated and the European nations were faced with the problem of their own recovery, and on the more political front, the Western nations were concerned to secure their common defence. Old ways were recognised as inadequate with respect to both these matters, but new ways were feared because of their implications for the sovereignty of nation states.

With respect to world trade, a return to the free market system and a *laissez-faire* international order was not a politically acceptable solution to those industrial nations that had been devastated by war since they had economies that were too weak to cope with the blast of competition from an open world economy. At the same time, however, there was the fear that, in the absence of this commitment to an open world economy, nations would retreat into the kind of protectionist and nationalist economic policies which had predominated in the 1930s – policies which had led to the breakdown of the international monetary system itself. If national solutions were feared with respect to the problem of economic trade, then they were recognised as inadequate with respect to the problem of defence. Looking backwards, the war itself stood as some kind of testament to the disasters of a rampant nationalism and, looking forwards, the size of the Soviet bloc seemed to defy the possibility of purely national defence arrangements in Europe. At the same time, however, the strength of national identities and fears meant that the conditions were no more ripe for a fully international solution to the problem of world security than they were for a fully-fledged system of free international trade. Compromise, then, was to be the order of the day with respect to the problems of both economic recovery and world trade, and Western defence. In both cases, however, the fact that the USA controlled almost 70 per cent of the world's gold and foreign exchange reserves and more than 40 per cent of industrial output meant that it was in the position to be the leader in fashioning the new arrangements for the international and political order of the Western world.

Britain depends on world trade and the organisations which support and sustain that trade at the same time as it is a member of the European Community (EC) and looks for security through her membership of the North Atlantic Treaty Organisation (NATO). Britain is also a member of the United Nations (UN), the Commonwealth, the World Bank, the International Monetary Fund (IMF), the International Civil Aviation Authority, the World Health Organisation (WHO), the International Atomic Energy Authority, the General Agreement on Tariffs and Trade (GATT), the World Meteorological Organisation, the World Intellectual Property Organisation, the Nordic Council, the European Space Agency, and a host of other international organisations of varying degrees of power and importance for British politics and policy-making. The post-war growth of international organisations is a response to the need for integration and co-operation for common purposes through voluntary participation. The sheer number and scope of those of which Britain is a member, highlights the extent to which much British policy-making takes place within the framework of international organisations that are able to exert varying kinds of authority on the international scene and within domestic politics. Some international organisations have a direct effect on Britain but many others have a decisive impact because they constrain the scope for choice in British politics. We clearly cannot assess the impact of all the international organisations of which Britain is a member, but it is especially important to attend to the ways in which the IMF, NATO and, above all, the EC have come to constrain and control crucial aspects of British politics and state activity.

The International Monetary Fund (IMF)

The IMF is a specialised agency of the United Nations. It aims to promote a smoothly functioning system of international trade and finance through the use of three basic mechanisms:

1 Provision of a forum for consultation and co-operation among member countries.
2 Provision of short-term credit and liquidity needed by national governments to stabilise their exchange rates and help with balance-of-payments difficulties.
3 Surveillance of exchange rate policies to ensure that they do not promote national interests at the expense of the world community.

The IMF, together with the International Bank for Reconstruction and Development (IBRD) – the World Bank – originated from the Final Act of the 1944 UN Monetary and Financial Conference, when the representatives of 44 countries met at Bretton Woods in America in order to fashion a new international monetary order different from that which had prevailed in the 1930s. The British negotiating position in 1944 was dominated by Keynes' utopian vision of a world with a central bank and free of economic nationalism. The Americans did not accept his idea of a powerful supranational agency because they had no wish to see international bureaucrats telling them how to manage their economic and financial affairs. This view was shared by other participants at the conference and reflected the general reluctance of nation states to surrender to a world bank their sovereignty over national economic policies. So, instead of an international central bank of real substance, the conference plumped for the IMF – an institution that was empowered to lend to deficit countries but which had no effective power to penalise surplus countries and so manage the structure of world demand. Through the creation of the IBRD and the IMF, the representatives at Bretton Woods hoped to establish institutions that would foster a measure of international political co-operation on monetary matters as the basis for a revival of world trade along lines where there would be free international economic competition. But in doing all this they stopped well short of creating international organisations that would eat into the formal sovereignty of the member states. Having said that, we shall see that the issue of sovereignty becomes somewhat academic once a state needs credit from the Fund because the 'conditions' which the Fund attaches to such a loan do much to constrain and even determine the realities of public policy-making by debtor states – and this notwithstanding any formal position with respect to the 'independence' and 'sovereignty' of the state in question.

Orginally, there were 30 member nations, but today membership of the Fund totals about 150 countries in widely different stages of economic development. Subscriptions to the Fund are related to a member country's wealth. Voting power within the Fund is determined by the size of these subscriptions, and so the USA (with roughly 20 per cent of total votes) is in a strong position to be able to shape Fund policies although the voting power of Germany, Japan and the Arab countries has increased over the years. Members of the Fund commit themselves to mutual collaboration to promote orderly exchange arrangements and a system of stable exchange rates. Also they are bound to supply such information as the Fund deems necessary for its operations; they must undertake certain specific obligations relating to domestic and external policies that affect the balance of payments and the exchange rate; they must secure IMF permission if they wish to adjust their exchange rates; and if they need a loan in order to cope with a serious balance-of-payments deficit then they must expect the IMF to impose conditions. The fact that the IMF imposes conditions before loans are granted gives it power to intervene in the domestic policy-making of individual countries. This has been of decisive importance at particular moments of British history as we shall now see.

In chapter 9 we saw that the British economy ended a period of rapid growth in 1963. Imports had increased much more rapidly than exports and, as a result, the balance of payments shifted from a surplus of more than $600 million in 1962 to a deficit of almost $650 million by 1964. In this situation sterling weakened on the foreign exchange markets – its value fell against the dollar – and as British reserves began to be used up so the Conservative government had to renew a standby credit of $1 billion from the IMF. Because a general election was due some time in 1964, the Conservatives were reluctant to act 'hard' and long term in order to stem the deteriorating balance-of-payments position but instead adopted short-term coping solutions that merely left the problem on hold.

Labour won the election in October 1964 on the basis of a promise to end the 'wasted years of Tory rule' and create a 'new Britain'. Economic growth through 'socialist planning' and an end to 'stop-go' economic policies was to be the priority, but the manifesto also committed the government to full employment and a vast series of social reforms ranging from a capital gains tax through to a guaranteed income for the retired and widows, as well as the abolition of charges within the National Health Service. Electoral promises by a party out of office are one thing, but the economic realities which confront a government once in office are quite another. Right from the start the Labour Government confronted a massive balance-of-payments deficit and there was uncertainty as to whether Britain would be forced to devalue the pound. The Prime Minister, Harold Wilson, chose to defend the value of sterling, in part because he did not want his party to be identified as the 'devaluation party', in part because the Americans were known to be strongly opposed to devaluation – and this at a time when the Prime Minister was anxious to strengthen the 'special relationship' with that country. In the event, the government sought to improve the balance of payments by imposing a temporary surcharge of 15 per cent on imported goods. However, the November budget, which promised increased pensions and the introduction of a corporation tax and a capital gains tax, inspired a massive movement of investors out of sterling. The Labour government now had little choice. It was forced to respond to the sterling crisis by increasing the bank rate by 2 per cent; by arranging a substantial standby credit of $3000 million with the central banks; and by going to the IMF in December for a further $1000 million. This package restored confidence; persuaded the foreign exchange markets that the value of sterling could be held; and so the crisis passed and sterling recovered. The respite was shortlived, however, as sterling weakened again in March 1965 and in May the government drew the remainder of its quota from the IMF.

Behind the scenes an active discussion was taking place both within the British government and between British and American officials on the need for a more stringent incomes policy that would hold down costs, curb inflation and, in cutting down demand, cut down imports. Gradually a programme was formulated involving an incomes policy 'with teeth' on the British side and, on the American, leadership in assembling an international rescue package for sterling. Notwithstanding a series of budgets which cut public expenditure and curbed the radical edges of Labour's election pledges, sterling remained under international pressure and by the end of 1967 the issue of devaluation was once again on the political agenda. If Britain was to hold the parity of the pound then the IMF made it clear that it would lend its support, and its dollars, but only on the basis of 'rigid restrictions' that the Prime Minister saw as leading to 'the most searching intrusions not only into our privacy, but even into our economic independence'. in fact, the government took the decision to devalue in November 1967 and a *Letter of Intent* was sent to the IMF outlining the proposals that had been hammered out in secret between the government and the IMF to restore a healthy balance of payments. On the basis of a promise to restrict the growth in the money supply, to raise taxes, and to cut public expenditure on health, education, and housing, the government secured an IMF standby in support of the new exchange rate. Despite the devaluation and the tough monetary and fiscal measures that were designed to ease the balance-of payments problem, sterling remained weak on the foreign exchange markets for much of 1968. By 1970, however, and with the help of the IMF, Labour in government had eventually achieved a measure of success with respect to financial policy. The pressure was off the pound; the current account of the balance of payments was in surplus; and, perhaps most notably, the budget deficit had been eliminated and the public sector borrowing requirement was negative. However, what was good for the Exchequer was not necessarily good for the Party (or its supporters) and Labour lost the election of 1970.

Harold Wilson, in his account of what it was like to lead a Labour government in the teeth of a sterling crisis, noted how in the early days of office:

> We were soon to learn that decisions on pensions and taxation were no longer to be regarded, as in the past, as decisions for Parliament alone. The combination of tax increases with increased social security benefits provoked the first of a series of attacks on sterling, by speculators and others, which beset almost every action of the government for the next five years.

In more concrete terms (and we have already touched on this in our discussion of the power of the Bank of England in chapter 6) Wilson also noted how the Governor of that Bank demanded all round cuts in public expenditure which led Wilson to write that

> not for the first time, I said that we had now reached a situation where a newly elected government with a mandate from the people was being told, not so much by the Governor of the Bank of England but by international speculators, that the policies on which we had fought the election could not be implemented; that the government was to be forced into the adoption of Tory policies to which it was fundamentally opposed. The Governor confirmed that this was, in fact, the case. I asked him if this meant that it was impossible for any government, whatever its party label, whatever its manifesto or the policies on which it fought the election, to continue unless it reverted to full-scale Tory policies. He had to admit that this is what the argument meant, because of the sheer complusion of the economic dictation of those who exercised decisive economic power.

Labour in office had discovered the vicious truth of Harold Wilson's warning to the Trades Union Congress just before the election of 1964:

> You can get into pawn, but don't then talk about an independent foreign policy or an independent defence policy. . . . If you borrow from some of the world's bankers you will quickly find that you lose another kind of independence because of the deflationary policies and the cuts in social services that will be imposed on a government that has got itself into that position.

Notwithstanding these gloomy assessments of the powerlessness of Labour in government, the Party won the election of 1974 on the basis of a series of policy commitments more radical in tone and in aspiration than any that the Party had endorsed since 1945. However, it won in the context of a situation where the balance of payments was a worsening problem given the reality of the rise in oil prices on world markets and our need to import the stuff. In his 1975 budget speech, Denis Healey, announced cuts in public expenditure arguing that 'we in Britain must keep control of our own policy', but in December of that year the government still had to resort to borrowing from the IMF. This loan did not stop the pound falling sharply against the dollar through the spring of 1976 and, under pressure, the government announced a further set of public spending cuts. By September, the government's reserves of foreign currency stood at the lowest level since 1971 and the government was again forced to accept an IMF investigation into its policies. A loan of $3.9 billion was negotiated from the IMF but, naturally enough, conditions were insisted upon by the IMF and the Americans and these were set out in the *Letter of Intent* despatched by the British government on 15 December 1976. That *Letter* stated that 'an essential element of the government's strategy will be a continuing and substantial reduction over the next few years in the share of resources required for the public sector' with the government going on to argue that 'it is also essential to reduce the PSBR in order to create monetary conditions which will encourage investment and support sustained growth and the control of inflation.'

All things considered, it was another period of extraordinary overseas influence on British economic policy. However, it was by no means clear that the Prime Minister and his chancellor were unwilling participants in the process leading up to the adoption of the IMF's harsh economic medicine. In an earlier speech to the Labour Party conference in 1976 the Prime Minister had already sounded the death-knell for Keynesian policies at the same time as he ushered in the new era of monetarism that was to flourish under the premiership of Margaret Thatcher in the 1980s:

> We used to think that you could just spend your way out of a recession, and increase employment by cutting taxes and boosting government spending. I tell you in all candour that that option no longer exists, and in so far as it ever did exist, it worked by injecting inflation into the economy. And each time that happened, the average level of unemployment has risen. Higher inflation, followed by higher unemployment. That is the history of the last twenty years.

It is hard to be precise as to the origins of the Labour government's late conversion to monetarism, but confidence in the pound returned, the balance of payments improved and even inflation began to fall. This was partly because of the economic measures imposed by the IMF, but also because there was the hope that North Sea oil would transform Britain's economy and her balance-of-payments problem and hence the 'need' for the kind of stop-go economic policies that were recognised as no basis for sustaining long-term growth.

North Sea oil production had commenced in 1976 and, by 1979 when the Conservatives were returned to office, was rising strongly. By the 1980s, oil self-sufficiency looked like removing the balance-of-payments constraint which had dogged successive British governments since the war at the same time as it provided a substantial and sustained revenue boost for the Exchequer. The fact that Britain was now an oil producer in the context of a world of rising oil prices transformed the pound into a petrocurrency that should have been strong on the world market. This was the case in 1980, but by the middle of 1981 the pound was falling and although there was a recovery, the pound weakened again shortly after the June 1983 election, partly because the Chancellor was too keen to reduce interest rates but also because the dollar was strong and there was anxiety about the implications of industrial action in Britain's coal mines. All in all, the pound still seemed to be as vulnerable to damaging waves of selling pressure as it had been under Labour in the mid 1970s. Perhaps it was the happy accident of North Sea oil; the related build-up in Britain's foreign exchange reserves during the 1980s; the larger recovery in the world economy; and the fact that the Conservative government was pursuing policies in line with those 'expected' by the IMF, which, taken together, allowed the government to escape from the need to approach the IMF for a loan.

The precise impact of the IMF on policy-making in Britain demands an appreciation of the policies which it seeks to impose as a condition for any loan. When a country starts to borrow a small amount then the credit is granted with no conditions save the need to repay within a period of between three and five years. But the more a country borrows, the more conditions are stipulated by the IMF before the funds are disbursed. These conditions concern the adoption of domestic policies that assure the country's ability to repay the loan in the future. In essence, the IMF seeks to eliminate the balance-of-payments deficit of a country to which it offers a loan but only on the basis of that country avoiding protectionist measures that restrict the freedom of world trade and going instead for financial discipline and deflationary policies which reduce consumption at the same time as the government adopts a 'hands-off' economic policy which leaves private firms free to increase investment. A 'standard' IMF package, therefore, involves a reduction in state expenditure (particularly in the provision of subsidies for the consumption of goods by low-income groups); some mechanism for reducing wages; and the dismantling of controls on the activities of private capitalists be they domestic or foreign. The effect of these policies is designed to reduce the level of consumption and therefore the level of imports, and to boost the rate of profit and the level of exports through reductions in taxes and in wages. Accepting an IMF loan involves accepting a massive international intrusion into domestic policy-making and national sovereignty in a way that hits at progressive taxation and policies for income and wealth redistribution, as well as policies involving state intervention in the economy.

For the most part, the IMF bears down on the policies of the poor countries of the Third World that import much but export little. However, we have seen that there have been specific occasions when Labour governments in Britain have found themselves at the mercy of IMF loan conditions in ways which seem to make a mockery of our claim to be a sovereign nation state. It is not surprising that those on the Left have railed against the 'power' of the IMF. The trouble is that such a view ignores the fact that we can look at this power and reality another way. If we do this, then we see not so much the power of the IMF but rather the more fundamental reality of a weak British economy being managed by Labour governments that have lacked the policies to secure the kind of economic strength that would preclude the IMF from ever being able to intervene to exert their power. Now, the fact that the Conservative governments of the 1980s have avoided the need to secure an IMF loan suggests that the Fund no longer constrains our domestic policy-making so that we are once again in charge of our own economic affairs and a truly sovereign state. At one level this is true, but, once again, things are not always as they appear. Indeed, it just might be the case that we are free to organise our own economic affairs precisely because Conservative governments have chosen to pursue a broad line of economic and monetary policy that is at one with the kind of policy perspective integral to the essence of IMF interventions into domestic policy-making. Conservative governments may have avoided coming up against the power of the IMF, but only because they have chosen to do things along IMF lines in the first place. Not for the first time in this book are you having to ponder on the meaning of power and freedom as well as the precise reality of choice and constraint.

The North Atlantic Treaty Organisation (NATO)

The North Atlantic Treaty Organisation (NATO) is a military alliance, linking 14 West European countries with the USA and Canada against the threat from the USSR. The North Atlantic Treaty was signed in Washington in April 1949 but it represented the outcome of initiatives taken on both sides of the Atlantic. In March 1948, Britain, Belgium, Holland, Luxembourg, and France, all signed the Brussels Treaty promising that all countries would come to the aid of any one of them that was attacked. The following April, the Canadian Secretary of State for External Affairs suggested that the Brussels Treaty Organisation be replaced by an Atlantic defence system including the countries of North America. The Berlin blockade by the USSR prompted the American Senate to express a view as to the virtues of developing 'collective arrangements' for 'collective self-defence' and this set in motion the negotiations on the drafting of the North Atlantic Treaty.

NATO was always something of an American project. The USA sought influence in Europe; it recognised that economic recovery there was keenly related to the problem of Western defence in that the domestic need to give priority to reconstruction precluded the European nations being able to afford their own defence arrangements. Hence, it stepped into the defence breach providing far and away the largest single contribution to NATO. For its part, Britain devoted 4.3 per cent of GDP to defence in 1988 (third in the NATO rankings) with 95 per cent of that expenditure being devoted to the NATO area. It is impossible to talk about the guts of Britain's defence policy outside of the context of NATO, and this notwithstanding the extent to which Britain has had to deal with disorders surrounding the remnants of her Empire. This being the case it is important to decide who makes NATO policy?

The Treaty deals very briefly with institutional aspects, mentioning only the establishment of a Council empowered to set up subsidiary organs, in particular a defence committee. In theory, NATO decisions are taken on the basis of consensus and the consent of all the member governments. This requires unanimity and therefore compromise, and if such a system were left entirely to itself not much would ever get decided. In reality, not all participants are of equal importance because NATO is less an equal partnership and more a system of highly dependent partnerships within which pressures can be applied to get the vastly complex organisation moving. According to Smith, in *Pressure: How America Runs NATO*, 'The USA is consistently able to prevail, to win on policies which are unpopular with allied governments or their electorates, or both. It is neither secret nor surprising. It is part and parcel of the USA being a superpower. It wins on such issues because it is a superpower; it is a superpower because it wins.' Now, the relative powerlessness of Greece and Turkey within the Alliance is one thing, but does not the fact that Britain has an independent nuclear deterrent and a 'special relationship' with the USA serve to give us extra clout within the alliance so that we assume a crucial role in shaping the defence policy of NATO?

Britain could have a nuclear capability without the assistance of the USA. However, the fact that Polaris and Trident are equipped with American missiles on the understanding that they are committed to NATO and the fact that they are targeted through information from American satellites makes it difficult to think of a situation in which Britain would, or even could, use its independent nuclear deterrent independently. The British view on the special relationship with the USA has tended to emphasise the extra influence which it is argued has enabled us to exercise in Washington and in NATO decision-making. The relationship does probably provide more opportunities for British influence than are available to other Western European states, but within the specific context of Anglo-American relations influence flows mainly from Washington to London and the relationship itself has not been without its costs for Britain. It has demanded a loyalty to American policy aspirations that has inhibited British independence in matters of defence and diplomacy.

Nations are sovereign to the extent that they possess the supreme authority to rule over their territory. This being the case, defence of territory and decisions about war and peace are central to the integrity, independence and defining essence of a nation state. The fact that we are members of NATO might help us to secure our territory but we pay a price. We have given up our sovereignty with respect to the making of our own defence policy and handed it over to the Americans who have sustained the NATO alliance on the basis of the Russian threat – a threat which, in easing, opens up the possibility of changes in international relations which have implications for the continuation of NATO itself.

The European Community (EC)

Right from the start the European Community (EC) has posed problems both for British politics and for those bent on making sense of the EC itself. We say this because the EC is different from most other international organisations. Not surprisingly, therefore, the institutions and legal capacity of the EC have confused British politicians. At the same time, they have confounded traditional academic distinctions between 'powerful' nation states and well-meaning, but relatively powerless, international organisations that never seem to be able to agree on, still less to implement, common policies of any real substance. The EC may not be a state in its own right – it has no territory of its own; no citizenry which is not a citizenry of the member states; and its 'government' has no powers except those defined by treaties agreed among the member states – but for all that the EC is powerful. It has the authority to legislate for the Community as a whole and it has money to back up its policies. Put another way, the EC can make laws that are binding on member states; these laws take precedence over national legislation where they are in conflict; and so the EC *is* in a position to make and implement policies for the Community as a whole – policies which can dramatically affect the lives of those within the individual member states.

On the one hand the EC can be seen as embracing a cluster of shared aims and common institutions geared to political integration. On the other hand the EC is also a political system that is made up of independent nation states that are jealous of their sovereignty. This combination is bound to cause tensions and political difficulties. Many of the aims and institutions of the EC are all about expansion, internationalisation, centralisation, and the 'progressive' integration of the member states into some kind of larger European political union. This being the case, we are forced to consider whether the EC, in biting into the legislative competence of member states, is slowly transforming itself into a federal state overseeing a future United States of Europe. But the states themselves are always concerned to secure what they see as their distinct national interests. They are often 'old-fashioned' in defending their own sovereignty and autonomy in a way which limits the very process of European integration of which they are the vital and determining part. When we deal with the EC, we are dealing with interdependent nation states where a shifting balance is constantly having to be struck between the maintenance of national sovereignty and the impetus for European integration. Moreover, this balance is struck, partly on the basis of the public clash of power politics, diplomacy and international relations, partly on the basis of more private negotiations by Eurocrats and politicians operating through a complex process involving EC institutions located in Brussels and Strasbourg.

History

The idea of a European-wide system of government can be traced back to medieval times but the rise of nation states in the eighteenth and nineteenth centuries meant that such unification was invariably attempted by force and conquest through empires based upon a single strong state. After the Second World War there were those who were concerned to prevent another war from breaking out in Europe and who took the view that it was important to pool resources and break with the traditional diplomacy of the past. At first the drive towards European union was simple, direct and highly political. But these early initiatives were blocked by nation states, concerned to maintain their political independence, and so the emphasis came to be placed on the creation of a more modest economic union. The European Coal and Steel Community was established by 'the six' – France, Germany, Italy and the Benelux countries – who signed the Treaty of Paris in 1951. It was seen as a block to a further war between the nation states of Western Europe and there was the hope that 'the pooling of coal and steel production will immediately provide for the setting up of common bases for economic development as a first step in the federation of Europe'. The principles tried and tested in the ECSC were extended in 1957 when the six signed the Treaty of Rome and established the European Economic Community (EEC) with a view to creating a Common Market and a set of targets for the establishment of common economic policies. The European Atomic Energy Commission (EURATOM) was also established in Rome on the same day in order to try and secure the safe development of nuclear energy for peaceful purposes. Strictly speaking, then, there are three European Communities but the institutions of the Communities were formally merged in 1965. Since then it has become common to refer to them collectively as the European Community (EC) even though legally they are still separate entities.

Britain stood aloof from these initiatives and declined to join the Community at the time it was first established because it persisted in the belief that it has a 'special relationship' with the USA and was a world power in its own right with its major interests outside of Europe. It was also caught up in the tricky process of losing an Empire whilst trying to find a new role for itself on the world stage. During the 1960s, however, pressing domestic concerns about economic growth and the need to modernise the British economy encouraged the governments of Harold Macmillan and Harold

Wilson to apply for entry to the Community in the hope that membership would unlock the door to the economic revival of modern Britain. Both of these applications were vetoed by General de Gaulle of France. He was anxious about the French national interest and the possible loss of French influence within the Community if it were extended to include Britain. It was not until de Gaulle retired in 1969 that the way was open for an enlargement of the Community. Britain, Denmark and Ireland finally became EC members in 1973 (and all three ratified the decision in popular referenda) and by 1986 Greece, Spain and Portugal were also members, producing a community of twelve nation states.

Britain's membership of the Community has been fraught with difficulties, not least because it joined late; not on terms of its own choosing; and at a time when energy prices quadrupled so that the world was tumbling into a recession in a way which encouraged protectionism and the pursuit of 'selfish' national interests – and this notwithstanding the aims and aspirations of the Community as a whole. Britain found itself having to work within an institutional framework which it had played no part in shaping and it had to confront established policies that were not of its making at the same time as the formula for national contributions to the Community budget was seen as disadvantageous to the interests of the British people. Public policies always have implications for budgets and public expenditure and so it should be no surprise for us to find the efforts to sort out Britain's contribution to the Community budget have been inextricably linked to efforts to reform the Common Agricultural Policy (CAP) – the only sector where the EC has had a genuine common policy.

The CAP was intended to support Europe's farmers and ensure food supplies through a system of guaranteed prices. In reality, the policy has kept part-time inefficient farmers (in France) in business in a way that has led to escalating costs and surplus production. Between 1979 and 1984 agricultural expenditure rose by 76 per cent, and by the beginning of the latter year the Community's excess of production over consumption was 15 per cent for cereals, 19 per cent for sugar, 27 per cent for dairy products and 27 per cent for wine. Much of this was stored in 'lakes' and 'mountains', but in order to dump some of these surpluses on world markets vast export subsidies have had to be paid to the advantage of our 'enemies' in the Soviet bloc. In early 1985 these subsidies were estimated to be running at an annual rate of £5 billion, or about 34 per cent of total agricultural spending through the Community budget. In 1973 the CAP was absorbing 80.6 per cent of the Community budget. It has been claimed that the average British family spends an extra £10 a week on food because of the CAP system of guaranteed payments to farmers; and even today the CAP takes up about 65 per cent of the entire EC budget.

The problem of Britain's contribution to the Community budget first emerged little more than a year after entry when the newly elected Labour government announced that it wished to renegotiate the accession agreement in order to secure a 'fair deal' because it was becoming apparent that

Britain would soon become a net financial contributor to the Community, and this in spite of the fact that it was one of the poorer member states. The Labour government secured Community agreement on a 'budgetary correcting mechanism', but the basic problem remained. The argument was taken up by the Conservative government in 1979 when there were fears that Britain might become a net contributor to the tune of nearly £1 billion a year. The European Commission, ever eager to extend the remit of the Community and hence its own power base, sought a solution by suggesting that the number of community policies be enlarged beyond agriculture. In this way Britain would qualify for more Community money through the adoption of common policies favourable to its own domestic interests. This, however, was not acceptable to the Conservative government. Margaret Thatcher was not happy at the prospect of more Community policies. She was anxious about empire-building by Eurocrats in Brussells at the same time as she was worried about the loss of national sovereignty and the entry of 'socialism' into Britain via the back door of Europe. This being the case, the Conservative government persisted in the view that any solution to the budgetary problem must come through a reform of the CAP before there were any further moves to extend Community policies and European integration. But this in its turn was not appealing to France and those member states which derived substantial financial and political benefits from the maintenance of the CAP.

Entrenched national interests were blocking a solution to what was seen as 'the British problem'. The stakes were high. The French spoke of excluding the British from various meetings of EC states and the British Cabinet actively discussed ways of unilaterally, and probably illegally, holding back payments to the EC. In the mid-1980s, President Mitterand of France realised that if some of the member states were to express support for a higher level of European integration this could put pressure on Britain to compromise on its budgetary grievance. In effect, there was a threat to move a core of member states to a higher level of integration, if necessary without Britain, and in a way that was designed to force the Convervative government to balance its concern for the specifics of budgetary reform as against its concern to secure the larger objective of staying within the developing Community game. A game that was seen as of increasing advantage to the British economy given the scale of the European market for British goods and services. Agreement on Britain's budgetary rebate was eventually reached at the European Council at Fointainbleau in June 1984 even though there was little movement on the matter of reforming the CAP. A Community which had been in the doldrums in the 1970s now found itself caught up in the process of trying to secure the ideals expressed by the founders of the EC and establish a single market, or an internal market, without frontiers and other barriers to the free movement of people, goods, services and capital – and all this by 1992.

The Single European Act and 1992

The Single European Act (SEA) came into force in 1 July 1987, after ratification by each member state. The Act carries forward the basic Community ideal and has its origin in a series of declarations by the European Council on the way forward for the Community, most notably that of December 1982 which instructed 'the Council to decide . . . on priority measures to reinforce the internal market.' Having said that, the programme only really began in earnest in 1985 when the European Commission published the White Paper on *Completing the Internal Market* by Lord Cockfield, the senior British Commissioner from 1985 to 1989 with specific responsibility for the internal market. This paper not only traced the consequences of the removal of each non-tariff barrier but also specified a follow-up programme of over 300 measures that were seen as necessary to ensure that the removal of the different barriers worked in a co-ordinated way. An *un*common market was seen as costly. It was calculated that the effective implementation of the White Paper's internal market programme would boost the Community's gross domestic product by some 5 per cent; would cause prices to be around 6 per cent lower than they would otherwise be; and would create around 1.8 million new jobs. There were, however, deep anxieties that the programme was but the thin end of a wedge that was designed to cut into the sovereignty of the nation states within the Community. Notwithstanding these anxieties, the White Paper was adopted by the European Council at Luxembourg in 1985; the Single European Act was born; and the Council of Ministers was instructed 'to initiate a precise programme of action, based on the White Paper . . . with a view to achieving completely and effectively the conditions for a single market in the Community by 1992 at the latest.'

The Single European Act amends the Treaty of Rome and other Community Treaties. Its main provisions involve the expansion of EC competence into new areas (including Research and Development, and environmental and social policies); the co-ordination of foreign policies; the extension of the range of subjects which can be dealt with by qualified majority voting in the Council of Ministers; the extension of the formal power of the European Parliament; the formalisation of the position of the European Council; and, most importantly, the completion of the internal market by 1992 as a way of 'making concrete progress towards European unity'. The Hanover summit of June 1988 recognised that the 1992 programme was 'irreversible' and there are those who see the completion of the single market as but a step towards a European union and then a federation. However, by May 1987 the European Council was still some 112 proposals behind the timetable specified by the White Paper for the completion of the internal market, and tax harmonisation will probably fall far short of what Lord Cockfield intended. British business has been urged to get ready for 1992 but there are those who doubt whether the European Community and the internal market will be ready for British business by that date given the inefficiencies and inadequacies of Community institutions and policy-making procedures.

Community institutions

The basic pattern of Community institutions was set by the ECSC, then modified in EURATOM, and the most important of the three, the EEC. All three Communities share the same institutions. The main ones are:

(1) *Commission* The Commission is the Community's executive and civil service. It is headed by a President and a number of Commissioners, one from each of the smaller states and two from each of the larger. The process of selecting the Commission President has been likened to a 'papal chimney smoke' but each of the Commissioners are nominated and appointed by the member governments, after consultation within the Community, for a four-year renewable term during which time they are sworn to abandon all national allegiances. The Commission takes decisions on a collegiate basis, but individual Commissioners are responsible for particular policy areas and are assisted by small personal staffs (known as 'cabinets') and a larger bureaucracy of around 12,000 officials (known as the secretariat) that is divided into directorate-generals (DGs) who broadly mirror the administrative responsibilities of Commissioners for particular policy areas. The Commission is the guardian of the Community ideal and has to implement Community policies and ensure that Treaty provisions and legislation are applied (and, if necessary, it can refer infringements to the Court of Justice). But the fact that the Treaty of Rome reserves almost exclusively for the Commission the power to initiate and propose legislation – proposals that are then sent to the Council of Ministers for final approval – serves to define what is the Commission's most vital and political function.

(2) *Council of Ministers* The Council of Ministers is the Community's legislature and it always meets in private, much to the chagrin of those who are concerned to champion the cause of democracy within the Community. It is composed of representatives (usually ministers accompanied by officials) from all the member states. In practice, the Council meets in about 20 different formations because the precise composition of each Council meeting is determined by the policy sector under discussion, with Ministers of Agriculture attending meetings when the CAP is being considered whilst other ministers attend those meetings that fall within their own particular policy competence. The 'senior' body is the Council of Foreign Ministers which is supposed to iron out the problems that the 'subject-matter Councils' have been unable to solve, as well as deal with matters falling specifically within the field of foreign affairs. The Council's chief role is to adopt, or reject, the legislative proposals that have been initiated and submitted by the Commission and so in acting as the EC's legislature it can be seen, formally at least, as the key decision-making body for all EC policy. The Council is not a collegiate body. It tends to embrace several (often twelve!) competing opinions as to what constitutes

an acceptable compromise on a draft Commission proposal. The turnover of national representatives attending the meetings does nothing to help foster a sense of common purpose. In reflecting and defending distinct national views, the Council of Ministers tends to curb the integrative momentum set in motion by the Commission and this tendency is buttressed by the Council's voting procedures which, in not allowing for simple majority voting, tend to block collective action.

In order to reject a Commission proposal the Council must be unanimous, and in order to accept a Commission proposal the Treaty of Rome requires unanimity for decisions considered decisive. However, even in the formal absence of the unanimity requirement, convention and political reality (entrenched in 'the Luxembourg Compromise' of 1966 – a compromise of no legal status) has allowed states the right of national veto so that 'where very important interests are at stake the discussion must be continued until unanimous agreement is reached'. Since ratification of the SEA, an increasingly broad range of decisions have been subject to 'qualified majority vote' – a vote weighted so that two of the larger states combined can be overruled by a unified vote of the other members. This decision rule was designed to facilitate action and end the Luxembourg Compromise, at least for 1992 issues. However, whether member states will be prepared to drop their right to use the national veto will only become clear in the course of time, and then only if member states cease to be concerned to defend their national interests in the face of the drive for Community integration. Given the difficulty of getting nation states to agree to common policies (a difficulty that finds expression in the decision procedures of the Council of Ministers) we should not be surprised to find that, on average, two to five years elapse between the submission of a Commission proposal and the emission of a Council decision. Moreover, this leaves aside those times when the Council of Ministers has simply postponed taking a decision on a contentious piece of legislation. The number of proposals awaiting decision by the Council has been variously estimated at between 300 and 600.

(3) *European Parliament* The European Parliament is not a legislature and so it can make no laws. It has its origins in the Assembly of the European Coal and Steel Community to which national MPs were seconded, but it has been directly elected since 1979 and is currently composed of 518 members (MEPs). Britain elects 81 MEPs and is alone in refusing to use some form of proportional representation. Parliament's formal role is to 'exercise the advisory and supervisory powers' conferred upon it by the treaties. It can offer 'opinions' on proposals before the Commission and the Council (which can be ignored); it has the power to demand, by a two-thirds majority, the resignation of the entire Commission (but it has never done so; it does not have the more useful power of being able to demand the resignation of an individual Commissioner; and the Commission does not derive from the Parliament in the way that a British cabinet comes from the House of Commons); it has a limited say with respect to the budget and the spending programme of the Community (but has no say with respect to spending for farm support which still accounts for some two-thirds of the budget); and it ratifies the Community's international agreements. The Single European Act has given the Parliament additional powers to involve itself in the adoption of Community legislation but we will be con-

sidering the implications of the 'assent' procedure and the 'co-operation' procedure in our discussion of democracy within the Community. In reality, there
is little scope for parliamentary institutions within the EC and the European
Parliament has had difficulty inserting itself into the Commission-Council
dialogue.

(4) *European Council* The European Council is the name given to the summit
meetings of the heads of government of the member states plus the Commission President. The practice of summits was started in 1969, but they were not
put on a regular basis until 1974 when President Giscard d'Estaing of France
proposed that they be held three times a year (twice per annum since 1987). The
European Council does not really enjoy any formal powers and until the SEA
there was no reference to the European Council in any of the Comunity
treaties. Under the treaties the ultimate decision-making authority within the
Community is the Council of Ministers but, notwithstanding the legal and
constitutional niceties, politically and in practice the European Council has
assumed an important 'motor' role in integration. It has agreed and launched
broad lines of policy for the Community; it has provided a forum within which
Community disputes can be resolved and policies co-ordinated; and it has
assumed a social function in providing an opportunity for the leaders of
member states to meet, fraternise, and posture to their own electorates back
home. The European Council has 'emerged' and has come to be the final
decision-making body even though it has no real treaty status.

(5) *The Court of Justice* The rulings of the Court of Justice are binding on
member states and so the European judges assume powers in British politics
akin to those enjoyed by the British judges that we discussed in chapter 6. The
Court of Justice has the right to interpret Community treaties and to rule on
the validity of EC law. More importantly, the Court has the right to interpret
EC law and so it is in a position where it can effectively make law, and this in
a situation where Community law assumes precedence over the national law of
the individual member states. Given this state of affairs, the Court gives
preliminary rulings on cases referred to it by national courts when a point
of EC law is at issue, and the national court then has to apply the ruling.
However, cases can also be brought directly to the Court by individuals, companies, governments or the Commission itself,which brings cases against both
companies and member states for the infringement of EC rules, including 1992
legislation. In the early days, the majority of actions to reach the Court were
almost all concerned with breaches of Community law with respect to free
competition and free trade. In the 1960s and 1970s the Court made a number
of landmark rulings and interpreted EC law in an expansive way that was
useful to the integrative ambitions of the Commission and the European
Parliament. Although the Court has been more circumspect in recent years, it
is bound to assume a higher profile as the the new laws necessary to create the
single market are enacted. The Court is composed of thirteen judges, one
appointed by each member government (with a thirteenth chosen in rotation).
The Court works in a similar way to appeal courts in member states. In common with most courts, the European Court is overloaded and so judgements
are delayed. In order to deal with this the Council of Ministers agreed to the

setting up of a lower-level EC Court of First Instance to sift cases before they reach the European Court proper.

(6) *Other Community institutions* In addition to the major Community institutions identified above there are also many other institutions of varying degrees of importance. The Court of Auditors is the EC's external financial conscience and is responsible for the audit of the legality, regularity and sound management of EC finances. The Economic and Social Committee, which has 189 members drawn from trade unionists, industrialists and other sectors of EC opinion, assumes a consultative and advisory role with respect to draft legislation. The Committee of Permanent Representatives, composed of the ambassadors to the Community backed up by officials and civil servants from the various national bureaucracies, acts as a gatekeeper between the supranational and national systems and prepares the ground for the Council of Ministers. Well over 700 Euro-interest groups are meshed into the work of the Commission in a way that has corporatist overtones.

Community policy-making

It is one thing to describe the institutions of the Community and to set down the treaties and the (constitutional) theory as to how they should work together in contributing to the making of Community laws and policies. It is, however, quite another matter to get on top of the reality of Community policy-making. In any political system there is always likely to be something of a 'gap' between theory and practice, constitutional niceties and political realities. In chapters 1 and 3 we made it clear that this was the case with respect to the British political system. However, the gap between theory and practice is likely to be especially acute in the case of international organisations precisely because the rough play of power politics between independent nation states is not easily contained within treaties and formal arrangements. Put another way, the pressing reality of international relations is always likely to intervene to disturb the 'proper' process of policy-making within international organisations and so we should not be surprised to find that the practice and politics of Community policy-making is at odds with the theory embodied in the Community treaties.

The problem of getting to grips with Community policy-making is compounded, however, once we face the fact that the authority of the various Community institutions and the relations between them are not fixed. They are subject to change in response to the shifting balance of power between the member states and in response to the particular Community issues under consideration. No single snapshot can ever do justice to the moving picture show of Community policy-making. In the early days of the Community and until the mid- to late 1960s the French determined the pace of integration; the West Germans were the decisive force from then until the late 1970s; since 1984 the stance of the British has been of particular significance; and developments in Eastern Europe look likely to condition the development of the Community into the 1990s. Against this backdrop of power politics is superimposed the position of the various Community institutions. In the 1950s the Commission enjoyed a supremacy and was able to pursue integration fairly free from government restraint; in the 1960s the Commission was upstaged by the Council of Ministers and integration was checked by intergovernmentalism. Then in the 1970s and 1980s the European Council came to prominence as the drive to advance the Community ideal was renewed by governments that were still concerned to protect national interests.

Making sense of Community policy-making, then, involves attending to theory and practice; to particular issue areas and policy sectors; and to the tussles between member states and Community institutions, between executives and parliaments, and between bureaucrats and politicians. All this in the context of a perspective that is attentive to change over time.

Traditionally and in theory, EC policy has been depicted as the outcome of a dialogue between the Commission and the Council of Ministers – a dialogue into which the European Parliament has had difficulty inserting itself in any meaningful way so that it is often portrayed as little more than a mere talking shop of no policy consequence. In effect, policy has been seen as the product of a process whereby the supranational Commission proposes legislation to the Council; the Council deliberates and decides upon its adoption; and then the Commission takes over and involves itself in the tasks associated with policy implementation, aided and assisted by the Court of Justice which rules on the fair and honest implementation of agreements once they are reached. More than this, the Commission has been portrayed as a collegiate body that is composed to represent 'Europe' so that it serves as the motor for European integration, whereas the Council is seen as composed to represent member governments in such a way that it tends to act as a brake on any progress towards integration. In bald terms, the Commission is frequently regarded as the active and progressive institution that proposes legislation for integration, whereas the Council is presented as the reactive and reactionary body that all too often disposes of these proposals in a way that hinders progress towards European union.

There is some truth in this kind of perspective on Community policy-making, but government expectations of ' their nationals in the Commission have undermined the ideal of the Commission as a collegiate body promoting the EC's collective interest'. A variety of developments have served to reduce the power and authority of the Commission so that it is now less a supranational Eurocracy and more a secretariat to the Council of Ministers. Developments which have reduced the power of the Commission might be construed as having enhanced the position of the Council of Ministers within the Community, but such a perspective would ignore the developing role of the European Council. The European Council was not even referred to within the EC treaties until the SEA. However, the power and authority attaching to the heads of the member states when coupled with the concern of states to defend 'their' interests has meant that this twice-yearly summit meeting has nevertheless come to assume a position of strategic significance. And, in a way which has done much to undermine the authority of the Council of Ministers as the legislature and the key decision-making body for the EC.

This kind of perspective on policy-making within the Community, whilst attentive to the position of Community institutions and mindful of the concerns and intrusions of member states, has rather ignored the part played by the informal activities of interest groups within the whole process. In chapter 4 we made it clear that interest groups were of significance within British politics itself, and so it should not surprise us to find that interest groups are active within the EC. Pressure groups enjoy ready access to EC decision-makers. The Commission itself has regular contact with the most important and even keeps a list of those it officially recognises. Indeed, such contacts have been fostered by the Commission and have been seen as especially important in developing two-way communication between the groups and the Commission. Moreover, the fact that the Economic and Social Committee also provides a forum through which economic and social interests are able to participate in discussions has encouraged commentators to suggest that there are elements of corporatism within the process of EC policy-making. There is some truth in this observation, but the corporatist features in the EC pertain more to policy implementation than to policy formulation although the push to 1992 is likely to affect the development of a 'partnership' between industry and labour and the Commission. In concrete terms, the agricultural lobby has been comparatively effective and the Commission has developed links with industry but until recently trade unions have tended to be more distant from Community discussions. Notwithstanding all of this, most commentators have tended to see Euro-pressure groups themselves as weak. They have further suggested that the limited direct influence of pressure groups on Community decisions has to do with the extent to which member governments are caught up in pressing the case for the interests dominant within their countries in a way which has pre-empted the need for a more direct pressure politics.

All things considered, Community decisions are taken by a complex process of bargaining, confrontation and compromise, in which the most important actors are the governments of the sovereign member states working in, against and outside the institutions of the Community. Many commentators have been critical of the process, regarding it as inefficient and slow at the same time as it fails to live up to those standards of democratic accountability which member states are accustomed to expect in their own domestic politics. Those committed to further political union have tended to see the process as a problem precisely because the development of common policies is inhibited, delayed, blocked and constrained by the member states and by those Community institutions – the Council of Ministers and the European Council – which represent the intergovernmental element within the Community. In fact, such a critical perspective tells us a lot about the integrationist sympathies of the commentators but it rather downplays the extent to which the member states have legitimate national interests and concerns about sovereignty. These concerns were present at the outset and led to the setting up of a policy process that was prepared to allow for co-operation and union only if there were devices to protect national interests. And these concerns are present today, encouraging states to intervene in the policy process in ways which are all too easily construed as blocking of 'progress' in the Community. We simply cannot escape the fact that Community policy-making will always be a slow and difficult business precisely because we are dealing with sovereign states. At the same time as they are trying to agree and get together, they are bent on protecting their own national interests in ways that can involve limiting EC policy-making itself. The extent of democracy within the Community is a different kind of problem. Developments on this front need to be considered before we tackle the more contentious 'problem' of national sovereignty – a problem that refuses to go away, and this notwithstanding the extent to which it dogs the attainment of the Community ideal.

Democracy

Concern about the extent of democracy within the Community and worries about the 'democracy deficit' tend to centre on a number of facets of the policy process. First, there is concern that Community policy-making takes place behind closed doors. The fact that the Council of Ministers – the legislature for the Community – meets in camera makes the public identification of individual states' positions difficult. So it is hard to tease out which states are responsible for the making, and delaying, of Community law. Second, the fact that EC policy-making processes are largely dominated by bureaucracies, Eurocrats and governments serves to marginalise the role of citizens working through parliaments. This is regarded as something of a problem by those who would wish to see a wider public involvement in, and knowledge of, Community affairs. Third, the 'messy' nature of the whole policy process – the fact that responsibilities are shared and divided between Community institutions and between those institutions and member governments – means that it is hard to scrutinise the process and quite impossible to identify the ultimate responsibility for particular Community decisions. This inevitablity means that no one is ever really held to account and blamed when something goes wrong, and yet the accountability of the powerful to the public is recognised as a crucial defining element of a healthy democracy. Fourth, there is concern that the European Parliament (EP) is allowed too little scope to intervene in the policy process and there are worries that national parliaments enjoy only limited rights of scrutiny and control. In bald terms, then, there hangs over the Community policy process the whole question of how European institutions and Community law-making can be subjected to popular and democratic control.

Attempts to reduce the democracy deficit and further the extent of democracy within the community have tended to centre on the position of the EP. This institution has become disruptive precisely because it is dissatisfied with the distribution of authority amongst the Community institutions. This is hardly surprising given the fact that it is not a legislature and has 'little scope' to intervene. Until the 1980s, the EP lacked many of the attributes typical of modern legislatures in West European liberal democracies but its influence has been extended beyond the negligible and deliberative constitutional position by MEPs who have sought to increase their authority. Almost alone among parliaments within the EC, the EP is struggling to increase its power. The Single European Act introduced two new procedures for involving the Parliament in Community affairs: the 'assent' procedure and the 'co-operation, procedure. Under the assent procedure Parliament has a final say in commercial agreements negotiated between the EC and non-EC countries, and a say in the admission of new member states to the Community. Under the co-operation procudure, the legislative process begins with the submission of a Commission proposal to the EP. The Council of Ministers may begin deliberating but may not *act* until after the EP has made its view known. After attending to the view of the EP, the Council then adopts a 'common position' by qualified majority vote and the Parliament has three months to accept the position. If it does so, or takes no action, the Council adopts the proposal according to the common position and it passes into law. If the EP proposes amendments, or rejects the bill, then the Council can only pass its original version by a unanimous vote, otherwise it must accept Parliament's version or drop the bill altogether. It is too early to pronounce on the implications of these procedures for the power of the Parliament. Expectations of what the co-operation procedure would deliver for the EP were modest and ill-defined but experience has shown that the procedure has augmented Parliament's role and made it one of a number of important players in policy-making. However, it has not put the EP on a co-equal footing with the Council and the Commission. Since proposals rejected by the Parliament can still become law, Parliament's role falls far short of the aspirations which it expressed in its 1984 draft Treaty on European Union. That Treaty, in proposing that 'the Commission shall be responsible to the European Parliament', pressed the case for the Community becoming a kind of parliamentary democracy. One not too dissimilar to the British constitutionmal system that we set down in chapter 1 when we discussed the growth of democracy and the developing position of Parliament, the Cabinet, and political parties. The Treaty proposed that the EP be given the right of co-decision in the appointment of the Commission; it required the Commission to secure a vote of confidence, based on its programme, before taking office; and it allowed the Parliament to remove the Commission following a motion of censure passed by a qualified majority. Member states have been wary about these aspirations of the EP, correctly seeing the development of fully-fledged parliamentary democracy at the European level as a precursor to the further transfer of national responsibilities to Community institutions over which they would have little control.

In fact, there are many models of democracy and hence a variety of perspectives on what it might mean to democratise the Community and solve the democratic deficit. First, there are those who reject the Parliamentary model because they are mindful of the problems of party organisation within the EP and hence of the limited possibilities for the development of responsible party government. Moreover, because they are eager for leadership to advance the cause of further integration, they consider that democracy and European integration can best be achieved if the Community were to adopt a presidential model of democracy. This would entail the direct election of the European Commission as the executive in a position analagous to the President of the United States. Second, and from a very different tack, there are many free marketeers within the Community who celebrate the market and applaud the virtue of decisions shaped by 'market forces' alone. They take the view that the market diffuses power, empowers consumers, controls businesses, and, by virtue of all of this, serves as a democratic system in its own right for the taking of decisions involving the allocation and use of resources within the Community. This being the case, there is less concern to reform Community institutions in order to advance political democracy than there is a concern to limit the power of these institutions in order that the system of economic democracy that is the free market can be left to work its efficient, responsive, and accountable magic unhindered by the rough intrusion of Community politics – be it democratic or otherwise. Third, and finally, states that are concerned about national sovereignty take the view that democracy within the Community means that popularly elected governments from the member states should be able to be decisive in the approval and delay of Community legislation through their involvement in the Council of Ministers and the European Council. From this point of view, alarm bells ring when there are proposals to increase the powers of the EP because this would weaken the power of the Council of Ministers and the European Council and this would mean that member governments would have to surrender much of their role in the determination of Community policy. Moreover, because these governments are popularly elected and responsible to their electorates back home any attempt to shift powers away from member states can itself be portrayed as undemocratic. And the more so since democracy is poorly developed within the Community itself, notwithstanding the fact that the British Parliament exercises no direct control over Community legislation and has had its powers weakened by the SEA.

Notwithstanding how we choose to define 'democracy' within the Community, it is clear that the problem is inextricably linked to the problem of national sovereignty. Does the answer to fears about our lack of control over political affairs within the Community lie in increasing the extent of democracy within the institutions of the EC, or does it lie in the robust defence of national sovereignty by popularly elected governments that are accountable to their electorates?

Sovereignty

The Community treaties have established a new and distinct system of law. This being the case, the member states of the Community are not entirely sovereign for, by Treaty, they have delegated a portion of their law-making powers to an external authority (the Community). At the same time they have consented to abide by Community law, give it precedence over domestic law, and enforce it in their own domestic courts. The very notion of the EC presupposes some transfer of powers from the member states to the Community, and hence a partial surrender of national sovereignty, but over the years national competence has declined just as Community competence has risen. Member states agreed to this when they signed and accepted the provisions of the founding treaties and new treaties. Treaties which have enabled the institutions of the Community to make laws in the form of regulations (which are binding in their entirety and are directly applicable in all the member states); directives (which are binding with regard to the goal to be achieved even though the member states are free to decide how to enact the directives); and decisions (which are binding in their entity on the member states to which they are addressed).

When Britain entered the EC it was necessary to pass the European Communities Act, 1972 in order to transform the treaty obligations into domestic law. Under section 2(1) of that Act the entire body of ECSC decisions and EEC and EURATOM regulations in force at the commencement of British membership automatically became part of the law of the United Kingdom. All decisions and regulations made *after* British membership were also destined to automatically become a part of the law of the United Kingdom just as soon as they were made; and so-called 'enforceable Community rights' were adopted. Such a situation clearly poses a challenge to Dicey's notion of parliamentary sovereignty since Community institutions are in a position where they can override the legislation of a 'sovereign' British Parliament and can make laws which Parliament cannot make or unmake. Of course, there is nothing to prevent a future Parliament from repealing the European Communities Act in its entirety so that the country is able to recover its full sovereignty to make its own laws. However, as long as the political reality remains membership of the Community then the transfer of sovereignty can be regarded as irreversible. It has to be assumed that Britain will honour the legal and constitutional obligations of membership so that our Parliament will have to refrain from passing legislation inconsistent with Community law just as our courts will have to accept that Community law is now a part of the law of the land and assumes precedence over domestic law.

The loss of national sovereignty consequent upon our membership of the Community has long been a source of concern to British politicians of all persuasions. Tony Benn, the veteran Left-wing Labour MP, addressed a letter to his constituents at the time of the referendum on membership in 1975. He advised them that we should withdraw because

> the power of the electors of Britain, through their direct representatives in Parliament, to make laws, levy taxes, change laws which the courts must uphold, and control the conduct of public affairs, has been substantially ceded to the EC, whose Council of Ministers and Commission are neither collectively elected, nor collectively dismissed by the British people, nor even by the peoples of all the Community countries put together.

In a similar vein, Enoch Powell, an ex-MP on the right of British politics, delivered a speech against the Community in 1986 arguing that 'our Parliament has formally and comprehensively renounced its old exclusive right to make laws and assent to taxation. We are only a sub-species now of the genus European. We live under a European Court, a European Council, and a European Parliament (so it calls itself); their rules override our laws, their verdicts override our courts, their legislature dictates to our Parliament.' In a slightly lighter vein, the tabloid newspaper *The Star*, carried a front-page story in August 1988 in which it argued that 'Mrs Thatcher does not run Britain anymore. Nor does the Government. The Civil Service is powerless, and the highest courts in the land can be overruled. This is not the nightmare scenario of George Orwell's *1984*, it is the amazing reality of what life will be like in 1992. For that is the year when Britain will virtually disappear into a United States of Europe.' We can discount the excesses of these kind of observations but that does not destroy the fact that membership of the EC has eaten into our sovereignty and reduced our capacity to govern ourselves. Having said that, there are many who would question the reality of national political sovereignty today in the context of an interdependent international economy where multinational companies have a clout that enables them to work around national borders in ways which reduce the extent to which nation states are masters of their own economic affairs and public policies. If it is the case that national political sovereignty is a hollow shell without real substance, then does this mean that we have to look beyond the nation state in order to assert an effective political control (even if international organisations like the EC are somewhat remote and undemocratic) or should we be content to leave international market forces unfettered by the play of politics in nation states or international organisations?

Conclusion

A number of things stand out from our discussion of the significance of the international level of politics for the British political system.

1 In crucial areas of policy, be they to do with defence, the economy, agriculture, social affairs, or the developing world, Britain just cannot be seen as self-governing or in control. It is in a position where it is constrained by the implications that flow from an involvement in a host of international organisations, an involvement which actually determines what the law should be in certain matters of enormous significance to the British people.

2 In so far as international organisations bear down on British politics then they bear very unevenly on the policies and programmes of the different political parties. International organisations have tended to constrain the aspirations of Labour governments more than those of a Conservative persuasion but as the EC seeks to develop a 'social dimension' so it challenges the limited state perspective that has been integral to the Conservatism of Margaret Thatcher.

3 It is easy to point to the constraining significance of international organisations for British politics but if we stress this too much then there is the danger that we lift these political organisations out of the larger economic context within which they themselves operate and take on their being. For example, the IMF has never been a completely free agent since it is subject to processes at work in the world economy, and when policies emerge from the EC then it is important to realise that they too are shaped by and have to operate within a world that is not entirely subject to their control. For us to say that British politicians are sometimes weak in the face of the power of international organisations should not mean that we fail to recognise that behind international organisations there is often the crucial constraining significance of an international economic order that is beyond the easy reach of political processes.

Works Cited and Guide to Further Reading

Bains, M. (1972) *The New local Authorities: Management and Structure*, London, HMSO.
The blueprint for corporate management methods within the reorganised local government system.

Benn, T. (1981) *Arguments for Democracy*, Harmondsworth, Penguin.
The fading star of the Left provides a powerful statement as to Britain's loss of sovereignty consequent upon our involvement in NATO, the IMF and the EC. The argument is similar to that of Enoch Powell, the fading star of the Right.

Birch, A. (1971) *Political integration and Disintegration in the British Isles*, London, Allen and Unwin.
A useful and sobre discussion of the national question within the UK written at a time when political controversy was at its height and when it seemed certain that something in the centralised United Kingdom state would have to give.

Boddy, M. and Fudge, C. (1984) *Local Socialism*, London, Macmillan.
A collection of articles discussing the changing pattern of central–local government relations and focusing in particular on the strategies of the 'new urban Left' at the local level. Includes interesting interviews with Ken Livingstone and David Blunkett

who were then leaders respectively of the Greater London and Sheffield socialist councils (both have subsequently become MPs).

Budd, S. and Jones, A. (1989), *The European Community: A Guide to the Maze*, 3rd edn, London, Kogan Page.
Good, clear, basic account with a bonus section at the end listing further 'sources of information'.

Cockburn, C. (1977) *The local State*, London, Pluto Press.
The classic, but perhaps too simple, Marxist analysis of local state activity and of the responses to it of local people in Lambeth.

Dearlove, J. (1979) *The Reorganisation of British Local Government*, London, Cambridge University Press.
Concerned to explore 'orthodoxies' about the problem of local government while also advancing a 'political perspective' on reorganisation itself. The basic argument still stands up.

Foot, P. (1989) *Ireland: Why Britain Must Get Out*, London, Chatto and Windus.
A short, passionate exposition of the history and politics of Ireland by a socialist who believes that Protestant workers in the north have been bamboozled by cunning capitalists who have disguised their economic objectives in religious dogma.

Grubel, H. (1984) *The International Monetary System*, 4th edn, Harmondsworth, Penguin.
Not an easy read, and half the book is concerned to provide 'a theoretical model of an efficient world monetary system', but provides useful chapters on the IMF and on the implications of the EC for monetary integration.

Gyford, J., Leach, S. and Game, C. (1989) *The Changing Politics of Local Government*, London, Unwin Hyman.
Based on research undertaken for the Widdicombe committee of inquiry into the Conduct of Local Authority Business, the book itself focuses on the political organisation of local authorities and deals with the 'politicisation' of local government.

Hogwood, B. and Keating, M. (eds)(1982), *Regional Government in England*, Oxford, Clarendon Press.
Still one of the best reviews available of government activity in the regions, although some chapters (such as that on the water industry) have now been superseded.

Lodge, J. (ed.)(1989), *The EC and the Challenge of the Future*, London, Pinter.
If you read only one book on the EC then read this one because it has a depth that is lacking in many of the more 'instant' books on the Community.

Moxon-Browne, E. (1983) *Nation, Class and Creed in Northern Ireland*, Aldershot, Gower.
Reports the results of an attitude survey in the province which conclusively demonstrates the lack of any basis for a political consensus and which shows that polarisation is as strong as it ever was. Warns against pursuit of short-term solutions.

Nairn, T. (1981) *The break-up of Britain*, 2nd edn, London, Verso.
One of the best Marxist analyses of the national question in the UK written by an old member of the New Left who is also a Scottish nationalist.

Owen, R. and Dynes, M. (1989) *The Times Guide to 1992*, London, Times Books.
There are many guides to 1992 and this is as good as any.

Redcliffe-Maud, J. (1969) *Royal Commission on Local Government in England*, Cmnd 4040, London, HMSO.
The report which recommended a system of unitary local authorities and which was subsequently ignored by the Heath government when it restructured the local government system.

Rhodes, R. (1988) *Beyond Westminster and Whitehall: The Sub-central Governments of Britain*, London, Unwin Hyman.
Massive and scholarly study that tells you more than you will ever need to know about sub-central government. Although Rhodes adopts a neo-pluralist framework, the overall argument tends to get lost in a mass of detail.

Ritchie, R. (ed.)(1989) *Enoch Powell on 1992*, London, Anaya.
Collection of speeches by a faded star of the Right hostile to Britain's membership of the EC on the grounds that it has destroyed parliamentary sovereignty and undermined national autonomy. Much in common with the line advocated by Benn, faded star of the Left.

Schiavone, G. (1986) *International Organisations: A Dictionary and Bibliography*, 2nd edn, London, Macmillan.
In describing hundreds of international organisations, Schiavone forces the reader to consider the impact which they have had on domestic British politics.

Smith, D. (1989) *Pressure: How America Runs NATO*, London, Bloomsbury.
Argues that, 'NATO is run by the USA; if it were not, it would not work.'

Stoker, G. (1988) *The Politics of Local Government*, London, Macmillan.
Best basic book on the subject with good chapters on non-elected local government, central–local relations, the battle over local spending, privatisation and Labour's urban Left.

Wallace, H., Wallace, W. and Webb, C. (eds)(1983), *Policy-making in the European Community*, 2nd edn, London, Wiley.
Anything on the EC dates quickly, but this holds up better than most because it goes behind the details and is concerned to develop theoretical perspectives on the Community.

Wilson, T. (1989) *Ulster: Conflict and Consent*, Oxford, Basil Blackwell.
An excellent guide to the political impasse in Northern Ireland. Helpfully avoids polemic and cliches. Premissed on a rejection of the 'map image' of Ireland which assumes that one land mass must conincide with just one nation.

Conclusions

We live in a world of rapid and dramatic social and political change. In Eastern Europe, a power bloc which seemed to be set in stone has crumbled. As we write, the Soviet Empire is falling apart, the Western European countries are moving rapidly towards closer economic and political integration, and fragments of the Berlin Wall are being sold to tourists. The geopolitical map of post-war empires, alliances and spheres of influence is being redrawn as nations which the world has forgotten for fifty years reassert their sovereignty. We live in dangerous yet exhilarating times.

This turmoil in international affairs serves to remind us of two crucial points when we come to consider politics in Britain. One is that (as we saw in chapter 12) it makes less and less sense to try to understand and analyse affairs in Britain without reference to developments beyond our shores over which we may have little influence or control. In the space of fifty years, Britain has moved from the position of a leading (if ailing) imperial power on the world stage to one of a somewhat peripheral and certainly rather small offshore island. Obviously the decisions made at Westminster, the judgements handed down in the British courts, the strategies pursued by pressure groups and the choices made by voters are still very important in shaping the lives we lead in Britain, but increasingly we are forced to recognise that some of the most crucial determinants of what happens here no longer originate from within our territorial boundaries.

The second point is that any account of British politics is time-bound. The world beyond the English Channel has been changing fast, but so too has the political situation within this country. When we wrote the first edition of this book, for example, it seemed that the Labour Party was in terminal decline and that a new centre force was redrawing the electoral map. Today the SDP has been wound up and the Labour Party is once more in serious contention for political power. To write a book about British politics is to aim at a moving target, and as the philosopher Karl Popper warned many years ago social scientists can easily go astray when they assume that current trends will continue into the future. Political developments can swiftly take new and unexpected directions which wreck the most assiduous and careful of analyses. Yesterday's textbooks, like yesterday's newspapers, can soon become little more than historical curios if they fail to maintain a healthy distance from the immediacy of political events.

Our task in concluding this book must therefore be to try to identify some of the general, and hopefully more enduring, features of the polity which we have been describing and analysing in earlier chapters. We need to present an overview and to escape from the detail. To achieve this, it is helpful first to extricate from each of the preceeding chapters the core propositions which helped structure our presentation and argument. We therefore present below a distillation of the basic propositions found in each chapter. Each set of propositions is then followed by a summary statement which seems to us to capture some fundamental lesson to be drawn from the chapter in question. These summary statements have deliberately been written as boldly and unambiguously as possible. They represent our attempt to identify the practices, the processes or the ideas which most succinctly define the contours of contemporary British politics. We cannot foresee the future and we do not claim to do so. But if the analyses of British politics developed in this book are broadly valid, then we should be able to draw some general conclusions about how political processes are likely to unfold.

Chapter 1 The Changing Constitution

Propositions

1.1 An understanding of the British constitution is fundamental to any analysis of British politics. The constitution sets the context within which politics operate; it is itself an object of political debate and conflict; and it provides a theory of how political processes should and do work.

1.2 The British constitution is, however, a rather nebulous thing, for there are few written rules. It is a constitution of convention which has evolved from the eighteenth-century 'balanced constitution' governing the relation between the Crown, Lords and Commons, through the nineteenth-century 'liberal constitution' which established the dominance of the elected House of Commons, to the twentieth-century 'liberal-democratic' constitution based on a universal adult franchise.

1.3 The contemporary theory of the liberal-democratic constitution is still grounded in the three principles indentified by Dicey a hundred years ago, viz.: the sovereignty of Parliament over all other institutions including the courts; the conventions of the constitution and the sanctity of the Rule of Law.

1.4 Developments in the twentieth century, notably the evolution of a strong party system, have necessitated revisions of some aspects of the liberal-democratic constitutional model. In particular, it is now recognised that the Prime Minister and his or her Cabinet control the Commons rather than vice versa. In Bagehot's terms, the Commons has become part of the 'dignified' constitutional apparatus.

1.5 Within the executive there are similarly signs that power may be concentrating more in the hands of the Prime Minister thus generating prime ministerial rather than Cabinet government. This tendency was strengthened during the Thatcher Premiership but may not be irreversible.

Summary statement

The Constitution does not determine what happens in British politics, but as a system of unwritten rules it does enable some things to happen while preventing others. Like the rules governing any game, the constitutional norms and conventions are constantly evolving, are always subject to renegotiation or challenge and may be interpreted in different ways according to the diverse interests and objectives of the participants.

Chapter 2 Perspectives on the Party System

Propositions

2.1 There has been a marked shift since the war away from constitutional perspectives on British politics as political science has come to address the central role of parties in the contemporary political system.

2.2 The 'Responsible Party Government' model developed as the dominant perspective on the role of political parties and as *the* explanation for British politics. This holds that strong parties enhance democracy by providing a link between electors and Parliament. Two main parties compete for electoral support and therefore seek to develop programmes which will maximise voter preferences. The winning party then carries out the mandate given it by the electorate.

2.3 Among the more serious problems with this model are the decline of two-party competition; the suspicion that parties do not always offer clear and contrasting choices of programmes; the failure of winning parties to deliver on their promises; and evidence that voters may not make their choices according to careful evaluation of party manifestos.

2.4 One alternative perspective is offered by the 'Adversary Party Politics' model. This holds that the party duopoly is only maintained through a biased and unfair voting system; that the two main parties are influenced by extreme views which are not reflected in the more moderate majority of voters; that party competition exaggerates party differences, artificially polarises political debate and undermines consensus; and that major discontinuities of policy following each change of government have contributed to Britain's decline.

2.5 A second alternative perspective is offered by 'Public Choice' theory. This holds that vote-seeking by parties results in crude attempts to buy votes through irresponsible promises, that voters are encouraged to develop ever more unrealistic expectations and aspirations, and that governments attempt to manipulate the economy for electoral advantage doing serious long-term damage.

2.6 All three models have strengths and weaknesses. The party system may be seen as both functional and dysfunctional as regards its contribution to democratic processes and economic well-being. Party competition does help transmit popular preferences into policies, but it does this in rough-and-ready fashion and it can lead to an inflation of popular expectations which cannot realistically be fulfilled.

Summary statement

The party system is changing. The Conservative and Labour Parties are in long-term decline as measured by their electoral support, their membership and their effectiveness in responding to new issues and policy agendas. Many voters are politically homeless and the electoral map seems increasingly complex and volatile.

Chapter 3 Explaining Voting Behaviour

Propositions

3.1 Like many other aspects of social life, voting behavior is patterned and, to some extent, predictable. The problem for political scientists is that the patterns are complex (many different factors need to be taken simultaneously into account) and predictability has become less reliable since the 1960s. Nevertheless, voting is not random. The task is to develop models which can identify the main factors and processes which influence how people vote.

3.2 Until the political turbulence of the 1970s, the principal model of voting was that of 'Party Identification'. This holds that for most people, party identification is a product of socialisation – we grow up to think of ourselves as socialists or Conservatives and this shapes how we vote and how we react to party programmes. We do not support a party because of its policies; rather, we support its policies because we already identify with the party.

3.3 This party Identification model did achieve a high degree of predictive accuracy, but important weaknesses have been exposed. The model overemphasises the importance of social class and related factors and fails to explain why class should influence voting in the first place. It fails to take account of new political and social cleavages in British society and it undervalues the importance of issues and policies in influencing voter choice. It also gave rise to a prediction regarding the strengthening of two-party politics which has been falsified by events since the sixties.

3.4 Since the 1970s, the pattern of voting have been changing. There has been a process of partisan dealignment in which increasing numbers of people are decoupling themselves from any strong party loyalty. There has also been a process of (absolute) class dealignment in which the link between social class and party voting has been weakened. Changes in the social structure (especially the erosion in the size of the working class) have also shifted voting patterns.

3.5 One response to these processes of dealignment has been a renewed emphasis on the importance of issues in shaping electoral choices. Attitudes to various policy items are a stronger indicator of voting patterns than class or other sociological characteristics. However, parties can and do still win elections despite rather than because of their policies.

3.6 A second response to dealingment has been to analyse changes in the social structure, in particular the emergence of new 'sectoral cleavages' structured around the division between state and private-sector employment and service provision. However, while production sector cleavages do seem pertinent (especially in the middle class), consumption effects appear weak. Furthermore, the dominant ideology thesis which is employed to explain these effects is crude and unsupported.

Summary statement

Most people are not very interested in politics, but nor are they totally ignorant of it. Their actions in voting, like their actions in many other areas of their lives, are influenced by social factors such as their class background or their exposure to media images, but are not detemined by them. Any explanation of voting behaviour must focus on individual *and* social factors. Attempts to reduce political behaviour to sociological variables are necessarily limited, for voters do make *political* judgements and are not simply creatures of habit or products of social conditioning.

Chapter 4 Perspectives on Interests and Groups

Propositions

4.1 The political process involves more than just governments, parties and voters. Modern democracies like Britain sustain a plethora of organised groups which attempt, not to run the government, but to influence it. Some of these groups are enduring and established; others arise around single issues.

4.2 Pluralist theories of politics hold that interest groups perform a crucial role in the democratic process. British society is said to be relatively open (in that any group is free to organise) and is comprised of many different interests. No one group is dominant, for winners on one issue may lose on another, and people who are allies in one context may line up against each other in another. Government functions as a neutral arena and responds to the relative weight of pressures exerted upon it. Competition between groups takes place against a backdrop of consensus over the basic framework of the society and polity.

4.3 Pluralist theories have been criticised from the Left. Plularism is said to ignore private power in its focus on public policy-making; to ignore the crucial question of who really benefits from government policies; to be blind to the favourable position of groups like big business which have the ear of government; and to ignore 'non-decision-making' – the subtle ways in which some issues are prevented from ever being aired and some interests routinely go unheard.

4.4 Pluralist theories have also been criticised from the Right. Pluralism is said to ignore the way in which state officials and bureaucrats can turn public policy to their own interests; to be blind to the unique power exerted by strong trade unions, professions and other sectional interests; and to neglect the way in which special interests are able to secure advantages for themselves at the expense of a disorganised majority.

4.5 Pluralist theories have also been challenged by corporatist theories of British politics which hold that big business and organised labour have become 'governing institutions' harnessed to government itself. These interests are directly and routinely represented within government and also act on behalf of government once agreements have been reached. Pluralist competition is bypassed and the competitive world of pressure groups plays second fiddle to the corporatist bias. Corporatist theories, strong in the 1970s, were however weakened by the Thatcher government's attacks on corporatist structures and processes in the eighties.

Summary statement

Organised interests can and do influence policy outcomes, sometimes openly and spectacularly, at other times more routinely and less obviously. In theory, any interest can organise itself to pressure government, but in practice some can achieve this much more easily and effectively than others. Major producer interests do often have an inside track, and other groups can easily become marginalised. When all this has been said, however, it is important not to exaggerate the significance of these pressures from outside the state system. Pluralist, Marxist and New Right perspectives have all been guilty of assuming that government and state are weaker than is the reality. The centre of political power and authority in Britain still lies within the state system, not outside it.

Chapter 5 The Constitution in Crisis

Propositions

5.1 Since the 1970s the constitution has become a central issue in British politics for the first time since 1922. Entry into the EC, unrest in Northern Ireland, nationalist pressures in Scotland and Wales, the strengthening of prime ministerial power and the growing unfairness of the electoral system have all contributed to pressures for change.

5.2 Much of the concern centres on the doctrine of the sovereignty of Parliament, for this has come to mean the virtually unchecked power of the majority party leadership. Mainstream proposals for reform advocated by various constitutional authorities since the seventies include: (a) limiting parliamentary power through a written constitution and Bill of Rights; (b) strengthening of countervailing powers of a new second chamber and the judiciary; and (c) strengthening the independence of the House of Commons from the executive. These ideas also often appear in proposals developed from various different parts of the political spectrum.

5.3 From the Left the concern has been to check the undemocratic exercise of power, whether by unelected judges and Lords, or by foreign powers such as the USA operating through NATO, or by unpopular and unresponsive governments. The emphasis is on broadening power to enable more surveillance of government and more effective participation in policy-making. To this end, the Labour Party favours a new elected second chamber, increased power for the Commons *vis-à-vis* the government, a Freedom of Information Act, and devolution to the regions together with a strengthening of local government.

5.4 From the neo-liberal Right the concern has been to safeguard individual liberties in the face of growing state power. Democracy and participation are no safeguard, for elected majorities can trample over fundamental freedoms of those whom they can out-vote. The task therefore is to limit Parliament's power to legislate in favour of specific interests by imposing the overriding principle of a 'blind' Rule of Law.

5.5 From the political centre the primary concern has been to introduce electoral reform so as to ensure that representation in Parliament reflects voting patterns. Together with a commitment to Proportional Representation (which would increase the political clout of the centre), the Liberal Democrats favour a Bill of Rights, devolution, reform of the Lords and the Civil Service and fixed elections as well as procedures designed to break the secrecy of government.

5.6 Although there is widespread agreement that the constitution is looking rather threadbare there is little agreement on what should be done. A fundamental problem in any attempt to bring about constitutional reform lies in the sovereignty of Parliament itself. How can future Parliaments be bound by new procedures agreed by a previous Parliament? And (more pragmatically) is any governing party likely to introduce changes designed to limit its own power and strengthen the position of potential or actual opponents?

Summary statement

Britain is in a period of constitutional transition every bit as significant as the transitions which occured from the balanced to the liberal, and from the liberal to the liberal-democratic constitutions. The theory of the liberal-democratic constitution no longer corresponds to the reality of political practice. Constitutional reform, however, is highly contentious and politicised, for the rules of the game are never neutral. Different proposed arrangements – PR, a Bill of Rights, an elected second chamber, etc. – always favour some parties and interests at the expense of others. This is why there is no consensus over the future direction of constitutional change. It is also why all proposals should be carefully examined with respect to the interests of those who support them.

Chapter 6 The Power of the Secret State

Propositions

6.1 The British state consists of much more than the government. While the government is democratically elected, much else in the state system is not. There is a crucial set of institutions beyond government which are non-elected, powerful, secretive and largely autonomous. These are the institutions of the 'secret state'.

6.2 The Civil Service exists to administer government policy but inevitably is caught up in making and influencing it. Ministers and senior civil servants are locked into an unequal but interdependent relationship in which the former can never match the power of knowledge and expertise enjoyed by the latter. The backgrounds from which senior civil servants are drawn, together with their long socialisation into a departmental ethos, tend to reinforce a conservative orientation to public affairs which can block or frustrate radical governments of Left *or* Right.

6.3 The Bank of England is a key financial institution which is expected to carry out Treasury policy but which is centrally involved in influencing and shaping economic policy. It is accountable to no one. It acts as banker to the government and to the commercial banks, and is in practice an important lobbyist for City opinion. Like the Civil Service it is conservative in its inclinations and maintains strong pressure against policies likely to prove inflationary. The fact that it has nevertheless failed to keep inflation in check has fuelled support for locking control of money supply into a new and even more independent European central bank.

6.4 The judiciary both applies statute law and creates common law through precedent. This latter function necessarily gives to High Court judges and the Law Lords a creative function involving inevitable value judgements. These values reflect both the selective recruitment of judges (who are mainly white, male and upper class) and a process of socialisation within the closed world of the legal profession. Again, therefore, the judiciary tends to reinforce a conservative force within the state system, and the principle of independence from Parliament and government (together with the fact that judges are not elected) means that the judicial power is exercised in a non-accountable manner.

6.5 The police, too, are only weakly accountable, for local police committees have little effective control over the policies pursued by Chief Constables. Policing inevitably entails widespread exercise of discretion, and this tends to reflect the values held in common by most police officers who are overwhelmingly white, male and conservative.

6.6 The armed forces have a long tradition of subordination to civil authority. There has been no military coup in Britain since 1688. The armed forces, in conjunction with the armaments industry, are nevertheless a centre of influence in the state system as regards pressures on spending and policy priorities. With 95 per cent of military spending devoted to NATO, British governments are in practice tightly locked into a voluntary but unequal relationship with the USA.

6.7 The security services are the most secret part of the secret state and their activities are generally hidden from view by the need to preserve 'national security'. This level of secrecy precludes the possibility of effective accountability to Parliament or anyone else. Virtually a law unto themselves, the security services mount surveillance on both real and imagined enemies of the state, and this has even extended to operations mounted against an elected Labour Prime Minister. The security services represent a major worry for those concerned about erosion of civil liberties in Britain.

Summary statement

The government is only one part of the state. Much of what the state does crucially affects everyday life in Britain yet is beyond the power of Parliament, or even government, to control, direct or monitor. Compared with, say, the United States, a remarkable cloak of secrecy envelopes great swathes of state activity in Britain. In general, the institutions comprising the secret state are not only unelected, powerful, autonomous and secretive, but are also conservative. As such, governments bent on change (whether radical Right or radical Left) will encounter massive obstacles of inertia when they run up against senior civil servants, top judges, M15 and M16, the Chief Constables, the military chiefs and the Governor of the Bank of England. Voters can throw out governments but much of the state system is immune to popular pressure or control.

Chapter 7 Capitalism, Marxism and Labourism

Propositions

7.1 Marxist approaches to the analysis of state power and political processes are premissed on the argument that political power is essentially an expression of economic power. The role of the state must above all else be to maintain and safeguard the interests of the dominant economic class.

7.2 Instrumentalist approaches within Marxist theory suggest that the state functions in the interests of the capitalist class because: (a) key positions are held by members of the bourgeoisie; (b) capitalist interests can wield the greatest pressure and influence upon government policy-making; and (c) those who run the state are aware of the need to maintain profitability in order to keep the economy growing (see, for example, Miliband's work).

7.3 Relative autonomy approaches within Marxist theory explain the class character of the state, not with reference to the actions of individuals, but by analysing the structural determinants of state outcomes. Seen in these terms, the state expresses the balance of forces between social classes, and it maintains the capitalist system by making short-run concessions to non-capitalist classes when they begin to get powerful.

7.4 A basic problem with instrumentalist theories is that they fail to explain the structural constraints within which powerful individuals must operate; a basic problem with relative autonomy theories is their failure to recognize that individuals' actions are not completely determined by the context in which they must operate.

7.5   The logic of Marx's original analysis of the state was that fundamental change could only be achieved by overthrowing the system. Today, however, the debate between insurrectionary and revisionist strategies has effectively been settled in favour of the latter. Socialism will come in Britain through parliamentary and democratic means or not at all. The only agency which could give effect to such a transformation is the Labour Party.

7.6   While nominally committed to socialism, the Labour Party has always been reformist in character and social democratic in its objectives. Its brief flirtation with a more fundamentalist form a socialism in the early eighties proved electorally disastrous and pushed the party back towards the centre ground.

7.7   It is doubtful whether there exists the basis for a stronger form of socialism to prevail in Britain in the future. The working class is fragmented and divided; is getting smaller; and is not 'naturally' inclined towards socialist values. Socialism (as opposed to reformist social democracy) is almost certainly now dead in Britain.

Summary statement

Marxism was always a weak influence in British politics and is now dead. Marxist analysis may still offer some insights into how the state system operates, but as a guide to practice it is now irrelevant. Socialism has a future in Britain only in the form of a social democratic agenda which seeks to make capitalism work better rather than to transform it. Britain is and will remain a capitalist democracy and this notwithstanding the tensions between capitalism and democracy.

Chapter 8 Liberalism, Conservatism and the 'New Right'

Propositions

8.1   Liberal approaches to the analysis of state power are premised on the view that individual freedoms and economic prosperity have been fundamentally threatened by the growth of state intervention. Minimal state activity is necessary in order to maintain and enforce law and order, to defend the realm, to support those who cannot maintain themselves, and to safeguard the conditions in which commerce and trade can flourish. Beyond this, state power becomes pernicious rather than beneficial.

8.2   Despite its historic opposition to conservatism, liberalism has re-emerged in British politics over the last twenty years through the agency of the Conservative Party. The phenomenon of 'Thatcherism' was an uneasy combination of key elements of both liberal and conservative thinking.

8.3 A key objective of the 'New Right' was to promote free markets in place of state provision and regulation. Free markets were seen as: (a) a condition of other liberties; (b) a means for ensuring progress and innovation; (c) the only efficient way of organising complex modern economies; (d) a safeguard against totalitarianism; (e) a means for giving ordinary people an effective voice; and (f) a just system of distribution of resources.

8.4 In economic policy the New Right emphasised monetary discipline, promotion of competition and low taxes. In practice, however, the Thatcher governments fell far short of the objectives in all three cases. In welfare policy the aim was to replace state provision in kind by private provision and market purchases, but again the changes introduced through the eighties fell far short of this. Just as Labour governments have often led socialists to despair of their timidity, so the Thatcher administrations were seen as a disappointment by most new-liberals.

8.5 Socialists and social democrats attacked the New Right as authoritarian; dismissed its emphasis on competition as a safeguard for ordinary people confronted by the power of big corporations; pointed to the inability of the poor to exercise effective market choices; stressed the need for continuing state provision and regulation of key areas of service provision; and criticised what they saw as the selfishness of the new values espoused by the New Right. Such points were countered by New Right advocates, though not always fully or convincingly.

8.6 The experience of the 1980s suggests that New Right ideas were often difficult to put into practice, were often unpopular with the electorate, and often failed to achieve their stated objectives. To some extent this experience bears out the saliency of Public Choice theories which New Right analysts have themselves done so much to develop.

Summary statement

The neo-liberal agenda has been exhausted. Taken together with the collapse of socialism, this suggests that British politics are headed for a new period of relative consensus in which the Left accepts private property and market competition while the Right accepts state regulation and widespread welfare provision. The growing significance of the EC, and possible future moves towards electoral reform, will only reinforce this consensus.

Chapter 9 Managing the Economy

Propositions

9.1 Although it has grown in absolute terms many times over, the British economy has been in relative decline as compared with the country's major industrial competitors for virtually the whole of the twentieth century.

9.2 Liberal orthodoxy dominated government's economic thinking until the

1930s. Central to this orthodoxy was a commitment to free trade and tight monetary discipline. Free trade exposed declining British industries to growing overseas competition while commitment to the Gold Standard priced British goods out of world markets and prevented action to reverse the inter-war depression.

9.3 For thirty years during and after the war, governments tried to manage the economy through Keynesian fine-tuning strategies coupled with a sizeable public sector. Such policies seemed to work in the short term but problems of inflation and inefficiency built up in the longer term. By the 1970s both inflation and unemployment were rising fast, and in 1976 a loan negotiated with the IMF finally put the brakes on the growth of deficit spending.

9.4 From the 1960s onwards, Labour and Conservative governments also tried to involve the state in planning the economy in co-operation with representatives of industy and organised labour. The history of such corporatist initiatives is littered with failure – most spectacularly, the collapse of the National Plan in 1966 and the chaos of the 'winter of discontent' in 1978/9.

9.5 The 1980s witnessed a return to liberal economic principles, at least in theory. Tight monetary discipline contributed to a major recession in the early eighties but also helped create the conditions for sustained recovery in the middle years of the decade. However, monetarism proved difficult to maintain and was effectively abandoned in 1986. Public spending, too, continued to grow despite efforts to cut back. Trade union reforms and the privatisation of state-owned enterprises were more successfully carried through, but ten years on, inflation, unemployment and economic growth rates were all looking little different from where they were when the Thatcher government first came to office.

Summary statement

Post-war British politics have been, and continue to be, dominated by the problem of the relative weakness of the British economy. Over fifty years, governments have tried virtually every feasible strategy, and none seems to have worked. In the future, with the EC committed to currency union and removal of all trade barriers, the economy will effectively be beyond the scope of any British government to influence or control. This may turn out to be good for the economy, but it will be bad for governments who will still be judged by voters on their economic record.

Chapter 10 Providing for Social Need

Propositions

10.1 One basic problem of welfare provision in a capitalist system is that state support undermines the system of market rewards and penalties. Ever since the days of the Elizabethan Poor Law, governments have wrestled with the problem of how to relieve genuine suffering while preserving the material incentives and inducements required to get people to work.

10.2 A second fundamental problem is that, in a capitalist country, economic inequalities are inherent. Although absolute standards of living rise for everybody, there will always be a stratum of people who, relative to others, are 'poor'. If the 'problem of poverty' is inherent, then pressure to expand welfare provisions will remain strong.

10.3 A third fundamental problem is that free goods and services are in infinite demand. No matter how large and fast the welfare state grows, demands on its services will remain as strong and urgent as ever.

10.4 The weakness of the British economy has meant that escalating welfare spending in the post-war years has become increasingly difficult to finance. However, voters want and expect expenditure on services like health and education to be increased, and state employees pressure the goverment to increase spending through their unions and professional associations.

10.5 The failure of the welfare state to 'eradicate poverty' despite a century of growing state activity and expenditure sustains both Left and Right critiques. In the 1980s the Right critique has been to the fore, but after more than ten years of a 'radical Right' government, the basic framework of the welfare state established after the war remains in tact and there has been no sustained move to privatise welfare other than in the field of housing.

10.6 As general living standards have risen, so increasing numbers of people have been able to provide for their own consumption in areas such as home ownership and private pension plans. Health and education, however, remain the core of a universalistic welfare system. These services are expensive, popular, but under constant pressure.

Summary statement

The British welfare state is expensive to maintain but is under constant pressure to expand. While it does provide a low-level 'safety net' for most people, it has failed to fulfil the hopes of egalitarians and collectivists. Equally, it has successfully resisted moves from the Right to dismantle or fundamentally reform it. The apparent inability of any party to countenance a major restructuring of the welfare system suggests that core elements of the system such as schools and health care may continue to decline in quality as they increase in cost.

Chapter 11 Maintaining the Social Order

Propositions

11.1 It is a fundamental responsibility of the state to maintain social order. This necessitates the use of force when necessary, but no social order can be maintained in the long term in the absence of some degree of consensus.

11.2 The state is unique as the only institution of modern society with the right to use force against its citizens. It is, however, also crucially involved in the maintenance of consensus.

11.3 The traditional agencies through which moral consensus is achieved and maintained have all been weakened. The patriarchal family structure is fraying with increases in working women, divorce rates, single parents, etc. The Church now challenges the established order as often as it endorses it. Community sentiment has been eroded and norms of 'responsible citizenship' appear weak. Governments have been able to achieve little in reversing these trends.

11.4 Modern agencies for mobilising consensus include the schools, the mass media and the social work agencies. The state is often centrally involved in these institutions, and government has recently attempted to increase its influence and control over both schooling and broadcasting, but all are relatively pluralistic as regards the moral values they endorse.

11.5 As moral consensus has weakened, so the need to resort to coercion has increased. Police powers have been strengthened as public confidence in the police has weakened. Crime rates have, nevertheless, continued to escalate and violent outbreaks of civil unrest have multiplied.

11.6 The Left sees in recent years the evidence of a drift into a more authoritarian form of government and society. The Right, by contrast, emphasises the deleterious effects of continued moral permissiveness and the weakening of rules. Both would probably agree that legitimation has become increasingly problematic.

Summary statement

Britain (as opposed to Northern Ireland) is still a relatively consensual political society and is not *fundamentally* threatened by major cleavages of interest or moral sentiment. Nevertheless, traditional moralities have lost the grip they once had over popular consciousness. With greater individualism and diversity has come new strains to the social fabric and a sense of ambivalence towards certain traditional values and core institutions. In a period of rapid change, old certainties have collapsed and the social order is now subjected to tensions and conflicts which cannot simply or easily be institutionalised or contained. There is no 'crisis' of legitimation, but popular consent is now more difficult to achieve than it once was.

Chapter 12 Government and Politics Beyond Westminster and Whitehall

Propositions

12.1 Britain is a 'unitary state' system. Nevertheless, not all state power is centralised, and important institutions operate both below the centre and beyond it which can and do challenge or modify the policies and strategies pursued by the central authority.

12.2 There has been a tendency through most of this century for central government to attempt to extend its control or regulation of local elected authorities. It has done this by removing responsibilities from local councils, by reorganising the structure of local government, by controlling local spending and the right to raise revenue through local taxation, and by use of formal and informal pressures. Local government still accounts for a major slice of state activity, but compared with the 1930s, local councils have lost power relative to the centre.

12.3 An important set of non-elected state agencies operates at a regional level between local authorities and central government. These regional bodies, the most important of which are arguably the Health Authorities, are more easily controlled from the centre. They also tend to be relatively immune to popular pressures while affording special sectional interests an inside track in policy formulation and implementation.

12.4 Taken as a whole, the United Kingdom consists of four nations. National identity is relatively weak in England and Wales but has fuelled a move for devolution or even separatism in Scotland which may yet pose a major challenge to the future of the Union. In Northern Ireland there is a fundamental cleavage between a majority favouring the Union and a minority whose aspirations and emotions lie in breaking from it.

12.5 The sovereignty of the UK state has progressively been eroded in the post-war period through participation in international agencies such as the IMF, NATO and, most crucially, the European Community. In certain core areas of policy, Britain can no longer be seen as self-governing.

Summary statement

There is a clear tendency in the post-war period for power to shift increasingly towards larger and more remote institutions. As local government powers have been lost to the centre, so central government powers have been ceeded to international organisations. Nevertheless, there are countervailing tendencies, most notably in the periodic resurgence of nationalist sentiment or separatist movements within the UK. Both these centrifugal and centripetal tendencies are likely to increase in the future, for as Britain's fate becomes ever more inextricably linked with that of Europe, so demands for some degree of autonomous self-direction and control are likely to bubble up from below.

We end with one final proposition. It is clear that events within Britain are increasingly being shaped by forces outside it. This suggests that the rationale for a book on British politics is becoming weaker as time goes by. In our introduction to the first edition of this book we quoted from John Steinbeck's *The Grapes of Wrath* to illustrate how, when we try to trace where power *really* lies, we find ourselves moving further and further away from the obvious targets. In the first half of this book, for example, we showed how power lies less in Parliament than with the Executive, how pressures from outside of government may influence policies adopted within it, and how the elected side of the state system can itself seem relatively weak or insignificant when set against the power of non-elected 'secret' agencies such as the Civil Service, the judiciary and the security services. In the later chapters, however, it has also become apparent that the whole state system in Britain is itself losing autonomy and power relative to organisations and institutions operating beyond our shores. The era of a world political system of sovereign nation states is drawing to a close. The perplexed tenant farmer of Steinbeck's novel, set in the 1930s, may be well advised today to put away his rifle and go home, for the centres of power which affect our lives are now beyond the reach of ordinary people. Certainly if he (or anyone else) really wants to know who, or what, is influencing his life, he is unlikely to get a satisfactory answer if he limits his investigations to books on political processes *within* nation states. For good or bad, British politics can no longer be contained within the increasingly anachronistic boundaries of the territorial nation state, and so narrow books on British politics seem destined ultimately for the dusty shelves of the antiquarian bookshops.

Index